THE ART OF THE SILVERSMITH
IN MEXICO

Text and Plate Volumes

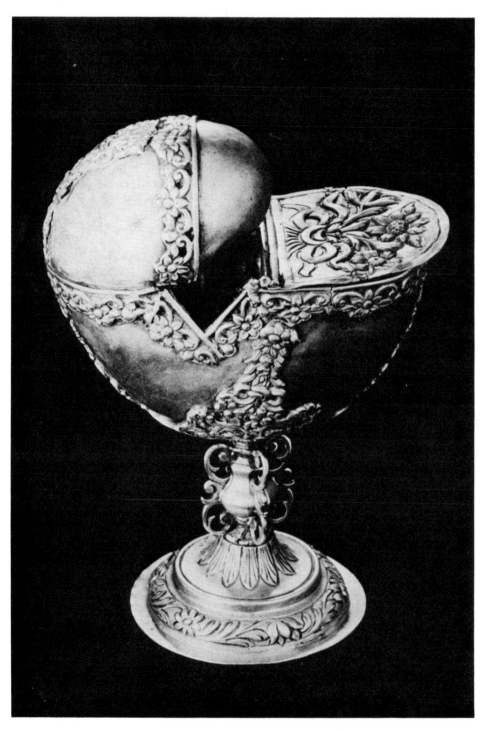

An incense boat of silver, of the XVII Century; height 8⅟₁₆ inches, length 6⅝₁₆, width 3⅜ and base 3⅟₁₆ inches in diameter. Author's collection.

THE ART
OF THE SILVERSMITH
IN MEXICO
1519-1936

BY LAWRENCE ANDERSON

Volume I
Text

Hacker Art Books
New York
1975

First published by Oxford University Press, New York, 1941.

Reissued 1975 by Hacker Art Books, Inc., New York.

Library of Congress Catalogue Card Number 73-81683 ISBN 0-87817-139-8

Printed in the United States of America.

This book is dedicated to the Mexican people with all affection and respect, and with the hope that it will contribute to the better understanding and appreciation of their artistic achievements.

Contents

THE ART OF THE SILVERSMITH
IN MEXICO

THE ART OF THE SILVERSMITH IN MEXICO

Introduction

Scope

THIS BOOK was written with two objectives: To awaken interest in a subject of considerable importance which has been ignored, and to serve as a guide for collectors.

Much of the material here presented is new, particularly that concerning hall-marks and the names of the silversmiths, these subjects apparently having failed to awaken in Mexico sufficient interest to warrant an investigation.

The usual difficulties inherent in an entirely new field of research were encountered. No landmarks had been established by previous investigators. Starting only with the knowledge that beautiful examples of plate of the Colonial period existed, it was necessary to follow up every possible clue that could be found and laboriously, step by step, unfold the history of the art. Hall-marks were a peculiarly difficult problem, for, apparently, the Government officials were interested in stamping plate only as proof that taxes had been paid. Hence they did not retain records of the marks, which were, moreover, frequently changed; and clever falsifications abounded.

Although ecclesiastical plate such as tabernacles, thrones, images and the like is interesting, little space is given to such objects, as the few remaining originals are not available to the collector; few photographs or drawings of them exist, and, moreover, full descriptions of the more important objects can be found in other works.

At first it was proposed to include in this study an examination of the silversmiths' art throughout Mexico, and some data to this end was gathered. I soon saw that the provincial work was not nearly as important as that of Mexico City and adjacent cities. Long visits to many places would have been necessary to include the work of the provinces, which for me were impossible and would have brought about an undesirable extension of this monograph. For these reasons, only the plate of Mexico City and adjacent cities is included.

It was intended to make this work comprehensive, but not exhaustive: new and valuable material will be found in the course of further investigations and in the cataloguing of the National Archives.

The Good Taste of the Mexican Silversmiths

Just as the strife and sophistication of Europe is felt in the ambitious, tormented, showy forms produced by those extravagantly rewarded pets of court favorites, the Continental silversmiths, so is the peace and simplicity of Colonial life faithfully reflected in the craft of Mexico. Even in plate completely covered by decoration, such as was produced in the third quarter of the eighteenth century, we see none of the intense craving for glory, none of the near-madness felt in similar forms of Continental Europe. It seemed impossible for the Mexican silversmiths to violate the canons of good taste. With a complete command of technique, they achieved, even in their most earnest attempts to reproduce current European forms, an almost Franciscan directness and simplicity.

Provincial Plate

To help the collector identify the plate of the provinces, data are offered on documents; hall-marks in Guatemala-Chiapas and San Luis Potosí; and plate of Puebla and other provinces.

A. *Documents*.

Prohibition (against making plate) outside Mexico City, 1563:

The Viceroy,[1] having been informed[2] that various natives, especially in the cities and places of Jochimilco, Tescoco, Cholula, Michoacán and other parts, work, cast and sell pieces of silver, failing to have the plate stamped with hall-marks and to pay the royal taxes, resolved to prohibit generally the making of silver plate with

---

1 Don Luis de Velazco.
2 Fabian de Fonseca, y Carlos de Urrutia, *Historia General de Real de Hacienda*, vol.I, p.391. Vicente García Torres, 6 vols. Mexico, 1849. The date of this prohibition is not given, but from the text it is inferred that it was about 1563.

the sole exception of those [silversmiths] who reside in this city and work in places designated [by the authorities]. These are obliged to declare the silver and gold which they desire to employ and like the Spanish silversmiths [in Spain] they must secure hall-marks from officials. They must observe the ordinances governing [the fabrication of plate] under pain of seizure of the plate, one hundred lashes in public and exile for six years from an area ten leagues around the place where the fraud was committed. This ordinance was published in those towns where it was considered necessary.

This prohibition did not apply to those towns where there were *Cajas Reales* [Royal strong boxes — fiscal agencies of the Viceroy]:

1570

Because fiscal agents of certain *cajas* or provinces[3] customarily visited other places where they hall-marked silver and gold, and because there were objections to this practice including risk of fraud, it was ordered, by royal decree dated in Madrid on the 10th August of 1570, that said fiscal agents should mark plate only within their own districts and in their own assay offices and *cajas reales*, regulating the tax according to the custom and rules which prevailed there.

1621

That the authorities continued their efforts to confine the making of plate to Mexico City and towns where there were *Cajas Reales*, is shown by a decree dated May, 1621. It was ordered:

That no Silversmith or other person whatsoever shall work a new piece of silver in the City of Puebla de los Angeles. They shall confine their activities to repairing old plate. Penalty: Forfeiture of the plate and permanent loss of the right to make plate. And the *Alcalde Mayor* shall exercise due vigilance that this decree is obeyed and enforced, investigating all denunciations to this effect.[4]

1644

In the *Instructions for Sr. Valerio Cortés del Rey, appointed Assayer of the Mines, in the Jurisdiction of Parral*, issued by Count de Salvatierra on the 9th January 1644, no mention is made of plate, but it is learned that the royal punch (die) was kept by the Mayor, who also

---

3 Ibid., vol.I, p.18.

4 Dr. Eusebio Bentura Beleña, *Recopilación Sumaria de todos los Autos Acordados de la Real Audiencia y Sala del Crimen de esta Nueva España.* vol.I, p.85. Felipe de Zuñiga y Ontiveros. 2 vols., Mexico, 1787.

collected the royal taxes, and that the assay office was always 'near the place where the royal punch (die) was kept.'

By 1733 this prohibition had been relaxed:

In those cities and towns where there are neither official assayers nor approved stampers of hall-marks, the most capable and honest silversmith in each place shall be chosen, so that he may assist in the monthly inspections as provided for in the decree.[5]

In 1746 the prohibition regarding those places where there were no *Cajas Reales* was still in effect:

Outside of this city, except where there are *cajas reales* and assayer, no silversmith could work gold or silver, either his property or of others, as it would not be of the quality provided by law or hall-marked unless the ordinances had been observed.[6]

The provisions of the *Caja Matriz* (Chief Royal strong box) of Mexico City applied to the provinces:

As these provisions[7] apply also to *cajas foráneas* [royal strong boxes outside Mexico City] they will not be detailed here, and reference will be made only to the sums charged as fees by the chief assayer of the *caja matriz* in this city, which are as follows. . . .

The *Ordinances of the Assayers*[8] of 1783, governing the assayers of the provinces of the interior, state that 'the duties of founder, marker and weighmaster being united in the hands of the assayers . . . who shall have their dwelling in the house of assays. . . .'

The Viceroy, Count Revilla Gigedo, in his advice to his successor[9] signed in 1794, leaves us important information on the character of the officials governing the provinces and of the lack of control everywhere:

The lack of control over the provinces . . . not having been able to make the governor and towns comply . . . and only the governor of Durango replied on the 15th March 1790 that he had executed his orders.

5 Fonseca y Urrutia, op.cit., vol.I, p.398. Royal Decree of 1st October 1733.
6 Ibid., vol.I, p.402.
7 Ibid., vol.I, p.48. Royal Decree of the 12th May 1779.
8 Ibid., vol.I, p.55. *Ordenanzas de Ensayadores*.
9 Count Revilla Gigedo, *Instrucción Reservada*, p.38. Calle de las Escalerillas, Mexico, 1831.

171 — All others asked to be excused. . . .

172 — Unless the necessary authority for these kingdoms is given to the viceroy so that he may force compliance with the necessary dispositions and issue those that are advisable, little profit will be obtained from the public wealth, and few public works of importance will be carried out.

The *Cajas Reales*, proposed by Count Revilla Gigedo and approved by His Majesty in 1792, were as follows:

878. I proposed three different classes . . . considering in the first class those of Mexico and Veracruz . . . in the second, those of Puebla, Guadalajara, Valladolid, San Luis Potosí, Durango, Zacatecas, Oaxaca and Mérida de Yucatán . . .

879. For the third class I proposed those of Bolaños, Zimapán, Pachuca, Acapulco, Chihuahua, el Rosario, Campeche, the disbursement office [pagaduría] of Arizpe, and the *caja* of Cardonál. . . .

880. Subsequently, the disbursement office of Saltillo was established. . . .

The Marks of the Mints from 1822 to 1853

The marks of the Mints, other than Mexico City, from 1822 to 1853, were as follows:[10]

YEARS	MINT	MARK
1824-53	Guanajuato	G with an o in the body of the letter
1824-53	Zacatecas	Z^s
1824-53	Guadalajara	G^a
1844-50	Guadalupe y Calvo	G C
1824-53	Durango	D^o
1832-53	Chihuahua	C^a
1846-53	Culiacán	C^n
1827-53	San Luis Potosí	$P^I.$

The Law of the 4th September 1839 ordered the establishment of Assay Offices at all points where considered necessary:

1. The government shall establish assay offices at all points where they are considered necessary; the report of the governors and departmental boards and the chief assayer should make recommendations as to the necessity for establishing [assay offices], as well as to the fixing of salaries of the employees, and the amount of the bonds. . . .

10 *Diccionario Universal de Historia y Geografía*, pp.391-956. F.Escalante y Cía., Mexico, 1854.

7. Ordinances, 9, 25, and 26 for silversmiths, on hall-marks and punches [dies], shall remain in force. In regulating this law, the government shall determine the manner of making inspections of the shops of silversmiths, *tiradores* [drawers of gold and silver wire] and *bateojas* [beaters of gold and silver] throughout the Republic, after hearing the chief assayer. . . .

And for due compliance with the preceding decree, by virtue of the provisions of Art.6 hereof, his Excellency the president of the Republic has ordered, after hearing the chief assayer and in agreement with the government council, that the following provisions be observed. . . .

Fourth. In order to collect the cost of smelting and assaying of the metals, in accordance with the provisions of Art.9 of the decree of the government board of 22nd November 1821, the assayers shall make every year a statement of the separate expenses of these operations. This statement shall serve as a guide for the offices [charged with collecting the 3 per cent tax and with supplying the expenses of the assay offices], in collecting the expenses of these operations. . . .

Eighth. . . . those [assayers] in outside [assay] offices, shall name two experts, or where there are none, two honest citizens to cooperate with them and shall inspect the silversmiths, *tiradores* [drawers of gold and silver wire] and *bateojas* [beaters of gold and silver], in order to verify whether the silver and gold being employed and which shall be weighed at once together with all that has not been hall-marked is found to agree with the assay certificates in his possession, and which shall be compared with the entries in the books which the assayers shall carry with them. The assayers shall also take from the metals being worked a small sample which, from the silver, shall not exceed in value one-eighth of a *real* and, from the gold, two-thirds of a *tomine*. On each piece the artificer shall stamp his mark, in order that once the assay has been made the metal may be returned to him if the metal is of the required standard: if it is not, in order that the responsible parties may be prosecuted in accordance with the provisions in force. Authenticity of the marks found on gold and silver shall also be examined, and if there should be pieces that have been adulterated . . .

Tenth. Those silversmiths, drawers of gold or silver wire, and beaters of gold and silver who have shops, or those who in the future may open shops, shall notify the chief assay office in this capital, and outside [of the capital] the corresponding assay offices, in order that they take due note for compliance with the ordinances.[11]

11 *Colección de Leyes y Decretos Publicados en el año de* 1839, pp.196-201. Printed at the Palace, Mexico, 1851.

B. *Hall-marks — Provinces of Guatemala-Chiapas*

Until 1823 what is now the State of Chiapas[12] was a province of Guatemala. For our purpose, therefore, they will be considered as a unit. Of the plate examined, unquestionably from these provinces, but few pieces are hall-marked. It is, however, easily distinguished from the plate of Mexico City, because of its marked indigenous influence and naïveté which makes it comparable to the plate of ancient Peru. Most of it was probably made by Indian silversmiths working under the supervision of Spaniards. *Plates* 1, 2 and 3 show plate made in Guatemala, and in *Plate* 4 is shown a delightful old bowl from Peru. The hall-mark shown in *Plate* 1 is that of Guatemala, according to don Manuel Romero de Terreros y Vinent, Marquis of San Francisco in *Las Artes Industriales in la Nueva España*.[13]

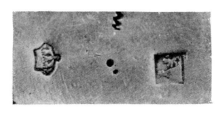

Hall-marks—Guatemala-Chiapas

C. *Hall-marks — San Luis Potosí*

The hall-mark of San Luis Potosí, shown below, is the mark of the Mint of San Luis Potosí, which was established 1st October 1827 and closed in 1853. Inspired by Tolsá, the plate of San Luis Potosí has a charming delicacy and a sophistication surprising in provincial work of that period. Examples are shown in *Plates* 7 and 8.

12 The discussion with reference to Chiapas, Session of the Constituent Congress of 10th July 1922, found in *Actas del Congreso Constituyente Mexicano*, vol.II, p.229, Alejandro Valdés, Mexico, 1922, is of interest. Excerpt reads: 'The Ancient kingdom of Goatemala, disorganized and dissolved, as stated before, made it possible for those provinces to express their wishes with entire liberty; therefore, the insurrection of the majority seeking annexation to the Mexican Empire could not have been more popular and widespread. The Province of Chiapas has indisputably declared its firm desire to be joined to the Mexican Empire, this wish having been accepted and proclaimed by the administrative board [*junta gubernativa*]. . . .'

13 Librería de Pedro Robredo, Mexico, 1923.

The marks[14] shown on these pieces are:

Actual Size   *Enlarged*

Actual Size

Enlarged

D. *The Plate of Puebla*[15]

As an Assay Office was never established in Puebla, the plate made there was stamped in Mexico City and it can be distinguished from that of Mexico City only by the marks of the silversmiths.

E. *The Silver of the Other Provinces*

Plate was made in Pachuca, Zacatecas and Guadalajara, and no doubt in all the provinces. It is probable that the hall-marks used after 1822 were those of the mints.

Cajas Reales

As many of the documents translated here refer to *Cajas Reales* it is advisable to explain what the latter were. The most detailed explanation is found in the *Recopilación de Leyes de las Indias*.[16]

14 Information on this mark was given to me by don Manuel Romero de Terreros, Marquis of San Francisco.

15 The construction of the City of Puebla de los Angeles of the then province of Tlaxcala, destined to be the second City in Mexico with respect to plate, began in 1530. R.P.Fr.Toribio de Benavente, o, Motolinía, *Historia de los Indios de la Nueva España*, p.237. Heirs of Juan Gili, Barcelona, 1914. The first church was constructed in 1531. [*Diccionario Universal de Historia y de Geografía*, F.Escalante y Cía., Mexico, 1854].

16 *Recopilación de Leyes de los Reinos de las Indias*, vol.II, book 4, tit.6. *Cajas Reales*. Boix, Madrid, 1841. 2 vols. divided into 4 books.

2nd LAW—That strong boxes be manufactured and the keys be distributed—Philip II, Ordinance 4 of the year 1579.

There being no strong boxes in the province for the payment of our royal revenue and all the treasure belonging to us or which may accrue to us, you will instruct our Officers to order the manufacture of a strong box (or two, if another were necessary), of a large size, of good quality lumber, heavy, thick, stout, and with the sides, corners and bottoms fastened with irons in order that our Royal Treasury be well protected. In the presence of the Governor or Chief Justice, Officers and Scrivener, who shall attest, the boxes shall be equipped with three locks with keys, of which one [key] will be held by the Treasurer, the second by the Reckoner and the third by the Factor wherever there is one. The box or boxes are to be placed and kept always in a strong and safe place, where our Royal Treasury may not be endangered.

3rd LAW—That the *Cajas Reales* be made and placed in accordance with this law.

Upon the installation of the *Cajas Reales* of our Royal Treasury, the Governor or Chief Justice shall have them opened in his and the Scrivener's presence and there shall be counted our Royal dies and the punches therein contained which are used to stamp and mark the gold and silver brought for hall-marking and for the payment of taxes. And after the counting, and after each punch is recorded, there shall be entered, counted and inventoried all the gold and silver, pearls and [precious] stones and all other things, therein contained in any way belonging to us. The number, weight, quality and value of the gold and silver, and the pearls and stones by weight, kind and lot of each shall be stated; and when all has been counted, weighed and inventoried, it shall again be placed in the box with three keys and the Treasurer shall take charge of all, entering first the entry in the general ledger of our Royal Treasury, which shall always be kept inside the box. After the entry has been made, and signed by all the said Officers, it shall be entered in each of the other private books which each Officer is to keep, as has been ordered.

4th LAW—That on the door of the room where the boxes are kept there be placed as many locks and keys as there are Officers.

That in the chamber and room where our boxes are kept, strong and safe doors be placed, with as many locks and keys as there are Officers, and that each one have his key, and when the gold and silver, stones and pearls are boxed for sending to these kingdoms, the boxes be placed in one room [which shall be] locked until the Officers dispatch them [to the king]. . . .

During the Colonial period the Mint in Mexico City, now the National Museum, was connected with the National Palace. The Ministers lived in the National Palace, and the Chief Assayer in the *casa del Real Ensaye* or Mint.

Disappearance of Plate

As in Spain, most of the old Mexican plate has disappeared.[17] Nearly all of the ecclesiastical plate of the seventeenth century and the first half of the eighteenth century, as mentioned in the inventories and descriptions of the times, was destroyed, either to make 'something better' or to replace stolen pieces indispensable in the service. Much of it was coined during the troublous times through which the country necessarily passed to gain its independence.

The disappearance of civil plate may be attributed to the excessive hardships suffered by its owners during the last century; pressing circumstances forced them to have it coined.

Acknowledgments

The cooperation given by the American Council of Learned Societies through its distinguished Committee on Research and Publication in the Fine Arts, which made possible the publication of this work, is gratefully acknowledged. It is a pleasure to record my thanks to Dr. Clarence H. Haring, professor of Latin American history, Harvard University; to Dr. George C. Vaillant of the American Museum of Natural History, New York City; to Dr. Leo S. Rowe, Director General of the Pan American Union, Washington, D.C.; to Dr. John C. Merriam, of the Carnegie Institute of Washington, D.C.; and to Lic. Luis Chico Goerne, Rector of the Universidad Nacional de Mexico, for their interest in and sympathetic estimate of this work.

Recognition of authors whose works have been freely utilized in the preparation of this book is duly made in the text. I am greatly indebted to friends who permitted reproductions of examples in their possession; to Don Federico Gómez de Orozco for the arduous task of the revision of the Spanish text, for the use of his library and many data; to Don Carlos Rincón Gallardo, Marqués de Guadalupe, for all of the material on the *Charro*; to Don Alberto María Carreño and to Father Jesús García Gutiérrez for their aid in the research conducted in the Mexican

17 Narciso Sentenach *Bosquejo Histórico sobre la Orfebrería Española*, pp.92, 93, 135 and 141. *Imp. de la Revista de Arch., Bibl. y Museos*, Madrid, 1909, and *Catálogo de la Exposición de Orfebrería Civil Española*, p.7, pub. by the *Sociedad Española de Amigos del Arte. Imp. Mateu, Artes e Industrias Gráficas*, Madrid, 1925.

National Archives; to Mr. E. R. Sutcliffe for the excellence of the photographs; to Mr. Severo Lopez, who, during my long absences, corrected the many proofs; to my late friend, Mr. William B. Stephens, to whom I owe lasting remembrance for his constant help and inspiration; and, finally, to my friend, Mr. J. S. Kunkle, who translated nearly all of the documents and helped me in many ways.

L.A.

Casa Alvarado,
    Coyoacán, D.F.
        1st September, 1936.

Chapter I

THE SILVERSMITHS' ART BEFORE THE CONQUEST

PART I

I. ORIGIN OF THE ART. 2. FIRST CONTACTS WITH THE SPANIARDS. 3. THE GIFT TO EMPEROR CHARLES V. 4. INVASION OF THE INTERIOR. 5. ENTRY OF THE SPANIARDS INTO MEXICO CITY. 6. DESCRIPTION OF THE CITY OF MEXICO. 7. THE INDIAN ORNAMENTS. 8. ADORNMENTS USED BY THE NOBLES IN WAR. 9. DISCOVERY OF MOCTEZUMA'S TREASURE. 10. VALUE OF THE TREASURE LOST ON THE NOCHE TRISTE.

1. *Origin of the Art*

THE AZTECS[1] attributed the origin of their silversmiths' art to the Toltecs,[2] their predecessors in the Valley of Mexico, and its development to Quetzalcoatl, the hero who later was made a god,[3] and whose principal temple was in Cholula.

We do not know when the Indian silversmiths attained the great skill that was theirs at the time of the Conquest; but from the descriptions of the objects of jade and gold recovered by Thompson[4] from the sacred well in Chichen-Itza, Yucatán, and from the jewels of Monte Albán discovered in 1932, now in the National Museum at Mexico City, we may safely conclude that they were accomplished masters of the art long before the Conquest.[5]

---

1 The Aztecs arrived at the Lake of Texcoco in A.D. 1325 and named their first king about A.D. 1376. Herbert I. Priestley, *The Mexican Nation*, New York, 1930, pp.22-3.

2 The Toltecs arrived in the Central Plateau at the end of the seventh century, Priestley, op.cit., p.18.

3 Marshall H. Saville, *The Goldsmith's Art in Ancient Mexico*, New York, 1920, p.117.

4 Edward Herbert Thompson, *People of the Serpent*, New York, 1932.

5 Ad.F.Bandelier, *On the Social Organization and Mode of Government of the Ancient Mexicans*, p.601, Salem Press, Salem, 1879, states that the Aztecs called gold 'teo-cuitlatl' and silver 'Iztac-teo-cuitlatl' and that the words are composed of 'Iztac,' white object, 'Teotl,' god, and 'Cuitlatl,' filth; therefore gold was 'offal of God,' and silver, 'white offal of God.'

2. *First Contacts with the Spaniards*

The expedition of Francisco Hernández de Córdoba[6] in 1517 discovered the coasts of Yucatán, the first land sighted by the Spaniards of what is now Mexico. Having defeated the Indians of Catoche, Yucatán, in the first battle, they examined the temples of the idols, of which Bernal Díaz relates:[7]

A little further on, where we had the affray of which I have spoken, there was a small square and three stone houses, which were temples of the idols, where there were many clay idols, some with faces like demons and others with the faces of women, with tall bodies, and others with very evil figures . . . and inside the houses they had some small chests made of wood, and inside them other evil idols and some medals, and some pendants and three diadems, and other small pieces in the shape of fishes and others in the shape of ducks, all of low-grade gold. And after we had seen this, the gold as well as the stone houses, we were very pleased to have discovered such a land, because at that time Peru had not been discovered, nor was it discovered until sixteen years later.

Grijalva — April 1518

After touching several points along the coast and suffering greatly in battles with the Indians, the expedition hastened its return to Cuba. Almost upon arrival Captain Francisco Hernández de Córdoba, seriously wounded, died[8] as a consequence of the wounds received in battles with the Indians. The gold brought by the expedition aroused the cupidity of Diego Velázquez, Governor of Cuba, who hastened to organize another armada,[9] naming as Captain his relative Juan de Grijalva. This second armada of four ships left Cuba on the 8th April 1518. They first touched the island of Cozumel, then various points along the coast, until they arrived at the mouth of the Tabasco River, where the Indians gave them some gold. Bernal Díaz says:[10]

6 Córdoba's expedition, the purpose of which was barter, consisted of three vessels and 110 soldiers. It left Havana, Cuba, on the 8th February 1517. Bernal Díaz, *Historia Verdadera de la Conquista de la Nueva España*, vol.II, p.2. *Biblioteca de Autores Españoles*, Madrid, 1858.

7 Díaz, op.cit., p.3.

8 Ibid., p.5: of the crew of the armada only one was not wounded, 57 Spaniards having perished in a single battle.

9 Ibid., p.8.

10 Ibid., p.10.

And then they placed on the floor some mats, which here are called *petates*, and on top a cloth, and they presented to us certain jewels of gold which were like ducks such as those of Castille, and other jewels resembling lizards, and three necklaces of cast beads, and other things of gold of little value, which were not worth more than two hundred *pesos*.

Beyond the coast, in the river which they named Banderas,[11] they were more fortunate, obtaining 'more[12] than fifteen thousand *pesos* in small jewels of low-grade gold of varied workmanship.'
Near the Tonalá River they found some gold:[13]

I also remember that a soldier, who called himself Bartolomé Pardo, went to a house of the idols on a high hill, I have said these were called *cues*—the house of their gods one might say. In that house he found many idols, and *copal*, like incense, and flint knives which they used for sacrifices and circumcision. Also there were wooden chests, and inside them many diadems and necklaces of gold, and two idols, and things like beads. The soldier took the gold for himself, and brought the idols to the captain. Someone saw him and told Grijalva, who wanted to take the gold from him; but we begged him, after taking His Majesty's part, to give the remainder to the poor soldier; and it was not worth eighty *pesos*.

After the Spaniards sailed from the small barren island which they named San Juan de Ulúa,[14] in front of what is now the port of Veracruz, the Indian governors took to Emperor Moctezuma a personal description, including paintings of men, ships and cannon, all so strange to them. Moctezuma consulted his court and soothsayers, and all agreed that this mysterious visitor could be no other than Quetzalcoatl, God of the Air, whom they had awaited for many years. They sent ambassadors with rich presents, but the ambassadors did not reach Grijalva.[15]

This expedition sailed along the coast to the Pánuco River, whence Grijalva, faithfully following his instructions, sailed for Cuba, although the soldiers wished to establish a colony.
Bernal Díaz estimated the total value of the gold brought by Gri-

11 Because of the banners of the *caciques* (chiefs) of the land. Ibid., p.11.
12 Ibid., p.12.
13 Ibid., pp.13-14.
14 Francisco J. Clavijero, *Historia Antigua de México y su Conquista*, Mexico, 1883, vol.II, p.6, says: '*Ulúa* was what the Spaniards understood for *Colhua* [Mexico].'
15 Ibid., vol.II, p.7.

jalva's expedition at $24,000 *pesos*,[16] of which His Majesty's fiscal agents took the Royal share.

Greatly impressed, Governor Velázquez immediately decided to send another armada. Grijalva, however, was discredited through the intrigue of Alonso de Avila and Francisco de Montejo, aided by the connivance of Andrés de Duero[17] [the Governor's Secretary], and Amador de Larez, His Majesty's purser. As a result, Velázquez accepted the nomination of Hernán Cortés for the post of Captain General of the new armada. Soon regretting his choice, he attempted to imprison Cortés and put Vasco Porcallo in his place. However, Cortés eluded him and sailed from Cuba for Yucatán on the 18th February 1519, with his armada of eleven vessels and 580 soldiers, ships' masters, pilots and seamen to the number of 109 men, together with 200 Indian servants of both sexes. In Cozumel Cortés had the great good fortune to rescue Jerónimo de Aguilar,[18] shipwrecked seven years previously, who because of his long sojourn in Yucatán was acquainted with the Mayan language. When the expedition reached the Grijalva River, the *Cacique* of Tabasco presented Cortés with twenty women, including the famous Malintzin, doña Marina, a Mexican Indian who also spoke the Mayan tongue, and who soon learned to speak Spanish.

Through these two faithful interpreters Cortés was able to communicate directly with the Indians, an advantage possessed by neither Córdoba nor Grijalva.

Cortés obtained little gold in Tabasco, and soon resumed his voyage. Following the coast to the north, he arrived in San Juan de Ulúa on the 21st April 1519.

Upon his arrival, the Indian *Cacique* of the coast sent two canoes with warriors to learn the purpose of his visit and to offer their services.[19] Through his interpreters, Marina and Aguilar, Cortés told the *Cacique* that he had come only to barter and discuss matters of importance with their King. Upon disembarking, two *Caciques* of the coast, Teuchtile and Cuitlalpitoc, vassals of Moctezuma, arrived with a large following of soldiers and servants. After an exchange of courte-

16 Díaz, op.cit., p.14.
17 Ibid., p.16.
18 An ecclesiastic, one of two survivors of a ship sunk while en route from Darien to the Island of Santo Domingo.
19 The Mexicans by this time knew that the Spaniards were not gods. Clavijero, op.cit., vol.II, p.12.

sies, Cortés spoke of the greatness and power of his King, who had
sent him to speak with Moctezuma of very important matters.

Gifts were exchanged; and Teuchtile, carrying paintings of the
Spaniards, their arms, and their strange horses, left to report to Moctezuma. The latter, after consulting his gods through the priests, was
advised not to allow the visitors to enter the capital. To soften his
refusal, he sent an ambassador to Cortés, presenting him with a gift
of many gold and silver objects, and telling him that a more valuable
gift would be sent for the King. Cortés, greatly pleased, reciprocated
to the best of his ability, but far from desisting from his purpose, he
told the ambassadors of the long voyage he had made to see Moctezuma, and of the certain displeasure of his King should he learn that
this had not been possible. He added that the character of the Spaniards
was such that they were discouraged neither by danger nor by the
fatigue of journeys. Shortly thereafter, Teuchtile left, promising to
advise Moctezuma of what Cortés said with regard to the refusal to
allow his party to enter Mexico and to return with Moctezuma's
answer. At the time another ambassador from Moctezuma, chosen
because of his resemblance to Cortés, delivered to him the promised
gift for the Catholic King. The naïve Aztec King thought that this
great treasure would satisfy the cupidity of the Spaniards, and that
they would gladly take their leave, never to return.[20]

The facile acquisition of such a treasure was not the sort of thing to
induce Cortés to desist from his invasion of the interior. After pacifying
the discontented followers of Velázquez, who desired to return to Cuba,
he elected himself Captain General and Chief Justice of this new land.
These acts he legalized with the foundation of a town which he named
Villa Rica de la Vera Cruz, where he installed a municipal government,
with a mayor, aldermen and constables.

He then marched to Cempoala where, profiting by the discontent
among the Totonacos who suffered under the rule of Moctezuma, he
persuaded them to revolt openly and become vassals of Charles V, and,
at the same time, represented himself to Moctezuma as a friend who
had rescued his collectors of tribute from harm at the hands of the
Totonacos.

20 Díaz, op.cit., pp.33-5, and Clavijero, op.cit., pp.14-16.

He forthwith put the Totonacos to work assisting the Spaniards in the construction of a fortress.[21]

His religious zeal, bordering on fanaticism, tolerated no delay. No sooner had he obtained the allegiance of a few of the Totanaco villages than he began to destroy their idols. Only the abject fear in which the Indians held the Spaniards prevented an armed clash, which might have terminated disastrously for the *Conquistadores*. And still more incredible; under his direction, these same Indians built an altar and decorated it with flowers.

His open defiance of Velázquez, who, he felt certain, would immediately endeavor to regain control of the expedition and imprison him for his disloyal acts, doubtless influenced Cortés to seek the protection of His Majesty.

As a first step towards this end, and despite the protests of his soldiers, and particularly those of the group loyal to Velázquez, Cortés sent all the treasure obtained up to that time to Charles V through His Majesty's fiscal agents, Alonso Hernández Puerto-Carrero and Francisco de Montejo. The ship sailed on the 16th July 1519.[22]

Touching Cuba, en route to Seville, Montejo, who bore a grudge against Cortés, communicated with Velázquez and the latter attempted to seize the ship. Failing, he began the organization of another armada to capture and punish Cortés.

Bernal Díaz did not remember details of this treasure because 'it was so long ago.' Fortunately an inventory[23] exists:

3. *The Gift to Emperor Charles V*

Report of the jewels, shields, and clothing sent to the Emperor Charles the Fifth by don Fernando Cortés and the Municipal Council of Veracruz with their proctors Francisco de Montejo and Alonso Hernández Portocarrero.

21 Regarding the site of Veracruz, Clavijero, op.cit., vol.II, p.20, says: 'Almost all historians are mistaken with regard to the founding of Veracruz, for when they say that the first colony of the Spaniards was the old one, founded on the banks of the river bearing the same name, they believe that there have been but two cities with the name of Veracruz, that is, the old and the new, built on the sandy ground where Cortés landed. But there is no doubt that there have been three cities bearing the same name: the first founded in 1519, near the port of Quiahuitztla, which later kept its name of Villa Rica; the second, the old Veracruz, founded in 1523 or 1524; and the third, the new Veracruz, which retains this second name, and which was founded by order of the Count of Monterrey, Viceroy of Mexico, at the end of the sixteenth century, and received from Philip III the title of city in 1615.'

22 Clavijero, op.cit., vol.II, p.23.

23 Ibid., vol.II, p.335.
    Also found in Lucas Alamán, *Obras de*, Mexico, 1899, vol.IV, pp.96-105. The translation is from Saville, op.cit.

The contents of this report are of the greatest interest, because they show the state of the fine arts of the Mexicans before they had any contact with the Europeans. D.Juan Muñoz compared, on March 30 1784, the following report of the presents sent from New Spain, with another which he found in the book called *Manual del Tesorero de la casa de la contratación* of Seville, and from this latter manuscript are the discrepancies which follow. [Given here as footnotes].

The gold and jewels and stones and feather-work (a) which they had in these newly discovered places (b), after we arrived here, which you, Alonso Fernandez Portocarrero and Francisco de Montejo, who go as custodians of this rich town of Veracruz, carry to the very high and very excellent princes and very Catholic and very great kings and lords, the Queen Doña Juana and Don Carlos her son, our lords, are the following:

First, a large circular piece with figures of monsters on it (c), and all worked with gold foliage, weighing three thousand eight *pesos* of gold; and in this wheel because it was the best piece which has been found here (d), and of the best gold, they took the fifth part for their highnesses, that was (e) two thousand *castellanos* that pertained (f) to their fifth and royal right according to the stipulations that captain Fernando Cortés carried from the fathers of San Jerónimo who resided on the island of Española, and on others; and all that goes to make up one thousand eight hundred *pesos*, the council of this town place at the service of their highnesses, with all the rest which is contained in this report, which belonged to those of said town. (a)

Item: two collars (b) of gold and stones, one of which (c) has eight strings, and in them two hundred and thirty-two red stones, and one hundred and sixty-three green stones; and hanging from the said collar (d) and from the border twenty-seven gold bells, and in the center of them there are four figures of large stones set (e) in gold, and from each of the two in the center (f) hang simple pendants, (g) and of those at the ends (h) each has four double pendants (i). And the other collar has (j) four strings that have one hundred and two red stones and one hundred and seventy-two stones that appear to have a green color, and around said stones twenty-six gold

(a) And feathers and silver that they found in these places, etc.
(b) Newly discovered by captain Fernando Cortés, sent from the rich town of Veracruz, with Alonso Fernandez Portocarrero and Francisco de Montejo for Their Catholic Majesties, and that were received in this *casa de la contrata-* *ción*[24] saturday, 5th November 1519, are the following.
(c) With a figure of (a) monster in the center.
(d) Which here had been had.
(e) Were
(f) Which belonged to them.

(a) Which belongs to them.
(b) Another item: two large collars.
(c) That the one of them.
(d) And hang from the said collar.
(e) Inlaid.
(f) And in the center of the one.
(g) Hang seven pendants.
(h) And in the ends of the two.
(i) Pendants.
(j) And one of them.

24 Tribunal for regulating trade and commerce in the Indies.

bells, and in the said collar ten large stones set in gold, from which hang one hundred and forty-two pendants (k) of gold.

Item: Four pairs of *antiparras* [leggings], two pairs being of yellow deerskin with a trimming of delicate gold leaf, and the other two [pairs], of white deerskin (l) with a trimming of thin silver leaf, and the others of red deerskin trimmed with feather-work (m) of different colors, and very well made, from each of which hang sixteen gold bells.

Another item: a hundred *pesos* of gold ore, so that their highnesses (a) might see how they get gold here from the mines.

Another item: a box (b) of a large piece of feather-work lined with leather, the colors seeming like martens, and fastened and placed in the said piece, and in the center (is) a large disc of gold (c), which weighed sixty *pesos* of gold, and a piece of blue stone mosaic-work a little reddish (d), and at the end of the piece another piece of colored feather-work that hangs from it (e).

Item: (f) a fly whisk of colored feather-work with thirty-seven small rods (g) covered with gold.

Another item: a large piece of colored feather-work which is to be worn (h) on the head, which is surrounded by (i) sixty-eight (j) small pieces of gold, each (k) of which is as large as a half copper coin, and below them are twenty little turrets of gold. (l)

Item: a mitre (m) of blue stone mosaic-work with the figure of monsters (n) in the center, and lined with leather which seems in its colors to be that of martens, with a small (piece) of feather-work which is, as the one mentioned above, of this said mitre. (o)

Item: four spears of feather-work (p) with their points of flint fastened with a gold thread, and a center of stone mosaic-work with two rings of gold, and the rest of feather-work.

Item: (a) an armlet of stone mosaic-work, and furthermore, a piece of small black feather-work (b) with other colors.

(k) Pendants.
(l) Of white deer [skin] the trimming (of silver).

(m) And the rest of feather-work.

(a) Their Royal Highnesses.
(b) In a box.
(c) Of large gold.
(d) And a little reddish, like a wheel, and another piece of blue stone mosaic-work a little red-dish.
(e) That hang from it of colors.
(f) Another item.
(g) Rods.
(h) Which put.

(i) And surrounding it.
(j) Sixty-eight.
(k) That each may be as large.
(l) And below them twenty little turrets of gold.
(m) A mitre.
(n) Monster.
(o) Which, and the one above which is mentioned are of this said mitre.
(p) Four spears of feather-work.

(a) Another item.

(b) Of feathers.

Item: a pair of large sandals of colored leather (c) that appears like martens, the soles white, sewed with threads of gold. (d)

Furthermore: a mirror placed in a piece of blue and red stone mosaic-work with feather-work stuck (e) to it, and two strips of red leather stuck (f) to it, and another skin that seems (g) like those martens.

Item: (h) three colored (pieces) of feather-work which are (pertain to) a large gold head like a crocodile.

Item: some leggings of blue (i) stone mosaic-work, lined with leather, of which the colors seem (j) like martens; on each (k) of them (there are) fifteen gold bells.

Item: (l) a *maniple* (standard) of wolf-skin, with four strips of skin like martens.

Furthermore: some fibers (m) placed in (the quills of) colored feathers, and the said fibers are white, and appear (n) like locks of hair.

Item: (o) two colored (pieces of) feather-work which are for two (pieces of) head armor (p) of stone mosaic-work, which is mentioned further on.

Also, two other (pieces of) colored feather-work which are for two pieces of gold which they wear (a) on the head, made like (b) great shells.

Also, two birds of green feathers with their feet, beaks, and eyes (made) of gold, which are put in a piece of one of those shell-like pieces of gold. (c)

Also, two *guariques* (ear ornaments) of blue stone mosaic-work (d) which are to be put in the big head of the crocodile.

In another square box a head of a large crocodile of gold, which is the one spoken of above, where the said pieces (e) are placed.

Also, another head-dress (f) of blue stone mosaic-work with (g) twenty gold bells which hang pendent at the border, with two strings (h) of beads which are above (i) each bell, and two *guariques* of wood with two plates of gold. Also a bird of green feathers and the feet, beak and eyes of gold.

Item: another head-dress (k) of blue stone mosaic-work with twenty-five gold bells, and two beads of gold above each bell, that hang around it with some (l) *guariques* of wood with plates of gold, and a bird of green plumage with the feet, beak, and eyes of gold.

(c) Item: a pair of shoes of a skin which in its colors looks like, etc.
(d) Some small *tiritas* (bands) of gold.
(e) Stuck.
(f) Stuck.
(g) Which appear.
(h) Another item.
(i) Furthermore, some leggings of blue stone-mosaic.

(j) Appear.
(k) With each.
(l) Another item.
(m) Furthermore in some *barbas* (fibers).
(n) And appear.
(o) Another item.
(p) *Capacetes* (head armor).

(a) Which are worn.
(b) Like.
(c) This part is lacking in the Sevillian manuscript.
(d) Of blue stone.
(e) For which are the pieces.
(f) *Capacete* (head-dress).

(g) In.
(h) With two beads.
(i) Which are in *canada* (pendant).
(j) Furthermore: a female bird.
(k) *Capacete* (head-dress).
(l) Some.

Item: in a reed basket, two large pieces of gold which they put on the head, which are made like a gold shell with their *guariques* of wood and plates of gold, and besides, two birds of green plumage, with their feet, beaks, and eyes of gold. (a)

Moreover: sixteen shields of stone-mosaic-work, with their colored feather-work hanging from the edge of them, (b) and a wide-angled slab with stone mosaic-work with its colored feather-work, and in the center of said slab, made of the said stone mosaic-work, a cross of a wheel (c) which is lined with leather, which has the color of martens.

Again, a scepter of red stone mosaic-work, made like (d) a snake, with its head, teeth, and eyes from what appears to be mother-of-pearl, and the hilt is adorned with the skin (e) of a spotted animal, and below the said hilt hang six small pieces of feather-work.

Another item: a fan (f) of feather-work, placed on a reed adorned with the skin of a spotted animal, after the manner of a weather-cock, and above it has a crown of feather-work, and finally (g) has all over it long green feathers.

Item: two birds made (h) of thread and feather-work, having the quills of their wings, tails, and the claws of their feet, and the eyes and the ends of the beaks made of gold, (i) placed on respective reeds, covered with gold, and below some feather down, one white, the other yellow (j), with certain gold embroidery between the feathers, and from each hang seven strands of feathers.

Item: four feet made (a) after the manner of skates (sea fish) placed on respective canes (b) covered with gold, having (c) the tails and the organs of respiration, and the eyes and mouths of gold; below (d) in the tails some green feather-work, and having toward the mouths of the said skates (e) respective crowns of colored feather-work, and on some of the white feathers are (hanging) (f) certain gold embroidery, and below hang (g) from each six strands of colored feather-work.

Item: a small copper rod (h) covered with a skin on which is placed (i) a piece of gold after the manner of feather-work, which above and below has certain colored feather-work.

Another item: five fans (j) of colored feather-work, four of them (k) have ten (l) small quills covered with gold, and the other has thirteen. (m)

(a) This part is lacking in the Seville manuscript.
(b) Around them.
(c) Of wheels.
(d) Like.
(e) With a skin.
(f) A fan.

(g) Which finally.
(h) Item: two ducks made.
(i) And they have the quills of the wings and the tails of gold and the claws of the feet and the eyes and the ends of the feet placed, etc.
(j) The one white and the other yellow.

(a) Item: three pieces made.
(b) Canes.
(c) And which have.
(d) And below.
(e) And toward the mouths of the said skates have, etc.
(f) Hang.

(g) And below the handle hang.
(h) *Vergueta* (rod)
(i) In a skin put.
(j) Item: four fans.
(k) Which three of them.
(l) And they have three each.
(m) And one has thirteen.

Item: four spears of white flint, (n) mounted on four rods of feather-work. (o)

Item: a large shield of feather-work covered on the back (p) with the skin of a spotted animal; in the center of the field of the said shield (is) a plate of gold with a figure, like those that the Indians make, with four other half plates of gold on the edge, which altogether form a cross.

Another item: a piece of feather-work (q) of divers colors, made like (r) a half chasuble, lined with the skin of a spotted animal, which the lords of these parts whom we have seen up to now, place (a) hanging from the neck, and over the chest they have thirteen pieces (b) of gold very well fitted (together).

Item: a piece of colored feather-work which the lords of this land are wont to put on their heads, (c) and from it hang two ear-ornaments (d) of stone mosaic-work with two bells and two beads of gold, and above a feather-work of wide green feathers, and below hang (e) some white, long hairs.

Also, four heads of animals: two seem to be wolves, and the other two tigers, (f) with some spotted skins, and from it hang (g) metal bells.

Item: two skins of spotted animals, mounted on some mantles of cotton (h), and the skins appear like those of the *gato cerval* (i) (wildcat).

Item: one reddish and brown skin of another animal and two other skins which seem to be of a deer. (j)

Item: four skins of small deer, of which they make here the small prepared gloves. (k)

Moreover, two books of those which the Indians have here.

Moreover, a half-dozen fans (l) of colored feather-work.

Moreover: a perfume censer of colored feathers, with certain embroidery on it. (m)

Again: (a) large circular piece of silver which weighed forty-eight *marcos* of silver; (a) moreover, some armlets and some beaten (silver) leaves, weighing a *marco* and five ounces, and four *adarmes* of silver. (b) And a large shield and another small one of silver which weighed four *marcos* and two ounces; and two other shields which appear to be of silver, weighing six *marcos*, two ounces. (c) And another

(n) *Pedrenal* (flint).
(o) Trimmed with feather-work.
(p) Trimmed on the back.

(q) Feather-work.
(r) Like.

(a) Which the lords of these parts, who until now were.
(b) And on the breast thirteen pieces.
(c) Like the helmet of one who plays at jousts.
(d) Ear ornaments.
(e) Hang from it.
(f) And the other two tigers.
(g) And from them
(h) Mantles of cotton.

(i) Which seems of *gato cerval* (wildcat).
(j) Of another animal, which seems to be a lion, and two other deerskins.
(k) Furthermore: four small tanned deerskins, and furthermore a half dozen (pieces) of stamped leather, which the Indians here make.
(l) Of fly whisks.
(m) This part is lacking in the Vienna manuscript.

(a) Which weighed by scale forty-eight *marcos* of silver.
(b) Furthermore: some armlets and some beaten

leaves, a *marco*, five ounces and four *adarmes*.
(c) Which weighed six *marcos* and two ounces of silver.

shield which appears to be also of silver, (d) weighing one *marco*, seven ounces: which (shields) altogether weigh sixty-two *marcos* of silver. (e)

Cotton Clothing (f)

Another item: two large pieces of cotton woven in patterns of white and black, (g) very rich.

Item: two pieces woven with feathers, (h) and another piece woven in various colors; (i) another piece woven in red, black, and white patterns, and on the back the patterns do not appear. (j)

Item: another piece woven with patterns, and in the center are some black wheels of feathers. (k)

Item: two white cotton cloths with some woven feather-work. (a)

Another cotton cloth with some colored cords attached to it. (b)

A loose garment of the men of the land.

A white (c) piece with a great disc of white feathers in the center.

Two pieces of grayish *guascasa* (d) with some circular pieces of feathers, and two others of tawny *guascasa*. (e)

Six painted pieces, (f) another red piece with some discs, and two other blue painted pieces, and two women's shirts.

Eleven sashes. (g)

Six shields, each having a plate of gold, that covers the shield, and a half miter of gold. (h)

Which things, each of them, as set forth by these chapters that declare and settle it, we, Alonso Fernandez Puertocarrero and Francisco de Montejo, the said custodians, certify it is true that we have received them, and they were delivered to us to carry to their highnesses, from thou, Fernando Cortés, Chief Justice for their highnesses in these parts, and from you, Alonso de Avila and Alonso de Grado, treasurer and *veedor* of their highnesses over here. And because it is true, we sign it with our names. Dated, the sixth of July of the year 1519. — Puerto Carrero. — Francisco de Montejo.

The things enumerated above in said memorial, with the aforesaid letter and report sent by the council of Vera Cruz, were received by our lord the King, Charles

(d) Which also seems of silver.

(e) This is lacking in the Sevillian manuscript, 'which are altogether sixty-two *marcos* of silver.'

(f) This title is lacking in the manuscript of Vienna.

(a) With some woven feather-work.

(b) Another mantle with some little colored pieces stuck on.

(c) Another piece.

(d) Two pieces of *guascasa*.

(e) *Guascasa.*

(g) Of white and black and tawny.

(h) Of feathers.

(i) And another woven piece in colored checkers.

(j) Another piece woven in black and white; on the back the patterns do not appear.

(k) Of feathers.

(f) Six painted pieces.

(g) This part is lacking in the manuscript of Vienna.

(h) Six shields, which each have a plate of gold covering all the shield. Item: a half miter of gold.

the Fifth, as has been beforesaid, in Valladolid during holy week, at the beginning of April, of the year of Our Lord, 1520. End of the inventory.

In place of the two preceding paragraphs which are not found in the manuscript of the *Manual del Tesorero de la casa de la contratación* of Seville, there is there the following:

All of those said things, as received, we send to His Majesty with Domingo de Ochandiano, by virtue of a letter which His Majesty commanded us to write, dated in Molins del Rey, the fifth of December of [year] one thousand five hundred and nineteen: and the said Domingo brought a decree of His Majesty, in which he commanded that the above mentioned things should be delivered to Luis Veret, keeper of His Majesty's jewels, and the receipt of said Luis Veret is in the keeping of said treasurer.

Don Juan Bautista Muños adds: It is stated in the same [*Manual del Tesorero*] that in fulfillment of the said decree, four Indians were richly dressed, two of them *caciques*, and two Indian girls, who were brought by Montejo and Puertocarrero, and sent to His Majesty in Tordecillas, where His Majesty was living. They left Seville, February 7, of the year 1520, and on the trip, and during their stay, and on the return, which was on the 22nd March they spent forty-five days. One of the Indians did not go to court, because he was taken sick in Córdoba, and returned to Seville. After coming from court, one died. The five remained in Seville very well taken care of until March 1521, the day on which they left on the ship of Ambrosio Sánchez for delivery to Diego Velázquez in Cuba, that he should do with them that which would be best for the service of His Majesty.

Notes by Mora

An explanation is here given of various words, in the foregoing report, which are no longer used. The *pujantes* or *pinjantes* that served to adorn the collars and other jewelry were pendants such as are now used in ear-drops and necklaces.

The *antiparras* or *antiparas* are described in this manner in the first dictionary of the Spanish language, published by the Academy in 1726, that gives the origin of the words and authorities in which the meaning is founded: 'certain kind of stockings reaching to the knees or leggings that cover the legs and the feet only, for the front part. . . .' The *patena* was a round adornment with some figures sculptured on it, that was worn hanging from the neck.

The *moscador* or *mosqueador* was a kind of feather fan, like those recently used by the women. It was used quite frequently among the ancient Mexicans, and there is hardly a painting of that time in which it is not found. They employed in making them the richest feathers and the handles were adorned with precious stones of which they had knowledge.

The *guariques*, I have not been able to discover what [this thing] was.

Caparetes were *capacetes*, a head-dress.

The *lizas* were an imitation of the fish of that name; placed in *sendas cimas*, that is, placed each on the extremity of a small rod. In this class of casting with divers metals, the mexican silversmiths were very skillful, like those here described, with the tails, and the sides of the heads of birds, the eyes and the mouths of gold, besides alternating the scales, some of gold and others of silver.

The *verjitas* were little rods of metal or other material like a cane or walking-stick, with some figure or feather worn in the end. They are frequently seen in the ancient Mexican paintings.

The prepared gloves are to be understood as tanned skin.

Their knowledge of weaving with a double woof is proof of the advancement they had made in the art of weaving, as evidenced by the pieces of cotton cloth with woven designs that do not appear on the reverse side.

The Indians who were taken to court, according to Bernal Díaz, were the four who were in Tabasco being fattened in 'bird cages' of wood, in preparation for sacrifice, and they were the first who were sent as examples of the inhabitants of the land.

Some of Velázquez' men planned to escape to Cuba in one of the ships.[25] Through a traitor among them, Cortés learned of the plan; some of the men were hanged; others mutilated.[26]

Cortés realized that while they had ships, it would be difficult, if not impossible, to control the many discontented members of the expedition, and prevent their deserting such a daring venture. As the only means of ending this constant danger once and for all, and at the same time strengthening the spirit of his men for the dangerous expedition to the interior by giving them the simple choice between victory and death, he resorted to what was perhaps one of the most daring acts in history: he sank his ships.

Cortés left a small garrison of the older soldiers and a few seamen in Veracruz, under the command of Juan de Escalante, and began his famous march to Mexico[27] on the 16th August 1519,[28] taking with him around 450 men, some small cannon, fifteen horses, and 1300 Totonaco Indians.

25 Under the command of the pilot Gonzalo de Umbría, perhaps an Italian, whom Cortés punished for his participation in the plot by having his toes cut off.
26 Clavijero, op.cit., vol.II, p.23. Díaz, op.cit., p.51. Priestley, op.cit., p.39.
27 Díaz, op.cit., pp.37-52.
28 Priestley, op.cit., p.39.

4. *Invasion of the Interior*

26TH SEPTEMBER 1519: SUBJECTION OF THE TLAXCALTECAS.

Following the advice of the Totonacos, the expedition took the road that led through the country of the Tlaxcaltecas,[29] mortal enemies of the Aztecs. After several important battles with the Tlaxcaltecas, all of which the Spaniards won, the former became vassals of the Catholic King and the faithful allies of the Spaniards.

Advancing toward Mexico City, the Tenochtitlán of the Aztecs, the Spaniards arrived in Cholula, an important sacred city allied with Moctezuma. Apparently they were well received, but the Cholultecas, knowing that Moctezuma did not want the Spaniards to enter Mexico, secretly[30] planned their destruction. Marina, ever faithful and vigilant, discovered the plot and revealed it to Cortés. With customary promptness, Cortés, after explaining his motives, killed thousands of Cholultecas. Historians universally condemn him for this massacre, but they omit mention of the only alternative—the loss of his life and those of his companions. The remaining Cholultecas promptly submitted to the Crown of Spain.

1ST NOVEMBER 1519

The Spaniards left Cholula for Tenochtitlán (Mexico City) on the 1st November 1519. Passing through the City of Texcoco, they spent the night in the City of Iztapalapan, in the gorgeous palace of Cuitlahuatzin, an enormous stone building surrounded by beautiful gardens. Next day they entered Tenochtitlán (Mexico City) over the great causeway which joined Iztapalapan with Tenochtitlán, 'paved, seven miles in length, built many years ago.'

5. *Entry of the Spaniards into Mexico City*[31]

8TH NOVEMBER 1519

Shortly before arriving in the city, Cortés was advised that the King of Mexico was

29 Cortés saw some silver and received gifts in Tlaxcala. Hernán Cortés, *Cartas de Relación de la Conquista de México*, Madrid, 1932, vol.I, p.56. Here Cortés did not forget his duty to convert the idolaters and wished to destroy their idols at once. However, Father Olmedo and other advisers dissuaded him. Clavijero, op.cit., vol.II, p.35.
30 Díaz, op.cit., p.74 and Clavijero, op.cit., vol.II, pp.39-40.
31 Clavijero, op.cit., vol.II, pp.46-48.

coming to receive him, and soon he appeared with a numerous and brilliant court. He was preceded by three nobles who carried in their hands staffs of gold, insignias of His Majesty, with which the presence of the sovereign was announced to the public. Moctezuma was richly dressed, and [travelled] on a litter covered with gold plates, carried on the shoulders of four nobles and under a parasol of green feathers, sprinkled with jewels. From his shoulders hung a blue cloak adorned with very rich jewels; on his head was a light gold crown, and on his feet were sandals, also of gold, tied with red leather thongs, and covered with precious stones. He was accompanied by two hundred lords, better dressed than the other nobles; but all barefooted, [walking] two by two, very close to the walls on either side of the street, to show their respect for the monarch. When the King and the Spanish general were face to face, they dismounted, the King from his litter and Cortés from his horse, and Moctezuma came to meet him leaning on the arms of the King of Texcoco and the lord of Iztapalapan. After bowing deeply, Cortés came near the King and placed around his neck a gold cord with glass beads, and the King bowed his head to receive it; but when Cortés wanted to embrace him, the two lords on whom the King leaned prevented it. The general stated, in a brief address, appropriate to the occasion, his affection, his veneration and his pleasure in knowing so great and powerful a King. Moctezuma replied in a few words, and after the usual ceremony, reciprocated the gift of the glass beads with two collars of beautiful mother-of-pearl, from which hung some large crabs of gold. He requested Prince Cuitlahuatzin to lead Cortés to his lodgings, and returned to his palace with the King of Texcoco.

The Spaniards were comfortably lodged in the large palace which had belonged to King Axayacatl, father of the Emperor Moctezuma.

6. *Description of the City of Mexico*[32]

The City of Mexico was then situated on a small island in lake Texcoco, fifteen miles to the west of the capital of Texcoco and four miles east of Tlacopan. The island was communicated with the mainland by three great causeways of earth and stone, constructed especially for this purpose across the lake: the one from Iztapalapan, on the south, was seven miles in length; that from Tlacopan, to the west, had a length of approximately two miles, while the one from Tepeyacac, to the north, was three miles long. All of these causeways were of sufficient width to accommodate ten horsemen abreast.

In addition, there was another causeway, slightly narrower, for the aqueducts from Chapoltepec. The perimeter of the city, not including the suburbs, was more than eleven miles, and the number of houses sixty thousand, at the least. The city

32 Clavijero, op.cit., vol.II, pp.52, 53.

was divided into four sections and there were four main streets, corresponding to the four gates of the atrium of the main temple. The first section, called Tecpan, now San Pablo, embraced that part of the city between the two streets corresponding to the southern and eastern gates. The second, Moyotla, now known as San Juan, included that portion between the southern and western gates. The third, Tlaquechiuhcan, now Santa María, that part between the western and northern streets. The fourth, Atzacualco, now San Sebastián, that between the northern and eastern gates. To these four parts, into which the city was divided since its founding, was later added, by conquest of the king Axayacatl, a fifth part, the city of Tlatelolco, which together with the four sections of Tenochtitlán formed the capital of the Mexican Empire.

Surrounding the city were many dikes and flood-gates, for holding back the waters in time of flood, and between these such a great number of canals, that there was hardly a section of the city that one could not traverse by boat. These canals not only contributed to the beauty of the city but at the same time afforded means of transportation for all kinds of products and protected the inhabitants against the attacks of their enemies. The principal streets were broad and straight. Some of the other streets were canals; others paved with stone were dry, and many consisted of a canal between two dikes, which either served for the convenience of passengers and discharge of merchandise or were planted with trees and flowers.

In addition to the many temples and palaces, there were other palaces or fine houses, constructed by the feudal lords for their use at such times as they were obliged to reside at the court. All of the houses, with the exception of those of the poorer class, had flat roofs with parapets, and some battlements and towers, although smaller than those of the temples; thus the temples, streets and houses were additional means of defense for the inhabitants.

Besides the great and famous plaza of Tlatelolco, which was the principal market place, there were smaller markets distributed throughout the city where ordinary food supplies were sold. In different parts of the city were fountains and pools, especially in the vicinity of the temples, and many gardens planted with flowers, some on the ground level and others on the flat roofs of the houses. The many beautiful, glistening white buildings, the high towers of the temples scattered throughout the city and the gardens and flowers formed a beautiful picture, greatly admired by the Spaniards, especially when viewed from the upper atrium of the main temple, which not only dominated the city of the court but the great and beautiful cities along the banks of the lakes as well. They were no less astonished upon viewing the royal palaces, and the infinite variety of plants and animals raised there; but nothing left them so amazed as the great plaza where the market was held. All of the Spaniards mentioned this with extravagant words of praise, and some, who had travelled over nearly the whole of Europe, asserted, according to Bernal Díaz, that they had never seen in any part of the world such a multitude of traders, variety of merchandise and general order and discipline.

When the conquerors arrived at the Capital, the emporium of the silversmiths' art was in Atzcapotzalco, located one league[33] to the north-west of Tenochtitlán; of which Bernal Díaz[34] says '. . . let us begin with the lapidaries, silver and goldsmiths and makers of all kinds of castings; the great silversmiths in our Spain could learn much from them. There were many skilled workmen of this class in the town of Atzcapotzalco, distant one league from Mexico.'

7. *The Indian Ornaments*

The good Friar Bernardino de Sahagún,[35] who arrived in Mexico in 1529, has left us a detailed description of the ornaments worn by the Indians:

They also wore gold bracelets on their arms [still used], and gold ear coverings: [not now in use], and fastened to their wrists a heavy black cord, soaked in balsam, from which hung a heavy bead [*cuenta*] of *chalchivitl* or other precious stone. They also wore a chin piece of *chalchivitl* mounted in gold [no longer used]. Some of these were made of long crystals, enclosing blue feathers giving them the appearance of sapphires. Many other kinds of precious stones were also used for chin pieces. Others had their thick lips perforated and from them hung, as though protruding from the flesh, pieces of gold like half-moons. The great nobles also had their noses pierced and very fine turquoises, or other precious stones, were worn in the orifices on each side. Strings of precious stones were worn around the neck. From a necklace of gold hung a medal with a flat precious stone in the center, and fringes of pearls around its circumference. They wore bracelets of mosaic, made with turquoise, bordered with fine feathers and gold and with rich feathers and strips of gold protruding from them higher than the head.

Below the knee they used greaves of very thin gold and in the right hand, a slender baton of gold with rich feathers at its upper end.

They wore, for a headdress, a bird of gorgeous plumage, with the beak toward the front and the tail of long feathers hanging down the neck, with the wings extended, giving the appearance of horns.

They also carried in the hand, fans for driving off flies, called *quetzallicasoaztli*, with strips of gold among the plumes. On the left hand, they wore simple, narrow bracelets of turquoise; they also wore necklaces of gold beads with small shells of

33 2.631 miles or 4.23 kilometers.
34 Díaz, op.cit., p.88.
35 Bernardino de Sahagún, *Historia General de las Cosas de Nueva España*, published by Carlos Maria de Bustamante, Mexico, 1829-30, vol.II, pp.289-90.

sea snails between each two beads. They used necklaces of gold made in imitation
of the joints of snakes; the men, at the feasts and dances, carried flowers in the hand
together with a reed from which they drew smoke. For adjusting their finery, they
used a mirror, which, after a careful inspection, was given to a servant for safe
keeping.

They used sandals of tiger-skin, fastened at the heel; the soles were of many
thicknesses of deerskin, sewed and painted. They used small and large drums; the
large drum reached to a man's waist, with a covering similar to the Spanish drums.
The small drum was of hollow wood, of the diameter of a man's body, three or less
hand breadths in length and brightly painted. These two kinds of drums are still
in use. They also used gold timbrels, some in the form of a turtle shell; today similar
timbrels are still used, but of wood or of the natural shell of the turtle. They used
masks, made of mosaic, with false hair, as are still used, and a crest of golden
feathers, fastened to the mask.

8. *Adornments used by the Nobles in War*

The nobles used in war a headdress of bright red plumes, called *tlauhquecholconoao*;
around the headdress, a crown of rich feathers, in the middle of which was a tuft
of beautiful feathers, called *quetzal* and pendant from this plumage, toward the
back, a tiny gilt drum[36] in a little gilt case, used for carrying things.

They used a corselet of bright red feathers that reached half way to the knees,
dotted with snail shells of gold, and short skirts of rich feathers: they carried shields,
bordered with gold, the field of which was of beautiful feathers, red, green, blue,
etc.; from the lower half of the circumference were hung fringes of bright feathers
with fringes and tassels, [and] of plumes. They wore necklaces of very fine precious
stones, all round and of the same size, and which were *chalchivites* and fine turquoises:
they wore long plumes instead of hair, with bands of gold interposed, or a corselet
of green feathers, and on the shoulders, a drum, also green and carried in a *cacaxtli*.
Together with the drum, they used short skirts of fine feathers and gold, and strips
of the same metal, scattered over the corselet: they carried another kind of insignia
and arms called *ocelototec* which were made of tiger-skin with scattered strips of
gold, and the drum, carried on the back, was painted in imitation of tiger-skin; the
short skirts of the drums were of rich plumes, with flashes of gold at the outer edges.
Another kind of shield of bright plumes was called *xiuhtotol*, in the middle of which
was a square of gold. They also carried on their backs green feathers in the shape
of butterflies and used a jacket, made of green feathers called *tocivitl* because these
were from the parrot. These jackets reached to the knees and were dotted with
bright pieces of gold. They used another kind of shield made of rich feathers, with
a circular piece of gold in the center, on which was engraved a butterfly. The nobles

36 Ibid., vol.II, pp.293-7.

also used other shields decorated with green feathers called *quetzatl*, in the shape of small huts and around all the edges a fringe of rich plumes and gold. They used a shirt of yellow feathers, and in war the nobles used a gold helmet with two tufts of feathers, placed to resemble horns, and with this helmet they wore the jacket above mentioned. They also used another kind of silver helmet and also carried another kind of insignia of rich plumes and gold. They also used with this helmet a shirt, made of the same plumes as mentioned, and with bright pieces of gold. Along with these, the nobles also carried in war a kind of baton, made of *quetzatl*, interlaced with strips of gold and at the end of which was a bunch of *quetzatl* forming a tuft; another kind of baton was made of silver with a tuft of plumes at the end. They also carried other batons made of strips of gold, with tufts of feathers at the outer end. The nobles wore on their backs a kind of insignia called *itzpapalotl*: of fine feathers, resembling the figure of the devil, it had the wings and tail in the form of a butterfly and the eyes, nails, feet, eyebrows, and all the rest was of gold and on the head they placed two tufts of *quetzatl* which resembled horns. The nobles often wore another kind of insignia on their backs, called *xochicuetzalpapalotl* also made to resemble the image of the devil, as it had the face, hands, feet, eyes, nails and nose in that likeness. The wings and tail were of the same feathers above mentioned and the body was adorned with gold and fine green and blue feathers, with horns of beautiful feathers like those of the butterfly. Another insignia called *quetzalpacatztli* was also used with a jacket of green feathers, and a circular shield of the same material, decorated with a round gold plate in the center. The insignia called *tozquaxolotl* was made of feathers in the form of a small basket, in which was a small dog with long feathers on the head, with eyes and nails of gold, etc.; with this they wore a jacket of yellow feathers, decorated with bright pieces of gold. Another insignia resembled the one just mentioned, with the exception that the feathers were blue and with much more gold ornament, and the corresponding jacket was also of blue feathers. There were other insignia like those mentioned, both in white and red feathers. Other insignia used was called *cacatzontli*, of rich yellow feathers, with feathered jacket of the same color. They also used other insignia called *toztzitzimitl* of bright colored feathers and gold, and the *toztzitzimitl* was like a monster made of gold, placed in the center of the insignia. The *toztzitzimitl* had a tuft of rich feathers. They also used another insignia called *xoxouhquitzitzimitl*, a devil-like monster, of green feathers with gold, which had at the top of the head a tuft of green feathers. They also used another insignia called *iztactzitzimitl*, like the ones above mentioned but with white feathers. They also wore cowls called *cuzticcuextecatl* with tufts of feathers at the point and a gold medal fastened to the cowl with a cord, giving the appearance of a circlet; the corresponding jacket was of yellow feathers with rays of gold. They wore half-moons of gold pendant from the nose and golden ear coverings which hung to the shoulders, made in the form of corn cobs. Another insignia, similar to that just mentioned was called *iztaccuextecatl*, while still another, *chictlapanquiavextecatl* because both cowl and jacket were half green and half yellow. Similar insignia were called *cuzticteucuitlacopilli* because the entire cowl was of gold with a cup full of feathers at the upper point. Other insignia of this kind were called *iztacteucuitlacopilli* being like the above mentioned but of silver. Sea shells and trumpets were used in time of war for the call to arms, and batons were raised in the hands as a signal for the soldiers to begin fighting. They also used a banner of rich feathers, like a large cart wheel, in the center of which was an image of the sun made of gold. They likewise used other insignia called *xilaxochipatzactli* made in the form of helmets with many tufts of feathers and two golden eyes. They also had wooden swords, whose cutting edges were of sharp stones fastened to the wood; these were like short swords. Other insignia used, of feathers and gold, were called *quetzalaztatzootli*. Other insignia called *acelotlachicomitl*: this is a jar covered with tigerskin from which extended a branch of flowers, resembling carnations, made of fine feathers.

Even Cortés, although he nearly always limited himself to mentioning *jewels of gold and silver*, nevertheless says:

Of Moctezuma's manner of living and the many things worthy of admiration which he had, due to his high rank and state, there is so much to be written, that I can assure Your Highness that I do not know where to begin . . . because, as I have said, what greater grandeur could there be than that a barbarian lord as this one should have jewels of gold and silver that no silversmith in the world could better; and as for the precious stones, one is at a loss to understand with what instruments they could have been made so perfectly; as to the feather-work, neither in wax nor embroidery of any kind could it be made so marvelously.[37]

9. *Discovery of Moctezuma's Treasure*

Soon after their arrival, the Spaniards began the search for the famous treasure[38] of which they had heard so much. Their efforts to locate it were soon successful.

Cortés,[39] although very reticent with respect to the treasure, quotes Moctezuma as follows:

. . . who I know have also told you that I have houses with walls of gold, and that the mats in my halls and other things in my household were likewise of gold and

37 Hernán Cortés, *Cartas de Relación de la Conquista de México*, Imp. Espasa-Calpe, S.A., Madrid, 1932, vol.I, p.106.
38 Clavijero believed that Moctezuma presented it to Cortés. (Clavijero, op.cit., pp.65-6)
39 Cortés, op.cit., vol.I, pp.78-9.

that I was and considered myself God and many other things. The houses are, as you see, of stone, lime and earth.' He then raised his vestments and showed me his body, saying to me: 'You here see that I am of flesh and bone like you and each one of you; that I am mortal and tangible.' Grasping my arms and body with his hands, he said: 'See how they have deceived you. It is true that I have a few things of gold that have been left me by my grandfathers. All that I have is yours any time you may demand it. I now go to other houses, where I live; here you will be provided with everything necessary for you and your followers, and have no sense of shame as you are in your own house and surroundings.'

Although not so romantic as the narrative of Durán,[40] that of Bernal Díaz is more explicit:[41]

. . . while we were looking for the best and most convenient site to place the altar, two of our soldiers, one of whom was a carpenter who called himself Alonso Yáñez, noticed on one of the walls signs indicating the former location of a door that had been walled up and carefully whitewashed and burnished. As . . . we had been told that in that chamber Moctezuma kept the treasure of his father, Axayaca, it was suspected that it might be in that hall which had been walled in and plastered within the past few days. Yáñez mentioned this to Juan Velázquez de León and Francisco de Lugo, who were captains and even relatives of mine. Alonso Yáñez, a servant of these captains who was there, told Cortés, and the door was secretly opened. When opened, Cortés with certain captains went in first and saw a great number of jewels, slabs and plates of gold and *chalchihuis* stones and other very great riches. It was soon known among all the other captains and soldiers and we went very secretly to see it. When I saw it I marvelled and as I was at that time a youth and had never in my life seen riches such as those, I felt certain that there could be no other such riches in the whole world. It was decided by all our captains and soldiers that none of us should even think of touching any part of it, but that the stones should be replaced and whitewashed in the same manner as we found it, and not speak of it, lest it come to the knowledge of Moctezuma.

On an island, difficult of egress, and surrounded by thousands of hostile Aztec warriors, the little band of *Conquistadores* was in a most perilous situation. Cortés, fully aware of the danger, by a ruse took Moctezuma prisoner and conducted him to the palace where the Spaniards were living. Moctezuma, subservient to Cortés' commands, called his principal nobles, ceded his kingdom to the Catholic king and

40 F. Diego de Durán, *Historia de las Indias de Nueva España y Tierra Firme*, Mexico, 1867-1880. Durán was not present at the discovery of the treasure.
41 Díaz, op.cit., pp.92-3.

ordered them to obey the Spaniards in all things.

Assured of the support of Moctezuma, it would have been possible for Cortés to continue with the conquest had not the alarming news reached him that Pánfilo de Narváez, sent by Velázquez, Governor of Cuba, had arrived at San Juan de Ulúa with eighteen[42] ships and 1,500 men with orders to relieve Cortés of the command and take him prisoner.

MAY 1520.

Cortés considered it imperative to face personally this grave danger, and leaving the most radical adherents of Velázquez and the less active of his soldiers under the command of Pedro de Alvarado, he began his march to the coast.

Promptly upon his arrival at Cempoala he executed a superb night attack and completely routed the greatly superior forces of Narváez. A still greater victory was his when he succeeded in persuading a great part of Narváez' forces to join him in the conquest. While preparing for the return march to Tenochtitlán, Cortés received the unwelcome and startling news of a serious uprising of the Indians and of the grave danger in which the small force left with Alvarado found itself.

After a forced march, he entered Tenochtitlán without encountering resistance.

The Indians soon began the attack, and notwithstanding the reinforcements brought by Cortés, his situation was still a most desperate one. Although thousands of Indians were slain, there were always more warriors to replace the dead. The Spaniards found the Indians, inspired by the valiant warrior Cuitláhuac,[43] no mean opponents but trained warriors as courageous as themselves. Having no other recourse, the Spaniards, on 1st July 1521, decided to abandon the city:[44]

   . . . Cortés ordered his chamberlain, who called himself Cristóbal de Guzmán, and others of his servants to remove, with the aid of many Indians from Tlascala, all the gold and silver and jewels from his chamber to the hall, and ordered Gonzalo

42 Certain discrepancies exist among authors as regards the number of ships, but Gomara, who took his data from Cortés himself, affirms that there were eighteen, eleven merchant ships and seven brigantines.
43 Who succeeded Moctezuma, slain by his own people.
44 Clavijero, op.cit., vol.II, p.81. Bernal Díaz gives the date as 10th July, but Clavijero states that this is a misprint. Priestley, op.cit., p.42 gives 'night of 30th June.'

Mejía to place in safety all the gold of His Majesty; and for carrying it, he gave them seven wounded and lame horses and one mare and more than eighty Tlascaltecan Indians. They carried the very wide, large gold bars which I have described in the chapter which refers to them, and there remained much more gold in the hall in piles. Cortés then summoned his secretary, who called himself Pedro Hernández, and others of the king's scriveners and said: 'Bear witness for me that I can do no more toward safeguarding this gold. We have here in this house and hall more than seven hundred thousand *pesos* and you can see we are unable to place in safety more than we have; to the soldiers, who may wish to take it out, I now give it, as otherwise it would be left here among these dogs.' On hearing this, many of the soldiers of Narvaez and even some of our own loaded themselves with it. I declare I had no craving for gold but only a desire to save my life, as we were in great danger, but I did not fail to pilfer from a bag four *chalchihuis*, which are stones very highly prized among the Indians, and which I quickly placed in my bosom under my armour; and just then Cortés gave orders to take the bag with the *chalchihuis* that remained so that his steward might guard it; and even the four *chalchihuis* that I took, had I not placed them in my bosom, Cortés would have demanded. These [later] served me very well for curing my wounds and eating from the proceeds of them.[45]

The retreat from the city was not as easy as the entry; still more difficult at night, as was attempted. Almost from the beginning of the retreat the Indian warriors were aware of the attempt and gave the cry of alarm. The portable bridge of the conquerors became mired in the mud on the bank of the first canal and there many soldiers perished.[46]

In this bloody battle, called the 'Sad Night,' so famous in history, Cortés says that all the treasure was lost; while Bernal Díaz affirms that 'The horses with the gold and the Tlascaltecas escaped in safety.'[47] But further on the good Bernal contradicts himself when, speaking of his encounter with the Tlaxcaltecan allies, he says:[48] '. . . and Cortés gave to . . . foremost men [of Tlaxcala] jewels of gold and stones of what had been saved, and to each soldier that which he was able and some of us gave of what we had to some of our acquaintances.'

From which it may be concluded that a very small part of the treasure was saved. On the march to Tlaxcala, where the Spaniards sought refuge with their Tlaxcaltecan allies, they had another unexpected

45 Díaz, op.cit., pp.133-4.
46 Cortés, op.cit., vol.I, pp.140-41.
47 Díaz, op.cit., vol.I, p.484, *Edición de Espasa Calpe*, S.A. Madrid 1928. This is the only reference to this edition.
48 Díaz, op.cit., p.138.

battle in the valley of Otumba. Probably the only thing that saved them from perishing there was the death of the Indian chief.

8TH JULY 1520.

Cortés, with those of his followers who escaped from Mexico City, finally arrived at Tlaxcala, where they were well received,[49] although many Tlaxcaltecas had perished during the retreat of the *Noche Triste*. With the aid of the Tlaxcaltecas, the Spaniards cured their wounds and later Cortés subjugated all the neighboring allies of Moctezuma, cut timbers for brigantines and made all preparations for the second invasion of the Capital. During his stay in Tlaxcala, he received reinforcements of other groups of Spaniards who had arrived at Veracruz. Finally, assisted by thousands of Indian allies, and by an epidemic of small-pox, brought into the country by the Spaniards, after seventy-five days of bloody battle, on 13th August 1521 the Spaniards again captured the City[50] of Tenochtitlán and destroyed it.

Never again were there dangerous uprisings of Indians and Cortés, on the completion of this heroic feat, promptly began the work of reconstruction of the City of Mexico, the discovery and opening up of mines and the definite conquest and pacification of the remainder of New Spain.

10. *The Value of the Treasure Lost During the Noche Triste*

From 'the evidence[51] of the Royal Officials against Diego Velázquez and Pánfilo de Narváez, relative to the gold and jewels for delivery to their Royal Majesties,' which was dated in Segura de la Frontera[52] on the 4th September 1520, we obtain an exact account of the value of the treasure lost in the retreat from Tenochtitlán. This document, slightly deteriorated, reads in part as follows:[53]

P.1./

/In/torn/Segura de la Frontera/torn/this New Spain of the sea, fourth day of the month of September year of the birth of our Saviour Jesus Christ of one thousand

---

49 Clavijero, op.cit., vol.II, p.84.
50 Ibid., vol.II, p.134.
51 *Archivo General de Indias*, 2-2-1/1, R° 2. *Patronato, Leg.* 180. Copy of this interesting document was furnished me by my friend, the distinguished historian, Federico Gómez de Orozco.
52 Near Puebla, now called Tepeaca. This was the second town founded in Mexico.
53 The punctuation is the author's.

five hundred and twenty years, before the Grand Lord Hernando Cortés, Captain General and Lord Chief Justice of this New Spain for the Emperor and King Don Carlos and the Queen Doña Juana, Our Lords, and in my presence, Geronimo de Alanys, scrivener of Their Majesties and notary public in their court and in all their kingdoms and possessions, scrivener of the court and tribunal of said Lord Captain, there appeared Alonso Davila, treasurer, and Alonso de Grado, reckoner, and Rrodrigo Alvares the younger, overseer of the melting of metals, and Bernaldino Velazques de Tapia, commissioner, officers of Your Highnesses in this said New Spain; these appeared before me the said scrivener and a document was made and certain questions the tenor of which, one after another, are those that follow:

Magnificent Sir:

Hernando Cortes, Captain General and Chief Justice in these parts of this New Spain: for Their Highnesses, Alonso Davila, treasurer, and Alonso de Grado, reckoner, and Bernaldino Vazques de Tapia, commissioner and Rrodrigo Alvarez, the younger, overseer, officials of Their Sacred Majesties; we appear in their royal name before Your Excellency in the manner prescribed by law and state that Your Lordship well knows and it is evident to him with/torn/of Their Royal Majesties Your Lordship/torn/going that in this manner in compliance with his [Cortés'] duty, he populated and pacified this land conquering in it many cities, villages and places; and brought to the service of the royal crown their nobles and inhabitants, giving themselves as they did as vassals of the Emperor and King and Queen Our Lords whom they served and contributed to with all that which in the royal name was ordered of them by Your Lordship, giving as they did much gold and silver and stones and jewels of gold of great worth and other jewels of various kinds whose worth could not be appraised; which said gold, once in possession of Your Lordship and in the presence of us the officers mentioned, was fifthed and in clean gold and molten there corresponded and belonged to Your Sacred Majesties as their fifth and royal right, thirty and two thousand and four hundred *pesos* of gold and in feather-work and other things that were for Your Royal Highness there were well one hundred thousand *pesos* of gold; and above and likewise from the fifth in silver there were well eighty and five thousand *marcos*, besides the jewels of various kinds that were for Their Majesties and of which here we are unable to appreciate their great value; all of which was entrusted by Your Lordship and by us said officers to Alonso Descobar, due to the treasurer being absent, and/which/he had under his care in the city of Thenustitan in a fortress . . . which through Your Majesty/torn/was assigned to him so as to have the aforesaid (p.2)./safe from all danger, and being, with all the aforesaid, waiting until there were ships or for the launching of one that Your Lordship had ordered to be built so as to send, in one or the others, all or the greater part of it to Spain to the Emperor and King and Queen our Sovereigns, with the account that Your Lordship and we the said officials should make for them of the land and dominions that Your Lordship in their royal name had conquered and pacified, and all being thus quiet and peaceful and Your Lordship occupied with things concerned with the service of Your Majesties, and the good handling and pacification of these said lands, in the past month of April of this present year of one thousand and five hundred and twenty, arrived at the port and bay of San Juan de Chalchicueto, which is in these lands, an armada of thirteen ships with many foot-soldiers and horsemen and well provided with artillery and all munition, which Diego Belazquez, Lieutenant-admiral in the Island Fernandona, was sending in the service of Your Majesties with an injurious and devilish thought, in which came as captain one Panfilo de Narvaez, resident of the village of San Salvador of the Island Fernandina and because of what Your Lordship well knows and [it] is manifest that the said Panfilo de Narvaez as soon as arrived at said port, certain native nobles of this land went to see him—[precisely] those to whom Your Lordship had issued orders, that each and every time that ships arrived there they should go to see them, and that the people that came on them should be provided with foods and of all that (p.2.rev.)/was necessary, and that they should make known to Your Lordship how they were; and said Panfilo de Narvaez, to manifest the ill will with which he was sent and came, or with which he set out from the said Island Fernandina, said to those nobles who went to see him, and made known to them and to other persons, that he came to this land to imprison Your Lordship and those that were with him in the service of Your Highnesses, and to liberate Moteçuma, Lord of the greater part of this land, whom Your Lordship held in prison, because of which imprisonment all the land was safe and peaceful and Your Majesties were well pleased; although said Narvaez stated that he came to free said Moteçuma and to imprison Your Lordship and those who were with him, he also said that he did not come for gold nor desired it but to carry out the aforementioned and return at once; and it being notorious and having learned the said Narvaez from many Spaniards who in company with Your Lordship in the name of Their Royal Highnesses had conquered and populated very quietly and peacefully this land, and parts of it, and that in them you were Chief Justice and Captain General in name of Your Majesties, not having taken into consideration any of the aforementioned, but determined to carry out his plan, many times sent word to Moteçuma that he was coming to free him and to carry out the aforesaid with the lords and persons who went to see him; from which we believed that the intent of said Diego Velazques was to do that which his said Captain Narvaez was doing, because without his approval and order he [Narvaez] would do nothing as he [Velázquez] was a strict man; (p.3) because of which the nobles seeing that it was better for them to be free as they were accustomed to be before and in their vices and idolatries, rather than under the yoke and servitude of the Royal Crown, as Your Lordship already held them all placed, and they desisted from giving what they were accustomed to give and from contributing to your Royal Highnesses with the gold they had or with anything that was requested of them in the name of Your Majesties; and Your Lordship well knows and it is evident to him that to prevent the aforementioned, jointly with us it seemed to him that it was most convenient and was necessary to set out from the said city of Thenustitan before the said nobles should be further aroused, so as to know what was the design of the said Captain Narvaez, and for Your Lordship to make provisions in that respect as would be most convenient for Your Highnesses; because of which it was necessary to leave in the said city of Thenustitan all the gold and the silver and all the other jewels which Your Lordship well knows of, and that Their Majesties held in keeping of the said Alonso Descobar and in guard of all the aforementioned, and for the safety of the said city and Moteçuma one hundred and fifty Spaniards; and since the said Moteçuma and the other nobles were already advised of the intention of said Narvaes wishing to separate himself from the service of Your Highnesses all [the Indians] jointly decided that, on the departure of Your Lordship, all should go and make war on said Spaniards, who in charge of the said gold and city and Moteçuma, had remained and this [plan] they put into effect — so much so that if God and Our Miraculous Lady had not wished to spare them all would have perished due to the violent war and battle that (p.3, reverse) they presented, in which they killed certain Spaniards; and at once, in order that all the above said be known to Your Lordship, he departed in much haste from the city of Cienpual [where he was arranging and despatching certain ships to Your Sacred Majesties in order to send in them all the greater part of the gold and jewels to Your Royal Highnesses with a report of all that which in these said parts had taken place] for the city of Thenustitan to assist and foresee and do that which was fit, in order to prevent the war already mentioned; so that he arrived there and entered safely said city of Thenustitan the day of Saint John in June of this year with the rest of the foot-soldiers, horsemen, and artillery that he was able to take; and as the said Moteçuma and the said nobles had already impressed on their minds the said words that the said Narvaes had told them and it being understood that he was intending to pursue his evil desire and thinking to complete that which he had already begun in the said city, the next day in the morning after Your Lordship arrived, daybreak showed all the bridges of said city raised and Your Lordship and those of us that are in your company, all surrounded by armed warriors with the idea of killing us; and thus they gave us battle in said city for six days and they fought our stronghold so valiantly and placed us in such a difficult position that they killed many Spaniards and nearly all or the greater part [of the remaining Spaniards] were wounded and could not fight and thus is seen by Your Lordship the great danger in which all of us were and that if the retreat had been delayed, not a single man would have remained alive and with your advice (p.4) and of all the others that were in the said city, it was advisable to leave [of necessity because no other thing was possible] for which cause was lost all the gold and silver and jewels and stones that already we have mentioned to Your Lordship and many soldiers and horses and all the artillery, for the retreat was so dangerous because this city is over the water and the bridges to it raised; moreover in all the land they waged war on us until we reached the province or dominions of Toscalteale which was in peace and under the command of the Royal Crown; whereby we could believe and hold in truth that those of us who reached there did so by divine mystery — all of which was and took place because of the fault of the said Diego Velazques and of his captain Panfilo de Narvaes and for sending the said armada, and for persuading and leading thus the native nobles of the land with the words and acts; that they had ill intent and an evil plan — all in disservice of Your Sacred Majesties, causing revolt of these said natives, as they did revolt against your royal service, and until this day on account of the aforesaid they are in arms and there were lost the said one hundred and thirty and two thousand and four hundred *pesos* of gold and all the other aforementioned jewels.

For which reasons and for each one of them, and for many others that in the prosecution of this case we are handling we say and claim, as officers of Your Sacred Majesties; of Your Lordship we ask, and if it is necessary we demand, that holding this our report as truthful, as it is, or a certain part of it which may be sufficient, so that in [view of] the said evidence you may order that it be proceeded against and you proceed against the aforementioned Diego Velasques and Panfilo de Narvaes with all rigor and justice, ordering the confiscation from them of all and any belongings, both goods and lands, that the aforementioned may have, both in these parts of this New Spain as well as in the island of Fernandina or in any others that may be, and once confiscated, order them inventoried and put in shares that we in the name of Your Royal Highnesses may be paid the said hundred and thirty and two thousand and four hundred *pesos* of gold besides all the jewels and other things that Your Majesties lose and might lose of the fifth that belongs to them of that which the said Indians would have given and contributed from the time that the said Narvaez came and made the revolt by land against the authority under which your lordship, in the name of your Royal Highnesses, held the land; for all of which [reasons] he should order in the name of justice, to all and any mayors and justices and judges who may be from these parts, as well as from the island Fernandina and the Española, so that whenever they may find possessions of the aforementioned they should confiscate them and put, as we have said, in shares and in keeping where they may be in safety until such time as they justly settle with us [and] this case be ended and finished; and of it to Your Highnesses we will make a report; thus Your Lordship by so doing will be doing justice, which is obligatory, and that which to a good judge and servant of Your Sacred Majesties is best fitting and ought to be done; if the contrary should be done, we [shall] protest in the said name, that it be to your charge and blame, and that we will collect all the aforesaid and (p.5.)/each thing and part of it from him and from his goods as from a judge who denies justice and we will complain against him to their Sacred Majesties; and as we ask and demand it we ask written testimony of the scrivener here present and if other petition should be necessary we ask fulfillment of justice, and of the magnificent office of Your Lordship we implore the things which we ask and declare: [signed] Alonso Davila, Alonso de Grado, Rrodrigo Alvares the Younger, Vernaldino Vasques de Tapia.[54]

By the following questions and articles will be interrogated and examined the witnesses and proofs that are, or were, presented in behalf of Alonso Davila, treasurer, and of Alonso de Grado, reckoner, and of Rrodrigo Alvares the Younger, overseer, and of Vernaldino Vazques, commissioner, officials of Your Highnesses, in the dispute with Diego Velasques and Panfilo de Narvaes.

V

Let them state if they know etc. that thus the said Monteçuma, as well as all his other vassals from other parts and territories and provinces that are subject to his dominion, gave and contributed to Your Highnesses and to the Lord Captain General in your name much gold and silver and jewels of many kinds, shields, plumages, necklaces and many other things of gold and stones of much value, of which corresponded to Your Highnesses, as their royal fifth, net thirty and two thousand and four hundred *pesos* of gold and eighty and five *marcos* of silver.

VI

Let them state if they know etc. that in the same manner Their Royal Highnesses had what the aforementioned had given to said Lord Captain General, in the said name, many jewels of gold and various kinds of stones and necklaces and shields and feather-work and other jewels, of which the gold that they contained was worth a hundred thousand *castellanos* of gold and over.

XXI

Let them state if they know etc. that the said cast gold that Your Highnesses lost, on account of the said Narvaes and of the said Diego Velazques, was thirty and two thousand and four hundred *pesos* of gold and in like manner the silver and stones and jewels and shields and featherwork and necklaces the gold of which was worth more than one hundred thousand *pesos* and in like manner they lost and lose Their Highnesses another hundred thousand *pesos* of gold which the said Indians would have given and contributed from the time the said Narvaes came to this land up to this day because the said Captain General would have discovered and pacified many lands very much richer, of which he had knowledge, by which Your High-

---

54 History places the blame for the insurrection on Alvarado, while from this document Diego Veláz-quez and Pánfilo de Narváez appear entirely responsible. Although there is little doubt that the direct cause was the action of Alvarado, in view of this new evidence it may be concluded that the uprising Alvarado suspected was not imaginary, but inspired by Pánfilo de Narváez.

nesses would have been very pleased and the Royal Crown increased, had it not been for the coming, as came, the said Narvaes in war-like mood and telling what he told to the said Indians.

From the foregoing it is concluded that the value of the Royal Fifth, the King's share of the accumulated treasure, consisted of:

1. The cast gold,
2. The gold contained in the feather-work,
3. The silver, and
4. The jewels.

Omitting the 'other hundred thousand *pesos* of gold which would have been given and contributed by the said Indians,' the testimony of the witnesses is in accord, except as to the value of 'the gold contained with the feather-work and others.' In connection with this, question VI gives it in *castellanos*, and Gerónimo de Aguilar also gives it in the same money unit, *castellanos*. The other witnesses give it in *pesos* and this appraisal is also given in question XXI.

Accepting the majority of the appraisals as correct, the calculable value of the lost Royal Fifth amounted to 132,400 *pesos* of gold and 85,000 *marcos* of silver.

The value of the gold mark, for the producer, was at that time[55] 105 *pesos*, 7 *reales*, 2 *maravedís*; therefore the equivalent of the 132,400 *pesos* of gold [taking the value at 106 *pesos*, in round numbers] was approximately 1249 *marcos*. Since one *marco* of gold was the approximate equivalent of 6.784 Troy ounces, the 1249 *marcos* had an approximate equivalent of 8,474 Troy ounces. And since the 132,400 *pesos* of gold represented the fifth part of the treasure, the total value of the lost gold was 42,370 Troy ounces of gold.

The silver *marco* contained 8 Spanish ounces, or 7.10548477 Troy ounces. Therefore the 85,000 silver *marcos* were equal to, approximately, 603,966 Troy ounces, and this being the fifth part of the total of the silver from the treasure, the total amounted to 3,019,830 Troy ounces.

The price of gold and silver[56] is as follows:

55 *Diccionario Universal de Geografía*, op.cit., vol.V, p.919.
56 20th February 1936.

MONETARY UNIT	GOLD	SILVER
	Per Troy ounce	*Per Troy ounce*
Mexican *Pesos*	124.07	1.595
Spanish *Pesetas*	254.316	3.004
U.S. Dollars	35.00	0.4475
Pounds Sterling	£ 7-1-1	£ 20 d.

From the foregoing is obtained the total value of the lost treasure in present day[57] currencies:

MONETARY UNIT	TOTAL VALUE OF THE TREASURE		
	Gold	*Silver*	*Total*
Mexican *Pesos*	5,256,845.90	4,816,628.85	10,073,474.75
Spanish *Pesetas*	10,775,368.92	9,071,569.32	19,846,938.24
U.S. Dollars	1,482,950.00	1,351,373.92	2,834,323.92
Pounds Sterling	£ 298,885-0-10-	£ 251,652-10-0	£ 550,537-10-10

57 February, 1936.

Chapter II

THE SILVERSMITHS' ART BEFORE THE CONQUEST

PART II

1. THE SPOILS OF THE CONQUEST. 2. INDIAN MINING. 3. THE TECHNIQUE OF THE INDIAN SILVERSMITHS. 4. CONCERNING THE GOLDSMITHS.

1. *The Spoils of the Conquest*

FROM 1524 to 1526 Cortés sent much treasure to Spain. Seven inventories have been published in the *Colección de Documentos Inéditos Relativos al Descubrimiento, Conquista, etc.*[1]

The eighth, discovered by Father Cuevas,[2] is found in the work *Cartas y otros Documentos de Hernán Cortés, etc.* Although all are of great interest, the brevity of this study permits only the inclusion of two: one from the *Colección*—the one taken by Diego de Soto, and that discovered by Father Cuevas.

LIST OF THE THINGS OF GOLD WHICH GO IN A BOX FOR YOUR MAJESTY, WHICH ARE BEING TAKEN IN CHARGE OF DIEGO DE SOTO.

No date[3]

A cannon of silver, called Fénix, that weighed twenty-two and a half *quintales* when delivered to the casting house.

IN THE FIRST PLACE

One mirror with two figures.
One mirror with a *guaxteca* figure.

---

[1] D. Luis Torres de Mendoza, *Colección de Documentos Inéditos Relativos al Descubrimiento, Conquista y Organización de las Antiguas Posesiones Españolas, sacados de los Archivos del Reino y muy especialmente de las Indias,* Madrid, 1869.

[2] Cuevas, S.J. Fr. Mariano *Cartas y otros Documentos de Hernán Cortés, novísimamente descubiertos en el Archivo General de Indias.* F. Díaz & Co., Seville, 1915.

[3] General Archives of the Indies. Patronato, Shelf 1, Box 1.

One *guaxteca* mirror with a crystal in the nostrils.

One round mirror, in the form of the sun.

One round mirror, large.

One mirror with the head of a lion.

One mirror with a figure of an owl, with some *chalchuys*.[4]

One mirror with a case of stones, used for knives.

Two *carnicles* with their tassels and on top a tree with a little bird.

One necklace with ten large beads.

One necklace of the same kind: twenty-two pieces with their fringes.

Another necklace with some round rattles.

One necklace with eighteen large pieces, of the head of an eagle, with their fringes.

One small necklace, of bent pieces [*piezas dobladas*] with their tassels.

One necklace of turtle shells, that has forty-eight pieces with their tassels.

One necklace with eight beads and ten hanging pieces in the form of turtles, with a figure of a man.

One necklace of eight pieces, with their tassels.

One necklace, like turtle shells, of fifteen pieces with their tassels.

One necklace like snail shells of fifteen pieces with their fringes.

One necklace like snail shells, that has forty pieces, without tassels.

One necklace of nine pieces like heads of a man with their tassels.

One small necklace like snail shells that has eighteen pieces.

One necklace with nine round beads and eight alligator teeth.

One necklace that has twenty-seven crickets, with their tassels.

One necklace like snail shells that has twenty-nine pieces without tassels.

One large necklace like a gold breast plate.

One large gold medal with a monster in the shape of a man.

Another similar gold medal.

Two gold flutes.

Three roses of gold in the form of artichokes.

Another gold rose with six leaves and six gold beads.

One gold rose with six leaves, three of silver and three of gold.

One piece of *chalchuy* mounted in gold in the shape of a bell, with a little bird and a cricket.

One flower of *chalchuy* encased in gold, and on top a little tree.

One turtle of gold, set with one *chalchuy*.

One head of gold, with the face of *chalchuy*, and one necklace of silver snail shells.

Three pieces in such manner, set with some *chalchuys*, and having other long *chalchuys* with the ends enclosed in gold.

One large piece, like a *Pora-Pax* with one large *chalchuy* in the center.

4 The *chachuí* or *chalcuite*, is a green stone which resembles the emerald.

One golden shield, with a small banner and three small rods fastened to the back part with their settings of stones.

One head of *chalchuy*, with eleven strings of *chalchuys*, in the end of each one a snail shell of gold.

One head of gold, with the face of green stone, with its ear coverings and tiny snail shells.

One head of green and white stone, that has a small tube of gold through the nostrils.

One head of an animal encased with gold with many tassels.

One head of green stone encased with gold, with some ears of snakes and some tiny snail shells at the ends.

One head of stone, that looks like porphyry, encased with gold, with four small emeralds.

One green head, encased in gold, that has hair fastened on, with a border and small gold ear coverings.

One head, that also looks like porphyry, encased in gold, with a wreath of gold, that has a snake's head in front.

One head of green stone, encased in gold, that has in the hair a twisted cord of gold.

One head of *chalchuy*, that looks like porphyry, wide, that has for ear coverings two small bells with two butterflies and rattles at the ends.

One piece of the same kind but with different ear coverings.

One gold skull.

One head of green stone, inclosed in gold, with feathers of gold hanging down.

One head, half of gold and half of green stone, with a mouth of a snake.

One head of gold and green stone.

One head of green stone and encased with gold, with mouth and beard of gold.

One head of green stone, inclosed in gold, with flowers of gold, at the ends of the tassels; sixteen heads of monsters, different one from the other, of gold.

Two monsters of gold, with a stone in the belly and four tassels.

One eagle of gold with four rattles on the tail.

Three small medals with their monsters.

One large medal with a monster and eight tassels.

One large stone, inclosed in gold and a flower of silver and gold.

Eight medals some with tassels others without, all with their green stones.

One purple-colored shell, with a green *chalchuy* in the center, inclosed in gold.

One piece of gold, with five hearts and one round green stone and another long one encased in gold.

One stone flower inclosed in gold, with a border of gold.

One flower of gold with six leaves and a green stone in the center.

One green stone encased with gold and in the base a stone of turquoise.

Three small flowers of gold and green stones, one with two beads and the other with a cross.

One large flower with three leaves and having within five other leaves that move.

Five butterflies, three of gold and stones and the other two of red and green shell.

Two earrings of gold with their tassels.

One head of a bird of gold.

Seventeen pieces of medals with their green stones, some with their tassels and others without.

Sixteen red shells, inclosed in gold.

Two white snail shells with their green stones fastened with their thread of gold.

Three flowers of land snails encased with gold.

Eight spindles with their knobs and a spinner in which the spindles are used, all of gold.

Nine spoons of gold.

One spoon of gold and silver.

One small duck of gold that comes out of a stone.

One face of gold and the front of precious stones.

Three tigers of gold.

Sixty-nine beads of gold and six *chalchuys*, and one tiger of gold, all strung on a string.

One rosary with seventy-seven beads and a rose of gold.

Eighteen skins with eagle talons of silver and gold in which there are seventy eagle talons.

Three bracelets with sharp points made of gold.

Six bracelets for the arms, of gold.

Fifteen strings in a necklace of green beads and of gold and of rattles.

One bracelet with the nails and fingers of gold.

One face of tiger-skin with the two ears of gold and precious stones.

One necklace for a greyhound, of turquoises.

Six rings[5] of gold that they used in the lower lips.

One lip ring of amber adorned with gold.

One lip ring of gold made the same as the one of amber.

One lip ring of silver and gold with *chalchuy*.

One long lip ring of gold.

Two hair ornaments of medals of gold and many *chalchuys* of green stones with their white hair.

Inventory: (the eighth), discovered by Father Cuevas:

5 The rings or ornaments that the Indians placed in their lower lips are called *bezotes*. This is a word derived from *bezo*, obsolete for *labio* [lip].

IV

JEWELS THAT HERNAN CORTES SENT TO SPAIN FROM MEXICO IN 1526 INVENTORIED BY CRISTOBAL DE OÑATE. MEXICO 25TH SEPTEMBER OF 1526.

This document is found in the section: *Papeles de Justicia de Indias*. Fiscal Edicts, Court of México. Shelf 47. Box 5. Bundle 1/35.

I, Christoval d'Oñate, Computor in this New Spain for the reckoner Rodrigo de Albornoz, state and swear that in the city of Tenuxtitán on the twenty-fifth day of the month of September of the year five hundred and twenty and six the Seño Governor don Hernando Cortés registered the following jewels:

One rapier guard that has two eagle's heads for pommels and two eagle's feet for the cross [piece] and a round handle and a network of two pieces through which the blade passed.

and one large *contera* [protective knob at the end of a sword scabbard] and one owl with six tassels

and one hanging ornament with six tassels and one little eagle and two rings fastened to the ornament

and two large ear coverings

and one Porta-Pax, stamped on it a Crucifix and images of the Virgin Mary and Saint John and also some strings of beads and some little birds and a large rose

and one shield with sixteen tassels

and one Flemish pouch with some little fish for tassels

and thirty-four large round beads and thirty-three beads on another string

and one necklace of turtles that has eighteen pieces with their tassels

and another necklace of little heads of lightning bugs that has thirty-five pieces

and two boxes of turtles and one large flying fish

and one alligator with wings

and one small necklace that has twenty-five pieces with their tassels

and one lightning bug inside of a turtle

and one snail shell with a *berineco*[6] and one small lion with a *chalchiui*[7] on the back

and one large eagle with a young one of the same kind on its back

and one lightning bug with a green stone in the belly

and one string of small tubes and of worms that has eighty pieces with their tassels

and one string of small beads with rattles for the points and one little medal at the ends with a *chalchiui*

and a rose with its tassels and a shield with arrows and fringes

and some strings of olive-shaped pearls and round ones and among them four butterflies and an eagle with tassels in the tail

6 *berineco*: semi-precious stone.
7 *chalchihui*: stone of bluish-green color.

and two butterflies with two *chalchiuies* on the backs

and forty-two long beads like little tubes with a large medal at the ends and plumes

and forty-six round beads and twenty-nine long ones on a cord and a lightning bug at the points

and two images

and one small shield a *chalchiui* at the point and two tassels of feathers hanging from it

and one rose of gold and silver with a *chalchiui* in the center

and another rose with a butterfly in the center

and one rosary that has seventy large beads on a cord and among them two large fish with wings and a large locust

and a cord that has twenty-two large beads and twenty and six round ones and a rose of gold and silver at the tip

and another large rose with a *chalchiui* in the center that has the figure of a man carved in the *chalchiui*

and twenty-five large tubes

and a little eagle with some *chalchiuies* and feather tassels hanging from the breast

and a string of large and round beads that has forty pieces

and a rose with a *chalchiui* in the center and ninety-six large round beads on a cord

and a little chain of long links with a Crucifix at the end

and a little frog and a lightning bug with a *chalchiui* in their breasts

and four hangings

and three rings with three little eagles

and two rings with two heads of owls

and two others with two roses

and one hanging ornament with four tassels

and thirteen rings with turquoises and one with a green stone and another with another red stone and two without stones and another with a little eagle and two heads of serpents

a jar with two bulges with its base [and] with two handles

one chocolate cup with its stirrer

one jar with a head of a tiger and an eagle on the spout

one cross with a Crucifix and its base

one small jar with one handle

one hanging ornament with tassels as mentioned, a rose and the head of a tiger in the center

a medal made to resemble the sun with a carved *chalchiui*, in the center a shield with thirteen tassels and some green stones in the center

a scorpion with a *chalchiui* in the body and a coiled serpent with a *chalchiui* in the center with nine tassels one rose with the head of an Indian and six tassels

a bird with a *chalchiui* on the breast

another coiled snake, with a *chalchiui* and a pearl in the center, and a cross on the back with its tassels

a tiger with eighteen beads on a cord

two large pouches with their tassels like medicine vessels

a little locust with two *chalchiuies* one on the head and the other in the body and with three turquoises in the tail

an eagle and a tiger joined one with the other and a carved stone in the breasts

a hanging ornament like a rose with five tassels and forty-four little tubes of gold

another hanging ornament with two tassels and sixty-four beads olive-shaped and round

fifty beads of little tubes and round [ones] and a fish of thin [metal]

an eagle with two heads and in the center of them a Crucifix with some tassels (and) forty-six round and olive-shaped beads

a lightning bug with some roses in the antennae and a hole in the belly

a tiger and two eagles and thirty-six beads all on a cord and a hanging ornament with nine tassels

a board of openwork and on it a Crucifix of silver and the Virgin Mary on the other side and four tassels

a rose with a *chalchiui* in the center

a coiled serpent with six tassels

another coiled serpent with a movable tail

thirty-nine olive-shaped beads and a hanging ornament with three tassels

a rose with a stem of tiny precious stones

one string of beads that has one hundred and five round and tube-like beads

another string that has twenty and six similar beads slightly smaller

another string of beads that has sixty-six little tubes and round ones and some little worms for hanging ornaments

and a small Crucifix with a cross

a tiny hand from which a tiger comes out

another large Crucifix with a twisted cross with three *chalchiuies* on the back of the cross and forty and eight beads like little bells

four little pieces each with two toothpicks

All of the gold which weighed two thousand and three hundred and fifty and nine *pesos*, of which was paid the fifth and taxes belonging to Your Majesty and to which I the said Christoval Doñate certify.

Dated the first of October of said year one thousand and five hundred and twenty and six.

Christoval de Oñate [rubric]

On the reverse side is read: the lords of the council ordered that I should place this attest in this process in Burgos on the XVIII of January MDXXVIII.

[There is a rubric]

The Lost Treasure

In addition, Cortés lost a very valuable treasure in the lake. Peralta says:[8]

CHAPTER XVIII

that treats of how Hernando Cortés, Marquis del Valle, desired to send to Spain to His Majesty a very great present of gold and silver, precious stones, and very fine pearls, and how it was lost in the lake: and of the arrival of his first wife, doña Catalina Suárez, and of her death. Being now Hernando Cortés at his leisure, having entrusted the towns of the New Spain to the conquerors, it seemed to him it would be well to send to His Majesty a present from his New World, of gold and silver and other fine things, of which he had in abundance, although he would have had more had it not been for the first war that the Indians had with the Spaniards during the feast of the idol, when the treasure of the King Monteçuma was lost, which was the greatest any lord had or ever had . . . Of that which afterwards he was able to obtain, he got together a great quantity of gold and silver, pearls and very fine precious stones, whose value was very great, and once collected he decided to load it in some canoes, and he with it, to take it to the port, where it was necessary to make a second loading on ships, and take it to Spain; it should be understood that these canoes had to go to Tezcuco, by the lake, and from there in packs to the port.

How was lost, in the lake at Mexico, the Marquis and the treasure, that he was sending to His Majesty: The canoes having set out from Mexico and begun to navigate with their oars and men, and the Marquis in them, already out in the widest part of the lake, having travelled some four or five leagues, and remaining for them to travel still another four, the weather became unsettled with [such] a very violent storm that they did not know what to do for their safety; nor did they know how to secure the canoes; and as these are of such small capacity, and long and narrow, and have no benches for the oarsmen to row [they have to stand up], they tried to join one [canoe] with another and fasten them, which would have been some help, as I say, had not the lake been so rough. The force of the water was such that they could not join them, and thus they went to the bottom, and all that wealth was lost. The Marquis and those that were with him escaped in other canoes, half swimming, holding on to them, and six or seven persons were drowned; this was a great loss that happened to Hernando Cortés. Reaching as he did the land, he returned to Mexico, and consulted with the Indians [to see] if it were possi-

8 Suárez de Peralta, *Noticias Históricas de la Nueva España*, published with the approval of the Minister of Agriculture and Development, by Justo Zaragoza, Madrid. Pub. Manuel G. González, 1878.

ble to help matters by recovering some of the treasure; and it was impossible, because it could be as readily saved as that which is lost in the middle of the sea, and he at once took steps to collect more gold and silver to send to His Majesty, which he did.

Of all the jewels and articles of gold and silver taken by the Spaniards, none now exist.[9]

The destruction of the gold and silver objects retained by the rough and ready *Conquistadores*, is, perhaps, excusable. They desired expendable wealth, and, naturally, they converted them into bullion. But it is difficult to understand why not a single piece remained in Spain, where the exquisites of the Court should have appreciated this exotic art.

Fortunately, some ancient jewels have been discovered in modern times. Of these, there are many specimens in the National Museum of Mexico.[10]

2. *Indian Mining*

The mining of the aborigines, due to the lack of iron tools, was necessarily very primitive. From the accounts of Cortés, it appears that a great part of the gold was taken from the sands and gravels of the rivers.

After I knew fully that he had much desire to serve Your Highness, I begged him [Moctezuma], that I might be able to render more fully an account to Your Majesty of the things of this land, that he show me the mines from which the gold was taken; he, with very good will, said this would please him. And at once he had come certain of his servants, and by two and two he divided them for four provinces, where he said it was taken out; and he asked me to give Spaniards to go with them, so that they might see it taken out; and thus I gave him, to each two of his own, two Spaniards. And some went to a province that is called Cuzula, which is eighty leagues from the great city of Temixtitán, and the natives of that province are vassals of said Moctezuma; and there they showed them three rivers, and . . . they brought me samples of gold, and very good, although taken out with few tools, because they had no tools other than those with which the Indians took it out; and on the road they crossed three provinces, according to what the Spaniards said, of very beautiful land and many villages and cities and other cities in such number and of such and

9 Saville, op.cit., pp.102-03.
10 Permission to photograph these was refused.

so fine buildings, that they say that in Spain there could be no better. Especially, they told me that they had seen a lodging house and fort that is larger and stronger and better built than the Castle of Burgos; and the people of one of these provinces, that is called Tamazulapa, were better clothed than any other that we have seen and, as it appeared to them, of much intelligence. The others went to another province that is called Malinaltebeque which is another seventy leagues from the said great city, that is more toward the shore of the sea. And likewise they brought me samples of gold from a great river that passes by there. And the others went to a land that is upstream from this river, of a people different from the language of Culúa, and which they call Tenis, and the lord of that land is called Coatelicamat and because his land is in some mountains, very high and rough, he is not subject to said Moctezuma, [and] the messengers that went with the Spaniards did not dare to enter into that land without making it known first to the lord of it and to ask permission, telling him that they were going with those Spaniards to see the mines of gold that were in his land, and that they begged him on my part and of said Moctezuma he consider this in order. The said Cuatelicamat replied to the Spaniards that he was very content that they should enter into his land and see the mines and all the rest that they might wish; but that those of Culúa, who are those of Moctezuma, should not enter into his land as they were his enemies. The Spaniards were somewhat in doubt if they should go by themselves or not, because those that went with them told them that they should not go; that they would kill them, and that in order to kill them they did not consent that those of Culúa should enter with them. And finally they decided to enter by themselves, and they were by said lord and those of his land very well received, and they showed them seven or eight rivers, from which they said that they took the gold, and in their presence the Indians took it out, and they brought me samples of all, and with the said Spaniards the said Coatelicamat sent me certain messengers of his, with whom he sent to offer his person and land to the service of Your Sacred Majesty, and he sent me certain jewels of gold and clothing of that which they have. The others went to another province that is called Tuchitebeque, that is almost on the same road toward the sea, twelve leagues from the province of Malinaltebuque, where I have already said that gold was found; and there they showed us two other rivers, from which they likewise took out samples of gold.[11]

As its extraction was more difficult, the relative value of silver to gold, at that time, was not the same as it is today. Alamán says:[12]

One of the things of most interest to Cortés were the mines. It may be said that the working of these and the extraction of their metals have been a work of the

11 Cortés, *Cartas de Relación de la Conquista de México*, Imp. Espasa-Calpe, S.A., Madrid, 1932, vol.I, pp.85-7.
12 Lucas Alamán, *Obras de*, vol.II, pp.111-12.

Conquest. Prior to this, the amount of silver extracted was very small, as the methods employed in getting it out were very inefficient. In the industrial arts, the results are necessarily in proportion to the methods and tools used. Having no knowledge of extraction by mercury, and as the smelters consisted merely of forges and small hearths, without other draft than that given through pipes in the mouths of men who were relieved from time to time, the ancient Mexicans were unable to utilize in any manner the greater part of the metals that we are familiar with, and the silver which they had was obtained either from that found in the native state, or from very rich ores that are very readily smelted. On this account, in all the data that we are able to obtain on that remote period, such as the presents from Moctezuma to Cortés, the tributes, and other data of this nature, we see that the gold and silver did not hold the ratio that today are found between these metals, not only in production but also in general use, the gold appearing in much greater quantity, not because there was more than today, but because there was a much less quantity of silver, which is more difficult to extract from its combinations than gold, which is found in a pure state and was collected in relatively greater quantity. The Spaniards introduced better methods of smelting, more powerful draft, and above all the use of mercury for amalgamation, to which discovery is due the great abundance of silver that has given so much activity to commerce, and which has changed the prices of all things.

Silver and probably some gold were obtained by the Indians from the placers that existed on the surface of the ground, or from excavations of slight depth; the underground mines were introduced by the Spaniards.

The Indians did have some knowledge of smelting, and the copper that they produced was so well finished that on one occasion it deceived the Spaniards:

. . . all the Indians of that province generally carried some hatchets of copper very well finished, as a mark of rank as well as arms, with handles of wood brightly painted, and we thought they were of low grade gold, and we began to barter for them; I say that in three days we collected more than three hundred of them, and we were very much satisfied with them, thinking that they were of low grade gold, and the Indians more so with the beads; but all turned out useless, as the hatchets were of copper and the beads a little of nothing.[13]

In addition, the first Spaniards that came found many jewels and ornaments of silver, of good quality:

13 Díaz, op.cit., p.13.

a. In the market of Tlaxcala,[14] on the way to Mexico, 'there are jewelers' shops of gold and silver.'

b. On his entrance into Mexico,[15] Moctezuma presented to him 'many and various jewels of gold and silver.'

c. Of the collection that, at the request of Cortés, Moctezuma sent to gather from the provinces:[16]

And thus it was, that all of those lords to whom he sent gave very plentifully of that which he asked of them; thus in jewels as well as sequins [*tejuelos*], and sheets of gold and silver, and other things of those that they had, that, melted all that was to be melted, there corresponded to Your Majesty's Fifth, thirty and two thousand four hundred and some *pesos* of gold, plus all the jewels of gold and silver, and feather ornaments and precious stones and many other things of value, which for Your Sacred Majesty I assigned and separated, and which could be worth a hundred thousand *ducados* or more; which things, apart from their value, were such and so marvellous, that considered for their novelty and rarity they had no price. Neither is it to be believed that any one of all the known princes of the world could have such things of such quality. And let it not appear fabulous to Your Highness that which I say, for it is true that [of] all the living things on the land as well as in the sea, of which the said Moctezuma could have had knowledge, he had [made] very natural images of gold and silver as well as of precious stones and of feather-work, in such perfection, that they looked almost real.

d. In the market of *Temixtitán*,[17] 'Jewels of gold and silver.'

e. The famous *Culebrina* of silver that Cortés sent to the King as a present and proof of the skill of the Indians.

. . . he sent also a *culebrina* [a small cannon] of silver in whose melting entered twenty and four *quintales* and two *arrobas*, although I believe part was lost in the casting, because it was made twice and although to me it was very costly, because, besides what the metal cost me, which were twenty and four thousand and five hundred *pesos* of gold, at the rate of five *pesos* of gold each *marco*, with the other expenses of melters and engravers and those taking it to the port, it cost me more than another three thousand *pesos* of gold; but for being a thing so rich and worthwhile seeing, and worthy of going before such a high and most excellent prince, I accepted the task and cost.

14 Cortés, op.cit., vol.1, p.56.
15 Ibid., vol.1, p.77.
16 Ibid., vol.1, pp.95-6.
17 Ibid., vol.1, p.99.

This magnificent piece, perhaps the first and last of its kind which has been cast of this metal, had engraved on it a phœnix and this *terzetto*:[18]

> Aquesta nació sin par
> Yo en serviros sin segundo,
> Vos sin igual en el mundo.

Cortés also mentions having obtained jewelry of silver on many other occasions, and Bernal Díaz refers to 'gold, half copper.'

As part of the spoils that resulted from the occupation of Mexico by the *Conquistadores*, in the year 1522 there were registered before Alonso de Vergara, Public Scrivener of the Villa de la Vera Cruz, the jewels and gold that Juan Bautista, master of the ship *Santa María de la Rábida*, was carrying to Spain, and on which Juan de Rivera, servant of Hernando Cortés,[19] was sailing.

Of this rich treasure the following items are of note:

Sixty *marcos* of silver that Cortés was sending to make some lamps for the monastery of *Nuestra Señora de Guadalupe*, *San Francisco de Medellín*, and for the shrine of *Nuestra Señora la Antigua de Sevilla*.

Alonso de Benavides manifested that he was taking 2500 *pesos* of his own, of gold melted and stamped, in addition to seven *marcos* of silver.

Francisco Rosales, sailor, manifested that five hundred *pesos* that he was sending should be delivered to Luis Hernandez or to Juan de Córdova, silversmiths, probably residents of Seville.

In the note relative to the Royal Fifth corresponding to the Emperor, of the gold and silver that was melted by the conquerors since 'we retreated defeated from the City of Temixtitan,' until the 16th May 1522 when this memorial was signed in Coyoacán, there appears:

There has belonged to Your Highness since the said day, until the date of this account, 35 *marcos* 5 ounces of silver, of the fifth of 178 *marcos* and 5 ounces that was taken. . . .

18 Alamán, op.cit., vol.I, p.280: 'after having it in his possession the Emperor Charles V presented it to his Secretary Francisco de los Cobos, who had it melted to turn it into doubloons. This cannot really be forgiven, as Cobos was a noble gentlemen. . . .'
   For further references to silver, see Cortés, op.cit., vol.I, pp.148-57, and vol.II, pp.54-70.
19 Luis Torres Mendoza, op.cit., vol.XII.

Item: two shields of silver decorated with gaudy ornaments, that weighed, one, twelve *marcos*, four ounces and four *reales*, the other eleven *marcos* five ounces; that are in all twenty-four *marcos* two ounces and four *reales*; which said shields were taken in the City of Temixtitán.

3. *Technique of the Indian Silversmiths*

Not only from the description of the jewels, but also from descriptions given by eye-witnesses[20] of the technique of the silversmiths, it is quite evident that the Indian silversmiths had attained a high perfection in the art.

A valuable account of how the Indian goldsmiths produced their magnificient works is preserved in the Florentine Codex. This is shown in *Plate* 9.

Silversmith[21] — The silversmith is a good judge of fine metal, and of it makes any kind of objects, cunningly and artfully. The good silversmith has dexterity, and all that he makes he does with scale and compass, and knows how to refine any kind of metal, and from castings to make flat and round pieces of gold and silver; he also knows how to make molds of charcoal, and pour metal in the fire for melting. The bad silversmith does not know how to refine silver, he leaves it mixed with ashes, and is clever in taking out and stealing some of the silver.

Goldsmith — Is he who sells beads of gold, silver, or copper, or deals in chains or necklaces of gold, and in bracelets for the wrists: he of this trade is at times a silversmith. If he is a good craftsman with fear and good conscience, he sells them according to what each may be worth, moderating its price; to him it is also advantageous to make and sell flat and round pieces of gold, and to make shrimps of gold; and he who is not such, at times mixes good gold with false gold, or with some low grade metal to give polish, with which he deceives those who buy, and in the price he usually haggles much, and nothing satisfies him; on the contrary, he is very stubborn.

Friar Toribio de Paredes or Benavente [called Motolinía], who was one of the first Franciscans who arrived in the country, in 1524, speaking of the handicraft of the Indians, says:[22]

They also learned how to beat gold, because a gold-beater who went to this New Spain, although he tried to hide his trade from the Indians, could not do so, because

20 Sahagún, op.cit., vol.III, p.18.
21 Ibid., vol.III, p.41.
22 Friar Toribio de Motolinía or Benavente, op.cit., pp.216-17. Apparently these lines were written prior to 1536, as this date is given on page 105 of his work.

they watched all the peculiarities of the trade and counted the blows he gave with the hammer, and how he turned the pattern, and before a year had passed they made beaten gold.

There have also been a few who make good stamped leather work, stealing the trade from the master, without his wishing to show th⸺ ⸺igh they had a difficult time in giving it the gold and silv⸺ ⸺ade some good bells with a clear tone: thi⸺ ⸺e out best. To be good silversn⸺ ⸺do not have, but with one ston⸺ ⸺ut in melting a piece and make ⸺ths of Spain, because they cast ⸺wings; and cast a monkey or o⸺ ⸺hands; and in the hands they pl⸺ ⸺and what is more they take a ⸺ ⸺ith all its scales, the one of gol⸺

Friar Jerónimo d⸺ ⸺rote:[23]

The silversmiths lack⸺ ⸺stone over another they made ⸺sting any piece or jewel they ⸺ause they cast a bird that mov⸺ ⸺st a monkey or other animal, t⸺ ⸺he hands they placed some tri⸺ ⸺d what is more, they took a p⸺ ⸺d cast a fish, the half of the sc⸺ ⸺f silver and another of gold at⸺

The reader will note tha⸺ work of Motolinía, above ⸺ the Indian silversmiths wer⸺ witness, and the actual gold⸺ seem to prove the contrary.

4. Concer⸺ ⸺ne Goldsmiths

Friar Bernardino de Sahagún,[25] commenting on the art of the Indian silversmiths, says:

23 Friar Jerónimo de Mendieta *Historia Eclesiástica Indiana*, pp.403-4, Published by Joaquín García Icazbalceta, Mexico, MDCCCLX. Printed by *Antigua Librería*.
24 Among the jewels of Monte Albán, there are objects half of silver and half of gold.
25 Sahagún, op.cit., vol.II, pp.387-9.

This chapter begins to deal with the workmen who make designs in gold and silver. The craftsmen who work gold are of two kinds, some of them are called hammerers or pounders, because these work with wrought gold, pounding it with stones or with hammers to make it thin as paper, others are called *tlatlaliani* which means that they work the gold or the silver or something [figure] in it. These are true artisans called *tulteca*; but they are divided into two classes, because they work the gold each one in his own manner. They had for a god, these artisans, in the time of their idolatry, a god who was called *Totec*; they held a festival each year in the *Cú* that was called *Yapico*, in the month that was called *Tlacaxipeoaliztli*: in this said feast many captives were skinned alive, for which cause it is called *tlacaxipeoaliztli*, which means: 'beheading of persons.' One of the Satraps clothed himself in a skin of those that they had stripped from the captives, and thus dressed, was an image of this god *Totec*. And they adorned themselves with their very precious ornaments: one of which was a crown made very neatly of fine feathers, and these same things served them as false hair: they placed in their nostrils a half-moon of gold, fastened in the gristle that divided the one opening from the other. They wore also some ear coverings of gold: they carried in the right hand a staff that was hollow inside and held rattles. . . .

Casting.

Friar Bernardino de Sahagún has left us complete data regarding the technique of casting of the Indian silversmiths. This is omitted in the abridged Spanish version of his work, published by Bustamante and Lord Kingsborough; but Seler has translated it from the original text and it can be found in *The Goldsmith's Art in Ancient Mexico.*[26]

26 Saville, op.cit., pp.125-41.

Chapter III

THE BEGINNING OF THE COLONIAL
SILVERSMITHS' ART

I. DESTRUCTION OF THE INDIAN CIVILIZATION. 2. SPANISH GREED. 3. THE RELIGIOUS INFLUENCE. 4. THE INFLUENCE OF THE SPANISH SILVER-SMITHS. 5. THE SKILL OF THE ANCIENT INDIANS.

1. *The Material and Moral Destruction of the*
Indian Civilization

HISTORY teaches us that, as a general rule, the nation that conquers another is satisfied with imposing itself politically, permitting the subjects of the conquered nation full liberty with respect to their religion, customs and the execution of their industrial arts. The Romans followed this plan in their many conquests, as did the Egyptians, the Moors in Spain, and the English in British-India.

Considering the intimate political-religious union of the Catholic Kingdom of that period, and the influence of religion in the intellectual life of the times, the slightest tolerance of idolatry was not possible. The Spaniard of the sixteenth century could not conceive of a conquest other than under the absolute domination of the Catholic religion, the establishment of his political organization, the integral application of his legislative[1] and administrative systems, and the imposition of his language.

Impelled by their fanaticism, friars, soldiers, administrators and simple citizens co-operated efficiently in the task of destroying the Indian civilization. Materially, they tore down the temples and idols and burned the old manuscripts. Morally, they destroyed the Indian insti-

[1] Later, the difficulties that were encountered in the application of the Spanish legislation forced the creation of laws to meet the special conditions of the Indies.

tutions, laws and religion. Nothing remained to impede the implanta-
tion of the Spanish civilization and its artistic expression. The silversmiths' art of the Aztecs was completely destroyed as soon as it came
under the influence of the art of Europe.

2. *Spanish Greed*

As greed for the precious metals inspired the Conquest, the *Conquistadores* possessed themselves immediately of all the bullion available,
leaving the Indian silversmiths a very limited amount of raw material.
So efficient were the methods employed that silver and gold soon became very scarce.

Cortés, when he was rebuilding Mexico, spoke of the then quite
notable scarcity of treasure: 'The truth is that neither of jewelry of
gold, nor silver, nor rich feathers, nor any rich thing, there is nothing
like the quantity there used to be; some small pieces of gold and silver
are obtained, but not as before.'[2]

3. *The Religious Influence*

When the construction of the Christian temples[3] and convents was
begun, the Church had urgent need of sacred vessels, jewelry and
images, for use in the churches and religious ceremonies. These objects
could have no forms other than those prescribed by the church of Spain.
The jewelry, the exquisite reproductions of animals and the ornaments
of the idols, in which the Indians excelled, were of no use to the missionaries. For the Spaniards, these were 'things worth seeing' and nothing more. This not only brought an end to the making of the exquisite
objects in which the Indians excelled; the Indians themselves could
not make the things required by the Spaniards without the instruction
and guidance of the Spanish silversmiths.

4. *The Influence of the Spanish Silversmiths*

There were silversmiths among the conquerors and the Spaniards who
arrived soon thereafter. These abhorred the Indian silversmiths on

2 Cortés, op.cit., vol.II, p.III.
3 'The principal church was in use in the year 1528.' José María Marroqui, *La Ciudad de México*,
   vol.III, p.470. 'La Europea,' Mexico, 1900. 3 vols.

account of the low price of their labor. The clergy, desiring their sacred vessels and other accessories as promptly and as cheaply as possible, and being protectors of the Indians by Royal warrants, were not content with the official criterion, but they could not ignore the laws and the power of the Spanish authorities.

When the conquerors established schools to teach the Indians the Spanish[4] arts, they began, as was natural, with the most skillful; but they also began to teach the children, who were soon converted to Christianity. Thus it came about that the teaching of Spanish art, gradually, perhaps unintentionally, obliterated that of the aborigines.

Friar Jerónimo de Mendieta[5] has left us a narrative that throws light on these two points:

5. The Skill of the Ancient Indians

How the Indians learned the mechanical trades of which they were ignorant, and perfected themselves in those that they formerly used.

INDUSTRIAL SEMINARY, CHAPEL OF SAN JOSE.

The first and only seminary that there was in New Spain for all kinds of trades and tasks [not only those pertaining to the service of the church, but also those that serve the laymen], was the chapel called San José, adjoining the church and monastery of San Francisco of the city of Mexico, where resided many years, having it in his charge, the very faithful servant of God and famous layman Friar Pedro de Gante, first and foremost master and industrious teacher of the Indians. He did not content himself with having a great school of children who were taught in the Christian doctrine, and to read and write and sing; he arranged that the young men should apply themselves to learn the trades and arts of the Spaniards, that their fathers and grandfathers did not know, as well as perfect themselves in those that they formerly used. For this he had at the end of the chapel several rooms and apartments used for this purpose, where he had them assembled, and he had them practice first in the most common trades, such as [those of] tailor, shoemaker, carpenter, painter and other similar ones, and afterwards in those of more skill, so that if by chance he did not employ them (. . . more especially in that time when they were timid and frightened of the past war, of the many of their own dead, of their ruined city, and finally, of such rapid change and such a difference in all things) without doubt they retained that which their forefathers knew. . . .

4 Icazbalceta believes that Friar Pedro de Gante taught also the adult Indians and even the old ones.
    J.García Icazbalceta, *Obras de*, p.26, vol.111. V.Agueros, Mexico, 1896.
5 Mendieta, op.cit., pp.406-7.

Moreover they began to develop with that ordinary exercise, and they coveted some advantage from [the knowledge] they were acquiring (in addition they were like monkeys: what they saw some do, the others wanted to do). In this manner they soon learned the trades better than our artisans desired. Because those who came fresh from Spain, and were thinking that as there were no others of their trade they were going to sell and earn as they might wish, soon found that the Indians excelled them on account of their great activity and talent and the excellent manner of their work, as . . . [did the Indian] who stole his trade from the first weaver of coarse stuff who came from Spain. . . . This same man was an overseer in the making of printed leathers, and he kept secret all possible from the Indians of that in which he worked, especially that they should not know how to apply the gold and silver colors. The Indians, seeing that he hid things from them, agreed to watch the materials that he was using, and they took a little bit of each thing, and they went to a friar, and said to him: 'Father, tell us where they sell this that we bring. If we may have it, however much the Spaniard conceals things from us, we can make printed leathers, and we will give them the gold and silver colors like the masters of Castille.' The friar (who must have been Friar Pedro de Gante, and who was pleased) told them where to buy the materials, and obtained, they made their printed leathers. When the Indians wished to imitate the saddles of the horsemen, that a Spaniard was beginning to make, they succeeded in all that was necessary for it, the breast plate, its overcovering and pads, except they did not know how to make the tree. And as the saddlemaker had a tree (as is customary) at the door of the house, they waited until he went inside to eat, and took the tree to make another. And once made, the next day at the same hour when he was eating they returned to replace the tree in its place. When the saddlemaker saw this, he at once feared that his trade would soon become commonplace in the hands of the Indians (like the other trades) and thus it turned out that after six or seven days an Indian came selling trees [saddle] in the street, and arriving at his house he asked him if he wished to buy those trees and others that he had made, on which the good saddlemaker was seized with anger and wanted to strike him on the head with them, because he, as he was the only one in the trade, sold his work as he desired, and placed in the hands of the Indians the price would come down very much.

The rulers of Spain, foreseeing that there would be no means of collecting their fifth of the silver and gold that the Indians might work, issued a Royal decree that was promulgated by the Municipal Council in Mexico on the 31st July 1527:[6]

. . . and that no person who might have been or who might be a miner for

6 Alamán. op.cit., vol.II, p.448 and *Actas de Cabildo del día 31 de julio de 1527.*

another shall dare to give to the Indian silversmiths of this New Spain, any jewelry of gold or sequins to make now or at any time. Penalty: loss of all their properties for the coffers of His Majesty and perpetual banishment from this New Spain.

Although the early settlers of Mexico paid little attention to many Royal decrees, this, which was pleasing to the Spanish silversmiths, was respected, and doubtless largely contributed to the destruction of the ancient art of the Indians.

The early decrees[7] prohibited anyone who was not a Spaniard of two generations to work even as a laborer in a shop of an accredited craftsman.

Not until 1776[8] did their Catholic Majesties graciously decree:

. . . limiting the third in the decree that denied the privilege of employing workmen of the Indians, Mestizos and Mulattos, of which class are nearly all the most skillful individuals of the guild.

Thus, the death of the Indian silversmiths' art and the lack of any Indian influence in the colonial silversmiths' art were due principally to the fact that the political-religious organization of the Spain of that period had decreed its death, and, in lesser degree, to the greed of the conquerors, who left the Indian silversmiths without raw material; to the urgent requirements for sacred vessels, etc., which made impracticable the production of the exquisite objects in which the natives delighted; to the desire of the Spanish silversmiths for a monopoly; and finally, to the degradation of the Indian from an honored master of his craft to a workman in the shops of the Spanish silversmiths.

Nevertheless, as an exception to this general rule, on several occasions the Spanish officials employed or forced the Indian silversmiths to make objects and jewels for them. The most celebrated of these was the celebrated scorpion of gold, emeralds, pearls and enamels that

7 *Ordenanzas de Batiojas,* 12th June 1598. *Ordenanzas de Gremios de la Nueva España,* p.142, also *Ordenanzas de Tiradores de Oro y Plata* p.139, 3rd January 1665, by Francisco del Barrio Lorenzot. Mexico, 1921. Published by the Secretariat of Industry, Commerce and Labor, under the direction of Genaro Estrada.

8 Antonio Xavier Pérez y López, *Teatro de Legislación Universal de España e Indios* Royal Ordinance, 12th October 1776, vol.XXIII, p.129, Madrid. Refers to Guatemala but applied to all the Indies.
   Even in 1746 the master silversmiths of Mexico were forbidden to accept as apprentice anyone who was not 'a Spaniard of good and worthy habits,' and forbade the admission of 'persons who might be of mixed color.' (Ordinances of the Viceroy Fuen-Clara of 1746. Ordinance No.36, *Ordenanzas de el Nobilissimo Arte de la Platería,* Mexico, 1746. Printed by María de Ribera.)

Hernando Cortés had made and taken to Spain in 1527 as an offering to the Virgin of Guadalupe in gratitude for his recovery from the effects of the bite of a poisonous scorpion, suffered in Yautepec, State of Morelos.[9]

Likewise are well known the inventories of jewels made by Indian silversmiths for Cortés and which he sent to Spain; those that Nuño de Guzmán ordered made for himself and those which the Spaniards demanded of the Indians of Tepetlaoztoc. These are reproduced in a Codice by means of which the Indians complained of their treatment.[10]

9 'This jewel is noteworthy due to the fact that it is the image of a scorpion or other insect that bit the famous Hernán Cortés, causing him a serious sickness, from which he was at the point of death during the time he was occupied in the campaign of Mexico. In his affliction he consecrated himself to the Virgin Mary of Guadalupe of his country, who heard his prayers. And the devout Cortés manifested his gratefulness by visiting his benefactress at this holy shrine seven years after he conquered Mexico, offering various gifts, one of which was this jewel, which is of gold with some enamel of green and other colors, with forty and three emeralds very clear, most of them large and beautiful, cut with much skill. It has also four pearls, two hanging and the other two fixed in the antennae. One emerald is missing.' (Vicente Barrantes,) *Virgen y Martir. Nuestra Sra. de Guadalupe*, Badajoz, 1895.

   These data and the photographs reproduced, *Plates* 10 and 11, were furnished me by my friend Don Federico Gómez de Orozco.

10 Francisco del Paso y Troncoso, *Memorial de los Indios de Tepetlaoztoc al Monarca Español contra los Encomenderos del Pueblo*. First Part. Printed by Hauser and Menet, Madrid, 1912.

Chapter IV

THE SILVERSMITHS' GUILD OF MEXICO

1. *Origin of the Legislation*

LEGISLATION and regulations relative to the silversmiths' art and the silversmiths' guild have existed since very ancient times in Spain,[1] where the collection of the Royal Fifth of the precious metals, the registration of the quality and fineness of the fabricated articles and many other minor details were fully treated in decrees and ordinances, which later served as a basis for legislation on this subject in the Indies.

2. *The Silversmiths' Guilds in Spain*

From ancient times the silversmiths were controlled, in common with the other industrial arts, by means of guilds. Sentenach says:[2]

The fraternity of the guilds already appear prominent and enjoying certain privileges towards the end of the fourteenth century, principally in Cataluña, because on the 30th May 1381 the *Infante* Juan de Aragón granted the guild the right to name its members on the day of Saint Eloy of each year, to which [privilege] was added another of 1394 setting the standard on gold and other particulars of the trade, continuing with other ordinances in subsequent years.

---

1 John II in Madrid, year of 1435, pet.31, and in Toledo, 1436, pet.1 and 2; Ferdinand and Isabella in Madrigal, year 1476, pet.14. *Novísima Recopilación de las Leyes en España*, vol.III, p.277. Madrid, 1805. Four vols.

2 Narciso de Sentenach, op.cit., p.75.

The Rulings of the Constitution of the guild members and brothers of the Guild and Fraternity of the Silversmiths of Toledo is dated 24th June 1423, renewed on the same day of the following year, and that of Seville, from John II, under *Title of the Gold Silversmiths,* dates from the 26th October 1425. The silversmiths' regulations were confirmed at Burgos by John II and Henry IV.

The Catholic Kings, so vigilant of all the industries in their kingdoms, also issued special orders relative to the jewelers, which are transcribed integrally in the Ordinances of Toledo, forming Chapters 33, on the embroiders; 48 on the assayers; 55 on the gilders; 90 on . . . and the hall-marks of the silversmiths and of the city . . . decree of October 6 1494, as well as other regulations tending to guarantee the standard of the metals, and likewise to allow certain privileges to the guilds and brotherhoods.

As we shall see further on, the system of guilds, among these that of the silversmiths, was established in Mexico soon after the conquest.

3. *Purpose of the Silversmiths' Guild in Mexico*

The guild, in addition to its effective control over the silversmiths' art, constituted a monopoly which regulated the output and the prices. Apprentices received no pay and their examinations for license to practice the art as a master were authorized by a master of the guild.

The silversmiths of Mexico, like those of France and Spain, had for their patron saint San Eligio, who, according to tradition, was once a silversmith. They organized a brotherhood within the guild and this had at its disposal funds for the protection of its members, forming an effective type of social insurance entirely independent of the State. This assisted them, not only in cases of sickness and death, but also extended its benefits beyond the guild, giving assistance to orphans, the destitute and the poor.

The *Monte Pio del noble Arte de Platería, Tiradores y Bateojas*, was organized on the initiative of Juan Antonio de Exija, a Director of the Board of the Guild, who drew up the petition for its organization, and the ordinances governing it, signing for the Board on the 7th December 1772. The Ordinances were approved by Diego González de la Cueva, *Juez Veedor* and *Ensayador Mayor* on the 16th December 1772, and with certain minor modifications, by King Charles III, in Madrid, on the 20th July 1777, and finally by the Viceroy and his Secretary, Juan

José Martínez de Soría, in Tacubaya (Mexico), on the 9th June 1784.[3]

By order of the King, the silversmiths handled the pension funds, 'without it being necessary that there intervene in matters relative to the Pension Fund any Ecclesiastical or Civil Judge, substituting the chief Assayer, *Juez Veedor*.'

According to Juan Antonio de Exija the scope of the Pension Fund was very broad: 'to give food to the poor, drink to the thirsty, clothe the naked, cure the sick, comfort the sad, assist the widow and with them her destitute orphans.'

In keeping with the Ordinances, the benefits were limited to members who had contributed and their families.

4. *The Influence of the Guild on the Silversmiths' Art in Mexico*

The few authors who have dealt with this subject differ in their opinions. The distinguished Mexican author, Luis González Obregón,[4] speaking of guilds in general says:

The guilds were similar to the modern unions, selfish and intransigent. They did not permit anyone to practice his art or trade who was not a member of their group. They became true dictators, for the artisans as well as for the public, as they fixed prices and customs to suit their will—to such a degree that the authorities were forced to intervene, naming inspectors and *veedores*, in order to insure compliance with the provisions of the decrees and ordinances that they had to issue for this purpose.

At the same time that such guilds exercised a monopoly prejudicial for the purchasers, they were an obstacle to the progress of the arts and trades, which were retarded, and a servitude for the apprentices, who served the masters free of charge during their apprenticeship, sweeping out the shops, running errands and being employed in other chores not too decent or becoming.

Marroqui[5] had a better opinion of the guilds:

3 *Archivo General de la Nación. Reales Cédulas* vol.143, Year 1775, p.225 reverse to 233.
    With the organization of this pension fund, the drawing of lots for orphans [*sorteo de huérfanos*] was abandoned. Of these drawings, that of *Nuestra Señora de las Lágrimas* was founded on the 26th June 1669; that of the *Purísima Concepción*, the 25th November 1743. Every member of the Guild contributed one *real* weekly to these funds, so that 'an orphan will be drawn by lot yearly on the day fixed and this to be done with all the silversmiths, beaters of gold and silver and drawers of gold wire who might have contributed their weekly alms taking part, and he who may be successful shall not bond her to any one other than a legitimate Spanish woman. . . .'
4 Luis González Obregón, *Las Calles de México*, vol.II, p.144. Manuel León Sánchez, Mexico, 1927. 2 vols.
5 Marroqui, op.cit., vol.III, p.197.

One of the purposes, perhaps the principal one, for the establishment of the guilds, was to bring about the perfection of their wares, using this word in its highest sense, for they took precautions not only in their perfection and beauty, but also intrinsically, taking care that the materials employed in the objects of art should be of the best quality, and that the work be done conscientiously with respect to its class and finish. For this reason they supervised the apprentices, instructed the workmen, required examinations of candidates who aspired to become masters, and only by complying with these requirements could they keep a shop. This supervision was exercised by the *veedores*, who were elected officials, chosen each year from among the masters to exercise this supervision. In the silversmiths' branch, therefore, it was necessary not only to pay attention to the beauty and perfection of the object, but to take care that the raw material, gold or silver, be of the required standard.

Manuel Romero de Terreros says:[6]

One of the things that influenced most the advancement of the industrial arts in New Spain, was, doubtless, the organization of guilds, that is, the legal classification of trades for the purpose of regulating the output and the respective taxes.

In all periods the principal factor and almost the only one that has had a decisive influence on the quality of plate, has been the price that the artisan has received for his wares. The concentration of wealth in the hands of the aristocratic class, appreciative of fine work and willing to pay the excessive prices that the artisan demanded and, indeed, required because of the time required to make a true work of art, was that which influenced most the advance of the silversmiths' art in Mexico. To this we may add the wealth of the church and the abundance of precious metals. For these reasons it is probable that competition, free from the control of the guild, would have been beneficial.

5. *The First Ordinances* (1524-1550)

CORTÉS' ORDINANCES — 1524

Cortés,[7] in his Fourth Descriptive Letter, signed on the 15th October 1524, informed his 'Most High and Most Powerful, Unconquerable, Lord Charles, Magnificent Emperor and King of Spain,' of having

6 Manuel Romero de Terreros, Marquis of San Francisco, *Las Artes Industriales en la Nueva España*, Pedro Robredo, Mexico, 1923.
7 Cortés, op.cit., vol.II, p.126.

issued certain ordinances. These are reproduced by Lucas Alamán[8] in his *Dissertations on the History of Mexico*, and none relative to silver[9] appear. Doubtless because the majority of these were regulations for the organization and good governing of the growing colony, they comprised only those essential at the time they were issued.

6. *The First Silversmiths in Mexico*

The great majority of the *conquistadores* were not professional soldiers, but ordinary citizens, and many of them were competent artisans.[10] Charmed with this rich and beautiful new world they had so boldly seized, they soon determined to settle there permanently. It is not surprising, then, that those not occupied in the conquest of the outlying regions, as well as those tired of war, should have returned to the arts and trades they knew best, dreaming of the great fortunes to be made in this new land where everything had to be made and competition was non-existent.[11]

Among the conquerors there was at least one silversmith, Gaspar de Garnica,[12] who soon established himself in Tenochtitlán.

With the Spaniards in pacific possession of the country and with the encouragement from the Crown,[13] mines began to be opened, assuring an abundance of the precious metals, necessary to meet the constant demand for jewelry, crosses and sacred vessels, which the clergy required in order to 'manifest the religious spirit of that period.'

Lucas Alamán[14] mentions two of the early silversmiths:

8 Alamán, op.cit., pp.105-148, Bib.

9 They might have existed, but if so they have not been discovered. Lucas Alamán obtained these from the private archives of Cortés, which were preserved by his descendants.

10 Marroqui, op.cit., vol.I, p.46.

11 In the *Diccionario Autobiográfico de Conquistadores y Pobladores de Nueva España* by Francisco A. de Icaza, Madrid, 1923, none admit being silversmiths. But this information was compiled for the purpose of asking help and reward for their participation in the conquest from Charles V. Therefore, it is not surprising that nearly all declared themselves 'poor and without apportionment of Indians, or trade.'

12 Díaz, op.cit., p.20, says that the Governor of Cuba, Diego Velázquez, 'sent his servant, who called himself Gaspar de Garnica, with orders and provisions so that by all means Cortés should be imprisoned, etc.' This when Velázquez was trying to prevent Cortés from leaving Cuba. The name of Gaspar de Garnica appears in the *Diccionario Universal de Historia y Geografía*, op.cit., vol.II, p.499, where it is mentioned that he came with Cortés.

13 By decree issued in Granada on the 9th November 1526, the Emperor Charles ordered that, without limitation, all kinds of people, Indians, Negroes or Spaniards, were allowed and should work the mines as their own, paying only the Royal Fifth.

14 Alamán, op.cit., vol.II, pp.445-6.

The lack of coins for currency was an obstacle for all business operations, as all transactions were accomplished by exchange for silver and gold by weight [*peso*], origin of the name of this money called *peso*. To overcome this inconvenience, it was ordered on the 6th April 1526 that all persons who might have gold from their labor in the mines, and wished to take it for melting in presence of the royal inspectors, might do so; it being returned to them reduced to small pieces or little plates of one *tomine*, and two *tomines*, and four *tomines*, and one *peso*, and two *pesos*, and four *pesos*. On each piece the number of carats would be stamped so that it would circulate in the land, and that they might buy and sell in small amounts. This matter they gave in charge of *Diego Martinez* and *Juan de Celada, silversmiths*, [who were in charge of the melting], so that the aforementioned might have charge of the work. It was also provided that they must give said men 'two gold *pesos* per hundred for that lost in making it into small [pieces] and for their work of assaying it four *pesos* per hundred, so that for each one hundred *pesos* that they may assay in the manner mentioned, they must have two-thirds in small pieces and one-third in [the larger pieces of] one *peso* up to four *pesos*.'

7. *The Prices*

Apparently the wealth of the colony and the lack of competition tempted the silversmiths to charge excessive prices, because on the 7th May 1527, the Municipal Council of the City of Mexico, in session of that date, acting on complaints of the high prices charged, issued the following regulations:

REGULATIONS FOR THE SILVERSMITHS: 7TH MAY 1527

. . . ordered and commanded that with respect to the silversmiths who practice their trade in this City and are charging very excessive and exorbitant prices for labor and wares that they make in the said trade; now henceforth shall comply with the impartial price rates that for their use are herein contained:

Firstly that for each silver *marco* of flat plate which includes plates and
    sweepings: one gold *peso*   ″1 ps.

For making each silver *marco* in plain jars or cups: two *pesos* gold   ″2 ps.

For making a jar or a kettle: two *pesos* and a half   ″2 ps. 4ts.

In case that on any of the aforementioned pieces they should make some design or guild them or enamel them or anything else besides the above mentioned, it shall be rated and appraised by the delegates and by one workman of his trade whom they will appoint and have sworn.

For making a plain ring with setting only, they should charge one *peso*
    and a half, or, if it be enamelled or   ″1 ps. 4ts.
    decorated, charge two *pesos* of gold   ″2 ps.

If it were without mounting one *peso* of gold   "1 ps.

That if anything of gold in jewelry, necklaces or mounting of stones or
 other things pertaining to the said trade were made by said silversmiths that the price for making such things be left for the appraisal of
 the said delegates and of one workman whom the said delegates shall
 name.

After saying which, the said Officials ordered the aforementioned silversmiths to
obey and comply with it, and that they should not go against it or exceed it, at
any time. Penalty: that for the first time they disobey they shall be subject to a
fine of fifty *pesos*, of which half shall be for the public works of this said city and
the other for the judge and denouncer. For the second and third time, double
penalty shall be applied in the same manner. And they ordered this proclaimed
publicly which was done on Monday the thirteenth day of May, being present at
the public square of this said City many people. Witnesses Diego Bezerra and
Angel de Villafaña and Juan Hernandez del Castillo, Public Scrivener.

DIEGO MARTINEZ *VEEDOR* OF THE SILVERSMITHS

The resolution of the Municipal Council had the desired result, as
shown in proceedings of the Assembly of the 17th May 1527:

On this day Diego Martínez, assayer, in his name and that of the silversmiths of
this City, presented a petition before the said officials in which he requested, for
certain reasons which he gave and that were contained in his said petition, that they
have the goodness to cancel the price tariff which they were ordered to make on
the things that they were to manufacture in their trade. Having been read by the
said Officials, they said that considering that the said Diego Martínez was a good
person and of good conscience and that he has always been so and held as such in
those places where he has been, and as it is public and well known among all those
who know him that he was appointed as *Veedor* of all the objects both of gold and
of silver that were made by all the silversmiths of this said City so that he might
appraise and set their price in accordance with God and his conscience . . . gave
the solemn oath that in such case is required.

THE FABRICATION OF GOLD AND SILVER IS PROHIBITED: 9TH NOVEMBER 1526

For fear that in these remote countries payment of the Royal Fifth
might be eluded by fabricating the precious metals, Charles V, by
Royal Decree dated in Granada on the 9th November 1526, and sent
to the authorities in Mexico, prohibited the fabrication of gold and
silver 'under penalty of death and loss of their properties.'

This decree was proclaimed in the City of 'Tenuxtitlán,' on the 22nd August 1527, '. . . in the principal church of this City, the Governor Hernando Cortés, the Magistrates, Councilmen of this said City and many other inhabitants being present. . . .'[15]

Notwithstanding the force of these restrictions, full compliance was not given, for in 1528 another Decree states: 'I [the King] am now informed that in this land there are silversmiths who fabricate gold and silver and publicly practice their trade and have shops for this purpose and have in their houses bellows and other apparatus for melting and you have and are permitting that which contributes to violation of our law . . . and with respect to this I send the order that applies so that henceforth this be not done, etc.'[16]

It appears that the Assembly itself considered it impossible to enforce such an absurd order. It is certain that little attention was paid to it, and finally the Queen, replying to letters from the Assembly, in Barcelona[17] on the 20th April 1533, modified the Royal Decree of the 9th November 1526. This, if it did not clearly authorize the free practice of the art, was sufficient to ease the conscience of the Second Assembly.

The Kings of Spain probably continued to harass the silversmiths, and the authorities of Mexico continued to protect them until the year 1559, when, in view of the fact that it was reported that silversmiths continued to work and evaded not only payment of the Royal Fifth but also the mining tax on gold and silver, Philip II abolished the prohibition against the making of plate.

The guild [by law] was bound to carry its patron saint, *el Señor Sant ypolito*,[18] in processions on the *fiestas* [feast days]:

THAT THE SILVERSMITHS CARRY SAINT YPOLITO IN THE PROCESSION OF CORPUS

On this day they said that inasmuch as the silversmiths of this city are bound to carry and they do so carry in the feast of Corpus Christi the Lord Saint Ypolito, [who is patron saint of this City of Mexico because on his day this city was taken],

15 *Cedulario de Puga*, vol.I, pp.27, 28. Edition of *El Sistema Postal*, Mexico 1878.
16 Ibid., vol.II, p.324.
17 Ibid., vol.I, p.293.
18 Patron saint of Mexico, and not of the silversmiths, who later chose St. Eligio as their patron saint.

and it is just to so honor and favor him. Wherefore they ordered and commanded that henceforth forever said silversmiths, carrying the said saint, shall go in the procession on the day of Corpus Christi next to the Blessed Sacrament. They shall be given preference above all other trades for reasons mentioned. . . .

PROCEEDINGS OF THE ASSEMBLY OF 18TH MAY 1537

Marroqui, speaking of the Chapel of San Eligio, patron saint of the silversmiths, says:[19]

This chapel is the third on the side of the Gospel and the first after the transept in relation to that of our Lady of the Antigua.

The Silversmiths' Guild, organized a few years after the reconstruction of the city, had for patron saint San Eligio, Bishop of Noyons, and in the first cathedral an altar was dedicated to him the decorations and maintenance of which was for their account. Annually on the first day of December a solemn festival was held with mass and sermon, and also a procession in the afternoon. As the Guild was wealthy, it made a silver statue of its patron saint, of medium size, with rich pontifical robes; the miter and staff were likewise of silver, but gold plated. This image was dedicated on its old altar the year 1618.

The silversmiths worshipped not only St. Eligio, but also the Mother of God, in Her Immaculate Conception, with a solemn festival on the eighth of December of each year.

It was necessary to demolish the existing cathedral and transfer to the new one everything contained in it; one of these things being the altar of St. Eligio; but on this occasion it was placed in a better site. . . . The silversmiths began to repair it, and when the work was well advanced, they fixed Wednesday, December 8, of the year 1648 for its dedication. The festival on this day was exceptional for its magnificence: Dr. Cristobal Gutiérrez de Medina, curate of the Sagrario preached; there was a jubilee during the entire octave, during which, in the afternoons, the Salve was sung by the Prelates.

Likewise endeavoring to improve their possessions, the silversmiths decided to make a silver image of the Immaculate Conception [*Purísima*]; this was made and weighed 243 *marcos*; it was dedicated in the year 1728. For more brilliant display of the new image, it was not dedicated in its chapel, but was placed at the right of the main altar of the cathedral, so that it might be admired during the service held by the Assembly. The carrying frames, used for the first time in the afternoon procession that year, were likewise of silver and weighed 100 *marcos*. This guild was generally very extravagant in all the festivals. . . . The silver images of patron saints of the guild were placed in the center of the principal altar, that of St. Eligio above and the Immaculate Conception below.

19 Marroqui, op.cit., vol.III, pp.448-9.

All this was established by the Regulations of the silversmiths' guild, and the silversmiths' art, so decadent at that time . . . improved. Artisans readily obtained work; they assisted each other in all their needs and provided for quite a few beggars. They also gave dowries to orphans and distributed alms. To fulfill these obligations they depended upon [the income from] twelve houses owned by them in this city, which together were worth $124,000.[20] Thus matters proceeded until the year 1861, when all these societies were abolished and their properties nationalized.

As, in the beginning, the Assembly was the body which by law controlled and commanded everything relative to the arts, including silver, it was hoped that many and valuable data would be found in its archives. Unfortunately this was not the case. Owing to their infrequent meetings[21] and the lack of order in handling the city records, there being no depository provided for them during the early years, there are many gaps in the history of the silversmiths' art.

In 1530, the City Council was at the point of losing nearly all its archives.[22] Later, the situation improved somewhat, but the archives were not placed in order until the reign of Philip II[23] who, with his characteristic energy and good judgment, commanded that the Archives of the City Councils in all the Indies be placed in order.[24]

The proceedings of the Assembly deal at length with dyers, shoe and glove makers, tanners, blacksmiths, confectioners, bakers, velvet weavers, etc., mentioning many of these by name and usually saying that they are 'poor ones who cannot pay for an examination for license,' and asking that provisional licenses be given them. Very little is said

20 These properties were:

No.12 Tiburcio Street	$ 13,000
No.13 Tiburcio Street	12,000
No.7 of the Segunda de las Damas	11,000
No.8 of the Segunda de las Damas	11,500
No.9 of the Segunda de las Damas	9,000
No.1 of the Segunda Estampa de Regina	10,500
No.2 Quesadas Street	11,000
Nos.10, 11 and 12 of San José el Real Street	24,000
No.16 Callejón de Lecuona	11,000
No.19 Mecateros	11,000
	Total: $124,000

21 Ibid., vol.I, pp.29, 30, 41, 44.
22 Ibid., vol.I, p.44.
23 Philip II ruled from 7th January 1556 until his death on the 13th September 1598. (Lucas Alamán, op.cit., vol.IV, p.400).
24 Ibid., vol.I, p.46.

of the silversmiths. Consistently, once a year, usually in January, the Assembly approved the appointment of *veedores* from different trades, for example, in the Proceedings of 23rd January 1612, the following appears:

This day there appeared in the assembly, to take oath of office, *Veedores* from the following trades:

The overseers from the trimmers and lacemakers' trades.

Those from the tailor trade.

Those from the trade of weavers of gold cloth.

Overseers from the ancient art of silk weavers.

Overseers from the cloth shearers' trade.

Those of silks and goods.

It is probable that the *veedores* of the silversmiths' guild were not named so regularly in the early days because of fear of the Royal wrath.

FIRST VEEDORES 1527

The Assembly first mentions silversmiths and ordinances, in the Proceedings of the 14th January 1527:

On this day the said members[25] appointed *alcaldes* and *veedores* of the silversmiths, Etor Mendez and Diego Martin,[26] so that henceforth they may have charge of examining the persons of said trade who might set up shops and watch over and enforce the ordinances which have been issued on this subject.

As confirmed by this record and others mentioned hereafter, the members of the guild had the obligation of meeting annually to appoint *veedores*. At the beginning, this election was confirmed by the Assembly and later by the Viceroy. At first, it appears that two were appointed.

Although, due to incomplete data, it is not possible to define precisely the duties of the *veedores* of that period, it is believed that they did not differ greatly from those of Spain, and from those mentioned in subsequent ordinances, which, in general, were the following:

To examine the applicants for the title of master silversmith.[27]

25 This refers to the members present in the Assembly on the 14th January 1627.

26 Or Martínez, because in the Proceedings of the Assembly of the 17th May of the same year the same man is so called.

27 For the technical part of the examination, see the resumé of the ordinances of the 15th July 1598 and of the 19th February 1599 [Indies] issued by the Viceroy, Count of Monterrey. These are the first data that we have encountered relative to the technique of the examination in Mexico.

Visit the shops to denounce falsifications, as well as frauds to the authorities.

In the beginning to hall-mark the silver.

The same Proceedings of the Assembly mention ordinances on other occasions, namely, that of the 26th May 1532:

This day there appeared in the assembly certain silversmiths and begged of said members that they appoint *alcaldes* and *veedor* from said trade as there are in other cities of Castille, that they see and examine the wares of gold and silver that are made in said trade (in keeping with the ordinances that this city has issued or may issue). The members then ordered them to give their opinion as to who should be selected and who is most intelligent and received their formal oaths to respect whomsoever they might vote for and judge worthy. It appeared that Francisco de Toledo had more votes. And then the members stated that they named and chose for *alcalde* and *veedor* from said trade of the silversmiths and jewelers for this present year Francisco de Toledo, from whom they received oath in the form required by law in such cases, by reason of which he promised to act well and faithfully in said office and to enfore the ordinances that the city might give him and thus having taken the said solemn oath they gave him power to exercise said office.

That of the 24th January 1533:

MARKER FOR THE CITY AND *VEEDOR* OF THE SILVERSMITHS, 1533

This day the said members, with the consent and approval of the artisans of silver and gold, said that they named and appointed for *veedor* and *alcalde* of said trade and for marker [hall-marker] of this city Pedro Despina,[28] assayer, as the person who had more votes from the artisans of said trade, and they received the solemn oath that in such cases is required, and which he gave in due form. Having given the oath they gave him power and authority to administer the offices and charges in keeping with the ordinances of this city. They then delivered to him the die[29] [punch] of this city which he received in his keeping and signed. Pedro Despina.

That of the 18th August 1536:

WITH RESPECT TO SILVERSMITHS

They said that inasmuch as this city has issued ordinances with respect to the practice of the silversmiths' trade, [to the effect] that if qualified [to practice] they

28 In the Proceedings of the Assembly of the 25th september 1528 it was decreed that Pedro de Espina 'shall assay and [hall] mark the carats of the gold which is cast in the mint,' things which, until that time, had not been done.

29 Note particularly the reference to the 'die of this city' — the first reference to a hall-mark which has been found in the records.

should give bonds as is provided in said ordinances; and they ordered Bartolomé Ruyz and Antonio Hernandez, silversmiths, *alcaldes* of said trade in this city that they present themselves; and being present that they take a copy of said ordinances and require that all artisans of said trade comply with the ordinances in such manner that they be enforced; with warning that if through not enforcing them some damage should result [to the treasury], they shall pay with their persons and properties; and, if to carry out the foregoing they should require help and aid, that they shall apply to the delegates of this said city and that in its name they will be given means to enforce the ordinances. They also said to Bartolomé Ruyz and Antonio Hernandez that they should observe closely the ordinances and fulfill that which city orders and commands therein.

That of the 23rd January 1537:

WITH RESPECT TO TAILORS AND SILVERSMITHS

This day they said that inasmuch as it is an ordinance of this city, confirmed and proclaimed, that no silversmiths, tailors, makers of chain-mail, or shoemakers may practice said trades without being examined and able to show the title of examination in this assembly, and give bonds as is provided in said ordinance; and because in the result and application of the aforesaid it has not been done according to the orders given the *alcaldes* of said trades, they ordered that notice be given said *alcaldes* for the first meeting of the assembly to give a record of the workmen in each trade, and which were or were not examined, and whether or not bonds were made and which persons are the bondsmen . . . so that after revision in the meeting of the assembly the necessary action may be taken which they are commanded to do under penalty of thirty *pesos* fine to each, one half for the treasury of His Majesty and the other half for the public works of this city. [Signed] Geronimo Ruyz de la Mota. Hernan Perez de Bocanegra. Gonzalo Ruyz. Joan de Mansilla. Miguel Lopez.

That of the 3rd July 1544:

This day the artificers of the silver art who are in this city presented to said assembly a petition in which they named as *alcalde*, *veedor* and marker of said trade Gabriel de Billasana. They begged that this be accepted and confirmed by said assembly and that the die [punch] of this city be ordered given him according to the long statement in said petition. Then the justices and assemblymen ordered that said Gabriel de Billasana present himself in the assembly and received from him the proper oath by law, which he gave in due form and promised to administer well and faithfully said office of *veedor* and marker [hall-marker] for the silver trade, obeying the laws and ordinances of Your Majesty and the ordinances[30] that said

---

30 The ordinances mentioned in these and prior Proceedings have not been found, despite a diligent search of the archives of the City Council and of the General Archives of the Nation.

city has and may issue relative to said trade and having taken the oath they accepted said individual as *veedor* and marker and gave him authority and delivered to him the die [punch] of this city so that he may place it on the pieces made in this city and he received it and accepted said charge. Witnessed and signed: Pedro de Sauzedo and Gonzalo Gil.

In addition to those already named, other *veedores* are mentioned at irregular intervals in the books of the Assembly.

From 1527 to 1557 in the Proceedings of the Assembly of Mexico there are registered as *veedores* and markers of silver and gold:

YEAR	DATE	NAME	
1527	14 January	Etor Mendez and Diego Martin	Named *veedores*
1532	26 May	Francisco de Toledo	Named *veedor*
1533	24 January	Pedro de Espina	" "
1536	28 July	Bartolomé Ruys and Antonio Hernandez	Named *veedores*
1537	13 March	Gonzalo Rodriguez	Named *veedor*
1537	6 April	Luys Rodriguez	" "
1538	6 May	Francisco Hernandez	" "
1538	10 February	Pedro Hernandez	" "
1542	11 July	Gomez de Luque and Gonzalo Gil	Named *veedores*
1544	3 July	Gabriel de Billasana	Named *veedor*
1546	9 February	Pedro de Sabsedo	Mentioned as *veedor*
1546	29 March	Enrique Baez and Ramon de Cardona	Named *veedores*
1551	24 July	Gabriel de Billanueva	Named Marker
1557	12 April	Miguel de Consuegra	" "

From the foregoing it is seen that, during a period of thirty years, the Assembly appointed or mentioned as exercising these offices, eighteen persons only;[31] stranger still is the fact that from the 15th January 1580 to the 9th February 1607, the Proceedings of the Assembly mention neither silversmiths nor the silversmiths' art. Perhaps the lack of confirmation of many elections of *veedores* during the first thirty years of the colony was owing to the slight importance given the silversmiths, who were allowed to practice their trade as they pleased.

The lack of confirmations since 1572 may be attributed to a change

31 We do not know whether those named markers were at the same time *veedores*. It is possible that they were markers and assayers for the Mint only.

of system, as it appears that from that year, at least, and possibly from 1558, the appointment was confirmed by the Viceroy. Fonseca and Urrutia say:[32]

The Viceroy, Martín Enriquez, following the example of his predecessors, confirmed on the 5th November 1572 the appointment of Gabriel Villasana as *veedor* of the silversmiths of this city. He was granted the authority necessary for the proper discharge of his office and an annual salary of one hundred and fifty *pesos* for this work.

It is certain that the Viceroy continued to appoint *veedores* during this period, because there appears, in the General Archives of the Nation, the appointment of this same 'Graviel de Villasana' as *veedor* for the goldsmiths in the year 1581.[33]

Marroqui[34] says that the silversmiths organized their guild about 1580, but it has not been possible to verify this date or confirm his statement.

8. *Legislation and Ordinances*, 1551-1600

On the 17th April 1551 the fabrication of gold was again prohibited, although silver was not mentioned. The prohibition against the fabrication of gold was not revoked until the 23rd May 1559 when the Princess Governess, by decree dated in Valladolid, commanded that the fabrication of gold be permitted, on condition that 'they keep and obey any other ordinances that we might issue on this subject.'[35]

Whether owing to the slight interest that the Assembly of Mexico took in the affairs of the silversmiths, or to the summary manner in which the energetic and competent Viceroy, Luis de Velazco,[36] sus-

32 Fonseca y Urrutia, op.cit., vol.I, p.393. It is probable that on account of the intervention of the Viceroy the *veedores* were no longer elected by the silversmiths but were paid employees of the Government.

33 *Archivo General de la Nación, Libro de Ordenanzas.* File O.O.O.O., p.61 reverse.

34 Marroqui, op.cit., vol.III, p.195.

35 *Cedulario de Puga*, op.cit., vol.II, p.324.

36 Fonseca y Urrutia, op.cit., vol.I, pp.390-1 say:
   On the 6th of July 1563, the Viceroy, Luis de Velazco, issued orders suspending the licenses given to the drawers of gold and silver wire for having frequently practiced their trade by working metals not manifested at the mint, and without being marked or assayed. Also for concealing their shops in different houses and streets, where they caused great damage to the Republic [sic] by selling the ounce of silver wire at four or five *pesos*, and leaf gold at no less excessive prices; for which he imposed on all the suspended artisans a cash fine, which was assigned by thirds to the treasury, the judge and the informant, and also that of exile from this capital; all of which was proclaimed so that no one might allege ignorance.

pended the licenses of 'the artisans who drew and beat gold and silver,' for having used metals that had not been assayed, we may conclude that the silversmiths' art received slight attention from the authorities during this period; and that the silversmiths, from 1524 to 1563, practiced their trade more or less as they pleased.

The *batiojas* (beaters of gold and silver) and the *tiradores* (drawers of gold and silver wire), after presenting various petitions and promising to obey faithfully the laws and ordinances that might be issued, finally succeeded in regaining their licenses and resumed work. The Viceroy, Luis de Velazco, issued the first silversmiths' ordinances of record, on the 30th October 1563:[37]

That before they may begin to practice their trade, they must give bond that they will not commit any kind of fraud against the royal Treasury.

That they must practice their trade in the mints, or in the shops designated by the royal officials and [that they must] contribute to His Majesty with the quota that will be assigned to each.

That while the shops are being built they may practice their trade in their own houses.

That when they may be required by the royal officials to report to the mint, they must do so immediately.

That thus the *bateojas* [beaters of gold and silver] and the *tiradores* [drawers of gold and silver wire] shall appoint each year a person from their trade so that, in the name of them all, he shall assay before the royal officials all the gold and silver that they might have for working, which is afterwards marked; and each person must have a book in which will be noted that which each gave for assay, and that delivered to him after being marked, so that he can give proof to the said agents when they demand it. Penalty: death and loss of their properties.

After the silver is assayed it must be cast in the casting house in the presence of the royal assayer and in no other place, under the same penalty; and this official must have another book in which he shall note that [metal] cast for each.

That all the tools for melting the metals, the molds into which the crucibles are emptied and in addition, everything connected with the casting must be done, precisely, within said house, from which they must not be taken to any other place. The silversmiths must not have in their houses bellows or forges, under penalty of loss of half of their properties, assigned to the coffers and treasury of His Majesty, the informant, and the judge who passes sentence, and of perpetual exile from the kingdom.

That they must not sell anything that they draw or beat from gold or silver,

37 Ibid., op.cit., vol.I, pp.391-3.

until they have again manifested it before the royal officials, or in the absence of these, the *veedor* of His Majesty, so that it be noted and signed in the book, in order that the account may be terminated at any time desired.

That each four months said officials must appear before the *veedor* to compare their books. Those of the assayer [shall be compared] with those of the persons. Everything assayed, marked, cast and fabricated, [shall be compared] that there may be no fraud. Penalty [for the official who fails to comply], loss of office in this city.

That none other than an actual artisan in these trades, married in this city, may practice such trade, under penalty of a fine of two hundred *pesos* distributed as mentioned.

That each year they must name the persons to assay the silver, rotating the position. . . .

THE STREET OF THE SILVERSMITHS

The Viceroy, Martín Enríquez,[38] having been informed that fraud by silversmiths was easier because of the fact that they were not segregated in one place, ordered, on the 23rd April 1580, that all silversmiths should have their shops in the street of San Francisco, 'one of the oldest of this city.'[39] This order was approved and confirmed by the Count of Monterrey, his successor, on the 16th December 1595.[40]

This idea of forcing all the silversmiths to have their shops in one street persisted. Ordinance 26 of the Ordinances of Cadereyta of 1638, not only ordered silversmiths to congregate in Calle de San Francisco, but specified what part of the street:

No gold or silversmiths, beaters of gold and silver and drawers of gold and silver wire from now henceforth shall have their shops in any part of the city other than in the street of San Francisco, where they must congregate and be together from the entrance and corner of the plaza to that of the houses that belonged to the General Secretary Ossorio to the street that turns at the girls' college. . . .

38 Ibid., p.393.
39 Marroqui, op.cit., vol.III, p.192: 'Rodrigo de Castañeada and Francisco Dávila had a shop on this street in 1539.'
40 They were following the example of Spain:
   'Inspired by these great masters, the silversmiths' art flourished in Madrid, many stores and shops congregated in Mayor street, at the place still known as [that of] the *Silversmiths Shops*. Here they had the opportunity to exhibit the extraordinary abundance and beauty of their wares on the occasion of the arrival of Queen Margarita of Austria, who later became the wife of the Monarch. The exhibition given by the silversmiths at that time was dazzling; to such a degree that as the retinue passed they were astonished by such magnificence. . . .' — [*Bosquejo Histórico sobre la Orfebrería Española*, p.137, by Narciso Sentenach *Revista de Arch., Bibl. y Museos.* Madrid 1909].

The King, by Royal Decree of the 1st October 1733,[41] issued the following instructions:

That having fixed the time limit you may consider advisable, arrange that, within the period established, the silversmiths of each city be induced to live within the same district in one or different streets, without mingling with other artisans or handicraftsmen, because in addition to being the most satisfactory for good order and in keeping with the custom in these kingdoms, it will better facilitate the sale and purchase of their wares, and the monthly inspection that should be made of the workmen and shops, and will eliminate many grievances and inconveniences that result from having their shops separated and secreted.

In the Ordinances[42] of 1746, for silversmiths, beaters of gold and silver and drawers of gold and silver wire, which were approved by the Viceroy, Count of Fuen-Clara, it was commanded:

That all silversmiths, beaters of gold and silver and drawers of gold and silver wire should congregate in San Francisco street and that they could not have shops in any other place.

These commands were obeyed in part only, Marroqui says:[43]

In the year 1755, it was called either street of the *Plateros* [Silversmiths] or San Francisco, which indicates that the first name, which became firmly established during the second half of the past century, was not at that time in general use.

In the census [44] of 1753, the first two blocks were called *San Francisco*, while in that of 1811[45] the same street was called Street of the Silversmiths, *Calle de Plateros*.

With respect to the number of silversmiths living in these blocks, as compared with those living elsewhere, the records reveal the following:

41 Fonseca y Urrutia, op.cit., vol.I, p.398.
42 Ibid., vol.I, pp.400-1, and *Ordenanzas de el Nobilissimo Arte de la Platería, Imp. Real del Superior Gobierno del Nuevo Rezado, de Doña María de Ribera*, Mexico, 1746.
43 Marroqui, op.cit., vol.III, p.198.
44 *Archivo General de la Nación, Empadronamiento de 1753.* The pages are not numbered.
45 *Archivo General de la Nación. Empadronamiento de 1811.*

SUMMARY OF THE SILVERSMITHS ESTABLISHED IN THE CALLE DE
SAN FRANCISCO OR PLATEROS

YEAR	NUMBER OF SILVER-SMITHS ON SAN FRANCISCO STREET	NUMBER OF SILVER-SMITHS ON OTHER STREETS	TOTAL
[46]1696	47	26	73
[47]1753	10	71	81
[48]1811	29	36	65
[49]1842	7	24	31
[50]1854	8	51	59
[51]1859	3	61	64
[52]1864	7	51	58
[53]1865	4	60	64
[54]1867	4	45	49
[55]1882	1	11	12

1598: ORDINANCES OF THE VICEROY COUNT OF MONTERREY

On the 15th July 1598, the Viceroy, Count of Monterrey, confirmed the Ordinances for the *bateojas*[56] (beaters of gold and silver) and on the 25th May 1599, the same Viceroy confirmed other Ordinances 'for beaters of thin sheets of gold,'[57] summaries of which are as follows:

ORDINANCES FOR *BATIOJAS*: BEATERS OF GOLD AND SILVER

Viceroy Count of Monterrey
15th July 1598

1. That the second day of the year the masters shall meet and appoint:

46 José Torre Revello, *El Gremio de Plateros en las Indias Occidentales*, p.25. Imp. de la Universidad, Buenos Aires, 1932.
47 *Archivo General de la Nación (Civil indiferente T.64) Empadronamiento de 1753.* Pages not numbered.
48 *Archivo General de la Nación. Empadronamiento de 1811. Cuartel menor núm.1.*
49 *Archivo General de la Nación. Padron de establecimientos industriales. 1842. Cuartel menor núm.1.*
50 *Guía de Forasteros en la Ciudad de Méjico, para el año de 1854.* Published by Mariano Galvan Rivera.
51 Juan N. del Valle, *El Viajero en México*, pp.381-3. Andrada and Escalante, Mexico, 1859.
52 Juan. N. del Valle, *El Viajero en México. Completa Guía de Forasteros para 1864.* Andrade and Escalante, Mexico, 1864.
53 *Archivo General de la Nación. Calificación de Establecimientos industriales.—1865.* Establishments of silversmiths.
54 *Directorio del Comercio del Imperio Mexicano para el año de 1867.* Printed by Maillefert, Mexico, 1867.
55 Ireneo Paz and Miguel Tornel, *Nueva Guía de México*, pp.883-4. Year 1882. I.Paz, Mexico.
56 Lorenzot, op.cit., p.142.
57 Ibid., p.145.

   a. An *Alcalde*.

   b. A *Veedor* of the Guild

   c. Some third person for cases of disagreement.

2. That no-one may have a shop without being [first] examined.

3. That no-one who is an Indian, Mulatto or Mestizo may be examined.

4. Any one not a Spaniard who may have learned the trade may work as a laborer in the shop of an examined master.

5. Apprentices:

   a. No time limit is prescribed for apprentices; they may take an examination (if they are skillful) at any time.

   b. He must be able to make a sheet of beaten gold from start to finish (in the shop of one of the *veedores*)

   c. Give bond before opening a shop.

6. Drawers of gold and silver wire:

   Shall not be allowed to beat sheets.

7. Beaters of gold and silver:

   Shall not accept the apprentices of another without his consent.

8. He shall not work except in his own shop or that of another beater of gold and silver on San Francisco Street.

9. None of them may weave, give metal to be woven, have woven materials in their shop or store, possess counterfeit silver or embroider on loose silk, twisted silk or any other kind of silk.

Ordinances for the Beaters of Sheets of Gold [gold leaf]
19th February 1599

VICEROY COUNT OF MONTERREY

1. That on the second or third day of the year they shall elect:
   a. *Veedores*.
   b. An assistant for cases of dispute before the Scrivener of the Assembly.
   c. One Deputy Councilman.

2. That none may have a shop without having been examined.

3. It is forbidden to examine: Indians, Mestizos, Negroes, Mulattos. These may, however, work as laborers in the shops of master silversmiths.

GUILD OF MEXICO   89

4. He shall not be examined until he has given bond.

5. He shall not live or have a shop except on San Francisco Street.

6. He who is examined:

   a. Must know how to draw and make two sheets into gold cloth.

   b. And after making, to finish for use in any design.

   c. He must be able to make a large metal blow pipe and an additional tip of a different size, which are used for gilding.

   d. He must know how to cast a bar of gold and one of silver, that the silver bar be of one ounce and the gold eight *castellanos*; and be able to forge a thin strip from them and solder them together.

In the Proceedings of the Assembly of the 9th February 1607, the following appears:

PROCEEDINGS OF THE ASSEMBLY
9th February 1607

This day was examined the ordinances of the beaters of gold and silver that was presented already drawn up by Francisco de Trejo[58] and after examination it was ordered signed and was signed.

These ordinances have not been found.

1619

In the *Ordenanzas Tocante al Arte de la Platería* (Ordinances Relative to the Silversmiths' Art), which the Marquis de Cadereyta, in 1638, ordered obeyed, it is stated that the silversmiths:

. . . presented me a petition and the order of the Marquis de Guadalcazar of the 7th September 1619,[59] with respect to . . . they shall have their shops and stores in the street of San Francisco, and the other things that it contains and thus also the ordinances that said guild had issued during the past year of 1623, for the good conduct and exercise of their trades and arts to provide better service . . . and in view of this the Marquis of Galvez confirmed and approved them and ordered that they be kept, fulfilled and executed, begging me that I see fit to order it thus, as said ordinances had been maliciously hidden and on account of not being carried out there had resulted. . . .

58 Trejo was an assemblyman in charge of administration of revenues.

59 This document, which is found in the *Archivo General de la Nación, Ordenanzas, vol.2, years 1590-1635, p.27-8,* is limited to ordering the concentration of the silversmiths in San Francisco Street.

From the foregoing, we may conclude that neither the command of the Marquis de Guadalcázar nor the Ordinances of 1623 were obeyed and that the first Ordinances that were effective in form and detail were those of the Marquis de Cadereyta, Viceroy, of 1638, *The Ordinances Relative to the Art of the Silversmiths*,[60] of which a synopsis follows:

SYNOPSIS OF THE

ORDINANCES RELATIVE TO THE SILVERSMITHS' ART

Ordered Obeyed by the Marquis de Cadereyta — 20th October 1638

Ordinance

SAN ELIGIO

1. The obligation to celebrate the festival of San Eligio, their patron saint, is approved.

THE OFFICIALS

2. That the officials selected be: one Rector, two Superintendents and five Delegates.

ELECTIONS

3. That the elections be held the first day of each year in the dwelling of the Rector.

4. That they shall not postpone the elections for another day nor shall those holding office be re-elected, except in the form provided.

DIFFERENCES

5. For any differences that might arise, they should get together the oldest members and be guided by them.

ACCOUNTS

6. The Superintendents should have three books in which they should record the members, alms collected, and how they were expended.

---

60 These ordinances were found only after a search of many months. They are the first in complete form and were never greatly modified. Because of their exceptional importance, the complete text is given in Appendix II.

THE TAX

7. That on all kinds of jewelry of gold and silver they must pay to his Majesty the Royal Fifth which is his due.

THE MARK

8. The law that must be obeyed, in order not to defraud the Royal Fifth, by the silversmiths as well as on the part of the *Veedor* and Royal Officials, is the following:

    a. Before working any silver or gold they shall be obliged to present it before the Royal Officials that they may verify that the bullion is assayed and marked.

    b. The Royal Officials shall weigh and register the bullion, returning it with a certificate.

    c. After the pieces are made they shall be taken before the same Royal Officials so that it may be verified that their weight is the same as the metal in bars [already registered] and that they are of the same standard.

    d. The *Veedor*, in the presence of the Royal Officials, shall mark it with the mark and stamp that he should have for this purpose.

THE GOLD STANDARD

9. They shall not, under penalty, work any gold of less than 22 carats standard.

10. The caster shall not cast any piece of gold of less than 22 carats standard.

11. That gold jewelry, not containing diamonds, rubies, emeralds or other precious stones, shall not be sold except by weight and the making considered separately.

12. That no jewel shall be made of silver or brass gilded with fine enamels.

13. That the jewelry made shall not contain any small pieces of silver or copper-gilt.

PRECIOUS STONES

14. That in these Ordinances there is nothing which changes or alters that ordered by the Decrees and Ordinances relative to the payment of the fifth on precious stones.

CHINESE JEWELRY

15. That the chains, necklaces, sashes, buttons and other jewels brought from China, shall pay the fifth.

LICENSES FOR GOLDSMITHS

16. That although their licenses may be approved by the *Veedor*, Rector and Superintendents, they shall not operate a shop without license from the Government.

THE SILVERSMITHS' MARKS

17. a. That the silversmiths must have a known mark and stamp to be placed on all pieces made by them.
    b. That this mark shall be registered with the Public Scrivener of the Assembly of the City of Mexico.
    c. That without this mark they shall not, under penalty, sell plate.

18. That the *Veedor* [Overseer] shall not receive any piece of gold or silver that does not have the stamp and mark of the artisan who made it.

INSPECTIONS

19. That the Rector, Superintendent and Delegates shall inspect the shops and stores of the silversmiths and see that they comply with their obligations.

20. That the *Veedor* see that full compliance is given Ordinance 19.

PROHIBITION OF BELLOWS, FORGES AND CRUCIBLES

21. That the silversmiths shall not have in their shops or stores bellows, forges or crucibles for smelting, under penalties.

22. That no goldsmith shall work any kind of silver, nor shall a silversmith work any kind of gold.

STANDARD OF SILVER

23. That no silversmith shall work silver of lower standard than eleven *dineros* and four grains.

STANDARD AND ASSAY

24. That no silversmith shall cast sheets [for forging from them any article] without the metal having been assayed.

STANDARD AND HALL-MARK

25. That the wares made shall not be sold without being of the proper standard, and being hall-marked.

STREET OF THE SILVERSMITHS

26. That all the silversmiths shall congregate in the *Calle de San Francisco* and that none shall have their shops outside of it, under penalties.

SALE OF SILVER

27. That in no other part of the city, except in the auction places, shall any article of silver be sold.

SALE OF SALVAGED OR DAMAGED METALS

28. That only the silversmiths may purchase salvaged or damaged gold or silver, and such pieces shall not be sold except in silver shops.

29. That the *Veedor* take special care not to stamp, without first seeing that they are of the required standard, loose pieces such as spouts, assembled and ready to solder, necks of vessels, small bottles, jars and flasks, tubes for candlesticks, ends of salt pans, perfume pots, pepper jars and sugar bowls. . . .

PLATE OUTSIDE THE CITY OF MEXICO

30. That no silversmith shall make any gold jewelry or article of silver outside of Mexico City.

MELTING OF COINS

31. That coins shall not be melted for the purpose of making from them any article of silver.

SILVER GILT

32.   That with respect to silver gilding they shall be guided by the provisions of the laws of the Kingdom as given in Laws 5, 6, 7, 8, 9 and 10, under heading 24, book 5, Recapitulation 4.

THE SCALES

33.   That the scales be adjusted by the inspector of weights and measures of this city and set up with a fulcrum.

OATH

34.   Before setting up a shop and obtaining a license, the silversmiths shall take oath to comply with these Ordinances.

35.   That these Ordinances be proclaimed and printed.

It will be noted that the Ordinances of Cadereyta of 1638 provide for the election of a Rector, Superintendents and Delegates but contain no provision for the election of *Veedor*. Ordinance 16 mentions *Veedor*, Rector and Superintendents and the 18 says: 'the *Veedor* shall not accept any article of gold or silver that does not bear the mark and stamp of the artisan who made it,' while Ordinance 18 reads 'the assayer, when articles are brought to the Royal Treasury to be fifthed . . . shall not accept them unless . . . they bear the mark . . . of the artisan. . . .' And further on: 'the assayer and marker shall not hall mark any articles. . . .' In the 19th, 'they shall advise the *Veedor* who will be the assayer and marker for the Royal Treasury and Mint of this City.'

From the foregoing it is concluded that during this period:

a. The Guild did not elect the *Veedor*.

b. The *Veedor* was an employee of the Government.

c. The *Veedor* was, at the same time, assayer and marker for the Royal Treasury and also for the Mint.

The Viceroy, Marquis de Mancera, saw fit to confirm the Ordinances[61] for *tiradores* [drawers of gold and silver wire] dated 19th October 1669. A synopsis of these follows:

61 Lorenzot, op.cit., p.139.

SYNOPSIS

Ordinances for Tiradores [drawers of gold and silver wire]
Viceroy Marquis de Mancera

19TH OCTOBER 1669

1. That on the 6th January all graduate masters shall meet to elect the two *Veedores*.

2. That no-one who has not been examined [to receive a license as Master Silversmith] shall be allowed to open a shop.

3. That in the future, no master shall teach or employ on bench work, a Negro slave or anyone of mixed color. Those who have already learned [the trade] may continue as workmen with the licensed masters.

4. That in order to take the examination:
   a. He must be a Spaniard
   b. He must have learned the art from books, [studying under] a licensed master who has a shop
   c. Know how to do the following:
      (1) To Cast.
      (2) To Forge.
      (3) To File.
      (4) To square, by hammering the four sides of a small silver ingot.[62]
      (5) To gold-plate with the necessary liquids.
      (6) To make a drill and with it drill two holes in the *hilera*.[63]
      (7) To make, from silver or gold wire, a perfect ribbon[64] the length of the long work bench.
      (8) With a new file to make four ounces of filings.

---

62 Small silver ingots, about twelve inches long, were cast in molds, that had the open side slightly wider than the bottom to facilitate emptying. The four sides of the ingot were then trued by hammering.

63 The *hilera* was a small steel plate, about three inches wide, eight inches in length and one-half inch thick, with several round and square holes of different sizes, through which the silver or gold was drawn forming wire of the desired shape and size. The wire-drawers made their own *hileras*.

64 As a test of skill, a wire the length of the work bench was transformed by hammering into a ribbon of uniform width and thickness.

(9) To set up and take apart two steel rolls[65] and with them make flat wire of gold or silver.

5. The widows of master-workmen shall enjoy the privileges of their husbands until they marry someone who is not a master.

6. He shall not draw wire, weave nor do brass work, because these are contrary to the ordinances.

The Guild of Silversmiths maintained at its own expense a Company of Grenadiers of one hundred men. The curious book *México en* 1768,[66] referring to the military organization in the Capital, gives us these data on the subject:

The regiment, formed by all the tradesmen, has up to one thousand men, who appear in red uniforms of the finest scarlet woolen cloth, coat and blue lining of the same material, yellow buttons. All wear a narrow sword of silver, sash, hat and coat embroidered with fine gold, white leggings with epaulets of black velvet, blue powder-box usually embroidered with embossed gold, caps of fur for the grenadiers, with the underfolds decorated and embroidered in gold on a blue background, and their corresponding tassels, and musket, bayonet and bullet pouch. The officers differ only in that their coats are embroidered with double gold braid, as in everything else of the fine uniform the lowest soldier can compete with his Colonel, who is today Manuel de Rivas Cacho, Brigadier of the Royal Army . . . who furthermore occupied for barracks a great and important house, which he paid for out of his own money.

Of the three companies the first is infantry, like that of the tradesmen, and composed of a hundred grenadiers,[67] from the Silversmiths' Guild. These cannot be told from the tradesmen, either by their appearance or by their uniforms except for the fact that they have three gold stripes on each arm; the other two [companies] of light cavalry, composed of Bakers' and Butchers' Guilds, similarly dressed, mounted and well equipped at their own expense; [all] graciously serve His Majesty whenever ordered, the uniform of the former being of fine blue felt with coat, lining, red cape, shoulder strap, hat and coat embroidered with fine silver, and the second [cavalry] wear the same red felt with coat, cape and blue lining, with similar gold embroidery.

65 The wire was passed between two small steel rolls, mounted on a shaft and turned by a hand crank. By adjusting the opening between the rolls, ribbons of the desired thickness and width were produced. These were used for embroidery or cut into short lengths for sequins.

66 Juan Manuel de San Vicente, *México en* 1768. *Exacta descripción de la Magnífica Corte Mexicana*, pp.72-5. Published in Cadiz, in the eighteenth century and now newly printed by Luis González Obregón, *Imp. El Nacional*, Mexico, 1897.

67 We know that Captain Diego González de la Cueva was a Captain of Grenadiers because he is mentioned as such in the *Archivo General de la Nación. Ordenanzas, vol.II*, 1723-63, *p.*320.

It appears that while the drawers of gold and silver wire and beaters of gold and silver continued to be served by two *Veedores* for each branch[68] of the industry, the silversmiths abolished the office of elective *Veedores*, possibly from 1580, when the Government began paying them, and were content until 1724 with *Mayordomos* and *Diputados* only. 'The silversmiths in olden times had no *Veedor*, but only *Mayordomos* and *Diputados* until in the year 1724, when Sergeant-Major Felipe de Ribas y Angulo, *Ensayador Mayor* of the Most Excellent Marquis de Casa Fuerte, requested that a new position be created so that he might perform the examination and inspections as done in the other Arts; the Most Excellent Lord saw fit to so order, as shown in the Book of election of the Silversmiths' guild.'

1733

The Royal Decree of the 1st October 1733[69] gave specific and interesting instructions to the silversmiths, which may be summarized as follows:

1. Having been notified that the silversmiths, wire-drawers and sheet-beaters malpracticed their arts without conforming to the ordinances and taking for themselves the tenths and corresponding taxes on the greater part of the gold and silver jewelry they fabricate, the recommendations of Viceroy Juan de Acuña, Marquis de Casa Fuerte, are hereby approved as follows:
   a. That a law on silver be published giving them [the silversmiths] a time limit to present to the royal treasuries the silver not hall-marked.
   b. That the Chief Assayer make more frequent inspections of silversmiths' shops, complying with the ordinances in this regard.
   c. That the number of silversmiths throughout Mexico be limited to a minimum.
   d. That for a period deemed advisable, no more apprentices be accepted.

68 Until 17th November 1762 when, at their request, the number was reduced to one for each branch. *Archivo General de la Nación. Ordenanzas. Vol.II*, 1723-63, *p.320.*

69 *Archivo General de la Nación. Reales Cédulas, vol.52, p.324, Exp.104. Año* 1733. It is also found in *Un Virrey Limeño en México*, pp.207-12 by José de J. Núñez y Domínguez. *Talleres Gráficos del Museo Nacional*, Mexico, 1927.

e. Penalty for fraud: loss of the silver or gold, fines, debarment from the trade, and exile from the kingdom.

f. That the silversmiths who need gold or silver shall obtain it on account from the royal officers of the treasuries who are charged with collecting the tax. That upon completion, the articles be presented so that these officials may place thereon the hall-mark. The articles must also be inspected by the Chief Assayer so that if all be of eleven *dineros* he may mark all the articles with the punch bearing his name.

g. Old gold and silver plate that individuals might sell to the silver-smiths must be registered.

h. Order published and enforce the royal order of the 28th February 1730 that regulates the laws relative to the fabrication of gold and silver jewelry.

i. In places where there may be authorized assayers they shall make monthly inspections of the silver shops.

j. In the cities and towns where there are no authorized assayers and markers: the most skillful and important one shall be chosen from among the artisans of each branch and appointed as in-spector.

k. The silversmiths of each city must live in the same district on one or several streets.

l. With respect to those of Mexico City: It is in accordance with the ordinances of this guild that they shall not sell plate lacking the mark of the artisan and the marker, as ordered by laws 1/a and 2/a of heading 24, book 5/o of the *Recopilación de Castilla*.

m. Demand reports as follows:

    a. By what ordinances are the silver-shops governed in other cities and towns?

    b. How many silversmiths are there in each place?

We were unable to find the document by which the Viceroy, Juan de Acuña, should have published this Royal Decree, neither is it mentioned by José de J. Núñez y Domínguez,[70] nor by Fonseca y Urrutia; but from a consultation by Chief Assayer Joseph Antonio Lince González

70 Op.cit.

with the Royal Governing Assembly, we learn that it was enforced.[71]

ORDINANCES OF THE COUNT OF MOCTEZUMA: 1701

From the title page of the Ordinances of 1746, it is learned that these were '*issued and ordered obeyed by the Most Excellent Marquis de Cade-reyta, Viceroy of this New Spain, revised and enlarged by the Most Excellent Count of Moctezuma,*[72] *likewise Viceroy of this New Spain . . . and finally revised, corrected and enlarged by the Most Excellent Viceroy, Count of Fuen-Clara. . . .*'

ORDINANCES OF FUEN-CLARA: 1746

The Ordinances of 1746 differ little from those of 1638. Therefore only the differences between them need be considered here. Nearly all were copied literally from those of 1638. The only differences of importance are that instead of a simple *Veedor*, paid by the Government, there appears the *Juez Veedor*, who at the same time is *Ensayador Mayor*. The *Ensayador Mayor* acted as *Veedor* from 1701 [although he was not called *Juez Veedor*], for on the title page of the book in which the Ordinance of 1746 was published appears the following:

Revised and Enlarged by the . . . Count of Moctezuma . . . at the request of Captain Nicolás González de la Cueva, *Ensayador Mayor, Valanzario* and *Marcador* of the *Real Caxa de Mexico, Abridor de Quintos, Sellos y Marcas Reales, Fundidor Mayor y Veedor* of said Art.

It appears that the Ordinances of 1746 were the last issued, because in 1790[73] Fonseca and Urrutia referred to *Ordinance No.29*, and from its contents it appears to refer to that published in 1746. The Decree of the 4th September 1839 refers to Ordinances 9, 25 and 26, of the year 1746.

With the publication of the very explicit *Ordenanzas de Ensayadores, formadas por el Lic. D. Joseph Antonio Lince González, ensayador mayor*

---

71 *Consulta hecha a la Real Audiencia Governadora por el Lic. Don Joseph Antonio Lince (González), Ensayador Mayor del Reyno y Juez Veedor del Noble Arte de la Platería sobre varios particulares respectivos al mismo arte mui interesantes al Real servicio y utilidad pública.* [From a manuscript in the author's possession with this title: *Documentos respectivos al Arte de Ensayar oro y Plata, Ordenanzas de Ensayadores y otros sobre el Govierno de la Platería, Batiojería, y Tiraduría de Oro y Plata que ofrece al Señor Don Vicente de Herrera Caballero etc. el Licenciado Don Joseph Antonio Lince González etc. en México, año de* 1786].

72 The date of notification was the 31st August 1701.

73 Fonseca y Urrutia, op.cit., vol.I, p.409.

del reyno y juez veedor del noble arte de la platería, batiojas y tiradores de oro y plata, confirmed by the Viceroy Matías de Galvez by Royal Decree of 30th December 1783, the Chief Assayer was reminded of his obligation to inspect the silversmith shops:

That the assayer should make, personally (without delegating this charge to another), frequent inspections at least four times yearly, in the stalls, arcades, markets, silver shops and other places where they trade or may trade in silver or gold; seizing that which may be found to lack hall-marks, if the piece is sufficiently large to permit this, so that action may be taken in accordance with the royal decrees, ordinances and orders, giving prompt report of the infractions he may find.[74]

By one of the provisions of these Ordinances the silversmiths were relieved of the obligation of paying for their examinations:

That on receiving the bits of metal taken for assay and all the other income pertaining to the royal treasury, as well as to other branches of same, the royal officials should take due precautions to prevent all fraud and misuse; all fees that they have been enjoying by reason of examination of assayers, master silversmiths and others are abolished; these he shall do free of charge and without any other taxes, under penalty of being deprived of office. The royal officials shall pay all expenses of salaries, wages, cupels, charcoal, crucibles, *aqua fortis* and others that may be necessary for the operation and work of the offices, economizing wherever possible.[75]

The Apprentices

Complying with the suggestion, dated 22nd July,[76] 1789, of Bernardo Bonilla, President of the Royal Academy of San Carlos, and after many consultations, the Viceroy, Count of Revilla Gigedo, modified Ordinance 36, which deals with the examination of apprentices, in an order addressed to Francisco Arance y Cobos, Lieutenant, acting as Chief Assayer, which reads as follows:

Instead of the methods of examination provided therein, there is established and shall be observed henceforth the appointment of sponsors for this purpose, and anyone desiring to employ an Apprentice shall first address himself in writing to you as *Juez Veedor,* so that you may name the two sponsors, who shall take oath to

74 Ibid., vol.I, pp.94, 95.
75 Ibid., vol.I, pp.46, 47.
76 *Archivo General de la Nación. Yndustria Artística y Manufacturera,* vol.5, 1746-92, Foj.224-43.

faithfully perform their commission and under it [oath] render their reports in full as outlined in your Report of 29th January last. . . .

The report of Francisco Arance y Cobos to which reference is made, says:[77]

Most Excellent Lord:

Having held, on the seventh of this month, the meeting of silversmiths that Your Excellency ordered, they have accepted the suggestion of the Prosecutor, agreeing to receive the apprentices after report of their ability in extra-judicial manner, and with the only modification that the notarial document be not omitted, as its cost will not exceed four *pesos* which may be divided between the apprentice and the employer or master who is to receive him; two *pesos* for each, which is a small matter. Moreover the silversmiths agree to pay in full the tax on the document if the poverty of the applicant is such that he cannot afford to pay.

. . . There remains only that the superior approval of Your Excellency be given thereby limiting the functions of the Chief Assayer as *Juez Veedor* of the Body, so that the silversmiths will know there is no change in this matter, and must give him notice of their intention before taking any action, so that, as formerly, he may receive the proofs by reason of the new methods, (which do not decrease his income). [Likewise that he may] name the officials so that they may be to his satisfaction, . . . notifying the same assayer promptly, that he may call the meeting wherein they should decide whether the applicant is to be admitted or rejected.

May God keep Your Excellency many years.

Royal General Assay Office of Mexico, the 29th January 1790.

Fran.co Aranze y Cobos

Most Excellent Viceroy Count of Revilla Gigedo.

The object was to oblige all apprentices to attend the drafting classes at the Academy of San Carlos and to refuse to admit to examination 'those whose ability was not accredited by a certificate from the Secretary of the Academy.'

It appears that this was not sufficient to force the attendance of the apprentices at the Royal Academy, because on the 17th May 1794, Antonio Forcada y la Plaza, Chief Assayer, 'having received notice that the Apprentices of the Silversmiths' Art do not attend the Royal Academy regularly,' summoned Alexandro Cañas, *Veedor*, to call a meeting of the 'Body of Directors' of the silversmiths and, also, José María Rodallega, as 'this person was one of those who was active in promoting all concerning the betterment of his art.'

77 Idem., Foj.237-8.

They met in the Royal Assay Office, the 19th May 1794.[78] As a result of this meeting the hour of attendance was changed from night to the afternoon. To pay the keeper, each silversmith who had a shop contributed half a *real* every week.

The distinguished Viceroy, Count of Revilla Gigedo, in his *Instrucción Reservada*[79] to his successor, the Marquis de Branciforte, signed on the 30th June 1794, referring to guilds in general, says:

337. The crafts and arts are very decadent, for lack of proper education of the artisans. In other times, it is known that greater care was taken in this respect, because in accordance with the ideas on arts prevailing at the time, efforts were made to draw up their respective ordinances and to establish different guilds.

338. There are fifty in this city, with their different ordinances, of which very few have been made in this century, many in the past century and the greatest part in the one prior to that.

339. For the very reason of their age they are full of defects, and contain provisions more likely to retard than to advance the arts. In the most part they are designed to retard the advance of the industry and to burden the artisans with charges and useless activities.

340. Thus it is seen that the decadence that was subsequently noticed in Spain, was, likewise, general in America, where the retrogression continued for a period of two and a half centuries. There were, at that time, several trades organized into a guild, for whom the issuance of certain laws was considered imperative, these now being about forgotten.

341. It would be very advisable to abolish several of the guilds which are no longer necessary, such as candy and candle-makers and other similar ones. In some cases it would be convenient, according to the present state of affairs in these kingdoms, that some of the guilds continue under revised laws, and although this work for all the guilds would be very long and difficult, at least a general law should be issued, based on sound principles, with the sole view of establishing uniform order and discipline among masters, workmen and apprentices, and that some general regulations should be issued on the essential points of each class of articles but without endeavoring to limit the shape, size and other details, which may at all times be changed according to the taste and fancy of the purchasers and makers.

In contrast with the other guilds, that of the silversmiths was now reorganized and progressive. The Viceroy, in his *Instrucción Reservada*,[80] says:

78 Idem., *vol.*23—1793-1805—*Foj.*59 to 71 reverse.
79 P.84. *Tip. de la Calle de las Escalerillas*. Mexico, 1831.
80 Ibid., p.85.

342. The founding of the Royal Academy of the Noble Arts of San Carlos, has provided many advantages in this respect: the silversmiths, in accordance with their by-laws, send their apprentices there; and this benefit might well be extended to other trades, to whom the principles of drafting would be very useful. At present the academy is well provided with very competent professors in architecture, painting, sculpture and engraving; and in order that the work of this latter course might be useful the director of engraving was given a pension of 300 *pesos* in order that he might teach printing to some of the students, the practice of which was very decadent. . . .

372. The silver art has advanced here proportionately more than any other trade, as silver is one of the principal products of the country, readily obtained in bullion, which is not the case in Spain, as there the manufacturing cost is very high, as it is necessary to take plate and recast it.[81]

According to Marroqui,[82] the Silversmiths' Guild was abolished in the year 1861 and its properties nationalized.

LIST OF VEEDORES

YEAR	NAME	REFERENCE
1527	Etor Mendez	*Actas de Cabildo*, 14th January 1527
	Diego Martín	" " " 14th January 1527
1532	Francisco de Toledo	" " " 26th May 1532
1533	Pedro de Espina	" " " 24th January 1533
1536	Bartolomé Ruys	" " " 28th July 1536
	Antonio Hernandez	" " " 28th July 1536
1537	Gonzalo Rodriguez	" " " 13th March 1537
	Luys Rodriguez	" " " 6th April 1537
1538	Francisco Hernandez	" " " 6th May 1538
	Pedro Hernandez	" " " 10th February 1538
1542	Gomez de Luque	" " " 11th July 1542
	Gonzalo Gil	" " " 11th July 1542
1544	Grabiel Billasana	" " " 3rd July 1544

81 Ibid., p.93.
82 Marroqui, op.cit., vol.III, p.449. Among the decrees of this period we have found none that refer especially to the Silversmiths' Guild; but as the Silversmiths' Brotherhood was closely associated with the church it is possible that it was abolished by the law of 12th July 1859 [Number 5053] *Ley de Nacionalización de los Bienes Eclesiásticos*, articles 5 and 6 which read: '5. The Religious orders that exist throughout the Republic are hereby abolished, whatever may be the denomination or purpose for which they were organized, likewise all fraternities, brotherhoods, associations or fraternal societies connected with religious communities, the cathedrals, churches or other places of worship. 6. The organization or construction of new convents, fraternities, brotherhoods, associations, or fraternal societies, in any name or form whatsoever, is forbidden, as is the use of robes and habits of the abolished orders.'

YEAR	NAME	REFERENCE
1546	Grabiel Billasana	*Actas de Cabildo*, 9th February 1546
	Pedro de Sabsedo	" " " 9th February 1546
	Enrique Baez	" " " 29th March 1546
	Ramon de Cardona	" " " 29th March 1546
1553	Pedro de Spina	" " " 24th January 1553
1572	Gabriel Villasana	Fonseca y Urrutia, *Historia de Real Hacienda.* vol.I, p.393.
1724	Ygnazio Ruis de Santiago	*Archivo General de la Nación. Ordenanzas.* vol. 11, p.9 reverse 1723-63.
1725	Joseph de la Porta Bargas	Ibid., vol.II, p.14. Bis. 1723-63.
1727	Manuel Marin (Alferez)	Ibid., vol.11, 1723-63.
	Fran.co Cruz	Ibid., vol.11, p.37. 1723-63.
1745	Adrian Ximenes	Ibid., vol.11, p.189, reverse. 1723-63.
1747	Adrian Ximenes	Ibid., vol.11, p.232. 1723-63.
1759	Cristobal Marradon	Ibid., vol.11, p.299 reverse. 1723-63.
1760	Francisco Peña Rosa	Ibid., vol.11, p.311. 1723-63.
1762	Manuel Salinas	Ibid., vol.11, p.324 reverse. 1723-63.
1764	Jps. del Castillo	Ibid., vol.16, p.1. 14th January 1764.
1765	Sebastian de la Parra	Ibid., vol.16, p.5 reverse. 11th January 1765.
1766	Pedro de Avila	Ibid., vol.16, p.10 reverse. 14th January 1766.
1767	Miguel Carlos de Rivera	Ibid., vol.16, p.14. 10th January 1767.
1768	Miguel Carlos de Rivera	Ibid., vol.16, p.16. 15th January 1768.
1769	Juan Antonio Exiga	Ibid., vol.16, p.19. 10th January 1769.
1770	Nicolás de Esprugas	Ibid., vol.16, p.22. 10th January 1770.
1771	Nicolás Esprugas	Ibid., vol.16, p.32. 9th January 1771.
1772	Francisco Setadul	Ibid., vol.16, p.42. 8th January 1772.
1773	Cristobal de Marradon	Ibid., vol.16, p.49. 9th January 1773.
1774	Manuel de Badillo	Ibid., vol.16, p.66 reverse. 21st April 1774.
1775	Juan Jph. Montes de Oca	Ibid., vol.16, p.70 reverse. 25th January 1775.
1776	Jph. Antonio del Castillo	Ibid., vol.16, p.79. 16th January 1776.
1777	Jph. Antonio del Castillo	Ibid., vol.16, p.90 reverse. 4th February 1777.
1778	Juan Antonio Exija	Ibid., vol.16, p.105 reverse. 30th January 1778.
1781	José María de Rodallega	Ibid., vol.16, p.117 reverse. 11th January 1781.
1782	Josep Yglesias	Ibid., vol.16, p.122. 11th January 1782.
1783	José María Rodallega	Ibid., vol.16, p.129 reverse. 9th January 1783.
1784	Eduardo Calderon	Ibid., vol.16, p.135 reverse. 9th July 1784.
1785	Manuel de los Ríos	Ibid., vol.16, p.145 reverse. 14th January 1785.
1786	Josep de la Torre	Ibid., vol.16, p.145 reverse. 29th January 1786.
1787	Manuel de los Rios	Ibid., vol.16, p.149. 16th January 1787.
1788	Fernando Samano	Ibid., vol.16, p.156. 11th February 1788.

YEAR	NAME	REFERENCE
1789	Joaquin Espejo	Ibid., vol.16, p.157. 14th January 1789.
1790	Eduardo Calderon	Ibid., vol.16, p.159. 13th January 1790.
1791	Miguel Ruiz Cano	Ibid., vol.16, p.162 reverse. 8th January 1791.
1792	José María del Castillo	Ibid., vol. 5, p.255. 29th December 1792.
1793	Joaquin Espejo	Ibid., vol.16, p.175. 3rd January 1793.
1794	Alexandro de Cañas	Ibid., vol.16, p.177 reverse. 9th January 1794.
1795	José María Guzman	Ibid., vol.16, p.179 reverse. 26th February 1795.
1796	José Cardona	Ibid., vol.16, p.181 reverse. 9th January 1796.
1797	José María Rodallega	Ibid., vol.16, p.183 reverse. 12th January 1797.
1798	José María Rodallega	Ibid., vol.16, p.184. 22nd January 1798.
1799	Joaquin Villarreal	Ibid., vol.16, p.185 reverse. 9th January 1799.
1800	Antonio Caamaño	Ibid., vol.16, p.186 reverse. 1st January 1800.
1801	Antonio Caamaño	Ibid., vol.16, p.190 reverse. 9th January 1801.
1802	Miguel María Martel	Ibid., vol.16, p.191 reverse. 8th January 1802.
1803	Jph. Guzman	Ibid., vol.16, p.192 reverse. 13th January 1803.
1804	Alexandro de Cañas	Ibid., vol.16, p.193 reverse. 7th January 1804.
1805	Fernando Samano	Ibid., vol.16, p.194 reverse. 11th January 1805.
1807	Francisco Galvan	Ibid., vol.16, p.196. 7th January 1807.
1808	Antonio Caamaño	Ibid., vol.16, p.197. 8th January 1808.
1809	Fernando Samano	Ibid., vol.16, p.198. 10th February 1809.
1810	José María Rodallega	Ibid., vol.16, p.199. 3rd January 1810.
1811	José María Rodallega	Ibid., vol.16, p.200. 5th January 1811.
1812	José María Rodallega	Ibid., vol.16, p.200. 7th January 1812.
1813	Fernando Samano	Ibid., vol.16, p.200 reverse. 8th January 1813.
1814	José María Bernal	Ibid., vol.16, p.200 reverse. 7th January 1814.
1815	Pedro Marquez	Ibid., vol.16, p.201. 14th January 1815.
1816	Miguel María Martel	Ibid., vol.16, p.201 reverse. 9th March 1816.

Chapter V

1. *The Branches of the Silversmiths' Art*: INTRODUCTION; THE BEATERS OF GOLD AND SILVER SHEETS; THE DRAWERS OF GOLD AND SILVER WIRE; DEFINITION OF THE BRANCHES OF THE ART. 2. *The Standard of Quality of Plate*: INTRODUCTION; THE SPANISH PRECEDENT; DOCUMENTS RELATIVE TO THE QUALITY OF METAL TO BE WORKED IN MEXICO; SUMMARY OF DOCUMENTS; SUMMARY. 3. *Taxes on the Precious Metals*: INTRODUCTION; THE MINING TAX OR ROYAL FIFTH; THE ASSAY TAX; THE KING'S TAX ON THE COINAGE OF MONEY; TAX ON PLATE; EXCISE TAX; CONCLUSION; AMENDMENTS; INDEPENDENT MEXICO.

1. *The Branches of the Silversmiths' Art: Introduction*

THE silversmiths in Mexico never divided themselves into as many technical groups as in Spain, where there were forgers, drawers of gold and silver wire, gold-beaters, spinners, refiners, casters, lapidaries, polishers, beaters of gold and silver sheets, filigree workers and makers of holy ornaments.

In Mexico City, from 1527 to 1563, judging by the records of the Municipal Council, all were called silversmiths. In 1563 these records begin to refer to *workmen who draw wire and beat sheets*, and in 1598 are found ordinances for sheet-beaters. It appears that these same ordinances applied also to the wire-drawers, because they forbade the wire-drawers to beat sheets. In 1599 ordinances were published for beaters of gold leaf who then had separate *veedores* (inspectors and overseers). Reference is made in 1730 to the Silversmiths' Guild, without mentioning the other branches. From 1743 to 1746 and thereafter, there were three divisions of the silversmiths' art, each with its own *veedores*.

The three divisions were: silversmiths, beaters of gold and silver sheets and drawers of gold and silver wire.

But the three groups during this period apparently were governed by the one Guild. The foregoing may be summarized as follows:

BRANCHES OF THE SILVERSMITH'S ART IN MEXICO

AUTHORITY	YEAR	SILVERSMITHS	BEATERS OF GOLD & SILVER SHEETS	DRAWERS OF GOLD & SILVER WIRE	SEPARATE BRANCH
Municipal Act Mexico City	1527-1563	Silversmiths			
Fonseca and Urrutia, op.cit., vol.I, p.391	1563		Beaters	Drawers	
Fonseca and Urrutia, op.cit., vol.I, p.390	1578		Beaters	Drawers	
Fonseca and Urrutia, op.cit., vol.I, p.393	1580	Silversmiths		Drawers	
Lorenzot, op.cit., p.142	1598		Beaters		
Lorenzot, op.cit., p.145	1599				Beaters of Gold Leaf
Lorenzot, op.cit., p.139	1669			Drawers	
Revello, op.cit., vol.XXVII	1685	Silversmiths	Beaters	Drawers	
Fonseca and Urrutia, op.cit., vol.I, p.131	1731	Silversmiths	Beaters	Drawers	
Fonseca and Urrutia, op.cit., vol.I, p.399	1746	Silversmiths	Beaters	Drawers	

NOTE: In many Directories of the nineteenth century, for example, in the *Directorio del Comercio del Imperio Mexicano para el año de 1867*, are found lists of the artisans of Mexico, and among them, silversmiths, beaters of gold and silver sheets and drawers of gold and silver wire. From this it is seen that the same divisions held down to modern times.

Batiojas—the Beaters of Gold and Silver Sheets

The Ordinances of 1598 required the apprentice on taking his examination 'To be able to make a beaten sheet of silver gilt from start to finish.'

In the lawsuit against the silversmiths in 1696,[1] the following appears: 'Make and draw up a list of all the master smiths of gold and silver that they call *Mazonería* [relief work] who have stores and shops publicly or secretly.'

Tiradores—the Drawers of Gold and Silver Wire

The Ordinances for *Drawers of Gold and Silver Wire* of 1669 required of the apprentice a full knowledge of the following:

a. Casting.
b. Forging.
c. Filing.
d. To square, by hammering the four sides of a small silver bar.[2]
e. To gold plate it with the necessary liquids.
f. To make a drill and with it drill two holes in the *hilera*.[3]
g. To make, from silver or gold wire, a perfect ribbon[4] the length of the long work bench.
i. To set up and take apart two steel rolls[5] and with them make flat wire of gold or silver.
j. He must not spin, weave or do brass work.
k. 'And the *veedores* will limit themselves to that corresponding to their trade which is: to spin, embroider, and to sell sequins to the lacemaker, because it belongs to this trade to provide the material required for weaving.'

1 Revello, op.cit., p.xxvii.
2 Small silver bars, about twelve inches long, were cast in molds with the open side slightly wider than the bottom to facilitate withdrawal from the mold. The four sides of the bar were then trued by hammering.
3 The *hilera* was a small steel plate, about three inches wide, eight inches in length and one-half inch thick, with several holes of different sizes, both round and square, through which the silver or gold was drawn, forming wire of the desired shape and size. The wire-drawers made their own *hileras*.
4 As a test of skill, a wire the length of the work bench was transformed by hammering into a ribbon of uniform width and thickness. These long ribbons were much more difficult to make than were those of short lengths.
5 The wire was passed between two small steel rolls, mounted on a shaft and turned by a hand-crank. By adjusting the opening between the rolls, ribbons of the desired thickness and width were produced. These were used for embroidery or cut into short lengths for sequins.

Fonseca and Urrutia[6] left us a definition of the drawers of wire (1783):

'With respect to the drawers of gold wire, it is silver that they work, which afterwards is plated with gold on the outside, from which comes the name drawers of gold and silver wire.'

Definition of the Branches of the Art

From the foregoing it is seen that, in general, from the year 1563 the silversmiths' art was divided into three technical groups: Silversmiths, *Bateojas* (beaters[7] of gold and silver sheets), and *Tiradores* (drawers of gold and silver wire).

Thus the work of each group may be defined as follows:

a. *Beaters of gold and silver*: made sheets of silver and gold, silver gilt, and relief work.

b. *Drawers of gold and silver wire*: artisans who reduced silver to a thread, for weaving and embroidery. It was usually plated with gold.

c. *Silversmiths*: to whom corresponded the execution of finished works, casting, relief work, engraving, enamelling, the mounting of precious stones and everything relative to the silversmiths' art in general.

2. *The Standard of Quality of Plate: Introduction*

Following the example of Spain, the quality of the metals employed in the making of plate was insured by means of visits of inspection made by officials or silversmiths appointed for that purpose. From each piece, the Assayer, a Government employee, took a tiny piece of metal with an engraver's tool, which was assayed for quality.

6 Op.cit., vol.I, p.90.

7 The Beaters of Gold Leaf was a separate branch, as it is today, and properly is beyond the scope of this work.

The Ordinance of 1599 required 'Beaters of Gold Leaf':

a. To know how to work and make a pair of circular pieces of metal into cloth.

b. And after making, to be able to perfect for use.

c. To know how to make a big soldering iron for making another thick one with which to gild plate iron.

d. They must know how to melt an ingot of unrefined gold and another of silver; the one of silver to be an ounce, and that of gold eight *castellanos*; and

e. Know how to forge a ribbon for use in soldering.

This art was then a series of operations by which they were able to convert the metal into very thin sheets, to which they give the name of gold leaf.

From the few complaints that are found in the records relative to the silversmiths' art and in the General Archives of the Nation, it may be concluded that the standard of quality was successfully maintained throughout colonial times.

The Spanish Precedent

The standard of quality of plate was regulated in Spain from very ancient times, as is shown by the following:

MONTHLY REPORT OF THE WEIGHTS OF GOLD AND SILVER MARK AND OF THEIR STANDARD OF PURITY BY TWO OFFICIALS OF EACH COUNCIL.

We command and order that in each city, village and place where there may be money-changers and silversmiths, the Council of each of them shall name and appoint each month two officials of the same Council, one to be the Mayor,[8] and the other a Councilman or a Magistrate; and take with them, if they wish, the marker who may have been appointed by said Council, and one day in each month, without mentioning or making it known beforehand, ask and demand all the scales and weights used for gold. Demand also the plate which should bear marks and which has already been sold, as well as the plate for sale by the money-changers, merchants and silversmiths . . . and who may be in the city, village or place . . . after notice has been given by common crier, see that the plate be of the standard of eleven *dineros* and four grains, and that the genuine hall-mark has been stamped on the plate and that the scales are rightful, and that they have the genuine marks; and if you should find that the said scales and weights are not just, or have not the said mark or the said silver is not standard, or that the weight with which they weigh is deficient, that you impose on those who may be found guilty the penalties provided for in said laws and contained in this our letter. . . .

Documents Relative to the Quality of Metal to be Worked in Mexico

Although all the Laws of the Indies[9] of the first period specified only that the silver and gold should be of the proper standard, without mentioning the *dineros* that the silver should have or the carats of gold, this standard was that of the money, or eleven *dineros* and four grains

8 John II in Madrid, year 1435, petition 31, and in Toledo, year 36, petitions 1 and 2 and Ferdinand and Isabella in Madrigal, year 1476, petition 14, *Novísima Recopilación de las Leyes de España*, vol.III, p.279. Madrid, 1805. 4 vols.
9 Among these the First Law, Heading 22, Book IV.

for the silver, and twenty-two carats for the gold. It appears that in 1581 the *veedor* had difficulty in enforcing the Ordinances for the silver-smiths, because in the General Archives of the Nation[10] is found the following:

DECREE THAT THEY RESPECT THAT COMMANDED BY HIS MAJ-ESTY RELATIVE TO THE ORDINANCES OF THE GOLDSMITHS (Year of 1581).

Lorenzo Suárez de Mendoza, etc. Inasmuch as Graviel de Villa Sana, *Veedor* of the goldsmiths of this city of Mexico, has reported to me that, by decree of the Very Illustrious Antonio de Mendoza Viceroy Governor, formerly in this New Spain, it is ordered that no goldsmith dare to work any gold of less than twenty-two carats under certain penalties, and further that by another decree it is ordered that no one shall have precious metal in his possession . . . without it first having been declared before the person who may be in charge of stamping the gold, and to [later] exhibit the pieces that they may have made of said stamped gold.

By other laws and decrees of His Majesty it is ordered that no silversmith shall dare to have a piece of plate on display that is not of the standard of twenty-two carats, under penalty for the first offense that the piece be broken and for the second the same and in addition one hundred *pesos* fine. He also reported that the silversmiths who reside in this city do not care to obey and respect the custom of not selling a *castellano* of gold plate at more than two *pesos* of common gold the *peso*, which is in force and respected in the Kingdoms of Castille, and he demanded of me that orders be given demanding compliance and . . . by the present I order the Justices of His Majesty of this New Spain . . . force them to obey and com-ply and execute . . . and if necessary proclaim it in public, and they may execute the penalties provided for those who are liable to them.

Dated in Mexico, on the twenty-sixth day of January of the year One Thousand Five Hundred and Eighty-one.

The Count of la Coruña. By command of His Excellency, Juan de Cuevas.

NOTIFICATION: In the City of Mexico, 25th April, of the year One Thousand Five Hundred and Eighty-one, the Very Excellent Lorenzo Suárez de Mendoza Count of la Coruña, Viceroy, Governor and Captain General for his Majesty in this New Spain and President of the Royal Court . . . said that in order that there may be better control on the sale of said gold and that none may be sold other than that registered at the declared price, he ordered and commanded that neither in this city nor outside of it any silversmith should sell any other than old gold. The gold plate having been registered it should be compared and duly proven as having covered the said amount which has been declared, so it may not be possible for them

10 *Archivo General de la Nación. Libro de Ordenanzas.* O.O.O.O., Fol.61, reverse.

to sell more . . . under penalty of losing the said gold which otherwise they would sell.

The Count of la Coruña. Before me, Juan de Cuevas.

The records show also:

1730-1731

V.[11] The standard that the silver should have that is not mixed with gold, that is the silver received in the coffers and the royal Mint, must be that of eleven *dineros*,[12] for although Law XII, heading 8, book 8, orders that it be of two thousand two hundred and ten *maravedis*, this corresponded to eleven *dineros* and four grains that was the standard of money and plate in those times; but as it was decided by royal mandates in the year 1730[13] that the standard be eleven *dineros*, the pieces should have this standard, and thus it is decreed in the second chapter of the seventh ordinance of the royal Mint.[14]

There is, also, among the regulations, an order that reads:[15]

COUNCIL OF COINAGE AND COMMERCE

1730

XX. — By royal decree given in Seville on the 26th January 1731, in which is inserted the royal decree of the 15th November 1730, it pleased His Majesty Philip V (who in glory may be) to create the royal council of coinage and commerce, so that they might have charge of and judge privately the affairs of the mint, silversmiths, beaters of gold and silver sheets and drawers of gold and silver wire, establishing their jurisdiction in these terms:

Which council was created for examining and deciding all transactions, lawsuits and affairs, civil as well as criminal, and their snares, connections, supplements and relations, in any form in all matters of justice and disputes, on matters relative to my royal mint above mentioned, silversmiths, beaters of gold and silver sheets, drawers of gold and silver wire, and all the other artisans who are occupied in the coinage of gold and silver and copper, and the handicrafts of the aforementioned gold and silver metals. [It is ordered] that you make them respect inviolably the standards of twenty-two carats of gold, and that of eleven *dineros* in silver, not

11 Fonseca y Urrutia, op.cit., vol.I, p.68.
12 Chapter 13 of Law XVIII, heading 22, book 4, of the *Recopilación de las Indias*.
13 Royal Decree of 28th February 1730.
14 Royal Decree given in Seville on 26th January 1731.
15 Fonseca y Urrutia, op.cit., vol.I, pp.92-4.

only when these two metals are to be reduced to coins, but also when bullion or powder are to be used in making plate, and of any kind of pieces large or small, and any handiwork without exception: in such manner that it is not permitted to any person, silversmith, beater of gold and silver, or any other artisan, or shop-keeper, to make designs of, stamp, or sell any article of gold of standard other than that fixed of twenty-two carats; nor may any work or piece of silver be made that be not of eleven *dineros*, under the penalties established by the laws of these my kingdoms, and the greater [penalties] that according to the character and circumstances of the cases the Council may consider necessary. . . .

And as regards weights and scales, it is the royal will that they be corrected and adjusted precisely to the weights of the Mint, and royal mark of Castille, granting in this the same private jurisdiction to the royal Council, manifesting, among other points, that the Assayer and Chief Marker of the kingdoms should carry out those ordinances in the inspections that they are obliged to make, with authority to imprison, embargo property, confiscate the weights and scales prohibited and not in order, and seize all the pieces and articles of gold and silver that they might find fabricated which are not of the required standard and weight, and bring suit against those who might have failed in their obligations. . . .

The Royal Decree of the 1st October 1733 specified that plate made shall be of eleven *dineros*, and gold of twenty-two carats.

The Ordinances of Fuen-Clara of 1746 (Ordinance II) specifies that gold of twenty-two carats shall be used.

From the *Ordinances of Assayers* of 1783 the following is taken:[16]

In the inspections[17] of the shops of silversmiths, beaters of gold and silver, and drawers of gold and silver wire the chief assayer will see that they show him the certificate for the hall-marks that each has, and bring with him the book of the silver shop in his charge, in order to find out from these documents if the silver and

---

16 Fonseca and Urrutia, op.cit., vol.I, pp.95-6.

17 These Inspections of the Silversmiths were not mere formalities but on the contrary effective measures taken against the possessors of silver from which the king's fifth had not been taken. In the records are found but few cases of discoveries of plate that was not tax-marked. Of these the following was taken from the *Archivo General de la Nación. Ordenanzas*. vol.II, pp.121-1723-1763:

   'Your Excellency orders the Royal Officials of this Court, in keeping with the higher decision that is mentioned in the warrants of inspection of the silver trade, to deliver to Juan de Soria the 13 *marcos* one ounce and four *reales* of his silver that is embargoed, paying double tax as is provided for.

   Juan Antonio, Archbishop, Viceroy, etc.—Inasmuch as Juan de Soria, an inhabitant of this city of Mexico and master silversmith in it, has stated that during an inspection of silversmiths there were taken from him 13 silver *marcos* that were found to lack the tax mark and that in consideration the charge was proven the return of said silver was ordered, paying to Your Majesty double tax; and since the same action has been taken with like violations he begged me to please order his silver

gold that is being worked corresponds to that hall-marked . . . If a surplus is found it shall be seized and the corresponding charge brought. Of the silver and gold that he may be working, take out a little piece [for assay], which may not have a value greater than one-eighth of a *real* of the silver, and two *tomines* of the gold. On the [plate being worked] the artisan will punch his mark, so that it will be known to whom it belongs. It will also be assayed and the standard of that which each was working will be ascertained, so that if it be not of the proper standard, action may be taken according to the laws and decrees. . . .

THE GOLD STANDARD

From 1499 the fabrication[18] of gold plate was allowed in Spain with three standards:

exquisite gold	24 carats
gold of lower grade	22 "
gold of still lower grade	20 "

But in practice of the silversmiths' art in Madrid, they began introducing corrupt methods with respect to the standard and quality of the metal and its fabrication, which brought about legislation on the subject, the most ancient ordinance being that given in Madrid for the good conduct of the industry on the 5th December 1695, confirmed later on by another of the 10th March 1771.[19]

PROCLAMATION OF 25TH APRIL 1785

By Proclamation of 25th April 1785, the Royal Order of the 15th August 1784 was published,[20] giving permission to work gold of twenty

returned . . . and in keeping with the report by the Royal Officers of this Court . . . and because this embargo is similar to that placed on Alonso de Avilés, and the silver was returned to the widow of the aforementioned, with the obligation of paying Your Majesty double tax on the silver that was not tax marked, in conformity with my superior decree of 17th August of this year, issued with approval of the Fiscal Agent of Your Majesty:

   . . . by virtue . . . I order the Royal Officers of this Court to deliver to the defendant said 13 *marcos*, one ounce and 8 *tomines* of silver, paying to Your Majesty double taxes in the same manner as has been done with the others.

   Mexico, 27th September 1736.

   Juan Antonio, Archbishop of Mexico.

   By order of His Excellency—Juan Martínez de Soria.'

18 See the summary at the end of this chapter.

19 See Larruga, vol.IV of *Memorias Políticas y Económicas Sobre los Frutos, Comercio, Fábricas y Minas de España*, Madrid, 1789, and *Bosquejo Histórico sobre la Orfebrería Española*, pp.139-40, by Narciso Sentenach. Printed by the *Revista de Arch. Bib. y Museos*, Madrid, 1909.

20 Beleña, op.cit., vol.I, p.283—third numbering of pages.

carats and a quarter of purity [which is twenty-carats plus one gram], although this was limited to the articles 'whose fabrication was difficult with gold of 22 carats.'

At the same time it was required that this work be distinguished from that of twenty-two carats by means of other marks.

SUMMARY OF DOCUMENTS

YEAR	THE LAW	REMARKS	Fineness Required	
			SILVER	GOLD
1435	Recopilación, book 5, heading 24, Law I. *Los Reyes Católicos en Madrigal*, year 1476, petition 14.	Spain	11 *dineros* & 4 grains	
1436	*Juan II en Madrid*, year 1435, petition 12, by Antonio Xavier Pérez and López, op.cit., vol.23, p.60.			
1488	Law 2. The same ones in Valencia, 12th April 1488, chap.10, Royal Ordinances. Pérez and López, op.cit., vol.23, p.60.	Spain	11 *dineros* & 4 grains	
1499	Law 3. The same ones in Granada 25th July 1499, chap.I, Royal Ordinances, Pérez and López, op.cit., vol.23, p.61.	Spain	11 *dineros* & 4 grains	
1499	Law 3. The same ones in Granada 25th July 1499, chap.I, Royal Ordinances, Pérez and López, op.cit., vol.23, p.61.	Exquisite Gold Gold of lower grade. . . . Gold of still lower grade.		24 carats 22 carats 20 carats
1581	*Archivo General de la Nación.* Book of Ordinances. O.O.O.O., p.61 reverse.	For Mexico		22 carats 24 carats
1730	*Autos Acordados.* Book 5, heading 24, decision 2. Philip V in Seville 28th February 1730. Pérez and López, op.cit., vol.23, p.65.	Included the Indies[21]		22 carats 20 carats

21 Although 'it included the Indies' it appears from the proclamations that follow that this law was not enforced in Mexico.

SUMMARY OF DOCUMENTS

YEAR	THE LAW	REMARKS	Fineness Required	
			SILVER	GOLD
1730	Royal Decree of 26th April 1730. Beleña, op.cit., vol.I, pp.281-2 (Proclamation of 30th December)		11 *dineros*	22 carats
1731	Royal Decree given in Seville on 26th January 1731. Fonseca and Urrutia, op.cit., vol.I, p.68.		11 *dineros* / 11 *dineros*	22 carats / 22 carats
1733	Royal Decree of 1st October 1733.		11 *dineros*	22 carats
1746	Ordinances of the Viceroy Fuen Clara of 1746.			22 carats
1772	Beleña, op.cit. vol.I, p.281, second enumeration of pages.		11 *dineros*	
1785	Proclamation of 25th April 1785. The Royal Ordinance of 15th August 1784 was made public giving permission to fabricate gold of 20 carats and one fourth of fineness (which is 20 carats and one gram).			

Summary: The Quality of the Precious Metals Employed and their Value in Modern Currency

SILVER

For determining the fineness, the *dineral* was the standard used. Each *dineral* was divided into 12 *dineros* of 24 grains each. From the time of the Conquest until the 9th June 1728, silver money of 11 *dineros* four grains was coined, and all the laws of that period required that plate should be of the same standard.

From 1728, money coined was of 11 *dineros*, and probably the plate was immediately reduced to the same standard, although authority for the reduction apparently was not granted until 1730.

Calculating this fineness in thousands:

	1535 to 1728	From 1728
1 *Dineral*	1,000	1,000
11 *Dineros* & 4 grains	930.5 +	
11 *Dineros*		916.6 +

GOLD

During the entire colonial period, gold of twenty-two carats,[22] that is, twenty-two parts of pure gold and two parts of alloy, or 916.6 parts of pure gold in each thousand, was employed.

On the following pages are shown tables of equivalences and values in modern currencies.

22 Although the use of gold of 20 carats was permitted 'in all those pieces whose fabrication was difficult with the standard of twenty-two.'

SILVER

TABLE OF EQUIVALENTS

1 Silver marco	1 Spanish ounce	1 Ochava	1 Tomine
8 Spanish ounces	8 ochavas	8 Tomines	12 Spanish grains
4608 Spanish grains			
7.10548477 troy ounces			
3278.8224 U.S. grains			

STANDARD FOR PLATE

a. Pure silver was 12 *dineros* or one *dineral.*
b. From the time of the discovery of the Indies until the 9th June 1728 the standard was 11 *dineros* and 4 grains.
c. Until the end of the colonial period the standard was 11 *dineros.*

Silver of 11 *dineros and 4 grains*	Silver of 11 *dineros*
.93055555 of pure silver	.9166-2/3 of pure silver

1 *Marco* = 6.6120476823 troy ounces pure silver	1 *Marco* = 6.5133610 4 troy ounces of pure silver
1 Spanish ounce = .8265	1 Spanish ounce = .8147 troy ounces of pure silver

VALUES IN MODERN CURRENCY[23]

SILVER OF 11 DINEROS 4 GRAINS

CURRENCY	VALUE TROY OUNCES	1 *Marco*	1 *Spanish Ounce*	1 *Ochava*	1 *Tomine*
Mexican *pesos*[24]	1.595	10.54621605	1.318277	.164784625	.0137320521
Spanish *pesetas*[25]	3.004	19.86259124	2.4828239	.310352987	.0258627489I
U.S.Dollars	0.4475	2.958891338	.36986I417	.046232677	I.0038572723091
Pounds sterling	£0.0.20	£0.11.0.24	£0.1.4.53	£0.0.2.06	£0.0.0.17

SILVER OF 11 DINEROS

CURRENCY	VALUE TROY OUNCES	1 *Marco*	1 *Spanish Ounce*	1 *Ochava*	1 *Tomine*
Mexican *pesos*[26]	1.595	10.38881086	1.29860135	.162325168	.0135279733
Spanish *pesetas*[27]	3.004	19.56613656	2.44576707	.305720883	.0254767402 5
U.S.Dollars	0.4475	2.914729065	.364341133	.045542641 6	.003795220133
Pounds sterling	£0.0.20	£0.10.10.26	£0.1.4.28	£0.0.2.03	£0.0.0.17

23 20th February 1936. The price of silver today is calculated on the basis of silver of 99% purity.
24 Based on New York price less 1% commission.
25 Based on London price.
26 Based on New York price less 1% commission.
27 Based on London price.

GOLD

TABLE OF EQUIVALENTS

1 Gold Marco	1 Castellano	1 Tomine	1 Spanish Grain
50 Castellanos	8 Tomines	12 Spanish grains	.74015625 U.S. grains
400 Tomines			.00154198732 troy ounces
4800 Spanish grains			
3552.75 U.S. grains			
7.401545136 troy ounces			
230 metric grains			

STANDARD OF FABRICATED GOLD; 22 CARATS DURING THE ENTIRE COLONIAL PERIOD

From 1758 it was permitted to fabricate gold of twenty carats

1. As pure gold is 24 carats, gold of 22 carats is 22/24 pure or .9166666 pure gold.
2. Therefore a gold *marco* of 22 carats contained 6.78474041975 troy ounces of pure gold.
3. And the gold *Castellano* of 22 carats contained .1356944 troy ounces of pure gold.

PRESENT-DAY[28] VALUES OF GOLD

Currency	Gold of 24 Carats per Troy ounce	1 Marco of 22 Carats	1 Castellano of 22 Carats	1 Tomine of 22 Carats	1 Spanish grain of 22 Carats
Mexican *pesos*[29]	124.07	841.7827439	16.83565487	2.10445685	.17537I404
Spanish *pesetas*[30]	254.316	1725.4680446	34.5093609	4.3136701I	.359472509
U.S. Dollars	35.00	237.4659147	4.74931829	.5936647786	.049472o655
Pounds sterling	£ 7.1.1	£ 47.17.2.56	£ 0.19.1.71	£ 0.2.4.71	£0.0.2.39

28 24th February 1936. Pure gold of 24 carats.
29 Per kilogram: $3,955 *pesos*.
30 Calculation based on price in London.

3. *Taxes on the Precious Metals: Introduction*

During the entire colonial period three separate taxes were imposed on gold and silver. These, modified during various periods, were at the beginning:

	Net
1. The tax on precious metal mined, called the 'Royal Fifth,' from the time of the Conquest	20%
2. The tax on smelting and assay, from 1552	1½%
3. The coinage tax, pertaining to the King, from 1567	3 *reals* for each silver *marco*

Such heavy taxes could never be made effective, and those concerned took the only course that permitted them to live: fraud. The miners presented a part of the silver for coinage and paid the corresponding tax; but on that sold for commercial purposes as well as that to be fabricated into plate and jewelry, a great part paid no taxes. This was one of the principal reasons for the great quantities of jewelry and plate found in Mexican homes. Nearly a fourth part of the value of the metal was thus saved and it was converted into objects readily saleable in emergencies.

That these exorbitant taxes were contrary to the best interests of the Government was made clear by the experiment of 1711, when, for the miners of Zacatecas only, the mining tax was reduced one-half. The result was an increase in the revenue of the Treasury, during the ten years 1711-1720, of $852,031 *pesos* greater than that for the similar prior period.

The Mining Tax or Royal Fifth: Its Origin, 1386

In 1386, in the *Cortes* that were held in Alcalá, Alfonso XI

. . . decreed by fundamental perpetual law that all the mines of gold, silver, lead and of any other metal that might be found in the territories of his Dominion, belonged exclusively to the crown: And he ordered that no subject should dare work them without his special permission and order.[31]

When the Americas were discovered, Ferdinand and Isabella, as the

---

31 Fonseca y Urrutia, op.cit., vol.I, p.3.

most efficient and practical means of profiting from the exploitation of the mines, by decree of the 5th February 1504, permitted[32] their subjects in the Indies to work them as though they were their own, with the sole condition that they should contribute the fifth part of the metal extracted, free of all cost, to the Royal patrimony.

One of the first matters that occupied the attention of Cortés was the appointment of officers of the Royal Treasury, with the obligation of collecting the Royal Fifth. These officials were Julián de Alderete, Alonzo de Grado, and Bernardino Vázquez de Tapia, who approved the *Third Descriptive Letter*, on the 15th May 1522.[33]

FERDINAND AND ISABELLA, 5TH FEBRUARY 1504. PHILIP II, 1572

The laws that established the bases for the utilization of the metals by the subjects of the Spanish Kings later formed the First Law of Book VIII, Heading X, of the *Recopilación de Indias*, which reads:

We order that all inhabitants and dwellers in our Indies who might come upon or extract in any province . . . gold, silver, lead, zinc, mercury, iron or any other metal, shall and must pay to us the fifth part of that which they come upon or extract, net, without any discount whatsoever, with the restrictions contained in law 51 of this heading and placed in the keeping of our Treasurers and Royal Officials of that province, with the understanding that it [metal] can not be collected or extracted by any person who, in accordance with our orders, are prohibited to do so, or to stay or dwell in the Indies.

Because it is our will to make them a grant of the other four parts, so that all may dispose of them as of their own personal property, freely, without hindrance or attachment, in consideration of the costs and expenses that they might have incurred, provided always that when collecting or extracting the metals mentioned they obey the orders and prescribed manner in which they are given . . . so that there be no fraud, or concealment of any kind, and all must pay the fifths, under the penalties imposed by the laws of this heading.[34]

The restriction of Law 51 of this heading, to which the foregoing refers, is the following:

And because our intention and desire is to assist, protect and make a gift to all our subjects and vassals that they be encouraged to continue the discoveries of

32 Ibid., vol.I, p.3. The decree was repeated on the 9th November 1525. Ibid., vol.I, p.6.
33 Ibid., vol.I, p.5.
34 *Recopilación de Leyes de Indias*, op.cit., vol.3, fol.55, reverse.

mines of said metals of lead, zinc, copper, iron and other similar ones, and to change their irregular methods to a fixed determination, we order that from the new mines that they may discover, those who extract these metals shall pay us during the first ten years, instead of the fifth, the tenth part, and no more.

1526-1568

Those who were authorized to extract gold and silver are specified by the First Law of Book IV, Heading XIX, which was compiled with decrees of Charles V on the 9th December 1526, and of Philip II on the 19th June 1568:

It is our will and pleasure that all persons of whatever civil state, rank, preeminence or grandeur, Spaniards and Indians our vassals, may extract gold, silver, mercury and other metals personally with their servants or slaves, in all the mines which they may find, or where they may desire or consider convenient. . . .[35]

On the other hand, the Eighth Law of Book III, Heading XIII, imposed nothing less than 'sentence of death and loss of property for all those who may exchange or barter gold, silver, pearls, precious stones . . . in the Indies, its provinces or ports, with foreigners of these our kingdoms of Spain, of whatever nation that they may be.'[36]

The Assay Tax

Once the metals were extracted from the mines, it was necessary to smelt and assay them, and therefore, to pay the taxes imposed by Law 2 of Book IV, Heading 22, compiled with decrees of Charles V on the 8th August 1551, and of Philip II, on the 8th July 1578 which reads:

We order and command that all the gold and silver that may be in the provinces of the Indies and which may be collected and extracted from the rivers and mines, be assayed and tested and marked with the carats and true standard and that which each contains be made known . . . and according to the standard and value they may have the Royal Officials shall collect for Us the fifths and the tax of one and a half per cent that corresponds to Us, and give account of all to the Treasurer in the Royal book, under penalty of loss of their positions and their properties for our Treasury.[37]

35 Ibid., vol.2, fol.118, reverse.
36 Ibid, vol.2, fol.16, reverse.
37 Ibid., vol.2, fol.123, reverse.

And Law 13 of the same heading orders:

'We command that in all the Royal Treasuries there be collected one and a half per cent as a fee for smelting, and for Assayer and Marker.'[38]

The King's Tax on the Coinage of Money

Once the silver was assayed, it was necessary to utilize it by converting it into coin, plate or jewelry, and in all cases a special tax applied. The King reserved the exclusive right to coin money, and when individuals coined the silver that they extracted from the mines they paid a tax called *señoreage* [coinage tax] required by Laws 7 and 8 of Book IV, Heading 23, *Recopilación de las Indias*.

Law 7 was compiled of decrees of Philip II, of the 15th February 1567, and of Philip III, of the 26th October 1613, the 20th January 1615 and the 1st April 1620, and reads as follows:

To us is due, according to law, the coinage tax or tax on the money that is made in the mints in these our Kingdoms of Castille, and it is just that those of the Indies pay us. And considering that in the [the Kingdoms of Castille] we collect fifty *maravedis* for each silver *marco*, for doing good and protecting our subjects and natives of the Indies and assisting them in every possible manner, we command that from each silver *marco* that is made into coins there be and remain one *real* for us for the tax of coinage or making of coins.

1565-1620

Law 8 was compiled of decrees of Charles V in 1535, of Philip II in 1565 and 1567 and of Philip III in 1620, and reads as follows:

Because, according to the ordinances of the mints of these Kingdoms of Castille there should be taken from each silver *marco* sixty-seven *reales* of which one is reserved for all the Officials, and as the expenses in the Indies are very high it is fitting to give them greater recompense that they may be more productive in their work and have competent sustenance, we order that the Officials of the Mints in the Indies may take and we permit them to take from each silver *marco* that there is fabricated, three *reales*, which they must give and divide among the aforesaid [officials] in the same manner as those of these kingdoms, unless it be otherwise agreed and approved by general consent . . . in such manner that the two *reales* be for the charges and expenses, and the other for the coinage tax.[39]

38 Ibid., vol.II, fol.125.
39 Ibid., vol.2, fol.130.

Tax on Plate

1578-1584

The silver employed in jewelry or plate paid the tax called *de vajilla* [of tableware] which was ordered by Law 34 of Book 8, Heading 10. This consisted of decrees of Philip II, of 8th July 1578 and 30th October 1584, and directed:[40]

We command that all the silver and gold that may be fabricated in any part of our Indies, from which they may make any kind of vessels, show cases, household ware, chests, desks, brasiers, or pieces of any class, quality and kind that it is customary to have for the trade, display, ornament of the houses or other purpose, and thus also the adornments and finery of images, altars, paintings, oratories, jewels, necklaces, belts, chains, medals, pouches, buttons, laces, rings and other classes or kinds of works fabricated of gold and silver, the fifth must be paid to us.

And in order that there be no fraud and it be certain that this is paid, we command that all persons who give to make and fabricate the above-mentioned pieces, or any one of them, or in other form, be obliged to take and must take to present before our Royal Officials of that district . . . to the nearest [official] the gold and silver bullion which is to be worked and fabricated. These will see that this is fifthed and stamped with the marks that it should have and if it has them, weigh it, note and register it in the special book that should be kept for this purpose.

They will note therein the amount and the pieces, jewels and other things that the exhibitor declares and may wish to make, and by the hand of which silversmith, and with this it be returned with the certificate and proof of the notation and register.

The exhibitor shall obligate himself to, within the period that appears sufficient for making the pieces, take them fc. inspection before the same Officials in order to compare their weight with that of the silver registered and place such small mark (which mark the official will make for this purpose), as he may elect on each piece; and once marked they shall return it to the interested parties. Without which mark they may not have [precious metals] or make use of them, nor may any silversmith fabricate metals without having complied with this procedure and having the certificate of our Officials showing that it has been registered before them and the fifth paid, under penalty of paying the full value for the first offense, (the owners and silversmiths are obligated jointly), and the second [time] to be liable to that reserved for those who defraud our Royal Fifth, fully applied as it is provided for and ordered.

This law attempted to eliminate the failure to pay the Royal Fifth,

40 Ibid., vol.3, fol.59, reverse.

and for this reason demanded, first, that the gold or silver bullion should be exhibited so that the royal officials might see if it were fifthed, and only in case it were not would they collect the tax of the Royal Fifth, and second, that after the bullion was fabricated into plate they should present it again in order that the royal officials might verify if the weight of the plate corresponded with that of the bullion presented for inspection. This, of course, was to prevent the paying of the fifth for a certain weight of bullion and making plate of a greater weight by adding metal on which the tax had not been paid. But if the bullion had already paid the 20% tax and the weight of the finished work corresponded to that presented for registry the tax, of course, was not again payable.

Excise Tax

If the owners of the silver did not wish to coin it or make it into plate but, on the contrary, desired to use it for commercial purposes, they paid the tax called *alcabala*, excise tax. Carreño says: 'The origin of the word *alcabala* . . . is to be found in the phrase *Dadme algo que valga* [give me something of value], which was the phrase used for the tax created to assist the Spanish kings' expenditures for war.'[41]

The decree of Philip II, November 1591, from which is taken the First Law of Book 8, Heading 13, reads as follows:

The excise tax on that which is universally sold and bought by all is a tax ancient and justified . . . and for this reason is imposed in the kingdoms of the Indies since the time that the union of the one was made with the other. . . .

From this came the regulation of excise taxes which specified how much should be paid, including such insignificant persons as rag-dealers and tramps.

Law 6 deals with the tax on plate:

On the silver that the silversmiths may buy of any person must be paid five *maravedis* per *marco* of excise tax, and no more, and if they should sell pieces of silver of one or two *marcos* they must pay another five *maravedis*, and if the sale be of less than a *marco* they must pay only the excise tax on that which they might

41 *Compendio de la Historia de la Real Hacienda de Nueva España*, written in the year 1794 by Joaquín Marian, with notes and comments by Alberto M. Carreño. *Imp. y Fototipia de la Sec. de Ind. Com. y Trab.* Pub. by the *Soc. Mex. de Geo. y Estadística*. México, 1914.

gain on that silver, deducting the cost, and they should be believed as to the sale and purchase by their oath, without any other proceedings: and of the gold of another that they fabricate they do not have to pay excise tax for the labor; but of the gold that they fabricate or may have fabricated to sell, and that which they may sell in any form, they must pay at the rate of two *maravedis* per ounce, but only on that [profit] which they gain on the gold, taking off in price what it cost them and no more. And they must pay to the collector at the end of each week.

1696

Notwithstanding the insistence of the Kings of Spain, efforts to collect the excise tax from the silversmiths were not successful, as is disclosed in the lawsuit of 1696 against the silversmiths of Mexico. Revello[42] says:

Philip II promulgated on the 1st November 1591 the tariff that ordered the payment of the excise tax on gold and silver, at the rate of five *maravedis* per *marco* on the last, and at two *maravedis* per ounce on the first. It was incorporated in the *Recopilación de Leyes de Indias*, in Book VIII, Heading XIII, Law VI.

Notwithstanding the *Recopilación de Indias* . . . the silversmiths' guild of Mexico, as it later contended toward the end of the seventeenth century, had not up until that time paid such tribute; which gave rise to a lawsuit brought by the Prosecutor of the Council of the Indies . . . with writ of execution of 11th May 1690,[43] 'which was circulated among all the authorities of the Columbian Continent.'

The text of the proceedings reads[44] in part:

I say that inasmuch as Your Majesty orders and commands by the Sixth law, heading thirteen, book eight of my recapitulation of the Indies that all the silversmiths who might buy any silver of any persons

must pay five *maravedis* per *marco* of Excise Tax, and if they should sell pieces of silver, one or two *marcos*, they must pay

another five *maravedis*.

And if the sale were for less than one *marco* of small things they must pay only the excise tax on that which they would gain on that silver, taking off the costs. . . . They must pay the said excise tax at the rate of two *maravedis* per ounce only on that which they gain on the gold taken out of the price that it cost them and no more. . . .

42 Revello, op.cit., p.15.
43 This appears to be a misprint and should be 1696.
44 Revello, op.cit., appendix p.xxvii.

Conclusion

Thus gold and silver were subject to the following taxes:

a. For right of extraction, the fifth part, or 20 per cent, which was called the Royal Fifth.

b. The right of smelting and assay, of 1½ per cent.

c. If the silver was used for the making of coins, they paid three *reals* [36 *centavos*] for each silver *marco*, of which one *real* [12 *centavos*] was for the coinage right and two *reals* [24 *centavos*] for the Officials of the Royal Mints.

To these statements it is necessary to add the following explanations:

a. The only persons who could mine gold and silver and traffic with them were subjects of the King, Spaniards and Indians.

b. The taxes on mining, smelting and assaying were paid to the Royal Officials of the Treasury, who were the Treasurer, Reckoner and Inspector (Book 8, Heading 3, Law 5).

c. The coinage tax was paid at the Mint; and

d. The excise taxes were paid to the Inspectors, who were subordinate to the Customs Officials.

Amendments

Although these taxes are set forth in the Recapitulation of Laws of the Indies, which were effective during all the colonial period, these laws were general and may have been strictly enforced in certain parts of the vast Spanish dominions; but with respect to New Spain, in the course of time they were modified. The principal modifications are the following:

From the beginning, the authorities in charge of collecting the taxes must have realized that the tax of the Royal Fifth, net and without deducting the cost of production, was excessive, because in 1530 and on various subsequent occasions they explained to the King that the mining costs were so high that the deduction of the Royal Fifth left no profit for the miners, and as a result, they often abandoned the mines with serious detriment to the Royal Treasury. For this reason they petitioned that the tax of one fifth be reduced to one tenth.

On the 17th September 1548, the King authorized this reduction for a period of six years, at the end of which it was extended for an additional seven years, which extension was legalized in 1569 and 1572.[45] Of exceptional importance were the ordinances issued by Philip II on the 22nd August 1584, by which it was decreed:

a. That those who might discover and those who, prior to this date, had already discovered mines, could hold them as their personal property and do with them as they pleased.

b. That if the mines produced one *marco* and a half of silver per hundred weight [of ore], they should pay the tenth part to the Royal Treasury.

c. That if they produced from a *marco* and a half to four *marcos* of silver per hundred weight, they should pay the half of the tenth part without discounting the costs; and

d. That the gold should always pay one half [of the gross], regardless of its standard, quality and quantity, and without deducting the costs.[46]

With the reduction of the mining tax to one tenth, the traders, merchants, and ore buyers were still obliged to pay the tax of one fifth [on metal for which the mining tax had not been paid] and this was the source of much fraud. For this reason, in 1700 the Count of Moctezuma petitioned the King that all taxes of a fifth, that were still effective on the silver, be reduced to a tenth. In view of the reasons set forth, the King granted to the mining industry and tradesmen of Zacatecas, the opportunity, 'as an experiment, for six or eight years, 'that the tax of the fifth that the tradesmen, merchants and refiners of silver of that mining town and its confines were paying be reduced, in accordance with their petition, to the tenth that the miners were paying.'

The result of this experiment was reported as follows:

. . . which statement, having been rendered, proved that during the time while the tenth was paid, which was in the years from 1711 up to 1720, an increase has resulted to my Royal Treasury of $852,031 *pesos* more than that of an equal preceding period when the fifth was paid.

From which the Marquis de Valero, who rendered the report, con-

45 Fonseca y Urrutia, op.cit., vol.I, p.15.
46 Ibid., p.16, xxxiv and following.

cluded that it was advantageous that the temporary reduction from the fifth to the tenth be made permanent, not only for Zacatecas but for the entire kingdom. Having studied and examined the proposal of the Marquis de Valero, the King replied to his successor, the Marquis de Casa Fuerte, on the 19th June 1723, as follows: 'I have decided that on all the metals of that land and kingdom of Mexico there be paid generally the tenth tax on silver (buyers of it, jewelers, and other persons), and that the same command apply and be effective also on the gold in said kingdom, likewise imposing on it the tenth tax as on the silver, having considered that the same reason apply to one as to the other.'[47] Marroqui, writing of the College of Mines, said: 'The Council and King being agreeable to this procedure, the reduction was approved and recorded by decree of the 19th June 1723, addressed to the Marquis de Casa Fuerte.'

The full text of this Royal Decree was published by Fonseca and Urrutia.[48] This remedy was not sufficient to prevent the defraudation of the Royal Treasury. The Marquis de Casa Fuerte (1722-1734) complained of 'how general and deep-rooted' was 'this pernicious practice,'[49] and in 1746 Juan Francisco de Güemes y Horcasitas stated that 'the practice of trading in plate lacking hall-marks was spreading to the gold in ingots, silver bullion and sheets.'[50]

King Charles III, desiring to correct these evils and eliminate the fraudulent trading in gold and silver, as well as to aid the miners and silversmiths, on the 1st March 1777 issued a Royal Decree as follows:

I have decided to fix, for the present, the taxes on gold for all my known kingdoms of the Indies, including that of Cobos that is paid in Peru, at three per cent at the same time the fifth is taken and two per cent on its introduction into Spain. This quota includes all the uncontrolled taxes that may be paid on this metal.[51]

In 1732 the coinage of metals for the account of the Crown was begun.[52] For this purpose the precious metals were purchased by the King, and for this reason, in some places, they began to collect taxes, both in the

47 Marroqui, op.cit., vol.I, p.383.
48 Ibid., vol.I, pp.32-5.
49 Ibid., vol.I, p.384.
50 Ibid., vol.I, p.384.
51 Fonseca y Urrutia, op.cit., vol.I, pp.34-9.
52 Until 1732 the privilege of coinage had been leased to the highest bidder.

Treasuries and the Royal Mints, thus doubling the tax. Fonseca and Urrutia say:

A Royal Decree was finally issued dated in Madrid on the 1st July 1776, in which His Majesty decided (among other things) that all the silver and gold should pay either the Royal Coinage Tax at the Mint at the time of coinage or the same tax in the Royal Treasuries on being registered for conversion into jewelry or plate, because these metals could have no other use than that of coinage, which is the principal and general one in which the tradesmen and State are interested, or being made into plate or jewelry, which is secondary and of less importance, and in which only the private interests of the owners are concerned.

The assembly, held on December 20 of the same year 76, in view of this Royal Command ratified the abolition of the double coinage tax and made payable at the Mint only the tax due on the gold and silver at the time of coinage. It was further ordered that the Royal Officials should collect in addition to the taxes of the tenth and one per cent, the *real* tax on plate and that corresponding to the gold on the metals that were registered for this purpose, issuing the regulations considered necessary in order to prevent frauds and losses. Of this a new report was rendered to His Majesty, with certified copy of the proceedings of the assembly and notification given the Treasury, Superintendents of the Mint, and Officials of the Royal Chests, both at home and in the foreign kingdoms.[53]

With regard to the number of assayers, on the 1st August 1750, the King commanded:

Whereas, the great number of bars and ingots of silver which are bought and coined in my Royal Mint in Mexico, and the administration of the assayers, due to their heavy and constant work, requires much diligence in order that they may comply and observe [the laws], I command that in the said mint, there be four assayers, two permanent employees and two substitutes instead of the two that are by general rule provided for in each one of my Royal Mints in Spain.

And with respect to the assay taxes, he repeated that which was already commanded, namely, that

from each gold assay, be the amount of metal large or small, there shall be taken for assay a half *ochava* of the same gold, and from each silver assay four *ochavas* of the same silver. And from the assays of loose metal, when its melting is entrusted to the clerk of the mint, the assayers shall take out only the *pallon* [button], returning to him exactly all the residuum of the loose metals[54] taken for assay.

53 Ibid., vol.I, p.403.
54 Ibid., vol.I, pp.263-4.

Concerning the taxes that were collected in the Royal Mint in Mexico, as fees corresponding to the office of Chief Assayer, and in the other mints of the Kingdom, as fees for their assayers, Fonseca and Urrutia say:

1st. The Royal Officials of the Royal Mint of Mexico should collect, and the owners or parties interested in the metals pay, at the rate of three *pesos* for each hundred *marcos* of pure silver. When mixed with gold a tenth should be taken on account of the casting, although the pieces brought should be already cast, as was mentioned in chapter I, paragraphs 2 and 3 of these ordinances.

A like tax shall be collected on all the silver bullion in possession of the silversmiths and which is melted or alloyed for them. . . .

The drawers of gold wire shall pay two *reals* for each silver *marco* that is stamped and melted and made into bars at the assay place itself: the same to apply on the fragments they bring from the filings and cuttings of the bars and spoiled pieces of the same sampled silver and which are returned to the assay to be melted and made into bars.

The beaters of gold and silver shall pay a *real* for each silver *marco* stamped and four *reals* for each gold *marco* reduced to the standard of twenty-two carats.

On all the gold bullion with carat mark that may be tenthed or sampled the declarants or silversmiths shall pay four *reals* per *marco*, reducing the carats marked on the piece to the standard of twenty-two carats, applying the same to the gold made into plate or other objects that they might declare requesting tax exemption.

On all assays that may be made of gold using *aqua fortis* they should pay two *pesos* for the assay.

The articles fabricated by the silversmiths will be charged a half [*real*] for each, be they large or small, and as they usually bring them in pieces before soldering and putting them together, calculate with good judgment that which corresponds to each piece.

Although law 16 of heading 22, book 4 commands that the sample for assay shall not exceed the weight of a quarter of an ounce, as conditions may have caused the application of higher taxes due to higher prices and costs of living, due to lack of employment and other conditions from immemorial times down to the present, the ounce has been generally maintained; wherefore this was one of the taxes considered just by the Chief Assayer, Diego González de la Cueva, in the draft he made of these for all the mints, and obedience to which was ordered by Royal Command of the 12th May 1779. By virtue of these a small sample should be taken from all the objects of eighty *marcos* or more, of one ounce, which will be proportionally smaller from those less than this weight down to fifty *marcos*, from which four *ochavas* should be taken, and this same from any other smaller object, of whatever size it may be, with exception of pieces of plate, from each of which shall be taken a tiny shaving or piece with a buril, and if the pieces are few, several should be taken to complete the assay.

From the ingots of gold an *ochava* should be taken for assay.

For the inspection of alloyed silver made for the silversmiths (in order to advise them what discount these are subject to) four *reals* for each.

From the re-assays that parties may request there shall be collected one half *ochava* sample of the gold plus the two *pesos* (fee on) assays of this kind.

From pure silver a sample of four *ochavas*, and from those of plate four *reals*.

The taxes corresponding to the other assays are stated in the draft prepared by the Chief Assayer, Diego González de la Cueva, approved by His Majesty and commanded respected by royal order of the 12th May 1779, which is in the following form:

ASSAY BY THE ROYAL MINTS[55]	MELTING TAX	SAMPLING SILVER	SAMPLING GOLD PURE, OR MIXED	ASSAY TAXES ON GOLD	SILVER TABLEWARE
Guanajuato	2 *pesos 4 reals* for each 100 *marcos*	1 ounce from 80 *marcos* &.	2 *ochavas* of	2 *pesos* for each assay	2 *pesos* for each lot
Guadalajara	3 *pesos* per 100 *marcos*	1 ounce	1 *peso*	2 *pesos*	2 *pesos* per lot
Zacatecas	3 *pesos* per 100 *marcos*	1 *peso* per piece		5 *pesos* per ingot of pure gold and 3 for mixed gold	1 *real* per *marco*
Bolaños	3 *pesos* for each 100 *marcos*	1 ounce			1 *real* per *marco*
Potosí	21 *reals* from 90 *marcos* and over and from there under, 13 *reals*	1 ounce		1 *peso* 4 *reals* for the test	
Pachuca	27 *reals* per 100 *marcos*	1 ounce			
Sombrerete	3 *pesos* per 100 *marcos*	1 ounce			
Alamos	Each ingot of gold 6 *pesos*: silver piece of 100 *marcos*, 6 *pesos*: from 50 to 90 *marcos* 3 *pesos*: from 20 to 50, 2 *pesos 4 reals*	1 ounce or one *peso*	2 *pesos 4 reals* or 2 *ochavas*		
Zimapán	3 *pesos* for each 100 *marcos*	4 *ochavas*	2 *ochavas*	2 *pesos*	
Durango	2 *pesos 4 reals* per 100 *marcos*	1 ounce	1 *ochava*	2 *pesos*	
Chihuahua	2 *pesos 4 reals* per 100 *marcos*	1 ounce			
Parral	2 *pesos 4 reals* per 100 *marcos*	1 ounce			

55 Fonseca y Urrutia, op.cit., vol.I, p.100.

To the foregoing it is necessary to add this paragraph from Fonseca and Urrutia:[56]

Regarding the pieces of private individuals, the Chief Assayer may likewise re-assay those he might consider necessary (chapter 15 of law XVII) of silver as well as of gold, without charging taxes to the interested parties other than the *ochava* on the silver, and, on the gold, only that amount required to perform the work; and were it necessary to repeat the assay on account of a difference, he should return to the parties that [metal] left in the pans; but if it were at the request of the parties, then they should pay the two *pesos* tax for the assay on gold for each of the pieces tested and the half *ochava* for the test sample of each, with exception of plate or coarse grains of gold, which, although they might be in various pieces, all should be taken together for the assay and should not pay more than the one tax and four *ochavas* for each sample of pure silver.

On the 17th October 1789 began the period of the government of the Viceroy, Vicente Güemes Pacheco de Padilla, second Count of Revilla Gigedo, who governed until the 12th July 1794. In compliance with the dispositions of Law 24 of Book 3, Heading 22 of the *Recopilación de las Indias*, he left to his successor most interesting confidential instructions, from which the following is taken:

The taxes on gold and silver, which are among the most ancient known in these kingdoms, in the beginning were very high but decreased until by Royal Decree of the 1st March 1777 the taxes were reduced to only three per cent which was imposed on gold presented in the Royal Mints. The double coinage tax was abolished, so that at present only one is charged at the Mint. . . . The total of this tax amounts to $2,000,000 and has no administrative costs other than $400, so that all that amount remains free of cost in favor of His Majesty.

The gold and silver plate presented for taking out the fifth at the places where there are collectors, stamps and punches pays three per cent and one per cent on the silver brought for taking out the tenth part and one *real*, on each *marco*, corresponding to . . . the coinage tax.

To avoid frauds practiced by workers of gold and silver it was decided by the Superior Assembly that they be provided at the Mint with the gold which they might require at the price of $128 and 32 *maravedis* per *marco* of 22 carats, and that the silver be furnished them from the Central Mints. The value of this tax increased to $14,977 *pesos* yearly, which entered intact into the Royal Treasury without any deduction, since there were no direct expenses.

For each assay of gold, pure or mixed with silver, two *pesos* shall be paid: each

56 Ibid., vol.I, p.84, iv.

gold *marco* that is tenthed or sampled, be it bullion or plate shall pay four *reals*, reduced to the standard of 22 carats; each piece of those the silversmiths make shall pay a half *real* because they stamp it for him and from each ingot of ten *marcos* or more, should be taken a sample of one *ochava*, and one half *ochava* when it weighs from three to five *marcos*.

There shall be collected also, as a fee for melting and assaying, on the silver brought in by the miners and the bullion or plate that the silversmiths present, three *pesos* for each 10 *marcos*; and there shall be taken a one ounce sample in addition, from each bar of over 100 *marcos*; one half an ounce when over 50 and two *ochavas* when it is smaller. The same three *pesos* are paid for each 100 *marcos* of silver that is sampled for the silversmiths, reduced to the standard of 11 *dineros*. That which is sampled for the wire drawers; 2 *reals* per *marco*, reduced to the standard of 12 *dineros*, and one *real* per *marco* for that sampled [for assay] for the beaters of gold and silver.

The silversmiths shall also pay half a *real* on each piece that is fifthed, for the stamp placed thereon, and 4 *reals* for the assay made of the silver and gold they present. The wire drawers pay also 2 *reals* for each *marco* for the small pieces they bring or send for melting, and the sheet beaters pay in the same case only one *real*.

This tax produces about $90,000 *pesos* annually, but from that the salaries of the assayers must be paid. These positions were formerly subject to sale and transfer, but they were later incorporated with the Crown. Their salaries at present will amount in the entire kingdom to about $35,000 *pesos* and $25,000 *pesos* being the expenses of the assays, there only remains for his Majesty $35,000 *pesos* net yearly.

The great number of taxes mentioned in connection with the Mint in Mexico and the great variety [of taxes] that exist in various others in the country, might have been the reason for the assays remaining such a long time in charge of private parties, who by all means endeavored to advance their own interests and find ways of increasing their income, although this might be to the detriment of the vassals.[57]

Independent Mexico

The amendments set forth in the foregoing were in effect until 1821. In that year the *Cortes* of Cadiz issued a very important decree which largely influenced the legislation on this subject in the period of independent Mexico. It reads as follows:

Abolishment of certain taxes on silver and gold &c. The *Cortes*, after having duly observed all the formalities prescribed by the constitution, have decreed the following:

Article 1. The taxes known as the fifth, one per cent and coinage tax are abolished.

57 *Instrucción Reservada*, op.cit., pp.310-13.

Article 2. These are substituted by a single tax of three per cent on silver and the same on gold, which shall be paid in the same form as the fifth was collected.

Article 3. The miners and refiners, as a class, shall not be subject to payment of any other tax, except those payable to the general mining tribunal, when they do not engage in any other industry or have another kind of business; but this shall not apply as regards general and municipal taxes to which the other class of citizens are subject.

Article 4. No charge shall be made for coinage other than the actual cost of the operation, reducing the two *reals* that are now paid to what the actual cost may be. To determine this the average expenses for each five year period shall be taken, and this shall be what is charged during the following five years, changing these averages in every period (of five years). In the Mints that may be newly established, an estimate shall be made that will be in effect during the first year, adjusting it at the end of the year in accordance with the result of their accounts, and be governed by this corrected estimate until at the end of the first five year period they can take the average. To the producers, in numerical order, without giving preference to one over another, shall be paid the value of their metals in cash, and without any unnecessary delay.

Article 5. The tax of eight *maravedis* per silver *marco* that is paid as refining charges is abolished, and likewise the twenty-six *maravedis* imposed on the same quantity of mixed bullion that is brought in for separation. . . .

Article 6. The increase in the standard of silver which might be obtained in refining and that which occurs in melting the ingots of silver and gold to mix them and make them into bars, deducting the costs of these operations, likewise the value of the underweight coins shall be added to the operating fund of the mining department, and the difference between the increase in gold and true losses in silver during the separation, shall be deducted from the costs of this operation.

Article 7. The separating costs shall not be more than two *reals* per silver *marco*, which are those that this operation now has after the deduction mentioned in the previous article, crediting the producers all the gold that their bullion might have contained. When with improved methods the costs may be less, a proportionate reduction to what the producers now pay will be made, crediting them the gold in the same proportion, and leaving them free to perform this operation by themselves or where they may desire.

Article 8. All that which has been said on silver is applicable to gold, charging the same for the coinage of one silver *marco* as for one of gold, cancelling the so-called sampling for assay tax, and reducing that of the assay to the cost that this operation might have, as with the silver.

Article 9.   Once payment has been made in the National Treasuries of the tax of three per cent on silver, and the same on gold, and the seals confirming this are placed on the bars and ingots of these metals, without price limit, their owners are free to sell or utilize them in any manner they may desire.

Article 10.   The Royal Decrees of 13th January 1784, the 12th November 1791, the 6th December 1796, relative to exemption from excise taxes allowed on articles for consumption in the mines, as well as the decree of the 13th January 1812, relative to salt, shall be strictly obeyed.

Article 11.   All the taxes created during the revolution, those on articles for consumption in mines as well as those on metals in bulk or coins by whatever name they may be known, are hereby abolished.

Article 12.   The government will endeavor to send as large a quantity as possible of mercury, consigning this to the mining agencies, that these may distribute it to the miners, so that in the future the shipments be sufficient to provide for all the necessities of the mines, maintaining in Mexico a sufficient supply, so that there may never be a lack of that ingredient, necessary for the refining process.

Article 13.   Hereafter the technical positions in the mints and smelters and those of assayers in the mints of the capital and interior, shall be filled exclusively by persons who, after undergoing examinations by masters in these sciences, may be found to have the necessary knowledge of physics, chemistry and mineralogy for filling them, and for those that may be progressive in the same establishments, preference shall be given, for the first vacancies, to the graduates of the Mining Seminary.

Article 14.   These regulations are applicable to North America only.

In view of the date of this decree, if it reached Mexico, it must have arrived about the middle of August 1821, when the national independence was practically accomplished, and the Spanish government had already lost control of nearly all of the territory. Thus it is probable that if this decree reached Mexico, it was not published, as the government was then busily concerned with more serious affairs.

But it was of such importance that, after the independence was declared, the Regency of the Empire accepted and promulgated it with some modifications, as can be seen from the following transcription:

The Regency of the Empire, governing provisionally in the absence of the Emperor, to all by whom these presents may be seen and understood, know ye:

That this Supreme Provisional Assembly, which from the first moments of its installation took into consideration the deplorable and declining state of the mining industry and the urgency of assisting this branch with the means at its control to contribute to its greater prosperity, on which that of the Empire depends; having duly studied the report rendered this Regency as a result of the deliberations held on 22 November last and the opinions given by the mining commission on this serious matter, by virtue of its authority and in keeping with the provisions of article II of Chapter II of its Regulations, has seen fit to decree and herein decrees:

1. The taxes of one per cent, the tenth and *real* for coinage are abolished.

2. Likewise, the tax of eight *maravedis* on each silver *marco*, that was charged for the refining of silver subjected to this operation.

3. Thus also is revoked, the tax of twenty-six *maravedis*, imposed on each *marco* of mixed silver, that was charged on account of shrinkage of silver in the smelter.

4. The tax of four *ochavas* on each piece of silver and that of one half *ochava* on the pieces of gold, collected for testing in the Mint, is also revoked.

5. Likewise are revoked all the taxes that were imposed on the silver and gold bullion and on coins during the revolution.

6. The only tax that will be charged is the three per cent on the true value of the silver and the same on the gold, paying this tax in the same manner as the one per cent and the tenth were paid.

7. In the Mint at the capital, two *reals* on each silver *marco*, and the same on each gold *marco* will be the only tax for the coinage of these metals; and in the others of the kingdom, because they are newly established, an estimate will be prepared which will be in force during the first year, and after correcting with the accounts of expenses at the end of the year, the corrected estimate shall be effective for the following year.

8. No charge shall be made for separating other than two *reals* for each *marco* of alloyed silver, instead of the five and one half *reals* that have been charged, and they shall set aside for the producers all the bullion that according to their gold content warrant this operation. The owners of alloyed silver are at liberty to perform this operation by themselves or wherever they may desire.

9. On outside assays [outside the capital] only the true costs of the assay operations shall be charged and those on the melting of the pieces that might require it, abolishing the sampling tax.

10. Once payment has been made in the National Treasuries of the only tax imposed by article six on gold and silver bullion and the stamps confirming this placed on the pieces of these metals, without price limit, their owners are free to sell or utilize them in any manner they may desire.

11. In the silver money there shall be allowed a deficiency of only eight and one half grains instead of eighteen as now permitted.

12. Hereafter the technical positions in the Mints and Smelters shall be limited exclusively to persons who may have the necessary knowledge of physics, chemistry and mineralogy for these positions.

13. Mercury in liquid state is left absolutely free of duty, whether coming from Europe or Asia, or whether produced in the Empire.

14. The powder which the miners might need to work their mines shall be provided by the government at cost plus expenses.

Let the Regency be duly informed and make necessary orders for its prompt compliance and that it be printed, published and circulated.

Mexico, 13th February 1822, second year of the independence of the Empire.

Juan José Espinosa de los Monteros	Vice-president
José Ignacio García y Llueca	Secretary
Isidro Ignacio de Icaza	Secretary
José María de Jáuregui	Secretary

To the Regency of this Empire.[58]

A decree dated June 1847, which likewise modified the taxes on metals, is as follows:

His Excellency, Provisional President, has been pleased to send me the decree which follows:

Antonio López de Santa Anna, General of Division, well deserving of the country and Provisional President of the United States of Mexico, to the people of the Republic, know ye:

That taking into consideration the reasons set forth by the board of promotion and administration of mining and by its creditors, considering the serious damages that would result to this important industry by making effective the decree of 30th April of the present year in the part that provides that, instead of the *real* per *marco* charged on the silver of eleven *dineros* which goes to that institution as its only fund, it shall hereafter receive only six grains, and the remaining six, as well as the other twelve increased by the aforementioned decree, shall be taken in to the general treasury, and considering as well the important services rendered by the aforesaid board, and providing the urgent assistance that the circumstances demand; in use of the faculties invested in me, I have seen fit to decree the following

Art. 1. Article 2 of the aforementioned decree of the 30th April, is hereby abrogated in that part which assigned to the institution of mining six grains, instead of the twelve which it received for each silver *marco*.

Art. 2. In consequence, said institution shall continue to receive the twelve grains per *marco* which corresponds to its total fund, in the manner established prior to the issuance of the above-mentioned decree, crediting it besides with that which it had not received for the six grains which were assigned

58 *Guía de Hacienda de la República Mexicana. Año de* 1826. Vol.II, pp.62-6. Legislative Part. 2 vols.

to the federal treasury in the decree mentioned from the date of its publication henceforth; and as regards the amounts that the respective offices may have delivered to the agents of said institution, as officials of the government, the part corresponding to the above-mentioned six grains said offices shall record as paid to the institution.

Art. 3. The increase of twelve grains in the tax mentioned in the same decree will continue in effect but only for the time necessary, not to exceed the year previously fixed, to apply on the debt to whose payment this has been assigned, and in which the credit and honor of the nation is compromised, for by no other means can this be paid and with the preference that its importance demands.

I, therefore, order this printed, published, circulated and duly complied with.

Palace of the Federal Government in Mexico, 16th June 1847, Antonio López de Santa Anna.

A.D.Juan Rondero.[59]

In 1863, Licentiate Benito Juárez increased the taxes of the fifth and the assay of silver:

The Citizen President of the Republic has seen fit to send me the decree which follows:

Citizen Benito Juarez, &, know ye:

That by reason of the authority in me vested, I have considered fitting to decree the following:

Only Article. The taxes of the fifth and of assay that the silvers pay are increased to ten per cent, instead of the three that formerly was paid.

Therefore, &c., Mexico, 22nd January of 1863 — Benito Juarez.[60]

The foregoing decree, far from producing beneficial effects that the government doubtless hoped for, was prejudicial to such an extent that one month after its promulgation it was found necessary to modify it, reducing the tax:

The Citizen President has seen fit to send me the following decree:

Citizen Benito Juárez, &c., know ye:

That reconciling private interests with those of the present conditions in the Republic, I have decided to decree the following:

59 Manuel Dublán y José María Lozano, *Legislación Mexicana*, vol.V, pp.285-6. *Imp. del Comercio*, Mexico, 1876.

60 Ibid., vol.IX, p.578.

Only Article. The taxes of the fifth and on assays on the silvers, which by decree of
the 22nd of last January were ordered increased to ten, instead of the
three that they had been paying, are reduced to six per cent.

Therefore &c., Mexico, 13th February 1863 — Benito Juárez.

To Citizen J.H.Nuñez, Minister of Finance and Public Credit.[61]

And even so, the preceding reduction was prejudicial and doubtless brought forth protests and claims, since the government was forced, fifteen days later, to cancel this decree and return to the former tax rate.[62]

The next decree on the subject is the following:

NUMBER 13,118[63]

20th July, 1895. Circular of the General Administration of the Stamp Tax. Establishes the fees for the mints, assay offices and Stamp office, from the sale of special stamps of the tax on precious metals.

Circular No.203. The Secretary of Finance and Public Credit, in order dated the 15th of the present month, notifies me:

In compliance with the provisions in art.3 of the Regulations of 26th June last, the President of the Republic has deemed fit to establish, in the following terms, the fees which from the sale of special stamps on the tax of precious metals, should be assigned to the corresponding mints, assay offices and stamp offices.

First. The Mint in Mexico should be provided with stamps directly from the General Stamp Administration Office and shall enjoy a fee of three-fourths of one per cent on the value of the stamps sold.

Second. The Mints of Zacatecas and Guanajuato will be given one and one quarter per cent (each of them), and the principal stamp official in such towns, one half per cent.

Third. The Mint in Culiacán will be allowed one and one half per cent, and the principal stamp official one half per cent.

Fourth. The Director General of the Mints, after hearing the opinions of the directors of the mints of Guanajuato, Zacatecas and Culiacán, will consult with this Secretariat as regards the distribution that should be made of the above fees assigned to the four mints, and among the employees of the same, who may be in charge of the sale of stamps or assume some responsibility because of their safe-keeping, their vigilance or their intervention in the handling of said stamps.

Fifth. The fee from the sale of stamps in the assay offices shall be the following: In the Monterrey Office, one per cent. In Chihuahua one and one half per cent.

61 Ibid., vol.IX, pp.586-9.
62 Ibid., vol.IX, p.597.
63 Adolfo Dublán y Adalberto A. Esteva, *Legislación Mexicana*, vol.XXV, pp.280-81.

In those of Guadalajara, San Luis Potosí and Durango, one and three quarters per cent. In those of Hermosillo, Alamos and Oaxaca, two per cent.

Sixth. The distribution of the fee fixed by the foregoing order shall be assigned: To the chief of the assay office, forty-five *céntimos*. To the assistant-chief, twenty *céntimos*. To the book-keeper, ten *céntimos*. To the principal stamp administrator, twenty-five *céntimos*.

Seventh. In the cases where one of the office employees be absent, the following rules should be observed:

I. The share that corresponds to the employee who is absent shall in no case be added to that of the stamp administrator and to that of the principal employees in the office; and only the lower employee who may be the substitute shall be entitled to it, and in such case he shall not receive the fee corresponding to his regular post.

II. In no case shall the fees be accumulative.

III. The fee corresponding to the employee who is substituting for another who occupies a higher position shall be assigned to the treasury; likewise that corresponding to an employee who has no substitute.

Eighth. The Secretariat shall fix in each case the fee that should be assigned to the employees of the special assay offices.

Ninth. The Director General shall consult the Secretariat with respect to all the doubtful points that may arise and the changes that may be advisable to introduce in the division of the fees from the sale of stamps, in accordance with the importance of the offices and the work and responsibility that the employees may have.

Which I communicate to you for your information and other ends.

I transcribe this to you for your information and effects.

Mexico, 20th July 1895. The general administrator, E.LOAEZA. To the principal stamp administrator in. . . .

The taxes from 1895 to present times underwent various changes, based always on a percentage of the value of the metal, but they are of slight interest and it is not necessary to mention all of them in detail.

The taxes for assay of plate effective since the 23rd February 1931 are as follows:

Pesos

On gold objects, including the mark [stamping of hall-mark] $5.50
On silver objects, including the mark [stamping of hall-mark]   3.50

The Director of the Mint says that today plate is very seldom presented for assay.

The law of 11th April 1935, establishing the present[64] taxes on the mining industry, reads as follows:

DECREE

FIRST ARTICLE. Subdivision B, article 8 of the Tax Law affecting the mining industry, dated 30th August 1934, is hereby modified to read as follows:

B. On the value of silver:

I. On minerals in their natural state	6.0%
II. On concentrates	5.0%
III. On precipitates or in ingots impure or alloyed	4.0%
IV. On refined	3.0%

When the value of silver in the New York market, converted to national money, may exceed $1.20 *pesos*, but not over $2.40 *pesos* per ounce [the tax] shall be increased one per cent for each $0.15 (fifteen *centavos*) or fraction of increase.

When it may exceed $2.40 *pesos* per ounce, without exceeding $3.60 *pesos*, the tax shall be paid on that corresponding to the initial price of $2.40 *pesos* in the manner established in the previous paragraph, and as far as the remainder, at the rate of fifty per cent of the amount of this.

When the value of the silver shall exceed $3.60 *pesos* per ounce, the tax shall be calculated in accordance with the preceding paragraph with respect to the first $3.60 *pesos* of the price, and of the excess there shall correspond to the Nation, as tax, seventy-five per cent.

The tax on silver and gold, contained in concentrates whose per cent of zinc be equal or greater than forty per cent, shall be fifty per cent of the corresponding tax (Article 50).

The tax on gold produced and ten per cent additional, shall be paid in kind.

The Secretariat of Finance is authorized to demand payment of the tax on silver produced and the corresponding additional tax, in kind.

64 26th March 1936.

Chapter VI

THE SILVERSMITHS' ART
1524-1600

1. THE IMPOSITION OF THE SPANISH ART. 2. SPANISH INSPIRATION. 3. CHARACTER OF THE SILVERSMITHS' ART OF THE SIXTEENTH CENTURY. 4. LIMITED PRODUCTION OF PLATE DURING THE SIXTEENTH CENTURY. 5. THE FIRST OBJECTS MADE.

1. *The Imposition of the Spanish Art*

WITH the destruction of the Aztec civilization, a clear field remained for the civilization of Spain, and the conquerors, with great zeal, began to implant the Spanish arts.

The missionaries converted the Indians by thousands. Materially, the curious tendency was to rebuild precisely on the sites of the ancient Aztec buildings and temples.[1] The best example of this was the reconstruction of the City of Mexico. Although the location of Tenochtitlán was bad, on low ground, subject to overflow and very difficult to drain, Cortés constructed his palace on the ruins of that of the Aztec Kings and the Cathedral on the former site of the temple of Huitzilopochtli, despite the fact that there were other advantageous sites near by, such as Coyoacán, much better located and more beautiful than the island on which Tenochtitlán stood.

This destruction of the Aztec civilization and the imposition of Spanish culture applied, as has been shown, to the arts as well as to architecture, religion and customs. Thus, for a full understanding of the colonial silversmiths' art it is necessary to bear in mind that the art of the Indian silversmiths was not absorbed but destroyed, and that

---

[1] Marroqui, op.cit., vol.I, pp.22-3. There were other examples, such as the church constructed on the ancient pyramid of Cholula.

the colonial silversmiths' art was a branch of the Spanish art without a trace of Indian influence.

2. *Spanish Inspiration*

Since plate made in Mexico was of purely Spanish inspiration, it may be useful to review briefly the character of this art in Spain during the sixteenth century.

The sixteenth century opened under favorable auspices. The famous Enrique de Arfe, who 'closed the *Ogival* style of gold and silver work in Spain,' was, in 1506, already producing important works. Sentenach[2] says: 'These, in many details, were the forerunners of the new Italian Renaissance art that was destined to bring about a brilliant resurgence of the goldsmiths' and silversmiths' art in Spain.'

Sánchez Cantón says:

ENRIQUE DE ARFE 1501-1524

In the following pages a history of a family of artists through three generations is given, whose work included all the prevailing styles of the Spanish Art during the XVI century.

With the arrival of the first of the Arfes in our country, the Gothic forms began to give way to the more graceful Italian styles.

ANTONIO DE ARFE 1539-1578

The second Arfe worked during the period of development of the Renaissance styles.

JUAN DE ARFE 1564-1602

The third Arfe, ardent admirer of ancient forms, opposed the extravagance of the Plateresque and endeavored to introduce the simple Graeco-Roman.

These three covered all the phases of our art in this progressive century in the life of Spain.[3]

The first Spanish silversmiths who came to Mexico left a country where their art was flourishing and where there was a great demand for their work. Hence it is unlikely that the more competent and prosperous ones would have abandoned an appreciative clientele in Spain to undertake such an uncertain adventure as that of establishing them-

2 Sentenach, op.cit., p.100. Enrique de Arfe worked from 1506 to 1524.
3 F.J.Sánchez Cantón, *Las Artes*, pp.7-8. Saturnino Calleja, S.A. Madrid, 1920.

selves in a new country. Therefore, it may be concluded that, in general, the silversmiths who came to Mexico during the sixteenth century were the less skillful ones, who lacked the ability to prosper in Spain. This, perhaps, together with the austere and severe character of the *Conquistadores*, explains why the silversmiths of Mexico, although they retained the Spanish feeling in their work, did not attempt to imitate the styles of the Arfes and the Becerriles, the great Spanish silversmiths of that period. As shown by the descriptions and the meager drawings of sixteenth century plate, their work assumed a different character for, although they produced pleasing objects, these were severe and unpretentious.

Very few silversmiths arrived from Spain during this period, if we may judge from the official lists of sailings for the Indies,[4] and records of those who applied to the Municipal Council for licenses to practice their art.[5] In addition to those referred to in previous chapters, the Notarial Archives mention the following silversmiths:[6]

BARTOLOME RUYS. SIGNED: BARTOLOME RUYS.

Record of the sale of silversmith tools, as well as of two female Indian slaves, Juana and Angela, and an Indian slave, Juan, a Silversmith worker, made to Francisco Ruys, Silversmith.

Know ye by these presents that I, Bartolomé Ruys, silversmith, resident of this great city of Tenextitlan, Mexico of this New Spain, of my own free will and accord hereby execute and agree in this letter to the sale, to you, Francisco Ruys, resident of this city, and now present in it, of two female Indian slaves named Juana and Angela, and an Indian slave named Juan, a silversmith, together with all the tools of my silversmith trade which I have in my shop . . . Mexico, on the first day of the month of December of the year 1536. Signed: Bartolome Ruys. (*Archivo de Protocolos de Notarías de la Nueva España. Lugar citado: Anónimos.* 1536-43.)

FRANCISCO RUYS

Promissory payment letter from Francisco Ruys, silversmith, in favor of Bartolome Ruys, concerning some slaves and tools of the silversmiths' trade:

4 *Pasajeros a Indias*, 1492-1592, 2 vols., forming vols.IX and X of the *Colección de Documentos Inéditos para la Historia de Hispano-América* by Luis Rubio y Moreno, Madrid. Cía. Ibero Americana de Publicaciones, S.A.

5 During this period, by law, a master silversmith who possessed a Spanish license could practice his art without the necessity of an examination in Mexico, by obtaining a license from the Municipal Council. It is not likely that the Silversmiths' Guild of Mexico would have permitted them to work without the required license.

6 Many of these data were furnished me by my friend Don Francisco Pérez Salazar, Mexico, D.F.

Know ye by these presents that I, Francisco Ruys, silversmith, resident of this great city of Temextitlan, Mexico of this New Spain, hereby accept and agree that I owe payment to you, Bartolome Ruys, resident of this said city, of two hundred *pesos* of fine gold of the required standard, covering payment of all the tools of my trade, which I own, and of an Indian slave workman who calls himself Juan . . . In the said city of Mexico on the first of December, year of Our Lord one thousand five hundred and thirty-six. There being present witnesses, Alonso Alavez, licentiate Diego Nuñez, residents of said city, Bartolome Ruys also being present, and as said Francisco Ruys stated he did not know how to sign, said licentiate Diego Nuñez signed for him at his request. Signature of Diego Nuñez follows. (*Archivo de Protocolos. Anónimos.* 1536-43).

JUAN NAVARRO

Letter power of attorney from Juan Navarro, silversmith, in favor of Gonzalo Narez, Mexico, 20th November 1536:

Know ye by these presents that I, Juan Navarro, silversmith, resident of this great city of Temextitlan, Mexico, of this New Spain, hereby assign and recognize that I give and grant full, free, complete and sufficient authority, which I may have, in order that I may more fully give and grant same and that by law it may be of more force and effect, to you, Gonzalo Narez, present in this said city, for its general effects in all my suits and actions . . . Mexico, on the twentieth day of the month of November, of the year of our lord one thousand five hundred and thirty six. Signed: Juan Navarro. There is also another signature: Diego Xuarez. (*Archivo de Protocolos. Anónimos.* 1536-43.)

COSME DE HORRANTYA

Promissory payment letter from Cosme de Horrantya, silversmith, executed in favor of Esteban Paez, resident of this city of Mexico, on 22nd January 1537. Signed: Cosme de Horrantya. (*Archivo de Protocolos. Anónimos.* 1536-1543.)

Letter power of attorney by Cosme de Orrantia [sic], silversmith, resident of this very noble and remarkable city of Mexico, in favor of Pedro de Aguilar, public prosecutor.

The form of this letter power of attorney is printed in gothic characters, probably from the printing-shop of Juan Pablos, first printer in America. Although it has no printed footnote of the printing-shop, the type is identical to those Pablos used. This class of blank forms began to make their appearance precisely in this year 1560, which is the date, in longhand, of this document. . . . This document is dated Mexico, 2nd May 1560, and signed: Cosme de Orrantia. Before me: Antonio Alonso. (*Archivo de Protocolos. Registro de Actas de Antonio Alonso, Escribano Público. Años* 1554-65, p.22.)

PEDRO GOMEZ

Promissory letter of payment executed by Pedro Gomez, silversmith, resident of this city of Mexico, of the New Spain, in favor of Alonso de Jaen, tradesman, present in this city of Mexico. Mexico, 21st October 1537. Signed: Pedro Gomez. (*Archivo de Protocolos. Anónimos.* 1536-43.)

LORENZO DE BUYTRAGO

Letter power of attorney granted by Lorenzo de Buytrago, silversmith, resident of this very noble, remarkable and very loyal city of Mexico, of this New Spain, in favor of Diego de Buytrago, to represent him in all legal actions and suits. Mexico, 11th January 1559. The witnesses were Juan Pablos and Juan Ortiz. Said letter is signed by Lorenzo de Buytrago. Before me, Antonio Alonso. (*Archivo de Protocolos. Actas de Antonio Alonso*, 1554-65. Page ccvii.) It is believed that this dealt with the famous printer Juan Pablos, and his workman, of French nationality, Juan Ortiz, printer, engraver and silversmith.

LORENZO BAEZ

Promissory letter of payment executed by Lorenzo Baez, silversmith, in favor of *Pedro de Beydacar*, silversmith, Mexico, 22nd June 1565.

Know ye by these presents that I, Lorenzo Baez, silversmith, resident of this city of Mexico, of the new Spain, obligate myself to give and pay you, Pedro de Beydacar, silversmith, a resident of this same city of Mexico, or whoever may hold your power of attorney, as agreed, thirty *pesos* of common gold of eight silver *reales* per *peso*, which are for account of certain silver that you gave me to fabricate and money for certain work which I was to do. . . . Mexico, on the twenty-second day of the month of June of the year one thousand five hundred and sixty-five. Signed: Lorenzo Baez.

Before me, Antonio Alonso, scrivener. (Form printed in gothic characters). (*Archivo de Protocolos. Actas de Antonio Alonso.* 1554-1565. DCCXXXIII reverse*).

1562. 29th October. *Antonio Cortés*, silversmith, appears before Jorge Cerón Carbajal, extending receipt for $44.00 (*Archivo de Notarías de México. Ante Antonio Alonso, Escribano Público.*)

1563. 15th July. *Diego Gentil*, goldsmith, resident of the City of Mexico, sells to Diego Hermoso, goldsmith, several houses, with lower and upper stories, in the suburb of San Pablo, which have adjoining them on one side *Vezero* and on the other Diego de Segouia, who bought from Alonso Franco. (Ibid.)

1563. 10th April. *Juan Martinez de Urroz*, goldsmith, obligated himself. (Ibid.)

1563. 27th January. *Andrés Gutierrez*, goldsmith, husband of Juana Martínez, *albacea* of Juan de Morales, silk weaver, dyer, and dealer in silks. (Ibid.)

1563. 9th November. Bernaldino Asencio, goldsmith. Power of attorney. (Ibid.)

1564. Bond extended by *Juan de Victoria*, Silversmith. (Ibid.)
1564. *Pedro Hernandez*, silversmith, acknowledges a debt. (Ibid.)

3. *The Character of the Silversmiths' Art of the Sixteenth Century*

We may be certain that during the sixteenth century the silversmiths were occupied almost exclusively in satisfying the enormous demand of the clergy for sacred vessels, jewelry, images and decorations. Moreover, the new inhabitants, when erecting their dwellings and haciendas, always built private chapels, which required great quantities of sacred objects. These, in view of the religious spirit of the times, were naturally given preference over plate for their own personal use.

Another reason for the lack of civil plate was the insistence of the kings of Spain that their subjects should avoid ostentation in their private lives. They particularly objected to the use of plate in the homes of their vassals.

Sentenach, speaking of Spain, although the laws embraced the Indies as well, says:

. . . apart from their personal jewelry, our wealthy class never displayed such wealth at their tables and in their chambers as the Italians and Flemish. This was the result, in part, of the laws against extravagances. These, under guise of moralizing the customs, tended principally to support these privileges [of the kings]. These laws, dating from the time of Alfonso VIII, were issued in an effort to suppress the craving for luxury; but not even in the time of the strict Philip II were they vigorously enforced, in spite of the efforts of the clergy to oppose the instinctive desire to display the newly acquired wealth.

In 1593, during the reign of that monarch, the moralizing influence reached the extreme of forbidding the fabrication of silver objects for any purpose other than for use in the churches. Neither do the guilds appear to have been very progressive during that period, as the only work done was by special contracts with the grandees.

4. *Limited Production of Plate during the Sixteenth Century*

The sixteenth century was a period of conquest and expansion. The *Conquistadores* were busily engaged in acquiring mines, lands and Indians. Women, whose demands always stimulate the arts, were lacking. These factors were all elements which were not propitious for the advancement of the arts, which require peace and leisure for their appreciation and development.

Although the treasure and ornaments of the Aztecs were of exceptional interest, their intrinsic value was relatively small—insufficient to pay even the cost of the Conquest. Thus, until the mines were in full production, the raw material for the use of the silversmiths was limited.

In 1536,[7] the Spaniards sent equipment for smelting operations to Mexico.

The rich mine of San Bernabé, in Guanajuato, was being successfully operated in 1549. The famous mines of Pachuca were discovered in 1551. With the discovery of the mercury process, the mining industry made rapid progress. In 1562, there were 35 reduction works operating in Zacatecas alone.

The first church in Mexico[8] was that of San Francisco, which was completed in 1525.[9] Building activities progressed so rapidly that by the year 1596: 'there were already nearly four hundred monasteries and a like number of convents, apart from the churches in the towns, of which there were, in the province of Santo Evangelio alone, nearly a thousand. This gives some idea of the great numbers in the other four provinces of the same category, in those of other provinces, and in the dioceses of the bishops.'[10]

During the sixteenth century, the Church in Mexico had not yet attained the wealth it acquired in the centuries that followed. García Icazbalceta says:[11]

In spite of everything and the fact that the money[12] at that time had greater value, the income [of the Church] was not sufficient to incite cupidity, even on the part of persons of the same cult. Some were satisfied with honor, without gain, and thus we see that on the 18th November 1539, Francisco Rodríguez Santos was given charge of a prebendary and informed that, as the Church had no money, he

7 Francisco Fernández del Castillo, *Algunos Documentos Nuevos sobre Bartolomé de Medina*. Mexico, 1927. The dates of the discovery of some of the first mines exploited by the Spaniards are as follows: Compostela (1543). Fresnillo (1568). Zacatecas (1548). Guanajuato (1549—San Bernabé).

8 Motolonía, op.cit., p.137.

9 Priestley, op.cit., p.166.

10 Barroso, op.cit., p.43.

11 *Biografía de Fr. Juan de Zumárraga, Obras de* J.García Icazbalceta, vol.V., pp.234-6. V.Agüeros, Mexico, 1897.

12 *México en 1554*. Three Latin dialogues written by Francisco Cervantes Salazar and printed in Mexico in that same year. These were translated into Spanish and reprinted with notes by Joaquín García Icazbalceta, Mexico, 1875, 8°, p.53.

would not be paid until such time as funds were available. Even the Bishop did not live in opulence but, on the contrary, spent more than his small income on charitable works, and assisted members of the cult and by so doing remained in want.[13]

Indeed, as late as the year 1582, when the wealth of the colony had increased notably, the church was still poor. The proceedings of the Ecclesiastic Council state that on the 3rd July 1582 notice was given to the musicians and choir that, 'if they desired to continue working, they would have to wait for their pay until funds were available and that they should not take this matter to court, as they had previously done, embargoing even the chalices and crosses, leaving the church without those things necessary for the performance of services.'

Nevertheless, in the principal houses, such as those of Cortés and the Viceroy, there was, from the beginning, great luxury. Of the feast offered by Cortés to Viceroy Mendoza to celebrate the peace between Spain and France, we are told:

The tables at which more than five hundred guests were seated, were sumptuously decorated and all the service was of gold and silver . . . more than a hundred silver *marcos* of plate [14] were stolen.

There were also, towards the end of the century, a few individuals who had enriched themselves by the discovery of mines:[15]

A Crœus of the Sixteenth Century in Mexico

Alonso de Villaseca was the most famous resident of that period on account of his great wealth and astonishing liberality. He was a native of Arcicola, a small village in the diocese of Toledo [Spain], son of the nobles Andrés de Villaseca and Teresa Gutiérrez de Foranzo. Although the date of his arrival in New Spain is not definitely known, it was prior to 1540. Here he was married to Francisca Morón, daughter of parents so wealthy that among their many haciendas there was one on which they branded annually twenty thousand head of cattle. Don Alonso became the rich man par excellence of the New Spain, and, to exaggerate the wealth of anyone, the saying was: *he is a Villaseca*. He did not increase his wealth by business dealings, nor did he make great efforts to collect the income from his properties: his *mayordomos* gave him what they desired and he accepted what they gave him. He pos-

13 Motolinía, op.cit., treatise 1, chap.3: 'Then he gave much care and diligence to the decoration of his cathedral, on which he spent during five years all the income from the bishopric.'
14 Luis González Obregón, *Las Calles de México*, vol.II, pp.48-53. Manuel León Sánchez, Mexico, 1927.
15 *Obras de J.García Icazbalceta*. Vol.II, *Opúsculos Varios* pp.435-6. V.Agüeros, Mexico, 1896.

sessed haciendas, some under cultivation and others with all kinds of livestock, many houses in Mexico and rich mines in Pachuca and Ixmiquilpan; his slaves were so numerous that he did not know them, and often asked them to whom they belonged. His wealth was estimated at a million and a half *pesos* and his income at a hundred and fifty thousand *ducados*; very great sums, considering the greater value of the money of that period. He was of an irascible character; he liked to give, but his countenance showed little pleasure when he was asked for anything, and less when thanked for any benefits received. He avoided all dealings and friendship with the grandees and persons of rank, and lived the greater part of the time in retirement at his mines in Ixmiquilpan, where death finally overtook him on the 8th September 1580. His body was embalmed and taken to Mexico, where it lay in state three days in the church of Our Lady of Guadalupe, while arrangements were being made for the burial, which was carried out with great solemnity, attended by the Viceroy, *audiencia*, *tribunales*, archbishops, and both the ecclesiastical and secular *cabildos*.

Terreros,[16] writing about Villaseca said:

About the middle of the sixteenth century, Alonso de Villaseca presented to the Shrine of Guadalupe an image of the Immaculate Conception that appears to be made of silver, embossed and adorned with precious stones.

Although in the following centuries there are many descriptions of the churches and their decorations, similar descriptions written in the sixteenth century contain very little with respect to jewelry and images, which together with the foregoing leads us to conclude that the production of plate in Mexico, during the sixteenth century, was limited.

5. *The First Objects Made*

11th JANUARY 1527

Although, prior to 1527, some church jewelry was doubtless made, there was a dearth of plate and this continued for some time, according to Motolinía[17] who, writing in 1538, says:

The Sign of the Cross is so revered in this land, in all the villages and on the roads, that it is said that in no part of Christendom is it more reverenced, and nowhere are there so many and such tall crosses, those in the patios of the churches, especially, are most solemn looking, and each Sunday and feast day they are adorned with

16 Romero de Terreros, *Las Artes Industriales en Nueva España*, op.cit., p.25.
17 Op.cit., pp.137-8.

many roses and flowers, cat-tails and bunches of flowers. Those used in the churches and on the altars are made of gold and silver and of feathers, not of solid metal, but of sheets of gold and feathers on wood. There are many other crosses made, and still being made, of turquoises, of which there are many in this country, although few round ones are found, nearly all of them being flat; these, after the cross has been carved or made in wood, and covered with a paste or glue and those stones have been cut, they cunningly soften the glue with fire and place the turquoises until they cover the whole of the cross and among these turquoises they place other stones of different colors. These crosses are very beautiful, very much esteemed by the lapidaries and said to be of great value. They also make crosses with their bases very well made from a clear, transparent, white stone; and these are used as *port-pax* at the altar, because they are made the size of a handbreadth or more.

On nearly all the *retablos* [pictures painted on wood] they paint the image of a crucifix in the center. As until this time they had no sheet gold they placed on the images of the many *retablos*, crowns of gold leaf. Other crucifixes are made in the form of statues, either of wood or some other materials, and are so made that although the crucifix may be the size of a man, a child can lift it from the floor with one hand. Before this sign of the cross various miracles have occurred, which I will not mention for lack of space. I will only say that the Indians hold it in such veneration that many of them fast on Fridays and abstain from touching their women for devotion and reverence to the cross.

The first silver objects made by the Spaniards in Mexico, of which we have record, were the city seals. Marroqui[18] relates:

The first seals used in that city [Mexico] were of silver, made by the silversmiths Diego Martinez and Etor Mendez; they were paid with two lots, which had been given to Gaspar Garnica, one of the conquerors and likewise a silversmith, who ceded them to his companions. The Municipal Council approved this cession and gave possession of the lots on the 11th January 1527, as may be read in the proceedings of the council of that date.

For the first flag four *varas* of damask were purchased from Alonso Montes and Diego González for sixteen *pesos* and this was sewn by a tailor named Portillo for one *peso*. All this was ordered paid by the municipal council on the 9th March 1528.

There is, in the archives of the Basilica, a book, handwritten in the Mexican Indian language, known as the *Anales de Juan Bautista*. On page 21 of this book there is a note, translated by a canon who was keeper of the files, which reads as follows:

18 Marroqui, op.cit., vol.I, p.46.

Sunday, 15th September of the year 1566, when the octave of our mother *Santa María de la Natividad* was held, and when the procession left that place in *Tepeyacac de Santa María de Guadalupe*. In which place Villaseca lives, who displayed an image of our mother, that is all of silver. . . .

Two years later, in 1568, the English pirate, Sir John Hawkins, was forced to abandon many of his followers on the coast near the Pánuco River, some of whom were captured and taken to Mexico. One of them, Miles Philips,[19] wrote an account of the hardships that they had suffered, and in this account, after saying that during the first days of November they arrived at Cuautitlán, he continues:

Early in the morning of the next day we started on foot for Mexico, until we were two leagues from the city, in a place where the Spaniards have built a magnificent church dedicated to the Virgin. They have there her image of silver gilt, as large as a tall woman, and in the rest of the church, there are as many silver lamps as there are days in the year, all of which are lighted during the solemn ceremonies.

The *Códice Sierra*,[20] gives us a rough idea of the articles made between 1551 and 1558.

19 This narrative of Philips was published for the first time in London and reprinted in 1812 by Evans. Joaquín García Icazbalceta translated Philips' narrative and published it in the *Boletín de la Sociedad Mexicana de Geografía y Estadística* (Year II, vol.I, p.193 and following. 1869), and it was reproduced by Licentiate Victoriano Agüeros in vol.14 of his *Biblioteca de Autores Mejicanos*. (J. García Icazbalceta, *Obras de*, V.Agüeros, Mexico, 1898. vol.VII — V — *Relación de Miles Philips*, 1582, p.183).

20 *Códice Sierra. Traducción al Español de su Texto Nahuatl y Explicación de sus Pintures Jeroglíficas* by Dr. Nicolas León. Mexico, 1933. *Imp. del Museo Nacional de Historia y Etnografía*. Published with an introduction by don Federico Gómez de Orozco.

Chapter VII

THE SILVERSMITHS' ART DURING THE
SEVENTEENTH CENTURY

I. WEALTH AND DEMAND. 2. THE FESTIVALS. 3. THE SILVERSMITHS OF
THE SEVENTEENTH CENTURY AND THEIR WORKS.

I. *Wealth and Demand*

BY THE end of the sixteenth century the period of Spanish conquest and expansion in Mexico was ended and the country was peaceful. The intense religious zeal which characterized the seventeenth century in Mexico, together with the ecclesiastical construction then at its height,[1] created an enormous demand for images, sacred vessels, and jewelry. Since there were not any banks, bills, bonds or shares, the only portable wealth was jewels, gold and silver. Because it was useful, decorative, and easily converted into currency, a great part of the treasure accumulated took the form of silver plate. The enormous riches of the Mexican mines, concentrated in a few hands, created a wealthy leisure class. Thus the requisites, peace, wealth and demand, were present, and it was not long before the necessary artisans were developed.

At the beginning of the century the number of silversmiths was evidently insufficient, because on the 17th April 1600, the Viceroy, Count of Monterrey, issued the following order:

Don Gaspar &. Whereas Canon Fran.co de Paz has informed me that the work on the image of Our Lady that is being made for the Cathedral of the City of Mexico, by Luis de Uargas, silversmith, is not being finished for lack of casters and that the only ones capable of doing it are two Indians named Pablo and Baltassar; and he requested me to order that for the month said work may last they shall take charge of it. Being duly informed, by these presents I order the tax assessor of the

1 More than 7,000 churches were erected in the seventeenth century alone.

districts of Mexico and Santiago of said city, and their governors and *Alcaldes*, that, as soon as this order is shown to them, they make said Indians Pablo and Baltassar take charge and work on it in the place where it is being made for a period of fifteen days and thereafter the time necessary, with good treatment and payment of the wages they are accustomed to earn, without accepting any excuse, and if necessary, compel and force them to it as deemed advisable.

Dated at Chapultepec on the twenty-seventh day of the month of April of the year one thousand six hundred, the Count of Monterrey, by order of the Viceroy. Pedro de Campos.[2]

2. *Festivals*

The festivals of that period were of great importance in the life of the Colony. They were generally organized on the recommendation of the Viceroy, and carefully planned by the Municipal Council. The program and its outcome were always recorded in the Proceedings of the Municipal Council, and to these records we are indebted for many curious details.[3]

The first account of an important festival recorded in the Proceedings of the Municipal Council of the seventeenth century was that of *San Ignacio*, approved by the Assembly of 5th July 1610 to be held the 30th of the same month and year:

That on the eve of the feast of San Ignacio, which is the 30th of this month, there be publicly proclaimed throughout this city a masked festival and for that night there be announced festive lights and general fireworks which shall begin at nightfall and last until ten o'clock at night. And that this same night there be in these buildings of the assembly a great number of festive lights so that no part remain unlighted and many flares in clay pans and in the usual form; distributed in the corridors [there shall be] twenty-four large candles of black wax and many firecrackers and firework wheels and on the plaza in front of the assembly buildings [there shall be] sixteen casks full of wood which shall be burned; all of which shall be in charge of Albaro de Castrillo and carried out with great brilliance and in such manner that these fireworks last as long as possible; and that on the roof of the assembly building there be trumpeters, and oboe and kettledrum players.

And on the saint's day all the city shall gather, without any being absent, dressed in their richest, most brilliant and elegant costumes with all the embroidery, adornments and jewels and the best that they may find, and, especially, that all the

2 *Archivo General de la Nación. General de Parte.* vol.5, p.177 reverse. 1599-1601.
3 Among the most interesting are those that appear in the proceedings of the Municipal Council corresponding to the 25th July 1624; 3rd July 1640 and 8th October 1642.

gentlemen councilmen shall wear white boots and shall gather at the assembly buildings, so that from there they may go in a body as ordered by the *corregidor* [Mayor].

On this same day, after dinner, the trumpeters, oboe and kettledrum players shall assemble on the roofs of the assembly buildings and during said day and night there [shall] be the same [type of] fireworks as on the previous night and in the same form, which shall be in charge of the same *comyssario* [assemblyman] Albaro de Castrillo.

And thus likewise the city approved that during the octave of the Blessed San Ignacio, on the 6th August, a ring tournament be held on the street of Casa Profesa, where it crosses in front of the church, for which this city names, for bearing the cost, Francisco de Solis y Barraza Alferes whom it offers to assist in the expense with one thousand *ducados* of castille, that with them the day may be more effectively celebrated without so much cost on his part. For which purpose Francisco de Solis y Barraza is appointed *comyssario* [assemblyman] to take charge of the stage covering and canvas enclosure in the manner that he may consider advisable.

And thus also the city approved that during the octave of said festival bulls be given free of charge to persons and their families who may desire to hold bull-baiting contests in their streets and neighborhoods.

And thus likewise, the city ordered that on the twenty-first of August the public square be arranged for fighting fifty bulls during the two days on which prizes should be given for the best lance thrust, and also, prizes for the best bull fighter on foot. And during these days there be races on the public square and gentlemen bull fighters and all other events that may be considered fitting to make these days joyful. The jurisdiction over the bulls in the public square should be given to Francisco de Solis Alferes, who, without cost to the city, may auction them off or have them cut up for meat, as he may see fit.

And the city likewise ordered that a repast be served on the day of the ring tournament and on the first day of the bull fight.

The works of Manuel Romero de Terreros, Marquis of San Francisco, give some details regarding the participation of the silversmiths in these festivals:[4]

From the beginning, the guild chose as patrons the Immaculate Conception and Saint Eligio, Bishop of Noyons, and as time went on fabricated their images in silver; that of the Bishop, of medium size, with rich pontifical vestments, the miter and staff of gold plated silver, which was first used in the year 1618, and that of the *Purísima*, weighing 243 *marcos*, in 1628. The following quatrain mentioned by Vetancourt, refers to this image:

4 *Las Artes Industriales en la Nueva España*, op.cit.

La platería os retrata
en plata, Virgen, y es bien
que en plata retrate a quien
es más pura que la plata.

Both statues were placed on the altar in the chapel of San Eligio in the Cathedral. . . .

Every 8th December the guild held a most solemn festival, of which one is described in the following paragraph of the *Diario de Guijo*:[5]

This same day (8th December 1662) the silversmiths celebrated with great pomp said festival in their chapel in the cathedral. They used for the first time a new *retablo* [figure painted on wood]. They cleaned the silver image and placed thereon rays radiating from the body, of silver gilt, and an imperial crown of precious stones and pearls, which in all amounted to 9,000 *pesos*. The procession left the cathedral, attended by the Municipal Council and clergy, and all the silversmiths bearing large tapers with four lighted wicks. Father Estéban de Aguilar, of the Jesuit Order, preached and the octave was celebrated with much splendor. The following Saturday bullfights were held on Plateros street, the entrances at the plaza and Casa Profesa being closed.

Neither the procession of Corpus, the Holy Sepulcher, nor similar ones passed without the silversmiths' erecting on their two streets an altar or stand, usually 'in the form of a castle (says Guijo), richly decorated on all four sides, with an image of San Eligio at the top;' and sometimes all the streets were decorated with silver plate and mirrors which produced a most surprising effect. They also took part in lay festivals and on the 24th January 1621 a masked festival was held on the streets of the city by the *artisans of the silversmiths' guild in Mexico and those devoted to the glorious San Isidro Labrador, of Madrid, in honor of his glorious beatification: given by Juan Rodríguez Abril, silversmith*. It left the houses of the Marshal of Castille; then located on San Juan de Letrán Street, and lasted from two in the afternoon until the angelus. The masked procession was led by an allegory of *Fame*, on a white horse, attired in rose-colored cloth with a beautiful head-dress. 'Then followed a gallant *labrador* [San Isidro], mounted on a coal black horse, the smallest to be found in New Spain, with the finest legs and appearance possible to depict, with a handsome mane, and rich and beautiful equipment. The man representing the *labrador* wore a silver mask, breeches and shirt richly fabricated of *agave* fiber [century plant]; hood, coat and leggings of dark cloth with the edgings trimmed with hyacinths [a precious stone of a yellow color] set in gold and the entire background covered with many other jewels of gold in such abundance that it is impossible to estimate their value. He carried a cast silver lance from which hung an excellent reproduction of the coat of arms of Madrid. Preceding the Saint, to give the

5 *Documentos para la Historia de México (Manuel Orozco y Berra) Diario de Sucesos Notables por el Lic. Gregorio Martin de Guijo*. Series I, vol.I, year 1650.

impression of grandeur and magnificence, were all the knight-errants, characters from books on knighthood, don Belianis de Grecia, Palmerín de Oliva, the Knight Febo, etc., the last, as the most modern, being don Quijote de la Mancha, all mounted and wearing red sleeveless jackets with lances, shields and helmets. . . .'

3. The Silversmiths of the Seventeenth Century and their Works

The roll of silversmiths of the seventeenth century is extensive; but there are few interesting details of their lives and but little data relative to their identification with the great quantity of plate made. Some among them were wealthy, such as Constantino de la Mota and Baltazar de Nava,[6] who donated an image to the church on the 20th November 1620. According to Guijo[7] some were thieves:

On Sunday the 15th of said month (January, 1651), Juan Manuel, *alcalde* of the court, caught Bernardo Moreno, master silversmith and [a man named] Grillo with a sackfull of plate. The latter opened the doors of the churches with a picklock and stole the silver candelabra and lamps, and Moreno melted them. These were found to be the products of the robberies of San Juan, Santa Clara and other convents in this city.

Father Tomás Gage[8] left an elaborate account of what he claimed to have seen:

The Indians and Chinese who have embraced the Christian religion and who visit the city every year, have perfected the Spaniards in that trade [silversmith's] and the latter now work with an admirable excellence.

The viceroy who arrived in New Spain in 1625, wishing to send the King of Spain a gift worthy of His Majesty, ordered a parrot of gold, silver and precious stones which was made to represent the natural plumage with such skill that the workmanship alone was valued at fifteen thousand *ducados*.

In the church of the Dominican convent, there is a silver lamp which has three hundred branches or holders for that number of candles, and a hundred small lamps . . . which is of such varied colors, rare and perfect workmanship that it is valued at four hundred thousand *ducados*. . . .[9]

Among the riches of this order are two remarkable things. . . . The first is a silver lamp which hangs before the main altar, so large that it required three men

6 *Archivo de Notarías de México*. Before Antonio Alonso, Public Scrivener.
7 Manuel Orozco y Berra, *Documentos para la Historia de México*. First Series, vol.I, *Diario de Sucesos Notables* by Lic. Gregorio Martin de Guijo. 15th January 1651.
8 Op.cit., vol.I. Written about 1625. The good father's stories are not always true.
9 Ibid., vol.I, p.176.

to raise it. The second, even more valuable, is an image of the Virgin Mary made of pure silver, as large as a woman of good height. It is placed in a tabernacle made especially for the chapel of the rosary, where there are at least twelve silver lamps which burn perpetually before this image. In fact, this convent is so rich that . . . a hundred thousand *ducados* could be obtained for the treasures it holds. Furthermore, in the cloister nothing is lacking that can contribute to the pleasures and recreation of the clergy. . . .[10]

The same author has left us some account of the life of that period:[11]

Although the inhabitants of that city are extremely given to pleasure, there is nowhere in the world a country where there is greater inclination to do good to the church and its ministers. Each vies with the other in making gifts to the monks and nuns, and to enrich the convents. Some erect, at their own expense, handsome altars in the chapels of the saints of their particular devotion; others present images of the virgin, crowns and gold chains, or give silver lamps; others erect convents or repair them at their expense; and still others give an income of two or three thousand *ducados*. Thus they imagine that by the good they do the churches, they will escape the penalty merited by their sins. . . .

In fact, as happens often in that populous city, alms and extraordinary liberality towards the churches and religious houses come from persons whose lives are as free as they are scandalous: its inhabitants, given to pleasures of all kinds, believe that such largesse causes their sins to disappear, and hence obstinately enrich the churches, which are so opulent and are built with such magnificence that no one can imagine anything more sumptuous.

There are only fifty parochial churches and monasteries and convents; but these are the best that I have known. The roofs and rafters are gilded; the greater part of the altars are adorned with columns of marble of various colors and the steps are of Brazil wood; in a word, the tabernacles are so rich that the meanest is worth twenty thousand *ducados*.

In addition to the beauty of the buildings, there is an enormous number of jewels and treasures which pertain to the altars, such as chasubles, capes, dalmaticas, canopies, hangings, altar ornaments, candelabra, jewels, gold and silver crowns, and gold and crystal monstrances, treasures which all together are worth as much as a silver mine, and could enrich the nation which took possession of them. . . .

In the *Misteca* range as far as *Guajaca* [Oaxaca] we saw nothing to attract our attention except a few villages or ranches of two or three hundred inhabitants, with many churches, very well built, adorned with silver lamps and candelabra, whose saints wear rich crowns. . . .

10 Ibid., vol.II, pp.25-8.
11 Ibid., vol.II, pp.180-182, 279.

Although the Proceedings of the Municipal Council of the period give little space to articles of fabricated silver, the following are mentioned:

. . . for many years there has been no inkstand or silver sandbox for the dispatch of business on the table of the Municipal Council. This is very unbecoming, and in view of the fact that Juan de Figueroa has offered to furnish one of silver and a sandbox for the [value of the silver bullion] weight only, it is ordered that the *mayordomo* shall weigh it and whatever it amounts to be paid for their own account and the inkstand, sandbox and bell delivered to the chief scrivener who will give a receipt and the auditor's office shall take note [of the transaction]. (28th May 1627).

A petition of Manuel Casasana was seen in which he states that because of the many favors received from the Virgin of the Remedies he wishes to serve her and does so with a silver perfumer which cost eight hundred *pesos* and weighs sixty *marcos* and that . . . this small service is performed with the understanding that it may not be mortgaged in any manner or loaned . . .

The city says that it appreciates the perfumer and accepts the offer of it on the terms made. (30th May 1636).

Manuel Romero de Terreros, Marquis of San Francisco,[12] describing a pyx made in 1655, as well as the famous *ciprés* which was first used in 1673 in the old tabernacle of the Cathedral of Mexico, says:[13]

In the cathedral of *Santo Domingo de la Calzada* there is a pyx sent from Mexico by Gaspar de Osio, an inhabitant of *San Miguel el Grande*. This monstrance, of silver gilt, bears red geometrical figures on a white enamel background and measures 1.20 meters in height. 'Its baroque decoration,' says Gascón de Gotor, 'is slight; the beautiful, severe, uncontaminated architectural lines of the rococo predominate.' It bears the following inscription: 'This monstrance was donated to the Cathedral of the City of *Santo Domingo de la Calzada* by don Gaspar de Ocio, in the year 1655.'

But, unquestionably, the most important work of the silversmiths in all New Spain was the *ciprés* that was placed on the ancient and magnificent high altar of the Cathedral. . . . This [ciprés] was designed by the Sevillian artist Jerónimo de Balbás. It was of solid silver and was dedicated on the 15th August 1673.

From the corners of a wide and decorated pedestal with three oval, ornamented plaques on each side, four brackets supported a number of statues of the Evangelists. On the corners of the pedestal and directly in front of these statues, were four small

12 *Las Artes Industriales de la Nueva España*, op.cit., pp.26-30.
13 Ibid., p.26.

pillars from which arose an equal number of projections [*juncos*] each upheld by two angels, and on the projections, the statues of the four Evangelists. These small pillars were united by oval, decorated plaques to as many other small pillars of a larger size, which supported the architrove and the cornice, and four arches with a number of angels from which many other oval plaques sustained the statue of St. John the Evangelist, which crowned the top of the *ciprés*. Well proportioned, very beautifully worked, and of the churrigueresque style, it measured more than six *varas* in height. It cost sixteen thousand *pesos* and was dismantled and melted about 1850.

In the center of this *ciprés* there was a temple in three parts, of silver gilt, of the Corinthian order and plateresque style. Above the base arose the first, composed of eight columns and many statues of the Prophets. The second part also had eight columns and at the base of these many statues of the Evangelists and Doctors of the Church; in the center was the place for the Host, in circular form, decorated with the *Agnus Dei* and surmounted by an imperial crown; and on the cornice, were four angels and eight 'pyramids.' The third part was formed of eight figures which supported a circular pedestal with the statue of Saint Michael. This temple was ordered by Archbishop Vizarrón y Eguiarreta, and later señor Rubio y Salinas and some capitulars had various changes made to it. It cost approximately thirty thousand *pesos*.

This piece, which disappeared in June 1867, was one of the few 'monstrances in the form of a temple or small tower' in Mexico, which is not the case in Spain where they still abound.

In the *Teatro Angelopolitano*[14] there are many descriptions of plate made in the seventeenth century for the Cathedral of Puebla:

We will describe the Sacristy of this Holy Church, which is one of the jewels of which it is justly proud. It is twenty *varas* in length by thirteen in width, in which space there are costly chests, for keeping the ornaments and sacred vestments, with exquisite fabrics on the walls and especially on the one in the center where there is painted the triumph of our Holy Mother Church and the Faith which we Christians profess, which with its gilded frames were hung the year of 1674 at the request of the Illustrious Doctor Juan García de Palacios, who was in charge of the collection of taxes for the repairs and maintenance of this Holy Church with which wealth only the sacristy of the Holy Cathedral in Mexico can compete. . . .

Three antependia, one bearing the image of St. Ildephonzo, donated through the magnificent generosity of the Illustrious Dr. Alonzo de Salazar Barona and first used on Holy Thursday the 25th March of the year 1660; the second was paid for by the school-teacher Dr. Joseph Ossorio de Cordova, the greater part of its fabric

14 Bermúdez de Castro, op.cit.

being of gold and in the center the image of his patron saint the Holy Virgin Mary of Defense; and the third of the same fabric with the keys of St. Peter in the center, donated by the Dean of this Holy church, Vicar-General and Governor of his Bishopric and formerly of His Majesty's Council and his minister in the Royal Audience of Guadalaxara, Dr. Gerónimo de Luna. . . .

Six silver jars, with nosegays of silver flowers, which with the missal stands for the pulpits on each side of the high altar, and the Gospel of St. John, reached a cost of eight thousand three hundred and ninety-seven *pesos* which sum was donated by the Dean Dr. Diego de Victoria Salazar as legacy of Dr. Silberio de Pineda. . . .

There is also a record of a silver throne made by Miguel de Olachea for the Cathedral of Puebla:[15]

This is a magnificent throne with a silver canopy adorned with angels, moldings, cornices and gilded figures of leaves. At the top of the canopy there is an angel in the center, and two jars with flowers on the corners, all weighing two thousand nine hundred and fifty *marcos*, and costing forty-two thousand three hundred and forty-two *pesos* and two *reals*. It was made by the master silversmith Miguel de Olachea in the year 1699.

The only complete list of silversmiths of the seventeenth century, which I have found, is the following:[16]

LIST OF THE SILVERSMITHS, AS TAKEN FROM THE

Decision handed down by the Royal Council of the Indies against the Silversmiths' Guild of Mexico, on the payment of the Excise Tax on all gold and silver purchased, sold or fabricated.

11th May 1696

Francisco Rendón, silversmith	Alcaizería.
Juan de la Cruz	San Francisco Street
Miguel de Pineda	San Francisco Street
Joseph de Medina	San Francisco Street
Andrés González Vezerra	San Francisco Street
Joseph de la Vega, goldsmith	San Francisco Street
Juan de Cuebas	San Francisco Street
Diego Ruiz de Santtos, goldsmith	Said street.
Alferez Alonso de Neyra, filigree worker	Said street.
Luis Anjel, goldsmith	Said street.
Joseph de Vergara, goldsmith	San Francisco Street

15 Echeverría y Veytia, op.cit., p.165.
16 Torre Revello, *El Gremio de Plateros en las Indias Occidentales*, op.cit., p.25.

Diego Zamunio, goldsmith	Said Street
Matheo Nuñez	San Francisco Street
Diego de Murria y Juan de Valdes	
Diego de Ignigo	San Francisco Street
Captain Francisco Vezerra	San Francisco Street
Alonso de Paris	Said Street
Captain Joseph Arias	San Francisco Street
Pedro Zedillo	Said Street
Xptóval Polanco	Said Street
Bartolome López	San Francisco Street
Gerónimo Pizerro	San Francisco Street
Manuel de Bergara, filigree worker	Said Street
Manuel de Luna	Said Street
Xptóval de León	Said Street
Joseph Reinosso	San Francisco Street
Joseph Reinosso	San Francisco Street
Joseph Sanchez	San Francisco Street
Miguel de Pedraza	San Francisco Street
Diego de Medina	Same Street
Mrs. María de Tolossa, widow of Polanco	
Ph(e). de Abrego	San Francisco Street
Thomas Moreno	San Francisco Street
Ramon Zauallos	San Francisco Street
Ambrossio Enomorado	San Francisco Street
Xptóval Campuzano [Cristóbal, was then written Xptóval]	San Francisco Street
Manuel Gomez	Same Street
Francisco de Otero	San Francisco Street
Nicolás de Valdés	Same Street
Juan de Marcarenas, goldsmith	Same Street
Xptóval del Carauajal	Same Street
Joseph Cortazar	Alcaizeria
Antonio Castaño	La Compañía Street
Juan de Peñalossa	Same Street
Diego Vazques	San Agustin Street
Antonio de Orozco	Same Street
Luis de Figueroa	Beneath the portal of the Cathedral
Gregorio Pardo, filigree worker	Relox Street
Diego de Aguilar	Same Street
Mrs. Maria Palazios, widow of Seuastian Garzia	Alcaizeria

Juan de la Vanquilla	La Palma Street
Benito Ro(ss)	San Francisco Street
Juan Manuel R.(ss)	Same Street
Nicolas de Vergara	Same Street
Saluador de la Cruz	Same Street
Mrs. Francisca de Vargas, widow of Diego Saldaña	
Juan de Castro	San Francisco Street
Pedro de Palazios	San Francisco Street
Nicolas Bernal	Empedradillo
Diego de Victorio	San Agustin Street
Martín Rodriguez	Alcaizería de lo Ancho
Joseph Saenz	Alcaizeria
Diego Vrttado	San Francisco Street
Francisco Ponze	San Francisco Street
Mrs. Ana de Adane, widow of Juan Tellez	Same Street
Mrs. Isabel de Cardenas, widow of Juan Calderon	
Joseph de Anaya	San Francisco Street
Mrs. Ana de la Vega, widow of Alonso de la Cueba	Same Street
Seu(n). Moreno	Same Street
Nicolas Polanco	At the Empedradillo
Juan de Vergara	San Francisco Street
Francisco Blanquetto	Santo Domingo Street
Mrs. Melchora de Cobarrubias, widow of Jacinto de Abiles	Same Street

Chapter VIII

THE SILVERSMITHS' ART DURING THE EIGHTEENTH CENTURY

1. WEALTH AND DEMAND. 2. FESTIVALS. 3. SILVERSMITHS OF THE EIGHTEENTH CENTURY AND THEIR WORKS. 4. THE SILVERSMITHS' ART AT THE END OF THE EIGHTEENTH CENTURY.

1. *Wealth and Demand*

THE intelligence, ability and activity of the Spanish kings of the eighteenth century, who, during that period, restored to Spain its old prestige, was reflected in Mexico by the character of their viceroys. These, with the exception of Branciforte, contributed in great measure towards the advancement of the country during that century.

The quantity of precious metals mined was enormous. From the time the Mint in Mexico City was incorporated into the Royal Crown in 1733 until the year 1790, the enormous sum of $810,905,885 *pesos* was coined.

The increase is shown by comparing the coinage of the year 1733, which was $10,175,895, with that of 1791, which amounted to $21,121,713, without adding to the latter two million *pesos*, value of the silver sent to Spain during that same year, for account of His Majesty.[1]

Thus there was an abundance of wealth, the main factor indispensable for the development of the silversmiths' art. The complementary factors — culture, religious fervor, and the demand for jewelry and precious stones — continued to increase and the descendants of the conquerors, although their power was waning, still demanded fabricated silver, in large quantity, to adorn their palaces.

Although in the eighteenth century the wealth of the clergy was

[1] All these figures were taken from Fonseca y Urrutia, op.cit., vol.I, pp.210-12.

not limited to the Cathedral of Mexico, which was rivalled by the Cathedral of Puebla and the Shrine of Guadalupe, nevertheless it was magnificent, as shown by the following descriptions of *La Catedral de México en* 1768[2] and the copy of the inventory made in 1807:[3]

In both the lateral naves, there are fourteen chapels, all with magnificent altars, paintings and other ornaments. These are enclosed by bars of fine wood, carefully worked, which reach to the height of the arches, leaving on the east side the very ample sacristy, whose walls are covered with very large paintings and large mirrors. All around [the sacristy] are tall, beautiful chests for safeguarding the sacred vessels with a sumptuous [baptismal] font in the center, of hammered silver, made in two parts, like a lectern; six large imperial torches, four larger tapers on tall supports commonly used for the services, all of which weigh one thousand and fifty-seven *marcos* of silver, as evidenced by an old pamphlet of their dedication, written by Dr. Isidro Sariñana, curate of the parish of the Santa Veracruz. . . .

In front, on the opposite side, is the *Sala Capitular* [chamber where the clergy meet] with hangings of crimson damask from Italy, the throne and seat of honor of embroidered velvet; and a variety of exquisite canvases of saints and ecclesiastical and secular princes. The other columns of the three open naves are covered, throughout their height and circumference, by two drapes, one, used on festive occasions, of crimson velvet adorned with braid and wide fringes of Milan gold, the other of plain crimson velvet and damask.

The main body [of the Cathedral] is lighted by one hundred and seventy-four windows, of beautiful, clear glass. Most of these have iron gratings. Free access [to the Cathedral] is by seven magnificent doors, with screens, one on the east and one on the west, decorated on the outside by various pillars with beautiful relief work, excellent images and passages from the life of Christ. It is understood that the number of doors mentioned does not include those of the sacristy, accounting office and *sagrario*, which, although indirectly, likewise permit access to the church from the street.

Two massive towers form the corners to the main façade; although neither of them is finished; one with many noteworthy bells of which the principal one weighs *cien quintales* [ten thousand pounds]. Outstanding among all are the small bells which are rung only as a manifestation of joy or thanksgiving for the health of our Catholic Majesty, when news is received from Spain, or when allegiance is sworn to Their Majesties and fair Princes. To their well-known chimes all the other churches immediately respond with such harmony that be it [an occasion] of general rejoicing or what is more probable and certain, [a demonstration] of the loyal worship prevailing among the vassals, it makes all rejoice whenever this novel event occurs.

2 Juan Manuel de San Vicente, *México en* 1768, op.cit., pp.28-44.
3 Manuscript in possession of my friend, Father Jesús García Gutiérrez.

For holy water there are eight great fountains of finest white stone that can scarcely be distinguished from marble. Of the same [material] are the magnificent pulpits, beautifully made and with gilded figures in relief, one for sermons, the others for chanting the Gospel and the Epistles. There is another fountain, enclosed by bars, where Saint Felipe de Jesús was baptized. . . .

Occupying the space between two arches on either side of the main nave, are two gigantic [pipe] organs, each with two exposures [the front and back the same] and four sections [in height] whose most beautiful housings, with the fine and delicately carved woods with gilded figures in relief, are seventeen *varas* in height and eleven in width. Towering from [the floor of] the choir gallery, these fill the whole space between the arches, exceeding in height the corresponding centers [of the arches]. [Equipped] with five hidden bellows for pumping air, they produce sweet notes from three thousand three hundred and fifty pipes, forming eighty-six chords, which have daily served for sacred services since they were erected on October tenth of the year 1736.

For offering the holy sacrifice of the mass, there are fifty consecrated stones on a like number of altars. The principal one is located between four arches in the main nave. It is in the shape of an artistic pyramid. The four sides are alike, each an altar, and it is supported by twenty-four marble pillars which embellish the four antependia. The book-stands and candelabra of each [altar] are of hammered silver. It is constructed in two sections and although it is so high that it almost reaches the dome, all the center part of the first section is of silver. Its magnificent projection serves as a shield or covering for another most beautiful section, gold plated and delicately worked and covered by a great canopy of heavy embroidered silk. Here the Holy Sacrament is placed, to which, on occasions, two magnificent figures of gold serve as atlantes, one embellished with pearls and emeralds, which weighs nine hundred and four *castellanos*, the other, somewhat larger, with a rich sapphire, valued at one thousand *pesos* but with few additional precious stones. For illuminating the Blessed Sacrament, there are countless candles in beautiful silver candle-sticks and four very exceptional gold ones.

On the fourteenth day of August of the year one thousand six hundred and ten there was placed on this altar, with great solemnity and display, the most sacred image of the Sovereign Queen of the Heavens, patroness of the Holy Church in her Divine Assumption. Both her Divine Image as well as the four angels that support it are of gold of many carats, with a weight of six thousand nine hundred and eighty four *castellanos*, adorned with very valuable precious stones. The value of the materials is so great that it is over twenty thousand *pesos*. No doubt the cost of its manufacture was greater on account of the delicate art embodied in this work. . . .

On the same altar, on certain appointed days, is displayed a most perfect cross of gold weighing three hundred and twenty-five *castellanos* which guards a piece of the True Cross. Serving as a base is a crystal case adorned with silver with various sacred objects and a great abundance of other beautiful ornaments, basins, plates, cruets, patens and chalices, the principal one of the latter being a paten whose weight is six hundred and forty three *castellanos* of gold. This, embellished with diamonds and richly enameled, is used only on great festive occasions, especially on Holy Thursday, when it is placed on the Sacred Monument which on this day is erected on the eastern side under a beautiful canopy that cost six hundred and fifty-eight *pesos.*

Tenebrario [triangular candlestick bearing fifteen candles] made of ebony and decorated with silver, first used in the year one thousand six hundred and eighty-five, which cost five thousand *pesos*, is used on the three days of the Passion [Wednesday, Thursday and Friday of Holy Week]. After this the great Paschal candle is lighted. The cost of this enormous object in spite of the fact that it weighs forty-five *arrobas* [1,125 pounds], cannot be exactly determined, due to the different prices of the wax [used]. It is well to state that its original cost was one thousand one hundred and eighteen *pesos.*

On this altar are venerated sixty life sized images, carved and perfectly finished. These represent the five members of the Sacred Family, the seven of the Angelic Hierarchy, the twelve Apostles, the four Evangelists, the four doctors and the principal patriarchs of the sacred religion. Included among them are eight of hammered silver and, in addition, four large ivory figures of the crucified Christ and many other half-size figures of different saints.

The presbytery is enclosed by a magnificent railing of the finest yellow metal, one *vara* in height and more than a sixth [of a *vara*] in width. This from the first step of the base supporting the main altar to the first step of the choir gallery, forms a railing one hundred and thirty-eight feet in length and terminates at the two ends of the front part of said choir gallery. There it forms another enclosure where the Most Illustrious Archbishop and the Venerable Ecclesiastical Council [Cabildo] are seated to hear the sermons. There are also, of the same [yellow] metal, equally spaced, sixty-two small pillars with the same number of full size statues with a cornucopia in the hands of each, which hold torches for illumination.

The space between the two vaults is occupied by the choir [gallery]. Its floor is at the same level as that of the presbytery, embellished by a magnificent row of seats of two kinds, high and low, made of precious woods. On the upper part of the back rest of each there is a beautiful, full length image, delicately carved and gilded; it is enclosed [the gallery] on three sides by a masonry wall, rising to a height of fifteen feet. On the upper part of this wall is a balcony [with a balustrade] of still finer materials than those of the presbytery and altar.

The length of these [balustrades] is such, that including the front railing (although this is much more elegant as will be described later) there are one thousand three hundred and thirty balusters, well separated, and of a thickness in proportion to the hand rail whose moulding has a width of one-sixth of a *vara.*

The above-mentioned railing that encloses the front of the choir [gallery] was inaugurated on the first day of May of the year one thousand seven hundred and thirty. It is one of the most noteworthy works of this cathedral, made of the exquisite metals, *tumbago* and *caláin* [equal parts of gold, silver and copper] fabricated in Macon, China, in Asia. It has a width of fifteen and a half *varas* and two inches and eleven and three fourths [*varas*] in height. It is fabricated in a composite style with fanciful figures, mouldings, reliefs, superimposed pieces, leaves and decorations, terminating in a marvelous image of the Assumption resting on a cloud and surrounded by cherubs within an oval on the upper part of which is a great image of the Crucified Christ. It has at its sides those [images] of the good and bad thieves, surrounded by other pyramidal shaped pieces having on their upper points two spheres with sixteen very fine bells. The cost of the whole is in keeping with its great magnificence. Considering the great distance from which it was brought, the excellence of the work, the quality of the metals [used], whose weight is fifty-three thousand pounds, and the fact that the Venerable Ecclesiastical Council advanced ten thousand *pesos* towards its fabrication, one may gain a fair idea of its great value.

Similar in elegance to the main altar is that of the Kings, which is located between the two doors on the north side. [This was] begun in the year one thousand seven hundred and eighteen and dedicated on the twenty-third day of September of [the year] one thousand seven hundred and thirty-seven. It is of great size, being thirty *varas* in height and fifteen in width, where many images of the Holy Kings are placed. Its chapel is in hexagonal form, covered by two domes on Attic columns enclosed by a railing like that of the altar. All of the other altars are like these two, many of them with their antependia of hammered silver. There is an image of the Immaculate Conception of the same metal [silver] which weighs one hundred and thirty-eight *marcos* without counting those on the other [altars]. . . .

The decorations are enhanced by forty great lamps and chandeliers of silver, used daily for services, without counting others used on special feast days, all of which are the height of a man. The principal one of these is the enormous chandelier that lights the main altar, noteworthy not only on account of its construction but for its size. It is ten *varas* and a half in circumference at the base and more than two *varas* in height. . . . And although it is true that when first used, on August fifteenth of the year one thousand seven hundred and thirty-three, it weighed only two thousand six hundred *marcos* of high grade silver, so many perfect pieces were later added that its weight has been increased and its cost now exceeds sixty-four thousand *pesos*. . . .

And since mention is made of the lamps for the service, no less worthy of mention are two magnificent lanterns inaugurated on the octave of Corpus, the fifteenth day of June, one thousand seven hundred and thirty. Added to others already installed, whose cost alone was one thousand five hundred *pesos*, one may imagine the total cost of what has been described. . . .

The Divine Sacrament, in a beautiful ciborium of gold, is taken from here on visits to the sick and those in prison, carried with great devotion in the hands of one of the curates, dressed with surplice, stole and cape, always seated alone on the rear seat of one of the carriages which have been provided for His Majesty for this purpose. This is surpassed only by the coach used on the most important feast days, and which was inaugurated on the sixteenth of June, [one thousand] seven hundred and twenty-nine, at a cost of two thousand five hundred *pesos*. It is drawn by six richly caparisoned mules (accompanying the curate and seated on the front seat are a priest bearing the consecrated stone and the Holy Oils and an altar boy with lighted lantern, both wearing surplices). It moves with a great escort of church dignitaries and other pious persons who, with lanterns, torches and candles light the way. Often, especially at night, they are joined by great numbers of musicians, who sing different hymns and play a variety of instruments, making the parade more praiseworthy. To all of which are added from each group of guards or place where there are troops that is passed, a corporal and four soldiers. These come out and with fixed bayonets escort His Majesty [the Host]. This by superior order of His Excellency, the Viceroy, issued to the sergeant-major of the Garrison. They reach such numbers that, at times, the coach is surrounded by fifty foot soldiers, noisy cavalrymen, sword in hand, who usually go clearing the way for the coaches. In addition, two altar boys dressed with robes usually go offering incense and two men always go at the head of the procession. One of these signals with a small bell, the other carries a table, covered and decorated, so that in case the dwelling of the sick person be of the most squalid class, the sacred ciborium may be exposed in a fitting manner, although such would be a very unusual case, for on account of the Catholic religiousness of the people, even the poorest, on such occasions, not only adorn the place where it is to be exposed but it is also wonderful to see how at night the neighbors place lighted candles at the windows on the streets through which the Lord passes . . .

JEWELS OF THE CATHEDRAL OF MEXICO

(Inventory made in 1807)

TABERNACLES AND CIBORIUMS

No.1. A tabernacle of gilded silver, beautifully worked, which served in olden times in the processions and is now placed on the main altar. Made in two sections it rests on a stand or base. It has four sides with a mask-relief on each: from its base rises the first section, with eight columns, two on each corner and eight prophets at the foot of them.

The second section follows, having likewise eight columns, two on each corner with the eight statues of the evangelists and doctors at their feet. On the upper part of this section there is, on each corner, an angel and back of it two pyramids.

The top is formed by eight pyramids distributed around the edge and, at their center, a pedestal made up of eight figures and on top of each a small pyramid supporting a statue of the archangel Saint Michael.

No.2. A tabernacle of silver in the center of which the above is placed, and which cost $29,628 *pesos*. It was made by [order of] the Most Illustrious and Most Excellent archbishop Dr. Juan Antonio Vizarrón, and to which were added (through the devotion of the Most Illustrious Dr. Manuel Rubio y Salinas and several other dignitaries of the church) the four doctors of the church and the pedestal or base with the Four Evangelists. This work was [ordered] done by Dr. Ignacio Ceballos, the Treasurer. The latter [figures] weighed 1,612 *marcos* and one ounce and cost $16,000 [*pesos*]

No.3. A tabernacle or repository of native silver, built on wood, with a statue of Faith at the top and on its door a picture of the Saviour, with its glass, and finished in white on its interior. The silver alone weighs 181 *marcos* and one ounce. This was made in the year [one thousand] seven hundred and seventy-seven by *Maestro* Montes de Oca, under the direction of the Treasurer, for use on Holy Thursday, at a cost of $2,175 [*pesos*] five and a half *reales*, the old one having been destroyed.

No.4. A small chest or repository made of silver with mouldings, gilded both outside and inside, with the coat of arms of the Most Excellent and Most Illustrious Juan de Ortega (y Montañes). Its weight is 43 *marcos* and 4 ounces.

No.5. A medium sized case of gilded silver, with an iron padlock, and a cross with two cherubs on the ends, both with two wings missing, which previously served as a repository.

NOTE: On the 12th January 1808 there was delivered to the silversmith Rodallega, as part of the cost of the gold cross with precious stones that he is making, the small chest or repository of silver with gilded mouldings bearing the coat of arms of the Most Illustrious Señor Ortega, [item] No.4, which item is omitted from this inventory.

KEYS

No.1. Three keys of gilded silver for the tabernacles.

No.2. One tabernacle key of gold and rose and flat diamonds, with a large chain of gold; and for making this key a pectoral and a small chain were delivered to Silversmith Rodallega.

No.3. Three tabernacle keys, gilded, which a benefactor donated for the tabernacle of the Main Altar, the altar used on Holy Thursday and that of the altar of the Kings.

No.4. Two tabernacle keys of white silver.

No.5. Two keys of Our Holy Father Saint Peter, of silver, with the key-eyes and guards gilded and weighing two *marcos* and three ounces.

NOTE: On the 12th January 1808 there were delivered to silversmith Rodallega as part of the cost of the gold cross with precious stones which he is making, the three keys of gilded silver [item] No.1 and the two of white silver [item] No.4, which are omitted from this inventory.

TABERNACLE SCREENS

No.1. One large tabernacle screen embroidered in gold with open-work, mounted on wood, with three bronze legs, which as it stands weighs 78 *marcos*.

No.2. One tabernacle screen made of native silver, purchased from [José] Borda, with gilded superimposed ornaments, with a weight of 2 *marcos* and 4½ ounces.

MONSTRANCES

No.1. The pyx of the large monstrance bought from José la Borda has on one side 4,107 diamonds of all sizes and on the other 1,757 emeralds. It weighs 895 *castellanos*. Its base, made for account of the church, has 3,219 stones in this manner: 1765 diamonds of all sizes, 896 emeralds, 544 rubies, 8 sapphires and 106 amethysts, weighing in all 3,506 *castellanos* and 2 *tomines*. And the angel [figures have] some strings of small pearls, according to a notation on the old inventory. One small emerald is missing from the pyx and two hyacinths from the bunches of grapes.

No.2. One monstrance of gold, donated by Dean Dr. Juan de Salcedo, with its base of gilded silver, with 47 superimposed pieces and weighs 13 *marcos*, 6 ounces and one *ochava*, and is little more than 2 *tercias* in height.

The cross has two rubies, 9 emeralds, 9 white amethysts on its base, 2 hyacinths, 1 topaz and 1 amethyst, 1 oriental topaz from Germany, 1 hexagonal emerald and 1 amethyst, 16 rubies on the upright section [*cañón*]; on one side 4 emeralds and on the other 4 amethysts, on the cross-piece 4 sapphires, 6 emeralds, 4 rubies, 4 topazes and on the upper vertical part 2 white sapphires and on the rays 17 emeralds, 8 topazes, 40 whole pearls, and weighs 287 *castellanos*, 2 *tomines*. This monstrance, which is used on ordinary occasions may be used on its own stand or on that of the major or great one, mentioned under the following item, which is adorned with 57 superimposed pieces of gold and no [precious] stones.

No.3. One monstrance of gilded silver with its pyx of gold, which has two stands, one larger than the other. The larger one has 57 superimposed pieces of gold without a single precious stone; the smaller, oval shaped one has 24 superimposed pieces of gold and on these 4 emeralds, no hyacinths and 4 fine white stones from Bohemia. On the 26 rays of the monstrance there are 16 cherubs of gold, and all three pieces weigh 23 *marcos* and 2 ounces.

No.4. Two cases for monstrances. One gilded with a weight of one *marco* five and one half ounces, and the other of silver, also gilded, weighing two *marcos* seven and a half ounces, both weighing four *marcos*, five ounces.

CIBORIUMS

No.1. One large ciborium of gold, bought from Borda, with 955 rose diamonds on the main piece, 693 of the same diamonds on the cover and 48 on the pall, making altogether 1696, and on the pall there are 9 pearls. It weighs 12 *marcos* of gold which represent 600 *castellanos*, in its case of crimson velvet. All this description according to examination made by silversmith Rodallega.

No.2. One small ciborium of gold, adorned with 60 small flat diamonds, 48 rubies and 62 emeralds. It has no pall.

It belonged to the college of Tepotzotlan and the Royal Assembly assigned it to this holy Church. It weighs 3 gold *marcos*, 5 ounces, 1 ochava and 4 *tomines*, representing 182 *castellanos*. This is according to the appraisal of the silversmith Rodallega.

No.3. One ciborium of gold filigree work, one *tercia* [one third of a *vara*] in height, excluding the cross, adorned with 268 small flat diamonds, 131 emeralds, 20 amethysts and 24 rubies on the main piece, 10 diamonds and 9 emeralds on the cross. It has no pall and weighs 8 gold *marcos*, which represent 400 *castellanos*.

It belonged to the *Colegio de San Pedro y San Pablo* and was assigned to this Holy Church by said Royal Superior Board of Assignations, and according to a description given when it was delivered, weighs 400 *castellanos*, as above stated, according to an examination and report of the silversmith Rodallega.

No.4. One ciborium of gilded silver, in the shape of a sea-shell, donated by the Most Illustrious Señor Rubio, weighing 5 *marcos* and one ounce, including the pall.

No.5. One small ciborium or vase, gilded, without top or pall, weighing seven and three-quarter ounces.

NOTE: On the 12th January 1808 there were delivered to silversmith Rodallega, as part of the cost of the cross with precious stones that he is making, the small ciborium of gold, with diamonds, rubies and emeralds which belonged to Tepotzotlan, [item] No.2 and the small gilded ciborium, without top or pall [item] No.5, which are omitted from this inventory.

CHALICES

No.1. One chalice of gold, with paten and small spoon, bought from Borda, with 1,616 rose diamonds, 216 of these flat, which altogether make up 1,832 and weighs six gold *marcos*, three ounces, five *ochavas* and one *tomin*, which represent 320 *castellanos*. It is in its case of crimson velvet. All as described by silversmith Rodallega.

NOTE: This chalice, monstrance [item] No.1 and ciborium [item] No.1, were bought for $34,500 *pesos* and the cost of the chalice was borne by Schoolmaster Dr. Cayetano de Torrez, that it may be used on the day of the Precious Blood of Christ.

No.2. One chalice of gold with paten and small spoon, with 77 small flat diamonds, 8 large rose diamonds, 82 rubies, and its gold weighs 4 *marcos* 7 ounces and 2 *tomines*, which represent 244 *castellanos*. It is placed in its chamois leather case and belonged to the *Casa Profesa* (now San José el Real) of the ex-Jesuit fathers, and was assigned to this Holy Church by the Royal Superior Board of Assignations. Its weight of gold and number of stones is according to examination and report rendered by silversmith Rodallega. It has some enamel work.

No.3. One large chalice of gold with paten, but without the small spoon, all enamelled, which is used for the altar Holy Thursday, with a weight of 526 *castellanos*, adorned with 122 flat diamonds, 143 emeralds and 132 rubies. Its cost was $3,438 [*pesos*] 7 *tomines* and 6 grains. It is dented at the base.

No.4. Another smaller chalice and paten of gold, all enamelled in green, white and red with no [precious] stones, and weighing 371 *castellanos* and 7 *tomines*. It has no small spoon. It is damaged at the base.

MARGINAL NOTE: On the 27th January 1815 it was delivered to shop-owner [silversmith] Alejandro Cañas [in exchange] for the chalice and cruets sent to His Holiness.

No.5. One chalice of gold adorned with 314 emeralds, with its paten, small spoon, platter, cruets and bell, the whole weighing 476 *castellanos*, donated to this Holy Church by the Most Illustrious archbishop Dr. Manuel José Rubio y Salinas, with the stipulations set forth in the proceedings of the [Ecclesiastical] council of 13th April 1756. It has on the outside several symbols of the Sacrament and the four Evangelists on the base, beautifully made and engraved. It was appraised by Francisco Peñaroja at $4,644 [pesos], *five reales*.

MARGINAL NOTE: The chalice corresponds to the inventory, but the cruets, the small platter and small bell were delivered to shop-owner Cañas for the chalice for His Holiness.

No.6. One chalice donated by Schoolmaster Dr. Francisco Navarijo, with paten and goblet of gold, weighing 59 *castellanos*, 4 *tomines*. The base, stem and lid of gilded silver with a weight of 2 *marcos*, 7 ounces and 1 *ochava*. It has an inscription on the base.

No.7. One chalice, all of gold with paten and small spoon, which weighs, according to the reckoning of the silversmith 215 *castellanos*, which at the rate of $4 [*pesos* per *castellano*] cost $860 *pesos*.

No.8. One chalice of gold with paten and small spoon of same, made in France. . . .

No.9. One chalice of gold, with paten and two small spoons, cruets, bell and small platter, all of gold, left to the church at the death of Sr. Haro. . . .

No.10. One chalice and paten of gilded silver with large goblet, octagonal base and relief-mouldings, with the four Evangelists with their emblems in the middle [of the chalice], made in Milan. . . .

No.11. One gilded chalice, engraved with the emblems of the Passion, and the paten with an engraving representing the Resurrection, with its platter and cruets to match, with the Apostleship engraved on them. This was left to the church at the death of the Most Illustrious Monsignor Rubio. It weighs 15 *marcos*, 6 ounces.

No.12. One chalice, gilded and engraved, with inlays of mother-of-pearl, with paten and bell. Also left to the church at the death of the aforesaid prelate.

No.13. One chalice with four cherubs, with paten and small spoon. There is doubt as to whether it came to the church at the death of Señor Rubio or was donated by Schoolmaster Dr. Francisco Navarijo.

No.14. One chalice and paten, both gilded, with twelve cherubs and bunches of grapes, which is now being used in the oratory of the Viceroy.

MARGINAL NOTE: The cherubs agree with the inventory, but instead of bunches of grapes there are some flowers and the lid is of filigree work.

No.15. Another gilded one, with its base carved in the form of a pineapple.

No.16. Six gilded and engraved ones, for the use of the higher classes, with patens and small spoons.

No.17. Twelve chalices with patens and small spoons, gilded, for the daily use of the Lords.

No.18. Another gilded [one] with carvings.

No.19. Twelve of plain white silver, with their patens, and the keys of Saint Peter engraved thereon, for the use of the chaplains.

No.20. One chalice of white silver for the dead.[4]

No.21. Another gilded, plain, with paten and small spoon, left to the Church at the death of Señor Haro.

No.22. Another of white silver, with paten and small spoon, platter, cruets and bell, left to the Church at the death of Señor Haro, and which he used in his portable oratory.

CRUETS, PLATTERS AND ALTAR BELLS

No.1. Two cruets, platter and altar bell, all of gold, left to the Church at the death of Señor Rubio, companion pieces of the chalice with the emeralds.

MARGINAL NOTE: These were delivered to shop-owner Cañas for the chalice for His Holiness.

No.2. Two cruets, platter and altar bell, all of gold, left to the Church on the death of Señor Haro.

No.3. Two cruets, platter and altar bell, all guilded, apparently matching the chalice of the Passion.

No.4. Six platters of native silver . . . for the use of the priests, with cruets of crystal and covers of native silver.

4 A chalice that, on the death of priests connected with the Cathedral, was placed in their hands until burial.

MARGINAL NOTE: One missing, which was stolen from Señor Mier, when saying mass, on 13th May 1811.

No.5. Seventeen platters of white silver for the chaplains, with crystal cruets. . . .

NOTE: On the 12th January 1808 there were delivered to silversmith Rodallega, as part of the cost of the gold cross with stones which he is making, the gilded platter No.8 and the loose, gilded altar bell No.11, which are deducted from this inventory.

INCENSORIES, CENSERS AND SPOONS

No.1. Two incensories of gold with their censers and spoons, in a very curiously made case, donated to this Holy Church by the Most Excellent Dr. and Master Juan Ignacio de la Rocha, Bishop of Michoacán, while he was Dean of [this Church], with a weight of 790 *castellanos*, 5 *tomines*, and cost, including the fire-pans and case, $2,731 *pesos 6 reales*.

No.2. Two incensories with their censers, chains and spoons, without hall-marks, gilded, with a weight of eleven *marcos*, three and one half ounces.

No.3. Two incensories of white silver, hall-marked, with chains and hooks, their main part being plain and their tops of open work, with one censer and one spoon.

No.4. Two incensories made while Señor Bruno was treasurer, in the year 1803, with their spoons and censers, all of white silver, and weighing eleven *marcos*, six ounces, four *ochavas* at $12 *pesos* which amounted to $141 *pesos 6 reales*.

No.5. Two large censers, with their spoons, for the perfumers, made by silversmith Rodallega in the year 1807, with a weight of six *marcos*, five ounces, six *ochavas* at $11 *pesos* per *marco* and which amounted to $73 *pesos*, 7 *reales*, Señor Gamboa being treasurer.

PACES

No.1. Two paces of silver gilt, hall-marked, bought from Borda, weighing 17 *marcos* and one half ounce.

No.2. One gilded pax, used for the viceroys, weighing five *marcos*, five and one half ounces. . . .

CROSSES

No.3. Another large [cross] of plain silver, with base of same, with gilded lines and mouldings, the crucifix being almost one *vara* [in height] made of copper gilt, crown and nails of silver gilt, all made while Señor Gamboa was Treasurer, by silversmith Rodallega, in the year 1807, with the following weight:

The cross, including the I.N.R.I., weighs 75 *marcos*, which at $16 [*pesos* per *marco*] amounted to $1,200 *pesos*. The base 111 *marcos* and 2 ounces, which at $18 [*pesos* per *marco*] amounted to $2,002 *pesos*, 4 *reales*. The crucifix with wooden model, lead mold, copper gilt, cost of hollow casting and its superfine gilt, and double gilt for longer duration, with crown and nails of silver gilt, weight 56 *marcos* and cost $1,400 *pesos*, and adding these three items the total amounts to $4,602 *pesos*, 4 *reales* which is what was paid to silversmith Rodallega.

No.7. One cross with crucifix and base of gold and precious stones which Treasurer Gamboa had made, and whose value, according to the account of silversmith Rodallega, who fabricated it in the year 1808, is as follows:

	Pesos	
In the center of the cross a large ruby, with circle of diamonds, worth	$ 500	
At the end of each arm a topaz with circle of diamonds, both worth	600	
Ten emeralds with circle of rose diamonds, in this manner: 4 in each arm and 2 in the center of the cross, which make a total of 10 emeralds, and are worth	520	
On the upright of the cross, from the feet of the crucifix down to the base there are 6 topazes bordered with diamonds and two small topazes which are worth	1,150	
The I.N.R.I. bordered with rose diamonds and the letters with rubies are worth	600	
On the four nails, four rubies	16	
On the main front of the base and on its back, four roses formed by 32 diamonds which weigh two carats, which at $100 per carat, are	200	
On the four sides of said base are distributed 385 rose diamonds totalling 40 carats, which at $40 are	1,600	
On said four sides 43 flat diamonds with a weight of 4 carats which at $16 are	64	
On said four sides 189 rubies with a weight of 50 carats, which at $3 are	150	
On said four sides 11 small emeralds with weight of 36 carats, which at $5 are	180	
At the center of the main front and the two sides 3 large amethysts which are worth	200	
In the center of the rear part of the base one large emerald, perforated, with two small diamonds, which is worth	40	
On the rim on top of the base 51 topazes with a weight of 64 carats, which at $4, 4 *reales* are	288	
On the lower rim of the base, on its main front, it has 14 medium sized amethysts, which are worth	140	
On said rim, on the other three sides, there are distributed 73 bullet-like stones, the color of amethysts which at the rate of five *reales* each, are	45	5 *reales*

The crucifix, cross and base have, of gold, 20 *marcos*, 7 ounces,
    or 1,043 *castellanos*, 6 *tomines*, which at the rate of $4 are   4,175

The under part of the base and a case are of silver gilt, and the
    bridges that hold the stones through the inside of the cross
    are of white silver, their total weight being 2 *marcos*, 6
    ounces, 2 *ochavas*, which make   26   6 *reales*

Value of the cross $10,495   3 *reales*

Hereto is added the case of fine wood, with lock and hinges,
    lined in crimson velvet where it [the cross] is placed, which
    cost   52

Total cost $10,547   3 *reales*

NUMBER OF STONES IN THE CROSS AND BASE

Diamonds in the cross: 287; in the base 32, which make	319
Rose diamonds in the cross 194; in the base 385, which are	579
Flat diamonds on the base alone	43
Topazes in the cross, 29; in the base 51; which are	80
Amethysts in the base alone	17
Emeralds on the cross 10; in the base 112; which are	122
Rubies in the cross and Crucifix 26; in the base 189, which are	215
Purple bullet-like stones on the base	73
Total stones	1,448

LARGE AND SMALL CANDLESTICKS

No.1. Four candlesticks of gold, of little more than one *tercia* [one third *vara*] in height, donated by the most Illustrious and most Excellent Archbishop Dr. Juan Antonio de Vizarrón, with a weight of 943 *castellanos* 6 *tomines*.

No.2. Six candlesticks of gold, three-fourths [of a *vara*] in height, donated by the Most Excellent and Most Illustrious Dr. Ildefonso Nuñez de Haro, with a cross, crucifix and its base also of gold, of the same height as the candlesticks, the whole weighing 92 *marcos* 4 ounces 4 *ochavas*, which should be used, as willed by the donor, on Holy Thursday, on the feast and entire octave of Corpus, Assumption Day, Guadalupe Day, Saint Joseph's, Saint Peter's and Saint Ildephonso's.

No.3. Six large altar candlesticks, mixed metal, hall-marked, bought from Borda, weighing 712 *marcos* 4 and one half ounces.

No.4. Six medium sized candlesticks engraved, hall-marked, left to the church at the death of the Most Illustrious Sr. Rubio.

No.5. Fourteen medium sized candlesticks from Tepotzotlan, with a [figure of] Jesus on the base and equal to the torch-holders, with a weight of 444 *marcos* 2 ounces.

No.6. Six large plain candlesticks of silver, hall-marked, of more than one *vara* [in height] with a weight of 264 *marcos*.

No.7. Six large candlesticks of silver not hall-marked, of one *vara* in height with [figures of] angels on the base and a weight of 196 *marcos*.

No.8. Twenty-four of the aforesaid, plain, hall-marked, with [a weight of] 263 *marcos* and 6 ounces [for the use] at mass of renovation.

No.9. Sixteen plain candlesticks, which are called *chatos* [short], of which there are 14 in the church and two at the house of the Viceroy, weighing, in all, 161 *marcos*.

No.10. Twenty-two candlesticks, hall-marked, which are used daily for mass with [a weight of] 88 *marcos*.

No.11. Two small candlesticks with their stands which weigh 7 *marcos*, 2 ounces.

No.12. Two large, round, candlesticks, engraved, which are called *chapines* [slippers] a half *vara* in [height] with [a weight of] 49 *marcos*, 4 ounces, for the choir.

No.15. Twenty-four large candlesticks of mixed metal, made by silversmith Rodallega in the year 1805.

No.16. Sixteen large candlesticks, somewhat smaller, made by Rodallega in the aforesaid year.

No.17. Twenty somewhat smaller, made in said year by Rodallega, so that those in this item added to those of the two previous ones make 60 large candlesticks.

No.18. Four small candlesticks, one *tercia* [third of a *vara* in height] with their cross, all of silver, from the portable oratory of Señor Haro.

NOTE: The 60 large candlesticks mentioned under items 15, 16 and 17 weigh 1,773 *marcos* two *ochavas*, which at $15 *pesos* amounted to $26,595 *pesos* 3 *reales* and ¾ *real* which were paid to silversmith Rodallega, part in money and part in old large candlesticks and torch-holders and other objects, in the year 1804 and 1805, Juan Bruno being treasurer.

ALTAR ORNAMENTS

No.1. Four clusters of flowers, of gold, donated by the Dean of this Holy Church Dr. Leonardo José de Terraya, which weigh 30 *marcos*, one ounce, 4 *ochavas* of 22 carat gold, making 1,509 *castellanos*, which at the rate of 29 *reales* per *castellano* amount to $547 *pesos*, 1 *real*, with additional 2 *marcos*, 2 ounces of silver of the screws and fastenings.

No.3. Six vases of silver alloy with their clusters [of flowers] all [ordered] made by Treasurer Bruno, with [a weight of] 254 *marcos*, 2 ounces which at $16 *pesos* total $4,068 *pesos* paid in *reales* and [payment was completed by] other old objects [given to] Rodallega.

No.4. Twenty-four vases of white silver for flowers, [ordered made] by Treasurer Bruno, with [a weight of] 177 *marcos*, 2 ounces, which at $12 *pesos* amounted to $2,127 *pesos* paid partly in *reales* and partly in old objects to Rodallega in [1]804 and [1]805.

No.5. Four large silver alloy vases, with their bases also of silver alloy, for the presbytery, which were made when Señor Bruno was treasurer, weighing 1,042 *marcos* which at $16 *pesos* amounted to $16,672 *pesos* paid to Rodallega, partly in *reales* and partly with other old pieces. Later on, when Gamboa was treasurer, they were changed into perfumers, in 1807, leaving the shape the same but changing their upper ends, and for this innovation said silversmith was paid $1,689 *pesos*, 6 *reales*, for the manufacture and silver that was added to them, weighing 93 *marcos*, 7 ounces at $18 *pesos* per *marco*.

MISSAL STANDS AND PRAYER FRAMES

No.1. Two missal stands and one prayer frame of 22 carat gold, donated by Dean Dr. Leonardo Taraya, with weight of 24 *marcos*, 7 ounces 5 *ochavas* which are equivalent to 1,247 *castellanos* and 5 *tomines*, which at 29 *reales* a *castellano* amount to $4,522 *pesos*, 5 *reales*, besides the frame work of very fine brass, fire gilded, at a cost of $16 *pesos* per pound, which has 25 pounds of this brass and amounted to $400 *pesos*, both items totalling $4,922 *pesos*, 5 *reales*, as evidenced by the account of José María Rodallega.

No.2. Two missal stands and one large prayer frame of engraved silver, in filigree work, their fronts gilded and the backs of white silver, donated to this Holy Church by Schoolmaster D. Navarijo, with a weight of 99 *marcos*, 22 ounces.

No.3. Three prayer frames, all alike, for the consecration, Gospel and lavatory, bought from José de la Borda, with a weight of 39 *marcos*, 2 ounces. They had their two missal stands to match but these were donated by order of the Venerable Council to the church in Lerma, in the year 1807.

No.5. Eighteen missal stands, which Treasurer Bruno ordered made for account of the church; two of silver alloy with the tiaras embroidered on crimson velvet; eight white ones, with the tiaras embroidered the same as the first ones and the other eight of white silver with the tiara and keys of silver gilt at the center.

NOTE: Of the eighteen missal stands of the preceding item, eight weigh 239 *marcos* 7 ounces, which at $12 *pesos* amounted to $2,878 *pesos* 4 *reales*.

Two others with gilded adornments weigh 64 *marcos*, which at $14 *pesos* amounted to $896 *pesos*. The remaining plain missal stands with gilded crests, weigh 254 *marcos* one ounce, which at $12 *pesos* amounted to $3,049 *pesos* 4 *reales*, plus $134 *pesos* of the gilding and $15 *pesos* for the velvet, and all these items together, had a cost of $4,094 *pesos*, 4 *reales* plus 70 *pesos* for embroidering ten crests and that sum was paid to silversmith Rodallega, partly in *reales* and partly in old missal stands and other things which were given him.

ALTAR ANTEPENDIA

No.1. Three antependiums of silver alloy, hall-marked, bought from José de la Borda. The largest with two panels, or portable frontals; which weighed 535 *marcos*, one ounce; the second one with [a weight of] 312 *marcos* one ounce and the third 294 *marcos* and 5 ounces and all three making [a total of] 1141 *marcos* and 7 ounces, but it must be taken into account that in the year 1807, Gamboa being Treasurer, one *sesma* [sixth of a *vara*] was added on each side, to the first one; and to the other two, one *tercia* [third of a *vara*] was added to each side; these additions involved 158 *marcos*, as follows: 44 *marcos* 2 ounces, 2 *ochavas* of [silver] gilt which, at $16 pesos per *marco*, amounted to $709 *pesos*, and 130 *marcos*, 5 ounces, 4 *ochavas* of white silver which, at the rate of $14 *pesos* per *marco*, amounted to $1,591 *pesos*, 5 *reales*, which, together with the $709 *pesos* mentioned above, make up the total of $2,300 *pesos*, 5 *reales*, same which were paid to silversmith Rodallega.

No.2. One antependium, called *El Lagar* [wine press] with the two explorers Joshua and Caleph, which weighs 424 *marcos*.

No.3. Another which they called the crucifix, with a weight of 408 *marcos*.

No.4. One antependium called the Supper with [weight of] 474 *marcos*.

No.5. One antependium of the main altar, with a gilded tiara in the middle.

LAMPS

No.1. The large lamp which is hung at the front of the main altar, taking the account of its first fabrication as given by *maestros* [master silversmiths] Francisco de Estrada and Francisco de la Cruz, has [a weight of] 2,663 *marcos* and half an ounce of white silver and 1,710 *marcos* one ounce and 5 *ochavas* of gilded silver, all hall-marked; both items totalling 4,373 *marcos* 2 ounces and one *ochava*, and as set forth in the report on this matter, as stated in the old inventory are in the archives of this church, its value is $71,343 *pesos*, 2 *reales*, 6 grains.

No.3. Two lamps of plain silver, hall-marked, both alike, made by Archdeacon Luis Antonio de Torres for the chapel of the Crucifix, out of the two old [lamps] which were there, with weight of 21 *marcos*, five and one-half ounces.

No.4. Three lamps, all alike, of silver, hall-marked, in the Chapel of Our Father Saint Peter, which were made over from the three old ones by Archdeacon Dr. Ignacio Ceballos, with a weight of 456 *marcos* and 7 ounces.

No.5. One lamp of silver, plain, donated by Rev. Dr. Joaquín Zorrilla, with a weight of 70 *marcos*.

CHANDELIERS

No.1. Two chandeliers of silver alloy bought from Borda, which are placed at the sides of the large lamp, and have a weight of 1,010 *marcos*, 2½ ounces.

No.2. Two chandeliers, both alike, which are located in front of the altars of the Holy Kings and that of Our Lady of Pardon, of plain silver, hall-marked, with a weight of 1,564 *marcos*.

No.3. Six chandeliers, all the same, distributed among both lateral naves of this Holy Church, each with 24 arms and of two *varas* in height, of plain silver, hall-marked, and all with [a total] weight of 1,784 *marcos* four and one-half ounces.

No.7. One chandelier of silver, hall-marked, which is found in the chaper of the crucifix for which it was donated by Archdeacon Luis Antonio de Torres, with a weight of 128 *marcos*, one and one-fourth ounces.

PECTORALS AND RINGS

No.1. One pectoral with 62 emeralds of all sizes and its 'wedding ring'[5] with one emerald of full color, a large one, with a thin gold chain; all with a weight of 39 *castellanos*, two *tomines*, which is of our Father Saint Peter.

No.2. One pectoral bordered on one side by 120 rose diamonds, large and small, and on the other by 100 rubies and in the center, in a crystal cross, a [piece of the] True Cross with its document of authenticity, which was in a box of silver gilt and weighs 7 ounces.

No.3. One pectoral with 20 amethysts and with two wedding rings of the same [stones].

MISCELLANEOUS OBJECTS

No.21. One girandole of ebony with inlays of silver and fifteen drip-pans of the same [silver] one larger than the others, all of which weigh 167 *marcos*, 7 ounces.

No.24. One paschal candlestick of polished wood with inlays and superimposed pieces and mouldings of silver alloy, and caryatids of the same metal which serve as its support and some figures of children, also of silver, on the pedestal. It contains 818 *marcos*, 7 ounces, 2 *ochavas* of silver, besides 258 *castellanos* of gold, and the total cost of the metal, wood, accessories, woodwork, silversmith's work and including the five flowers for the paschal taper, was $15,424 [*pesos*] which was paid to silversmith Rodallega, the Most Illustrious Señor Omaña being treasurer.

No.25. One fountain of silver, which is in the sacristy of this Holy Church, which is made up of the following sections: The first is a large vessel, of more than one *vara* in diameter, plain, with engraved rim, its base is square and engraved, of three fourths [of a *vara*] in height, with four handles and four large flowers in relief on its copper base. It weighed 347 *marcos*.

The second is another medium sized vessel, which forms the second section, with four caryatids and in the center four faces, from which four serpent heads protrude where the spigots for the pipes to the wash-stand are located, and at the top there are four sea-shells with four handles, all engraved, of silver, not hall-marked. It weighs 145 *marcos*.

The third an eagle with a crown, on a column or pedestal, on whose breast is the coat of arms of the Church, gilded. This forms the third section and weighs 77 *marcos* and 6 ounces. All three sections totalled 569 *marcos* and 6 ounces.

MARGINAL NOTE: This was broken up, except the vessel and the pedestal, and a new one [fountain] was made by order of the Venerable Council. This con-

5 The pastoral ring, often called the 'wedding ring' because it symbolizes the mystic wedding of the Bishop and the Church.

sists of a bowl with its pedestal with four holders for four cups; the small vessel with a rod that supports a cushion with the tiara and the keys and weighs 219 *marcos*, 7 ounces, not including the old large vessel or the pedestal.

GOLD IMAGES

No.1. One image of Our Lady of the Assumption, of enamelled gold, with the following adornment: It has 24 emeralds on the body, a jewel of gold, set alone on the breast, with a hexagonal emerald of one inch in size; an enamelled half moon at the feet, separated by a large one, 20 garnets, 27 white stones, 5 deep diamonds, two narrow belts one of emerald and the other of topazes, 10 false red stones, a gold crown with a topaz, two flat diamonds, three rubies, three emeralds and 17 false stones. [It has] four figures of angels of gold on a pedestal of enamelled gold with eight stones of rock crystal and the wings of gold.

MARGINAL NOTE: In accord. However there are missing on the Virgin two amethysts of such low price that they are probably worth one *real*; the crown is of gilded brass, the Holy Ghost is of silver gilt, the *imperiales* also; the superimposed pieces are of enamelled gold; the knobs of the base are of brass, of which two are missing.

No.2. Four statues of silver, hall-marked, representing Saint Louis, King of France, Saint Aloysius, Saint Rosalie, and Saint Rose of Lima, with their authentic relics, donated by Archdeacon Dr. Luis de Torres and Schoolmaster Dr. Cayetano de Torres, which [statues] are placed in the four niches of the two altars to the sides of the chapel of the Holy Kings, which cost was defrayed by said gentlemen. [The statues] have a weight of 160 *marcos* 2 and one half ounces.

ACCOUNT OF THE SILVER *MARCOS* OF SOME OF THE JEWELS OF THIS HOLY METROPOLITAN CHURCH AS TAKEN FROM THE INVENTORY

Twelve platters with their holders with covers of silver	0031 ms.[5a] 03 ozs. 4/8
Two incensories with their censer	0011 ms. 03.1/2 ozs.
Two ditto ditto	0011 ms. 06 ozs. 4/8
Two large censers	0006 ms. 05 ozs. 6/8
Two Porta-Paces	0005 ms. 02 ozs. 1/8
Fourteen medium sized candlesticks from Tepotzotlan	0444 ms. 02 ozs.
Six plain, large candlesticks	0264 ms. 00 ozs.
Six large candlesticks with figures of angels	0196 ms. 00 ozs.
Twenty-four medium sized candlesticks, plain	0263 ms. 06 ozs.
Sixteen candlesticks called *chatos* [short]	0161 ms. 00 ozs.
Twenty-two candlesticks	0088 ms. 00 ozs.
Two small candlesticks with their stands	0007 ms. 02 ozs.

5a *Marcos.*

Two *chapines* [slippers]	0049 ms. 04 ozs.
Twenty-four large candlesticks	
Sixteen smaller ones	1773 ms. 00 ozs. 2/8
Twenty smaller ones	
Six large clusters of flowers	0254 ms. 02 ozs.
Twenty-four bowls or flower vases	0177 ms. 02 ozs.
Four vases with their pedestals	1042 ms. 00 ozs.
Two missal stands and one prayer frame	0099 ms. 02 ozs.
Three missal stands	0039 ms. 02 ozs.
Two missal stands and one prayer frame	0015 ms. 00 ozs.
Eighteen missal stands	0558 ms. 00 ozs.
One small antependium	0003 ms. 12 ozs.
One silver cross for processions	0027 ms. 07 ozs. 4/8
Two tall candlesticks	0052 ms. 01.1/2 ozs.
Three pedestals	0747 ms. 00 ozs.
One pedestal for his Most Illustrious[6]	0071 ms. 04 ozs.
Two ditto from Tepotzotlan	
Four torch holders from Tepotzotlan	0851 ms. 03 ozs.
Four ditto which are called *burritos* [saw-horses]	0768 ms. 00 ozs.
One pitcher	0006 ms. 04 ozs.
Two said [pitchers]	0012 ms. 03 ozs.
One ditto for daily use	0005 ms. 07 ozs.
One ditto from Señor Haro[7]	
Another ditto which was donated by D. Ventura[8]	
Thirty-one fountains	
Two wash-bowls	
One Host box of filigree work	0003 ms. 00 ozs.
Another ditto	0002 ms. 00 ozs.
Another ditto plain	
Another from Señor Haro	
One font [for Holy Water]	0006 ms. 04.1/2 ozs.
Another ditto from Señor Haro	
One small candlestick, snuffers and two pointers	0003 ms. 02 ozs.
One ditto	
Another ditto with snuffers	
Two pointers[9]	0001 ms. 04 ozs.

6 That is, the pedestal where the archbishopal cross is placed.

7 The Most Excellent and Most Illustrious Alonso Nuñez de Haro y Peralta, who was Archbishop of Mexico from 1771 to 1800.

8 Probably Father Buenaventura López, who in 1807 was chief Sacristan of the cathedral, as proven by some inventories taken at that time.

9 The pointer is a short stick, about ten inches long, usually having on one end a small hand with the index finger extended; it is used by the masters of ceremonies in the cathedrals to point out the prayers in the missal and the priests at the altar whose turn it is to perform a certain ceremony.

One ditto	0001 ms. 03 ozs.
The large lamp	4373 ms. 02 ozs.
The lamp of the Wise Men	
Two lamps from the Chapel of the Crucifix	0021 ms. 05.1/2 ozs.
Three lamps from the Chapel of Saint Peter	0456 ms. 07 ozs.
One lamp from the Chapel of Saint Ann	0070 ms. 00 ozs.
One ditto in the Chapel of Our Lady of Sorrows	0145 ms. 00 ozs.
One lamp from the Chapel of Saint Michael	
Another lamp from the Chapel of Saints Cosme and Damian	0064 ms. 06 ozs.
Another lamp from the Chapel of Saint Joseph	
Three ditto from the Chapel of Our Lady of Solitude	
One lamp in the Chapel of Saint Philip of Jesus	
Another ditto from the altar of Our Lord of Good Dispatch	
Another ditto from Saint Joseph	0025 ms. 00 ozs.
Two chandeliers, alike, from the [altars of] the Wise Men and Pardon	1564 ms. 00 ozs.
Six chandeliers from the naves	1784 ms. 04 ozs.
One chandelier in front of the choir	
Another from inside the choir	
Six small chandeliers	
One in the Chapel of the Crucifix	0128 ms. 01 ozs. 2/8
One large wash-bowl	
Another ditto from Señor Rubio[10]	0051 ms. 06 ozs.
One bowl to wash purificators	0014 ms. 06 ozs.
One throne with steps	0161 ms. 06 ozs.
Another throne from the 'Ecce Homo' in the Sacristy	0125 ms. 00 ozs.
Six urns	
Two ditto from Señor Haro	
Three ditto from Señor Rubio	
Two bowls for holy oil with their plate with border in the center	
One small chest with bowls for holy oils from Señor Lizana[11]	
One *crucero* [holder for carrying the cross] from Señor Rubio	
One staff from Señor Haro	
One ditto from Señor Lizana	
One large missal stand that is in the choir	0297 ms. 02 ozs. 2/8
Another ditto	0031 ms. 01 ozs.
Three scepters[12]	0024 ms. 06 ozs. 4/8

10 The Most Excellent and Most Illustrious Señor Manuel Rubio y Salinas, who was Archbishop of Mexico from 1749 to 1765.

11 The Most Excellent and Most Illustrious Señor Francisco Javier de Lizana y Beaumont, who was Archbishop of Mexico from 1802 to 1811.

12 Scepters are a kind of baton or short staff somewhat less than the height of a man, used by the prelates in the cathedrals on certain major festivals for vespers and masses where they serve in the choir, wearing capes.

Six scepters	0074 ms. 00 ozs. 4/8
Six scepters	0076 ms. 06 ozs.
The lantern	0203 ms. 06 ozs.
Two ditto with silver bases	0113 ms. 02 ozs.
One base of [the statue of] Saint Joseph	0009 ms. 02 ozs. 7/8
Eight poles from the pallium	0146 ms. 00 ozs.
Twenty-eight drip pans	0017 ms. 00 ozs.
Six ditto from Our Lord[13]	
One silver glass from the Sacristy	0001 ms. 03 ozs. 4/8
Two large goblets	0009 ms. 07 ozs. 4/8
One tray with six goblets	
One shell with its plate	0009 ms. 07 ozs. 4/8
One ash-tray and four plates	0009 ms. 05 ozs.
One extra plate [which was melted]	
One small plate, cross and glass to bless the water	0005 ms. 00 ozs.
A pair of candelabra from Saint Joseph	
The branching candlestick[14] with its fifteen drip-pans	0167 ms. 07 ozs.
The fire-pan used on Holy Saturday[15]	0008 ms. 06 ozs.
The staff of the [three] Marys[16]	0012 ms. 04 ozs.
The stand for the taper[17]	0818 ms. 07 ozs. 2/8
The wash-stand from the Sacristy	0569 ms. 06 ozs.
One holder for flowers of the taper[18]	0010 ms. 00 ozs.
SUM TOTAL	19666 ms. 07 ozs. 6/8

NOTE: The candelabra of Saint Joseph and those of the *Ecce Homo* in the Sacristy, which have no weight [registered] were omitted.

2. *Festivals*

The first festival of importance recorded in the Proceedings of the Municipal Council of the eighteenth century, was that commemorating the 'happy and desired birth of our Prince and Lord don Luis Fer-

13 That is, the Blessed Sacrament.
14 *Tenebrarium* is a candlestick in the shape of an isosceles triangle, that has seven candles on each side and one on the top angle, and is used in the cathedrals for matins on Wednesday, Thursday and Saturday of Holy Week, which are called matin services.
15 The fire-pan which is used in the services of Easter Saturday to light and bless the new fire.
16 The staff on which during Holy Saturday services the tripartite candle is placed. That is, three candles twisted to form a single one at the base but separated at the upper ends. They are a symbol of the mystery of the Blessed Trinity, but are usually called the Three Marys, referring to the Holy Virgin, Mary Magdalen and Saint Mary of Cleophs, whom the Gospel mentions as having been on Mount Calvary at the foot of the Cross.
17 That is the pedestal where the paschal candle or taper is placed.
18 When the paschal candle is blessed on Holy Saturday five grains of incense are placed on it in the form of a cross, but since the taper mentioned herein was of extraordinary size, the grains of incense had to be in proportion to make them visible, and hence they are called the flowers of the taper.

nando . . . Prince of the Asturias.' The Council[19] was advised of the event on the 4th February 1708, by the Viceroy, Duke of Alburquerque, who at the same time ordered the festival which the occasion demanded:

The glorious event of the happy birth of the Prince of Asturias with which heaven has rewarded the justice and heroic virtues of our loved monarch and lord Philip V and perpetuated the hope of such loyal vassals as the Spaniards, demands demonstrations of joy and celebration to complement the hearts full of love and fidelity of the inhabitants of these distant lands. So that this joy may not be deferred I have decided that Monday the sixth of the present month, the festivals in question shall begin with a solemn novena of thanksgiving to the miraculous image of Mary Most Holy [Virgin] of the Remedies in this cathedral; that every night of these nine days there shall be general illumination, fireworks and theatricals in this royal palace and that the bull-fights and other amusements and public demonstrations shall continue during the remaining days up to Ash Wednesday. Other days [of rejoicing] are to be set aside after Easter Sunday, all of which I inform this very noble and loyal city for its attendance at everything, carrying out the ceremonies which on similar happy occasions have been observed. Signed with the rubric of His Excellency. Mexico, 4th February 1708. And below it says: to this very noble and loyal city. . . .

The Council convened that same day and recorded in the proceedings, the following:

That in [acknowledgment] with much rejoicing and the esteem due Your Excellency the [motion] was approved that in compliance therewith and in obligation thereto during the nine days this very noble city shall attend the novena·made to Our Lady. Everyone [shall appear] fully apparelled and wearing jewels, and every night at the royal palace shall be present at the fireworks and theatricals to which Your Excellency invites them. On the Monday assigned, the formal good wishes shall be given my Lady the Duchess, fully complying with all due outward formalities.

And in order that the expenses during the nine days of the novena for tapers and decoration of the altar, and his excellency the Archbishop's royal attendance at the Holy Church and other tribunals, may be borne equally, this very noble city shall defray the latter, closing [the festival] with a procession in the church carrying the Most Holy Virgin's image of Our Lady of the Remedies. The total expense of tapers, fireworks and other [costs] necessary shall be for their account [Municipal Council] and Pedro Jimenez is hereby commissioned to attend to this and with his

19 Proceedings of the Council of 4th February 1708.

order or warrant the city steward shall give and pay everything demanded of him.

Having held conferences . . . the following is resolved:

That the entire nine nights there be lights and illumination on the council build-ings and on the last night closing the festival the best fireworks that can be made be set off, the Mayor [*Corregidor*] being in charge. . . .

It is likewise approved that robes or loose gowns of the best quality be made for the *porteros almotacenes* at the command of Pedro Jimenez who shall have suits made for their use, of whatever he deems best, and hereby he is formally commis-sioned [to do so].

Likewise it is approved that a canopy be ordered for the council hall and that it be purchased with city funds at the will of the Mayor [*Corregidor*], and that His Lordship shall direct everything else which concerns the grandeur of these festi-vals, their expenses and all else relating to the functions, as one who considers them among the most important. All the expenses are for account of the city and said steward shall make them up and the bill shall be included with his own.

The Mayor said that for the festival, provided for according to the plan and made known to the guilds, the chief scrivener of the municipal council, who is present, is requesting the greatest assistance from them [the guilds] because only those considered financially able to take part are to participate and only by grouping three or four guilds together, so that many of the poorest ones will not be included. The idea of the division of the groups is as follows:

First, a car representing a ship made by the *pulque* [a drink prepared from the *agave* plant] vendors dressed in their sailor suits, and in the car an image of Neptune signifies the one who brought the news of the successful delivery of the Queen Our Lady.

Another car follows representing the arms of the city of Goajaca [Oaxaca] and Suchimilco [Xochimilco]. The moon is assigned to the group of bacon-vendors and youths dressed in white and saffron color shall ride therein and everything else pertaining thereto.

Another car follows with the arms of the city of Valladolid, its planet Jupiter. This [car] was alloted to the tanners, foremen and founders, and sellers of clothing.

The car of the city of Mérida, Yucatán, follows with its image of Saturn. This is assigned to the candlemakers, confectioners and dyers.

Another car made of the arms of the city of Guadalajara with its image of Mercury. This corresponds to the architects, wagon-makers, carvers, painters and gilders and the groups are advised to dress according to the images.

This is followed by [the car] of the city of Veracruz with its image of Mars. This is given to the silk-mercers, cap-makers, silk twisters and lace-makers. They are all dressed as Spanish soldiers.

The city of Puebla has Venus for its image and this fell to the bakers.

The car of this imperial city of Mexico follows, which is assigned to the silversmiths, who dress as politicians with all their corresponding followers, and in the car the Prince our Lord. Everything depicts this city as head of the others and their mother, with everyone and the whole kingdom paying homage to our beloved Prince, as all will be explained in the paper drawn up concerning this and because therein appear all the *veedores* [inspectors] of said guilds and all have been shown drawings of the design of the cars and costumes which are to be worn and are being made and provided for; and the occupations and worries of the Mayor [*Corregidor*] do not permit him to visit or assist them in whatever is required, as he is working most of the time and this very noble city is the master of the function, names commissioners to assist said guilds.

And having been heard by said gentlemen it was approved that commissioners be named as requested by the Mayor and the following are appointed.

With Señor Cuevas the silk-mercers, cap-makers, twisters of silk and lace-makers who all together form a group.

With the aforesaid [Señor Cuevas] the candlemakers, confectioners and dyers.
The bacon dealers,
The pulque vendors,
The tanners, overseers, foundrymen and dry goods dealers.

With Señor Jimenez the bakers,
The architects, carriage makers, the wood-carvers, painters and gilders.
The Mayor [*Corregidor*] is given charge of the workers of the silversmiths' art and in the manner mentioned, they are appointed to assist, in every way possible, the guilds and overseers and to carry out any orders that may be given for which they are commissioned in due form.

And all that was agreed upon and decided in this [municipal] council was approved by the Mayor and they signed it. . . .

PROCESSION FOR SWEARING ALLEGIANCE TO THE PATRONAGE OF THE VIRGIN OF GUADALUPE

On the 16th of May the *Corregidor* [Mayor] published[20] a proclamation that the solemn taking of the oath would occur on the 26th day and ordering that [during] the three previous [days] all citizens adorn [the front of] their houses during the day and illuminate them at night, threatening to impose fines upon those who did not follow his orders. This was an unnecessary threat, because in reality the true devotion there was and always has been towards the Virgin of Guadalupe spread throughout all classes of society, and during those unfortunate times, although a few dissenters were not lacking, it may be said with some exaggeration that everyone favored the proclamation of homage to this protectress the Blessed Virgin Mary, although without this [proclamation] the festivals would have been equally splendid.

There was not a balcony, window or door that was not richly adorned, luxuri-

20 Marroqui, op.cit., vol.I, p.154.

ously, or with simple taste, according to the possibilities of its owners. It was wonderful to see the multitude of altars, superb or humble, which were erected in balconies and windows, with the image of the new patron, adorned with garlands, ribbons, flowers, curtains, and whatever hangings imagination and good taste could suggest. The illumination during the three nights was general and splendid; there was no house or church that lacked lights; the cathedral surpassed all buildings, its tower being covered with lights and its domes with torch holders, shining as though it were molten gold.

Through printed invitations, dated the 22nd of the same month of May, the *Comisarios* of the city, Felipe Cayetano de Medina and Francisco Espinosa y Aguirre, requested the corporations and many distinguished private individuals to contribute with their presence to form the procession which should start from the Metropolitan Church at half past three in the afternoon on Saturday the 25th of this month.

The procession did not travel a long distance. It left from the gate on the eastern side of the church, moving to the front on *Empedradillo* Street, going from there towards the south as far as the corner of the *Diputación* [House of Deputies], turning in front of it as far as the Palace and going towards the north, proceeded as far as the western door of the church, through which it entered. But in such a short distance, how much richness was congregated: Five altars were distributed in it [the procession]. One was erected by the guild of the wax candle-makers at the place where the procession turned on *Empedradillo* Street in addition to the one that each had at the door of his shop. Thus the whole sidewalk looked like one long solid altar, with one step running along its front. The second was put up by the guild of the silversmiths, in the corner of their street and the Arcade. Towards the center of this arcade, the merchants and market-vendors set up theirs. The city, in the arcade of its buildings, set up the fourth, near the entrance of the *Alhóndiga* [public market]. The fifth was set up by several people on the lower floor of the Royal Palace, near the corner of the *Volador* in the portal where judicial auctions are held.

It is no easy task for us to render a detailed description of each of these altars; reading them [descriptions] we have been persuaded that they were all large, beautiful, rich, profusely illuminated, and with slight variations the one of the silversmiths was, without doubt, the richest of all, because on its steps and tables there was an abundance of silver objects for ornament, and also because they took out from their chapel in the cathedral, the two images of their patron saints, which they had of said metal. The one of the Immaculate Conception occupied the center and Saint Eligio and Saint Felipe de Jesus were at the sides. Although in all the altars there were many lights, in this respect, and with reason, all were surpassed by the candle-makers who went further, setting up a sort of wooden fence the length of the space assigned to them in the *Empedradillo*, and on top of same, here and there, placed thick tapers which were lighted the whole afternoon.

Participating in the procession, were the brotherhoods, fraternities and confederations with their standards and pennants, the guilds, a scattering of natives and the religious orders with their crosses and candle staffs, presided over by the Ecclesiastical Council. There followed an image of the Virgin of Guadalupe, full size, on silver *andas* [stretcher-like frame, carried on the shoulders of men] [the image] resting on a base resembling a hill, adorned with moss, plants and flowers. Starting upward from the rocks of the hill and all around the image, there was an arc, like a rainbow, with innumerable fine pearls simulating dew drops. The mantle of the Virgin was adorned with a thousand precious stones and from the bracelet hung a large pearl, of more than three carats.[21]

Following the image there were the *Audiencia* [ministers], all the *Tribunales* [judges], public officials and the *Consulado* [consul] with the Archbishop Viceroy presiding; then followed the nobility of the City, and private individuals who had been invited. Presiding over all was the *Ayuntamiento* [Municipal Councilmen] as lords of the festival. Heading the procession were Indians, dancing in the manner in which they were accustomed to dance when they were heathens.

It was the custom in Mexico to set arches of flowers and bright cloth across the streets through which the procession passed and often they hung banners with their ends tied, or other decorations they called *mundos* [globes] filled with flowers, or thin bits of paper of varied colors. By pulling a rope; these [*mundos*] opened, letting a shower of objects fall over the image, object of the celebration. On this occasion the *mundos* were not lacking, and they were somewhat unusual. Some of them, of the ordinary shape, contained pigeons and other birds, while others resembled the figure of an Indian holding his *tilma*[22] in his hands. When this was spread open, flowers would fall, disclosing the figure of the Virgin of Guadalupe, in which manner, according to legend, the vision appeared [leaving a portrait of the Virgin thereon].

Balconies, windows and flat-roofs were filled with people and the streets were extremely crowded. In front of the Arcade of the Flowers, where there are no buildings, wooden stands were set up, covered with branches and flowers, from which to admire the procession. Although the distance covered by this [procession] was short, it lasted the entire afternoon and entered the Cathedral at nightfall.

That night, on the *plaza* beautiful fireworks were lighted. So much care was taken, that as there was a man in Puebla who has fame as a good maker of fireworks, he was brought from there, so that he would make those for this festival. Those on the Plaza of Mexico City were not the only ones lighted, as there were

---

21 Father Cabrera y Quintero, from whom this description is taken, says: 'one pearl of such considerable weight, that it lacks only three carats to equal the famous Margarita.' *Escudo de Armas de la Ciudad de México*, vol.IV, chap.x, No.929, p.471.

22 A short blanket worn by the Indians, covering the front and back, with a slit in the center through which the head protrudes.

also others in the town of Guadalupe, in front of the Church of the Virgin. All of them were for account of our Municipal Council.

At dawn on the 26th, the city was equally embellished. After the *Tercia* [nine o'clock], mass began, which was sung by Precenter Dr. Alonso Moreno de Castro, served by chaplains of the cathedral assisted by a numerous group of musicians and singers. When the gospel was ended, Dr. Francisco Jimenez Caro, one of the four curates from the *Sagrario*, ascended the pulpit and read the edict from the Archbishop Juan Antonio de Vizarrón y Eguiarreta, declaring the patronage and instituting a holy day of obligation for the 12th December of each year. When the reading of the edict was finished, the sermon followed, given by Dean Dr. and Master Tomas Montaño. This was printed at the end of the book by Cayetano Cabrera. . . . The mass ended, a magnificent *Salve Regina* was sung, thus terminating the services.

The decoration of the church was in accord with the magnificence of the entire festival. The eight isolated columns and the four next to the walls which form the cross naves, were hung with crimson velvet and strips of gold braid. On the vaults and arches there was hung a multitude of pennants of rich silk cloths. More than forty *arrobas* [weight of 25 pounds] of wax in candles of different thicknesses and sizes were distributed among chandeliers, and on the altar, between columns, frieze and cornices.

FLOAT EXHIBITED BY THE SILVERSMITHS IN CELEBRATION OF THE CORONATION OF FERDINAND VI

Most solemn festivals were held in the City of Mexico, in February 1747, in celebration of the coronation of Ferdinand VI, King of Spain. These were described at length and with an abundance of detail by Father José Mariano de Abarca, S.J., Professor of Philosophy and Literature in the *Colegio Máximo de San Pedro y San Pablo*:

FINE FLOAT EXHIBITED BY THE SILVERSMITHS, SHEET-BEATERS AND DRAWERS OF GOLD WIRE

On Thursday the 9th, it was the lot of the [guilds of] the silversmiths' art, sheet-beaters and drawers of wire to participate in the celebration with their floats. Although theirs was placed last in the parade, in richness, daintiness and magnificence the general opinion was that it was second to none. As a prelude to the splendors, the night previous to Wednesday the three guilds referred to placed tapers of four wicks in all their balconies and windows, not excepting those of the members of these committees appointed to render their monarch this showy tribute, no matter how badly fortune may have treated them. More than the wax, the spirit of this court was burning with a desire to rejoice at the sight of that well finished float, masterpiece of such skilled [artisans] who give lustre to the silver-smiths' art in these kingdoms. It seems that the heavens, not to defraud the people of such just rejoicing, willed that Thursday dawn other than did the previous days for, while those were very stormy and rainy, this day was calm, without gray, heavy clouds. In opposition to its well reflected lights, this costly display could be admired by all when the sun's rays began softly to gild the lofty summits of the *Nabateos*.

Provided for its magnificence, the sweet attraction of all mortals, the white lucid metal—silver—of which it was made and in whose fabrication entered more than nine hundred and seventy-two *marcos*. Its ingenious form was in the Corinthian style with engraved plates of this metal [silver] placed on wood. And although the material from which it was made was so precious, it was nevertheless surpassed by the delicate art of its manufacture, to such an extent that the same may be said of this float as was sung by Jason about the gates of the sun, study of Vulcan: *Materiam superabat opus* [the work surpassed the material].

Its length was five *varas* from front to back, its width two [*varas*] at the front and one [*vara*] at the rear; its height from the canopy to the ground was five [*varas*].

From the upper part of the throne a gallant cherub was poised, holding in its hands an imperial gold crown, covered with many emeralds. In the center was a silver chair very well fabricated, on which sat a handsome youth who represented his August Majesty, Ferdinand, and on its sides there were the two well known columns with which the Theban Hercules made *Calpe* and *Avila* famous from whose arrogant inscription *Non Plus Ultra* the negative was erased by the public, in view of the fact that their glories had been diminished by the unconquerable Spaniards by discovering another more extensive and wealthy world which, many centuries before it was made known by the immortal Columbus, was already conceived in the minds of wise men as evidenced by that sentence, which some consider a prophecy of Seneca:

> . . . venient annis
> Secula feris, quibus Oceanus
> Vincula rerum laxet, et ingens
> Pateat Tellus, Tiphus que novos
> . . . Detegat orbes.

(There will be a time, centuries hence, when the Ocean will break its bounds, disclosing a great continent, and *Tifón* will discover new worlds.)

And with greater reason *there is nothing further to add* could be engraved on this silver float as being the only one, among so many that were built through the loyalty of the people [towards] their new monarch, and in noble praise of his triumph [also engraved thereon] the following lines, which were sung, I do not know by which Muse, alluding to the discovery of the Indies by the valiant Spaniards:

> El que hay mas mundos verás
> En la inscripción española,
> Y en el carro advertirás
> Cuando el primor lo acrisola,
> Que como aqueste no hay más.

Two well polished statues of cast silver, on each side of the chair supported the two columns with their heads, each holding with one hand a huge lion, at the feet of our invincible *Alcides*, and embracing with the other its corresponding sign, also of hammered silver. Here in black, well formed letters, the motto and poem alluding to the symbol represented by the float were sculptured.

The statue on the right, with its crowned wild brute represented loyal Spain, happy throne of her kings, whose generous sons, no less vigorous than lions in loyalty to their homes as well as fortitude and valor, with these attributes are faithful custodians of their princes, vigilantly guarding their persons and domains, in spite of enemy invasion.

The statue on the left, with its lion, was symbolic of imperial America. . . .

At the feet of the chair was a sign with this Latin motto: *Alterutro commoveor inspecto*, showing that our beloved monarch with equal solicitude and care pays attention to both Spains, setting the light of his eyes with no less attention on one as on the other.

At the back of the float was the statue of Fame, also of silver, enlivening her sounding trumpet with the warm breath of her lips. Several war implements were spread at her feet; plumed helmets, flags, spears, head armor, breast-plates and cannon. Further down the Mexican eagle could be seen, showing by the depression of her imperial wings that she has never been higher than when overcome by the rays of the hesperial sun, noble trophy of her arms.

As part of the emblem, in front of Fame, imitated in green enamel was a plant, commonly called *siempreviva* [forever living]. . . .

All the splendor of such gallant arrangements was due to Sr. Francisco Sánchez de la Rosa, member of the *Santo Oficio* [Inquisition] and at present *Mayordomo* [steward] of San Eligio, appointed by his guild as *Comisario* [manager] of the festival, together with Eligio Solis, now Secretary of the board, and Andrés de Segura, several times *Mayordomo* and *Veedor* and now deputy.

The magnificent float, thus arrayed, commenced to move at three o'clock in the afternoon, taking its course through the wide streets of this court. It encountered no little difficulty at the start because from two o'clock so many people had gathered on the street of the silversmiths that neither the Royal Cavalry Guards nor those of the art [of silversmiths] were sufficient to disperse the crowds, made enthusiastic by the richness and beauty of the float and the elegant damask and Turkish hangings with which balconies and windows were gaily adorned.

At this hour, Alonso Perez Calderon ascended the float to occupy the chair. He was a more fortunate youth than *Ida's*, for, if that one was fortunate enough to attract Jupiter's attention to become his table-servant, this one had the fortune of taking away from the people the privilege of such a high post as substitute for His Most High Majesty, representing the person of Ferdinand. This gallant youth wore a rich suit of blue velvet with golden stripe; the coat and cape of beautiful red cloth; blue stockings embroidered in gold; and around his neck a chain of very high carat gold, and hanging from this the [emblem of the] Royal Order of Philip the Good, covered with costly diamonds.

The parade formed, lead by six trumpeters with silver bugles whose loud notes were followed by seventy shop-owners of the aforementioned guilds, mounted on spirited and richly caparisoned horses. Each had as footmen two officials of their guild, uniformly dressed in white cambric shirts, red bands, short silk skirts trimmed with gold lace from Milan, blue stockings, red shoes and berets of velvet on the front of which was the coat of arms of His Majesty in hammered silver, with the two columns of Hercules with two lions at its sides. Back of them all went Francisco Cruz who has been *Mayordomo* and *Veedor* several times, and is now deputy and Lieutenant Captain of His Majesty's Corps of Grenadiers.

The image of their glorious patron, Saint Eligius, made in solid silver, served as page bearing aloft the royal standard on one side and on the other the arms of this Most Noble City. Protecting the standard were two Guards de Corps at the side of the aforesaid Señor Francisco, and behind followed four master silversmiths acting as escort. Immediately following His Majesty's float, drawn by six sturdy mules, handled by Miguel Puerta as chief coachman and as assistant coachman Antonio Fernandez. Both wore rich suits and held their hats beneath their arms, in reverence to His Majesty. At the sides of the float were twelve halberdiers with red uniforms and blue capes, with gold braid, and the blades of their halberds were of polished silver. Their captain was Manuel Benitez de Aranda, who, because of his rectitude, had held various posts on the board, and through his skill in fulfilling them, had deserved the singular attention of his guild. The post of groom was held by Adrian Jimenez de Almendral, several times *Mayordomo*, now *Veedor* and *Alferez* for His Majesty in the company of Grenadiers, and *Alferez de Alabarderos*, Nicolas de Rojas, now *Mayordomo* of our Lady of Tears, both in parade uniforms. Following the float were 28 officials as body-guard to the image of our King. These went sword in hand, riding beautiful horses, with blue saddles, red uniforms, the linings, jackets and flags all in blue adorned with rich gold stripes. The Captain of the horsemen was Salvador Montenegro; [also being present] *Alferez* José de Esquivel, Lieutenant Manuel de Rivas and Sargent Francisco Infanta, who closed the assemblage in the parade.

This parade, as justly demanded by the royal representation, with pomp and solemnity moved along until it reached the Palace, where it halted at four o'clock and with His Excellency and noble family listening, an ingenious poem was recited, well delivered, with the proper gestures, by a young man from the *Coliseo* [school], and on its termination, amid loud musical compositions and cheerful cries of *Long Live Ferdinand!* bade farewell to His Excellency to continue its rejoicing throughout the entire city. Thence it immediately went by the Municipal Palace, then to the Archbishop's Palace, afterwards to the Inquisition Building and from there, making its way through other streets, finally, before night-fall, returned to the place from which it started, thus terminating the festival of these aforementioned guilds, whose loyalty (if it were possible) would have torn from the heavens the flashing chariot driven by *Bootes* in the *Triones* [Ursa Major] for the use of their beloved monarch.

They have furnished ample proofs of this truth whenever some service to their Monarch is concerned, and to show the attitude of these kingdoms on such matters, as in the present case. . . . Noticing that the 12th of this month was not taken, that is that no festival had been planned, they decided to repeat the procession, as was done with great rejoicing of the city. In the morning all the apprentices of the silversmiths assembled, dressed as on the day of their parade and forming a colorful group composed of several companies and corresponding officers, thus marching down the streets, some of them discharging their guns at every step amid repeated cheers of *Long Live Ferdinand!* thus announcing their coming; others by the sound of the instruments, and all those who hastily came out to enjoy the antics, were given new cause to applaud the ascension to the throne of their beloved prince. They followed the same procedure throughout the afternoon until night buried in the west the last rays of day, but not their shining display, which lives and will always live in the Hall of Fame, as an example to all loyal vassals.

SOLEMN CEREMONIAL TO CELEBRATE THE CONFIRMATION OF THE PATRONAGE OF [THE VIRGIN OF] GUADALUPE

The confirmation by the Holy See of the patronage of the Most Blessed Virgin of Guadalupe was solemnized in Mexico by religious festivals held on the 9th, 10th and 11th days of November 1756. One of the ceremonies of this solemn occasion was a most magnificent procession, which José Manuel de Castro y Santa Anna, an eyewitness, describes in his 'Diary' in the following terms:

The morning of the 9th, the day appointed for the announced celebration, this imperial court of Mexico made a display of her wealth, and its inhabitants of their generosity. The spacious arches and cupolas of the Holy Church [cathedral] were crowned with beautiful flags and pennants, the entire city transformed as by the brush of an artist, [both] its districts and suburbs, and in most houses there were beautiful altars with an abundance of silver plate, mirrors and shades, and the most beautiful and rich [altars] were those from the *Casas Arzobispales* [Archbishops' Palaces], houses of Dr. Francisco Jiménez Caro, penitentiary canon of this Holy Church; Manuel Cosuela, of the order of Santiago, Attorney José Volado, Marshal of Castille; and of the count of the Valley of Orizaba; Regidor José Cuevas Aguirre, Francisco de Castro, and many others which, due to competition [among their owners] were exquisitely made, as was the case with those of the silversmiths' guild, whose entire street was hung with silver objects and four of its balconies constructed of hammered silver.

The attendance on this day, to view such splendor, was very numerous, as most of the people from places and towns nearby came, attracted by the magnificence of the display.

At the noon hour, the small bells [*esquilas*] of the Holy Cathedral rang out followed by all the other bells in this city, and at half past three in the afternoon, the procession began to emerge from said Holy Church. It was headed by all the flags and banners of the societies and brotherhoods of the guilds, carrying wax-candles in their hands. Following, was the *Orden Tercera de Nuestra Señora de la Merced* [Order of Our Lady of Mercies] carrying its patroness, Saint Mary of Mercy, with a rich dress of gold embroidered silk adorned with pearls and diamonds; then followed the *Orden Tercera* of our father Saint Augustine, with their patron [saint] adorned with exquisite and costly jewels; next the *Orden Tercera* of our father Saint Francis, carrying Saint Louis, King of France, their patron [saint], with his royal apparel so covered with diamonds, rubies, emeralds and pearls, that they appraised his costume at more than $300,000 *pesos*. The aforementioned three *Terceras Ordenes* are composed of the shopkeepers, merchants and store-owners, a very numerous and wealthy group for which reason they had a prominent part.

Then followed, headed by the cross and candle-poles, the order of Bethlehem, of more than one hundred members, accompanied by seven boys richly dressed, representing the seven princes before Our Lady of Bethlehem. This [the Virgin's statue] had a dress of silver embroidered silk adorned with many jewels, precious stones and pearls; following with the cross was the order of *San Hipolito* carrying their patron saint dressed as a captain and (the costume) being made of rich cloth adorned with diamonds, emeralds, rubies and pearls; then followed the order of the great father of the poor, San Juan de Dios, carrying their blessed patron with the vestments decorated with similar [precious] stones and pearls. Next with its cross and candle-poles, the militant religious order of Our Lady of Mercy, with several boys dressed as captives, adorned with many [precious] stones and pearls and [carrying] their patron, Saint Peter Nolasco, with like adornments of very high worth; then followed the Carmelite Order, with a hundred members, carrying the mystic doctress Saint Therese with the habit made of silver embroidered silk adorned with diamonds and rubies and the tassel of the cap made of large, whole pearls estimated to be worth over $100,000 [*pesos*]. Then came the order of the Augustines, in large numbers, carrying their patron saint with the habit of black velvet embroidered with gold, [decorated] with many jewels of [precious] stones, and the miter and staff adorned with pearls. Then followed the *Orden Seráfica de Observantes Dieguinos Cosmistas y Apostólicos*, of more than three hundred members, who carried their patron dressed in rich robes of heavy silk which cost $50 [*pesos*] a *vara*. The rays and standard, which he carried in his hand, adorned with diamonds and large whole pearls, was estimated as worth more than $400,000 [*pesos*]. Then came the order of the Dominicans, carrying their patron saint with the habit of silk embroidered in silver and the cape of black velvet adorned with gold braid from Milan. Then followed the cross of the Holy Church, with the clergy to the number of 680, carrying in their midst the most glorious patriarch Saint Joseph, decorated with rods and necklaces of gold and diamonds and many [precious] stones. Next came the groups [of Indians] from [towns of] San Juan and of Santiago with their governors, principal chiefs, *alcaldes regidores* and all the other representatives of their race. They were dressed in their native costumes with wraps of cloth, embroidered with jewels and their hats adorned with pearls. They were given this place [in the procession] considering that this festival was very much their own, because of the Divine Lady having made her appearance before the happy Indian Juan Diego. Then came all the music of the Holy Church followed by some children in native costumes, richly garbed with clothing and (adorned with) jewelry, and in their hands baskets with flowers of the season, which they were spreading through the streets. One of them carried a bowl of hammered silver, from which sweet and delicate odours escaped. Next followed the curates of the parish of the *Sagrario*, the Reverend Dean and the *Cabildo* [Council], presided by His Most Illustrious Prelate Manuel Rubio y Salinas, wearing pontifical robes. Then came the Divine Lady, Most Holy Mary of Guadalupe, on a beautiful painting of oval shape, surrounded by very rich flowers from Italy and decorated cards under a pallium, whose poles were held by the nobles and lords of this capital. These were followed by the members of the Medical Examiners and Commerce, the Staff of the Royal University, with their maces, with 80 doctors with their insignia of tassels and cloaks, presided by their Rector. Then came the most noble city [officials] with all the nobility and *Ayuntamiento* [Municipal Council] which was led by the *Corregidor* [Mayor]; then the Tribunal of the Royal Coffers, Collectors of excise-tax and tributes, Tribunal of the Royal Treasury, presided by its Regent, the Royal Board of Crime [criminal court], the *Fiscales* and *Oidores* presided by His Excellency, the Viceroy, marquis of the *Amarillas*, then his family, *Relatores* [Spokesmen], Scriveners of the Chamber and porter, the infantry of the Royal Palace, Halberdiers and Cavalry Guards. . . .

Words fail to describe the throngs at the windows, in the streets and on the flat-roofs. Also noticeable, in addition to the richly decorated images, were all the women in the procession of both the upper and middle classes, adorned with all their ear rings and finery.

The entire Holy Church was illuminated and the outside of the tower and the edges of the domes [were decorated] with draperies. When the procession ended, at seven o'clock at night, the entire city had torches in all balconies and windows, its altars were illuminated and on its flat-roofs and streets, there were bonfires. Many and beautiful fancy fireworks were burnt in front of the aforesaid Holy Church of the Royal Palace, and of the *Casas Arzobispales* [Archbishops' Palaces] and of the *Ayuntamiento* [Municipal buildings]. In front of the aforesaid Royal Palace, and towering as high as the building itself, was set up a flaming tower made up of large wheels at the base and gradually diminishing in size towards the top. Inside these wheels there were bowls filled with resin and pitch and all these were connected by a wick. Once lighted there was disclosed a tower of fire that lasted over three hours, giving the appearance of a flaming *ciprés* [tabernacle].

PREPARATIONS FOR THE FESTIVAL OF THE 12TH DECEMBER IN THE COLLEGIATE CHURCH OF GUADALUPE[23]

In the Sanctuary and Royal College of Our Lady of Guadalupe, on the 9th [of December] it being near [the date] for celebrating the confirmation of her patronage and miraculous appearance, they began to adorn and place hangings on her magnificent church, and cleaning its rich and beautiful treasures of lamps, chandeliers, torch-holders, *blandones* [large candlesticks] vases and *crujía* [railings] all of hammered silver, and its showy *retablo* [painting on wood]. On its altars there were polished jugs, with beautiful bouquets of flowers, very much like those from Italy. On its choir could be seen the costly rows of chairs of red mahogany, all engraved with reliefs representing the various miracles. There were in like material and fashion, the two rostrums or pulpits, which were built up at the sides of the presbytery for the purpose of chanting the Epistle and the Gospel. In the village, [the people] adorned the façades of their houses, setting up many beautiful altars. There was a large attendance both from this city as well as from many other places. On the 11th day the festival began with the solemn vespers, and at night-fall illuminations, fire works and the *monomaquia* [flaming tower] which was moved to that village from this court.

3. *Silversmiths of the Eighteenth Century and their Works*

The number of silversmiths of the eighteenth century was very great

23 Castro y Santa Anna, op.cit.

and descriptions of their works abound. Among the most noted are the following:

ALONSO DE AVILES

Alonso de Avilés, gold- and silversmith, was also an able politician and received many favors from the Municipal Council of Mexico City, as shown by the many instances where his name is mentioned throughout many years in the Acts of the Municipal Council. For this reason it was only natural that he should have been named to fabricate plate which the Municipal Council gave to the Most Excellent and Most Illustrious Lord Juan Ortega y Monañez, who being Archbishop of Mexico, was for a second time appointed Viceroy of New Spain:[24]

. . . and having discussed who was competent, Alonso de Avilés, gold- and silversmith, was called into this Council Hall. He brought a *salva* [horn] and a seashell of mother-of-pearl, the *salva* of silver gilded both inside and out. The seashell was gilded on the outside, with four baskets of fruits and flowers in relief filigree work superimposed on the outside; both pieces for hunting, and [also brought] statues and birds and a variety of boxes, mouldings and edges with their case.

A desk, made in Naples, of tortoise-shell adorned with relief filigree work, with white and gilded superimposed pieces, with birds, fruits and flowers. Its mirror was inside, adorned like the outside, with the five senses painted on the frame. Its drawers at the far end on the inside where the inkstand, sand-box, bell and seal are, all of white and gilded silver, and others [drawers] for paper and accessories, in their box.

A holy water font of gilded silver, two *tercias* [two-thirds of a *vara*] long, adorned with filigree work and superimposed flowers and birds, and at the center, an image of Our Lady of Guadalupe in a panel with its gilded doors. This serves as a background for a [gilded] rose of Castille, [the font] having at the center and higher up a gilded pectoral cross outlined in diamonds, and a gilded top in the form of a cluster of flowers and fruits, in its case.

Some flat baskets, three-fourths [of a *vara*] and a half in length and two-thirds [of a *vara*] in width, filled with flowers and flemish buds, with a card in the center bearing a portrait of our King on horseback and a Turk at his feet, all of white [silver] and gilded, with their cases.

After having seen these jewels, their exquisite [workmanship] and beauty, the price with said silversmith was settled for three thousand two hundred *pesos*. After the silversmith was dismissed, the members [of the Council] said that payment and satisfaction for the aforesaid three thousand two hundred *pesos* should be made

24 *Actas de Cabildo de México*, 5th November 1701.

from the city's own funds and revenues, which are exempt from any additional charges. Therefore it is approved and decided that Juan Antonio Vasquez, *Mayordomo* [steward], should request and deliver them to the aforementioned Alonso, and not having such funds [in the Treasury] that Pedro Jimenez supply them as promised, so that payment may be made as soon as possible.

And as this City desires to aid its treasury and one of the city's revenues is four thousand *pesos* from the slaughter house stands, [it is hereby agreed] that an increase in revenue be sought when fixing the taxes for the coming year, whether or not there is need therefor, so that the amount in excess may cover some or the greater part of this expenditure, and against the receipt of the said Alonso the aforesaid three thousand two hundred *pesos* be turned over to the account of said *Mayordomo*.

THE DE LARIOS, SILVERSMITHS, OF PUEBLA

Diego Martín de Larios and his son Diego Matías, the former, son of Pablo de Larios, all silversmiths, fabricated many important works during the period between 1721 and 1768.[25]

Another canopy of modern workmanship, that is little more than two *varas* in height, with mouldings and gilt decorations weighing ninety-five *marcos* and five ounces, fabricated by shop-owner Diego Matías de Larios in the year 1768, which cost one thousand five hundred and five *pesos* and five and one half *reales*.

It has six silver statues, as follows: one of Our Lady of the Conception, placed in the third niche of the processional nave [on the side] of the Epistle, referred to in chapter VII of this book, donated to this church by Licentiate Antonio Fernández de Olivares y Franco, priest in charge of the Inquisition in the village of Atlixco, [it] measures one *vara* and three fourths [of a *vara*] in height; it is adorned with embroidered edging on the mantle, and both the clothing and base are adorned with flowers and gilded decorations. It weighs three hundred and sixty-one *marcos*, four ounces and costs five thousand nine hundred and thirty-eight *pesos* and one *real*, not including the value of one good sized topaz mounted in gold in the middle of the statue's breast. It was made in this city by Diego Martín de Larios.

Another [statue] of the apostle Saint Paul, like the other, although heavier, as it weighs four hundred *marcos*, including the wood on which the base is mounted. It was made in this city by the two shop-owners Juan María de Ariza and Diego Martín de Larios in the year 1721 and its cost exceeded seven thousand *pesos* which was paid by precentor Dr. José Tomás de Luna y Arias, who donated it to the church so that it would accompany the statue of Saint Peter.

. . . which, because of its size was dismantled in the year 1743 and another

25 Echeverría y Veytia, op.cit., pp.165, 166, 169.

corresponding to the size of the altar was made by shop-owner Diego Matías de Larios, which was also gilded here and there and in the center had a medallion with the holy image of Our Lady of Solitude.

With the part taken from this antependium and an old canopy the church had, the same shop-owner made five small antependiums, each a *vara* in length, which are used to hold the silver statues on the altars set up on the four pillars of the presbytery for the octave of Corpus Christi. . . .

. . . the principal lamp hanging in front of the main altar, is one of the richest and most delicate jewels in this church. It is hexagonal in form, with six chains hanging from the vault to hold the weight and each hexagon is divided into five angles, its entire circumference thus consisting of thirty angles. Its height is nine and a half *varas*, from the head of the angel that surmounts the top, to and including the sphere which hangs beneath the bowl. Each hexagon rests on a hook from which the chain starts and [the chain] ends at the top, inside the mouth of a dolphin. Each chain is one *sesma* in width, and each link is a rose, alternating white and gilt. Riding on the six dolphins at the top are an equal number of figures of boys in graceful poses, with a light in each hand, making twelve in the circle. The hooks on the bowl support six cornucopias with three lights each. At the center of the bowl stands a beautiful jar that holds the [oil] lamp chimney. From around this mouth of the jar protrude six additional cornucopias, each with two lights, so that, when the whole lamp is lighted it has forty-three lights. At both the base and the top are superimposed gilded adornments, beautifully fabricated. On its top is the statue of the Archangel Saint Michael, and beneath the bowl hangs a sphere of white silver, surrounded by gilded snakes, all interwoven, which form a grille. The entire weight of the silver is three thousand six hundred and eighty-six *marcos*, two ounces and four *ochavas*; corresponding to one thousand six hundred and forty-eight *marcos* four ounces and four *ochavas* of white silver content, and one thousand nine hundred and thirty-seven *marcos*, six ounces of silver gilt. It cost sixty-six thousand nine hundred and eighty-three *pesos*, including two thousand *pesos* which the chapter gave to shop-owner Diego Martín de Larios, who fabricated it in this city, for account of the Holy Church, and the [lamp] was first shown on Corpus Christi day, the 10th June of the year 1751.

In the cost is not included the iron frame work which is equally beautiful and so artistically arranged that without any of it showing it supports the entire mass, with no strain on the silver. The base or lower bowl is supported by a mahogany frame made in six pieces, hinged at the center, one beveled edge resting against the other so that by fastening one angle with its peg the others are held firmly. This entire mass hangs from an iron chain, very well finished and gilded, which is caught on a small lantern carved above the keystone of the arch next to the cupola. The weight of the iron in the frame work and chain is forty-six *arrobas* and five pounds, and the mahogany frame weighs five *arrobas*.

Before this lamp was made, another very good one (although old fashioned), which hung in front of the main altar, was moved over to the vault back of the presbytery to be used for the chapel of the Kings. It is five *varas* in height and the lower bowl is more than one *vara* in diameter. It is all hand hammered and very well finished, and weighs seven hundred and twenty-six *marcos*.

In front of the altar of Saint Michael, where the silver image of the Immaculate Conception stands, hangs another beautiful lamp of modern workmanship, that was first shown on the 8th December of the year 1766. It is also hexagonal in shape and from the top ornament, which is a palm, down to the handle under the lower base, its height is four and one half *varas*, and the base a little less than one *vara* in diameter. From its center rises a jug from which seven arms extend, [to hold] other oil lights [lamps] of very fine glass. It contains six hundred and forty-four *marcos* and five *ochavas* of silver, and its total cost was seven thousand one hundred and thirty-four *pesos*, six and a half *reales*. This includes fifty *pesos* which the chapter gave as a present to shop owner Diego Matías de Larios, son of the former [Larios] who made it, but does not include a hundred and fifty-two *pesos*, seven *reales*, which was the cost of its iron ornaments and the chain from which it hangs, which is equally well finished.

On the sides of the lamp of the presbytery and closest to the altar, hang two lamps, both alike, hand-hammered, three *varas* in height, with thirty lights each, distributed through their two sections, and both together weigh six hundred and eighty-seven *marcos*, six ounces, and cost eight thousand, nine hundred and forty *pesos* six *reales*. They were made by shop-owner Diego Martín de Larios in the year 1741.

Four other smaller [lamps] all alike and of modern workmanship, hang in the lateral naves, two in each, conveniently placed for lighting them. They are a little less than two *varas* in height, each with eight lights on a single section. They were made by Diego Matías de Larios in various years; all four weighing five hundred and seventy-seven *marcos*, four ounces one *ochava* and cost six thousand six hundred and fifty-eight *pesos* three *reales* which were paid from the church funds.

The three stands, also triangular in shape, where the candle poles and high cross are placed, were made by the same Diego Martín de Larios and weigh 501 *marcos* and 6 ounces of silver, not including the iron in their frame work.

There are such great numbers of large candlesticks to adorn the altars, of various sizes and workmanship, both to hold torches and for candles, that it would be superfluous to mention them. However I cannot refrain from referring to six, of more than one *vara* in height, which are known as the imperials, because they were gifts sent from Spain, just as they are, by Emperor Charles V. Including the iron and wood in their frame work, they weigh three hundred and sixteen *marcos*.

There are six jars with their bunches of flowers, also of silver, donated by Dean Dr. Diego de Victoria de Salazar as executor of the estate of Silverio de Pineda, Secretary and Intendant of the Most Illustrious Lord Palafox and later Treasurer and Dignitary of this church. These, together with the missal stands for the pulpits at each side of the main altar which he likewise donated, cost $8,397 [*pesos*].

For the consecration of Oils, there are four amphoras and a jar in which the balsam for confirmations is prepared. The two large amphoras, together with their spatula or spoon, were made by the same shop-owner Diego Martín de Larios in the year 1736. The amphoras weigh 147 *marcos* 5 ounces and two *ochavas* and the spoon one *marco* four ounces and seven *ochavas* and cost $608 [*pesos*] 7 *reales*. The other two are older and smaller; weigh 72 *marcos* 5 ounces and the jar weighs 6 *marcos*, 6 ounces.

There are some *andas* [stretcher-like platforms with shafts, carried on men's shoulders] of silver, on which the saints are carried in processions, donated by the Most Illustrious Alonso de la Mota, whose coat of arms is seen on one of the sides, on a gilded shield, and on each of the other three sides there is a jar with Easter lilies, which is the shield of the church. On these [*andas*] the Most Blessed Sacrament was also carried. They were donated by Señor Mota for this service so that He may be carried in the processions of Corpus, until Dr. Domingo Pantaleón Alvarez de Abreu donated others of modern workmanship and very well made by Diego Martín de Larios, which weigh 202 *marcos* and one ounce of silver, not including the iron and wood of their frames, and cost $2,500. He later ordered made by shop-owner Antonio Fernandez six poles to be held by those carrying the *andas*, which weigh 30 *marcos* of silver and were also donated by him.

In the south corner, between the door of the Council Hall and that leading to the Cloister, in the year 1765 a fountain was placed, the old one on the same site having been removed, so that the prelates might wash their hands before celebrating [Mass]. The basin of this [fountain] is made in one solid piece of *tecali* marble, round in form, one *vara* and a half in diameter; from its center rises a reversed pyramid of silver that holds a cup of the same material surmounted by an angel, also of silver, half a *vara* in height, the gilding on the entire piece greatly beautifying it. The angel is old and was used to carry the train of Our Lady of the Defense, in processions, placed on the same *andas*, and weighs twenty *marcos* one ounce and one *ochava*. The remaining plate was fabricated in this city by shop-owner Diego Matías de Larios in the said year [1] 765 and weighs 273 *marcos*, five ounces and five *ochavas* and cost four thousand *pesos*, not including the value of the angel, which, as stated before, was old.

THE LARGE MONSTRANCE

The large monstrance where the Most Divine Sacrament is exposed on the feast of Corpus, is made in two pieces: the sun or rays in whose center the Lord is placed, and the base on which it stands. The sun weighs seven *marcos* and four *ochavas* of gold and is adorned on one side with two hundred and ninety-seven diamonds. [Of these] seven are large ones, thirty-five medium sized, eighty-eight are smaller and the remainder are small. The majority are flat stones. On the other side it is adorned with emeralds numbering three hundred and fifteen: three large ones and of good color, sixteen medium sized; one hundred and thirty-seven somewhat smaller and the remainder small. The circle [rim] holding the crystals is adorned on both sides with whole pearls, large and of good quality, numbering fifty-eight on each side, making a total of one hundred and sixteen. The points of the rays end with stars formed of the same whole pearls, numbering two hundred and thirty-five in all. This sun or rays has been appraised at twenty-four thousand *pesos* and was a gift from Ana Francisca de Córdova, widow of general Diego Ortiz de Lagarchi, Knight of the Order of Santiago, concerning whose liberality we shall hear more in this history. The stem of the sun, which fits into the base, bears this sign: *A devoción de Doña Ana Francisca de Córdova año de* 1693 *la hizo Roque Benitez.* [Through the devotion of Mrs. Ana Francisca de Córdova, year of 1693, made by Roque Benitez]. Bermúdez says in his manuscript that she put her own jewels into this piece of jewelry [the monstrance].

The base was not in accord [with the rays] and therefore the chapter decided to have another made for account of the church in the year 1727. It was inaugurated on Corpus day, the 12th June of said year. It was made by shop-owners Juan María de Ariza and Diego Martín de Larios. It weighs forty-one [*marcos*] of gold; is lined and framed on the inside with gilded silver, weighing six *marcos*, six ounces and four *ochavas*.

It is likewise adorned with diamonds and emeralds. There are eight hundred and seventy-two diamonds, most of them rose diamonds and one yellow brilliant, of good size. There are fifty-four of four carats; eighteen of three; four hundred and seventy-four of one carat and the remainder are eight and ten to a carat. There are four hundred and seventy-seven emeralds: eighteen of three and a half carats; nine of two and half; a hundred and fifty-one of two carats and the remainder somewhat smaller. This base has been appraised at eighty-three thousand, two hundred *pesos*.

Such excessive riches went into the base that the sun or rays above mentioned were no longer in accord with it, either in value or size, and this was the reason why the Chapter decided (without breaking up the other) to have a larger sun made, that would correspond in size and value to this base. In consequence it was begun and was very finely fabricated by shop-owner Diego Matías de Larios, son of Diego Martín who made the base. [The new sun] was inaugurated on Corpus day, the 10th June of the year 1772. It has fifteen *marcos*, three ounces and three *ochavas* of gold and is adorned with diamonds on one side and emeralds on the other. The diamonds number one thousand nine hundred and seventy-one, all flat and rose diamonds of various sizes, in good proportion to the places where they were set, all weighing three hundred and forty-nine carats.

The emeralds are all of a fine color and clear, and many are large. Their number reaches one thousand seven hundred and seventy-two. This sun has been appraised at forty thousand *pesos*; it was also made for account of this Holy Church.

MISCELLANEOUS JEWELS[26]

There was a collection of 48 silver torch holders with superimposed pieces of artistic workmanship; one *vara* and a third in height and four two *varas* in height, very plain, but also of silver.

Eight large candlesticks for tapers, weighing one *arroba* with ornaments of silver gilt two and three-fourths *varas* in size.

Twenty-five silver chandeliers among which are two of three *varas* in size.

Six lamps of the same metal, among which one hung from the small lantern of the main cupola. It was made of one thousand and four pieces, with gilded ornaments with candelabra for forty-two lights and was eight *varas* five *sesmas* in height and two *varas* and a third in diameter. It was inaugurated on Corpus Thursday of the year 1751; weighed 3,686 *marcos*. It cost $67,000 and was made by Diego Larios.

JOSE DE LA BORDA'S MONSTRANCE

One of the most famous jewels in Mexico was the great monstrance belonging to José de la Borda, who accumulated great wealth from the mines in Taxco.

It was of gold, one *vara* and an eighth in height, weighing 88 gold *marcos*, and had 5,872 diamonds, 2,653 emeralds, 544 rubies, 106 amethysts and 28 sapphires. Sedano says:[27]

. . . it formerly belonged to the parish church of Taxco and was owned by the miner, José de la Borda, who loaned it for use, but reserved the rights of ownership. It is adorned with diamonds on one side and emeralds on the other, and the cross above has nothing but diamonds on both sides, [this monstrance] cost more than one hundred thousand *pesos*. It was bought by the Holy Cathedral and was inaugurated on Corpus day of the year 1773 on the 10th June; that is, only the sun

26 *Capilla de la Soledad*, Echeverría y Veytia, op.cit., vol.II, pp.154, 349, 350.
27 Francisco Sedano, *Noticias de México*, op.cit., p.180.
   Note: It was impracticable to mention the enormous number of descriptions of silver plate available. For those who may be particularly interested in this subject, the following references are given:
   Bermúdez de Castro, op.cit., pp.125, 230, 235, 243.
   Romero de Terreros, op.cit.
   Alamán, *Disertaciones*, op.cit.
   Gaceta de México, August 1729.
   García Gutiérrez, *Historia de la Virgen de los Dolores*, p.31 and following.
   Echeverría y Veytia, op.cit., pp.162, 166, 168, 169.
   P.Pérez Rivas, op.cit.

or circle; and on the second June 1774 of the following year, also on Corpus day, the base, likewise adorned with precious stones, was inaugurated.

This jewel disappeared on the night of the 17th January 1861, and is reported to be in the Cathedral of Paris, lacking the diamonds.

PRESENT FOR THE KING OF SPAIN

April 18. His Excellency ordered made by Manuel Vallido, master silversmith, two statues of cast silver, each one *vara* and a half in size, not counting the bases. The faces and the workmanship were beautiful. One was of Saint Theresa and the other of Saint Anthony; together they weighed 655 *marcos* and cost, including their manufacture, $16 per *marco*. It is believed that the bases exceeded 200 *marcos* in weight and were of beautiful workmanship. Likewise His Excellency ordered made by the same master three gold writing desks; the three weighing 56 *marcos*. They were beautifully finished, and [their cost] amounted to a large sum of *pesos*. They were sent packed in cases to Veracruz, so that they could go to Spain in the fleet. The two statues and one of the gold writing desks were presented to the King our Lord. It was not known to whom the other two writing desks were sent. Both silver and gold are hall-marked. . . .[28]

MISCELLANEOUS OBJECTS

The six torch-holders for placing torches on the steps of the presbytery are nearly three *varas* in height. They are triangular in shape, of modern fabrication, with some gilded coats-of-arms on the three sides of the base, with the insignia of the Church. They were made by shop-owner José de Barrios and were inaugurated on Corpus day, the 15th June of the year 1775. Their net weight is 2,531 *marcos* and seven ounces in white silver at ten grains per *marco*. The remaining 99 *marcos*, which the gilded superimposed pieces weighed, at 18 grains [per *marco*]. Both items amounted to $27,100 *pesos* 6 *reales*, which was the entire cost of the silver. To cover this, six other smaller [torch holders] which were there were melted down. To this cost should be added that of the iron on which they are mounted, supporting the entire weight, without any strain on the silver.

On the same day a stand was inaugurated, on which the large candlesticks are placed on the altar, made of silver sheets, with the sides carved and gilded, weighing 238 *marcos* 1½ ounces; of which 159 *marcos*, 4 ounces are gilded and the remainder is white. It all cost 3,681 grains [sic] 7 *reales* and was made by the same shop-owner Barrios.[29]

THE MONSTRANCE *LA TORRECILLA*

Second chapel. Of the Virgin of the *Antigua*. It has an altar with nothing worthy of note; it is new, made in the year 1852.

28 Castro Santa Anna, *Diario*, op.cit. (*El Platero D. Manuel Vallido*) year of 1758.
29 *Alhajas de la Catedral de Puebla*, op.cit. (*El Platero D. José de Barrios, de Puebla*).

On it was the monstrance called *Torrecilla* [small tower] because it is of that shape and two *varas* and five *sesmas* in height, divided into four sections, in addition to the base which was added later. Its base is hexagonal and the architecture is Corinthian. The first section is formed of twelve columns, grooved two-thirds of the way up. The lower part is decorated with fine drawings in pairs, on joint pedestals and they support a cornice and panelled dome. The pedestals extend forward, serving as supports for the statues of David, Melchizedech, Zachary, Ezekiel, Habacus and Michaes. On the front of said [bases] it has bas-reliefs of the patriarchs and in the middle [base] deeds from the Holy Scripture. On the protuberances of the cornice are other passages from the life of Jesus Christ and crowning the cornice are the statues of St. John the Baptist, St. Peter, St. Paul and St. Andrew. Back of these are graceful pyramids in pairs. Occupying the center of this section is a Last Supper, of much artistic merit.

The second section is similar to the other. Its statues are of Solomon, St. Elizabeth, St. Zachary, St. Joachim, St. Ann and St. John the Evangelist. The dome is gilded and panelled. At its center is a stand with bas-reliefs of holy doctors and angels, and on top is an elegant stand on which the beautiful sun of the monstrance formerly was placed.

The third section has only six columns on their pedestals which hold a cornice of seraphs and foliage on the base. At the top are six statues, four of the cardinal virtues. In the middle is the Immaculate Conception and in the center is the Eternal Father.

The fourth section has a stand and six stems with busts of angels receiving a crown and a graceful dome on whose top is a beautiful small statue of Christ after the Resurrection, of fine and perfect sculpture. In the center is another of St. Joseph.

This entire rich composition is a masterpiece of art. It is made of silver with gilt ornaments of the same metal and was made by the Mexican silversmith Miguel Torres. It weighs 157 *marcos* 6 ounces and cost $15,672 *pesos* 2 *reales*, 6 grains.

In the year 1854 this precious jewel was hidden because from 1847 it began to arouse the greed of some government officials. The Chapter was forced to give sums of money in addition to loans imposed, in order to save it, until Bishop Pelagio Antonio de Labastida y Dávalos decided to put it out of sight and it was removed from the chapel of the Antigua.[30]

STATUE OF THE APOSTLE SAINT PAUL IN THE CATHEDRAL OF PUEBLA

About 1721 there was inaugurated in this Holy Church the rich statue of the Apostle of the People, St. Paul. Even his face was like that of his prince, St. Peter. . . .

This magnificent and exquisite image was made by the noted master silversmith

30 A. Carrión, "Historia de la Ciudad de Puebla de los Angeles," vol.I, p.388-9. (*El Platero D.Miguel Torres de México*, 1751.)

and lapidary, Juan María de Arista, native of this city . . . surpassing in its well finished and unique workmanship the statue of St. Peter. Its cost exceeded seven thousand *pesos*.[31]

THE SILVERSMITHS JUAN MARIA DE ARISSA, JOSE ISUNZA, ANTONIO VILLAFAÑE Y NICOLAS MORA

. . . The never sufficiently praised work of a base of gold, emeralds and diamonds, made in the year 1727, for account of this Holy Church, by the noted artist Juan María de Arissa, was inaugurated on the 12th June of said year, on the feast of Corpus . . . this monstrance, one *vara* in height, and of the finest gold, has one of its two sides entirely covered with rich diamonds and the other with high priced emeralds. This [object] because of the wealth of its stones, richness of material, beauty of manufacture and cost, can only be duly praised by those who on seeing it can appreciate it. For this reason and for others which I omit, it is the most valuable jewel of this Holy Church and the best made monstrance of all those venerated in New Spain, there being sufficient reason to doubt that another can be found among those proclaimed by the trumpets of Europe, which in workmanship, size and richness may surpass it. The appraisal of its value is more than eighty-eight thousand *pesos*.[32]

Another modern chalice, of gold of [different] colors, beautifully engraved. It was made by José Isunza, son of [the city of] Puebla.

Three monstrances. The *Torrecilla*, which has been described; another all of gold, one side of the sun adorned with selected diamonds and the other with very large emeralds. It was first used on the 1st June of the year 1727. Another monstrance, smaller than the previous one, all of gold, having the sun decorated with a circle of black pearls and the rays with white pearls, decreasing in size from the center outward. The base was of gold of various colors and was very tastefully decorated with diamonds, emeralds, topazes, amethysts, garnets and pearls. It was first used in September 1803 and was the last piece of work made by José Isunza. He was unable to engrave it because of his advanced age, so this was done by Antonio Villafañe.

The greater part of the antependiums of all the altars of the Cathedral were of silver, some beautifully engraved. Among them, one which attracted attention was that used when 34 gilded busts of wood with relics in the breast, were placed on the main altar, which busts were paid for by the Most Illustrious Señor Vasquez. This antependium was transferred to the *Sagrario*, from where it disappeared at the same time that a silver throne [vanished]. Both pieces were substituted by others of gilded metal, made by Nicolás Mora.

31 Diego Antonio Bermúdez de Castro, *Teatro Angelopolitano*, op.cit., pp.240-1. (*El Platero D. Juan María de Arissa*).
32 Diego Antonio Bermúdez de Castro, op.cit., p.243.

In the *Archivos de Tlaxcala*, Volume 242, corresponding to the 7th October 1788, the following is found:

Contract between José de Isunza, master of the silversmiths' art, and Antonio de Pineda, Chaplain of the Temple of Ocotlán, to the effect that the former will make a triangular niche of silver for the Virgin, for which the Chaplain delivered to him 214 *marcos*, 5 ounces, Isunza obligating himself to deliver the work in May 1789.

This niche still exists.

RODALLEGA AND OTHER SILVERSMITHS

The [lamp] of the Cathedral of Mexico, from the bottom to the ring at the top, measures eight and one half *varas*; it is ten and one half *varas* in circumference and three and one half *varas* in diameter. Its branches have 54 candlesticks for an equal number of lights. It weighs 4,373 *marcos*, amounting to 2,186 and a half pounds or 87 *arrobas*, 11½ [pounds]. It is all of silver, the greater part doubly gilded and cost $71,343 [*pesos*] 3 *reales*, which amount to more than $16 [*pesos*] per *marco*. The iron chain from which it hangs weighs 62 *arrobas*, 10 pounds [1,560 pounds]. Said lamp was first used on the eve of the Assumption of Our Lady, 14th August 1733.

LAMPS OF THE CATHEDRALS OF MEXICO AND GUADALAJARA

	MEXICO	GUADALAJARA
Height	8½ *varas*	9 *varas*
Diameter	3½ *varas*	3 *varas*
Circumference	10½ *varas*	9 *varas*
Marcos	4,373	4,704 3½ ounces
Cost	$71,343 3 *rs.*	

The one from Guadalajara weighs 331 *marcos*, 3½ ounces more, which amounts to six *arrobas*, 15 pounds, 11½ ounces.

On 1st April 1806, in the parish church, the Sagrario of the Cathedral, the new silver lamp was hung and it was inaugurated on the 3rd, Holy Thursday. It measures eight *varas* from the hook above to the bottom: its bowl is 2 *varas* and 1/3 in diameter and 7 *varas* in circumference; it weighs 717 *marcos*, 6 ounces [14 *arrobas*, 8 pounds, 14 ounces], at $12 [*pesos*] 4 *reales* and ½ per *marco*, makes $9,004 [*pesos*] 5 *reales*. It has eighteen branches for candles.

COMPARISON BETWEEN THE LAMPS OF THE CATHEDRAL AND OF THE SAGRARIO

	THAT OF THE CATHEDRAL	THAT OF THE SAGRARIO	DIFFERENCE
Height	8½ *varas*	8 *varas*	½
Diameter	3½ *varas*	2-1/3 *varas*	1 *vara* 6 inches

Circumference	10½ *varas*	7 *varas*	3½ *varas*
Marcos	4,373	717 ounces 6	3,665 ounces 2
Value	$71,343 *rs.* 3	$9,004 *rs.* 5	$62,338 *rs.* 6

The one of the Cathedral weighs 73 *arrobas*, 2 pounds, 10 ounces more than the one of the Sagrario and has 36 more branches. It was inaugurated on the 14th August 1733.

The one of the Sagrario is worth one eighth of that of the Cathedral.[33]

SANTA MARIA DE GUADALUPE

Since the Collegiate Church of Guadalupe was, after the Cathedrals of Mexico and of Puebla, the richest in New Spain, it is of interest to give at least an idea of its magnificence:[34]

Although some parts of the church still had to be finished, the [people's] devotion already fervently desired to adorn the interior in a manner in keeping with the sumptuousness of the buildings and the majesty of the Holy Image to which it was dedicated. For this purpose they hastened the termination of the beauties of art in sculpture, wood-carving, reliefs and adornments of three gilded *retablos* [rich altar ornaments] so that they would decorate the front of the presbytery and the entire width of the church.

The first and largest [*retablo*] which rises from the presbytery itself is twenty-five *varas* and two thirds in height. It was made in four sections in the Corinthian style. The two colateral ones are nineteen *varas* and two-thirds high, their width corresponding to that of the naves they occupy. The one on the gospel side was a gift of Licentiate Ventura de Medina and the one on the epistle [side] was donated by the Most Excellent and Most Illustrious Lord Juan de Ortega Montañes, Archbishop and Viceroy. Both have excellent statues, carved and painted, and decorations of jewels.

In the center of the larger is a tabernacle where the Holy Image was placed. It is entirely of hammered silver, doubly gilded. It is four *varas* and one-eighth in height, and fourteen and a half in width and is composed of sixteen columns covered with vine leaves and bunches of colored grapes embossed and enamelled. On the architectural base there are distributed fifteen statues of various sizes, ranging from one *vara* down to one-third [of a *vara*] perfectly finished. There are fifty-one angels and eight plates whose relief work portrays the apparitions and other wonders of the [life of] the Most Holy Image. Eighty-eight figures all, as said, are of doubly gilded silver, forming a place for the solid gold frame for the most beautiful image of the

33 Sedano, op.cit., pp.349-50 (*Lámpara de la Catedral, y Lámparas de las Catedrales de México y Guadalajara*).
34 Ignacio Carrillo y Pérez, *Pensil Americano*, p.34 and following.

Virgin whose appearance is [venerated]. [The frame] is two *varas* and a fourth in height, one and a half in width, the moulding being one *sesma* in width. In the fabrication of the tabernacle alone three thousand two hundred fifty-seven *marcos*, three ounces and four *ochavas* of silver were used, which by including the gold used in its gilding, made its cost amount to seventy-eight thousand, one hundred and seventy-eight *pesos* and four *reales*, as shown by the letter of payment extended by its maker, Father Antonio Tura, Benedictine monk, which is kept in the archives of the shrine.[35]

35 In the archives of the Basilica of Guadalupe inventories are found which were made about the year 1750, from which my friend Father D.J.García Gutiérrez took and passed to me the following data which complete Carrillo y Pérez' remarks concerning the main altar:

'On the *retablo* of the main altar . . . is placed the Most Holy Image of Our Lady of Guadalupe at the center and in the principal place as patroness of the shrine. It is in a silver, circular-shaped niche which measures fourteen and a half *varas* in height and four *varas* and one *ochava* in width. It is entirely gilded and in its fabrication 3,257 *marcos*, 3½ ounces were used. At the rate of 16 *pesos* per *marco*, this makes the cost of fabrication 52,119 *pesos*, besides the value of the silver that was turned over to its maker, Father Antonio de Tura, a monk of [the order of] the great father Saint Benedict. This is proven by a final receipt and letter of payment extended in the city of Mexico on the 20th day of the month of April of the year 1709, by and before Juan de Ancibay y Anaya, Royal and Provincial Scrivener, exhibited by said Bachelor José de Lizardi y Valle, who said it was in his keeping as steward and administrator of said shrine. The niche was made and decorated with silver jewels as follows:

'On the top is a statue of Esther, which, together with the base on which it stands, is one *vara* and three-fourths in height.

'Item, another statue of the holy king David, which, together with its base, without the crown on the head, is one *vara* in height.

'Item, at the sides of said Holy King are two plates engraved with [an image of] Our Lady of Guadalupe.

'Item, on the same sides of said Holy King, other statues which, including their bases, are each one *vara* less one *ochava* [in height].

'Item, the frame in which Our Lady is placed, is two *varas* and one fourth in height and one *vara* and a half in width. The width of the moulding is one *sesma*. It is embossed with eight images at the ends and rests on a stand which is also of silver, one *vara* and two-thirds in length, and one *sesma* in width, with nineteen flesh-colored enamelled angels.

'Item, on said stand are four nude angels holding instruments in their hands: a harp, a guitar, a bass viol and a violin, each a fourth of a *vara* less two fingers in height.

'Item, 28 angels, some seated and others standing, distributed in various parts of the entire niche; two at the sides of the first statue—their dresses made of silver. Including their bases, each is one-third [of a *vara*] in height. There are two others at the sides of the second statue, similar in form and distribution to the previous ones. There are two nude angels which, seated, measure a fourth of a *vara* in height, and six of one *sesma* in height. . . .

'Item, on the right side of the frame of Our Lady are two statues like the aforementioned and two others on the left. Those on the upper part, on both sides, including their bases, are one *vara* two fingers in height; and those on the lower part, one *vara* less two fingers.

'Item, below said frame and stand is a repository where the Most Blessed Sacrament is exposed. Inside is a statue of St. John the Baptist, which, including the base and diadem, is one *vara* less an *ochava* in height.

'Item, at the sides of said Repository and statue of St. John are two other statues which, including their bases, are each three fourths of a *vara* and two fingers in height.

'Item, at the top of said Repository or niche of St. John, is a [statue of] St. Raphael, also of silver, dressed, which is one *ochava* in height.

'Item, on said sides, like those of the Repository where the cup or ciborium is, are four engraved plates; two showing the apparitions of Our Lady, one of the Assumption and one forming a map of said shrine.

The frame of the glass case was donated by Señor Garabito, dignitary of this holy metropolitan church, with its six gold candelabra. The interior frame of the same material was donated by Señores Torres, dignitaries of the said metropolitan church, and all three donations (interior and exterior frames and candelabra) weigh 4,050 *castellanos* and one fourth, which estimated at a reasonable price, amount to 14,175 *pesos* and seven *reales*.

The sheet of silver which serves as a guard to the holy cloth at the back, has an approximate value of 2,000 *pesos*.

The border, or top piece of silver, donated by the Most Excellent Antonio María de Bucareli, which was taken down and placed at the foot of the tabernacle because of the shadow it cast on the face of the Most Holy Image, cost 1,209 *pesos*. Adding these amounts to the cost of the tabernacle, its silver and gold content has a value of approximately 95,362 *pesos*.

The glass protecting the Most Holy Image is in one piece, of incomparable smoothness and clearness.

DECORATIONS OF THE ALTAR OF THE COLLEGIATE
CHURCH OF GUADALUPE

Six large candlesticks on the stand, with a weight of *marcos* of silver of	555 ms.[1] 1 oz.
The clusters of flowers and jugs	440 ms. 1 oz.
Two large vases, donated by Juan de Santillán	220 ms. 1½ oz.
The stand and antependium—I do not know their weight.	
The railing surrounding the presbytery extending in front of the choir is not entirely terminated; and not including the statues or figures, the amount that has been invested in it is	8,609 ms. 2 oz.

'Item, the aforesaid niche, ends with the Repository for the chalice and is one *vara* in height and more than a third [of a *vara*] in width. The little door which closes it has on the outside an image of the Saviour and on the inside another similar one with the apostolate engraved thereon.

'Item, sixteen columns holding the frame of Our Lady and niche of the holy king David, each two-thirds [of a *vara*] in height, with vine leaves and bunches of grapes embossed and enamelled [thereon].

'Item, in addition to the aforesaid angels, distributed throughout the niche, are eighty figures; 49 superimposed and the others of flesh-colored enamel.

'Item, on the frame of Our Lady, [there is] an image of God the Father, superimposed, which is one-third [of a *vara*] in height.

'Item, serving as a back to the frame of Our Lady is a sheet of silver two and a half *varas* in length and one *vara* and a half in width, apparently a little thicker than a *peso*, which, according to the estimate of said master (the *Alférez* Manuel Marín, master silversmith named for that purpose) weighs 200 *marcos*.

'Item, preserving the sovereign image of Our Lady is a [case] of fine crystal, two *varas* less one eighth [of a *vara*] in length and one *vara* and a little less than a fourth, in width; which, including the silver frame is two *varas* and a fourth in length, one and a half *varas* and two fingers in width.'

1 *Marcos*.

The statues should be 32, but nine are missing. For this reason
and because of their varying weights, it is not possible to
show with certainty [their exact weight] but estimating the
32 by the first six of the twelve that were donated by the
Most Excellent Knight Father Antonio María de Bucareli,
since the six cost 4,448 *pesos*, the cost of the 32, when completed, will amount to 23,919 *pesos*, which reduced to *marcos*,

gives a value of	2,646 ms. 4 oz.
Two large imperial candlesticks and four side [candlesticks]	1,236 ms. 1 oz.
Total number of *marcos*	13,707 ms. 2½ ozs.

Hanging in the presbytery are several silver and crystal chandeliers and two of
gold of fine foliage and majestic design; one was donated by Fernando José Mangino
and weighs one thousand one hundred and six *castellanos* and a half. This was
paired by the Royal College with another of equal weight and design, and the two
together weigh two thousand two hundred and thirteen *castellanos*. Since it is not
my intention to make an inventory of the sacred treasures in this wonderful shrine,
which are duly appreciated and show the [people's] devotion, even from far distant
lands, to this marvelous image, I shall not enumerate the monstrances, chalices and
other sacred vessels of gold and [precious] stones and other beautiful silver jewels
in chandeliers, candle poles, thrones, lamps, etc. However, something should be
said regarding the two lamps, the old and the new, because of their perfect and
beautiful workmanship.

The first, placed in front of the presbytery on the 11th August 1729, from the
knob at its end to the hook from which it hangs, measures five *varas* and weighs nine
hundred *marcos* of silver, of which two hundred and seventy-four are gilded. To
add to its decoration on the top thirty-one *marcos* of silver were added, making its
total weight nine hundred and thirty-one *marcos*. Distributed in the circle are fifty-
four candelabra.

The second [lamp] which was hung before the main altar while the Holy Image
was in the church of the Reverend Capuchin Nuns, on the 10th December 1792,
has seven hundred and fifty *marcos*, three and three sixteenths of silver. It is six
varas and two-thirds in length, two [*varas*] and an eighth in diameter and six *varas*
and three-eighths in circumference. Adorning it in the center is a vase with twelve
candelabra and on the lamp's circumference are forty-two [candelabra]. In addition
to these, it has forty-six gilded stars and at the top, a sun half a *vara* in diameter,
also of doubly gilded silver.

Among the many varied and beautiful curtains which adorn the frame and cover
the image of the Most Holy Virgin, unparalleled are some forming a canopy covering
almost two sections of the main *retablo* which were donated by Count of Reparad,
who had great devotion towards the Virgin of Guadalupe. When he donated them
I heard that they had been tapestries from the chamber of the Mother Queen María

Amalia, Princess of Parma, and were bought at a very low price, $14,000 *pesos*. The entire tapestry has a background of silver brocade with such high and beautifully embossed columns and lions that it is the admiration of all who are authorities [on the matter].

The choir, whose pavement in front is enclosed by a silver railing, is all of first class work and in fine taste. The grille and rows of chairs are of mahogany, the former with superimposed pieces of silver, on which eight hundred and ninety-nine *marcos*, five ounces [of silver] were employed. This piece is of a most graceful mixed style, with a full sized image of the [Virgin of] Guadalupe[36] at the top.

The rows of chairs are divided into two groups, the upper for the Rector of the Parish and members of the Chapter, the lower for the chaplains and ministers of the choir. Although most of the material of which it is made is mahogany, ebony and other fine woods are also used. The litany of the Virgin, with symbols alluding to the attributes and pre-eminence of Our Lady and other sacred passages, are represented thereon in high and bas relief, the carvings, drawings and idea being carried out with skill and beauty.

The upper choir has a very famous [pipe] organ, whose notes are so lively, sonorous and strong that they fill the church with their music and the hearts [of the people] with joy, particularly when accompanying the *Salve Regina*, which is sung each afternoon after the canonical hours.[37]

SILVERSMITHS WHO PRACTICED THEIR TRADE DURING THE EIGHTEENTH CENTURY

There are lists, supposedly complete, which give the names of all the silversmiths of the year 1753. These will be quoted later.

In 1768 there were, according to San Vicente,[38] fifty-three silversmith shops, an enormous number compared to other establishments which the same author mentions:

This seems sufficient to give an idea of how much is spent on other things. It is impossible to ascertain the amount of vegetables, fruits, seeds and similar things, as loads of such articles, even of flowers, are constantly coming in by land and water

---

36 This grille of the choir is the one mentioned by Romero de Terreros in *Las Artes Industriales en la Nueva España*, and is now at the entrance of the Sagrario.

37 To what Carrillo y Pérez said must be added the following narrative furnished me by my friend Father J.García Gutiérrez:
'The grille enclosing the choir of the canons was similar to that of the cathedral choir, except that instead of being of metal it was of mahogany with superimposed pieces of silver, in which 899 *marcos* and 5 ounces were employed and instead of having a group of the Assumption at the top it had an image of the Virgin of Guadalupe in an oval.'

38 Juan Manuel de San Vicente, *México en 1768. Exacta descripción de la Magnífica Corte Mexicana.* Published in Cadiz in the eighteenth century and reprinted by Luis González Obregón. Mexico, 1897. *Tip. El Nacional*, pp.86, 87.

in numerous small boats, called *canoas*, each brought by one or two Indian rowers from near-by towns, coming through the canal which starts at the Chalco lagoon and goes as far as the market-place called the *Volador* and the Public Market. This trade is constant, rich and amusing, as the aforesaid canal is seen packed with so many canoes of various sizes, filled with such a variety of things for sale, and there is such an immense number of stands, both in the markets and on the streets. As concerns the remaining noble merchandise of this kingdom and of the other three parts of the world, there are very many stores and tradesmen's shops, as may be surmised merely by listing the following:

Dry goods stores	098
Stores of merchants [handling drygoods]	350
Stores of food supplies	353
Wine stores	410
Sugar stores	040
Wax [candle] stores	038
Bakeries	080
Butcher shops	046
Pharmacies	040
Silversmith shops	053
Tailor shops	120

The complete list taken from the Census of 1753, is the following:[39]

SAN FRANCISCO STREET

7. Single room, Diego Sánchez, silver-shop owner.
8. Two-story house. Mrs. Inés de León, widow of Joaquín Pérez, silver-shop owner, and one brother, Manuel Pérez, silversmith, 25 years of age and José Rojas of the same trade, 23 years of age; one apprentice, Antonio Córdoba, 14 years of age.
9. Single room. Silver-shop of Antonio Fernández.
12. Tenement house. Manuel Paniagua, silversmith, married to Micaela de Paya.
14. Tenement house. Miguel Sánchez, silversmith, 36 years of age, married to Josefa de León. Sons: Agustín, 11 years of age; Vicente, 9 years of age and Pablo, 6 years of age.
16. Single room and two story house. José Barrientos with silver-shop; 30 years of age, married to María Lazcano. Sons: Manuel, 2 years of age and José 3.

39 *Archivo General de la Nación. Civil indiferente.* T.64. Year 1753. Proceedings which by virtue of decree of His Excellency Juan Francisco Guemes y Horcasitas, Count of Revilla Gigedo, Viceroy, Governor and Captain General of this New Spain, were carried out by Francisco Orozco Manrique de Lara, of His Majesty's Council, Criminal Judge of the Royal Hearings of this city of Mexico. (These proceedings were a census. The book has no folio numbers.)

24. Two story house and a single room. Silver-shop of José Rodríguez, married to Josefa Larrimbe, with one son, single, 20 years of age, silversmith, and two apprentices, José Vega 14 years of age and Joaquín Presa, 18.

25. Two story house and single room. Silver-shop of José de Mesa, 35 years of age, married to Micaela de Vergara. Son, José, 3 years of age.

SECOND BLOCK, SAME STREET.

7. Single room. Silver-shop of Pedro Avila.

12. Two story house and single room. Silver-shop of Manuel Salinas, 45 years of age, married to María Guerrero. Son, José, 11 years of age.

15. Two story house and single room. Silver-shop of Manuel Contreras, single, 25 years of age. Has two apprentices, José Campuzano, 18 years of age and Vicente Paredes, 12.

16. Two story house and a single room. Silver-shop of Juan de Aguilera, 40 years of age, married to María Rodriguez.. Son, Ignacio, 7 years of age.

FIRST BLOCK ACROSS FROM THE CONVENT OF SANTA ISABEL, FACING NORTH

2. Two story house. In the lower apartment, Ana Sánchez, with one son named Miguel, silversmith, 18 years of age.

BLOCK WHICH TURNS AT THE ALLEY CALLED CONDESA, FROM NORTH TO SOUTH.

5. Single room. Joaquín López, silversmith, 25 years of age.

6. Single room. Jorge Saavedra, silversmith, 35 years of age.

CORNER OF VERGARA STREET FROM NORTH TO SOUTH

6. Single room. Antonio Meneses, silversmith, 30 years of age.

THE NEXT BLOCK FROM SOUTH TO NORTH

11. Single room. Manuel Barrera, silversmith, 28 years of age.

SANTA CLARA ALLEY FROM SOUTH TO NORTH

15. Tenement house. José de Rojas, silversmith, 48 years of age.

16. Two story house. Antonio Salinas, silver-shop owner, a native of Seville, age not stated.

16. Nicolás Avalos, silversmith, a native of Seville, 50 years of age, and 30 years resident in the kingdom.

STREET OF THE COMPAÑIA DE JESUS FROM SOUTH TO NORTH

25. Tenement house. Juan Beltrán, silversmith, 30 years of age.

SIXTH BLOCK OF TACUBA STREET FROM WEST TO EAST.

2. Two story house. Pablo León, silversmith, 35 years of age.

SEVENTH BLOCK OF TACUBA STREET FROM EAST TO WEST

7. Government Building. Felipe Castillo, silversmith, 36 years of age.

CENTER OF THE MARKET PLACE FOR RAW SILK STARTING FROM THE ENTRANCE TO TACUBA STREET

1. Single room. Juan Centeno, silversmith, 50 years of age. Married to María Escoto. Son, Pascual, 18 years of age, in the same trade.
6. Two story house. Agustin de Herrera, silversmith, 26 years of age. Son, Andrés, 5 years of age.
12. Two story house. Manuel de Rivera, owner of the silver-shop, 40 years of age.
13. Tenement House. Manuel Casillas, silversmith, married to María Berdiguel, a mulatto; 36 years of age. Son, José, 17 years of age, silversmith.
16. Tenement house. Jacinto Cruz, silversmith, 36 years of age.
22. Tenement house. Antonio Aguiar, 32 years of age. Owner of the silver-shop.
26. Tenement house. Agustín Suárez, silversmith, 30 years of age.
30. Single room. José Estrella, silversmith, 42 years of age.
32. Two story house. Isidro de la Cueva, owner of the silver-shop. More than 30 years of age.
36. Single room. Silver-shop of Juan de Sierra, 26 years of age, a bachelor. He has an apprentice, Francisco Rivera, 12 years of age.
37. Single room. Tomás Cueva, owner of the silver-shop, 55 years of age, a bachelor.
62. José Esquivel, owner of the silver-shop, 40 years of age. His daughter María Herrera, married to Miguel de Oviedo, silversmith; 25 years of age.
69. Single room. Antonio de Córdoba, silversmith, 40 years of age.
74. Single room. Joaquín Aróstegui, silversmith, 30 years of age.
101. Two story house. Juan de Córdoba, 53 years of age, a bachelor, silversmith.
104. José de Sendejas, 25 years of age, silversmith, with one son 6 years of age.
117. Two story house. José de Olivera, owner of the silver-shop, 36 years of age.
118. Two story house. Francisco González, owner of the silver-shop, 50 years of age.
128. Two story house. Valentin de Soto, owner of the silver-shop, 32 years of age. Son, José, 13 years of age.
141. Two story house. Cristobal Garrido, owner of the silver-shop, 30 years of age.
142. Two story house. Rafael Roto, 30 years of age, silversmith.

FIRST BLOCK OF TACUBA STREET EAST TO WEST

5. Two story house. José Cruz, owner of the silver-shop.

SECOND BLOCK OF TACUBA STREET FROM EAST TO WEST

34. Two story house. Pedro de Avila, owner of the silver-shop, married to Ana Flores. Two apprentices, Pedro Fuentes, 15 years of age and Tomás Tenorio, 14 years of age.

THIRD BLOCK OF DONCELES STREET FROM WEST TO EAST

8. Single room. Juan de Argumedo, 36 years of age, married to Ana Cadeña. Sons, Marcos, 10 years of age and José, 6 years of age. Silversmith and owners of a cigarette shop.

FIRST BLOCK OF DONCELES STREET

41. Single room. Juan de Estrada, 50 years of age. Married to Andrea de Araujo. Son, Juan, 15 years of age.

55. Two story house. Francisco de la Peña, assayer of the Royal Mint, married to María Soroaide y Palacios. Sons, Francisco, 25 years of age; Mariano, 18 years of age and José, 16 years of age.

SECOND BLOCK OF LA CANOA STREET

21. Juan de Ontiveros, silversmith, 50 years of age.

AGUILA STREET FROM WEST TO EAST

19. Tenement house. Pedro Castillo, silversmith, 31 years of age. Son, Ignacio, 1 year of age.

28. Two story house. José Salinas, silversmith, 26 years of age.

FIRST [BLOCK] OF MEDINAS STREET

13. Single room. Juan Montiel, silversmith, married to María Pereira.

22. Two story house. Mariano Góngora, silversmith, 30 years of age, married to Juana Montiel. Son, Fermín, 5 years of age.

AGUILA STREET

11. Tenement house. Joaquín Medina, silversmith, married to Manuela Urisa.

22. Tenement house. Agustin Acha, silversmith, 30 years of age, married to Francisca Flores. Sons, José, 6 years of age; Bernardino, 5 months.

STREET WHICH GOES FROM THE CHAPEL TO LOS DOLORES TO THE CONVENT OF LA CONCEPCION

1. One story house. José Vallejos, silver-shop owner, married to Josefa Monroy. Son, José, three months old.

STREET RUNNING EAST AND WEST ACROSS FROM THE ORCHARD OF THE CONVENT OF SANTO DOMINGO

2. Single room. Juan de Soria, 30 years of age, silversmith, married to Antonia.

FROM THE CONVENT OF SANTO DOMINGO TO PILA SECA STREET

27. Two story house. Manuel Taña, married to Gertrudis Ruiz. Son, Pedro, 16 years of age. With a silver-shop.

LITTLE PARK OF THE CONVENT OF LA CONCEPCION

2. Single room. José Leñigo, a bachelor, 57 years of age, a silversmith.

ACROSS FROM THE CHURCH OF LA MISERICORDIA

4. Tenement house. Miguel Arenas, 60 years of age, a silversmith, married to Gertrudis García. Son, Joaquín, 32 years of age, a silversmith.

FIFTH BLOCK AS FAR AS THE MISERICORDIA BRIDGE

3. Tenement house. Cristobal Martínez, a silversmith, married to Manuela Osorio.

FIFTH BLOCK GOING TOWARDS THE CORNER OF SANTA CLARA

5. Single room. Sebastian Rodríguez, 50 years of age, a silversmith, married to María Zúñiga. Sons: José, 12 years of age and Sebastian, 8.
6. Two story house. Felipe Pérez, silversmith, married to María Montoya.

BLOCK WHICH GOES TOWARDS THE AMAYA BRIDGE

9. Tenement house. José Oliver, silversmith, 50 years of age, married to Ignacia Mascareñas.

FOURTH BLOCK OF SANTO DOMINGO STREET

3. Two story house. José Salvatierra, 30 years of age, owner of silver-shop, married to Ana Cabrera, Sons: José, 6 years of age and Santiago, 5.

SECOND BLOCK OF SANTO DOMINGO

2. Single Room. José Cabrera, with silver-shop, fifty years of age, married to María de Aro. Sons: José, 15 years of age, Mariano 12, José de San Agustin, 6.

FIFTH BLOCK WHICH FOLLOWS

Pedro Quiros, silversmith, 31 years of age, married to Mariana Moreno. Son: Dionisio, 5 years of age.

Juan de Rojas, silversmith, 26 years of age, married to Bernarda de León.

THIRD BLOCK OF RELOJ STREET

3. Single room. Juan López, master silversmith, a native of Cadiz, 28 years of age, and four residing in the kingdom, married to Clara Lodos. Son: Hilarión, 2 years of age. Apprentice Manuel Osorio, 12 years of age.
7. Single room. Ignacio Toriz, silversmith, 25 years of age, married to María Rincon.

SEVENTH BLOCK OF RELOJ STREET

2. Single room. Silversmith shop of Pedro Limas, 50 years of age, married to Feliciana González. Apprentice, Ventura Zúñiga, 12 years of age.

LAS MORAS STREET

4. Tenement house. Salvador Sixmundo (Sejismundo?) silversmith, 25 years of age, married to Ana Tellez.
10. Two story tenement house. José Brito, silversmith, 50 years of age, married to María Saens.
12. Single room. Juan Cásares, silversmith, 55 years of age, married to Catarina Ponce.

LA ENCARNACION STREET

9. Single room. Micaela Rodriguez, mother of Antonia, married to Anselmo, a silversmith.

CORDOBANES STREET

5. Single room. Antonio Romero, silversmith, 36 years of age, married to María Barrios, Sons: Santiago, 8 years of age; Ignacio, 4; José, 1.
9. Tenement house. José Arenas, silversmith, 50 years of age, married to María García.
30. Tenement house. Raimundo Escobar, silver-shop owner, 24 years of age, married to Ana Barrera.

The following is quoted from a document signed by the *Veedores, Mayordomos* and *Diputados* of the Guild in 1790:[40]

In compliance with the Superior Order of the Viceroy, Count of Revilla gigedo, of the 12th March, 1790, the signatures of the *Veedores, Mayordomos* and *Diputados* of the Silversmiths, *Batiojas* and *Tiradores*, are shown as follows:

Eduardo Calderón, *Veedor**	José Antonio del Castillo
Gregorio Vasques	José Antonio de las Cassas
Fernando Samano*	Josef María Rodallega*
Alejandro Antonio Cañas*	Mathias Vilches
Manuel de los Ríos	Miguel Ruiz Cano
Joaquín Esveje	Josef María Guzman
José Ygnacio de la Peña	Ygnacio Barrera
José Yglesias	Joachin Perez de Billa Rl.* (Villareal)
José Felipe Cardona	José Bera
José Licona	José Antonio Villegas

40 *Archivo General de la Nación. Industria Artística y Manufacturera.* vol. V. 1746-92, pp.241-3.

Tomás Chamuzgado	José Anastasio Garsia Villegas
Manuel Montes de Oca*	Manuel Apase*
Sebastian Rodríguez*	Miguel Lozano
Josef de Berta (Verta)*	José Herebalo
Miguel Rojas	Ramón Sánches de Almazán.*

Those marked with an asterisk were master silversmiths, concerning whom we have information from other sources.

The following is a list of silversmiths, dated 29th December 1792:[41]

List of silversmiths who are deemed worthy of a license to practise their trade: the first eight will soon take their examination, and the others, although skillful, are not yet ready for it.

1.	Rogelio Cárdenas	27.	José Caraballal
2.	Vicente León	28.	José Hipólito Mencera
3.	José María Guzmán	29.	Mariano Moroso
4.	José Ignacio Chamusgado	30.	Manuel Torralba
5.	Francisco Galván	31.	Pedro Estrada
6.	José Figueroa	32.	Ignacio Romero
7.	Manuel Villarreal	33.	Juan Díaz de la Cueva
8.	Ignacio Noriega	34.	José Mariano de la Cueva
9.	Nicolás Ramirez	35.	Ignacio Ramirez
10.	Juan Villarreal	36.	Ignacio Mendoza
11.	Cristóbal Senteno	37.	José Tello Meneces
12.	Marcelo Polanco	38.	Luis García
13.	Lorenzo Velázquez	39.	José García
14.	Lorenzo Plaza	40.	Miguel Oropeza
15.	José María Castro	41.	Mariano Perez
16.	Pedro Velasco	42.	Manuel León
17.	José Olaez	43.	Rafael de Urbina
18.	José Martinez	44.	Martín Carmona
19.	José Noriega	45.	Ignacio Maure
20.	Felix Romero	46.	Agustín Villegas
21.	Ignacio Negrete	47.	Francisco Mascareñas
22.	Jerónimo Cortés	48.	Pedro Mexía
23.	Mariano de la Torre	49.	Rafael Pérez
24.	Manuel Leal	50.	Joaquín Fuentes
25.	José María Vallín	51.	Manuel Tineo
26.	Manuel Prieto	52.	José Uribe

41 *Archivo General de la Nación. Industria.* vol.5, p.255.

53. Antonio Concha
54. Francisco de la Torre
55. Agustín Rodriguez
56. Manuel Rodriguez
57. Cristobal Barbabosa
58. Martín Bustos.
59. José Barrientos
60. Miguel Torres
61. José Manzano
62. Pedro Márquez
63. Mariano Velasco
64. Santiago Contreras
65. Ignacio Barbabosa
66. Rafael Mondragón
67. Antonio Quintana
68. Pedro Vélez
69. Ignacio de la Maza
70. José Robledo
71. Manuel Chirlin

72. Francisco Ugía
73. Ignacio Ruiz
74. José San Ciprian
75. Francisco Godoy
76. Francisco Villegas
77. Pedro Pierola
78. Felipe Espinosa
79. José Antonio Aguirre
80. Miguel Castera
81. Miguel Picazo
82. Juan Antonio Rodríguez
83. Francisco de la Fuente
84. Ignacio Bárcenas

México, 29 December, 1792. [Signed] Antonio Forcada y la Plaza. José María del Castillo, *Veedor*. Joaquín Espejel, *Mayordomo*. Miguel Ruiz Cosío, *Diputado*. [Rubrics].

4. *The Silversmiths' Art at the End of the Eighteenth Century*

Although the advancement of the silversmiths' art during the entire eighteenth century as regards technique as well as production was not neglected, during the second half and particularly in the third part of that century it received new and vigorous support. This movement continued up to the nineteenth century and was divided into very different phases: the first, essentially Mexican, which, judging from the existing examples, probably lasted from around 1750 until about 1795; and the second, when the influence of the Academy and particularly of Manuel Tolsá commenced to be felt, from about 1795.

FIRST PHASE OF THE MOVEMENT
1750-1795

As time passed, artists were developed. There was an enormous increase in the production of precious metals during the second half of the eighteenth century. Several centuries of peace and idleness in a land where practically the entire wealth of the country was held by

a very few aristocrats developed discriminating connoisseurs of beautiful things. This ideal combination of circumstances produced a noted
group of master silversmiths. Judging from the objects available for
study, the movement which I have classified as the first phase began
about 1750 and continued to increase in strength until it reached its
maximum during the ten years preceding the great increase of influence of the Academy of San Carlos, around 1795.

The lack of direct contact with European culture helped to produce
a phase of the art which, despite its European origin, was essentially
Mexican. It achieved an air which owed nothing to Europe, which
consistently avoided the air of the boudoir, which is felt in the plate
of Spain and Italy of that period, and possesses an air of peace and quiet
reflecting, perhaps, the magnificent simplicity of the lives of the rulers
of Mexico. One feels that its decoration, however ornate, is functionally
so — that precisely the decoration it bears was necessary to express the
feeling of the artist, and not designed merely to impress or catch the
eye of the buyer.

Many examples of this period are shown. Among these, those worthy
of special mention are the cruets, altar bell and small platter, *Plate* 107,
work of the noted master José María Rodallega, made towards the
end of the eighteenth century. This exquisite work may well be pointed
out as a perfect example of this period.

Others worthy of study are shown in *Plates* 104, 105, 106, 108, 109
112, 113 and 114.

SECOND PHASE OF THE MOVEMENT
1795-1862

1. *The Academy of St. Charles of New Spain*

A project of the Superintendent of the Mint at that time, Fernando
J. Manjino,[42] was approved by the King by Royal Ordinance of the
25th November 1785 and the Academy of St. Charles of New Spain
was founded, and the four masters who came from Europe were installed on the 18th September 1786.[43]

42 Or Mangino.
43 *El Viajero en México*, op.cit., pp.355-60.

This is the first instance where Mexico endeavored to import European culture in a systematic way. The European masters of the Academy immediately began to exercise a most profound influence, destined to change forever the trend of the arts in Mexico, replacing the colorful and genuinely Mexican forms by the classical style, which never felt at ease in Mexico.

The influence of the Academy on the silversmiths' art was not felt until 1789, when the second Count of Revilla Gigedo (1789-1794) one of the most vigorous and enthusiastic Viceroys that Spain sent to Mexico, heeded the suggestion of Bonilla, then Superintendent of the Academy of St. Charles, and insisted that silversmiths' apprentices should attend the drawing classes at the Academy.

Imbued with classicism, the apprentices of the time, who were destined to be masters later on, were taught the merits of the classical style and contempt for the truly Mexican forms being produced by Rodallega and his contemporaries.

2. *Manuel Tolsá*

At the death of José Arias,[44] Manuel Tolsá was named to succeed him. Tolsá was born in the village of Euguerra, Province of Valencia, Spain, on the 24th December 1757, and studied in the Academy of the Three Noble Arts of St. Charles in Valencia, where later he was an instructor. Tolsá left Valencia the 24th December 1790, bringing with him 76 cases of models, forms and books. After a long journey, with stopovers in Cadiz and Havana, he arrived in Mexico on the 22nd July 1791. Already a celebrated master and a man of great energy and enthusiasm, he took particular interest in the silversmiths' art. Not only the apprentices but the old masters very soon abandoned their current forms, so lovely and peculiar to Mexico, which they had followed until then, and adopted the classical renaissance style which Tolsá introduced. Escontría says:[45]

At the time Tolsá arrived in Mexico there was a great demand for copper-gilt, as these ornaments were the style; and although there were gilt artists here of

44 The greater part of this information was taken from the work of the architect Alfredo Escontría entitled: *Breve Estudio de la Obra y Personalidad del Escultor y Arquitecto Manuel Tolsá*. Mexico, 1929. Imp. El Progreso. *Boletín de la Sociedad Mexicana de Geografía y Estadística.*
45 Alfredo Escontría, op.cit.

great merit, like the famous Luis Rodríguez de Alconedo, creator of the magnificent coat of arms formerly on the main gates of the cathedral of Mexico, Tolsá soon surpassed them in this kind of work, which in addition to the excellence of the sculptor and the gold and silversmith, included the difficult technique of fire gilding where the polish or dullness of the pieces gilded require great skill on the part of the artisan who must make the principal parts stand out, as several complicated operations are required to achieve the final effect.

Of this type of work he made several noted pieces, among which we should mention first the beautiful statue of the Immaculate Conception which is at the top of the tabernacle of the Cathedral of Puebla, modelled and cast by Tolsá and gilded under his supervision by the noted silversmith of Puebla, Simón Salmón. This piece, as José Manzo says, 'is surprising in its beauty and symmetry, something difficult to accomplish in a piece of such great size and enormous weight.' It is a pity that because of the height and position of this statue its details cannot be admired.

For the same Cathedral of Puebla, Tolsá modelled and designed all the pieces of bronze adorning the aforesaid tabernacle. These consist of seraphs, festoons, brackets, rosettes, crosses, capitals and bases of columns and some large monograms of Mary, all of which show the good taste and skill of Tolsá as well as their marvelous fire gilt made under his supervision by the silversmith Antonio Caamañò.

Beautiful examples of superb workmanship under Tolsá's influence may be found in *Plates* 119, 120, 123, 124, 146, 147, 149 and 150.

As proven by the numerous pieces bearing a hall-mark other than the silversmith's own, the requisite established in 1701 that the silversmith should stamp his own hall-mark on the fabricated silver was never fully complied with.

This was probably due to the fact that the only purpose of marking in Mexico was to aid in discovering frauds and once the plate was taxed and assayed the authorities considered the stamping of the name of the silversmith no longer essential.

Whether for this or for other reasons, less than 25 per cent of the antique silver which I have seen bears the name of the maker. When hall-marks of silversmiths are found on plate the name is stamped in full or abbreviated. When the piece is made in two or more parts, in some cases the full name is found on one and the abbreviation on the others. Initials alone were not used.[46] Furthermore, the name stamped on plate indicated the silver-shop where the piece was fabricated. Thus

46 Only in plate made after 1840 have I seen the initials of the silversmith, although in these cases they also bear his name.

the piece may have been made by a silversmith, an employee of the same shop, a partner or a member of the family.

MIGUEL MARÍA MARTEL

Miguel María Martel was born in Andalucía in the year 1769,[47] and his examination to become a master and to open a shop was confirmed in 1794.[48] He was elected *Veedor* in 1802[49] and in 1816.[50]

Many pieces which bear his name are falsifications. His genuine mark is the following:

The best of the falsifications of Martel's mark, made by Apolonio Guevara:

JPH. MARIANO ABILA

1784

Abila's examination to be licensed as a master and to open a shop was confirmed on the 27th September 1784,[51] and we have no other information about him. However his mark is frequently found and is as follows:

From the official marks accompanying his own, I judge that he worked until around 1810.

47 *Archivo General de la Nación. Empadronamiento de 1811.*
48 *Archivo General de la Nación. Ordenanzas.* vol.16, p.156 reverse. 1764.
49 Ibid., vol.16, p.191 reverse. 1764. 8th January 1802.
50 Ibid., vol.16, p.201 reverse. 1764. 9th March 1816.
51 Ibid., vol.16, p.136 reverse. 1784.

ALEJANDRO ANTONIO DE CAÑAS

Born in Aculco in 1755,[52] Cañas' examination to be licensed as a master and open a shop was approved on the 27th September 1786.[53]

In 1794 he was elected *Veedor*[54] and again in 1804.[55] As late as the year 1831 reference is made to him, and his hall-mark, which frequently appears, is the following:

JOSE LUIS RODRIGUEZ ALCONEDO

Famous silversmith at the end of the eighteenth century and beginning of the nineteenth. A street in Mexico bears his name. Marroqui[56] says concerning him:

ALCONEDO STREET

This street runs from East to West, next to that of *Rebeldes*.

It owes its name to José Luis Rodríguez Alconedo, silver-shop owner, whose shop was on Plateros Street. His work was outstanding among other silversmiths. In the year 1805 he was a worthy member of the Academy in the branch of embossed work. He was in charge of making the fire-gilded bronze letters which were placed on the gates of the *Plaza de Armás*, decorated by the Marquis de Branciforte, to erect therein the equestrian statue of Charles IV. The shop where this work was done was at his home, located on the street which still bears his name.

He was also renowned for his work in copper gilt.

According to Romero de Terreros y Vinent[57] he was accused of having made the crown that José de Iturrigaray was to wear when proclaimed King of Mexico. He enlisted in the insurgent army of Morelos and was shot.

I have seen no plate bearing his mark.

52 *Archivo General de la Nación. Empadronamiento de* 1811.
53 *Archivo General de la Nación. Ordenanzas.* vol.16, p.146. 1764.
54 Ibid., vol.16, p.177 reverse. 1764. 9th January 1794.
55 Ibid., vol.16, p.193 reverse. 1764. 7th January 1804.
56 Op.cit., vol.I, p.282.
57 *Las Artes Industriales en la Nueva España*, p.40.

EIGHTEENTH CENTURY

EIGHTEENTH CENTURY

EIGHTEENTH CENTURY

EIGHTEENTH CENTURY # EIGHTEENTH CENTURY

EIGHTEENTH CENTURY

THE SILVERSMITHS CARDONA
1755-1811

Felipe, the father of the silversmiths Cardona, was born in Mexico City in the year 1755 and his sons, José María, Antonio and Agustín, had their shop at No.7 in the first block of Alcaicería Street. Their work is beautifully executed. Their genuine mark:

JOSE MARIA RODALLEGA
1772-1812

José María Rodallega, famous silversmith who worked around the end of the eighteenth century and the beginning of the nineteenth, was born in Guadalajara in 1741. His examination to be licensed as a master and open a shop in the City of Mexico was confirmed on the 22nd October 1772.

As early as 1780 he began to fabricate works of importance for the churches of New Spain; in 1781, 1783, 1810 and 1811 he was elected *Veedor* of the Silversmiths' Guild.

His last known work was completed in 1807, but in 1811, at 70 years of age, he was still managing his silver-shop at No.16 Plateros Street, now Francisco I. Madero Street.

There are many descriptions of the noted works of this great master. One of the first, made approximately in 1780 was 'a key for the repository, made of gold, used by the one carrying [the repository] on Holy Thursday, which has the handle adorned with a hundred and twenty-seven rose diamonds and three flat diamonds mounted on silver. This key hangs from a thin chain of Chinese gold three *varas* long.'[58] Thirteen years later he made a silver lamp, with superimposed pieces of the same metal, for the Profesa, principal church of the Jesuits in Mexico, then in the hands of the Philippian Fathers.

The documents of the time and the inventories mention 59 pieces

[58] Manuscript loaned to me by Federico Gómez de Orozco: *Inventario de los vasos sagrados, alhajas de esta Santa Iglesia Metropolitana de México, siendo Tesorero el Sr. Doctor Don Félix Osores, año de 1843.* All these descriptions were taken from the same source.

fabricated by this master for the Metropolitan Cathedral between 1780 and 1807. The cost of these, as given in the inventories, was $67,077 *pesos*. One of the most beautiful was a cross with crucifix and base of gold, which cost $10,547 *pesos*. It was inlaid with approximately a thousand precious stones, including about 120 emeralds, 213 rubies and 575 diamonds.

The largest piece made by him was 'a candlestick for the Paschal candle, of a compact wood, with superimposed pieces and moldings of mixed silver, figures of the same material that serve as legs, with figures of children, also of silver, on the pedestal. According to the old inventory it has 818 *marcos*, seven ounces, two *ochavas* of white silver and two hundred and fifty-eight *castellanos* of gold. It cost $15,424 *pesos*. . . . With the candle on it, it forms a column nine full *varas* in height, whose value is estimated at more than thirty thousand *pesos*. For this reason we believe that it is hardly possible for any other to be lighted which is as majestic and rich in the entire Christian world.'

Rodallega was paid about two *pesos* an ounce for his works for the Cathedral, a large part of which payment he received in the form of old plate belonging to the Cathedral.

He produced a great quantity of plate, many examples of which still exist and are in the hands of private collectors. Examples are shown in *Plates* 107, 114 and 149.

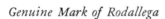

Genuine Mark of Rodallega   *Forged Mark*

Genuine Mark Enlarged

Chapter IX

THE SILVERSMITHS' ART 1800-1936

I. THE BEGINNING OF THE NINETEENTH CENTURY. 2. THE INDEPEN-
DENCE AND THE SILVERSMITHS' ART. 3. THE FRENCH INVASION. 4. ORIGIN
OF THE MEXICAN CHARRO AND HIS EQUIPMENT. 5. THE SILVERSMITHS
OF THE NINETEENTH CENTURY AND THEIR WORKS. 6. THE TWENTIETH
CENTURY.

I. *The Beginning of the Nineteenth Century*

FROM the beginning of the nineteenth century, the Mexican silversmiths formed a school in which the master was followed with such zeal that a style, known in Mexico since that time as 'Tolsá' was created. This industrious artist influenced the silversmiths of that period through his works and his personality to such an extent that even after his death, in 1816, and until the time of the French invasion, in 1863, his style continued to dominate the imaginations of the Mexican silversmiths.

During that period, the demand for artistic objects and the wealth of individuals as well as of the Catholic Clergy seem to have been but little affected by the disturbed condition of the country during the war for its independence (1810-1821).

Even the numerous robberies of the period stimulated the silversmiths' art, as the clergy tried to replace their lost treasures. From the time nationalization of church properties began in 1859 until the present, there have been no great pieces of plate fabricated for the church. Since the fall of General Porfirio Díaz in 1911, the only movement of importance has been the sale of plate belonging to individuals who have been forced by circumstances to part with it.

2. *The Independence and the Silversmiths' Art*

We have already seen that the laws and ordinances of Spain forbade anyone of 'broken color' to practice the silversmiths' trade. Until 1821 the silversmiths were Spaniards or the descendants of Spaniards. For this reason, while the original works they produced were unmistakably Mexican, they were European in feeling.

The Independence opened the gates of the art to all. The Indian artisan of that period, as well as those of today, when given sufficient time for his work, is as competent as, or superior to, any other; for in addition to his natural aptitude he has an almost unbelievable patience which is lacking in many other races. In spite of this, the Indian could not be expected to produce original works in a style foreign to his own feelings. Owing to the demand for objects in the 'Tolsá' style, those of Indian blood who entered the trade made reproductions. For this reason the only silversmiths who produced original works, after 1821, were the experts of Spanish blood of the old school, or new arrivals from Europe, the latter very few in number.

Doubtless for this reason, a decadence in technique is noted during the period from 1840 to 1863. However, it must be borne in mind that some of the sons of the master silversmiths of colonial times, inspired by the masters themselves, continued working until the middle of the nineteenth century, faithfully following their traditions. Prominent among these were José María Folco, who worked until 1847, Pedro Ochoa who still worked in 1852, Antonio Carillo who remained working in 1864 and Pedro Cañas, whose shop was open, still, in 1865.

3. *The French Invasion*

The French invasion deeply affected the cultural life of the country, dominating completely the conceptions of the patrons of the arts of that time. Beautiful old colonial furniture and objects were soon re-placed by French things while the former were sent to the store-rooms, or turned over to the servants or to the second hand dealers. Although, with the death of Emperor Maximilian in 1867, the political aspect of the French invasion ended, it was not so as regards the Mexican people, among whom this cultural influence unfortunately persists today.

If the Tolsá style did not lend itself to the naïve yet regal air which the Mexican silversmiths imparted to their work, the boudoir-like style of France was even more fatal to it. While the duration of the

French invasion was much too brief to impose a new school it helped, nevertheless, to give the final blow to the already decadent colonial art of the Mexican silversmiths. No original plate of artistic merit has been produced in Mexico since 1863. L'Enfer, a silversmith of the City of Puebla, who worked about the year 1852, apparently was the only one who tried to do original work. Unfortunately his taste was very bad indeed.

4. *Origin of the Mexican Charro and His Equipment*[1]

'The Mexican *charro* originated in Salamanca, Spain, where the peasant is called by that name.

The Mexican cattle-saddle is a modification of the Spanish and Arabian saddles.

The Conquerors brought the first horses, of Arabian origin, and Bernal Diaz del Castillo has left us a description of them. In the *Lienzo de Tlaxcala* and in the *Colección de Codices* published by the *Junta Colombina* in 1892 may be seen the marks of the branding iron . . .

The horse, an animal unknown to our natives, multiplied rapidly in the immense Mexican pasture lands and finally became an absolute necessity to the farmer. The first *charros* were the cattle ranchers and their farm hands, who had to handle wild animals. . . .

As the landholders began to breed both horses and cattle on the open ranges, the necessity to lasso, ride broncos and break them to rein and saddle, etc. became more urgent and in order to catch the broncos, the *charros* resorted to the rope and soon became expert. As a result, it was necessary to modify the saddle in order to perform these feats, replacing the front bow of the saddle by the saddle horn, which has rendered such good service. The Spanish head piece and mouth loop were replaced by the nose band of horse hair or hemp rope such as used for breaking horses for the saddle. Saddle bags of hairy goat skin, were invented, which are fastened to the saddle-tree, one hanging to each side. These are large pouches where the lasso is kept to protect it from the sun and rain and where the tie ropes are carried. The tail piece of the saddle was also invented. This is a short

1 For this valuable contribution I am indebted to don Carlos Rincón Gallardo, Marquis of Guadalupe

skirt of heavy stamped leather, that covers the hind quarters of the horse. Its lower edge is bordered with artistically cut rings, from which are hung small ornaments called charms and knobs and the entire set is known as the fringe, which common ranchers call, and not without reason, clatters. . . .

The Mexican saddle is, for our needs, far superior to any other in the entire world. The *machete* is also carried on the saddle, and is very useful to make one's way through the brush, to chop wood, and even on occasion as a weapon. The Mexican stirrup is likewise of Arabian and Spanish origin. The Arabian stirrup covers much of the foot as a protection, the Spanish stirrup covers it even more and the Mexican *charros* added to their stirrups the coverings made out of stamped leather, lined with sole-leather, that completely cover the feet, protecting them against rain, cold weather, thorns, kicks, bull's horns and falls. The Salamancan jacket and trousers were also handed down to our *charros* who gradually modified and adorned them with artistic embroideries and buttons. The *chaqueta* [jacket] retained its name, but the trousers are called *pantaloneras* when the seams are sewed and *calzoneras* when they are buttoned. The primitive *charro* hat resembled that used nowadays by the *picadores* in the bull-ring and the one with high crown and turned-up brim was first worn by Pedro Romero de Terreros y Gomez de Parada who, although he was not a great *charro*, was however a great personage who stood out among his contemporaries as a man of unique elegance.

The bit which we consider strictly Mexican and *charro*, the one with the lower jaw ring, is really Arabian. The Spanish spurs were gradually modified into our present type which are now classified into two groups: those of the ranchers with their long points and large wheels and those for bull-throwing with short points and small wheels. The *chaparreras* [chaps] are the Spanish *zahones* somewhat modified, as the *charros* lengthened them to protect the shins when *coleando* (this maneuver is unknown in Spain), adding to them two *rozaderas* [rubbing pieces] one on each leg to resist the *chorreadas* [friction] of the lasso. The *sarape* [blanket] and the *jorongo* are modifications of the Spanish *manta* [blanket]. The *jorongo* is a short blanket with *bocamanga* [slit to let the head through]; from this comes the proverb: *Cualquier sarape es jorongo abriéndole bocamanga*. [Any *sarape* becomes a *jorongo* if a *bocamanga* is opened in it]. The *ruano* is a *charro* cape from the Mother Country. Even the Spanish *faja* [sash] was inherited by the *charro*, who calls it *ceñidor* [belt].'

5. *Silversmiths of the Nineteenth Century and their Works*

MANUEL MARIANO FERNANDEZ Y CARTAMI

Born in Mexico in 1770,[2] his examination to become a *maestro* and to open a public shop was confirmed on the 1st October 1808.

No falsification of his mark, here illustrated, has been discovered:

Actual Size

ANTONIO CAAMAÑO

From 1799 to 1811 are found references to this prolific artisan who was born in Europe and who was elected *Veedor* in the years 1800, 1801 and 1808. In 1811 he had his shop in the 1st Street of the Alcaicería No.2, and his mark was the following:

Actual Size

There are many falsifications of his mark as shown below:

Enlarged

CARLOS PERALTA

No references to this *Maestro*, whose mark appears on plate engraved

2 Interesting examples of plate fabricated in Mexico during the time of Maximilian are shown in *Plates* 171 and 172. One of the few examples of the French style which subsisted after the fall of Maximilian, and which proves that the improved dies were not destroyed until later, is shown in *Plate* 173. *Archivo General da la Nación*, Census of 1811. Cuartel Menor, No.1 Calle de La Aguila No.24 (vivienda) 2a.

by Buitrón,[3] are found until 1831. Unfortunately, the rare examples I have seen, which bear Peralta's mark, are very much worn.

Enlarged

JOSE MARIA FOLCO

As may be seen from the census, references to Folco appear between the years 1842 and 1859. At this latter date he had his silver-shop on the 1st Calle de Plateros. He must have been a prominent *maestro*, as he served as appraiser for an inventory of the jewels of the Cathedral, made in 1844.

His mark is the following:

Actual Size

JOSE MARIA LARRALDE

References to this silversmith are found during the years 1854-1867, when he had his shop on Arquillo Street.

He made a chalice for the Church of Huehuetoca, prior to 1842, and in the Cathedral exists a stand for a monstrance, of gilded silver, which bears this inscription: *Lo hizo José María Larralde*. 1868. (This was made by José María Larralde. 1868.) His mark was his initials, 'J.M.'

EDUARDO L'ENFER

This silversmith had his shop with five workmen on San Pedro Street, in Puebla, in the year 1852. His mark is an odd one:

Actual Size

It appears that L'Enfer was one of the few silversmiths of the time

3 Mrs. C. H. E. Phillips, of Mexico City, very kindly loaned me a small spoon which bears Peralta's mark, here reproduced.

who endeavored to produce original works, but unfortunately, although of interest to the collector, they lack artistic merit. Two of them are reproduced in *Plates* 167 and 168.

MARIANO BARRAGAN

The first available reference to this *maestro* is in 1854, although he was established in Mexico prior to that date. In 1867 he was located on Olla Street No.2, having been on the 2nd Street of Plateros No.7 during the year 1864.

He was one of the two hundred and fifteen who formed the *Junta de Notables* [Board of the Noted Ones] of the Empire in 1863.

His mark, frequently found, is the following:

Actual Size

JOSE MARIA MARTINEZ

He probably began work prior to 1819, as his mark is frequently found with that of Forcada.

Prior to 1823 he fabricated works of importance as proved by the following quotation:[4]

A gold chalice with paten and two small spoons, altar bell, small platter and two cruets, all of gold, left to the Church at the death of Señor Haro.

This chalice was in the Archbishop's house when the previous inventory was taken, and therefore, omitted, but on the sixth of August of the year one thousand eight hundred and forty two, Atilano Sanchez, who previously had been Attorney-in-Fact to His Excellency Pedro José de Fonte, former Archbishop of this diocese, in the name of the executors of the estate of said prelate, delivered to this Holy Church one chalice with paten, small spoon, cruets and small platter, all of gold, beautifully fabricated, stamped, and with a weight of nine *marcos*, and which, with its manufacture, cost two thousand *pesos* as per the account of silver-shop owner José Ma. Martínez. With this chalice, Señor Fonte considered that [the Church] was reimbursed for the chalice, mentioned among the first items of this inventory, and two or three chasubles with boxes for ornaments and other minor articles which

4 Pages 14-15 of a manuscript, copy of the *Inventario de las alhajas de la Santa Iglesia Metropolitana, levantado por D. José Miguel Abarca, siendo Tesorero el Dr. D. Félix Osores, México, 26 de Dic.* 1844.

His Excellency took with him, when he left for Spain in 1823, and he formed his opinion or judgement, after appraising what he took, which was much less than two thousand *pesos*.

In 1831 he is mentioned as paying taxes[5] and in 1842 had his silver store with shop, on the *Callejon de Mecateros. Accesoria* 19.[6] Curiously, Martínez himself seems to have forged the punches of the authorities to evade payment of taxes, because his genuine hall-mark is found with both genuine and false official marks, as may be seen from the following illustrations which appear on authentic plate:

Martínez' genuine mark with the genuine official marks. Enlarged

Martínez' genuine mark with false official marks. Enlarged

There were also other silversmiths who, during the first quarter of that century, forged Martínez' marks as may be seen:

Actual Size

MARIANO DE LA TORRE

As will be seen from the references corresponding to the census of silversmiths, Appendix I, the examination of Mariano de la Torre to become a *Maestro* and open a public shop was confirmed on the 4th October 1799.

The following is a description of one of his most important works:

The master silversmith, Mariano de la Torre, has also presented today to His Excellency the Vice-President, the sword which should be given as a present to General Bravo in compliance with the decree issued by the congress of the Union that ordered this present made to him. The sword is magnificent, fabricated with exquisite taste and delicacy, and according to the opinion of intelligent men, it

5 *Archivo General de la Nación. Ramo de Hacienda.* Book that reads: *Casa de Ensaye de México.* 1830-1831. *Paquete* 45.
6 *Archivo General de la Nación. Padron de establecimientos industriales. Cuartel menor No.*1. 1842.

could not have been better fabricated in any other country where the arts have made so much progress. It has on the handle a figure in beautiful relief that, resting on military trophies, represents Victory and is adorned with diamonds, delicately mounted; and at its end is a head of Hercules symbolic of strength. The handle is formed by two cornucopias from which fruits and flowers are pouring and these are beautifully made. On the scabbard are shown the national arms, all of precious stones; the eagle is made of diamonds with a most beautiful solitaire in the center; the cactus leaves with emeralds and the cactus fruit of rubies. The entire handle is of gold as well as the scabbard; and on the blade is engraved with acid the inscription ordered by congress. This work is most magnificent and gives great credit to the Mexican arts.[7]

On the 21st January 1836,[8] the records show Mariano de la Torre as silver-shop owner, with a store in house letter B of the first Street of *Plateros*, where he had been established for several years.

His mark was often imitated and I have not been fortunate enough to find any object marked with his original die. That reproduced here is one of the common imitations:

Actual Size   *Enlarged*

Complete lists of silversmiths of various periods of the nineteenth century are as follows:

PLATEROS. 1811
(*Archivo General de la Nación*
Census of 1811)

ARQUILLO STREET

7. Joaquín García. Son of Antonia Mora, 19 years of age. [Born in] Guanajuato.

---

7 *Registro Oficial del Gobierno de los Estados Unidos Mexicanos — Año* 2° *Tomo V — Núm.*32, *del Miércoles* 1° *de Junio* 1831.
8 *Escritura* loaned to me by my friend Federico Gómez de Orozco.

SMALL ARCHWAY ENTERING THROUGH EMPEDRADILLO STREET

8. Lower floor. Andrés Ladrón de Guevara. Valladolid, 32 years of age.
   Antonia Gutiérrez, his wife, 28 years of age.
   Miguel Guevara, his son, Mexico. 10 years of age.
   Mariano Guevara. His son. 4 years of age. Mexico.
9. Joaquín Martínez, son of Mrs. María Arcos. Puebla. 15 years of age.
10. Agustín Herrera, son of Rafaela Arana. Mexico. 18 years of age.
11. Anselmo Aguilera. Mexico. 15 years of age.

NORTH SIDE OF DONCELES STREET

25. Silver-shop. Mrs. María Antonia González. Cuernavaca. 45 years of age
    José Madariaga. Veracruz. 40 years of age.
25. Entrance Hall. Pedro Aviles. Pachuca. 23 years of age.

SOUTH SIDE OF TACUBA STREET

13. Lower floor. Agustín Ruiz. Mexico. 45 years of age.
    María Avila, his wife. Tlaxcala. 46 years of age.
    José Mariano, his son. Mexico. 14 years of age.
6. Miguel Aguirre, Mexico. 30 years of age.
   Joaquina Vargas, his wife. Mexico. 22 years of age.
7. José Contreras. Mexico. 65 years of age.

NEAR SANTO DOMINGO STREET

5. Juan Herrera, son of Mrs. María Pizaño. Mexico. 18 years of age.

NORTH SIDE OF STREET. TENEMENT LA MERCED

16. Domingo Soto. Born in Temascaltepec. 30 years of age.
    María Bueno, his wife. Temascaltepec. 28 years of age.

TENEMENT OF SAN JOSE DE LA PILA

Manuel Portugues. Guadalajara. 31 years of age.
María Josefa Ruiz, his wife. Mexico. 25 years of age.

SECOND BLOCK OF PILA SECA STREET

3. Inn of Our Lady of Guadalupe. Apartment No.6 on second floor.
   Martín Cariñona. Mexico. 40 years of age.
   Mrs. María del Carmen Elizalde. 38 years of age.

ESCLAVO STREET

9. Victoriano Perusquía, son of Mrs. María Solís. Mexico. 16 years of age.

MISERICORDIA STREET

7. José María Camacho. Querétaro. 39 years of age.
   María Dolores Yociar, his wife. Querétaro.
   J.Buenaventura, his son. Querétaro. 10 years of age.
   Gumersindo, his son. Mexico. 8 months old.
9. Marcos Gutiérrez. Guanajuato. 33 years of age.

SECOND BLOCK OF SAN LORENZO STREET

7. Miguel Alvarado. Mexico. 37 years of age.
   Ignacia Cerero, his wife. Mexico. 33 years of age.
   Antonio Alvarado, his son. Mexico. 10 years of age.
   José Alvarado, his son. Mexico. 6 years of age.
17. Vicente Castro. Ixmiquilpan. 34 years of age.
    Guadalupe Cenil. Ixmiquilpan. 29 years of age. His wife.
18. Miguel Pavia. Mexico. 40 years of age.
    María Hernández, his wife. Mexico. 38 years of age.
    José Miguel Pavia, his son. Mexico. 16 years of age.
    Nestor Pavia, his son. Mexico. 5 years of age.
    José María, an orphan. Guanajuato. 18 years of age. Silversmith.
22. Rafael Artega. Mexico. 18 years of age.

AGUILA STREET. SOUTH SIDE

1. Ramón Sánchez Almazán. Mexico. 65 years of age. Owner of silver-shop.
3. Mariano Manzanar. Mexico. 24 years of age.
   Nicolás Manzanar. Mexico. 21 years of age.
House without a number. Mariano Rodríguez. Apam. 34 years of age.
   Mrs. Agustina Colima, his wife. Apam. 28 years of age.
10. Second floor. Luis López Puentes. Mexico. 68 years of age. Owner of silver-shop.
    María Araujo, his wife. Mexico. 40 years of age.
10. Ground floor. Juan José Barrios. Mexico. 54 years of age.
    María Tejadilla, his wife. Mexico. 50 years of age.
    Juan José Barrios, his son. Mexico. 5 years of age.

AGUILA STREET. NORTH SIDE

18. José Mariano Gallo. Tlaxcala. 45 years of age.
    María Guadalupe Cordero, his wife. Mexico. 32 years of age.
    José María, his son. Mexico. 4 years of age.
    Juan Pedro, his son. Mexico. 2 years of age.

19. Manuel Estrada. Mexico. 16 years of age.
24. Manuel Cartami. Mexico. 41 years of age. Owner of silver-shop.
    Bernabé de Lara, his wife. Mexico. 38 years of age.
Room No.4. José Luis Pardo. Puebla. 22 years of age.
Room No.5. Gabriel Díaz Varela. Puebla. 34 years of age.
            Josefa Ruiz, his wife. Tepozotlán. 30 years of age.
            José, his son. Mexico. 16 years of age.
            Manuel, his son. Mexico. 12 years of age.
            Gregorio, his son. Mexico. 6 years of age.

SAN JOSE EL REAL STREET

9. Room No.2, ground floor. Miguel Oropeza. Mexico. 45 years of age.

CANOA STREET

10. Room 5 ground floor. José Guzmán. Mexico. 73 years of age.
10. Rooms 2 and 3 second floor. José Luis Ordaz. Mexico. 13 years of age.

VERGARA STREET

8. Room 2, ground floor. José Manuel García. Mexico. 28 years of age.
   María Antonia Ximenez, his wife. Mexico. 26 years of age.

THIRD BLOCK SAN FRANCISCO STREET

1. José Ignacio Ochoa. Valladolid. 34 years of age.

SANTA CLARA STREET

5. Lower floor. José Morales. Veracruz. 24 years of age.
   José María Herrera, step-son. Mexico. 14 years of age.
6. Room 3 lower floor. José Castillo. Mexico. 29 years of age.
   Ana Ximénez. Mexico. 22 years of age.
5. Lower floor. Vicente Martínez. Querétaro. 31 years of age.
   Josefa Fernández, his wife. Mexico. 20 years of age.
   Agustín Martínez, his son. Mexico. 4 years of age.
   Ignacio Martínez, his son. Mexico. 3 years of age.
30. Room 4 lower floor. Miguel Potestad. Mexico. 12 years of age.
30. Room 6 lower floor. José Masardua. Mexico. 30 years of age.
    María Garibay, his wife. Mexico. 21 years of age.

BILBAO ALLEY

2. Room No.4 lower floor. José Bellido. Mexico. 32 years of age.

FIRST BLOCK PLATEROS STREET

7. Alejandro Cañas. Aculco. 56 years of age.
   María Josefa Andrea Villegas, his wife. Mexico. 54 years of age.
   Gumersindo Cañas, his son. Mexico. 28 years of age.
   Mateo Cañas, his son. Mexico. 11 years of age.

8 & 9. Miguel María Martel. Andalucía. 42 years of age.
   Maxima Fernández, his wife. Mexico. 30 years of age.
   José Joaquín Martel. Mexico. 15 years of age.
   Miguel Martel. Mexico. 13 years of age.
   Manuel Félix Martel. Mexico. 11 years of age.
   Joaquín Eduardo Martel. Mexico. 10 years of age.
   Antonio Martel. Mexico. 7 years of age.
   Juan Martel. Mexico. 2 years of age.

10. Miguel Cruz, Andalucía. 34 years of age.
    Margarita Calderón. Mexico. 25 years of age.
    Matías Gómez. Santander. 29 years of age.
    Pedro Trueva. Mexico. 22 years of age.

11. José Vera. Tulancingo. 45 years of age.
    Rosalía Bais. Mexico. 40 years of age.
    Patricio Vera. Mexico. 40 years of age.
    Jerónimo Vera. Mexico. 19 years of age.

12. Mariano Ignacio Martínez. Puebla. 36 years of age.
    María Dolores Caro. Mexico. 40 years of age.
    Francisco María Martínez. Mexico. 18 years of age.
    Francisco Dávila. Puebla. 46 years of age.
    Ursula Plol. México. 44 years of age.

13. Pedro Varela. Italy. 39 years of age.
    Ana Morzagaray. Mexico. 30 years of age.
    José Varela. Mexico. 12 years of age.
    Mariano. Mexico. 4 years of age.
    Agustín Varela. Mexico. 5 years of age.
    Fernando Varela. Mexico. 1 year of age.
    José María Cadalso. Mexico. 17 years of age.

14. José Bernal. Mexico. 53 years of age.
    Ana Mansilla. Mexico. 40 years of age.
    Ignacio Cristóbal Bernal. Mexico. 14 years of age.

15. Francisco Galván. Mexico. 44 years of age.

16. José María Rodallega. Guadalajara. 70 years of age.

17. Marcelo Polanco. Mexico. 52 years of age.
    Juan José Polanco. Mexico. 26 years of age.
    María San Ciprian. Mexico. 28 years of age.
    Vicente Bermudes. Mexico. 13 years of age.

SECOND BLOCK OF LA PALMA STREET

2. Pedro Marquez. Mexico. 47 years of age.
   Josefa Alarcón. Mexico. 40 years of age.
4. Single Room. José Angel Fernández de Lara. Zapotlán. 45 years of age.
4. Tenement house. María de la Luz Pierda. Mexico. 40 years of age.
   Mariano Fernández. Mexico. 11 years of age.
   Martín Fernández. Mexico. 10 years of age.
   Mariano José Fernández. 4 years of age.
   Miguel Fernández. Mexico. 3 years of age.
   Juan Fernández. 12 years of age.
5. Tenement No.8. Miguel Ruiz Cano. Mexico. 30 years of age.
4. Tenement No.21. José Valero. Mexico. 30 years of age.
4. Tenement No.23. Manuel Ayala. Mexico. 39 years of age.
   Gregorio Ayala, his son. Mexico. 10 years of age.
   Luis Ayala, his son. Mexico. 9 years of age.
   José Astores. Mexico. 30 years of age.
4. Tenement No.27. José Rafael Amaya. Potosí. 48 years of age.
   Gertrudis García, his wife. Potosí. 38 years of age.
4. Tenement No.30. Joaquín Crespo Contreras. Mexico. 30 years of age.
   Feliciana Fuentes, his wife. Mexico. 40 years of age.
4. Tenement No.31. Vibiano Marchena. Mexico. 24 years of age.
   Magdaleno Marchena. Mexico. 18 years of age.

SECOND BLOCK OF PLATEROS STREET

11. Pedro Escusa. Vizcaya. 44 years of age.
    Simón Salmón. Santander. 36 years of age.
    Gregorio Cortazar. Alava. 53 years of age.
    Fermín de Urcaga. Vizcaya. 29 years of age.
    Carlos Peralta. Mexico. 22 years of age. Apprentice.
    Manuel Rodríguez. Mexico. 20 years of age. Apprentice.
    Manuel Rodríguez. Real del Oro. 16 years of age. Apprentice.

COLISEO VIEJO STREET

Tenement without number. José Ignacio López. Mexico. 61 years of age.
Jerónimo Cortés. Oaxaca. 60 years of age.
Fernando Moctezuma. Mexico. 15 years of age.
José María Dávila. Sierra de Pinos. 32 years of age.

REFUGIO STREET

19. José Manuel Peña. Mexico. 35 years of age.
    José Rafael Pérez. Mexico. 45 years of age.

CADENA STREET

11. José Antonio Espínola. Mexico. 18 years of age.

LIST OF SILVERSMITHS

The lists of silversmiths and silver shops of the nineteenth century are more complete. There are lists for the years 1811, 1842, 1852, 1854, 1859, 1864, 1865, 1867 and 1882, as follows:

ARCHIVO GENERAL DE LA NACIÓN
Census of 1811
Cuartel menor No.1

1st block Tacuba Street No.25 — Tenement No.4.	José Marques. Mexico. 40 years of age. Widower. Silversmith.
1st block Tacuba Street No.25 — Tenement No.2, on ground floor.	Lorenzo de Alba. Mexico. 23 years of age. Silversmith.
	Dolores Serrano. Guadalajara. 25 years of age.
	Juan Alba. Mexico. 3 years of age.
1st block San José el Real Street No.11 — Tenement No.3 on ground floor.	Miguel Malcampo. Mexico. 25 years of age, a bachelor.
1st block Plateros Street No.4. Room No.2, on ground floor.	José Mariano Urruchi. Toluca. 48 years of age. Silversmith.
	Gertrudis Jurado. Atlixco. 43 years of age.
	Mariano. Mexico. 6 years of age.
1st block Plateros Street No.5. Tenement No.2.	Vicente Nuñez. Mexico. 58 years of age. Silversmith.
	María Cruz. Mexico. 57 years of age.
1st block Alcaicería Street No.24.	Manuel Garnote. Mexico. 36 years of age. Guest. Widower. Silversmith.
1st block Alcaicería Street No.2.	Antonio Caamaño. European. 46 years of age. Silversmith.
	Juana Díaz. European. 26 years of age.
1st block Alcaicería Street No.7.	Felipe Cardona. Mexico. 56 years of age.
	Mariana Josefa Alfaro, Mexico. 44 years of age.
	José Marticorena, his son. Mexico. 34 years of age.
	José María Cardona. Mexico. 25 years of age. Silversmith.

Antonio Cardona. Mexico. 24 years of age, silversmith.

Agustín Cardona. Mexico. 22 years of age, silversmith.

José María Gregorio. Mexico. 15 years of age, silversmith.

1st block of Arquillo Street No.5, single room B.

José María de la Torre. Cuautitlán. 26 years of age. Silversmith.

1st block of Arquillo Street No.18, Tenement No.2a.

Miguel Quiroga — Amecameca. 50 years of age. Silversmith.

Cazuela Alley — Letter A.

José María Trujeque. Pachuca. 20 years of age. Silversmith.

1st block Arquillo Street No.4, Tenement No.2a.

Ignacio Ibañez. Mexico. 40 years of age. Silversmith.

1st block Arquillo Street No.4, Room 40.

Bartolo Arauz. Mexico. 40 years of age. Silversmith.

Francisca López. Mexico. 28 years of age.

Ignacio Arauz. Mexico. 9 years of age.

1st block Arquillo Street No.4, Room No.5.

José María Rivera. Zacatecas. 35 years of age. Silversmith.

1st block Arquillo Street No.4, Room No.8.

Francisco González. Mexico. 52 years of age. Silversmith.

María Valero. Mexico. 40 years of age.

Gregorio González. Mexico. 25 years of age. Silversmith.

Joaquín González. Mexico. 18 years of age. Silversmith.

1st block Arquillo Street No.5

Manuel Reyes, Mexico. 50 years of age. Silversmith.

Single room.

Isidro Reyes. Mexico. 30 years of age. Silversmith.

1st block Arquillo Street No.3, without letter.

Francisco Cadalzo. Mexico. 55 years of age. Silversmith.

Guadalupe Rosales. Mexico. 30 years of age.

Cayetano Cadalzo, his son. Mexico. 19 years of age. Silversmith.

1st block Arquillo Street No.7, Room No.7.

Joaquín García. Mexico. 19 years of age. Silversmith.

1st block Arquillo Street No.8, Tenement b.

Miguel Guevara. Mexico. 19 years of age Silversmith.

1st block Arquillo Street No.9, Principal Tenement.	Joaquín Arcos. Puebla. 15 years of age. Silversmith.
1st block Arquillo Street No.10, Room No.20.	Agustin Herrera. Mexico. 18 years of age. Silversmith.
1st block Arquillo Street No.11, Room No.3.	Anselmo Aguilera. Mexico. 15 years of age. Silversmith.
2nd block Donceles Street No.25.	Pedro Avilés. Pachuca. 23 years of age. Silversmith.
2nd block Donceles Street No.25, Letter A.	Pedro Aviles. Pachuca. 23 years of age. Silversmith.
2nd block Donceles Street.	José Paolo, his son. Mexico. 5 years of age.
2nd block Tacuba Street No.13, ground floor No.2.	Mauricio Meza. Xochimilco. 28 years of age. Silversmith.
	Carmelita Montezuma. 26 years of age.
	José, son. Mexico. 11 years of age.
2nd block Tacuba Street No.13, ground floor No.3.	Agustín Ruis. Mexico. 45 years of age. Silversmith.
	María Avila. Tlaxcala. 46 years of age.
	José Mariano. Mexico. 14 years of age.
2nd block Tacuba Street No.6.	Miguel Aguirre. Mexico. 30 years of age. Silversmith.
2nd block Tacuba Street No.7.	José Contreras. Mexico. 65 years of age. Silversmith.
	Ildefonso, son of Neira. 3 years of age.
1st block Santo Domingo Street No.5-A.	Juan Herrera. Mexico. 18 years of age. Silversmith.
4th block Santo Domingo Street.	Domingo Soto. Temascaltepec. 30 years of age. Silversmith.
1st block La Pila Seca Street No.10.	Juan Ignacio Medel. Zempoala. 22 years of age. Silversmith.
Misericordia Street No.7—Interior No.9.	José María Camacho. Querétaro. 39 years of age. Silversmith.
	María Dolores Yrciar. Querétaro. 24 years of age.
	José Buenaventura, son. Querétaro. 10 years of age.
	Gumesindo. Mexico. 8 months old.
Misericordia Street No.9, Letter C.	Marcos Gutiérrez. Guanajuato. 33 years of age. Silversmith.
2nd block San Lorenzo Street No.9—Letter C.	Miguel Alvarado. Mexico. 37 years of age. Silversmith.

	Antonio, his son. Mexico. 10 years of age.
	José, his son. Mexico. 6 years of age.
2nd block San Lorenzo Street No.17, Interior 11.	Vicente Castro. Ixmiquilpan. 34 years of age. Silversmith.
2nd block San Lorenzo Street No.18 B.	Miguel Pavía. Mexico. 40 years of age. Silversmith.
	María Hernández. Mexico. 38 years of age.
	José Miguel, his son. Mexico. 16 years of age.
	Nestor, his son. Mexico. 5 years of age.
	José María, an orphan. Guanajuato. 18 years of age. Silversmith.
2nd block San Lorenzo Street No.22, Tenement on second floor.	Rafael Ortega. Mexico. 18 years of age. Silversmith.
Aguila Street No.1 — Tenement on second floor.	Ramón Sánchez Almazan. Mexico. 65 years of age. Owner of silver-shop.
Aguila Street No.3 — Interior — 9.	Mariano Manzanar. Mexico. 24 years of age. Silversmith.
	Nicolás, his brother. Mexico. 21 years of age. Silversmith.
Aguila Street — Interior No.6.	Mariano Rodríguez. Apam. 34 years of age. Silversmith.
	Agustina Colima. Apam. 28 years of age, his wife.
Aguila Street No.10 — Tenement on second floor.	Luis López Fuentes. Mexico. 68 years of age. Owner of silver-shop.
Aguila Street No.10. Room No.9.	Juan José Barios. Mexico. 54 years of age. Silversmith.
	María Tejadilla. Mexico. 50 years of age.
	Juan José, her son. Mexico. 5 years of age.
Aguila Street No.18 — Room No.15.	José Mariano Gallo. Tlascala. 45 years of age. Silversmith.
	María Guadalupe Cordero. Mexico. 32 years of age.
	José María, her son. Mexico. 4 years of age.
	Juan Pedro, her son. Mexico. 2 years of age.
Aguila Street No.19 — Room 6.	Manuel Estrada. Mexico. 16 years of age. Silversmith.
Aguila Street No.24 — Tenement 2a.	Manuel Cartami. Mexico. 41 years of age. Owner of silver-shop.
	Bernavela de Lara. Mexico. 38 years of age.

Aguila Street No.24 — Room 2.	José Bazan. Colima. 36 years of age. Silversmith.
	María Guadalupe Martínez. Guadalajara. 24 years of age.
Aguila Street No.24 — Room No.4.	José Luis Pardo. Puebla. 22 years of age.
Aguila Street No.24 — Room No.5.	Manuel Díaz Varela. Puebla. 34 years of age. Silversmith.
	Josefa Ruiz, his wife. Tepozotlan. 30 years of age.
	José, his son. Mexico. 16 years of age.
	Manuel, his son. Mexico, 12 years of age.
	Gregorio, his son. Mexico. 6 years of age.
San José el Real Street No.19, Room No.2.	Miguel Oropeza. Mexico. 45 years of age. Silversmith.
San José el Real Street No.19, Tenement No.7.	Joaquín Torrez. Mexico. 14 years of age. Silversmith.
Canoa Street No.10 — Room No.5.	José Guzman. Mexico. 73 years of age. Silversmith.
Canoa Street No.10 — Tenement 3.	José Luis Ordaz. Mexico. 13 years of age. Silversmith.
Vergara Street No.8 — Room No.2.	José Manuel García. Mexico. 28 years of age. Silversmith.
	María Antonia Jimenez. Mexico. 26 years of age.
3rd block San Francisco Street No.8.	José Ignacio Ochoa. Valladolid. 34 years of age. Silversmith.
	María Josefa Valle. Valladolid. 33 years of age.
Santa Clara Street No.5.	José Morales. Veracruz. 24 years of age. Silversmith.
Santa Clara Street No.5.	José María Herrera, step-son. Mexico. 14 years of age.
Santa Clara Street No.6 — Room 3.	José Castillo. Mexico. 29 years of age. Silversmith.
	Ana Jimenez. Mexico. 22 years of age.
Santa Clara Street No.4 — Room 5.	Vicente Martínez. Querétaro. 31 years of age. Silversmith.
	Josefa Fernández. Mexico. 20 years of age.
	Agustin Martínez. Mexico. 4 years of age.
Santa Clara Street No.10 — Room 6.	José Basardua. Mexico. 30 years of age. Silversmith.

ARCHIVO GENERAL DE LA NACIÓN
Census of Industrial Establishments
Cuartel menor No.1
1842

MECATEROS ALLEY

Single Room 19	Silver-store with work-shop	José María Martínez

ALCAISERIA STREET

Single Room A	Silversmith shop	Antonio Ibarra
Single Room 2	Silversmith shop	Hilario de la Maza

MECATEROS ALLEY

No.1	Silver-work shop	Luis Coto

ALCAISERIA STREET

House No.13	Silver-work shop	Francisco Zabala
House No.13-B	Silver-work shop	Balente Cortés
Single Room B of No.6	Silver-work shop	Antonio Muicelo

MEDINA STREET

Single Room A	Silver-shop	Juan Montes de Oca

SAN JOSE EL REAL STREET

Cellar of No.18	Silver-work shop	Trinidad Contreras

SANTA CLARA STREET

Single Room 21	Silver-work shop and lathe shop	Ramón Bernal

VERGARA STREET

House No.9	Silver-work shop	Cristóbal Cardoso

MANRIQUE STREET

Single Room A	Silver-work shop	Juan Rubio

SAN LORENZO STREET

No.1	Silver-shop	Antonio Morales
Letter A	Silver-shop	Joaquín Díaz de la Cueva

MISERICORDIA STREET

Letter A	Silver-shop	Felipe Gómez
Letter C	Silver-shop	Rafael Gómez
Single Room 7	Silver-shop	Seberiano Velasco
Single Room A	Silver-shop	Francisco Jimenez

MARISCALA Y ESTAMPA DE SAN ANDRES STREETS

| Number 20 | Silver-shop | Eusebio Trejo |

LA PALMA STREET

Number 11	Silver engraver	Antonio Guzman
Letter B	Silver-shop	Joaquín Chozne
Number 14	Silver-shop	José María Marcheni

PLATEROS STREET

Letter D	Silver-shop	Pedro Marquez
Letter A	Silver-shop	José María Folco
Letter D	Silver-shop	Ignacio Vieira
Letter A	Silver-shop	Rumesio Urbina (Frumencio?)
No number	Silver-shop	Camilo Rubin

ESPIRITU SANTO STREET

| Letter A | Silver-shop | Florencio Ortiz |

PLATEROS STREET

| Letter B | Silver-shop | Vicente Ibarra |
| Letter B | Silver-shop | Sebastián Sánchez |

ESTAMPA DE REGINA STREET

| Letter B | Silver-shop | Francisco López y Rosas |

1852

JEWELRY AND SILVER SHOPS[9]

FROM PUEBLA

| Antonio Beltrán, | 4 unlicensed silversmiths, 3rd block Real de San José Street |
| Manuel Robles, | 3 " " 3rd block Real de San José Street |

9 *Guía de Forasteros de la Capital de Puebla, para el año de 1852, dispuesta por Juan N. del Valle, Puebla: Imprenta del Editor.* pp.163-4.

Manuel Mateos,	1 unlicensed silversmiths,		Estanco de las Mugeres Street
Antonio Castro,	3 "	"	Estanco de las Mugeres Street
Mariano Hernández,	2 "	"	Santa Clara Street
Ignacio Escalona,	2 "	"	Santa Clara Street
Juan Ruiz,	2 "	"	Santa Clara Street
Alejandro Ruiz,	2 "	"	Santa Clara Street
Guadalupe Patiño,	6 "	"	2nd block Mercaderes Street

Feliciano Ruiz, 2nd block Mercaderes Street

Messrs. Alemanes,	3 unlicensed silversmiths,		2nd block Mercaderes Street
Juan Ochoa,	4 "	"	Las Cruces Street
N. Quiroz,	2 "	"	Ravozo Street
Eduardo L'Enfer,	5 "	"	San Pedro Street
José María Cao Romero,	4 unlicensed silversmiths,		Aduana Vieja Street
José María Soriano,	2 "	"	Parean Street
Antonio Romero,	3 "	"	Parean Street
Félix Sierra,	3 "	"	Mesones Street
José María Castillo,	2 "	"	Cholula Street
Pedro Ochoa,	4 "	"	Herreros Street
Teófilo Idrac,	3 "	"	Herreros Street
Joaquín Velarde,	3 "	"	Micieses Street
Francisco Velarde,	4 "	"	San Agustín Street
José María Altamirano,	3 "	"	Victoria Street
Juan Arce,	3 "	"	Peñas Street

NOTE: In addition there are a considerable number of freelance, unlicensed silversmiths, who work either in their homes or in different silver-shops: there might be 50.

1854

SILVER-SHOPS[10]

José María Acosta, Jesús María Street.

José Andrade, bridge of San Dimas

José María Baez, bridge of San Dimas Letter A.

Mariano Blanco, San Agustin Street Letter G.

Andres Baric, 2nd block Plateros Street No.7

Andres Baric, 2nd block Plateros Street No.7

Victor Baric, 2nd block Plateros Street

Mariano Barragan, Olla Alley

Mariano Barragan, 2nd block Plateros Street

José A. Berdejo, Tacuba Street

Francisco Castañeda, bridge of Balvanera.

10 *Guía de Forasteros en la Ciudad de Mégico, para el año de* 1854. Published by Mariano Galvan Rivera, with the authorization of the Government and examined by the Chancery. Mégico.

Pedro Cañas, Arquillo Street Letter B.

Juan Castañeda, Aguila Street Letter A.

Joaquín Chorne, Palma Street No.2

Juan Colin, Montealegre Street Letter A.

José María Cordero, 2nd block Santo Domingo Street

Luis Coto, Mecateros Alley.

Ignacio Durán, Sepulcros de Santo Domingo Street

José María Folio, 1st block Plateros Street

Antonio García, 5th block Relox Street

Angel Gomez, Amargura Street Letter C

Pablo Guerrero, 2nd block Relox Street

Victoriano Guerrero, Alcaicería Street

José Marcelo Gutierrez, 1st block Plateros Street No.9

Luciano Guzman, pulque shop on Palacio Street

Antonio Herrera, Estanco de Mugeres Street

Francisco Herrera, 6th block Relox Street

Jesús Huerta, Hospicio de S. Nicolás Street

Antonio Ibarra, Alcaicería Street

Juan Colin, Montealegre Street

José Lawarde, 2nd block Santo Domingo Street

Miguel León, 1st block Rastro Street Letter B.

Pomposo Lira, San José el Real Street

Casimiro Lopez, Puente Quebrado Street No.24

Susano Molina, Santa Teresa la Antigua Street

Manuel Moreno, Mecateros Alley

Antonio Masa, Palma Street No.6

Dionisio Noriega, Zuleta Street No.22

Francisco Ortega, San Ramón Street

Florencio Ortiz, San José el Real Street

Luis Páramo, 3rd block San Juan Street

José María Perez, Puente Blanco Street No.2

Maximino Ramirez, Tiburcio Street No.16.

José María Reyes, 2nd block Vanegas Street

Anacleto Saldivar, 1st block Santa Ana Street

José María Sanchez, 2nd block San Ramón Street

Sebastian Sanchez, 2nd block Plateros Street No.7

Pascual Sarcedo, Damas Street No.3

Bernabé Soriano, Puente de Peredo Street No.3

Cristóbal Solorzano, 1st block Ancha Street

Mariano Soto, Ortega Street No.22

Miguel Tobar, San Agustin Archway

Melesio Trujano, Puente de Rosario Street No.12
Francisco Vargas, Mecateros Street No.1
Emilio Vega, Esquiveles Alley
José Velasco, Santa Clara Alley, No.14
Joaquín Villavicencio, San José el Real Street No.11
Perfecto Zárate, 2nd block Damas Street No.4
Joaquín Zendejas, Alcaicería Street No.10.

SILVER-SHOPS IN THE CITY OF MEXICO IN 1859[11]

José Velasco, diamond-setter.
Aristeo Verdeja, Tacuba Street Letter B
Victoriano Guerrero, Alcaicería Street Letter A. Diamond-setter.
Teófilo Hidrad, Alcaicería Street Letter A. Diamond-setter.
Bernardo Dufourg, Mecateros Street Letter B.
Manuel Moreno, Mecateros Street No.4 Diamond-setter
Antonio Maza, San José Real Street Letter A. Jeweler.
Pomposo Lira, San José Real Street
Jesús Concha, San José Real Street
Pedro Cañas, Arquillo Street No.5
Filomeno Zuleta, near Santo Domingo Street Letter B.
Ponciano Mateos, Santa Clara Street No.19.
Cecilio Zendejas, 2nd block San Lorenzo Street No.23.
Felipe Lopez, Aguila Street Letter C.
Antonio Herrera, Puerta Falsa de Santo Domingo Street
Miguel Mascareño, 1st block of Amargura Street
José Montufar, Estanco de Mugeres Street
José María Falco, 1st block Plateros Street
Mariano Blanco, San Agustin Street
Miguel Tovar, Archway of San Agustin Street
Guadalupe Carrillo, Corchero Street
Mariano Barragan, 2nd block Plateros Street
José Sanchez, 2nd block Plateros Street
José Chorriel, Palma Street
Julian Lara, San Felipe Neri Street
Francisco Romero, Regina Street
Máximo Ramirez, Ortega Street No.13
Dario Noriega, Zuleta Street No.15
D.N.N., Portal de Tejada Street Letter A.
Hilario Salazar, Venero Street

11 Juan N. del Valle: op.cit., pp.381-3.
   The name of José María Folco is spelled *Falco* in the work mentioned.

D.N.N. 2nd block Damas Street
Francisco Ranjel, Acequia Street
Baltasar Orduño, Puente de Jesús María Street
Ignacio Lara, Puente Balvanera Street
Romualdo Resinas, Puente Balvanera Street
José María Perez, Puente Balvanera Street
Casimiro López, Puesto-Nuevo Street
Miguel León, 1st block Rastro Street
Vicente Usegueda, 1st block Relox Street
José María Larralde, 1st block Santo Domingo Street
Pablo Guerrero, 2nd block Relox Street
José Cardoso, 2nd block Santo Domingo Street
Manuel Coto, Cocheras Street
Ignacio Durán, Sepulcros Street
Juan Castañeira, Cocheras Street
Lorenzo Rodríguez, Cocheras Street
Tranquilino Medina, Moras Street
Angel Zaldivar, Parados Street Letter D.
Anacleto Zaldivar, Tesontlale Street Letter A.
Susano Molina, Palacio Pulque Shop
José María Ponce, Cuevas Alley
Miguel Millan, Recabado Alley.
Agustin Rodriguez, Recabado Alley.
José Castro, Alegría Alley
Manuel Huerta, 1st block Vanegas Street Letter B.
Francisco Rangel, Santa Inés Street
José María Reina, Hospicio de San Nicolás Street
Manuel Rodriguez, corner of Santa Ana Street
Mrs. Ana Dominguez, Peralvillo.
Teófilo Marquez, Peralvillo.
Pioquinto Campuzano, Peralvillo.
Jacinto Gris, Garita Street
Faustino Díaz, Garita Street
José María Azcárate, Peralvillo.

EL VIAJERO EN MEXICO
Completa Guía de Forasteros para
1864
By Juan N. del Valle
Silver-Shops

Antonio Alvarez, Puerta Falsa de Santo Domingo Street
Mariano Barragan, 2nd block Plateros Street No.7

Miguel Berdeja, 1st block Indio Triste Street No.9

Mariano Blanco, San Agustin Street No.15

Juan Calvillo, bridge of Santa Ana Street No.2

José María Cardoso, Sepulcros de Santo Domingo Street.

Antonio Carillo, Ortega Street No.30

Pedro Cañas, 1st block Plateros Street No.9.

José María Castro, Machincuepa Street No.9

Jesus Concha, San José el Real Street No.11

Bernardo Dufourg, Mecateros Street No.5

Ignacio Durán, Sepulcros de Santo Domingo Street No.6

Quirino Galván, Alcaicería Street

Pedro Gallegos, Correo Mayor Street No.1

Rafael Guevara, Manrique Street No.4

Antonio Guevara, Seminario Street No.3

Victoriano Guerrero, Alcaicería Street No.14

Pablo Guerrero, 2nd block Reloj Street No.7

Alejandro Gutiérrez, 1st block Plateros Street Nos.14 and 15.

José María Juarez, Alcaicería Street No.5

Julian Lara, 2nd block San Ramón Street No.2

José María Larralde, Alcaicería Street

Francisco López, Montealegre Street No.9

José López, Puerta Falsa de la Merced Street No.4

José Marchena, Alfaro Street No.2

Ponciano Mateos, Santa Clara Street No.19

José (de la) Maza, San José el Real Street No.13

Susano Molina, 2nd block Santo Domingo Street No.1

Manuel Moreno, Mecateros Street

Darío Noriega, Zuleta Street No.7

N.N., San Lorenzo Street

N.N. Merced Street

Susano N., Acequia Street

Ignacio Olaez, 2nd Plateros Street

Ignacio Olaez, Tacuba Street No.23

Baltasar Orduño, bridge of Jesús María Street No.3

Florencio Ortiz, San José el Real Street No.9

Pedro Páramo, 3rd block San Juan Street

Julián Peñuela, 2nd block Mesones Street

Cruz Pizarro, Hospice of San Nicolás

Teodoro Prado, Ortega No.15

Francisco Ramirez, Balvanera Street

Antonio Ramirez, Ortega Street No.27

M. Reinol, 1st block Plateros Street Nos.10 and 11
José María Reina, Migueles Street
Lorenzo Rodriguez, Cocheras Street No.20
Domingo Rosellon, Aguila Street No.5
José Sanchez, Puesto Nuevo Street No.4
Miguel Sandoval, Merced Street No.28
Miguel Tovar, Archway Letter G.
Eusebio Trejo, Donceles Street Letter A
Ignacio Vega, Estanco de Hombres Street
Pomposo Vega, Cocheras Street
N. Verdeja, Puente de Jesús Street Letter M
Marcos Villanueva, Cadena Street No.20
Nemecio Urbina 1st block Plateros Street No.3
Ruperto Urbina, 1st block Indio Triste Street
Luis Zamora, Santo Domingo Street
Joaquín Zendejas, Small Archway of Alcaicería Street.

ARCHIVO GENERAL DE LA NACIÓN

Classification of Industrial Establishments—1865

Silversmiths' Establishments

Alcaicería Street which connects with Plateros Street 5-B	José María Juarez
Alcaicería Street which connects with Plateros Street 5-B	Quirino Gaitan
Ollas Alley No.2-B	Mariano Barragan
Tacuba Street No.25-B	Aristeo Berdeja
Mecateros Street No.5-B	Bernardo Dufourg
Mecateros Street No.5-B	Manuel Moreno
Alcaicería Street which connects with Tacuba Street No.9-A	Joaquín Sendejas
Alcaicería Street which connects with Tacuba Street No.14	Victoriano Guerrero
Small Archway Profesa Street—E	José María Lamalde (Larralde)
San José el Real Street No.9	Florencio Ortiz
San José el Real Street No.10	Jesús Concha
San José el Real Street No.11	Joaquín Villavicencio
San José el Real Street No.13-A	Antonio de la Maza
Cazuela Alley Small Archway Profesa Street Letter A	Luis Portocarrero
Manrique Street No.4	Rafael Guevara

Aguila Street No.4½	Felipe López
1st block Amargura Street No.12-C	Nicanor Tobar
Puerta Falsa de Santo Domingo Street, Letter A	Antonio Alvarez
Estanco de Mugeres Street No.8	José María Montufar
1st block San Lorenzo Street No.13	Martín Esteves
Santa Clara Street Letter B.	José Velazques
2nd block Plateros Street No.5	Ignacio Olaes
1st block Plateros Street No.18	Pedro Cañas
1st block Plateros Street No.15	Alejandro Gutierrez
Archway San Agustín Street Letter C	Miguel Tovar
2nd block Plateros Street No.7	Mariano Barragan
Las Ratas Street No.14	Julian Peñuelas
Zuleta Street No.17-A	Dario Noriega
Ortega Street No.16	Teodocio Prado
Victoria Street Letter A	Antonio Ramirez
Victoria Street 30-B	Antonio Carrillo
Damas Street No.4	Perfecto Zárate
Alfaro Street No.3	José Anarchena
Colegio de Santos Street No.26	Susano Rosel
Puente de Jesús María Street No.3	Baltazar Orduña
Puente de Correo Mayor Street Letter A	Pedro Gallegos
Balvanera Street No.18	Francisco Ramirez
Balvanera Street No.18	José María Reina
Merced Street Letter H.	Anselmo Cosío
San Ramón Street Letter A	Julian Lara
2nd block Reloj Street Letter C	Pablo Guerrero
2nd block Santo Domingo Street Letter IE	José María Cardoso (Today Susano Molina)
Cocheras Street No.19-A	Lorenzo Rodriguez
Sepulcros Santo Domingo Street No.7	Ignacio Durán
1st block Indio Triste Street No.9	Miguel Berdejas
Hospice San Nicolás — Letter A.	Cruz Pizano.
(Sta. Ana) Puente Tezontlale Street 6-B	Anacleto Zaldivar
(Sta. Ana) Puente Tezontlale Street No.2	Tomás Calvillo
Moras Street No.12-G	Gabino Ramires
San Miguel Alley — Letter C	José Salazar
Machincuepa Street Letter A	José María Castro
3rd San Juan Street No.4	Pedro Páramo
Calle Ancha Street No.9	Cristobal Solorzano
Santa Clara Street No.12	Francisco Yoppe

Sepulcros de Santo Domingo Street, without   José María Cardoso
   number
San Felipe de Jesús Street No.24   Simón Mascareño
Puente de Balvanera Street No.10   Romualdo Recinas
Parados Street Letter D   Felipe Arroyo
4th block Reloj Street No.4   José Cerezo
Refugio Street No.19   G. Mastral
1st Venegas Street No.3   Próspero Vera
Moras Street Letter C   Antonio Alvarez
Ratas Street No.14   Jesús Carrillo
Verdeja Alley No.3-E   Jesús Oliva.

1867

According to the *Directorio del Comercio*[12] the silver shops in 1867 were:

Antonio Alvarez, Puerta Falsa de Santo Domingo Street
Antonio Alvarez, Moras Street
Mariano Barragan, Olla Street No.2
Mariano Barragan 2nd block Plateros Street No.7
Aristeo Berdeja, Tacuba Street No.25
Miguel Berdeja, 1st block Indio Triste Street
Pedro Cañas, 1st block Plateros Street No.18
Antonio Carrillo, Ortega Street No.30
Jesús Carrillo, Ratas Street No.14
J. María Castro, Machincuepa Street
Joaquín Cendejas, Alcaicería Street No.9
José Cereso, 4th block Reloj Street No.4
Jesús Concha, San José el Real Street
Anselmo Cosio, Merced Street
Bernardo Dufourg, Mecateros Street No.5
Ignacio Durán, Sepulcros de Santo Domingo Street No.7
Martín Esteves, 1st block San Lorenzo Street No.13
Quirino Gaitan, Alcaicería Street No.5
Victoriano Guerrero, Alcaicería, 14
Pablo Guerrero, 2nd block Reloj Street
Rafael Guevara, Manrique Street No.4
Alejandro Gutierrez, 1st block Plateros Street No.15
Julian Lara, San Ramón Street
J. María Larralde, Arquillo Street

12 *Directorio del Comercio del Imperio Mexicano para el año de 1867.* Mexico. Imp.E.Maillefert.

Felipe Lopez, Aguila Street No.4½
Antonio Masa, San José el Real Street No.13
G. Mastral, Refugio Street No.19
Susano Molina, Santo Domingo Street
Manuel Moreno, Mecateros Street
Dario Noriega, Zuleta Street No.17
Ignacio Olaez, 2nd block Plateros Street No.5
Jesus Oliva, Verdeja Street No.3
Baltazar Orduña, puente Jesús María Street
Florencio Ortiz, San José el Real Street
Pedro Páramo, 3rd block San Juan Street No.4
Julian Peñuela, Ratas Street No.14
Cruz Pizarro, Hospice of San Nicolás
Teodosio Prado, Ortega Street No.16
Francisco Ramíres, Balvanera Street No.18
Lorenzo Rodriguez, Cocheras Street
Susano Rosel, Acequia Street No.23
José Salazar, San Miguel Alley
Anacleto Saldivar, Puente Tezontlale Street
Cristobal Solorzano, Ancha Street No.9
Miguel Tovar, Archway of San Agustin Street Letter C
Nicanor Tovar, 1st block Amargura Street No.12
José Velazquez, Santa Clara Street
Prospero Vera, 1st block Vanegas Street No.3
Joaquín Villavicencio, San José el Real Street No.11
Francisco Yopp, Santa Clara Street No.12
Perfecto Zárate, Damas Street No.4

SILVER-SHOPS IN THE YEAR 1882[13]

Joaquín Villaseñor, San José el Real Street
Francisco Aranda, Alcaicería Street No.17
Apolonio Velarde, San Felipe Neri Street No.1
Pedro Cañas, 1st block Plateros Street No.8
Guadalupe Carrillo, Ortega Street No.9
Jesus Carrillo, Puente Quebrado Street No.30
Sóstenes Saldivar, Balvanera Street No.18
Antonio Ponton, Donceles Street No.13
J.Nieva, Alcaicería Street No.13
J.Llop, Santa Clara Street No.7
Alejandro Cosío, Hospicio San Nicolás Street No.1
Jesús Cherlin, 1st block Independencia Street No.3

13 *Nueva Guía de México. Por Irineo Paz y Manuel Tornel.* Year 1882. Mexico. *Imp. de I. Paz*, pp. 883-4.

6. *The Twentieth Century*: 1900-1936

At the beginning of the twentieth century there was a great demand for old Mexican plate, which resulted in a great number of imitations, many of them very well made. Unfortunately, forged hall-marks were stamped on many of these reproductions. Indeed, some dealers were so zealous that, not satisfied with stamping forged hall-marks on the imitations, they also used imitation dies on old plate which lacked hall-marks.

At the present time, the demand from tourists has created a movement of slight importance, limited in great part to the copying of old pieces. This movement is doomed to failure, due to the difficulties with workmen and present-day buyers' resistance to the excessive prices that works of art demand.

The silversmiths of today lower both the value and appearance of their reproductions by decreasing the percentage of pure silver used.[14] For this reason, comparing the modern plate with antique silver pieces, the former seem to be made largely of tin. Those dealers who by their sales support the present silver trade would do a great service to the silversmiths by insisting that the metal used be of the old standard of 916 *milésimos*.

With the exception of Apolonio Guevara, the present-day operators of silver-shops have become Superintendents of Factories of Silver Objects. They no longer work personally; the workmen do not even consider the possibility of creating original works; urged by the owner, who in turn is compelled by the necessities of modern life, they merely try to produce as many copies as possible in the shortest possible time.

THE *MAESTROS* GUEVARA

One of the two remaining descendants of the line of great *maestros* of the colonial tradition, Apolonio Guevara, son of Rafael of the same name who worked about the middle of last century and who was the son of Miguel, silversmith of 1811, is still living[15] and works in Mexico City, 24 Mina Street.

---

14 I sent a modern piece of silver, from a prominent silversmith, to the Mint for assay and it proved to be of 860 *milésimos*. I have one piece made by Carrillo Mendoza, a more trustworthy modern silversmith, that assayed 900 *milésimos*.

15 1st September 1936.

Apolonio was born on the 10th April 1856 and at the age of nine, that is in 1865, began work in his father's shop. He recalls that in his first year of apprenticeship he worked on silver objects for Emperor Maximilian and the Empress Carlota.

He has consistently refused to operate 'a factory of silver objects,' with modern machinery. He produces his works in the same manner he learned in his youth: with hammer, chisel, and his own hands. He does what he can, preferring to remain in poverty and obscurity rather than to employ machinery.

He seldom used his mark:

Enlarged

Don Apolonio says he is now the only person in Mexico who can gild by fire, using the same methods as in colonial times. The last piece he fire-gilded was a staff for Monsignor Silva, some thirty years ago. He also said that the last silversmiths who did fire-gilt, besides himself, were Barragán and Cañas. It was Apolonio's privilege to fire-gild the baptismal fountain of the *Sagrario Metropolitano*, still in use.

In order that the colonial technique of fire-gilding might not be lost, I arranged with Don Apolonio that he fire-gild a piece of plate, under the observation of a chemical engineer, who made an exact description of the process, as follows:

FIRE-GILDING PROCESS

In order to calculate precisely the materials required per square centimeter, it was decided to use a piece of silver plate of 25 square centimeters.

First of all, the silver plate is flattened with a small hammer against an iron anvil and then polished with emery to obtain a perfectly smooth surface. The piece of silver is placed in a weak solution of sulphuric acid and water, at room temperature, in an earthenware container.

The next step is to prepare the gold. This is done by cutting into small pieces with scissors the gold leaf that is to be used for gilding. The bits of gold are then placed in a small, new crucible, about 6 centimeters high and 3 centimeters in diameter, and in another crucible of like size is placed the mercury that is to be used.

Four fire bricks are first placed on the hearth of a brasier charged with burning charcoal. Then the crucible containing the bits of gold is placed on the fire, and burning charcoal is heaped around it. After four minutes, when the gold is beginning to shine [*espejear*] but is not yet melted, mercury is added and stirred with an iron rod for two minutes, still keeping the crucible on the fire. The hot mixture of mercury and gold is then transferred to another earthenware receptacle filled with cold water, in order to cleanse the metals.

After the mixture of gold and mercury has been washed, it is transferred to a glass mortar, the gilder adding five cubic centimeters of water and grinding the mixture until free from lumps. This operation results in an amalgamation of gold and mercury.

The amalgam and the water, left in the mortar, are by means of a string passed through a piece of very thin chamois, making a bag the size of the amalgam. This bag is squeezed to separate the gold amalgam from the free mercury and the water which go through the chamois, leaving within the pure amalgam of gold and mercury which is then ground in the glass mortar until perfectly smooth.

A spatule is made from a strip of polished copper with a spoon-like cavity at one end. Both the spatule and the piece of silver to be gilded are then washed in water with a slight solution of *tequexquite*, which is a natural caustic soda with chemical properties corresponding to an impure carbonate of sodium. To complete this operation both spatule and the piece of silver are scrubbed with a wire brush. The piece of silver is treated with mercury bichloride applied with a piece of cotton, to prepare the surface for the mercury bath. Then in a small porcelain vessel are added two cubic centimeters of nitric acid to one drop of mercury. Using the spatule the piece of silver is then coated with a mixture of mercury and acid. Once the piece has been coated with mercury the coating is evenly spread with a piece of cotton, washed with alkaline water and polished with a fine fiber brush.

The amalgam of gold and mercury to which two cubic centimeters of mercury are added to soften the paste is transferred by means of the spatule to a clean and porous piece of cotton cloth.

Then a bag is made out of the cotton cloth packed with the amalgam, applying this with the bag on the piece of silver, spreading it evenly with a rather stiff shaving brush, allowing the free mercury to drip down on to the spoon of the spatule. The operation is continued, evenly spreading on the surface and rubbing anew with the cotton, applying several coats of mercury and carefully letting the free mercury drip down on each application.

When the application of the amalgam has been completed, the piece is then placed on the burning charcoal and heated, to evaporate the mercury that continues dripping and begins to be expelled in the form of vapors. Simultaneously the amalgam is evenly spread with the shaving brush and a wad of cotton. The piece is again heated in a moderate fire, placing it on the charcoal and treating it again with the brush and wad of cotton, but being careful to remove it from the fire when the first mercury vapors begin to escape. The piece of silver gradually looses the brilliancy characteristic of the mercury, turning a dull silver color, and then slowly acquires a yellowish tinge. When the firm yellow color has appeared the piece is polished with the shaving brush to take out the white silver spots and the drying on the burning charcoals continues until the object acquires a golden color.

To terminate the process, the piece is placed in an earthenware container filled with boiling water slightly acidified with sulphuric acid, the purpose of this being to cleanse the silver and intensify the gold color. Finally the piece is washed in alkaline water and polished with a soft wire brush.

The actual working time to complete the gilding process of the silver plate with an area of 25 square centimeters was 5 hours. The materials employed were as follows: a silver plate, two millimeters in thickness and area of 25 square centimeters; weight 55 grams; purity of the silver 0.900.

One sheet of 24 carat gold; purity of the gold 0.9996.

Pure Mercury 57 grams.

In order to obtain an idea of the cost of gilding, it must be borne in mind that only one fifth of the amalgam was used, and after weighing what remained, it was found that 15.36 grams of pure gold are used for every 100 square centimeters of surface gilded.

THE SILVERSMITHS OF TODAY

The silversmith shops at the present time[16] are the following:

Salvador y Hnos. Alday	Escobedo 36
Benjamín Carrillo	Bolivar 41
Manuel Severo Carrillo y Mendoza	Rep. del Salvador 42
'Centro Platero' Margarita Roma	Calzada Piedad 101
Apolonio Guevara	Mina 24
Orf-Mex	Gral. Prim Street No.13
Alfredo Ortega, Jr.	5 de Mayo 3
'Platería Maciel,' Luis Maciel	Sadi Carnot 6

The two silver-shops 'Carrillo,' above mentioned, belong to the direct descendants of the famous 'Carrillo' family of silversmiths of the eighteenth century.

16 30th June 1936.

Chapter X

MARKS ON MEXICAN SILVER

1. INTRODUCTION: *General; the Assay Mark; Individual Owners' Marks; the R Crowned.* 2. HALL-MARKS BETWEEN 1524-78: *the Laws of the Indies; Proceedings of the Municipal Council; First Law of the Indies on Plate; Summary: 1524-78; the First Mark Stamped on Precious Metals; the First Marks Stamped on Plate.* 3. MARKS BETWEEN 1579-1732; 4. MARKS BETWEEN 1733-1820; 5. SUMMARY OF MARKS ACCORDING TO DOCUMENTS: 1524-1820; 6. THE CHIEF ASSAYERS; 7. MARKS AND FORGERIES: *Marks on Silver Between 1733-82; the Chief Assayer, Captain of Grenadiers Diego González de la Cueva, 1733-78.* 8. MARKS BETWEEN THE YEARS 1783-1823; 9. CHIEF ASSAYER JOSE ANTONIO LINCE Y GONZALEZ, 1779-88; 10. CHIEF ASSAYER FRANCISCO ARANCE Y COBOS, 1789-90; 11. CHIEF ASSAYER ANTONIO FORCADA Y LA PLAZA, 1791-1818; 12. CHIEF ASSAYER JOAQUIN DAVILA MADRID, 1819-23; 13. MARKS AND THE CHIEF ASSAYERS, 1823-95; 14. CHIEF ASSAYER CAYETANO BUITRON, 1823-43; 15. CHIEF ASSAYER SEBASTIAN CAMACHO, 1856-60, 1863-67; 16. CHIEF ASSAYER ANTONIO DEL CASTILLO, 1861-2, 1867-8; 17. CHIEF ASSAYER JOSE ANTONIO MUCHARRAZ, 1868-81; 18. CHIEF ASSAYER FRANCISCO MORALES, 1882-9; 19. CHIEF ASSAYER FERNANDO SAYAGO, 1890-3; 20. CHIEF ASSAYER ROMUALDO OBREGON MORALES, 1894-5; 21. HALL-MARKS BETWEEN 1895-1936; 22. SUMMARY OF GENUINE HALL-MARKS 1524-1936.

1. *Introduction*

General

NO DATE-MARKS were stamped on Mexican plate. The colonial authorities employed official marks only to signify that the taxes had been paid and that the precious metals used were of the required standard. Furthermore, to make the task of identification more difficult, much of the colonial silver was not hall-marked. The following factors, especially during the sixteenth and seventeenth centuries, contributed to this omission, so deplored by collectors:

The silversmith, by saving the tax, could sell to his clients at a discount, an advantage to both.[1]

The marks did not contribute to the beauty of the piece and many clients objected to them.

On the greater part of the silver made outside of the City of Mexico, as well as that destined for the Catholic service, the tax was not paid. The lack of marks is explained by Lic. Joseph Antonio Lince González in his *Consulta hecha a la Real Audiencia . . .* :[2]

Paragraph 21. This Kingdom was endowed by the Most High with the richest minerals in the world. It is filled with many cities, villages and opulent places, where there are wealthy natives who regularly acquire silver. Many, it is true, obtain it in [the City of] Mexico, taxed and with all obligations satisfied, but others go to the silversmiths. These are found everywhere, although not licensed, as licensed artisans are exceedingly rare, except in Puebla, where they are regulated like those in this jurisdiction in the form best suited to that city.

Paragraph 22. All the plate made where there are neither strong boxes nor assayers is not usually of legal standard, nor has the 20% tax thereon been paid. It is brought to Mexico because the owners come to reside in this city, or send it here to be renovated.

The Assay Mark

Before beginning a discussion of the hall-marks, it is well first to explain and clarify a point which frequently confuses the novice:

The inspectors of silversmith shops and later the assayer, took with a burin, from each piece made, a small sample of the metal. This sample was tested[3] to determine whether the metal used in the work was of the

---

1 As proved by many complaints made by the authorities and controversies. Pérez and López, op.cit., vol.23, pp.136-7, say: 'It having been taken into consideration that not all silversmiths and sheet-beaters of this Kingdom have the capital to supply their requirements of gold and silver, many are compelled to work on orders for private individuals who do not want to pay the tax and those who perform this work having the assurance that it will not be manifested for the tax, adulterate it and use alloy in excess. . . .' *Reales Resoluciones no recopiladas de Indias. Real ordenanza de 12 de octubre de 1776.*

2 Op.cit.

3 *Las Ordenanzas del Virrey Fuen-Clara de 1746,* give the following details: Ordinances of 1746. Ordinance No.30. 'Attention must be given by said *Juez Veedor* that said pieces be of the required purity. As they cannot be assayed, he must take from each a shaving and compare it with another from the paragon, a piece of silver whose assay shows it to be of the legal standard, and each must be refired. If the sample taken from the piece becomes blacker than that from the paragon, it is not standard; and it will be well to use the nitric acid and color tests, although both are doubtful because subject to sight and not to truth, etc.'

required standard. This was done during the entire period in which silver was hall-marked. The assayers were under obligation not to damage the plate in this operation and therefore nearly always the sample was taken from underneath. The mark left by the burin is called the *burilada*. This mark, which is often confused with the hall-mark, is always a zig-zag line like those here reproduced.

Actual Size

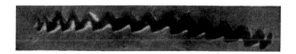

Enlarged

This mark, in genuine colonial plate, is rather deep and not a superficial scratch like that made at present by some silversmiths, many of whom do not know what this mark means.

The *burilada* generally appears on genuine pieces bearing other marks and is not usually found on those not hall-marked, because plate was assayed and hall-marked at the same time. Nevertheless, I have seen genuine pieces which are hall-marked and not marked by the burin. Therefore, to identify colonial silver the mark made by the burin has no value and the only general rule of any value is, that if a mere superficial line is found, one can be sure that no one in authority made it and that it was made to deceive the buyer.

The following excerpts are from Fonseca and Urrutia:[4]

ASSAY AND TAX

As regards pieces made both of gold and silver which the silversmiths bring to be assayed and taxed, a sufficient amount cannot be taken from each to perform the operation, nor is it possible to submit them to the comparison with the paragon, which the authors point out, because this is very fallible. The practice which should be observed is to take from each piece a bit of thread with the burin, put aside those from pieces called plated, which are hammered into shape and require a finer silver, and therefore are usually of standard quality, and those which are cast, in which it

4 Op.cit., vol.I, p.91. *Ordenanzas de Ensayadores de* 1783.

is often easier to find a defect. Both shall be assayed in the manner best suited and if all are of the standard of eleven *dineros* of silver and twenty-two *quilates* of gold, they shall be approved as good pieces, and the corresponding hall-marks shall be placed thereon; but if a difference is found, it shall be made known that there are pieces of different standards. This they shall try to ascertain so that the good ones may be hall-marked and the bad ones broken up. Those broken shall be melted by the silversmith and after assaying the resulting mass, and the amount lacking is known, calculation shall be made of the amount of fine silver to be combined with it so that it will conform to the standard of eleven *dineros*. This shall be observed with all old silver which the aforesaid artists use in order that any defect therein, caused by soldering or by the tax-mark, may be overcome. This should be performed with all the care the examination requires, using for this purpose the assay, the nitric acid or color tests and other methods and procedures which should be applied as best suited to the form of the piece and jewels of gold or silver, in accordance with the usage in the mints for purchases of plate. When, after the nitric acid and color tests of the sample taken with the burin, their standard is definitely established and there is no doubt of their quality, they may be accepted at their true value and payment made, provided the owner of the gold and silver agrees, but not otherwise. If they wish to deliver it for assay, or if the assayers consider this necessary, they may proceed as with ingots, and as ordered in chapter 4, and fulfill the requirements so that no damage is done.

Individual Owners' Marks

Many individuals had dies made and stamped their silver with their name. This is confusing, but when the mark on the piece is that of a known silversmith, it can be readily distinguished. Usually the owners' dies are more elaborate and therefore can be readily identified, as those of the silversmiths were always simple.

Typical examples of the individual owners' marks:

The 'R' Crowned:

The documents I have found referring to this mark are:

The[5] order to be followed in the silver paid by the miners for mercury which is given them:

Don Martín Enriquez etc.

As regards the order to the *alcaldes mayores* of the mines of this New Spain for them to have a chest with three keys, where the silver given them in payment of mercury should be deposited and kept. One of these keys shall be held by the said *alcaldes mayores*, one by the scrivener of their jurisdiction and the other by the deputies of the mines. I am informed that this is not complied with and that some times the silver given them in payment is taken out for their own use and profit, which is forbidden. This results in harm and risk to His Majesty's Royal Treasury as well as to the miners, and in order to avoid and overcome said improprieties and others which are followed, I order that from now henceforth, until either His Majesty or I in his name shall order and command otherwise, that in the chests of said mines, where the silver should be kept, there be a die with the word *Rey* [King] surmounted by a crown and the name of the mines, which die shall be stamped on all the silver which the miners pay for mercury, given them either by the former *alcaldes mayores* or by the present ones, and that it be stamped thereon in the presence of said *alcaldes mayores*, scrivener and deputy and of the person making payment. The scrivener shall record it in the book and certify it, and on this silver the 10% tax-mark shall not be stamped, but only the aforesaid mark and the die of the miner who makes the payment. This silver shall not be used or contracted until it is taxed and the tax-mark stamped thereon by the officials of said Royal Treasury under penalty of forfeiture in favor of His Majesty's treasury for anyone in whose possession it may be found, and such person shall be prosecuted as a thief. The judge who fails to proceed against him . . . shall be deprived of office and shall not be given another for a period of ten years and shall be fined five hundred *pesos*, half for His Majesty's exchequer and treasury and the other half for the informer and the judge who prosecutes. The miner who permits them to stamp the 10% tax-mark on the silver instead of his own shall not be credited with his payment, even though it be recorded in the book and indicated with the tax-mark, and he shall be obliged to pay again. This shall also be done if he allows his own mark and the 10% tax-mark to be stamped on the silver.

And so that it may come to the attention of all, I order that it be announced by

5 *Archivo General de la Nación. Ordenanzas* O.O.O.O. p.46 reverse.

crier in all the mines of the kingdom of this New Spain, and, after having been announced, His Majesty's Justices shall take special care to keep and comply with the command.

Dated in Mexico, the second of March, one thousand five hundred and eighty.

Don Martín Enriquez:

By order of His Excellency, Juan de la Cueva.

Declaration[6] for marking silver with the 10% tax mark.

Don Martín Enriquez etc.

With regard to a command signed with my name and by the subscribing notary, issued in this city the 2nd March last, this year, I ordered that in the chests of the mines of this New Spain where silver is collected from the sale of His Majesty's mercury, there be a die which reads *Rey* [King] surmounted by a crown and the name of the mines to be stamped on all silver the miners pay for mercury and that this be done in the presence of said *alcaldes mayores*, scrivener and deputy and of the person making payment. The scrivener shall record it in the book and this silver shall not be stamped with the 10% tax-mark, but only with the aforesaid mark and that of the miner making the payment, and other things contained in said command. That if the tax-mark is stamped on the silver paid for said mercury, proceedings might be instituted, in view of which command, by these presents I order that the command in question be kept as regards everything else. I declare and order that on each ingot of silver paid by the miners for mercury the 10% tax-mark and the others referred to shall be stamped and that all silver collected and received by the *alcaldes mayores* of the mines in payment of mercury shall be stamped with the 10% tax-mark, and silver offered to the officers of the Royal Treasury in payment of mercury which does not have this 10% tax-mark shall not be received.

Dated in Mexico, 20th August, one thousand five hundred and eighty.

Don Martín Enriquez

By command of His Excellency, Juan de la Cueva.

From the 'Consultation[7] made to the Royal Governing Tribunal by Lic. Joseph Antonio Linze, Chief Assayer of the Kingdom and *Juez Veedor* of the Noble Art of Silversmiths, regarding various details of this art, of much interest to the Royal service and public use:'

Paragraph 43: Since the incorporation into the mint of [the smelter] another

---

6 *Archivo General de la Nación.* Ordinances O.O.O.O. p.58.

7 Found in a book in the author's possession, entitled *Documentos respectivos al Arte de Ensayar Oro y Plata, Ordenanzas de Ensayadores, y otros sobre el Gobierno de la Platería, Batiojería y Tiraduría de Oro y Plata que ofrece el Señor Don Vicente de Herrera, Caballero, etc. . . . Lic. Joseph Antonio Lince González.* In Mexico, year 1786.

practice has been established; that is, that the silver mixed with gold as purchased or sent to the chest, is stamped with the mark of the smelter. As it is for His Majesty's account, after the metals have been separated they are not again manifested to the Royal officers or marked in the Treasurer's office but at the mint another mark—*Rey*—[King] is placed thereon and they may then be coined into money.

Paragraph 44: The mark *Rey* is the mint's certificate, although not outside the mint. It is very easily forged and can be put on any gold, which can be marked without payment of the taxes as it is believed that these have been paid, as is done when the gold is separated in the smelter.

Paragraph 45: The solution proposed . . . that a die be made like that stamped on all silver and gold which is sent to the Royal Treasury from all the chests outside of this Head Office, which reads *Rey* with a Crown above it, which die shall remain in my possession as do the others. . . .

This mark of the *R* surmounted by a crown appears on plate made at the end of the eighteenth century and beginning of the nineteenth century. It is not common.

From the foregoing it is assumed that this mark indicated that the piece was made of silver on which the tax had been paid, in order to prevent the Royal Officers collecting the tax a second time.

In any case this mark is of no value in determining the date of the silver, and its use for identification purposes may well be ignored by the collector.

2. Hall-marks Between 1524-78
The Laws of the Indies

ASSAYING, SMELTING AND HALL-MARKING GOLD AND SILVER

First Law[8]

The Emperor Charles in Barcelona on the 14th September 1519.

That the gold, taken in barter from the Indians, made into plate, be assayed, smelted and taxed. Knowing that a great quantity of fabricated gold is passing from the possession of the Indians to the Spaniards, obtained by payments, purchase and trade, in different pieces and makes of patens, ear-rings, beads, tubes, small bars, strings, bracelets, breast-plates and various other forms, which were formerly called *guanin*, a very low-grade gold alloyed with copper, and unless melted and assayed for value its standard cannot be determined. We command that

---

8 *Recopilación de Leyes de los Reinos de las Indias, mandada imprimir y publicar por Su Magestad Católica el Rey Don Carlos* II. *Nuestro Señor*, p.142. 5th edition. Vol.2. Madrid, 1841. Boix Editor.

this gold and pieces be assayed, melted and the 20% tax paid in the following manner:

The Governor or chief authority shall order that, in the presence of our Royal Officers, and melter, or his substitute, and the assayer and chief scrivener of mines and registers, or his substitute, all the gold obtained by barter made into pieces be brought and the larger, better pieces and those of higher standard be separated from the others and melted, and separate those not of the required standard. The tubes, beads and small pieces shall be set aside, so that there shall be four classes; the good pieces, those of higher standard which the Governor considers should not be melted for assay to determine their value, the assayer to apply the nitric acid test to the piece, as it is not possible to take out enough for an assay; and after paying the value, settle and pay the 20% tax, pay the assayer's fees and give the interested parties a certificate so that they may be at liberty to melt or exchange them for pearls or [precious] stones from the Indians or any other persons.

The other pieces in the second class which the Governor considers should be melted because they are not well made, or because it will be better than to leave them as they are, shall be melted and the taxes thereon be paid to us, and to the assayer and melter, and the remainder delivered to whom it belongs, as is customary.

The third class, composed of beads and tubes and other small pieces, if well made and cannot be assayed or marked because they would be dented, or because it would be best for them to remain as they are, shall be tested and assayed at the ends in order to determine their standard, fix their value and take our taxes and the fees of the assayer and marked. The remainder shall be distributed and returned to the owners, the assayer giving a list of the small pieces signed by the Governor, certifying to the aforesaid, so that the owners may make use of them and sell them if they desire.

The low-grade gold which has no known standard, and constitutes the fourth class, shall not be melted, but weighed, after which taxes shall be paid the assayer and our treasurer, which are our due. The remainder shall be distributed among the owners, and if some pieces are better fabricated than others let them be auctioned and sold to the highest bidder, because in this manner their price will be increased and more advantage gained, than if they were melted.

Low-grade gold in quantity without being divided and having a definite owner shall by no means be melted but after payment of the taxes, if in the hands of private individuals, the owners may melt it, mixing it with other gold, if desired, in order that it may come up to the required standard, and it may be assayed and marked, but not otherwise, because it is our will that no gold shall be melted that does not have a known standard and a definite price, and that the melting be done in the presence of our Royal Officers in the smelter.

When anyone wishes to melt any pieces of the aforesaid gold, whether of high quality and well made and of legal standard, or of lower quality, they may do so, and the melter shall be obliged to melt them, charging his fee for the process, provided they are of the required standard, and assay, but not otherwise. It is our intention that all gold melted have a known standard, and be done at the wish and election of the owners of such pieces, combining with them more melted gold to raise the standard, provided this gold is not from the mines, because that must be melted separately, as is commanded. On this gold that is melted, which is thus mixed with that from said pieces, and low-grade gold to raise its quality, fees shall be paid the melter although these have already been paid, because this is a remelting, and the melter performs the work and bears the cost.

If there be any bracelets, belts or collars or other jewels, which often have tubes or pearls mixed with the white and colored stones, they shall not be broken up to melt them, but an estimate shall be made of the gold, pearls and stones, and on payment of our taxes and fees of the assayer the certificate should be given. However, if afterwards these things should come into possession of an individual who wishes to break them up and melt them, he may do so, provided the certificate he received as proof of having paid the taxes, is destroyed.

And because some with importunity, whenever they desire, wish to melt pieces and things already assayed and marked, and give work to our officers at inopportune times, we command that only on the days and in the hours when our smelters are working in accordance with the regulations, shall this be done.

After the required procedure, such pieces of gold of whatever standard having been assayed and marked, and bearing our Royal Mark, may be withdrawn by anyone owning them, from the province where they are, and bring them to these our kingdoms, or send them to other provinces or islands of the Indies, and not to any other place, with a certificate furnished by the assayer of their value and standard, provided at the time they are taken from the province they are registered before a chief scrivener of mines and mining registers, and when brought to these kingdoms, register them with our Royal Officers in the ports of departure. If they are taken to any of the islands of the Indies register them with Our Officers in the port of departure and in the Island where they are brought.[9]

THE ROYAL TWENTY PER CENT TAX[10]

1543-1563

The Emperor Charles and governing Prince in Valladolid, 24th July 1543. Philip II in Madrid, 18th July 1563.

When payment of the 20% tax on gold and silver is made the hall-mark shall be stamped thereon.

9 See the royal command of 15th July 1790, ordering that the laws of this section be strictly observed. Another royal command revoked article 134 of the Intendents of Peru in that part relating to the incorporation of these trades which it regulated.

10 *Recopilación de Leyes de los Reinos de las Indias*, vol.3, p.63

We command that in all the islands and provinces of our Indies, at the time payment of the 20% tax is imposed on gold or silver, the hall-mark be placed thereon so
that its value may be known. Penalty: loss of favor and a thousand *ducados* fine
for our exchequer and treasury for those violating it.

LAW XII[11]

1550-1561

The Emperor Charles and the Queen of Bohemia, Governess in Valladolid, year
 1550, chapter of instructions. Philip II in Toledo 15th March 1561. See law 27,
 section 10, book 4.
That on Mondays and Thursdays the royal officials shall remain three hours witnessing
 payment of the 20% tax on gold and silver.
Our royal officials shall be present three full hours Monday and Thursday mornings
of each week that are not holidays, to wait on those who come to make payment of
the 20% tax on silver and gold, giving preference of seniority to those arriving first.

MINTS AND THEIR OFFICIALS

LAW XV[12]

1550-1563

The Emperor Charles and the Queen of Bohemia, governess in Valladolid, 16th
 April 1550.
Philip II ordinance II of 1563. Charles II and the reigning Queen.
That the officials of the mint shall not trade in silver and the manner in which the
 marking should be done.
We prohibit and forbid any officials of the mint to trade and bargain in fine or low-
grade silver, hall-marked or taxed, lacking hall-marks or with taxes unpaid, under
penalty of loss of office, of the silver, as well as all of his property. Two-thirds of
such fine to be applied to our exchequer and treasury, and the other to the judge
who passes sentence and to the informer, a half to each. And we command that
none of the aforesaid may enter the mint, although the 20% tax be paid, nor any
other person, unless for the purpose of coining money, under the same penalty. And
we command that whoever wishes to coin money, shall first take the silver to the
officials of our royal treasury, residing in that city or village who shall have it
hall-marked and payment of the 20% tax made, if it has not already been paid,
mark and record in the book to whom it belongs and the quantity and how it was
marked to coin into money; and after coinage its weight and quantity be ascertained.
And it is our will that the marking shall not be done by the officials of the mints,
nor by other persons, nor in another place, but by said royal officials, under penalty

11 Ibid., vol.II, p.145.
12 Ibid., vol.II, p.152.

of the owners losing the silver, two-thirds of which shall be applied to our exchequer and the other to the informer; and he who marks it shall be deprived of office and shall incur the penalty of forfeiture of all his property, and perpetual exile from the province. And we command our royal officials, that they be present when payment of the 20% tax is made and the marking is done on the days appointed, and shall receive the taxes pertaining to us, under penalty of a fine of twenty thousand *maravedis* for anyone violating this command.

THE TWENTY PER CENT ROYAL TAX

LAW IV[13]

1557

Philip II and the governing Princess in Valladolid, 17th May 1557.
That those obtaining gold and silver by barter shall manifest it and give bond for the payment of the 20% tax.
Whenever traders introduce gold or silver into Spanish towns, they shall go without delay to the authorities before taking it to their home or any other place, and manifest it and give bond that within the first thirty days following they will make payment of the 20% tax, under penalty of forfeiting it as well as an additional fourth.

LAW X[14]

1573

Emperor Charles year 1531. Philip II in Madrid, 10th April 1573. See law 8, sec.6, book 8.
That the hall-marks be uniform and that they be kept under three keys.
The hall-marks on gold and silver of the mints of the Indies, and smelters therein shall be uniform, and shall be kept in a place safe from fraud, very well guarded in the chest with three keys, so that they cannot be stolen or lost. And we command that they be placed and kept in the royal chest, and when it is required to use them to mark gold and silver, this be done by the royal officials and in no other way, and that afterwards they be returned to their place.

LAW II[15]

1578

Emperor Charles and the governing prince in Lérida, 8th August 1551. Philip II in Pardo, 8th June 1578. See law 24, sec.10, book 8.
That gold and silver be assayed and melted and used according to its value and standard.
We order and command that all the gold and silver there may be in the provinces

13 Ibid., vol.III, p.60.
14 Ibid., vol.II, p.145.
15 Ibid., vol.II, pp.143-4.

of the Indies, and which can be collected and taken from the rivers and mines, be assayed and hall-marked showing the true and known purity of each and according to said standard and assay, be used, and not in any other form, notwithstanding any order or custom, appeal or supplication against the sentences which our judges and justices pronounce on this matter; and according to the standard and value they might have, the royal officials shall collect for us the 20% tax and tax of 1½% which pertain to us, and deliver all to the treasurer for record in the royal books, under penalty of losing their offices and half of their property to our exchequer.

It must be borne in mind that the laws of the Indies quoted in preceding paragraphs of this chapter refer only to metals obtained by barter or bullion.

Excluding the metals obtained by barter, the laws on hall-marks of silver bullion mentioned, may be summarized as follows:

(Omitting Law I, Section 22, Book IV and Law IV and Law IV, Section X, Book VIII, which treat of gold bartered from the Indians.)

DATE	LAW	
1543-63	Book VIII Section X Law XXVIII	'At the time payment is made of the 20% tax on gold or silver, the hall-marks shall be stamped thereon.'
1550-63	Book IV Section 23 Law XV	'These marks [those to be stamped on the silver] shall not be stamped by the officials of the Mint nor other persons . . . but by the said royal [Treasury] officials.'
1578	Book IV Section 22 Law II	'It shall be assayed and marked with the true and known standard.'

Proceedings of the Municipal Council of the City of Mexico

ASSAY-MASTER OF THE CITY AND VEEDOR OF THE SILVERSMITHS

The earliest information I have found on hall-marks on silver in Mexico, in the Proceedings of the Municipal Council, appears in those of the 24th January 1533:

On this day said gentlemen, in conformity and agreement with the silversmith and goldsmith officials, said that they would name and did name as *veedor* and *alcalde* for said trade and as assay-master of this city Pedro Despina, assayer, as the person having the most votes of the officials of said trade and administered the solemn oath required in such cases in due form and after taking the oath he was empowered to use said offices and charges according to the ordinances of this city and then they delivered to him the mark and die [punch] of this city which he received and signed for. — Pedro Despina.

SILVERSMITHS' DIE [PUNCH] 17TH JULY 1536

Either the die was changed or for some reason it was taken from the marker, because it is so recorded in the Proceedings:

This day Antonio de Carbajal, Assemblyman, brought to this Municipal Council the die of this city which the silversmiths are to stamp on the pieces they make and which remained in the box which is in this council-hall.

MARKER AND ALCALDE OF THE SILVERSMITHS. 6TH APRIL 1537

On other dates the die of this city is mentioned:

This day they named for *alcalde* of the silversmiths' trade, Luis Rodríguez, silver-smith, and they also named him marker for this city, of the silver fabricated here. They summoned [him] to said council and administered the oath and formalities required by law in such cases and he promised to perform said offices well and faithfully and *the die of the city was delivered to him*. On this day it was proclaimed by town crier Montilla that he had been made marker. — Luis Rodríguez. (A rubric).

ALCALDE FOR THE SILVERSMITHS. 10TH MAY 1538

This day by request and supplication of the silversmiths of this city Francisco Hernández, silversmith, who was present, was named *alcalde* of the silversmiths for this year, in place of Luis Rodríguez, silversmith, who held the office last year, as he was selected by the silversmiths for *alcalde* and he was received as such. He was ordered to perform said office and took the oath as prescribed by law. The die of this city which had been in possession of Luis Rodríguez was then delivered to him and said Francisco Hernández signed for same.

ALCALDE FOR THE SILVERSMITHS. 10TH FEBRUARY 1538

This day they received as *alcalde* of the silversmiths Pedro Hernández, silver-smith, and he took the oath prescribed by law to perform said office well and faith-fully and he was empowered to make use of the office and *the die of the city was given to him* and he received it and signed for same. Pedro Hernández.

ALCALDE OF SILVERSMITHS IN JULY 1544: GRABIEL DE BILLASANA

This day the silversmith officials in this city presented in said council a petition naming *alcalde* and *veedor* of said trade and marker, Grabiel de Billasana [sic], silversmith, and asked that he be received and confirmed by said council and that the die of this city be ordered delivered to him, according to the lengthy contents of said petition. And then said justices and councilmen summoned Grabiel de Billasana to appear before said council receiving his oath as required by law. He promised to perform well and faithfully said office of *veedor* and marker of silver, keeping the laws and ordinances of His Majesty governing same and the city ordinances now in force and to be issued regarding this office. After giving the oath he was received as *veedor* and marker and empowered and *the die of this city was delivered to him* to be stamped on the pieces fabricated in this city and he received it and accepted said charge. Witnesses, Pedro Sabzedo and Gonzalo Gil, and he signed same.

TAKING OF THE OATH AND DELIVERY OF THE DIE
4TH JULY 1551

This day, by request and supplication of the silversmiths, Gabriel de Villasana was received as marker of silver[16] for this current year, and he was summoned to appear before this Municipal Council and take the solemn oath required in such cases. He appeared at once and took the solemn oath and promised to perform well and faithfully said office of marker of silver, keeping the service of His Majesty and good of the republic, and after said oath *the die for said silver was delivered to him*.

MARKER OF SILVER MIGUEL DE CONSUEGRA
2ND APRIL 1557

This day, by request and appointment of the silversmiths, Miguel de Consuegra, silversmith, was received as marker of silver pieces to whom the oath was administered in the form prescribed by law and under said oath he promised to perform well and faithfully the office of marker of silver keeping the service of God our Lord and of His Majesty and of the royal treasury and good of the republic and after taking the oath *the die of said office* was ordered delivered to him.

The fact that the silversmiths themselves were commissioned to mark silver is proved not only by the Proceedings of the Municipal Council referred to, but by the Ordinances of Sheet-beaters and Wire-drawers of 30th October 1563, in which the following appears:[17]

16 It is probable that he was *veedor* also.
17 Fonseca y Urrutia, op.cit., vol.I, p.393.

That each year, the persons who are to receive payment of the 20% tax on silver shall be appointed, this charge rotating among all to avoid fraud.

The First Law of the Indies on Plate

The law of 1578 expressly referred to silver plate:

THE TWENTY PER CENT ROYAL TAX
LAW XXXIV[18]

1578-1584

Philip II in the Pardo 8th July 1578. And 30th October 1584.

That gold and silver in ingots, jewels and pieces be marked in the form prescribed by this law.

We command that the 20% tax shall be paid to us on all silver and gold fabricated in any part of our Indies into plate, cabinets, furniture, chests, writing-desks, braziers, or pieces of any kind whatsoever, quality and species which it is usual to have for service, ostentation or ornament of the houses, or other purposes: and also the finery and adornments of images, *retablos*, paintings, oratories, jewels, collars, belts, chains, medals, bracelets, buttons, embroidery, rings, and other kinds or species of work, made of gold and silver. And in order that there be no fraud and there be a record that payment has been made, we order that all persons who have the aforesaid pieces made . . . be obliged to take and shall present to our royal officials of this district, and if there are none, the ones nearest, the gold and silver bullion from which they are fabricated. These shall see that the 20% tax is paid thereon and that they are marked with the marks they should have, and if they are [already] marked to weigh them and record same in the private book which they must keep for the purpose, stating the quantity involved, and the pieces, jewels and other things which the individual states and desires to have made and by which silversmith. After which they shall be returned to him with a certificate and testimonial of the statement and registry. The individual obligating himself to take them, within the time required to fabricate the pieces, to be registered with our officials, so that their weight may be compared with the bullion registered, and a *small symbol or mark* selected by them be stamped on each piece which shall be made for this purpose. After marking they shall be returned to the owners. Without [the marks] they can not be held or used or fabricated by any silversmith unless this proceeding has been followed and the certificate of our officials of having been registered with them and the 20% tax paid. Penalty: the owners and silversmith shall have to pay the total value for the first infraction, the obligation being mutual. For the second, the penalty imposed upon those who defraud payment of our 20% royal tax. All to be applied as prescribed and ordered.

18 *Recopilación de Leyes de los Reinos de las Indias*, vol.III, p.64.
   (Note: This law applied to Mexico. See Fonseca y Urrutia, op.cit., vol.I, pp.20-1, 389-90.)

Summary: 1524-78

1. The marking of plate:
   a. From the Proceedings of the Municipal Council it is proved that the silversmiths themselves marked it, at least until the year 1563.
   b. As there was no specific law on the marking of plate until the year 1578, it is probable that the silversmiths continued marking it up to that year.
   c. It is almost certain that after 1578, the royal officials marked the plate, complying with Law XXXIV, Section X, Book VIII, *Leyes de Indias*.
2. Number of marks:
   Both the Proceedings of the Municipal Council and Law XXXIV, Section X, Book VIII, clearly refer to one mark only.

The First Mark Stamped on Precious Metals in Mexico

Bernal Díaz, speaking of Moctezuma's gold which was melted, gives us information regarding the first mark stamped on gold and silver in Mexico:[19]

'. . . and the mark was the royal arms like a *real* and of the size of a fifty cent piece of four [*reales*].'

This mark was for use on bars of precious metals. It was, of course, too large for plate.

In the General Index of the Documents of the Board of the Indies, Codex of the Royal Library of History, Madrid, don Federico Gómez de Orozco found and gave me the following drawing and description with reference to the first mark used on gold in New Spain:

19 Op.cit., p.106.

Year MDXXV. *New Spain*

65. For gold which is melted the device of two columns and a band across two serpent's heads and the lettering *Plus Oultre* and beneath some water and as a border the New Spain, as shown on the margin—

Indice General de los Papeles del Consejo de Indias — Códice de la R. Bib. de la Hist. Madrid.

The First Marks Stamped on Plate

The hall-mark of plate stamped in Madrid was first an M, 'afterwards surmounted by a crown.' It is not known when it was first used.

By the middle of the sixteenth century the name of the City of Tenochtitlán was slowly being changed to Mexico City.[20]

In the Proceedings of the Municipal Council of 15th September 1559, speaking of 'all the marks and measures which up to now have been given by the faithful of this city,' there appears the following:

'. . . that a die shall be made with an M and an O above which means *Mexico* and that one be stamped on weights and the other on measures.'

Furthermore, the M with a small o above (M̊) appeared on money coined in Mexico from 1538 to 1821. From the Proceedings of the Municipal Council previously mentioned and the fact that the Council was entrusted with the regulation of the Silversmiths' Art until 1578, we have seen that the mark during this period was 'the mark and die of this city.'

Thus, it is quite possible that the mark first used on plate consisted of an M with or without an O beneath or to one side.[21] It is likely that the die was a rough one.

---

20 Motolinía, op.cit., pp.178-9, so stated, writing about 1536. Marroqui, op.cit., vol.I, p.18 says: 'Already in 1554 the change of the name of Tenochititlán to Mexico [City] was slowly beginning.'

21 Not, perhaps, above because it is scarcely likely that they would have made it identical with that for weights and measures.

One of the oldest pieces of plate that I have seen, bears such a mark.
It is shown in its original size:

3. Marks between 1579-1732

L A W VI[22]

1579

Philip II there. Ordinance 60 of 1579.
That in the marking of gold and silver the form prescribed by this law be observed.
Because after the gold and silver is melted, and payment of the duties and 20% tax
have been made, the parties return it to the smelter to be made into bars, plates
or large ingots, or fabricate it, and it is taken to our royal officials for marking and
to remove and destroy the note on the certificate recording this same quantity in
a different form. This can cause much harm and fraud to our royal treasury, if this
gold or silver should be of higher standard or carats. Therefore we command that
all silver and gold on which the 20% tax has been paid, in whatever form it be taken
for remelting, be presented to all our royal officials, and with the day, month and
year, in the presence of the parties, the royal officials shall record the quantity,
standard and carats in the book of marks, and the entry signed by all the aforesaid. It may then be melted and they shall not mix with it any other gold or silver.
After melting and assaying, they shall collect for us one and a half [per cent] tax
for melter, assayer and chief marker, and on the remainder the mark shall again be
placed, recording in the same book its quantity, legal standard after remelting,
so that the decrease or increase may be shown and that part of the one and a half
per cent that belongs to us. This shall be kept and complied with under penalty of
a fine of one hundred thousand *maravedis* for our exchequer.

From the year 1579 there were rules for safeguarding the dies used
for stamping silver:

THE ROYAL CHESTS

L A W VIII

That in the Treasurer's office there be a chest, with marks, and dies, and its key
    shall be held by the oldest Official.
(On the margin. Philip II Ord. 5th of 1579).
To avoid the damage and inconveniences that might result from the dies and

22 *Recopilación de Leyes de los Reinos de las Indias*, vol.II, p.144.

punches being separated, and not kept together in our royal chest with the gold and silver, and other things therein contained, it is ordered by law 10, section 22, book 4, that which was deemed suitable for their safety. And for further precaution and safety we command that the dies and punches shall always be kept in a small chest, of proportionate size, that has a good lock and key, from which they shall be taken in the presence of the officials, to mark gold and silver on which payment of the 20% tax is made. After using they shall be returned to the chest and it shall be locked with the key to be kept by the oldest official and he must not give it to anyone if not in accordance with the provisions, and the chest shall again be placed in the Royal Chest, from which it cannot be removed for any reason, or remain outside, under penalty of a fine of one hundred thousand *maravedis* for our Exchequer.

Section IV of Book XIII treats of Royal Officials. Law II says:

For the prompt and skillful execution of meltings, payment of the 20% tax, auctions, collections and payments to our royal treasury and other business, our royal officials shall live in the mint, wherever it is, and our Principal royal chest shall be kept there as well as the other things entrusted to them and the books and taxes, and there they shall perform their duties by order and in the form prescribed by our laws and ordinances.

LAW 12 states: We declare and command that the oldest royal official at least, shall live at our Mint, whether he be accountant or treasurer, and if there are no mints, after our royal chest is placed in the safest house in the city, the Treasurer shall live and stay wherever the chest is, even if he is not the oldest official.

In Mexico City, the Mint was in the building now occupied by the National Museum of History and Archaeology, for which reason the street is still called the Street of the Mint, and old lithographs exist in which the forges for smelting may be seen. The Mint formed part of the National Palace.

About the year 1606 the following proclamation appeared:[23]

10TH APRIL 1606

'That no Silversmith or any other person of whatsoever state or condition, shall buy or sell any silver acquired by barter or in any other manner, unless it is first assayed . . .'

23 Beleña, op.cit., vol.I, p.90 reverse.

In the 'Orders to the Fleet,' dated in Madrid the 12th July 1622, the following appears:

THE KING

TWENTY PER CENT TAX 1622

Because I have been informed that notwithstanding the provisions and order that no gold in bars or cones of silver to be taxed can be taken or brought from one place to another in my west Indies or to these kingdoms, and if any of such things be found without the 20% tax thereon having been paid or marked, in any port of the Indies where there is no smelter they shall be forfeited. Excessive amounts have been found in the past and frequently in the port of Callao and others of the provinces of Peru much gold and silver has been found without having been marked or the 20% tax thereon paid and because it is my will it is hereby provided and ordered that this command be kept and strictly observed.

By these presents I command my Viceroys, Tribunals, Governors and officials of my Royal Treasury and each and every part of my Islands of the Indies and land and sea that whenever in any part or place of their districts they find any gold, silver cones[24] or bars wrought or to be wrought into jewels, plate or other pieces, or gold in powder or in bars without the 20% tax having been paid thereon and marked shall be forfeited and seized, carrying out [this command] in accordance with the law and the provisions of laws and Royal Ordinances as this is my will.

I, THE KING[25]

By command of the King our Lord.

Juan Ruyz de Contreras.

All gold and silver found in whatever part of the Indies where no smelter exists, on which the 20% tax has not been paid shall be forfeited.

By decision of the Council—(Rubrics)

1619

The 'Ordinances Relative to the Silversmiths' Art,' commanded observed by the Marquis of Cadereyta in 1638, state that the silversmiths' guild:

presented to me a petition and the *command of the Marquis of Guadalcazar of 7th September* 1619, regarding which . . . they shall have their operators and stores on San Francisco Street and all the rest contained therein and therefore *the ordinances which said guild had drawn up last year*, 1623, for proper use and exercise of

---

24 Porous silver mass in conical form which remains in the crucibles where it is melted in the furnaces; the mass extracted from silver ore.

25 Philip IV.

their trade and art for the greater service . . . and in attention to this the Marquis of Gelves confirmed and approved them and ordered that they be complied with and executed, requesting me please to issue the order as said ordinances had been maliciously hidden and the order not having been issued had resulted in. . . .

1623

From the foregoing we may conclude that neither the command of the Marquis of Guadalcazar nor the Ordinances of 1623 were observed, and that the first effective Ordinances giving detailed instructions on marks, were those of Cadereyta, of 1638.[26]

The Ordinances of the Marquis of Cadereyta with respect to marks may be summarized as follows:

1. Ordinance 8.
   a. Present to the Officials of the Royal Treasury the silver and gold that is to be fabricated.
   b. That said Royal Officials ascertain whether the 20% tax thereon has been paid and marked, and if not, to collect the tax, weigh, record and register. . . .
   c. After this has been done, it shall be returned with a certificate . . . the person obligating himself to bring the pieces when finished to be registered by the same Royal Officials so that their weight may be compared with that of the ingots which they had marked.
   d. And to ascertain whether they are of the same standard, and if so, the *Veedor*, in the presence of the royal officials, shall mark them with the mark and symbol which should be kept for this purpose, which shall be in proportion to the size of the piece, regardless of how small it might be, so that the mark will indicate forever that they are of the required standard and that the 20% tax thereon has been paid.

2. Ordinance 17.

   So that fraud may be avoided and it may be easier to punish the silversmiths who make pieces of gold and silver not of the re quired standard, they shall have a known symbol or mark or their name, that shall be registered with the Public Scrivener

---

26 For complete text of these Ordinances see Appendix II.

of the Municipal Council of the City of Mexico. And without this the plate cannot be sold.

3. Ordinance 18.

That the *Veedor* shall not receive gold and silver plate unless it bears the symbol and mark of the artisan who made it.

It will be noted that in 1638 the *Veedor*, a silversmith employed by the Government and not one elected by the silversmiths, still marked the silver in the presence of the royal officials.

From the records it is clearly seen that until 1638 *only one mark* was required, a mark which indicated that the metal used in making the piece was of legal standard, and likewise that the records showed that the 20% tax on silver ingots had been duly paid. From these ordinances it is learned that from 1638, two marks were required: one indicating payment of the tax and the legal standard of the metal, and the second that of the silversmith.

Although promulgated for Peru, the Ordinances for Assayers of 1649-1651 contain clauses which are interesting:

LAW XVII[27]

1649-1651

The same in Madrid, 7th January 1649. In Buen Retiro, 6th May, 1651.
Ordinances which must be observed by the assayers of Peru.
First, the chief assayers, working together, or one alone in cases where permitted, must be informed that these offices were created so that they may endeavor by every possible means and methods they consider effective, to see that the silver and gold in use in all the provinces of Peru, whether in bars or ingots, money, plate and jewels, is of the legal standard, conforming to the laws of these our kingdoms of Castille, ordered observed in the Indies. Also that in the assay of these metals in ingots, coins and other pieces fraud shall cease, and that they be made as legal, certain and promptly as required, in view of its importance. Whatever error, carelessness or negligence in the assay occasions much damage and injury to public and private interests. [They shall] thus carry out all that is commanded, with the honesty, legality and intelligence which is expected of them, and if they find that by other means the damage may be overcome, they shall propose them to the Viceroy of those provinces, so that having the information he may decide what is to be done, and advise us.

27 *Recopilación de Leyes de los Reinos de las Indias*, vol.II, p.146.

CHAPTER XXIV[28]

1649-1651

The chief assayer shall be in charge of inspecting all those engaged in the trade of silver-shop keepers and gold beaters in the places where silver shops exist. And we command that no one may practice said trades in any other manner, notwithstanding any custom or privilege of the city, village or place.

CHAPTER XXV

We command that each silversmith who makes pieces of gold or silver, [shall] have his private mark which he shall record with the justice or scribe of the Municipal Council of the place where he resides. This mark shall be stamped on the pieces he makes so that if they are found not to be of the legal standard for silver and gold, the silversmith shall be prosecuted with the full force of the law. The Chief Assayers shall proclaim by public crier this chapter in all the cities, villages and places which they inspect, bearing the Viceroy's special order for the purpose, as provided for in chapter 22.

Summary of Documents on Marks

1579-1732

YEAR	DOCUMENTS	SUMMARY
1638	Ordinances of Cadereyta	Hall-mark: signifying payment of tax and quality of metal. Mark of the silversmith.
1640	Proceedings of the Municipal Council of 15th December	Assayer 'is given the privilege of inspecting the silver and its quality.'
1649-51	'Ordinances for Assayers of Peru,' Chapter I	'These offices have been created for enforcing . . . the legal standard . . . of silver and gold.'
	'Ordinances for Assayers of Peru,' Chapter XXV	'Each silversmith . . . shall have his private mark . . . and this mark shall be stamped on the pieces made by him so that if they are not of the legal standard . . . the silversmith may be prosecuted. . . .'
1622	'Orders to the Fleet'	'whenever . . . they may find any gold, silver . . . wrought or to be wrought into jewels, plate or other . . . without the 20% tax having been paid and hall-marked it shall be forfeited. . . .'

28 Ibid., vol. II.

1701   From the Ordinances   That the artisan stamp his mark on the
            of 1746   wrought silver. (Although I have not found
                                       the Ordinances of 1701, from the slight dif-
                                       ference between the Ordinances of 1638 and
                                       1748, we may be certain that they are similar.)

From the foregoing it is seen that in Mexico from 1638 it was commanded that in addition to the hall-mark certifying the quality and
the payment of the 20% tax (both by a single mark) the artisan should
stamp his private mark on plate. Therefore, two marks should appear
on plate made since 1638, and only one on plate made prior to 1638.

Hall-marks between 1579-1637

As we have seen, from 1579 to 1638 Government employees stamped
the silver with only one mark, which signified two facts: that the silver
was of legal standard and that the taxes had been paid.

Of the many pieces of silver of this period which I have examined
there are a few on which the hall-marks are barely legible. The others
either were never hall-marked or show only an impression proving that
they bore marks, erased by time and use. Although so faint that it does
not reproduce well, the hall-mark illustrated is of the Royal Arms, the
columns of Hercules and between them an M surmounted by a crown.

Hall-mark 1579-1637   *Hall-mark* 1579-1637
Original size   *Enlarged*

Hall-marks between 1638-1732

As we have seen, between 1638 and 1732 it was ordered that two marks
be used: one signifying that the metal used was of the required standard
and that the taxes had been duly paid, and the other that of the
artisan.

The marks reproduced below were used between 1638-1732. One is of the same form used between 1579 and 1637, that is to say, the Royal Arms, the columns of Hercules with an M surmounted by a crown between them, but is of a smaller size. The other is the mark of the artisan.

STANDARD AND TAX MARK

MARK OF THE ARTISAN
(TORRES)

Enlarged

Enlarged

4. *Hall-marks between* 1733-1820

No additional provision on hall-marks appears until the Royal Order of 1st October 1733, a summary of which, as regards hall-marks, is as follows:

MARK OF THE TWENTY PER CENT TAX

a. That, when finished, the pieces be taken so that 'these officials' (those of the Royal Treasury)[29] may place thereon the stamp of the 20% or 10% tax.

NAME OF ASSAYER

b. The Chief Assayer also shall inspect the pieces and if found to be of 11 *dineros*, he shall mark all of them with the punch bearing his name.

ARTISAN'S MARK

c. In keeping with the ordinances of this Union, no plate may be sold unless it bears the artisan's mark and the hall-mark, according to

---

29 *The Royal Officials.* Section III of Book VIII treats 'of the Tribunals of the Royal Treasury' and Law V stated: '. . . the offices of Treasurer, Accountant and Factor performed by our Royal Officials. . . .'

Law I stated: 'We order and command that our Royal Officials shall not be called Official Justices, or have any title other than that mentioned in this our Law of Royal Officials or of our Royal Treasury, and we permit and consider it in order that the room of their office be called Tribunal when they perform their duties therein together.'

the provisions of these laws: 1st and 2nd of Section 24, Book 50, of the *Recopilación de Castilla*.[30]

1746

The Ordinances of the Viceroy Fuen-Clara of 1746, as regards marks, are the same as those of 1638, as will be seen from the following excerpt:

ORDINANCE 9

TWENTY PER CENT TAX MARK

When finished . . . they shall be brought for registration to the same Royal Officials so that the weight may be compared with that of the ingots, which were marked, the entry being noted on the margin . . . and ascertain whether they are of the same standard, and if they are, the *Juez Veedor* [the Chief Assayer] in the presence of said Royal Officials shall stamp thereon the hall-mark, and symbol which he has for this purpose, and it shall be in proportion, so that regardless of the smallness of the piece, it shall be hall-marked. . . .

ORDINANCE 18

a. That the gold and silversmiths shall have marks of a known symbol, which they shall stamp on the pieces they make.[31]
b. That they register the mark with the Scrivener of the Chief Assayer.

From this, it is concluded that from 1733 three marks were stamped on silver:

a. Mark of the 20% tax. . . . (showing that taxes had been paid.)
b. Mark of the Assayer. . . . (showing that the metal was of legal standard.)
c. Mark of the artisan. . . . (solely to avoid fraud.)

It must be borne in mind that the Ordinances of Fuen-Clara of 1746

30 These laws are as follows: 'Section Twenty-four—Of Silversmiths and Gilders—Law I. John II, Madrid 1435 and Ferdinand and Isabella, Madrigal, 1475. Silversmiths who fabricate silver to be hall-marked with the standard of 11 *dineros* and 4 grains under penalty for falsification of sevenfold payment of the silver for the exchequer and accuser. They must have a known symbol which shall be shown to the Scribe of the council where they reside to be stamped on the silver they fabricate under the Mark of the city or Village where it is made. Those who go from one place to another to work are obliged to show and declare to the Scrivener of the council of that place, the symbol and mark they wish to put on the silver, under penalty of incurring the penalties prescribed for those who use false weight.
    Law 2. Ferdinand and Isabella. Valencia, 12th April 1488. No piece of silver shall be hall-marked that does not contain 11 *dineros* 4 grains under the penalties referred to in the preceding law, and the marker shall not accept more than the duties under penalty, for the first infraction, of paying the required duty sevenfold and for the second, loss of office and of half his property.'
31 Reason: to avoid fraud and make it easier to punish the silversmiths who might use a metal inferior to the legal standard.

do not command that the name of the Chief Assayer be used as a mark, although it was commanded in the Royal Order of 1st October 1733 that the Chief Assayer stamp his name on plate.

The silversmiths often fraudulently omitted payment of the 20% tax, which explains the lack of marks on much of the plate of that period.

This is confirmed by the following document and many others not mentioned for lack of space:

Carlos Francisco de Croix, Marquis of Croix, Knight of the Order of Calatrava, Knight Commander of Molinos y Laguna Rota of the same Order, Lieutenant General of the Royal Armies of His Majesty, Viceroy, Governor and Captain General of the Kingdom of New Spain, President of his Royal Tribunal, General Superintendent of the Royal Treasury and Tobacco Branch thereof, President of the Board of Judge Conservator of this Branch, general Sub-delegate of the Maritime Post Office Establishment in this same Kingdom.

In view of the limited number of silver and gold marks which on plate, jewelry and other wrought pieces have been manifested for payment of the 10% tax and the regular Royal Taxes thereon to the Royal Treasurer's Office of this capital during the first six months allowed as a privilege this year for [manifesting] . . . who still have plate and other pieces of gold and silver in their homes and service without the tax having been paid thereon, have not, perhaps, been able within that time to acquire the amount of the respective Royal taxes which should be paid his Majesty . . . but can, if given an additional period within which to make payment. I have decided to extend this six months' period designated in the aforesaid proclamation which was published, for the payment of ordinary and simple taxes for four additional months, which by cancellation of the other on this subject, shall be counted from the 26th day of the present month. It is well understood that at the expiration of this period the pieces of silver and gold which are manifested and on which the 10% tax is paid during the following six months, shall pay double taxes. And those which at the expiration of these last six months are found without the royal mark of the 10% tax, shall be forever forfeited, as prescribed in the first proclamation published to this effect, and again I declare that they incur the penalty. And so that it may be known by all and no one may allege ignorance I order that this be published by proclamation and others may be sent out for the same purpose, as was done with the first. Mexico, seventeenth of September, 1767.

> The Marquis of Croix
> By order of His Excellency.
> (Signatures missing)[31a]

1783

From the Ordinances for Assayers, prepared by Lic. José Antonio

[31a] *Archivo General de la Nación.* Proclamations, vol. VI. Proclamation 79.

Lince González, Chief Assayer of the Kingdom and of the Principal Royal Mint in Mexico, Weigher, Melter and Chief Marker, Receiver of 20% Tax Payments and Royal Hall-marks, and *Juez Veedor* of the Noble Art of the Silversmiths, Sheet-beaters and Wire-drawers of gold and silver, issued in Mexico on the 7th July 1783 by the Viceroy Matías de Gálvez,[32] and of the ordinances of the Mint,[33] issued at Buen Retiro, 1st August 1750, detailed data are found regarding marks:

1. *How the Royal Marks were Stamped*

XXVI

The Chief Assayer is the stamper of the hall-mark, seals and royal marks in accordance with his title, not because he actually does this or understands this art, which is foreign to his profession, but because special confidence is placed in this employment. Therefore he has in his possession the dies, characters, abc's, numbers and moulds with which these marks are stamped on ingots, plate, royal seals, paper bearing a seal, bulls and others, and whenever one is needed he issues the superior orders required to call an artisan to stamp them. The artisan's work is paid by the royal officials from sworn statements of the assayer. All of which shall thus be done, eliminating the pernicious abuse introduced some time ago in these parts of having *these marks made by an artisan, making dies for the purpose at his will*, as is done for the royal lottery, tobacco bureau and other bodies, with grave risk that these seals, the 20% tax-mark and royal marks[34] may thus be forged.

2. *Obligations of the Marker*

Marks[35] to be stamped on silver or gold, whether in bars and ingots or *pieces made into plate*, Laws I, section 22, book 4, and VIII, section 6, book 8, provide that they must be kept with the greatest care in a chest whose key is in the possession of the oldest royal official, which shall be kept in the chest with three keys, and that they cannot be taken out except when marking and taxing has to be done and all the officials are present. Therefore, they cannot be used except when the assayer is present, so that after the standard and weight of the pieces are declared, they shall be ordered stamped by the artisan spoken of in the preceding Ordinance, by hammering those that require it, after which the marks shall be returned to their chest, and the taxes having been paid by the parties, the 10% as well as the fees for assay and melting, the silver and gold shall be delivered to their owners who may then freely dispose of it.

32 Fonseca y Urrutia, op.cit., vol.I, pp.52-108.
33 Ibid., vol.I, pp.221-96.
34 Ibid., vol.I, pp.96-7. *Ordenanzas de Ensayadores de* 1783.
35 Chapter 6, paragraph V.

3. *Porter and Marker: Their Duties*

In the receiving and paying office of the royal mint there shall be a porter and a marker, who must be of well known fidelity and perfectly trustworthy, both entrusted with receiving in that room and caring for the pieces of gold and silver in ingots and plate which private individuals bring for sale, advising the treasurer. They must ascertain to whom each piece belongs and guard them during the interval before they are assayed and weighed and the treasurer receives them for my royal account. Both should have a key and the treasurer another, to the aforesaid office. Here both morning and afternoon the porter and marker shall be present; the latter, or in his absence the former, shall listen to the judge of weights when he weighs the metals, designate or mark with ink the standard and weight of each piece, as well as the weight of every thousand *pesos* counted and sacked, for making payments. One or the other shall inform as to the number of empty sacks, and shall watch to see that nothing is missing from the office. The porter shall attend to the cleaning of the office and of the tribunal, and both shall be held responsible for everything pertaining to said office that has been entrusted to them, which shall be received by them under inventory. They shall carry out the orders of the superintendent, accountant and treasurer of the service of said mint.

The porter and marker shall be provided by agreement between the three officials mentioned, or alternately, and be appointed by the superintendent.[36]

4. *Receiving Precious Metals in the Mint*

Manner of receiving in the office of the mint the pieces of gold and silver, of taking and weighing the small samples which the assayers together should remove for assay, and remuneration for the assay.

The gold and silver in ingots or plate which may be taken for sale to the said Royal Mint must have paid the royal taxes thereon to my Royal Treasury. And if through ignorance or inattention the owners should come to sell one or more of the bars or ingots without the usual marks which certify that my royal Treasury has been paid, the superintendent, with someone of the same mint, shall send them to the Royal Treasury of that city, so that my Royal Officials may exact the amount of the respective taxes. And all the metals mentioned of gold and silver in ingots or plate, *shall be received in the receiving and paying office* of the mint, by the porter and marker of said office, who must inform themselves of the number of pieces belonging to each owner, and advise the assayers of the mint so that they may present themselves to take the small samples for assay. The aforesaid porter and marker are entrusted with the care and safety of the pieces of gold and silver remaining in the office until they are assayed, and after weighing by the judge of weights, they are delivered to the treasurer for my Royal Account, having them placed in the treasury.

36 Ibid., vol.I, pp.276-7. *Ordenanzas de la Casa de Moneda de* 1750.

And notice is hereby given that at least one assayer shall be present at the time the small samples are taken in the receiving office where they are to be weighed by the judge of weights or his assistant, *at the rate of half an ochava of gold in each piece of this metal*, and for silver *four ochavas in each piece*, which is the fee the assayers should receive for these assays, so that by thus weighing the small pieces neither the owners of the pieces nor the assayers shall be harmed in the duties the former pay and the fees the latter receive for the assay.[37]

Chapter VIII of the aforesaid *Ordenanzas de Ensayadores de* 1783, referring to *los Ensayadores de Cajas Marcas* [Assayers where there were no Royal Chests] states:

After[38] the silver or gold is melted and assayed and stamped with the *hall-mark and name of the assayer*, they shall send the pieces to the justice of the district so that he may make note of them in his book which should be kept for the purpose. After each piece *is stamped with the mark of the place and the royal crown* which shall be sent him from this head treasurer's office (provided it is necessary) and the interested parties have fulfilled the obligations prescribed by Law IV, section 10, book 8, that they be taken for payment of the 20% tax within the succeeding first thirty days, they shall be given the certificate or list prescribed by Law XI of the same section, stating the pieces, their number, standard and weight, addressed to the respective royal treasurer's office, so that having fulfilled these requisites the gold or silver may be freely conducted until it is presented to the aforesaid royal treasurer's office, and the royal taxes thereon having been paid the marks certifying same shall be stamped thereon, under the penalties the same laws contain, of forfeiture of the silver, beasts of burden, and all else stated therein.

The above order is important because it is proof that the *Royal Crown was used as a certificate of quality*, and although it more specifically refers to the metal melted and assayed before being fabricated, it is quite probable that the Royal Crown was also used to certify the quality of silver plate.

The Royal Order of 15th August 1784, published by Proclamation[39] on 25th April 1785, contains provisions covering marks for gold and silver which may be summarized as follows:

Formerly gold and silver which was to be used for making plate was taken to the royal officials so that they might see:

37 Ibid., vol.I, pp.228-9. *Ordenanzas de la Casa de Moneda* issued at Buen Retiro 1st August 1750.
38 Ibid., vol.I, pp.77-8. *Ordenanzas de Ensayadores*, 1783.
39 Beleña, op.cit., vol.II.

a. Whether they are marked, and if not they should be marked, and

b. Their weight be recorded in the books (certificates being furnished them).

c. After fabrication:

    (1) They shall again be manifested.

    (2) The pieces presented shall be marked.

d. Gold of 22 carats:

    Shall be stamped with the *three marks* which up to this time *has been the custom.*

e. Gold of 20 carats: the same marks, plus a number '20.' The pieces which because of their small size or because of their workmanship do not allow 4 *marks*, shall be stamped with only one which shall be a *Royal Crown.*

It will be noted that in the Proclamation previously made the *Imperial Crown* appears as a *symbol of quality.*

This somewhat contradicts what was said by the Chief Assayer Joseph Lince González in 1779:

Paragraph 44: 'The Treasurer's Office[40] cannot make use of the 10% tax-mark which consists of the Royal Arms as this can only be used in the Treasurer's Offices by the Royal Officials. . . .[41]' Regarding marks, significant data is found in the 'Consultation[42] made the Royal Tribunal . . .' by Lic. Joseph Lince González. . . .

Paragraph 4: After the pieces are fabricated they shall again be brought for assay, tying together those of legal standard, they shall be passed to the Royal Treasurer's office so that they may be marked. They shall also be stamped with my name which certifies that they are of the required standard, and when by the Assay I find that they contain less than the eleven *Dineros* which by Royal commands they should have, it is ordered that they be broken up, in accordance with Chapter 23, Law 17, Section 22, Book 4, and ordinance 19 of the silversmiths' art and after I have regulated the alloy, they shall again be melted and fabricated.

The Viceroy Revilla Gigedo[43] speaking of the royal chests said:

1790

886. The poor distribution of work, and the fact that it all comes at once, without any order or method, causes the same inconveniences in the treasurer's office as in

40 *'Consulta hecha a la Real Audiencia*, etc.,' op.cit.
41 Of the Treasury.
42 Op.cit.
43 Op.cit., p.224.

any other. To prevent this I ordered by decree of 12th March [17]90, that Monday, Wednesday and Friday mornings be set always for payment of salary warrants, pensions, annuities, and other similar payments, and the afternoons for payment of the 20% tax, 10% tax on silver which the miners manifest, and pay and receive payments from outside treasurer's offices. Tuesday, Thursday and Saturday mornings for receiving payments of all branches of the royal treasury, and the afternoons for the 20% tax and hall-marks for silversmiths and sheet-beaters. The first six days of the third [week of the month] for all payments of salaries, wages and widows' pensions, and the first two days of the month for the same payments.

The foregoing may be summarized as follows:

1733-1820

YEAR		
1733	Royal Order of 1733	a. The mark showing that payment of the tax had been made. Stamped by the Royal officials.
		b. Name of Chief Assayer: quality of the metal used.
		c. Artisan's mark: for identification of maker.
1746	Ordinances	The same as the Royal Order of 1733. While the 'mark' of the Chief Assayer is mentioned, it is not specified that this mark shall be the name of the Chief Assayer.
1779	'Consultation made the Royal Tribunal etc.'	'The mark of the 10% Tax which is the Royal Arms.'
1783	Ordinances of Assayers	a. In the Royal Treasurer's Office: the marks which proved that the 20% tax had been paid.
		b. The name of the Chief Assayer: a mark which indicated by whom assayed and that the metal was found to be of the required standard.
		c. Mark of the place and Royal Crown: certificate of quality by the justice of the District.
		d. Artisan's mark: nothing is said regarding this mark. Nevertheless, as the Ordinances of 1746 were still in force, a repetition of this order was unnecessary.
1785	Royal Order of 15th August, 1784.	States that on gold of 22 carats there should be three marks.

5. *Summary of Marks According to Documents:* 1524-1820

1524-1637	One mark:	Certifying that tax was paid and that the metal used was of the required standard.
1638-1732	Two marks:	1. Certifying that tax had been paid and that the metal used was of the required standard.
		2. Artisan's mark.
1733-1782	Three marks:	1. Certifying that the tax was paid.
		2. Mark of the name of the Chief Assayer: certifying that the metal used was of the required standard.
		3. Artisan's mark.
1783-1820	Four marks:	1. Certifying that the tax was paid.
		2. Mark of the Chief Assayer: indicated who assayed it and that he found it to be of the required standard.
		3. Mark of the place and the Royal Crown: certificate of quality by the Justice of the District.
		4. Artisan's mark.

The Ordinances of 1746 were the last because in 1790[44] reference is made to 'Ordinance 29' of the Ordinances of 1746, and in 1839[45] reference is made to Ordinances 9, 25 and 26, of the same Ordinances of 1746.

In 1809-1811, the *Cortes* of Spain attempted to collect funds for war expenses, confiscating gold and silver plate from private individuals and churches. In 1811 'establishment[46] of a mark on jewels of gold and silver of the Church and of private individuals, and other measures to collect more easily the share demanded of them' was decreed. That is to say, it was ordered that the part of the silver returned to the owners should be marked. In the same decree these provisions were declared extensive to all the provinces of America and Asia. They did not specify the mark which the authorities should stamp on the part returned as this was evidently left to their judgement. I have not found any record that this decree was made effective in Mexico, and in view

44 Fonseca y Urrutia, op.cit., vol.I, p.409.
45 Decree of 4th September 1839.
46 Decree LXV. *Colección de los Decretos y Ordenes que han expedido las Cortes Generales y Extraordinarias desde su instalación de 24 de septiembre de 1810 hasta igual fecha de 1811*, vol.I. Ordered published by the same. Madrid, 1820. *Imp. Nacional.*

of the situation in that period, it is probable that the authorities did not dare to attempt to force compliance with such an absurd order.

6. *The Chief Assayers*

The office of Chief Assayer was created in Mexico at the time of the Conquest. According to Alamán,[47] Francisco de Cobos was the first[48] Chief Assayer, in 1522, and according to F. Fernández del Castillo, in his work *Algunos Documentos nuevos sobre Bartolomé de Medina*, published by the Scientific Society, Antonio Alzate, *Talleres Gráficos de la Nación*, Mexico, 1927, 'the first silversmith assayer who came to Mexico was Pedro Gómez, arriving with Pánfilo de Narváez. . . .'

The office of Chief Assayer was abolished in 1895, Romualdo Obregón being the last Chief Assayer in Mexico.

The following list of Chief Assayers during the years prior to 1731 may be of interest to future investigators:

LIST OF CHIEF ASSAYERS

YEAR	CHIEF ASSAYER	REFERENCE
1522	Francisco de los Cobos	Lucas Alamán *Obras de*, vol.I, p.248.
1552	Diego de los Cobos	Fonseca y Urrutia, op.cit., vol.I, pp.116-17.
1589	Luis Nuñez Pérez	*A.G. de la N. Libro General de la Contaduría del Rey*, p.200.
1628	Melchor de Cuellar	*A.G. de la N. Casa Moneda. Registro de Nombramientos*, pp.528 and following.
1632	Diego de Godoy	Lieutenant acting as Chief Assayer, do. p.281.
1649	Francisco de Ena	*A.G. de la N. Reales Cédulas 1645-1651*, v.15, p.48 reverse.
1673	Juan de la Fuente	Chief Assayer of the Kingdom and of the Royal Mint, *A.G. de la N. Ramo de la Inquisición*, vol.838, p.15. His lieutenant was Gerónimo Becerra.
1701	Nicolás González de la Cueva	*Ordenanzas de Plateros de Fuen-Clara* 1746. *Pregones.*
1704	Nicolás González de la Cueva	Fonseca y Urrutia, op.cit., vol.I, p.86. *Ens. y Fundidor de la Casa Moneda.*
1709	Nicolás González de la Cueva	*A.G. de la N. Inquisición, vol.838, p.82.*

47 Alamán, Lucas, op.cit., vol.I, p.248.
48 Cobos was the Secretary of Charles V and upon being appointed Assayer, he was also authorized, in enjoyment of the privilege, to name a person to represent him in New Spain.

1713	Nicolás González de la Cueva	*Defensa Jurídica de las Misiones de las Californias como Herederos de Dña. Gertrudis de la Peña Vda. del Maestre de Campo D. Francisco Lorens de Rada.* Mexico 1759, paragraph III, p.65.
1722	Juan de Cueva Sandoval — Assistant	*A.G. de la N. Ramo de Inquisición,* vol.838, p.2.
1723	Capt. Felipe Rivas de Angulo[49] — Assistant	*A.G. de la N. Ramo de Inquisición,* vol.838, p.2.
1724	Capt. Felipe Rivas de Angulo — Assistant	*A.G. de la N. Ordenanzas,* vol.II, 1723-63. p.320. Was Chief Assayer to His Excellency the Marquis de Cadereyta.
1729	Domingo García de Mendiola	Chief Assayer and Weigher of the Royal Mint of this Court. Fonseca y Urrutia, op.cit., p.89.

It was the duty of the Chief Assayer to examine (to make certain that the Royal tax had been paid) all the precious metals which were brought for assay, whether later to be made into ingots or plate or coined.

At times other similar work was assigned to them, such as 'Stamper of Hall-marks, Seals and Royal Marks, *Juez Veedor* of the Noble Silversmiths' Art.' The Chief Assayer was the most important authority for the silversmiths.

From 1522 to the 22nd July, 1783,[50] when it was incorporated into the Crown, the office was sold to the highest bidder and profits were for the benefit of the holder.

As seen by the Laws of Spain and the Indies the kings gave few detailed instructions regarding the manner of stamping the marks. Usually it was left to the judgement of the Chief Assayer 'as he deems best.' Therefore, as 'Stamper of Hall-marks' everything pertaining to the kind of marks, their design and execution, was in the hands of the Chief Assayer.

As has been seen in the Royal Order of the 1st of October 1733, issued by the Viceroy Juan de Acuña, Marquis of Casa Fuerte, it was commanded that, after examination of the pieces of plate, if they were of the required standard, 'he [the Chief Assayer] shall stamp all the pieces with the punch bearing his name.'

49 He took his examination for Assayer and was approved the 29th May 1669. (*A.G. de la N. Reales Cédulas,* vol.27, p.12, 3rd book). Therefore he must have been very old in 1724.

50 Fonseca y Urrutia, op.cit., vol.I, p.47.

As this was the first order to this effect, we can identify any piece of silver bearing the name of an Assayer and may safely conclude that:

a. It was made subsequent to the year 1733.
b. Pertains to the period between the year the Assayer took office and the year he left it, and
c. In order to date Mexican plate, the names of Chief Assayers beginning with the year 1732 are necessary.

7. *Marks and Forgeries*

There are many falsifications of old Mexican plate, especially of small brasiers, candlesticks, trays and bowls. Probably at least half of the objects now offered for sale are not genuine.

For many years the Mexican silversmiths' production has consisted almost exclusively of copies of colonial silver. The hall-marks were so little known that dealers had only to forge the marks to convert the piece into colonial silver for the great majority of their customers.

The reproductions which do not bear false hall-marks, although they may not have been originally represented as colonial plate, must be taken into consideration, as they are frequently offered for sale as antiques. Usually some defect may be found which does not appear in colonial silver. The copy always lacks the spirit of the original. Any intelligent observer who examines these objects feels that their maker produced exclusively for gain, did not enjoy making the objects and was not proud of them after they were made. Practically, it is seldom that one does not find the impression of the hammer, that is to say, it is poorly and coarsely finished. This is due to the high cost of labor and the unwillingness of the public to pay high prices rather than to lack of skill on the part of the silversmiths of today.

The reproductions made by Apolonio Guevara,[51] Master Silversmith, who is now very old and unable to work effectively, although he still tries, are the most difficult to distinguish from the genuine. His work is so similar to that of the colonial silversmiths that the collector who is deceived is not defrauded in acquiring them.

I have never seen a forgery of silver-gilt, and the cost of such reproductions would be so great that it is unlikely that any exist.

51 At the age of 80, in March 1936, he was still working.

Imitations with forged marks abound. It is now easier to distinguish them, as on subsequent pages are shown photographs of the genuine marks as well as of many forgeries.

Genuine pieces with forged marks are rare. Apparently forged marks were first stamped on genuine pieces during the first years of this century, when there was apparently a great demand for old plate, and antiquaries like Rolleri, Gendrop and Riveroll Sr., had difficulty in selling genuine pieces lacking hall-marks. For this reason they stamped old plate with false marks. This, of course, does not impair the value of the plate.

Master Silversmith Martínez, who worked at the beginning of the nineteenth century, must have had a set of forged punches which he used to avoid payment of taxes, because his genuine mark appears with forged official marks of the period, as well as with genuine official marks. In *Plate* 165 is shown a piece marked about 1810. The official marks stamped on it are forgeries, while Martínez' mark is genuine.

No great quantity of Mexican plate bears forgeries of the silversmiths' marks. Some falsifications, however, are found more often than are the genuine marks. Among these are the marks of Martínez, Torres, Martel, and Rodallega.

The difference between certain forgeries and the genuine marks is very difficult to detect. Perhaps satisfactory proof could never have been presented had it not been my great good fortune to find one of the old punches at the Mint. This punch has been in use since the Independence, the following[52] Chief Assayers having used it:

Buitrón — 1823-1843
Morales — 1882-1889
Sáyago — 1890-1893
Obregón — 1894-1895.

Having at hand one of the genuine marks, the tax mark and the other marks which appear with it necessarily must be genuine also. This being true, Buitrón's genuine punch and the genuine hall-mark of standard of quality in use at that time were established. To facilitate comparison, the genuine marks as well as each mark of the forgeries

52 From 1856 until about 1881, the assayers used other marks, but these, fortunately, were never forged.

were enlarged five diameters and then printed on transparent material. These enlarged prints were then compared over opaque glass, with a strong light underneath. It was found that, however excellent the forgery, it could not resist this test.

As Buitrón did not use the punches of his predecessors it was more difficult to secure satisfactory proof as to the genuineness of the older marks. Some silversmiths owning dies made for use in imitating the old marks, as a trade-mark or sometimes as a decoration, helped by furnishing bits of metal stamped with these dies. The most important of these were those which I bought from Apolonio Guevara. These are shown below, together with those of other silversmiths.

*Marks from Punches in possession of
the Silver Shop 'Maciel'
Actual size*

 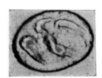

*Enlarged marks from punches used by Carillo y Mendoza
as decorations.*

*Marks from Apolonio
Guevara's forged punches
Actual size*

The second step was to classify as forgeries the electro-plated objects which bear marks, which furnished another collection of forged marks. The third and last step was to establish a '*standard*,' selecting great works of art not susceptible of forgery. For greater certainty, the marks appearing on objects of silver-gilt, the reproduction of which is so costly that it is not profitable, were chosen as standards. For example, when studying the marks of Diego González de la Cueva (1732-1778), the cruet, bell and small tray which are shown in *Plate* 107, the work of the famous Master Silversmith José María Rodallega, were selected as indubitably genuine. Using the marks on these pieces, the genuineness of six marks which appear thereon was established.

Chief Assayer José Antonio Lince González, who succeeded González, continued to use the die with the 'M' surmounted by a crown[53] which belonged to the latter. This aided greatly in establishing the genuineness of Lince's marks. In addition, another 'standard' was established, using the marks on the piece shown in *Plate* 109.

Chief Assayer Forcada's marks (1791-1818) were easier to distinguish, because they appeared next to the genuine marks of silversmiths, the genuineness of whose marks were already established because they appeared with older Government marks already established as authentic. In addition, of all the assayers' punches, his were the most skillfully engraved—far better than the imitations.

Care is advised in the examination of small pieces which do not bear the tax mark and which bear inscriptions. Many of these are forgeries. Due to their minor intrinsic value, inscriptions are placed on them to increase their sale price.

FORGERY OF '*MUNDOS Y MARES*'

This forgery merits special mention. Almost from the beginning of the Conquest the arms of Spain were stamped on precious metals and a shield bearing the same arms appeared on money coined in Mexico called *macuquina* (applied to coins with the milled edges cut away), until the year 1732. From that date to 1771 money was coined called

Obverse   *Reverse*

53 A fact established by the transparent paper test.

Columnaria ó de Mundos y Mares (Columnar or of Land and Seas), the reverse side of which was not changed during this period.

Probably through ignorance false marks were made bearing the shield of *Mundos y Mares*. There were no genuine marks bearing this device.

Marks on Plate between 1733-1782

As it was ordered in 1733 that the Chief Assayer should stamp his name on silver, the list of these assayers and the period of years each served are of great interest because with this information the approximate date the plate was marked can be determined.

The Chief Assayers between 1731-1782 were:

YEAR	NAME	REFERENCE AND SOURCE OF DATA
1731	Diego González de la Cueva	Fonseca y Urrutia, op.cit., vol.I, p.89.
1732	Diego González de la Cueva	*Archivo General de la Nación, Ramo de Inquisición*, vol.838, p.21.
1745	Diego González de la Cueva	*Archivo General de la Nación, Ordenanzas.* 1723-1763. vol.II, p.187 reverse.
1746	Diego González de la Cueva	*Ordenanzas de Fuen Clara de* 1746, op.cit.
1747	Diego González de la Cueva	*Archivo General de la Nación. Ordenanzas*, vol.II, p.232. 1723-1763.
1751	Diego González de la Cueva	Fonseca y Urrutia, op.cit., p.73.
1762	Diego González de la Cueva	*Archivo General de la Nación. Ordenanzas*, vol.II, p.320. 1723-1763.
1775	Diego González de la Cueva	*Calendario Manual y Guía de Forasteros para el año de* 1775.
1777	Diego González de la Cueva	*Calendario Manual y Guía de Forasteros para el año de* 1777.
1778	Diego González de la Cueva	*Calendario Manual y Guía de Forasteros para el año de* 1778.
1779	Joseph Antonio Lince González	*Calendario Manual y Guía de Forasteros para el año de* 1779.
1780	Joseph Antonio Lince González	*Calendario Manual y Guía de Forasteros para el año de* 1780.
1782	Joseph Antonio Lince González	*Calendario Manual y Guía de Forasteros para el año de* 1782.

Chief Assayer, Captain of Grenadiers
Diego González de la Cueva

1731-1778

By referring to the summary of the list of Chief Assayers it is seen that, between the years 1731 and 1778, the Chief Assayer was Captain Diego González de la Cueva. It is not possible to assure the reader that during those years for which no record was found there might not have been another assayer, but it is scarcely probable for these reasons:

a. Until 1783 the office was purchasable. It is not likely that Diego González de la Cueva sold and repurchased the office during this period.

b. The office, according to Fonseca and Urrutia, was sold for the last time in 'February 1730,' and as he held it in 1731, it is scarcely probable that another should have bought[55] it for 'the last time' in 1730.

MARKS DURING THE TIME OF DIEGO GONZALEZ DE LA CUEVA

1733-1778

As has been seen, in order to distinguish genuine marks from clever forgeries, 'standard' marks were established by selecting those appearing on works so beautifully wrought that they were not susceptible of successful imitation. Further, that for greater certainty only objects of silver gilt (fire-gilt) were used.

55 De la Cueva must have bought the office from the Carmelite Fathers of the *Santo Desierto*: Melchor de Cuellar, in the year 1628, (*A.G. de la N. Casa de Moneda. Registro de nombramientos*, p.582 and following) was the owner of the offices of melter and Chief Assayer of the Mint, having bought them for $150,000 *pesos* in gold, ceded them to the former in perpetuity so that they might 'perpetually enjoy the sale, rights and privileges of said office.'
1632
In 1632, through the death (*A.G. de la N. Casa de Moneda. Registro de nombramientos*, p.281) of Melchor de Cuellar, the Viceroy Marquis of Cerralvo named Diego de Godoy, who was Cuellar's assistant, to serve as Chief Assayer at the same time 'ordering the Treasurer to retain for him the rights belonging to said office now vacant, so that I may apply them to whom they pertain.'
1723
The Carmelite Fathers of the *Santo Desierto* still had possession of these rights in the year 1723 (*A.G. de la N. Ramo de Inquisición*, vol.838, p.2) because on the 18th December of that year the Marquis of Casafuerte confirmed the appointment made by the Rev. Father Martín de la Madre de Dios, Provincial of the Holy Province of San Alberto of New Spain, in charge of the spiritual and temporal government of *Santo Desierto*, of Captain Rivas de Angulo as Assistant Assayer and chief melter of the Royal Mint, 'the Fathers of the *Santo Desierto* being the owners thereof.'

The piece shown in *Plate* 107 possesses all these requisites. It is beautifully wrought, of silver gilt (fire-gilt) and bears the genuine mark of the Master Silversmith Rodallega.[56] The marks shown on this piece are the following:[57]

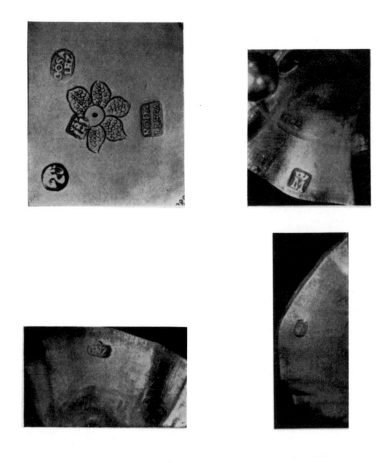

Actual Size

56 There are imitations of Rodallega's marks, but on pieces so badly made that none can be confused with his great original works.

57 As the mark of the Eagle appears on all silver, the origin of this insignia in the arms of Mexico may be of interest. Marroqui (op.cit., vol.I, p.46) says: 'As soon as the rebuilding of this city had been decided upon and when it had barely begun, Francisco de Montejo and Alonso Fernández de Puerto Carrero went to the Court as Attorneys thereto and for all New Spain. One of the instructions they

These same marks, enlarged:

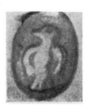

carried with them was to request the Emperor in the name of the COUNCIL, JUSTICES, GOVERNORS, KNIGHTS, GENTLEMEN, OFFICIALS AND GOOD MEN OF THE GREAT CITY OF TENOCHTITLAN, to designate a coat-of-arms that they might carry on their pennants, place on their seals and other places where cities and villages of those kingdoms customarily use them. The Emperor, by order signed in Valladolid, the 4th July 1523, also signed by the Secretary General, Francisco de los Cobos, granted one which represented the location of the city, its ancient grandeur and commemorated the victory obtained there by the Spanish arms. This shield had in the center a blue field of water, a golden castle, with three bridges of coarse-grained granitic stone. . . . On each was a lion rampant holding the castle in his claws, his paws supported on the end of the bridge. As a border there were ten leaves of the cactus plant on a field of gold. This shield was used by the city during the period of Spanish domination, but in the midst of this time of ordinary tranquility, an incident occurred mention of which should not be omitted. The shield which Charles granted did not have a crest or top, and perhaps because they were accustomed to see them on all or almost all shields this one seemed slighted by not having it, or for some other reason, it happened that at the end of a few years they began to use the traditional eagle and serpent thereon.'

In the old archives of the General Treasury collection of the 'taxes on gold applied by mercury' is many times mentioned, that is to say, on gold incorporated into a piece of silver; among others,

If all the above marks are genuine, then the presence of one of them on an object, authenticates the remainder of the marks. Comparing the above shown marks of Rodallega with others, various pieces were found which bear genuine marks of Rodallega and the mark 'Gõsalez.' This established the genuineness of the mark 'Gõsalez' — Diego González de la Cueva, of the Columns of Hercules, crowned, with the *M* between the Columns, and other marks, both contemporary with the period of González de la Cueva and earlier.

the following: *Archivo General de la Nación. Libro Mayor o Guía del cargo de la Tesorería General*, 1796, p.1, which shows that José María Rodallega, Master Silversmith, paid 'taxes on gold applied by mercury' on the gold contained in a piece of silver. [Gold plate]

It is logical to assume that a special additional mark used to signify that the 'tax on gold applied by mercury' had been paid, but if this is so I have not been able to confirm it.

The Eagle used by the Chief Assayer Diego González de la Cueva in the mark shown in *Plate* 30, I have been unable to find on plate other than silver gilt, and perhaps it was used in the period to which I refer for the 'tax on gold applied by mercury.'

GENUINE AND FORGED MARKS OF THE PERIOD OF CHIEF ASSAYER DIEGO GONZÁLEZ DE LA CUEVA
1733-1778

NO.	DESCRIPTION	MARK OF THE CHIEF ASSAYER	HALL-MARK (QUALITY)	TAX MARK	*Enlarged* REMARKS
4	Genuine				
5	Genuine				
6	Genuine				

GENUINE AND FORGED MARKS OF THE PERIOD OF CHIEF ASSAYER DIEGO GONZÁLEZ DE LA CUEVA
1733-1778

NO.	DESCRIPTION	MARK OF THE CHIEF ASSAYER	HALL-MARK (QUALITY)	TAX MARK	*Enlarged* REMARKS
6-A	Forgery				Forgery
6-B	Forgery				Forgery
6-C	Forgery				Forgery

GENUINE AND FORGED MARKS OF THE PERIOD OF CHIEF ASSAYER DIEGO GONZÁLEZ DE LA CUEVA
1733-1778

NO.	DESCRIPTION	MARK OF THE CHIEF ASSAYER	HALL-MARK (QUALITY)	TAX MARK	*Enlarged* REMARKS
6-D	Forgery		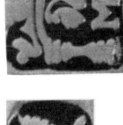		Forgery
6-E	Forgery				Forgery. From punches of Apolonio Guevara

8. *Marks between the Years 1783-1823, and the Chief Assayers during these Years*

Chief Assayers and the Years They Held Office:

YEAR	NAME	REFERENCE AND SOURCE OF THE DATA
1783	Joseph Antonio Lince González	*Calendario, Manual y Guía de Forasteros para el año de 1783.*
1784	Joseph Antonio Lince González	*Calendario, Manual y Guía de Forasteros para el año de 1784.*
1786	Joseph Antonio Lince González	*Archivo General de la Nación. Indice General de los Ramos*, etc., p.1 reverse.
1787	Joseph Antonio Lince González	*Archivo General de la Nación. Indice General de los Ramos*, etc., p.1 reverse.
1788	Joseph Antonio Lince González	*Calendario, Manual y Guía de Forasteros para el año de 1788.*
1789	Francisco Arance y Cobos 'Assistant Chief Assayer who is *Juez Veedor* of the Silversmiths' Art in general.'	*Archivo General de la Nación. Industria Artistica y Manufacturera*, vol.II, 1746-1792, 3rd October.
1790	Francisco Arance y Cobos	*Calendario, Manual y Guía de Forasteros para el año de 1790.*
1791-1818 inc.	Antonio Forcada y la Plaza	*Calendario, Manual y Guía de Forasteros para el año de 1791.* *Calendario, Manual y Guía de Forasteros para el año de 1818.*
1819	Joaquín Dávila Madrid	*Calendario, Manual y Guía de Forasteros para el año de 1819.*
1820	Joaquín Dávila Madrid	*Calendario, Manual y Guía de Forasteros para el año de 1820.*
1821	Joaquín Dávila Madrid	*Calendario, Manual y Guía de Forasteros para el año de 1821.*
1823	Joaquín Dávila Madrid	It appears that Dávila died in 1823.

9. *Chief Assayer José Antonio Lince y González, 1779-88*

Licentiate José Antonio Lince y González succeeded Captain Diego González de la Cueva in office in the year 1779. He held it until 1789, on which date Francisco Arance y Cobos took his place. For this

reason silver stamped with the punch of Lince y González was marked
between the years 1779 and 1788, both inclusive.[58]

Lince learned the trade from Diego González de la Cueva, and it is
probable that he entered office during González de la Cueva's absence
from the kingdom. In the *Consulta hecha a la Real Audiencia Gobernadora* (Consultation made the Royal Governing Body), by Licentiate
Joseph Antonio Lince, Chief Assayer of the Kingdom and Juez Veedor
of the Most Noble Silversmiths' Art, 'regarding various things concerning the said art, very interesting to the Royal Service and public
service,'[59] paragraph 3, Lince González says: 'following the practice
which I learned from my zealous predecessor Sergeant-Major Diego
González de la Cueva. . . .'

[58] *Consulta hecha a la Real Audiencia*, etc., op.cit., paragraph 32, states that the Chief Assayers, approximately in 1779, in addition to their wages as such were paid four hundred *pesos* a year for their
work as *Jueces Veedores* of the silversmiths' art.

[59] Op.cit.
As a result of this consultation the Viceroy, Martín de Mayorga, published his Proclamation of the
20th February 1780, which is here omitted because it contains only Ordinances and Laws with
which we are already familiar.

GENUINE AND FORGED MARKS OF THE PERIOD OF CHIEF ASSAYER LIC. JOSÉ ANTONIO LINCE GONZÁLEZ
1779-88

NO.	DESCRIPTION	MARK OF THE CHIEF ASSAYER	HALL-MARK (QUALITY)	TAX MARK	*Enlarged* REMARKS
7	Genuine				
8	Genuine				
8-A	Forgery				
8-B	Forgery				

GENUINE AND FORGED MARKS OF THE PERIOD OF CHIEF ASSAYER LIC. JOSÉ ANTONIO LINCE GONZÁLEZ
1779–1788

Enlarged

NO.	DESCRIPTION	MARK OF THE CHIEF ASSAYER	HALL-MARK (QUALITY)	TAX MARK	REMARKS
8-C	Forgery			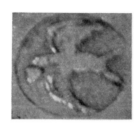	
8-D	Forgery				

GENUINE AND FORGED MARKS OF THE PERIOD OF CHIEF ASSAYER LIC. JOSÉ ANTONIO LINCE GONZÁLEZ
1779–1788

NO.	DESCRIPTION	MARK OF THE CHIEF ASSAYER	HALL-MARK (QUALITY)	TAX MARK	*Enlarged* REMARKS
8-E	Forgery				From punches of Apolonio Guevara  
8-F	Forgery				

10. *Chief Assayer Francisco Arance y Cobos*, 1789-90

Francisco Arance y Cobos succeeded Lince in 1789, having served many years as First Class Assayer in the Mint. He served as Lince's assistant in the year 1788, holding the office of Acting Chief Assayer during the years 1789 and 1790. Therefore, all silver bearing his mark may be considered of that period, although, because of the short time he held the office, his mark is rarely seen.

I have not seen a genuine mark stamped by Arance y Cobos. All of those I have studied were poorly made forgeries, similar to that shown below:

FORGERIES OF THE MARKS OF THE CHIEF ASSAYER
FRANCISCO ARANCE Y COBOS
1789-90

*Mark of the
Chief Assayer*

Tax-mark

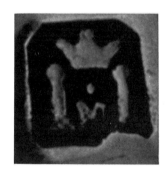

Hall-mark

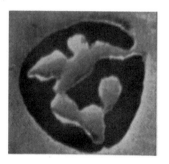

Actual Size

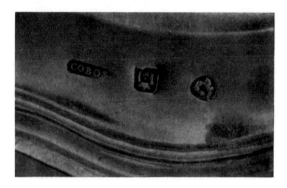

11. *Chief Assayer Antonio Forcada y la Plaza*, 1791-1818

Because of his long period in office, Forcada's marks abound. They consist of an Eagle in two forms: one flying over a cactus, which I have called the first of his marks; and the other an eagle in the attitude of flying, without the cactus, and which I have called his second mark. He also used various types of crowns. The lion rampant, which he also used, is skillfully made and similar to that seen on *cuartillas* (three cent pieces) first coined in the year 1794.

Obverse   *Reverse*

He also used a special mark as a hall-mark, which was stamped with a badly made die. I have not been able clearly to identify this mark, which I have found on objects of silver-gilt. It appears to be a man on horseback. (Mark number 13)

Genuine and Forged Marks of the Period of Chief Assayer Antonio Forcada y la Plaza

1791–1818

NO.	DESCRIPTION	MARK OF THE CHIEF ASSAYER	HALL-MARK (QUALITY)	TAX MARK	*Enlarged* REMARKS
10	Genuine				Another type of crown used with the same marks:
11	Genuine				Quite common
12	Genuine				Rare
13	Genuine				Rare

GENUINE AND FORGED MARKS OF THE PERIOD OF THE CHIEF ASSAYER ANTONIO FORCADA Y LA PLAZA
1791-1818

NO.	DESCRIPTION	MARK OF THE CHIEF ASSAYER	HALL-MARK (QUALITY)	TAX MARK	Enlarged REMARKS
14	Genuine				
14-A	Forgery				
14-B	Forgery				

12. *Chief Assayer Joaquín Dávila Madrid*, 1819-23

Dávila succeeded Forcada in the year 1819, having served as Assistant Chief Assayer from 1797 to 1818 with the exception of the years 1812 to 1815, both inclusive. I do not know precisely when he surrendered the office, but it is assumed that he died in 1823, because in 1824 the following appears:[60]

ORDER

Pension to the children of Joaquín Dávila Madrid.

In view of what has been stated by the officials of the treasury and exchequer regarding the petition of Mrs. Mariana Aspiros, relative to giving her son employment as assayer with a salary of one thousand five hundred *pesos*, the sovereign congress has seen fit to decide as follows:

1. The children of Joaquín Dávila Madrid are hereby granted a pension of eight hundred *pesos* annually, half of this sum to each, so that when the right of either shall cease, the other shall be given only four hundred *pesos*.

2. The right of the son to the pension shall cease when he secures employment equivalent thereto or when he is twenty-five years of age. The daughter's right thereto shall cease when she marries. 8th October, 1824.

The existing data regarding Dávila's marks are unfortunately deficient. All those that I have found, in my opinion, are forgeries.

It is logical to assume that from 1819 to 1821, Dávila's mark, the lion rampant and the *M* surmounted by a crown used by Forcada, should have been used and that with the Independence in 1821, he should have ceased using the mark of the lion rampant from the arms of Spain and probably replaced it with the 'Eagle,' also Forcada's. On a punch, one crown looks like another, so it is probable that he did not make a new die with the crown of Emperor Iturbide, but continued to use Forcada's crown.

The forged mark, which probably more closely resembles Dávila's genuine one, together with the others which appear with it, is this:

Actual Size

60 *Colección de Ordenes y Decretos de la Soberana Junta Provisional Gubernativa, y Soberanos Congresos Generales de la Nación Mexicana*, vol.III, p.108. Second Edition, Mexico, 1829. *Imp. Galván, a cargo de Mariano Arévalo.*

My reasons for believing that these marks, although from admirably engraved punches, are not genuine, are:

a. The *M* surmounted by a crown is quite similar to Mark No.13 (See Summary of Marks) used by Forcada and at a glance they appear to be alike, but enlarged five diameters and employing the 'transparency test,' it is clearly evident that they were not punched with Forcada's die.

    Assuming that all the dies of the time of Forcada were lost, which is improbable, why should Dávila have tried to imitate in every particular a die of Forcada's?

b. The lion rampant reproduced above, and other pieces marked by Forcada, subjected to the transparency test, show that in this also an attempt was made to imitate Forcada's mark. Forcada's figure of the lion is skillfully engraved and designed to make the figure appear in relief, while that of Dávila is outlined only. Furthermore, Dávila's die is oval, while the one used by Forcada is octagonal. It is probable that the genuine marks of Dávila's period consist of his name, more or less in the form shown below, of the crown used by Forcada, and the lion rampant, also Forcada's.

FORGERIES OF MADRID'S MARKS
1819-1823

MARK OF THE CHIEF ASSAYER	HALL-MARK (QUALITY)	TAX MARK	REMARKS
			Forgeries
		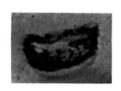	Forgeries

13. *Marks of the Chief Assayers of the Period from the Years 1823-95*

YEAR	NAME	REFERENCE AND SOURCE OF DATA
1823	Cayetano Buitrón	See text regarding Cayetano Buitrón.
1828	Cayetano Buitrón	*Calendario, Manual y Guía de Forasteros para el año de* 1828.
1829	Cayetano Buitrón	*Calendario, Manual y Guía de Forasteros para el año de* 1829.
1830	Cayetano Buitrón	*Archivo General de la Nación. Ramo de Hacienda.* Bundle No.45. Book which says: *Casa de Ensaye de México.*
1831	Cayetano Buitrón	Ibid.
1842	Cayetano Buitrón	*Archivo General de la Nación. Ramo de Hacienda.* Lower floor. Bundle 161. Years 1842, 1843. *Ensaye Mayor de la República.*
1843	Cayetano Buitrón	Ibid.
1856	Sebastián Camacho	*Memoria de Hacienda por el período de Dic.* 1855 *a Mayo* 1856, by Manuel Payno. Mexico, 1857. *Imp. Cumplido.*
1857	Sebastián Camacho	Ibid.
1861	Antonio del Castillo	21st January 1861 to 13th March 1862. From *Diario Oficial* of 13th June 1868, p.3.
1862	Sebastián Camacho	From 13th March 1862. See text.
1863	Sebastián Camacho	*Periódico Oficial del Imperio Mexicano*, No. 67, vol.I, p.3. Mexico, 24th Dec. 1863.
1864	Sebastián Camacho	Deducted.
1865	Sebastián Camacho	Deducted.
1866	Sebastián Camacho	*Almanaque Imperial para el año de* 1866. Mexico, 1866. *Imp. de J. M. Lara.*
1867	Sebastián Camacho	Until 30th June, 1867. *Diario Oficial* of 7th June 1868.
1867	Antonio del Castillo	June 1867 until Feb. 1868. From *Diario Oficial* of 13th June 1868, p.3.
1868	José Antonio Mucharraz	*Diario Oficial* of 16th June 1868, p.3.
1870	José Antonio Mucharraz	*Guía de Forasteros para el año de* 1871, by Juan E. Pérez. Mexico, 1871.
1871	José Antonio Mucharraz	*Almanaque de Oficinas y Guía de Forasteros*, by Juan E. Pérez. Mexico. *Imp. del Gobierno en el Palacio Nacional.*

1873	José Antonio Mucharraz	*Almanaque estadístico de las Oficinas y Guía de Forasteros*, by Juan E. Pérez, Mexico. *Imp. del Gobierno en el Palacio Nacional.*
1876	José Antonio Mucharraz	*Almanaque estadístico de las Oficinas y Guía de Forasteros y del Comercio de la República*, by Juan E. Pérez. Mexico. *Imp. del Gobierno en el Palacio Nacional.*
1882	Francisco Morales	*Cuenta del Tesoro Federal. Tip. de Gonzalo A. Esteva.* Mexico. 1885.
1883	Francisco Morales	*Cuenta del Tesoro Federal. Tip. El Gran Libro*, of F. Parres and Co. Mexico, 1885.
1884	Francisco Morales	*Cuenta del Tesoro Federal. Tip. El Gran Libro*, of F. Parres and Co. Mexico, 1886.
1885	Francisco Morales	*Cuenta del Tesoro Federal. Tip. El Gran Libro*, of F. Parres and Co. Mexico, 1887.
1886	Francisco Morales	*Cuenta del Tesoro Federal. Tip. El Gran Libro*, of F. Parres and Co. Mexico, 1888.
1887	Francisco Morales	*Cuenta del Tesoro Federal. Tip. El Gran Libro*, of F. Parres and Co. Mexico, 1889.
1888	Francisco Morales	*Cuenta del Tesoro Federal. Tip. El Gran Libro*, of F. Parres and Co. Mexico, 1890.
1889	Francisco Morales	*Cuenta del Tesoro Federal. Tip. El Gran Libro*, of F. Parres and Co. Mexico, 1892.
1890	Fernando Sáyago	Ibid.
1891	Fernando Sáyago	*Cuenta del Tesoro. Tip. de la Oficina Impresora de Estampillas.* National Palace. Mexico, 1893.
1892	Fernando Sáyago	*Cuenta del Tesoro. Tip. de Oficina Impresora de Estampillas.* National Palace. Mexico, 1894.
1893	Fernando Sáyago	*Cuenta del Tesoro.* Mexico, 1896. *Tip. de la Oficina impresora del Timbre.* National Palace.
1894	Romualdo Obregón Morales	Documents shown to me by Don Romualdo.
1895	Romualdo Obregón Morales	Ibid.

14. *Chief Assayer Cayetano Buitrón*, 1823-43

Chief Assayer Cayetano Buitrón served a number of years in different positions in the Departments of Assay. In 1809 he was Assayer in Pachuca. During the years 1812 to 1815 inclusive, he was assistant to Chief Assayer Antonio Forcada y la Plaza. From 1820 to 1822 he held the same position under Joaquín Dávila Madrid, the Chief Assayer. He lived at No.8 Mesones Street.

The 5th October 1821, by Decree IV,[61] 'all the authorities were empowered and their positions confirmed,' and the 26th February 1822, by Decree of the same date,[62] 'Civil authorities then in office were again confirmed.' Chief Assayers and their assistants must have been included.

The records of the year 1823 were not found, but it is believed, for reasons already stated, that Chief Assayer Joaquín Dávila Madrid died in that year or at the beginning of 1824. Buitrón's marks must have begun to appear about the middle of 1823, the date on which he took office because of the illness or death of Dávila Madrid.

In 1828 and 1829 he is named in the records as Assistant Chief Assayer 'performing the duties of Chief Assayer,' and like his predecessors still connected with the Treasury.

On the 29th September 1829, the following Circular of the Secretariat of the Treasury appeared:[63]

That all pieces of gold and silver shall be taken to the *Comisaría General* so that a small sample may be taken [for assay] and payment of the respective taxes.

His Excellency the President has seen fit to order that until a silver and gold assay office may be established in that city, you shall have all pieces of said metals taken to the *comisaría general*, and, removing a small sample therefrom, it then be sent with a statement of the weight of said pieces to the mint in this capital in a sealed folder, so that an assay can be made and the corresponding taxes calculated and collected. This decision having been communicated to the substitute director of the mint in the federal district for his information and guidance, as a command of His Excellency I hereby inform you for compliance with that part which concerns you.

61 *Colección de Ordenes y Decretos de la Soberana Junta Provisional Gubernativa y Soberanos Congresos Generales de la Nación Mexicana*, vol.I, p.8. Mexico, 1829. *Imp. Galván*. Second Edition.
62 *Actas del Congreso Constituyente Mexicano*, vol.I, pp.12-13. Mexico, 1822. *Imp. de Alejandro Valdés*.
63 Lic. Basilio José Arrillaga. *Recopilación de Leyes, Decretos, Bandos, Reglamentos, Circulares y Providencias de los Supremos Poderes, etc.*, p.245. Mexico, 1836. *Imp. J.M.Fernández de Lara*, January to December, 1829. 29th September, 1829.

It is believed that the office of Chief Assayer was not abolished, because in October 1830[64] the control of said office passed from the Treasury to the *Comisaría General*:

The Law regulating the General Treasury is dated 26th October 1830, and its Article 19 mentioned in the foregoing circular is as follows:

19. The lesser branches of the federal district, the royal mining branch and any others outside of the federal treasury, as well as the principal warehouses of the army and public treasury, and the taxes on silver and gold, shall in the future be in charge of the principal *comisaría* of Mexico. Consequently the assayer shall be subject to said *comisaría*.

It is assumed that 'Chief Assayer' is meant. There were various Assayers in the Mint.

The *Guía de Forasteros*[65] for the year 1832, does not give the name of the Chief Assayer subordinate to the Department of the Treasury of the Nation, as customarily, the omission being explained as follows: 'New personnel was assigned [to the Treasury of the Federation] by Law of 26th October 1830; but the only employees who have been appointed up to the present time are two Treasurers. . . .' Nor in this same '*Guía*' does a Chief Assayer appear in the list of Employees of the Chief Commission of the Federal District. However it is believed that Buitrón continued performing the duties of his office, because during the years 1842 and 1843[66] he is definitely mentioned as Chief Assayer.

In 1837 the old system of collection of taxes by the 'Royal Officials' was abandoned. After the Independence, taxes were paid to the Treasury, and from 1837 all taxes were collected in the Legal Assay Offices,[67]

64 Lic. José Basilio Arrillaga, op.cit., p.487. Year 1831.
65 Mexico (no date), *Imp. Galván*.
66 *Archivo General de la Nación*. Treasury Branch (Lower Floor), Bundle of papers 161. Year 1842 to 1843. Chief Assay Office of the Republic.
67 The Decree relative thereto says: 'As none of the revenues of the Treasury now belong especially to the departments of the Republic for at present all compose the National Exchequer, and the President having been informed that in some of said departments the practice is continued of collecting for their account the three per cent tax, levied on gold and silver by Article 6 of the Decree of the Sovereign Provisional Governing Board, dated 22nd November 1821 (Compilation of August 1835, p.375), which later pertained to the states by virtue of decree of classification of revenue issued the 24th August 1824, (this is a mistake; it is not the 24th but the 4th and it is found in the Compilation of 1832, p.62) for metals from mines in their respective territory. His Excellency has seen fit to decide that collection of the said tax in the departments in the manner customary up to the present time, shall cease; and in accordance with the Chief Assayer's statement concerning this matter, has

and all marks were stamped by the Chief Assayer or his deputies.

The Decree of 4th September 1839 states:

'7th. Ordinances 9, 25 and 26 on Silversmiths relative to the Tax [on Plate] and marks shall remain effective. . . .'

Although the decree does not so state, it refers to Ordinances of 1746:

9th. Before fabrication gold and silver must be taken to the Royal Officials so that they may see that the tax on plate has been paid, and if so, register it. On completion of the piece it shall be again taken to the Royal Officials so that they may compare its weight with that of the bullion, and the *Juez Veedor* [Chief Assayer] shall stamp it with the mark and symbol kept for this purpose.

25th. Silversmiths are forbidden to work with ingots on which the tax has not been paid.

26th. Fabricated pieces which lack the mark certifying their quality or the payment of the tax, cannot be sold.

In the same decree the following appears:

8th. The *Chief Assayer* in this capital, and those in the Treasurer's Offices outside of the capital, shall name two experts, and where such cannot be found, two honest residents, who with them shall inspect the silversmiths, wire-drawers and sheet-beaters, in order to ascertain whether the *silver* and gold *which is used*, and which shall be weighed immediately together with all on which the tax has not been paid, is found to agree with the *tax statements* each may have. These they shall present so that they may be checked with the entries in the books kept by this branch which the assayers shall have with them. Furthermore they shall remove from the metals being used a small sample not to exceed one *ochava* of the silver, and two *tomines* of the gold. The artisan shall stamp his mark thereon so that when the assay has been made the gold or silver resulting from the assay may be returned to him if the standard is correct, and if it is not, that he may be prosecuted according to provisions in force against infractors. The genuineness of the marks on the *silver* and gold on which the *tax* has been paid shall be ascertained. [It shall also be ascertained] whether there are pieces that have been alloyed.

seen fit to command that the aforesaid tax in future shall be collected in the legal assay offices, where the ingots or bars of said metals shall be presented for inspection, and when their standard is ascertained the hall-marks may be stamped thereon. For this purpose the collectors of revenues or taxes on the respective metals shall issue the corresponding certificates of the pieces inspected, stating their weight, so that they may be presented to the nearest legal assay office. (It was circulated by the Chief Treasury Office of the Department in Mexico on the 17th of said month). (Lic. José Basilio Arrillaga, op.cit., pp.450-51, *Todo el año de* 1837.)

The foregoing proves that the tax on silver was still paid in 1837 and that the Chief Assayer in Mexico continued to be responsible for collections.

Marks of Buitrón

As Mexico was an empire during the first months of Buitrón's occupancy of the office and it was left to his judgement what die he should use, Buitrón must have used the *M* surmounted with a crown. It is probable that he discarded the lion rampant of the Spaniards but continued to use Forcada's eagle. Genuine examples are lacking but there are many forgeries which strengthen the belief that the crowned *M* was used by him. One of the many forgeries of this type is shown below:

Actual Size

Enlarged

The mark *BTON* resembles somewhat Buitrón's genuine mark, and the eagle is an imitation of that used by Forcada, but the *M* surmounted by a crown is so well made that only by enlarging it and comparing it carefully can it be distinguished from the genuine mark stamped by Forcada, shown in the Summary of Marks as No.14. If there was such a group of marks, as I believe, they must have been Forcada's *M* surmounted by a crown, Forcada's or Buitrón's 'Eagle' and Buitrón's genuine punch.

Buitrón's Second Mark — 1824-42

From the establishment of the Republic in 1824, it was, of course, necessary to abandon the use of the Spanish crown. To certify the quality of the metals employed, the *M* with a small *o* above it was used. This mark appeared on money, coined in the Mint in Mexico from 1522 until 1824, without variation.

Buitrón's second mark is easily identified as it always accompanied the eagle of the Independence, erect and with the head towards the left, as shown in the following typical example:

Original Size   *Enlarged five diameters*

Genuine and Forged Marks of the Period of Chief Assayer Cayetano Buitrón
1823-43

NO.	DESCRIPTION	MARK OF THE CHIEF ASSAYER	HALL-MARK (QUALITY)	TAX MARK	*Size Enlarged* REMARKS
16	Genuine				These are the only genuine marks of the period of Buitrón that I have found. This is, by far, the most common of all authentic marks found on Mexican plate.
16-A	Forgery				Forgery. Frequently found.
16-B	Forgery				The *M* with the small *o* above is an excellent forgery.
16-C	Forgery				Poor forgery. Quite common.
16-D	Forgery				Rare

GENUINE AND FORGED MARKS OF THE PERIOD OF CHIEF ASSAYER CAYETANO BUITRÓN
1823-1843

NO.	DESCRIPTION	MARK OF THE CHIEF ASSAYER	HALL-MARK (QUALITY)	TAX MARK	*Size Enlarged* REMARKS
16-E	Forgery				With these same punches of 'Bton' and the 'Eagle' the following was also used: Rare
16-F	Forgery				Very rare
16-G	Forgery				Forgery found in abundance.
16-H	Forgery				The forgery of the *M* crowned is remarkably well made.

15. *Chief Assayer Sebastián Camacho*, 1856-60
1863-1867

The *Guía de Forasteros*[68] for the year 1852, stated that the Mexico City Mint was leased in 1847, and that in 1852 the Government Assayer was Joaquín González, who lived at No.4 Puente del Cuervo Street, and that the 'Company' Assayer was Sebastián Camacho, who lived at No.30 Puente de Alvarado Street.

The mint (Casa de Moneda) was operated by the Government, until the month of February 1847 when it was leased for ten years to Messrs. Mackintosh, Belangé and Company, for the sum of $174,100 *pesos* and an additional 1% of the amount coined annually.[69]

In the year 1854 the same *Guía* states[70] that the Mint was still leased and that the Government Assayer was Joaquín González. Further, that the 'Company's' 'Assayer' was Sebastián Camacho, No.39 Puente de Alvarado Street. 'He is also Professor in the College of Mining.'

In 1851[71] the *Comisarías*, including the principal one, were abolished. The Chief Assayer was connected with this office and the 20th July 1852 General Mariano Arista, then President of the Republic, by Decree No.3680,[72] re-established the Chief Assay Office, again subordinate to the Secretariat of Finance.

It is not known precisely when Camacho first entered the service, but in 1856 he held the position and it is probable that he held it as early as 1851, when the Chief Assay Office was again established. Perhaps he replaced Buitrón.

The *Memoria de Hacienda por el período de Diciembre de 1855 a Mayo de 1857*,[73] contains a letter from Sebastián Camacho to Payno, dated as follows: 'Chief Assay Office, 9th June, 1857.' This letter was in answer to a question of Payno's referring to a certain authorization in effect on the date when the latter resigned as Minister of Finance, in May, 1856. Thus, Camacho was Chief Assayer in 1856-1857.

68 By General Juan Nepomuceno Almonte, Mexico, 1852. *Imp. I. Cumplido.*
69 Juan N. del Valle, *El Viajero en México*, pp.367-8. Mexico, 1859. *Tip. de M. Castro.*
70 Guía de Forasteros para el año de 1854, p.229, published by Mariano Galván Rivera, Mexico (no date). *Imp. Librería Núm.7.*
71 By Decree of Congress No.3524, of 12th February 1851—Licentiates Manuel Dublán and José María Lozano—*Legislación Mexicana*, vol.VI, pp.18-19. Official Edition. Mexico, 1877. *Imp. de Comercio.*
72 Congressional Decree No.3680, of 20th July 1852, *Legislación Mexicana*, vol.VI, p.223.
73 By Manuel Payno, Mexico, 1857. *Imp. Cumplido.*

The controversy regarding various phases of the lease of the Mint (Casa de Moneda) to Alejandro Belangé and Juan Temple disclosed the fact that after the death of the latter Camacho served as Assayer 'the first six months of the year 1867,' or until June 30th of that year, the date on which he terminated his services with the Independent Government.[74]

Sebastián Camacho took the oath of allegiance to the Empire the 18th December 1863, as Chief Assayer,[75] and it is probable that he succeeded del Castillo on the 13th March 1862. As late as 1866, Camacho, Official of the Imperial Order of Guadalupe, who at that time lived at No.8 San Fernando Street, was still Chief Assayer.[76]

During the period of Maximilian's rule the following Decree appeared:

MANUEL G. AGUIRRE, Mayor of Mexico, to its inhabitants, know ye:

That the Secretariats of State and of Finance and Public Credit have informed me of the following decree:

Palace of the Regency of the Empire, Mexico, 8th August 1863. The Regency of this Empire has seen fit to send me the following decree:

THE REGENCY OF THE EMPIRE, to the inhabitants of the Nation, know ye:

That it has decreed the following:

Art. 1. The temporary personnel in the Chief Assay Office of this Capital shall be the following:

Chief Assayer with an annual salary of	$2,400
Clerk with a salary of	600
Minor office expenses	200
	$3,200

Art. 2. Employees appointed by virtue of the present decree shall be temporary, and shall receive the salary assigned them from the day they take possession.

Therefore, I order that it be printed, published, circulated and due compliance given. Issued in the Palace of the Empire in Mexico, 8th August 1863. Juan N. Almonte. José Mariano Salas. Juan B. Ormaechea. To the Undersecretary of State and of the Office of Finance and Public Credit.

And I inform you for your information and guidance. The Undersecretary of State and of the Office of Finance and Public Credit, M. de Castillo. Mayor of Mexico.

74 *Diario Oficial* of 7th June 1868.
75 *Periódico Oficial del Imperio Mexicano*, No.67, vol.I, p.2. Mexico, 24th December 1863.
76 *Almanaque Imperial para el año de* 1866, Mexico, 1866. *Imp. de J. M. Lara.* The last Chief Assayer, Romualdo Obregón, told me that Camacho died in 1916 or 1917.

And so that it shall come to the attention of all, I order that it be printed, published and circulated to whom it may concern. Mexico, 19th August 1863.

Mayor   Secretary of the Mayor's Office
Manuel G. Aguirre   José M. de Garay[77]

MARKS OF CAMACHO'S PERIOD, 1856-60

December 1863-June 1867.

It is certain that the marks shown are genuine, because on many pieces marked by Camacho, Castillo, etc., which have passed through my hands, I have never seen a variation or a forgery.

Enlarged

MARK OF THE CHIEF ASSAYER	HALL-MARK (QUALITY)	TAX MARK	REMARKS
			I have never seen a forgery or any variation of these marks.

16. Chief Assayer Antonio del Castillo

1861-1862
1867-1868

Diarios Oficiales from January to June 1868, mention the dispute[78] over the dismissal of Antonio del Castillo, then Chief Assayer and Government Inspector of the Mint, which was leased during this period. In the *Diario* of 23rd February 1868, and that of 27th March of the same year, an energetic protest, presented by the miners against

77 *Colección Completa de los Decretos Generales expedidos por el Exmo. Sr. Gral. Forey*, p.139. Mexico. *Imp. de A. Boix*, in charge of M. Zornoza, 1863.
78 On the 21st February 1868. The dispute was started by Deputy Mirafuentes.

his dismissal, was published. This was followed by another of the same force and tenor on the 28th of April 1868.

In the *Diario Oficial* of the 13th June 1868, page 3, it is stated that Castillo served as (Chief) Assayer from 21st January 1861 to the 13th March 1862 and from June 1867 to February 1868.

MARKS OF THE PERIOD OF CHIEF ASSAYER ANTONIO DEL CASTILLO 21ST JANUARY 1861 TO 13TH MARCH 1862 AND FROM JUNE 1867 TO FEBRUARY 1868.

The marks as they appear on a typical example are:

Enlarged

MARK OF THE CHIEF ASSAYER	HALL-MARK (QUALITY)	TAX MARK	REMARKS
			I have never seen either a forgery or any variation of this mark.

17. *Chief Assayer José Antonio Mucharraz*
1868-1881[79]

José Mucharraz succeeded Camacho in 1868. His mark is so rare that there are no forgeries.

In *Diario Oficial* of 16th June 1868, page 3, there is published a certificate signed by him as Chief Assayer of the Republic, dated 29th April of that same year.

---

79 I am not certain of the date he relinquished the office of Chief Assayer, but, from data that I have, it was learned that he was Chief Assayer from 1868 to 1876, inclusive, and in 1881 he still held the office.

MARKS OF THE PERIOD OF CHIEF ASSAYER
JOSÉ ANTONIO MUCHARRAZ
1868-1881

Mucharraz' genuine marks are the following:

Actual Size

MARK OF THE CHIEF ASSAYER	HALL-MARK (QUALITY)	TAX MARK	REMARKS
			I have found no forgery of any of these marks.

18. *Chief Assayer Francisco Morales*, 1882-1889

Francisco Morales, who lived at Number 20, Donceles Street, served as assistant for many years to Chief Assayer José Antonio Mucharraz. The first exact data relative to Morales having held the office of Chief Assayer is for the year 1882, but he may have held it some years prior to this date. It is known that he left office approximately in December 1889. Note that Morales returned to the use of Buitrón's dies, substituting only his own mark for that of Buitrón.

MARKS OF THE PERIOD OF CHIEF ASSAYER FRANCISCO MORALES
1882-1889

The marks as they appear on a typical example are:

Enlarged

MARK OF THE CHIEF ASSAYER	HALL-MARK (QUALITY)	TAX MARK

REMARKS

I have found no piece bearing a forgery of this die.

19. *Chief Assayer Fernando Sáyago*, 1890-1893

Sáyago succeeded Chief Assayer Francisco Morales in the year 1890, and held the office until his death, early in January 1894.[80] I have found no plate marked with Sáyago's die, but Romualdo Obregón, who was his assistant, states that on plate marked during this period Morales'[81] punch was used.

20. *The Last Chief Assayer, Romualdo Obregón Morales*, 1894-1895

Romualdo Obregón,[82] who still lives in the City of Mexico, after serving some years in the Chief Assay Office, became Sáyago's assistant in 1890. After the death of Sáyago in January 1894, he held the position of Chief Assayer until, by Decree of 15th June 1895,[83] various Mints were closed, the Chief Assay Office was abolished and creation of Special Assay Offices was ordered. From that time 'it was also the duty of the same assayers to fix the standard of the pieces manufactured of gold or silver which the public might present for that purpose.'

Consequently, Obregón was the last Chief Assayer, and, when he ceased using his die, silver no longer bore the mark of the Chief Assayer. It is, therefore, impossible to date plate stamped later than 1895.

During Don Romualdo's period no fee was charged for marking plate. Only plate voluntarily presented for this purpose by the interested parties was marked, as proof that the metals were of the required standard. Therefore very few objects were presented to be marked.

80 *El Tiempo*, Tuesday 9th January 1894.
81 That is to say the eagle used by Buitrón.
82 March 1936; who very courteously showed me a number of documents and other data.
83 Dublán y Esteva, op.cit., vol.XXV, p.227, Decree No.13,074.

Upon asking Don Romualdo why, in addition to his name, the 'Eagle' and the *M* with the small *o* above were used, he replied that it was the custom, but that none of the marks signified anything other than the fact that the metal was of the required standard.

Obregón informs me that he did not make new dies of the marks mentioned above, but used those that had belonged to Morales and to Sáyago. When the Chief Assayer's office was closed, he said, all the old dies were delivered to the Mint.

MARKS OF THE PERIOD OF CHIEF ASSAYER

ROMUALDO OBREGÓN MORALES

1894-1895

The marks as they appear on a typical example, are:

Actual Size   *Enlarged*

MARK OF THE CHIEF ASSAYER	HALL-MARK (QUALITY)	TAX MARK	REMARKS
			I have not seen any forgeries of Obregón's mark. The 'Eagle' is from the die used by Buitrón, Morales and Sáyago.

Obregón examined the photograph of plate marked with his die, and affirmed that it was stamped with the genuine die. It should be noted that the 'Eagle' is from the die used by Buitrón and Morales.

21. *Marks between 1895 and 1936*

From the Decree of 15th June 1895 which has already been mentioned, up to the present time, 'fabricated silver' may be marked at the Mint, as seen from the Presidential Resolution[84] of the 28th of the same month and year, by which the Secretariat of Finance issued provisional instructions for the Mints. The reference to marks on plate is as follows:

> 25th. Every piece of fabricated silver presented for this purpose shall be assayed and its standard up to the thousandth, the abbreviation of the State where the office is established and the national arms shall be marked thereon with a die, by hammer strokes. For this service the fees assigned in the respective tariff shall be charged.

In talking with one of the Assayers of the Mint, who has been in service since before 1895, I was informed that silver is rarely presented for marking. Although subsequent changes have been made in the laws, paragraph 25th., quoted above, has never been revoked, and anyone who desires may present silver for assay and marking[85] today.

I presented a piece of silver to the Mint for assay and the marks stamped on it, which have been used since 1895, are as follows:

Enlarged

The *L* means *Ley* [standard], and the number 860 denotes the parts of silver per thousand the piece contains. The 'Eagle' represents the 'National Arms.' It is interesting to note that this 'Eagle' is from the die in use for more than 100 years, used by Obregón, Morales, Sáyago and Buitrón. Thus it may be said that, from 1895 to the present time, plate has not been marked.[86]

84 Dublán y Esteva, op.cit., vol.XXV, pp.260-5, Decree No.13,095.
85 24th March 1936.
86 I make the statement that it was the same 'Eagle' because they are identical. After taking a photograph of the modern piece, being careful that it be of the exact size, it was enlarged five times its original size, developed on transparent negatives and superimposed on those of the other pieces photographed and enlarged in the manner indicated. All were identical.

22. SUMMARY OF GENUINE MARKS STAMPED ON MEXICAN SILVER
1524-1936

PERIOD	NO.	MARK USED FOR STANDARD (OF QUALITY) AND OF THE TAX (20%)	*Enlarged*	REMARKS
1524-1578	1			It is possible, but not certain, that this mark is the one used prior to 1578. The mark is enlarged, its actual size being the following:
1579-1637	2			Although worn, which makes its reproduction difficult, the following mark is: the columns of Hercules crowned (adapted from the Spanish Arms), with an *M* between, which means 'Mexico.'
1638-1732	3			This mark is similar to the preceding one but smaller.

SUMMARY OF THE GENUINE MARKS STAMPED ON MEXICAN SILVER
1524-1936

PERIOD	NO.	MARK OF THE CHIEF ASSAYER	HALL-MARK (QUALITY)	TAX MARK	*Enlarged* REMARKS
	4	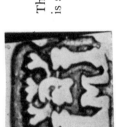	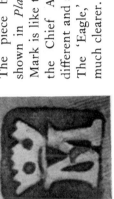		The piece bearing these marks is shown in *Plate* 107.
Of Chief Assayer González 1733-1778	5				The piece bearing them is shown in *Plate* 107. The Tax Mark is like that of No.4, but the Chief Assayer's is now different and spelled 'Gõzalez.' The 'Eagle,' being larger, is much clearer.
	6				These marks appear on the piece shown in *Plate* 114, made by the famous Master Silversmith, José María Rodallega: and are the same as those on piece 9133 at the Metropolitan Museum of Art in New York City.

SUMMARY OF THE GENUINE MARKS STAMPED ON MEXICAN SILVER
1524-1936

PERIOD	NO.	MARK OF THE CHIEF ASSAYER	HALL-MARK (QUALITY)	TAX MARK	Enlarged REMARKS
Of Chief Assayer Lince 1779-1788	7		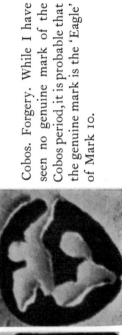		Marks used on medium sized and large pieces. From the year 1783 the *M* crowned was used as a hall-mark. This *M* crowned was stamped with the same punch as that of Mark No. 5 the 'Tax Mark.' The 'Eagle' was also stamped with the same punch as hall-mark No.6.
1779-1788	8		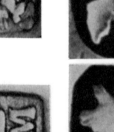		Small marks used on small pieces.
Of Chief Assayer Cobos 1789-1790	9			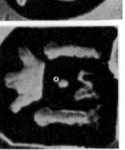	Cobos. Forgery. While I have seen no genuine mark of the Cobos period, it is probable that the genuine mark is the 'Eagle' of Mark 10.

SUMMARY OF THE GENUINE MARKS STAMPED ON MEXICAN PLATE
1524–1936

PERIOD	NO.	MARK OF THE CHIEF ASSAYER	HALL-MARK (QUALITY)	TAX MARK	*Enlarged* REMARKS
Of Chief Assayer Forcada 1791–1818	10				Marks found only on large pieces.
Of Chief Assayer Forcada	11				Marks used on pieces of ordinary size.
	12				Marks used on small pieces.
	13				

SUMMARY OF THE GENUINE MARKS STAMPED ON MEXICAN PLATE
1524-1936

PERIOD	NO.	MARK OF THE CHIEF ASSAYER	HALL-MARK (QUALITY)	TAX MARK	*Enlarged* REMARKS
1791-1818	14				
Of Chief Assayer Dávila 1819-1823	15				
Of Chief Assayer Buitrón 1823-1843	16				Forged marks. I have not seen Davila's genuine marks.

SUMMARY OF THE GENUINE MARKS STAMPED ON MEXICAN PLATE
1524-1936

PERIOD	NO.	MARK OF THE CHIEF ASSAYER	HALL-MARK (QUALITY)	TAX MARK	*Enlarged* REMARKS
Of Chief Assayer Camacho 1856-1860 1863-1867	17				Camacho. No forgeries are found.
Of Chief Assayer Castillo 1861-1862 1867-1868	18				Castillo. No forgeries are found.
Of Chief Assayer Mucharraz 1868-1880	19				Mucharraz. No forgeries are found. The 'Eagle' used by Morales is from Buitrón's punch, which is still in use in the Mint in Mexico.
Of Chief Assayer Morales 1881-1889	20				I have not found Sáyago's mark. Chief Assayer Obregón told me that Sáyago used Morales' punches the *M* with a small *o* above it and the 'Eagle.'
Of Chief Assayer Sáyago 1890-1893	21				

SUMMARY OF THE GENUINE MARKS STAMPED ON MEXICAN PLATE
1524-1936

PERIOD	NO.	MARK OF THE CHIEF ASSAYER	HALL-MARK (QUALITY)	TAX MARK	REMARKS *Enlarged*
1894-1895 Of Chief Assayer Obregón	22				
1895-1936	23	Not Used 	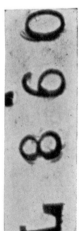		On the Hall-mark the *L* means '*Ley*' (standard) and the number 860 indicates the pure silver content in thousandths of the piece assayed. The Eagle is from the same punch used by Chief Assayers Buitrón, Morales, Sáyago and Obregón.

Appendix I

LIST OF SILVERSMITHS IN MEXICO

NAME	YEAR	SOURCE OF DATA AND REMARKS
Abalos, Juan de	1730	*Archivo General de la Nación. Ordenanzas*, vol.11, p.57. 1723-63. Examination 27th May. Master silversmith.
Abila, Jph. Mariano	1784	*A.G. de la N. Ordenanzas*, vol.16, p.136 reverse. 1784. Examination 27th September. Master silversmith.
Abiles, Melchora C., widow of	1685	*El Gremio de Plateros en las Indias Occidentales*, by José Torre Revello, p.xxix.
Abrego, Ph(e). de	1685	*El Gremio de Plateros en las Indias Occidentales*, by José Torre Revello, p.xxix. Silversmith.
Abril, Juan Rodríguez	1621	*Torneos en la Nueva España*, by Manuel Romero de Terreros, p.30. Silversmith.
Acha, Agustín	1753	*A.G. de la N. Civil indiferente*, vol.64. *Empadronamiento de* 1753. The pages of the book are not numbered. Silversmith.
Acosta, José María	1854	*Guía de Forasteros en la Ciudad de Mégico, para el año de* 1854. Silversmith.
Aguiar, Antonio	1753	*A.G. de la N. Civil indiferente*, vol.64. *Empadronamiento de* 1753. The pages of the book are not numbered. Owner of silver-shop.
Aguilar, Diego	1685	*El Gremio de Plateros en las Indias Occidentales*, by José Torre Revello, p.xxix. Silversmith.
Aguilar, Francisco Xavier de	1730	*A.G. de la N. Ordenanzas*, vol.11, p.61 reverse. 1723-63. Examination 24th August. Master silversmith.
Aguilar, Juan Jph. de	1770	*A.G. de la N. Ordenanzas*, vol.16, p.26. 1764. Examination 17th August. Master silversmith.
Aguilar, Manuel	1795	*A.G. de la N. Ordenanzas*, vol.16, p.179 reverse. 1764. Examination 21st March. Master silversmith.
Aguilar, Pedro de	1535	*Colección de Documentos Inéditos para la Historia de Hispano América*, by Luis Rubero y Moreno, vol.11, p.292. Silversmith.
Aguilera, Anselmo	1811	*A.G. de la N. Empadronamiento de* 1811. *Cuartel menor núm.*1. Silversmith. (15 years of age.)

Aguilera, Juan de	1753	*A.G. de la N. Civil indiferente*, vol.64. *Empadronamiento de* 1753. The pages of the book are not numbered. Silver-shop. (40 years of age.)
Aguirre, José Antonio	1792	*A.G. de la N. Industria*, vol.5, p.255. Unlicensed silversmith.
Aguirre, Miguel	1811	*A.G. de la N. Empadronamiento de* 1811. *Cuartel menor núm.*1. Silversmith. (30 years of age.)
Alba, Cayetano de	1742	*A.G. de la N. Ordenanzas*, vol.11, p.159. 1723-63. Examination 12th April. Master silversmith.
Alba, Lorenzo de	1811	*A.G. de la N. Empadronamiento de* 1811. *Cuartel menor núm.*1. Silversmith. (23 years of age.)
Aldaco, Manuel de	1757	*Documentos para la Historia de México*, by Manuel Orozco y Berra. Series 1, vol.6, p.87. Silversmith.
Alemanes, Messrs.	1852	*Guía de Forasteros de la Capital de Puebla, para el año de* 1852, by Juan N. del Valle. Silversmiths.
Alfaro, Diego Rodríguez	1623	Proceedings of Municipal Council, 15th December, 1623. Examined in Seville. Silversmith.
Almazán y Flores, Ramón	1778	*A.G. de la N. Ordenanzas*, vol.16, p.112. 1764. Examination 6th October. Master silversmith.
Almazán, Ramón Sánchez	1811	*A.G. de la N. Empadronamiento de* 1811. *Cuartel menor núm.*1. Owner of silver-shop. (65 years of age.)
Altamirano, José María	1852	*Guía de Forasteros de la Capital de Puebla, para el año de* 1852, by Juan N. del Valle. Silversmith.
Altrador, Ygnacio	1807	*A.G. de la N. Ordenanzas*, vol.16, p.196. 1764. Examination 10th June. Owner of silver-shop.
Alvarado, Miguel	1811	*A.G. de la N. Empadronamiento de* 1811. Cuartel *menor núm.*1. Silversmith. (37 years of age.)
Alvarez, Antonio	1865	*A.G. de la N. Calificación de establecimientos industriales.* Silver-shop. 1867 *Directorio del Comercio del Imperio Mexicano para el año de* 1867. Silver-shop.
Alvarez, Antonio	1864	*El Viajero en México*, by Juan N. del Valle. Silversmith. 1865. *A.G. de la N. Padrón de Establecimientos industriales.* Silver-shop. 1867 *Dir. del Comercio del Imperio Mexicano.*
Alvarez de Puente, Pedro J.	1731	*A.G. de la N. Ordenanzas*, vol.11, p.76 reverse. 1723-63. Examination 18th November. Master silversmith.
Amaya, José Rafael	1811	*A.G. de la N. Empadronamiento de* 1811. Silversmith. (48 years of age.)
Anaya, Joseph de	1685	*El Gremio de Plateros en las Indias Occidentales*, op.cit., p.xxix. Silversmith.
Andrade, José	1854	*Guía de Forasteros en la Ciudad de Mégico, para el año de* 1854. Silversmith.

Andrés e Ysaura, Manuel de	1805	*A.G. de la N. Ordenanzas*, vol.16, p.194 reverse. 1764. Examination 10th July. Owner of silver-shop.
Angel, Antonio del	1730	*A.G. de la N. Ordenanzas*, vol.11, p.57 reverse. 1723-63. Examination 2nd June. Master silversmith.
Angel, Luis	1685	*El Gremio de Plateros en las Indias Occidentales*, op.cit., p.xxix. Goldsmith.
Angeles, Simón de los	1676	*Indice de Documentos de Nueva España existentes en el Archivo de Indias de Sevilla. México. Monografías Bibliográficas Mexicanas. 1931. vol.4, p.174. Imp. Sría. R. Exteriores.*
Apaes, Manuel de	1782	*A.G. de la N. Ordenanzas*, vol.16, p.122 reverse. 1764. Examination 19th January. Master silversmith. 1798 *A.G.P. de la N. Guía de cargo y data de la Tesorería Gral. E. y R. Hda.*, p.9.
Aranda, Francisco	1882	*Nueva Guía de México en inglés, francés y castellano, etc.*, by Ireneo Paz y Manuel Tornel. p.833. Silver-shop.
Araujo Guerrero, Ysidro	1731	*A.G. de la N. Ordenanzas*, vol.11, p.65 reverse. 1723-63. Examination 18th January. Master silversmith.
Arauz, Bartolo	1811	*A.G. de la N. Empadronamiento de 1811. Cuartel menor núm.1.* Silversmith. (40 years of age.)
Arce, Juan	1852	*Guía de Forasteros de la capital de Puebla, para el año de 1852*, op.cit. Silversmith.
Arcos, Joaquín	1811	*A.G. de la N. Empadronamiento de 1811. Cuartel menor núm.1.* Silversmith. (15 years of age.)
Arellano, Marcos	1774	*A.G. de la N. Ordenanzas*, vol.16, p.66 reverse. 1764. Examination 21st April. Owner of silver-shop.
Arenas, Joaquín	1753	*A.G. de la N. Civil indiferente*, vol.64. *Empadronamiento de 1753.* The pages of the book are not numbered. Silversmith. (32 years of age.)
Arenas, José	1753	*A.G. de la N. Civil indiferente*, vol.64. *Empadronamiento de 1753.* The pages of the book are not numbered. Silversmith. (50 years of age.)
Arenas, Juan de	1721	*A.G. de la N. Ordenanzas*, vol.10, p.110. 1714-22. Examination 15th December. Master silversmith. *1724 y 1725 A.G. de la N. Ordenanzas*, vol.11, pp.9 reverse and 14 bis. 1723-63. *Mayordomo.*
Arenas, Miguel	1753	*A.G. de la N. Civil indiferente*, vol.64. *Empadronamiento de 1753.* The pages of the

book are not numbered. Silversmith. (60 years of age.)

Arevalo, José	1799	*A.G. de la N. Guía de cargo y data etc. para la cuenta del año de* 1799. Silversmith of this city.
Arias, Cap(n). Joseph	1685	*El Gremio de Plateros en las Indias Occidentales*, op.cit., p.xxix. Silversmith.
Arisza, Juan María de	1721	*Historia de la Fundación de la Ciudad de la Puebla de los Angeles en la Nueva España*, by Lic. Mariano Fernández Echeverría y Veytia, vol.11, p.168. Owner [of silver-shop].
Argumedo, Juan de	1753	*A.G. de la N. Civil indiferente*, vol.64. *Empadronamiento de* 1753. The pages of the book are not numbered. Silversmith and owner of cigarette shop. (36 years of age.)
Armas, Francisco Xavier de	1723	*A.G. de la N. Ordenanzas*, vol.11, p.95. 1723-63. Examination 4th May. Master silversmith.
Armendariz, José Fran.co. de	1782	*A.G. de la N. Ordenanzas*, vol.16, p.124 reverse. 1764. Examination 18th July. Master silversmith.
Armenta, José María	1800	*A.G. de la N. Ordenanzas*, vol.16, p.186 reverse. 1764. Examination 2nd April. Owner of silver-shop.
Armijo, Joaquín Antonio	1761	*A.G. de la N. Ordenanzas*, vol.11, p.319 reverse. 1723-63. Examination 3rd August. Master silversmith.
Aróstegui, Joaquín	1753	*A.G. de la N. Civil indiferente*, vol.64. *Empadronamiento de* 1753. The pages of the book are not numbered. Unlicensed silversmith. (30 years of age.)
Arriola, Antonio de	1736	*A.G. de la N. Ordenanzas*, vol.11, p.116 reverse. 1723-63. Examination 6th March. Master silversmith.
Arroyo, Felipe	1865	*A.G. de la N. Calificación de Establecimientos industriales*. Silver-shop.
Arteage, Jerónimo López de	1613	*Indice de Documentos de Nueva España existentes en el Archivo de Indias de Sevilla*. op.cit. Silversmith.
Asencio, Bernaldino	1563	*A. de Notarías de México*. Before Antonio Alonso, Public Scrivener. Goldsmith.
Astores, José	1811	*A.G. de la N. Empadronamiento de* 1811. Silversmith. (30 years of age.)
Avalos, Nicolás	1753	*A.G. de la N. Civil indiferente*, vol.64. *Empadronamiento de* 1753. The pages of the book are not numbered. Silversmith. (50 years of age.)
Avila, Francisco Antonio de	1737	*A.G. de la N. Ordenanzas*, vol.11, p.124. 1723-63. Examination in September. Master silversmith.

Avila, José María de	1786	*A.G. de la N. Indice Gral. de los ramos que comprenden el Libro Mayor de esta Real Casa Matriz*, p.13. No year is given but the seal on the paper is for 1786-7. Silversmith mentioned.
Avila, Pedro de	1753	*A.G. de la N. Civil indiferente*, vol.64. *Emp. de* 1753. The pages of the book are not numbered. Owner of silver-shop. 1766 *A.G. de la N. Ordenanzas*, vol.16, p.10 reverse. Election 14th January. *Veedor* of silversmiths.
Aviles, Alonzo de	1746	*Pregones de Ordenanzas de el Nobílissimo Arte de la Platería. México. Imp. de María de Ribera. Mayordomo* of the Silversmiths' Art. Proceedings of the Municipal Council of 7th November 1701.
Aviles, José Francisco	1803	*A.G. de la N. Ordenanzas*, vol.16, p.192 reverse. 1764. Examination 10th February. Owner of silver-shop.
Avilés, Pedro	1811	*A.G. de la N. Empadronamiento de 1811. Cuartel menor núm.*1. Silversmith. (23 years of age.)
Ayala, Manuel	1811	*A.G. de la N. Empadronamiento de 1811.* Silversmith. (39 years of age.)
Azcárate, José María	1859	*El Viajero en México*, op.cit. Silversmith.
Badillo, Manuel de	1774	*A.G. de la N. Ordenanzas*, vol.16, p.66 reverse. 1764. Election 21st April. *Veedor* of silversmiths.
Baez, Enrique	1546	Proceedings of Municipal Council of 26th and 27th March 1546. Silversmith.
Baez, José María	1854	*Guía de Forasteros en la Ciudad de Mégico*, op.cit. Silversmith.
Baez, Lorenzo	1565	*Archivo de Protocolos. Actas de Antonio Alonzo*, p.dccxxxiii reverse. 1554-65. Silversmith.
Barbabosa, Cristobal	1792	*A.G. de la N. Industria*, vol.5, p.255. Unlicensed silversmith.
Barbabosa, Ignacio	1792	*A.G. de la N. Industria*, vol.5, p.255. Unlicensed silversmith. 1798 *A.G. de la N. Ordenanzas*, vol.16, p.185. 1764. Examination 6th November. Owner of silver-shop.
Bárcenas, Ignacio	1792	*A.G. de la N. Industria*, vol.5, p.255. Unlicensed silversmith.
Barea, Mig.(l) Jph. Antonio	1776	*A.G. de la N. Ordenanzas*, vol.16, p.80. 1764. Examination 23rd May. Owner of silver-shop.
Baric, Andrés	1854	*Guía de Forasteros en la Ciudad de Mégico* op.cit. Silversmith.
Baric, Victor	1854	*Guía de Forasteros en la Ciudad de Mégico* op.cit. Silversmith.
Barragán, Mariano	1854	*Guía de Forasteros en la Ciudad de Mégico*, op.cit. Silversmith. 1859 *El Viajero en* México, op.cit. 1863 *C. Completa Decretos Grals. expedidos*

		Exmo. Sr. Gral. Forey, p.48. *Imp. cargo M. Zornosa.*
Barragán, Mariano	1864	*El Viajero en México*, op.cit. 1865. *A.G. de la N. Padrón de Est. industriales.* Silver-shop. 1867 *Directorio del Comercio del Imperio Mexicano*, op.cit. Silver-shop.
Barreda, Bartholomé	1778	*A.G. de la N. Ordenanzas*, vol.16, p.106 reverse. 1764. Examination 28th March. Owner of silver-shop.
Barreda, Ignacio	1764	*A.G. de la N. Ordenanzas*, vol.16, p.1. 1764. Examination 28th January. Master silversmith.
Barreda, Manuel	1753	*A.G. de la N. Civil indiferente*, vol.64. *Empadronamiento de 1753.* The pages of the book are not numbered. Unlicensed silversmith.
Barreda, Manuel de la	1725	*A.G. de la N. Ordenanzas*, vol.11, p.14 bis. 1723-63. Election 9th January. *Mayordomo.*
Barrientos, José	1753	*A.G. de la N. Civil indiferente*, vol.64. *Empadronamiento de 1753.* The pages of the book are not numbered. Silver-shop.
Barrientos, José	1792	*A.G. de la N. Industria*, vol.5, p.255. Unlicensed silversmith.
Barrientos, Manuel	1779	*A.G. de la N. Ordenanzas*, vol.16, p.113. 1764. Examination 8th January. Master silversmith.
Barrio, Juan Joseph del	1732	*A.G. de la N. Ordenanzas*, vol.11, p.82 reverse. 1723-63. Examination 7th June. Master silversmith.
Barrios, Francisco de	1725	*A.G. de la N. Ordenanzas*, vol.11, p.19. 1723-63. Examination 17th July. Master silversmith.
Barrios, Jph. Antonio	1769	*A.G. de la N. Ordenanzas*, vol.16, p.19 reverse. 1764. Examination 8th March. Master silversmith.
Barrios, José de	1774	*Historia de la Fundación de la Ciudad de la Puebla de los Angeles etc.* op.cit., vol.11, pp.164-5. Owner [of silver-shop] 1798 *Diccionario Universal de Geografía e Historia*, vol.6, p.484. Silversmith.
Barrios, Juan José	1811	*A.G. de la N. Empadronamiento de 1811. Cuartel menor núm.1.* Silversmith. (54 years of age.)
Barrios Carballido, Joseph	1725	*A.G. de la N. Ordenanzas*, vol.11, p.18 reverse. 1723-63. Examination 24th July. Master silversmith.
Basardua, José	1811	*A.G. de la N. Empadronamiento de 1811. Cuartel menor núm.1.* Silversmith. (30 years of age.)
Basurto, Miguel	1751	*A.G. de la N. Ordenanzas*, vol.11, p.261. 1723-63. Examination 15th December. Master silversmith.
Batan, Eugenio	1750	*Las Artes Industriales en la Nueva España*, op.cit., p.30. Silversmith.

Bazan, José	1811	*A.G. de la N. Empadronamiento de* 1811. *Cuartel menor núm.*1. Silversmith. (36 years of age.)
Bellica, García de	1535	*Colección de Documentos Inéditos para la Historia de Hispano América,* op.cit. Silversmith.
Bellido, José	1811	*A.G. de la N. Empadronamiento de* 1811. Silversmith. (32 years of age.)
Bello, Antonio	1779	*A.G. de la N. Ordenanzas,* vol.16, p.113 reverse. 1764. Examination 23rd February. Master silversmith.
Beltrán, Antonio	1852	*Guía de Forasteros de la Capital de Puebla, para el año de* 1852, op.cit. Silversmith.
Beltrán, Juan	1753	*A.G. de la N. Civil indiferente,* vol.64. *Empadronamientos de* 1753. The pages of the book are not numbered. Unlicensed silversmith. (30 years of age.)
Benítez, Roque	1693	*Las Artes Industriales en la Nueva España,* op.cit. Silversmith.
Berdeja, José Aristeo	1817	*A.G. de la N. Ordenanzas,* vol.16, p.202. Examination 10th June. Owner of silver-shop. 1854 *Guía de Forasteros en la Ciudad de Mégico,* op.cit. Silversmith. 1859 *El Viajero en México,* op.cit. Silver-shop.
Berdeja, José Aristeo	1865	*A.G. de la N. Calificación de Est. Industriales.* 1867. *Directorio del Comercio del Imperio Mexicano para el Año de* 1867, op.cit. Silver-shop.
Berdeja, Miguel	1864	*El Viajero en México,* op.cit. Silversmith. 1865 *A.G. de la N. Calificación de Est. Industriales.* Silver-shop. 1867 *Directorio del Comercio del Imperio Mexicano,* op.cit. Silver-shop.
Bergara, Man.(l) de	1685	*El Gremio de Plateros en las Indias Occidentales,* op.cit. p.xxix. Filigree worker.
Bernal, Gaspar	1606	*A.G. de la N. Reales Cédulas,* vol.5, p.57 reverse. 1605. (Planta alta) Examination 6th October. Master silversmith.
Bernal, José María	1791	*A.G. de la N. Ordenanzas,* vol.16, p.162 reverse. Examination 25th January. Master silversmith. 1811 *A.G. de la N. Emp. de* 1811. (53 years of age.) 1814 *Ord.,* vol.16, p.200 reverse. Elected *Veedor.*
Bernal, Nicolás	1685	*El Gremio de Plateros en las Indias Occidentales,* op.cit:, p.xxix. Sheet-beater.
Bernal, Ramón	1842	*A.G. de la N. Padrón de establecimientos industriales. Cuartel menor núm.*1. Silver-work shop and lathe shop.
Beydacar, Pedro de	1565	*Archivo de Protocolos. Actas de Antonio Alonso,* p.dccxxxiii reverse. 1554-65. Silversmith.
Bira, Pedro de	1745	*A.G. de la N. Ordenanzas,* vol.11, p.189 reverse. 1723-63. Election 11th January. *Mayordomo.*

Blanco, Mariano — 1854 — *Guía de Forasteros en la Ciudad de Mégico, etc.*, op.cit. Silversmith. 1859 and 1864 *El Viajero en Mexico para los años de 1859 y 1864.* op.cit. Silversmith.

Blanquetto, Francisco — 1685 — *El Gremio de Plateros en las Indias Occidentales*, op.cit., p.xxix. Silversmith.

Bolibar, Juan de — 1618 — Proceedings of Municipal Council, 29th January 1618. Sheet-beater.

Bonilla, Matheo — 1752 — *A.G. de la N. Ordenanzas*, vol.11, p.263 reverse. 1723-63. Examination 29th May. Master silversmith.

Borja y Villalón, Juan A. de — 1741 — *A.G. de la N. Ordenanzas*, vol.11, p.261. 1723-63. Examination 28th December. Master silversmith.

Bovis, Lorenzo — 1832 — *Registro Oficial del Gobierno de los Estados Unidos Mexicanos. Año 3°*, vol.9, No.47. 17th October 1832. Silversmith and diamond-cutter.

Brito, José — 1753 — *A.G. de la N. Civil indiferente*, vol.64. *Empadronamiento de 1753.* The pages of the book are not numbered. Unlicensed silversmith.

Buitrano, Andrés de — 1535 — *Colección de Documentos Inéditos para la Historia de Hispano América*, op.cit., vol.XIII, Vol.11, p.288. Silversmith.

Buytrago, Lorenzo de — 1559 — *Archivo de Protocolos. Actas de Antonio Alonso*, p.ccvii. 1554-1565. Silversmith.

Caamaño, Antonio — 1799 — *A.G. de la N. Guía de cargo y data etc. para la cuenta de 1799. Señoreage*, p.37 reverse. Silversmith of this city. 1800 *Ord.* vol.16, p.186 reverse. Election 1st January. *Veedor* of silversmiths.

Caamaño, Antonio — 1801 — *A.G. de la N. Ordenanzas*, vol.16, p.190 reverse. Election 9th January. *Veedor* of silversmiths. 1808 *Ord.*, vol.16, p.197. Election 8th January. *Veedor* of silversmiths. 1811 *Emp. de 1811. Cuartel menor núm.1.* European silversmith.

Cabrera, Joseph Ignacio de — 1737 — *A.G. de la N. Ordenanzas*, vol.11, p.123 reverse. 1723-63. Examination 27th July. Master silversmith. 1753 *A.G. de la N. Civil Ind.* vol.64. *Emp. de 1753.* With silver-shop.

Cadalzo, Cayetano — 1811 — *A.G. de la N. Empadronamiento de 1811. Cuartel menor núm.1.* Silversmith (19 years of age.)

Cadalzo, Francisco — 1811 — *A.G. de la N. Empadronamiento de 1811. Cuartel menor núm.1.* Silversmith (55 years of age.)

Calderón, Eduardo — 1769 — *A.G. de la N. Ordenanzas*, vol.16, p.19 reverse. Examination 22nd June. Master silversmith. 1784 *Ord.* vol.16, p.135 reverse. Election 14th January. *Veedor* of silversmiths.

Calderón, Eduardo	1790	*A.G. de la N. Ordenanzas*, vol.16, p.159. Election 13th January. *Veedor* of silversmiths. Romero de Terreros, op.cit., p.24. 1796 *A.G. de la N. Derechos de oro de fuego*. Silversmith.
Calderón, Ysabel C. widow of J.	1685	*El Gremio de Plateros en las Indias Occidentales*, op.cit., p.xxix.
Calvillo, Juan	1864	*El Viajero en México*, op.cit. Silversmith.
Calvillo, Tomás	1865	*A.G. de la N. Calificación de establecimientos Industriales*. Silver-shop.
Camacho, José María	1811	*A.G. de la N. Empadronamiento de 1811. Cuartel menor núm.1*. Silversmith. (39 years of age.)
Camaño, Manuel	1819	*Diccionario Universal de Historia y Geografía*, vol.6, p.484. 1820 *Las Artes Industriales en la Nueva España*, op.cit. Silversmith.
Cambria, Bartolomé	1724	*A.G. de la N. Ordenanzas*, vol.11, p.9 reverse. 1723-1763. Election 8th January. *Diputado*.
Campos, Antonio Féliz de	1779	*A.G. de la N. Ordenanzas*, vol.16, p.114. 1764. Examination 27th May. Master silversmith.
Campuzano, Pioquinto	1859	*El Viajero en México*, op.cit. Silversmith.
Campuzano, XP(l).	1685	*El Gremio de Plateros en las Indias Occidentales*, op.cit., p.xxix. Silversmith.
Cano, Francisco	1754	*A.G. de la N. Ordenanzas*, vol.11, p.270. 1723-63. Approved 7th March. Master silversmith. (Examined in Seville.)
Cañas, Alexandro Antonio	1786	*A.G. de la N. Ordenanzas*, vol.16, p.146. 1764. Examination 27th September. Master silversmith. 1794 *Ord.*, vol.16, p.177 reverse. 1764. Election 9th January. *Veedor* of silversmiths.
Cañas, Alexandro Antonio	1798	*A.G. de la N. Manual Común de 1798*. The pages of the book are not numbered. Owner [of silver-shop] 1804 Ord., vol.16, p.193 reverse. Election 7th January. *Veedor*. 1811 *Emp*. de 1811. Silversmith. (56 years of age.)
Cañas, Alexandro Antonio	1819	*Manuscript, copy of Inventario de las alhajas de la S.I.Catedral Méx. 26 Dic. 1844, p.41*. Silversmith. 1831 *A.G. de la N. Ramo de Hda. 1830-31*. Bundle 45. Silversmith.
Cañas, Gumesindo	1811	*A.G. de la N. Empadronamiento de 1811*. Silversmith. Son of Alejandro Cañas. (28 years of age.)
Cañas, Mateo, Mariano	1818	*A.G. de la N. Ordenanzas*, vol.16, p.202 reverse. 1764. Examination 22nd July. Owner of silver-shop.
Cañas, Pedro	1854	*Guía de Forasteros, etc. para 1854*, op.cit. Silversmith. 1859 and 1864 *El Viajero en México para 1859 y 1864*. Silversmith.
Cañas, Pedro	1865	*A.G. de la N. Padrón de Est. Ind.* Silver-shop.

		1867 *Directorio del Comercio del Imperio Mexicano*. Silversmith. 1882 *Nueva Guía de México*, by I.Paz and M.Tornel, p.833.
Cao Romero, José María	1852	*Guía de Forasteros de la Capital de Puebla, para el año de* 1852. Silversmith.
Caraballal, José	1792	*A.G. de la N. Industria*, vol.5, p.255. Unlicensed silversmith.
Carauajal, Xp(l).	1685	*El Gremio de Plateros en las Indias Occidentales*. p.xxix. Silversmith.
Cárdenas, Rogelio	1792	*A.G. de la N. Industria*, vol.5, p.255. Unlicensed silversmith.
Cardeña, Ygnacio	1731	*A.G. de la N. Ordenanzas*, vol.11, p.69. 1723-63. Examination 12th April. Master silversmith.
Cardona, Agustín	1811	*A.G. de la N. Emp. de* 1811. *Cuartel menor núm.*1. Silversmith. 1829 *Correo de la Federación Mexicana*, 16 de agosto de 1829. Silversmith.
Cardona, Antonio	1811	*A.G. de la N. Empadronamiento de* 1811. *Cuartel menor núm.*1. Silversmith. (24 years of age.)
Cardona, Felipe	1811	*A.G. de la N. Empadronamiento de* 1811. *Cuartel menor núm.*1. Silversmith. (56 years of age.)
Cardona, José	1796	*A.G. de la N. Ordenanzas*, vol.16, p.181 reverse. 1764. Election 9th January. *Veedor* of silversmiths. 1798 *A.G.P.N. Guía de cargo y data etc. para la cuenta de* 1798, p.12. Silversmith of this city.
Cardona, José María	1811	*A.G. de la N. Empadronamiento de* 1811. *Cuartel menor núm.*1. Silversmith. (25 years of age.)
Cardona, Ramón de	1546	*Actas de Cabildo*, 29 de marzo de 1546. Named *Veedor*.
Cardoso, Cristóbal	1842	*A.G. de la N. Padrón de establecimientos industriales. Cuartel menor núm.*1. Silver-work shop.
Cardoso, José María	1859	and 1864 *El Viajero en México para los años de* 1859 *y* 1864. op.cit. Silversmith. 1865 *A.G. de la N. Calificación de Est. Industriales*. Silver-shop.
Careaga, José	1790	*A.G. de la N. Ordenanzas*, vol.16, p.159. 1764. Examination 10th April. Master silversmith.
Cariñona, Martín	1811	*A.G. de la N. Empadronamiento de* 1811. Silversmith. (40 years of age.)
Carmona, Martín	1792	*A.G. de la N. Industria*, vol.5, p.255. Unlicensed silversmith.
Carrillo, Agustín	1730	*A.G. de la N. Ordenanzas*, vol.11, p.58 reverse. 1723-63. Examination 22nd June. Master silversmith.
Carrillo, Antonio	1864	*El Viajero en México*, op.cit. Silversmith. 1865 *A.G. de la N. Padrón de Est. Indust.* Silver-shop. 1867 *Directorio del Comercio del Imperio*

		Mexicano, etc. op.cit. Silver-shop.
Carrillo, Guadalupe	1859	*El Viajero en México*, op.cit. 1882 *Nueva Guía de México* by Ireneo Paz and Manuel Tornel, p.833. Mexico. Silver-shop.
Carrillo, Jesús	1865	*A.G. de la N. Padrón de Est. Indust.* Silver-shop. 1867 *Directorio del Comercio del Imperio Mexicano*, op.cit. Silver-shop. 1882 *Nueva Guía de México*, op.cit., p.833. Silver-shop.
Carrillo, Juan Jph.	1765	*A.G. de la N. Ordenanzas*, vol.16, p.9 reverse. 1764. Examination 15th June. Master silversmith.
Carrillo, Mariano	1788	*A.G. de la N. Ordenanzas*, vol.16, p.156 reverse. 1764. Examination. Master silversmith.
Cásares, Juan	1753	*A.G. de la N. Civil indiferente*, vol.64. *Empadronamiento de* 1753. The pages of the book are not numbered. Silversmith. (55 years of age.)
Casas, Josep de	1779	*A.G. de la N. Ordenanzas*, vol.16, p.114 reverse. 1764. Examination 14th June. Master silversmith.
Casillas, José	1753	*A.G. de la N. Civil indiferente*, vol.64. *Empadronamiento de* 1753. The pages of the book are not numbered. Unlicensed silversmith. (17 years of age.)
Casillas, Manuel	1753	*A.G. de la N. Civil indiferente*, vol.64. *Empadronamiento de* 1753. The pages of the book are not numbered. Silversmith.
Castañeda, Bernardo de	1730	*A.G. de la N. Ordenanzas*, vol.11, p.58 reverse. 1723-63. Examination 14th June. Master silversmith.
Castañeda, Juan	1854	*Guía de Forasteros en la Ciudad de Mégico.* Silversmith. 1859 *El Viajero en México.* Silversmith.
Castañeda, Francisco	1854	*Guía de Forasteros en la Ciudad de Mégico, para el año de* 1854. Silversmith.
Castaño, Anti.(o)	1685	*El Gremio de Plateros en las Indias Occidentales*, op.cit, p.xxix. Silversmith.
Castera, Miguel	1792	*A.G. de la N. Industria*, vol.5, p.255. Unlicensed silversmith.
Castillo, Cristóbal del	1735	*A.G. de la N. Ordenanzas*, vol.11, p.112 reverse. 1723-63. Examination 20th October. Master silversmith.
Castillo, Domingo	1744	*A.G. de la N. Ordenanzas*, vol.11, p.182. 1723-63. Examination 29th May. Master silversmith.
Castillo, Felipe	1753	*A.G. de la N. Civil indiferente*, vol.64. *Empadronamiento de* 1753. The pages of the book are not numbered. Unlicensed silversmith. (36 years of age.)

Castillo, José   1811   *A.G. de la N. Empadronamiento de* 1811. *Cuartel menor núm.*1. Silversmith. (29 years of age.)

Castillo, Joseph del   1735   *A.G. de la N. Ordenanzas,* vol.11, p.109 reverse. 1723-63. Examination 15th August. Master silversmith. 1764 *y* 1792 *Ord.,* vol.16, pp.1 and 170 reverse. Elected *Veedor* 14th January – 1st July.

Castillo, Jph. Antonio del   1776   and 1777 *A.G. de la N. Ordenanzas,* vol.16, pp.79 and 90 reverse. 1764. Election 16th January, 1776. Reelection 4th February, 1777. *Veedor* of silversmiths.

Castillo, José María del   1784   *A.G. de la N. Ordenanzas,* vol.16, p.136. Examination 4th March. Master silversmith. 1792 *A.G. de la N. Industria,* vol.5, p.255. Master [silversmith] and *Veedor.*

Castillo, José María   1852   *Guía de Forasteros de la capital de Puebla, para el año de* 1852. Silversmith.

Castillo, Juan Manuel del   1763   *A.G. de la N. Ordenanzas,* vol.11, p.323 reverse. 1723-1763. Examination 16th April. Master silversmith.

Castillo, Pedro   1753   *A.G. de la N. Civil indiferente,* vol.64. *Empadronamiento de* 1753. The pages of the book are not numbered. Unlicensed silversmith.

Castro, Antonio   1852   *Guía de Forasteros de la capital de Puebla, para el año de* 1852. Silversmith.

Castro, José María   1792   *A.G. de la N. Industria,* vol.5, p.255. Unlicensed silversmith. 1859 and 1864 *El Viajero en México, para los años de* 1859 *y de* 1864, op.cit. Silversmith.

Castro, José María   1865   *A.G. de la N. Calificación de Est. industriales.* Silver-shop. 1867 *Directorio del Comercio del Imperio Mexicano para el año de* 1867, op.cit. Silver-shop.

Castro, Juan de   1685   *El Gremio de Plateros en las Indias Occidentales,* op.cit., p.xxix. Silversmith.

Castro, Pedro Antonio   1771   *A.G. de la N. Ordenanzas,* vol.16, p.41 reverse. 1764. Examination 11th December. Master silversmith.

Castro, Vicente   1811   *A.G. de la N. Empadronamiento de* 1811. *Cuartel menor núm.*1. Silversmith. (34 years of age.)

Celada, Juan de   1526   Lucas Alamán, vol.11, p.445. Silversmith. Together with Diego Martínez, was in charge of the smelter.

Centeno, Juan   1753   *A.G. de la N. Civil indiferente,* vol.64. The pages of the book were not numbered. Unlicensed silversmith. (50 years of age.)

Centeno, Pascual   1753   *A.G. de la N. Civil indiferente,* vol.64. The pages of the book are not numbered. Unlicensed silversmith. (18 years of age.)

Cerdeño, Juan	1587	*A.G. de la N. General de Parte*, vol.3, p.40. Years 1587-8. Examination 28th February. Master silversmith.
Cerezo, José	1865	*A.G. de la N. Calificación de Est. industriales.* Silver-shop. 1867 *Directorio del Comercio del Imperio Mexicano para el año de 1867.* op.cit. Silver-shop.
Coba, Francisco Xavier de la	1731	*A.G. de la N. Ordenanzas*, vol.11, p.74 reverse. 1723-63. Examination 7th November. Master silversmith.
Colín, Juan	1854	*Guía de Forasteros en la Ciudad de Mégico, para el año de 1854.* op.cit. Silversmith.
Comont, Pedro	1761	*A.G. de la N. Ordenanzas*, vol.11, p.313. 1723-63. Examination 12th June. Master Silversmith. (Born in the city of Figeno, France.)
Concha, Antonio	1792	*A.G. de la N. Industria*, vol.5, p.255. Unlicensed silversmith.
Concha, Jesús	1859	and 1864 *El Viajero en México. Años de 1859 y 1864.* Silversmith. 1865 *A.G. de la N. Cal. de Est. Indus.* Silver-shop. 1867 *Directorio del Comercio del Imperio Mexicano*, op.cit. Silver-shop.
Condarco, José	1727	*A.G. de la N. Ordenanzas*, vol.11, p.40. 1723-63. Examination 6th March. Master silversmith.
Consuegra, Miguel de	1557	*Actas de Cabildo, 12 de Abril de 1557.* Silversmith, named marker.
Contreras, José	1811	*A.G. de la N. Empadronamiento de 1811. Cuartel menor núm.1.* Silversmith. (65 years of age.)
Contreras, Manuel	1753	*A.G. de la N. Civil indiferente*, vol.64. *Empadronamiento de 1753.* The pages of the book are not numbered. Silver-shop. (25 years of age.)
Contreras, Santiago	1792	*A.G. de la N. Industria*, vol.5, p.255. Unlicensed silversmith.
Contreras, Trinidad	1842	*A.G. de la N. Padrón de establecimientos industriales. Cuartel menor núm.1.* Silver-work shop.
Corballo, Antonio	1564	*A.G. de la N. Inquisición*, vol.26. Silversmith.
Cordero, José María	1854	*Guía de Forasteros en la Ciudad de Mégico, para el año de 1854.* op.cit. Silversmith.
Córdoba, Antonio de	1753	*A.G. de la N. Civil indiferente*, vol.64. *Empadronamiento de 1753.* The pages of the book are not numbered. Unlicensed silversmith.
Córdoba, Juan de	1753	*A.G. de la N. Civil indiferente*, vol.64. *Empadronamiento de 1753.* The pages of the book are not numbered. Unlicensed silversmith. (53 years of age.)

Córdova, Juan Miguel de	1721	*A.G. de la N. Ordenanzas*, vol.10, years 1714 to 1722. Examination. Master silversmith.
Córdova, Lorenzo de	1724	*A.G. de la N. Ordenanzas*, vol.11, p.9 reverse. 1723-63. Election 8th January. *Mayordomo.*
Cortazar, Gregorio	1811	*A.G. de la N. Empadronamiento de 1811.* Silversmith. (53 years of age.)
Cortazar, Joseph	1685	*El Gremio de Plateros en las Indias Occidentales*, op.cit., p.xxix. Silversmith.
Cortés, Antonio	1562	*Archivo de Notarías de México*. Before Antonio Alonso, Public Scrivener. 29th October. Silversmith.
Cortés, Balente	1842	*A.G. de la N. Padrón de establecimientos industriales. Cuartel menor núm.1.* Silver-work shop.
Cortés, Jerónimo	1792	*A.G. de la N. Industria*, vol.5, p.255. Unlicensed silversmith. 1811 *A.G. de la N. Empadronamiento de 1811.* Silversmith. (60 years of age.)
Cortés, Jph.	1772	*A.G. de la N. Ordenanzas*, vol.16, p.42 reverse. 1764. Examination 10th January. Master silversmith.
Cosío, Alejandro	1882	*Nueva Guía de México* by Ireneo Paz and Manuel Tornel. op.cit., p.834. Silver-shop.
Cosío, Anselmo	1865	*A.G. de la N. Calificación de Est. industriales.* Silver-shop. 1867 *Directorio del Comercio del Imperio Mexicano para el año de* 1867, op.cit. Silver-shop.
Cosme, Francisco	1606	*A.G. de la N. Reales Cédulas* (Planta alta). vol.5. 1605 Examination 6th October. Master silversmith.
Coto, Luis	1842	*A.G. de la N. Padrón de establecimientos industriales. Cuartel menor núm.1.* Silver-work shop. 1854 *Guía de Forasteros en la Ciudad de Mégico, etc.* op.cit. Silversmith.
Crespo, Gregorio	1723	*A.G. de la N. Ordenanzas*, vol.11, p.7. 1723-63. Examination 11th June. Master silversmith. 1727 *Ordenanzas*, vol.11, p.37. 1723-63. Election 13th January. *Mayordomo.*
Crespo Contreras, Joaquín	1811	*A.G. de la N. Empadronamiento de 1811.* Silversmith. (30 years of age.)
Cruz, Francisco de la	1724	*A.G. de la N. Ordenanzas*, vol.11, p.9 reverse. 1723-63. Election 8th January. *Mayordomo.* 1727 *Ordenanzas*, vol.11, p.37. 1723-63. Election 13th January. *Veedor.*
Cruz, Francisco de la	1733	Marroqui, vol.3, p.380. Silversmith. 1745 *A.G. de la N. Ordenanzas*, vol.11, p.189 reverse. 1723-63. Election 11th January. *Diputado.* (Lieutenant captain.)

Cruz, Jacinto	1753	*A.G. de la N. Civil indiferente*, vol.64. *Empadronamiento de* 1753. The pages of the book are not numbered. Unlicensed silversmith. (36 years of age.)
Cruz, José	1753	*A.G. de la N. Civil indiferente*, vol.64. *Empadronamiento de* 1753. The pages of the book are not numbered. Owner of silver-shop.
Cruz, Juan de la	1685	*El Gremio de Plateros en las Indias Occidentales*, op.cit., p.xxix. No.9. Silversmith (sergeant).
Cruz, Miguel	1811	*A.G. de la N. Empadronamiento de* 1811. Silversmith. (34 years of age.)
Cruz, Saluador de la	1685	*El Gremio de Plateros en las Indias Occidentales*. op.cit., p.xxix. No.9. Silversmith.
Cueba, Ana de la Vega, widow of	1685	*El Gremio de Plateros en las Indias Occidentales*, op.cit., p.xxix. No.9.
Cuebas, Juan Jph. de	1778	*A.G. de la N. Ordenanzas*, vol.16, p.111 reverse. 1764. Examination 22nd August. Master silversmith.
Cuebas, Juan de	1685	*El Gremio de Plateros en las Indias Occidentales*, op.cit., p.xxix. No.9. Silversmith.
Cuebas, Pedro de las	1550	*Actas de Cabildo*, 20 *de Febrero*. Mentioned as a silversmith.
Cuebas, Thomas de	1731	*A.G. de la N. Ordenanzas*, vol.11, p.76. 1723-63. Examination 17th November. Master silversmith. 1753 *Civil indiferente*, vol.64. *Emp. de* 1753. The pages of the book are not numbered. Owner of silver-shop. (55 years of age.)
Cuellar, Manuel de	1725	*A.G. de la N. Ordenanzas*, vol.11, p.18. 1723-63. Examination 20th July. Master silversmith.
Cueva, Isidro de la	1725	*A.G. de la N. Ordenanzas*, vol.11, p.15. 1723-63. Examination 20th February. Master silversmith. 1753 *Civil indiferente*, vol.64. *Emp. de* 1753. The pages of the book are not numbered. Owner of silver-shop.
Cueva, José Mariano de la	1792	*A.G. de la N. Industria*, vol.5, p.255. Unlicensed silversmith.
Cuevas, José	1784	*A.G. de la N. Ordenanzas*, vol.16, p.136. 1764. Examination 23rd July. Master silversmith.
Cuevas, Juan de	1564	*A.G. de la N. Inquisición*, vol.26. Silversmith.
Chamusgado, José Ignacio	1792	*A.G. de la N. Industria*, vol.5, p.255. Unlicensed silversmith.
Chamusgado, Thomas	1765	*A.G. de la N. Ordenanzas*, vol.16, p.10. 1764. Examination 29th July. Master silversmith.
Chávez, Juan Antonio de	1758	*A.G. de la N. Ordenanzas*, vol.11, p.298 reverse. 1723-63. Examination 11th December. Master silversmith.

Chávez Jugurron, Antonio de	1759	*A.G. de la N. Ordenanzas*, vol.11, p.302 reverse. 1723-63. Examination 28th June. Master silversmith.
Cherlin, Jesús	1882	*Nueva Guía de México*, op.cit., p.834. Silver-shop.
Chirlin, Manuel	1792	*A.G. de la N. Industria*, vol.5, p.255. Unlicensed silversmith.
Chorriel, José	1859	*El Viajero en México* by Juan N. del Valle. Year 1859. Silversmith.
Chozne, Joaquín	1842	*A.G. de la N. Padrón de establecimientos industriales. Cuartel menor núm.1.* Silver-shop. 1854 *Guía de Forasteros en la Ciudad de Mégico*, op.cit. Silversmith.
Dávila, Francisco	1811	*A.G. de la N. Empadronamiento de 1811.* Silversmith. (46 years of age.)
Dávila, José María	1811	*A.G. de la N. Empadronamiento de 1811.* Silversmith. (32 years of age.)
Díaz, Cayetano	1747	*A.G. de la N. Ordenanzas*, vol.11, p.235 reverse. 1723-63. Examination 8th July. Master silversmith.
Díaz, Diego	1746	*Pregones de Ordenanzas de el Nobilissimo Arte de la Platería. México. Imp. de* Doña María de Ribera. *Mayordomo* in the Silversmiths' art.
Díaz, Faustino	1859	*El Viajero en México* op.cit. Silversmith.
Díaz, Juan	1576	*Actas de Cabildo, 20 de Febrero 1576.* Silversmith.
Díaz, Luis	1595	*Proceso que formó la Inquisición a Luis Carbajal el Mozo*, p.413. Silversmith. 1597 *A.G. de la N. Inquisición*, vol.161. Accused of being heretic.
Díaz, Miguel	1788	*A.G. de la N. Ordenanzas*, vol.16, p.156 reverse. 1764. Examination 20th February. Master silversmith.
Díaz de Anaya, Manuel Antonio	1779	*A.G. de la N. Ordenanzas*, vol.16, p.114. 1764. Examination 27th May. Master silversmith.
Díaz de Anaya y Priego, Joseph	1758	*A.G. de la N. Ordenanzas*, vol.11, p.296. 1723-63. Examination 2nd March. Master silversmith.
Díaz de la Cueva, Joaquín	1842	*A.G. de la N. Padrón de establecimientos industriales. Cuartel menor núm.1.* Silver-shop.
Díaz de la Cueva, Juan	1792	*A.G. de la N. Industria*, vol.5, p.255. Unlicensed silversmith.
Díaz Varela, Gabriel	1811	*A.G. de la N. Empadronamiento de 1811.* Silversmith. (34 years of age.)
Díaz Varela, Manuel	1811	*A.G. de la N. Empadronamiento de 1811. Cuartel menor núm.1.* Silversmith. (34 years of age.)
Domínguez, Ana	1859	*El Viajero en México*, op.cit. Year of 1859. Silver-shop.
Domínguez, Francisco Xavier	1780	*A.G. de la N. Ordenanzas*, vol.16, p.116. 1764. Examination 29th May. Master silversmith.

Domínguez, Jph.	1766	*A.G. de la N. Ordenanzas*, vol.16, p.12. 1764. Examination 3rd September. Master silversmith.
Dufourg, Bernardo	1859	and 1864 *El Viajero en México*, op.cit. Silversmith. 1865 *A.G. de la N. Calificación de Est. Indust.* Silver-shop. 1867. *Directorio del Comercio del Imperio Mexicano*, op.cit. Silver-shop.
Dueñas, Jph.	1779	*A.G. de la N. Ordenanzas*, vol.16, p.114 reverse. 1764. Examination 10th December. Master silversmith.
Durán, Ignacio	1854	*Guía de Forasteros en la Ciudad de México, etc.*, op.cit. Silversmith. 1859 and 1864 *El Viajero en México. Años de 1859 y 1864.* op.cit. Silversmith.
Durán, Ignacio	1865	*A.G. de la N. Calificación de establecimientos industriales.* Silver-shop. 1867 *Directorio del Comercio del Imperio Mexicano, para el año de 1867.* op.cit. Silver-shop.
Eguiluz, José Antonio	1788	*A.G. de la N. Ordenanzas*, vol.16, p.156 reverse. 1764. Examination 20th February. Master silversmith.
Ena, Diego de	1725	*A.G. de la N. Ordenanzas*, vol.11, p.14 bis. 1723-63. Election 9th January. *Mayordomo.* 1746 *Pregones de Ordenanzas de el Nobilissimo Arte de la Platería. Mayordomo* in the Silversmiths' Art.
Enomorado, Ambrosio	1685	*El Gremio de Plateros en las Indias Occidentales*, p.xxix. No.9. Silversmith.
Escalona, Francisco J. de	1734	*A.G. de la N. Ordenanzas*, vol.11, p.102 reverse. 1723-63. Examination 5th May. Master silversmith.
Escalona, Ignacio	1852	*Guía de Forasteros de la capital de Puebla, para el año de 1852.* op.cit. Silversmith.
Escamilla, Manuel Antonio	1800	*Padrón de la Parcialidad de S. Juan de México*, vol.9, p.140 front and reverse. *Padrones Núm.105. A. G. de la N.* Silversmith. (Spanish.)
Escobar, Juan de	1576	*A.G. de la N. General de Partes*, vol.1. *Años* 1575-76. License 3rd July. Silver-shop.
Escobar, Manuel Alejo de	1759	*A.G. de la N. Ordenanzas*, vol.11, p.303. 1723-63. Examination 30th October. Master silversmith.
Escobar, Raimundo de	1753	*A.G. de la N. Civil indiferente*, vol.64. *Emp. de* 1753. The pages of the book are not numbered. Owner of silver-shop. 1754 *Ordenanzas*, vol.11, p.270. 1723-63. Examination 22nd March. Master silversmith.
Escobar Salcedo, Juan de	1625	*Archivo de Notarías de México*. Before José de la Cruz, Public Scrivener. 14th May 1625. Goldsmith.

Escusa, Pedro	1811	*A.G. de la N. Empadronamiento de* 1811. Silversmith. (44 years of age.)
Espejo, Joaquín	1778	*A.G. de la N. Ordenanzas*, vol.16, p.111 reverse. 1764. Examination 25th September. 1789 and 1793 *Ord.*, vol.16, pp.157, 175. 1764. Election 14th January, 1789 and 3rd January, 1764. *Veedor* of silversmiths.
Espinosa, Bartolomé	1784	Inscription on a bronze washbowl in the Sacristy of the Chapel of the *Pocito*, in the town of Guadalupe. Silversmith(?)
Espinosa, Felipe	1792	*A.G. de la N. Industria*, vol.5, p.255. Unlicensed silversmith.
Espinosa, Joseph	1723	*A.G. de la N. Ordenanzas*, vol.11, p.8. 1723-63. Examination 11th October. Master silversmith.
Espinosa, Ygo.Jph. de	1780	*A.G. de la N. Ordenanzas*, vol.16, 1764. Examination. Master silversmith.
Espinosa de los Monteros, Blas	1753	*A.G. de la N. Ordenanzas*, vol.11, p.263. 1723-63. Examination 25th June. Master silversmith.
Esprugas, Nicolás de	1770	*A.G. de la N. Ordenanzas*, vol.16, p.22. 1764. Election 10th January. *Veedor* of silversmiths. 1771. *Ord.* vol.16, p.32. 1764. Election 9th January. *Veedor* of silversmiths.
Esquivel, José	1753	*A.G. de la N. Civil indiferente*, vol.64. *Empadronamiento de* 1753. The pages of the book are not numbered. Owner of silver-shop. (40 years of age.)
Esteves, Martín	1865	*A.G. de la N. Calificación de establecimientos industriales*. Silver-shop. 1867 *Directorio del Comercio del Imperio Mexicano*, op.cit. Silver-shop.
Estienne, Luis	1847	*El Monitor Republicano* (principal newspaper of that time) 1st January 1847. Owner of silver-shop. Silversmith and diamond-cutter.
Estrada, Francisco de	1728	*A.G. de la N. Ordenanzas*, vol.11, p.50 reverse. 1723-63. Examination 16th December. Master silversmith. 1733 Marroqui, vol.3, p.380.
Estrada, Juan de	1738	*A.G. de la N. Ordenanzas*, vol.11, p.126. 1723-63. Examination 21st April. Master silversmith.
Estrada, Juan de	1753	*A.G. de la N. Civil indiferente*, vol.64. *Empadronamiento de* 1753. The pages of the book are not numbered. Silversmith. (50 years of age.)
Estrada, Manuel	1811	*A.G. de la N. Empadronamiento de* 1811. *Cuartel menor núm.*1. Silversmith (16 years of age.)
Estrada, Miguel de	1721	*A.G. de la N. Ordenanzas*, vol.10, years 1714 to 1722. Examination. Master silversmith.
Estrada, Pedro	1792	*A.G. de la N. Industria*, vol.5, p.255. 29th December. Unlicensed silversmith.

Estrada y Escobedo, Juan	1721	*A.G. de la N. Ordenanzas*, vol.10, p.110. 1714-22. Examination 11th November. Master silversmith. 1727 *Ord.* vol.11, p.37. 1723-63. Election 13th January. *Mayordomo.*
Estrella, José	1753	*A.G. de la N. Civil indiferente*, vol.64. *Empadronamiento de 1753.* The pages of the book are not numbered. Unlicensed silversmith. (42 years of age.)
Exiga, Juan Antonio	1769	*A.G. de la N. Ordenanzas*, vol.16, p.19. 1764. Election 10th January. *Veedor* of silversmiths. 1778 *Ord.* vol.16, p.105 reverse. Election 30th January. *Veedor* of silversmiths.
Fernández, Antonio	1731	*A.G. de la N. Ordenanzas*, vol.11, p.76. 1723-63. Examination 17th November. Master silversmith. 1741 *Historia de la milagrosa imagen de N.Sra. de Occotlan*, by Manuel Loayzaga.
Fernández, Antonio	1753	*A.G. de la N. Civil indiferente*, vol.64. *Empadronamiento de 1753.* The pages of the book are not numbered. Silver-shop.
Fernández, Francisco	1795	*A.G. de la N. Ordenanzas*, vol.16, p.180. 1764. Examination 27th March. Master silversmith.
Fernández, Jph.	1780	*A.G. de la N. Ordenanzas*, vol.16, p.115 reverse. 1764. Examination 26th February. Master silversmith.
Fernández, Manuel	1724	*A.G. de la N. Ordenanzas*, vol.11, p.9. 1723-63. Examination 8th January. Master silversmith.
Fernández, Francisco	1731	*A.G. de la N. Ordenanzas*, vol.11, p.69 reverse. 1723-63. Examination 3rd July. Master silversmith.
Fernández de Lara, J. Angel	1811	*A.G. de la N. Empadronamiento de 1811.* Silversmith. (45 years of age.)
Fernández de la Maza, Mariano	1788	*A.G. de la N. Ordenanzas*, vol.16, p.156 reverse. 1764. Examination 23rd August. Master silversmith.
Fernández de Villegas, Joseph	1745	*A.G. de la N. Ordenanzas*, vol.11, p.195. 1723-63 Examination 25th May. Master silversmith.
Fernández y Cartami, Manuel M.	1808	*A.G. de la N. Ordenanzas*, vol.16, p.197. 1764. Examination 1st October. Owner of silver-shop. 1811 *Empadronamiento de 1811. Cuartel menor núm.1.* Owner of silver-shop (41 years of age.)
Ferreira, Jph. Ant.o	1765	*A.G. de la N. Ordenanzas*, vol.16, p.9 reverse. 1764. Examination 1st July. Master silversmith
Figueroa, Antt.o Sebastian de	1694	*A.G. de la N. Ordenanzas*, vol.6, p.16. Years 1686 to 1689. License 10th May. License for a silver-shop.

Figueroa, Felipe	1752	*A.G. de la N. Ordenanzas*, vol.11, p.263 reverse. 1723-63. Examination 4th September. Master silversmith.
Figueroa, José	1792	*A.G. de la N. Industria*, vol.5, p.225. Unlicensed silversmith.
Figueroa, Luis de	1685	*El Gremio de Plateros en las Indias Occidentales*, op.cit., p.xxix. No.9. Drawer of gold wire. 1694 *A.G. de la N. Ordenanzas*, vol.6, p.16. Years 1686-98. 10th May, license for a silver-shop.
Filio, Juan de Dios	1776	*A.G. de la N. Ordenanzas*, vol.16, p.85. 1764. Examination 6th December. Master silversmith.
Flores, Joseph Manuel	1748	*A.G. de la N. Ordenanzas*, vol.11, p.247. 1723-63. Examination 27th August. Master silversmith.
Folco, José María	1842	*A.G. de la N. Padrón de establecimientos industriales. Cuartel menor núm.1*. Silver-shop. In 1842 and 1844 he served as expert in the inventory of the jewels of the Metropolitan Church, 26th December.
Folco, José María	1847	Marroqui, vol.III, p.380. 1854 *Guía de Forasteros en la Ciudad de Mégico*, op.cit. Silversmith. 1859 *El Viajero en México*, op.cit. Year of 1859. Silversmith.
Franco, Estevan	1543	Receipt given by the Marquise del Valle on this date. From a manuscript in a private collection. Cuernavaca, 18th December 1543.
Frías, Bernardo	1745	*A.G. de la N. Ordenanzas*, vol.11, p.189 reverse. 1723-63. Examination 2nd January, 1745. Sheet-beater.
Fuente, Francisco de la	1792	*A.G. de la N. Industria*, vol.5, p.255. Unlicensed silversmith.
Fuentes, Joaquín	1792	*A.G. de la N. Industria*, vol.5, p.255. Unlicensed silversmith.
Galesio, Miguel	1694	*A.G. de la N. Ordenanzas*, vol.6, p.16 reverse. Years 1686 to 1698. License 10th May. License for a silver-shop.
Gallo, José Mariano	1811	*A.G. de la N. Empadronamiento de 1811. Cuartel menor núm.1*. Silversmith (45 years of age.)
Gallo Espinosa de los Monteros, Ant.	1763	*A.G. de la N. Ordenanzas*, vol.11, p.323. 1723-63. Examination 18th January. Owner of silver-shop.
Gallegos, Pedro	1864	*El Viajero en México*, op.cit. Silversmith. 1865 *A.G. de la N. Calificación de establecimientos industriales*. Silver-shop.
Galván, Francisco	1792	*A.G. de la N. Industria*, vol.5, p.255. Unlicensed silversmith. 1798 *Ordenanzas*, vol.16, p.185. 1764. Examination 6th November. Owner of silver-shop.

Galván, Francisco	1799	*A.G. de la N. Guía de cargo y data etc. para la cuenta del año de* 1799, p.12 reverse. 23rd November. Silversmith. 1807 *Ord.*, vol.16, p.196. 1764. Election 7th January. *Veedor* of silversmiths.
Galván, Francisco	1807	Marroqui, vol.III, p.360. 1811 *A.G. de la N. Empadronamiento de* 1811. Silversmith. (44 years of age.)
Galván, Quirino (Gaitán?)	1864	*El Viajero en México*, op.cit. Silversmith. 1865 *A.G. de la N. Calificación de Est. Indust.* Silver-shop. 1867 *Directorio del Comercio del Imperio Mexicano*, op.cit. Silver-shop.
García, Antonio	1854	*Guía de Forasteros en la Ciudad de Mégico, para el año de* 1854, op.cit. Silversmith.
García, Carlos José	1818	*A.G. de la N. Ordenanzas*, vol.16, p.202 reverse. 1764. Examination 22nd July. Owner of silver-shop.
García, José	1792	*A.G. de la N. Industria*, vol.5, p.255. Unlicensed silversmith.
García, José Manuel	1811	*A.G. de la N. Empadronamiento de* 1811. *Cuartel menor núm.*1. Silversmith. (28 years of age.)
García, Joaquín	1811	*A.G. de la N. Empadronamiento de* 1811. *Cuartel menor núm.*1. Silversmith. (19 years of age.)
García, Juan	1800	*A.G. de la N. Ordenanzas*, vol.16, p.186 reverse. 1764. Examination 1st May. Owner of silver-shop.
García, Luis	1792	*A.G. de la N. Industria*, vol.5, p.255. Unlicensed silversmith.
García, María P. widow of S.	1685	*El Gremio de Plateros en las Indias Occidentales*, op.cit., p.xxix. No.9.
García, Phe.	1773	*A.G. de la N. Ordenanzas*, vol.16, p.54 reverse. 1764. Incorporation 8th July. Owner of silver-shop. (City of Seville.)
García, Ygnacio	1739	*A.G. de la N. Ordenanzas*, vol.11, p.132 reverse. 1723-63. Examination 10th July. Master silversmith.
García de Arellano, J. Mariano	1784	*A.G. de la N. Ordenanzas*, vol.16, p.136 reverse. 1764. Examination 11th August. Master silversmith.
García de Fuenlabrada, Juan	1738	*A.G. de la N. Ordenanzas*, vol.11, p.126. 1723-63. Examination May, 1738. Master silversmith.
García de León, Pedro Jph.	1741	*A.G. de la N. Ordenanzas*, vol.11, p.151 reverse. 1723-63. Examination 22nd June. Master silversmith.
García Maldonado, Joseph	1730	*A.G. de la N. Ordenanzas*, vol.11, p.58. 1723-63. Examination 5th June. Master silversmith.
García Villegas, J.Anastacio	1790	*A.G. de la N. Ordenanzas*, vol.16, p.159. 1764. Examination 22nd March. Master silversmith.

García Ynfante, Joachin Jph.	1765	*A.G. de la N. Ordenanzas*, vol.16, p.10. 1764. Examination 3rd December. Master silversmith.
García Ynfante, Juan	1729	*A.G. de la N. Ordenanzas*, vol.II, p.55 reverse. 1723-63. Examination 13th December. Master silversmith.
Garnica, Gaspar de	1527	Marroqui, vol.I, p.46. *Conquistador*. Silversmith.
Garnote, Manuel	1811	*A.G. de la N. Empadronamiento de 1811. Cuartel menor núm.1*. Silversmith. (36 years of age.)
Garrido, Bartholome	1770	*A.G. de la N. Ordenanzas*, vol.16, p.24 reverse. 1764. Examination 16th February. Master silversmith.
Garrido, Cristóbal	1753	*A.G. de la N. Civil indiferente*, vol.64. *Empadronamiento de 1753*. The pages of the book are not numbered. Owner of silver-shop. (30 years of age.)
Gentil, Diego	1563	*Archivo de Notarías de México*. Before Antonio Alonso, Public Scrivener. 15th July. Goldsmith.
Gentyl, Melchor	1542	*Actas de Cabildo, 30 de Junio de 1542*. Silversmith.
Gil, Gonzalo	1542	*Actas de Cabildo*, 11 de Julio de 1542. Appointed *Veedor* of silversmiths.
Gil de Arebalo, Jph. Bernardo	1780	*A.G. de la N. Ordenanzas*, vol.16, p.116 reverse. 1764. Examination 17th June. Master silversmith.
Gil de Arebalo, Paulino	1782	*A.G. de la N. Ordenanzas*, vol.16, p.122. 1764. Examination 11th January. Master silversmith.
Gilforte, Justo Pastor	1734	*A.G. de la N. Ordenanzas*, vol.11, p.110. 1723-63. Examination 6th September. Master silversmith.
Goderes, Antonio	1831	*A.G. de la N. Ramo de Hacienda*. Book which says: *Casa de Ensaye de México*. 1830-31. Bundle 45. Payment to silversmiths for stamping marks.
Godoy, Francisco	1792	*A.G. de la N. Industria*, vol.5, p.255. Unlicensed silversmith.
Godoy, Juan Carlos	1720	*A.G. de la N. Ordenanzas*, vol.10, Years 1714 to 1722. Examination. Master silversmith.
Gómez, Angel	1854	*Guía de Forasteros en la Ciudad de Mégico, para el año de* 1854. op.cit. Silversmith.
Gómez, Felipe	1842	*A.G. de la N. Padrón de establecimientos industriales. Cuartel menor núm.1*. Silver-shop.
Gómez, Juan Antonio	1724	*A.G. de la N. Ordenanzas*, vol.11, p.25 reverse. 1723-63. Examination 14th May. Master silversmith.
Gómez, Manuel	1685	*El Gremio de Plateros en las Indias Occidentales*, op.cit., p.xxix. No.9. Silversmith.
Gómez, Matías	1811	*A.G. de la N. Empadronamiento de* 1811. Silversmith. (29 years of age.)

Gómez, Pedro	1537	*Archivo de Protocolos, Anónimos.* 1536-43. Silversmith.
Gómez, Rafael	1842	*A.G. de la N. Padrón de establecimientos industriales. Cuartel menor núm.*1. Silver-shop.
Gómez, Ypolito Mariano	1757	*A.G. de la N. Ordenanzas,* vol.11, p.292 reverse. 1723-63. Examination 10th February. Master silversmith.
Gómez Maldonado, Juan	1591	*A.G. de la N. General de Parte,* vol.4, p.119. Years 1590-91. 8th April. License for public store. (Inhabitant of the city of Los Angeles.)
Góngora, Mariano	1753	*A.G. de la N. Civil indiferente,* vol.64. *Empadronamiento de* 1753. The pages of the book are not numbered. Unlicensed silversmith. (30 years of age.)
Góngora, Miguel de	1713	*Pleito de Rada de* 1713, pp.65-6, paragraph 3. Silversmith. 1727 *A.G. de la N. Ordenanzas,* vol.11, p.43 reverse. 1723-63. Examination 12th May. Master silversmith.
González, Francisco	1753	*A.G. de la N. Civil indiferente,* vol.64. *Empadronamiento de* 1753. The pages of the book are not numbered. Owner of silver-shop. (50 years of age.)
González, Francisco	1811	*A.G. de la N. Empadronamiento de* 1811. *Cuartel menor núm.*1. Silversmith. (52 years of age.)
González, Gregorio	1811	*A.G. de la N. Empadronamiento de* 1811. *Cuartel menor núm.*1. Silversmith. (25 years of age.)
González, Joaquín	1811	*A.G. de la N. Empadronamiento de* 1811. *Cuartel menor núm.*1. Silversmith. (18 years of age.)
González, María Antonia	1811	*A.G. de la N. Empadronamiento de* 1811. Silver-shop. (45 years of age.)
González Beserra, Fran.co.	1694	*A.G. de la N. Ordenanzas.* Years 1686 to 1698. vol.6, p.16. 10th May. License for silver-shop. (Capt.)
González del Castillo, Joseph	1778	*A.G. de la N. Ordenanzas.* 1764. vol.16, p.112. Examination 6th October. Master silversmith.
González Pesquera, Joseph	1753	*A.G. de la N. Ordenanzas.* 1723-63. vol.11, p.263. Examination 7th June. Master silversmith.
González Vezerra, Andrés	1685	*El Gremio de Plateros en las Indias Occidentales,* op.cit., p.xxix. No.9. Silversmith.
Gonzalve, Antonio	1772	*A.G. de la N. Ordenanzas,* 1764. vol.16, p.47. Examination 8th October. Master silversmith.
Gregorio, José María	1811	*A.G. de la N. Empadronamiento de* 1811. *Cuartel menor núm.*1. Silversmith. (15 years of age.)
Gris, Jacinto	1859	*El Viajero en México,* op.cit. Year 1859. Silversmith.
Guerrero, Pablo	1854	*Guía de Forasteros en la Ciudad de Mégico,* op.cit. Silversmith. 1859 and 1864. *El Viajero en México. Años* 1859 y 1864, op.cit. Silversmith.

Guerrero, Pablo	1865	*A.G. de la N. Calificación de establecimientos industriales.* Silver-shop. 1867. *Directorio del Comercio del Imperio Mexicano para el año de 1867,* op.cit. Silver-shop.
Guerrero, Victoriano	1854	*Guía de Forasteros en la Ciudad de Mégico,* op.cit. Silversmith. 1859 and 1864. *El Viajero en México,* op.cit. In 1859 setter [of precious stones] and 1864 silversmith.
Guerrero, Victoriano	1865	*A.G. de la N. Calificación de establecimientos industriales.* Silver-store. 1867 *Directorio del Comercio del Imperio Mexicano,* op.cit. Silver-shop.
Guerrero y Peralta, Jph. Ant.	1797	*Gazetas de México. Compendio de Noticias de Nueva España, de los años de 1796 y 1797,* by Manuel Antonio Valdés. vol.8, p.268. 3rd March 1797.
Guevara, Antonio	1864	*El Viajero en Mexico. Completa Guía de Forasteros para 1864,* op.cit. Silversmith.
Guevara, Miguel	1811	*A.G. de la N. Empadronamiento de 1811. Cuartel menor núm.1.* Silversmith. (19 years of age.)
Guevara, Rafael	1864	*El Viajero en México,* op.cit. Silversmith. 1865 *A.G. de la N. Calificación de Est. Indust.* Silver-shop. 1867 *Directorio del Comercio del Imperio Mexicano,* op.cit. Silver-shop.
Gutiérrez, Alejandro	1864	*El Viajero en México,* op.cit. Silversmith. 1865 *A.G. de la N. Padrón de establecimientos industriales.* Silver-shop. 1867 *Directorio del Comercio del Imperio Mexicano,* op.cit. Silver-shop.
Gutiérrez, Andrés	1563	*Archivo de Notarías de México.* 27th January. Goldsmith.
Gutiérrez, Francisco	1863	*Colección Completa de los Decretos Generales expedidos por el Exmo. Sr. General Forey, 1863.* p.48. Silversmith.
Gutiérrez, Marcelo José	1854	*Guía de Forasteros en la Ciudad de Mégico, para el año de 1854,* op.cit. Silversmith.
Gutiérrez, Marcos	1811	*A.G. de la N. Empadronamiento de 1811. Cuartel Menor núm.1.* Silversmith. (33 years of age.)
Guzmán, Antonio	1842	*A.G. de la N. Padrón de establecimientos industriales. Cuartel menor núm.1.* Silversmith, Engraver.
Guzmán, José	1796	*A.G. de la N. Derechos de oro de fuego,* p.7. Silversmith. 1799 *Guía de cargo y data etc. cuenta año* 1799. 13th September. Silversmith. 1811 *Emp. de 1811.* Silversmith. (73 years of age.)
Guzmán, José María	1792	*A.G. de la N. Industria,* vol.5, p.255. Unlicensed silversmith. 1795 y 1803 *Ordenanzas,* vol.16,

pp.179 reverse and 192 reverse. 1764. Election 26th February 1795 and 13th January 1803. *Veedor.*

Guzmán, Luciano	1854	*Guía de Forasteros en la Ciudad de Mégico, para el año de* 1854, op.cit. Silversmith.
Guzman, Ygnacio	1783	*A.G. de la N. Ordenanzas*, vol.16, p.129 reverse. 1764. Examination. Master silversmith.
Heredia, Manuel de	1731	*A.G. de la N. Ordenanzas*, vol.11, p.72 reverse. 1723-63. Examination 27th September. Master silversmith.
Hermoso, Diego	1563	*Archivo de Notarías de México.* 1563. 15th July. Goldsmith.
Hernández, Antonio	1536	*Actas de Cabildo* 28 *de Julio. Alcalde* of Silversmiths and marker in the smelter of this City, 1537. *Actas de Cabildo* 13 *de Marzo*, 1537. *Veedor.*
Hernández, Francisco	1738	*A.G. de la N. Ordenanzas*, vol.11, p.126 reverse. 1723-63. Examination 14th May. Master silversmith.
Hernández, Francisco	1535	*Actas de Cabildo*, 30 *de Enero* 1535. Became a citizen and presented a license. 1538 *Actas de Cabildo* 10 *de Mayo* 1538. Named *Alcalde* of Silversmiths and received the die of this city, etc.
Hernández, Joaquín Bartolomé	1758	*A.G. de la N. Ordenanzas*, vol.11, p.296. 1723-63. Examination 14th February. Master silversmith.
Hernández, Manuel	1808	*Las Artes Industriales en la Nueva España*, op.cit. Silversmith.
Hernández, Mariano	1852	*Guía de Forasteros de la capital de Puebla, para el año de* 1852, op.cit. Silversmith.
Hernández, Pedro	1564	*Archivo de Notarías de México.* 1564. Silversmith.
Hernández y Benítez, Jph. M.	1767	*A.G. de la N. Ordenanzas*, vol.16, p.14 reverse. 1764. Examination 23rd June. Master silversmith.
Hernández Ecifar, Mariano J.	1793	*A.G. de la N. Ordenanzas*, vol.16, p.175 reverse. 1764. Examination 15th October. Master silversmith.
Hernández López, Antonio	1731	*A.G. de la N. Ordenanzas*, vol.11, p.74 reverse. 1723-63. Examination 7th November. Master silversmith.
Herrera, Agustín	1753	*A.G. de la N. Civil indiferente*, vol.64. *Empadronamiento de* 1753. The pages of the book are not numbered. Unlicensed silversmith. (26 years of age.)
Herrera, Agustín	1811	*A.G. de la N. Empadronamiento de* 1811. *Cuartel menor núm.*1. Silversmith. (18 years of age.)

Herrera, Antonio	1854	*Guía de Forasteros en la Ciudad de Mégico,* op.cit. Silversmith. 1859 *El Viajero en México,* op.cit. Silversmith.
Herrera, Francisco	1854	*Guía de Forasteros en la Ciudad de Mégico,* op.cit. Year 1854. Silversmith.
Herrera, José M. Faustino	1817	*A.G. de la N. Ordenanzas,* vol.16, p.202. 1764. Examination 11th August. Owner of silver-shop.
Herrera, Juan	1811	*A.G. de la N. Empadronamiento de 1811. Cuartel menor núm.*1. Silversmith. (18 years of age.)
Herrera, Juan Agustín de	1726	*A.G. de la N. Ordenanzas,* vol.11, p.33 reverse. 1723-63. Examination 29th July. Master silversmith.
Hidalgo, Miguel	1748	*A.G. de la N. Ordenanzas,* vol.11, p.239. 1723-63. Examination 8th May. Master silversmith.
Hidrad, Teófilo	1859	*El Viajero en México,* op.cit. Silversmith.
Horrantya, Cosme de	1537	*Archivo de Protocolos. Anónimos.* 1536-43. Silversmith.
Hoyos y Acuña, Miguel de	1761	*A.G. de la N. Ordenanzas,* vol.11, p.311. 1723-63. Examination 15th January. Master silversmith.
Huérfano, José María	1811	*A.G. de la N. Empadronamiento de 1811. Cuartel menor núm.*1. Silversmith. (18 years of age.)
Huerta, Jesús	1854	*Guía de Forasteros en la Ciudad de Mégico, para el año de 1854,* op.cit. Silversmith.
Huerta, José Mariano de la	1784	*A.G. de la N. Ordenanzas,* vol.16, p.135 reverse. 1764. Examination 14th January. Master silversmith.
Huerta, Manuel	1859	*El Viajero en México,* op.cit. Year 1859. Silversmith.
Ibarra, Antonio	1842	*A.G. de la N. Padrón de establecimientos industriales. Cuartel menor núm.*1. Silver-work shop. 1854 *Guía de Forasteros en la Ciudad de México,* op.cit. Silversmith.
Ibarra, Vicente	1842	*A.G. de la N. Padrón de establecimientos industriales. Cuartel menor núm.*1. Silver-shop.
Ibañez, Ignacio	1811	*A.G. de la N. Empadronamiento de 1811. Cuartel menor núm.*1. Silversmith. (40 years of age.)
Idrac, Teófilo	1852	*Guía de Forasteros de la capital de Puebla, para el año de 1852,* op.cit. Silversmith.
Infante, Francisco	1727	*A.G. de la N. Ordenanzas,* vol.II, p.37. 1723-63. Election 13th January. *Mayordomo.*
Infante, José Manuel	1790	*A.G. de la N. Ordenanzas,* vol.16, p.159 reverse. 1764. Examination 16th September. Master silversmith.
Izunza, Joaquín de	1819	*Diccionario Universal de Historia etc.,* op.cit., vol.6, p.484. Silversmith.
Izunza, José de	1788	*Archivo de Tlaxcala,* vol.242. 7th October 1788.

Master of the Silversmiths' Art. 1803 *Las Artes Industriales en la Nueva España*, op.cit. Silversmith.

Jaimes de Vea, Francisco	1754	*A.G. de la N. Ordenanzas*, vol.11, p.270. 1723-63. Examination 27th March. Master silversmith. (Examined in Guadalajara.)
Jardel.	1861	French silversmith who in 1861 was arrested for having bought jewels stolen from the *Colegiata de Guadalupe*. (Newspapers of that period.)
Jerónimo, Miguel	1576	*A.G. de la N. General de Parte. Años 1575-6.* vol.I, p.228. License 30th August. License for silver-shop.
Jiménez, Francisco	1842	*A.G. de la N. Padrón de establecimientos industriales. Cuartel menor núm.1.* Silver-shop.
Jordanes, Ignacio	1724	*A.G. de la N. Ordenanzas*, vol.11, p.9 reverse. 1723-63. Election 8th January. *Diputado.* 1725 *Ord.* vol.11, p.14 bis. Election 9th January. *Mayordomo.* 1745. vol.II, p.189 reverse. 11th January *Diputado.*
Juárez, José María	1864	*El Viajero en México*, op.cit. Silversmith. 1865 *A.G. de la N. Calificación de establecimientos industriales.* Silver-store.
Jura, Fray Antonio de	1710	*Las Artes Industriales en la Nueva España*, op.cit. Silversmith.
Jura, Fr. Francisco de	1667	*Baluartes de México*, p.39. Silversmith.
Ladrón de Guevara, José And.	1807	*A.G. de la N. Ordenanzas*, vol.16, p.196 reverse. 1764. Examination 6th November. Master silversmith. 1811. *Empadronamiento de 1811.* Silversmith. (32 years of age, From Valladolid.)
Lara, Ignacio	1859	*El Viajero en México. Año de 1859.* op.cit. Silversmith.
Lara, José	1799	*A.G. de la N. Guía de cargo y data etc. para la quenta del año de 1799*, p.9. August 27. Silversmith of this city.
Lara, Julian	1859	*El Viajero en México*, op.cit. Silversmith. 1864. Ibid. Silversmith. 1865 *A.G. de la N. Calificación de Est. Indust.* Silver-shop. 1867 *Directorio del Comercio etc.* Silver-shop.
Larios, Diego Martín de	1721	1736 and 1751 *Historia de la Fundación de la Ciudad de la Puebla de los Angeles, etc.*, op.cit., pp.168, 170 and 174, vol.II. Owner [of silver-shop]. 1751 *Diccionario Universal etc.*, vol.6, p.487.
Larios, Diego Matías de	1741	1743, 1768 and 1776 *Historia de la Fundación de la Ciudad de la Puebla de los Angeles en la Nueva*

		España, su descripción y presente estado, op.cit., vol.II, pp.166, 169, 171 and 172.
Larralde, José María	1854	*Guía de Forasteros en la Ciudad de Mégico, etc.* Silversmith. 1859 and 1864 *El Viajero en México*, op.cit. Years 1859 and 1864. Silversmith.
Larralde, José María	1865	*A.G. de la N. Padrón de Establecimientos industriales*. Silver-shop. 1867 *Directorio del Comercio del Imperio Mexicano*, op.cit. Silver-shop.
Lasano, Josep	1784	*A.G. de la N. Ordenanzas*, vol.16, p.137. 1764. Examination 20th December. Master silversmith.
Leal, Manuel	1792	*A.G. de la N. Industria*, vol.5, p.255. Unlicensed silversmith.
Lecadreu, Juan Bapta.	1773	*A.G. de la N. Ordenanzas*, vol.16, p.61. 1764. Examination 9th October. Master silversmith. (License for store. French.)
Leiba, Joseph de	1728	*A.G. de la N. Ordenanzas*, vol.11, p.48 reverse. 1723-63. Examination 18th June. Master silversmith.
L'Enfer, Eduardo	1852	*Guía de Forasteros de la capital de Puebla, para el año de* 1852, op.cit. Silversmith.
Leñigo, José	1753	*A.G. de la N. Civil indiferente*, vol.64. *Empadronamiento de* 1753. The pages of the book are not numbered. Silversmith.
León, Juan Antonio de	1721	*A.G. de la N. Ordenanzas*, vol.10. Years 1714 to 1722. Examination. Master silversmith.
León, Manuel	1792	*A.G. de la N. Industria*, vol.5, p.255. Unlicensed silversmith.
León, Miguel	1854	*Guía de Forasteros en la Ciudad de Mégico, etc.*, op.cit. Silversmith. 1859 *El Viajero en México*, op.cit. Year 1859. Silversmith.
León, Nicolás de	1720	*A.G. de la N. Ordenanzas*, vol.10. Years 1714 to 1722. Examination. Master sheet-beater.
León, Pablo	1753	*A.G. de la N. Civil indiferente*, vol.64. *Empadronamiento de* 1753. The pages of the book are not numbered. Unlicensed silversmith (35 years of age.)
León, Vicente	1792	*A.G. de la N. Industria*, vol.5, p.255. Unlicensed silversmith.
León, XP(l).de	1685	*El Gremio de Plateros en las Indias Occidentales*, op.cit., p.xxix, No.9. Silversmith.
Leturriondo, Baltazar Jph. de	1732	*A.G. de la N. Ordenanzas*, vol.11, p.82. 1723-63. Examination 6th June. Master silversmith.
Limas, Pedro	1753	*A.G. de la N. Civil indiferente*, vol.64. *Empadronamiento de* 1753. The pages of the book are not numbered. Silver-shop of. (50 years of age.)

Lino, Pedro de	1723	*A.G. de la N. Ordenanzas*, vol.11, p.3. 1723-63. Examination 18th March. Master silversmith.
Lira, Antonio de	1731	*A.G. de la N. Ordenanzas*, vol.11, p.73. 1723-63. Examination 8th October. Master silversmith.
Lira, Pedro Nolasco de	1723	*A.G. de la N. Ordenanzas*, vol.11, p.6. 1723-63. Examination 11th June. Master silversmith.
Lira, Pomposo	1854	*Guía de Forasteros en la Ciudad de Mégico*, op.cit. Silversmith. 1859 *El Viajero en México. Año de 1859*, op.cit. Silversmith.
Liveran, Aph. Antonio	1784	*A.G. de la N. Ordenanzas*, vol.16, p.137. 1764. Examination 20th December. Master silversmith.
Llana, Manuel Ignacio de la	1759	*A.G. de la N. Ordenanzas*, vol.11, p.301. 1723-63. Examination 14th May. Master silversmith.
Loaeza, Julio Antonio de	1737	*A.G. de la N. Ordenanzas*, vol.11, p.122 reverse. 1723-63. Examination 8th May. Master silversmith.
Loaiza, Francisco de	1757	*A.G. de la N. Ordenanzas*, vol.11, p.293 reverse. 1723-63. Examination 2nd September. Master silversmith.
Llop, J.	1882	*Nueva Guía de México. Año de 1882*, by Ireneo Paz and Manuel Tornel, p.833. Silver-shop.
López, Bar.me	1685	*El Gremio de Plateros en las Indias Occidentales*, op.cit., p.xxix. No.9. Silversmith.
López, Casimiro	1854	*Guía de Forasteros en la Ciudad de Mégico* op.cit. Silversmith. 1859 *El Viajero en México*, op.cit. Silversmith.
López, Christoval	1782	*A.G. de la N. Ordenanzas*, vol.16, p.122 reverse. 1764. Examination 12th March. Master silversmith.
López, Felipe	1859	*El Viajero en México*, op.cit. Silversmith. 1865 *A.G. de la N. Calif. de Est. Indust.* Silver-shop. 1867 *Directorio del Comercio del Imperio Mexicano*, op.cit. Silver-shop.
López, Francisco	1592	*Indice de Documentos de Nueva España existentes en el Archivo de Indias de Sevilla*, op.cit., vol.IV, p.227. Silversmith.
López, Francisco	1864	*El Viajero en México Completa Guía de Forasteros para 1864.* Silversmith.
López, Joaquín	1753	*A.G. de la N. Civil indiferente*, vol.64. *Empadronamiento de 1753.* The pages of the book are not numbered. Unlicensed silversmith.
López, José	1864	*El Viajero en México. Completa Guía de Forasteros para 1864.* Silversmith.
López, José Ignacio	1811	*A.G. de la N. Empadronamiento de 1811.* Silversmith. (61 years of age.)

López, Juan	1579	*A.G. de la N. General de Parte. Años* 1579-80, vol.II, p.88. Examination 18th November. Perform his trade and have a public store.
López, Juan	1750	*A.G. de la N. Ordenanzas,* vol.11, p.260 1723-63. Examination 7th July. Master silversmith. 1753 *Civil indiferente,* vol.64. *Emp. de* 1753. The pages of the book are not numbered. Master silversmith. (Cadiz.)
López de Fuentes, Luis	1780	*A.G. de la N. Ordenanzas,* vol.16, p.115 reverse. 1764. Examination 7th January. Master silversmith. 1811 *Empadronamiento de* 1811. *Cuartel menor núm.*1. Owner of Silver-shop. (68 years of age.)
López García, Pedro Gerardo	1745	*A.G. de la N. Ordenanzas,* vol.11, p.211 reverse. 1723-63. Examination 24th November. Master silversmith.
López y Rosas, Francisco	1842	*A.G. de la N. Padrón de establecimientos industriales. Cuartel menor núm.*1. Silver-shop.
Lozano, Luis Antonio	1780	*A.G. de la N. Ordenanzas,* vol.16, p.116. 1764. Examination 12th May. Master silversmith.
Lozano, Miguel	1781	*A.G. de la N. Ordenanzas,* vol.16, p.121 reverse. 1764. Examination 26th November. Master silversmith.
Luna, Man.l de	1685	*El Gremio de Plateros en las Indias Occidentales,* op.cit., p.xxix. No.9. Silversmith. 1693 *A.G. de la N. Ordenanzas,* vol.6, p.14. 1686-98. License for Silver-shop.
Luque, Gomez de	1542	*Actas de Cabildo,* 11 *de Julio de* 1542. Named *Veedor* and silversmith.
Luys, Grabiel	1542	*Actas de Cabildo* 7 *de Noviembre* 1542. Silversmith.
Machado, Gerónimo	1730	*A.G. de la N. Ordenanzas,* vol.11, p.56 reverse. 1723-63. Examination 25th February, Master silversmith.
Madero, Bernabé	1780	*Las Artes Industriales en la Nueva España,* op.cit. Silversmith.
Madriaga, José	1811	*A.G. de la N. Empadronamiento de* 1811. Silversmith.
Malcampo, Miguel	1811	*A.G. de la N. Empadronamiento de* 1811. *Cuartel menor núm.*1. Silversmith. (25 years of age.)
Manzanar, Mariano	1811	*A.G. de la N. Empadronamiento de* 1811. *Cuartel menor núm.*1. Silversmith. (24 years of age.)
Manzanar, Nicolás	1811	*A.G. de la N. Empadronamiento de* 1811. *Cuartel menor núm.*1. Silversmith. (21 years of age.)
Manzano, José	1792	*A.G. de la N. Industria,* vol.5, p.255. Unlicensed Silversmith.

Marcarenas, Juan de	1685	*El Gremio de Plateros en las Indias Occidentales*, op.cit., p.xxix. No.9. Goldsmith.
Marchena, Bibiano	1811	*A.G. de la N. Empadronamiento de* 1811. Silversmith. (24 years of age.)
Marchena, José María	1831	*A.G. de la N. Ramo de Hacienda.* Book which says: *Casa de Ensaye de Mexico.* 1830-31. Bundle 45. Silversmith. 1842 *Padrón de Est. industriales. Cuartel menor núm.*1. Silver-shop.
Marchena, José María	1864	*El Viajero en México para* 1864, op.cit. Silver-shop. 1865 *A.G. de la N. Calificación de establecimientos industriales.* Silver-shop.
Marín, José Rafael	1800	*A.G. de la N. Ordenanzas*, vol.16, p.190. 1764. Examination 17th December. Owner of silver-shop.
Marques, José	1811	*A.G. de la N. Empadronamiento de* 1811. *Cuartel menor núm.* 1. Silversmith. (40 years of age.)
Márquez, Juan José	1810	*A.G. de la N. Ordenanzas*, vol.16, p.199 reverse. 1764. Examination 10th May. Owner of silver-shop.
Márquez, Pedro	1792	*A.G. de la N. Industria.* vol.5, p.255. Unlicensed Silversmith. 1811 *Emp. de* 1811. Silversmith. 1812 *Ordenanzas*, vol.16, p.200 reverse. Examination 15th May. Owner of silver-shop.
Márquez, Pedro	1815	*A.G. de la N. Ordenanzas*, vol.16, p.201. Election 14th January. *Veedor* of Silversmiths. 1829 *Correo de la Federación Mexicana*, 16 de Agosto de 1829. Appointed by comission.
Márquez, Pedro	1831	*A.G. de la N. Ramo de Hda.* Book which says: *Casa de Ensaye de Mexico.* 1830-31. Bundle 45. Silversmith. 1842 *Padrón de establecimientos industriales. Cuartel menor núm.*1. Silver-shop.
Márquez, Teófilo	1759	*El Viajero en México* by Juan N. del Valle. Year 1859. Silversmith.
Marradon, Cristóbal	1759	and 1773 *A.G. de la N. Ordenanzas*, vol.11, p.299 reverse and vol.16, p.49. Election 13th January, 1759 and 9th January 1773. *Veedor* of silversmiths.
Marrason, Cristóbal	1745	*A.G. de la N. Ordenanzas*, vol.11, p.205 reverse. 1723-63. Examination 1st July. Master silversmith.
Martel, Miguel María	1802	*A.G. de la N. Ordenanzas*, vol.16, p.191 reverse. Election 8th January. *Veedor* of silversmiths. 1811 *Empadronamiento de* 1811. Silversmith. (From Andalucía. 42 years of age.)
Martel, Miguel María	1788	*A.G. de la N. Ordenanzas*, vol.16, p.156 reverse. Examination. Master silversmith. 1816 *Ordenanzas*, vol.16, p.201 reverse. Election 9th March. *Veedor* of silversmiths.

Martínez, Andrés	1641	*Las Artes Industriales en la Nueva España*, op.cit. Silversmith (from Guatemala.)
Martínez, Cristóbal	1753	*A.G. de la N. Civil indiferente*, vol.64. *Empadronamiento de 1753*. The pages of the book are not numbered. Silversmith.
Martínez, Diego	1527	*Actas de Cabildo*, 14 *de Enero*, 1527. Named *Veedor*. And Marroqui, vol.I, p.46. Silversmith.
Martínez, José	1792	*A.G. de la N. Industria*, vol.5, p.255. Unlicensed silversmith.
Martínez, José María	1831	*A.G. de la N. Ramo de Hacienda*. Book which says: *Casa de Ensaye de Mexico*. 1830-31. Bundle 45. Silversmith. 1842 *Padrón de establecimientos indust*. Silver-store with workshop.
Martínez, José María	1844	Manuscript copy of the inventory of jewels of the Holy Metropolitan Church, taken by José Miguel Abarca, pp.14-15. México, 26th December 1844. Silversmith.
Martínez, Mariano Ignacio	1811	*A.G. de la N. Empadronamiento de* 1811. Silversmith. (36 years of age.)
Martínez, Pedro Jph.	1780	*A.G. de la N. Ordenanzas*, vol.16, p.116. 1764. Examination 2nd June. Master silversmith.
Martínez, Vicente	1811	*A.G. de la N. Empadronamiento de* 1811. *Cuartel menor núm.*1. Silversmith. (31 years of age.)
Martínez de Rivera, Manuel	1765	*A.G. de la N. Ordenanzas*, vol.16, p.9 reverse. 1764. Examination 14th June, 1765. Master silversmith.
Martínez de Urroz, Juan	1563	*Archivo de Notarías de México*. Before Antonio Alonso, Public Scrivener. 10th April. Goldsmith.
Masa, Antonio	1854	*Guía de Forasteros en la Ciudad de Mégico*, op.cit. Silversmith. 1859 *El Viajero en México*, op.cit. Jeweler. 1865 *A.G. de la N. Padrón est. indust*. Silver-shop.
Masa, Antonio	1867	*Directorio del Comercio del Imperio Mexicano para el año de* 1867, op.cit. Silver-shop.
Mascareñas, Francisco	1725	*A.G. de la N. Ordenanzas*, vol.11, p.17. 1723-63. Examination 14th July. Master silversmith.
Mascareñas, Francisco	1792	*A.G. de la N. Industria*, vol.5, p.255. Unlicensed silversmith.
Mascareñas, Juan de	1694	*A.G. de la N. Ordenanzas*, vol.6, p.14 reverse. Years 1686 to 1698. 21st April. License for silver-shop.
Mascareño, Miguel	1859	*El Viajero en México*, op.cit. Year 1859. Silversmith.
Mascareño, Simón	1865	*A.G. de la N. Calificación de establecimientos industriales*. Silver-shop.
Mastral, G.	1865	*A.G. de la N. Calificación de establecimientos*

industriales. Silver-shop. 1867 *Directorio del Comercio del Imperio Mexicano*, op.cit. Silver-shop.

Mateos, Manuel	1852	*Guía de Forasteros de la Capital de Puebla, para el año de* 1852, op.cit. Silversmith.
Mateos, Ponciano	1859	*El Viajero en México*, op.cit. Silversmith. 1864. Ibid Silversmith.
Maure, Ignacio	1792	*A.G. de la N. Industria*, vol.5, p.255. Unlicensed silversmith.
Mayo, Joseph de	1734	*A.G. de la N. Ordenanzas*, vol.11, p.101 reverse. 1723-63. Examination 9th March. Master silversmith.
Maza, Hilario de la	1842	*A.G. de la N. Padrón de establecimientos industriales. Cuartel menor núm.1.* Silver-work shop.
Maza, Ignacio de la	1792	*A.G. de la N. Industria*, vol.5, p.255. Unlicensed silversmith.
Maza, José de la	1864	*El Viajero en México Completa Guía de Forasteros para* 1864. Silversmith.
Medel, Juan Ignacio	1811	*A.G. de la N. Empadronamiento de* 1811. *Cuartel menor núm.1.* Silversmith. (22 years of age.)
Medina, Diego de	1685	*El Gremio de Plateros en las Indias Occidentales*, op.cit., p.xxix. No.9. Silversmith.
Medina, Francisco Xavier de	1723	*A.G. de la N. Ordenanzas*, vol.11, p.92. 1723-63. Examination 21st January. Master silversmith.
Medina, Joaquín	1753	*A.G. de la N. Civil indiferente*, vol.64. *Empadronamiento de* 1753. The pages of the book are not numbered. Silversmith.
Medina, Joseph de	1685	*El Gremio de Plateros en las Indias Occidentales*, op.cit., p.xxix. No.9. Silversmith.
Medina, Tranquilino	1859	*El Viajero en México*, op.cit. Silversmith.
Mejía, Antonio	1724	*A.G. de la N. Ordenanzas*, vol.II, p.9 reverse. 1723-63. Election 8th January. *Mayordomo*.
Mejía, Felipe	1831	*A.G. de la N. Ramo de Hacienda*. Book which says: *Casa de Ensaye de Mexico.* 1830-31. Bundle 45. Payment for stamping silversmiths' marks.
Mejía, widow of	1831	*A.G. de la N. Ramo de Hacienda*. Book which says: *Casa de Ensaye de Mexico.* 1830-31. Bundle 45. Payment for stamping Silversmiths' marks.
Mellado y Arenas, Joseph Joaq.	1758	*A.G. de la N. Ordenanzas*, vol.11, p.296. 1723-63. Examination 14th February. Master silversmith.
Mencera, José Hipólito	1792	*A.G. de la N. Industria*, vol.5, p.255. Unlicensed silversmith.

Méndez, Etor	1527	*Actas de Cabildo*, 14 *de Enero* 1527. Named *Veedor*, Marroqui, vol.I, p.46 and *Las Artes Industriales en la Nueva España*, op.cit. Silversmith.
Mendoza, Ignacio	1792	*A.G. de la N. Industria*, vol.5, p.255. Unlicensed silversmith.
Meneses, Antonio	1753	*A.G. de la N. Civil indiferente*, vol.64. *Empadronamiento de* 1753. The pages of the book are not numbered. Unlicensed silversmith. (30 years of age.)
Meoño	1750	*Las Artes Industriales en la Nueva España*, op.cit. Silversmith. (From Guatemala).
Meras, Joaquín de	1747	*A.G. de la N. Ordenanzas*, vol.11, p.236. 1723-63. Examination 17th July. Master silversmith.
Mesa, José de	1753	*A.G. de la N. Civil indiferente*, vol.64. *Empadronamiento de* 1753. The pages of the book are not numbered. Silver-store. (35 years of age.)
Mexia, José Felipe	1815	*A.G. de la N. Ordenanzas*, vol.16, p.201. 1764 Examination 23rd February. Owner of silver-shop.
Mexía, José Miguel	1791	*A.G. de la N. Ordenanzas*, vol.16, p.162 reverse. 1764. Examination 8th February. Master silversmith.
Mexía, Pedro	1792	*A.G. de la N. Industria*, vol.5, p.255. Unlicensed silversmith.
Meza, Mauricio	1811	*A.G. de la N. Empadronamiento de* 1811. *Cuartel menor núm.*1. Silversmith. (28 years of age.)
Millán, Manuel	1859	*El Viajero en México. Año de* 1859. By Juan N. del Valle. Silversmith.
Miranda, José Antonio	1800	*A.G. de la N. Padrón de la Parcialidad de S. Juan de México*, vol.9, p.140 front and reverse. *Padrones Núm.*105. Silversmith. (Indian.)
Miranda, Manuel	1815	*A.G. de la N. Ordenanzas*, vol.16, p.201. 1864. Examination 10th July. Owner of silver-shop.
Molina, Susano	1854	*Guía de Forasteros en la Ciudad de Mégico*, op.cit. Silversmith. 1859 *and* 1864 *El Viajero en México Años de* 1859 y 1864. op.cit. Silversmith.
Molina, Susano	1865	*A.G. de la N. Calificación de establecimientos industriales*. Silver-shop. 1867 *Directorio del Comercio del Imperio Mexicano para el año de* 1867, op.cit. Silver-shop.
Mongragón, Rafael	1792	*A.G. de la N. Industria*, vol.5, p.255. Unlicensed silversmith.
Montenegro, Salvador	1745	*A.G. de la N. Ordenanzas*, vol.11, p.189 reverse. 1723-63. Election 11th January. *Diputado*.

Montero, Gabriel de	1694	*A.G. de la N. Ordenanzas*, vol.6, p.16 reverse. Years 1686 to 1698. 10th May, 1694. License for silver-shop.
Montes, Pedro	1798	*Diccionario Universal de Historia, etc.*, op.cit., vol.6, p.484. Silversmith.
Montes de Oca, Juan Joseph	1758	*A.G. de la N. Ordenanzas*, vol.11, p.295 reverse. 1723-63. Examination 11th February. Master silversmith. 1775 *Ord.* vol.16, p.70 reverse. Election 25th January, *Veedor* of silversmiths.
Montes de Oca, Juan Joseph	1777	Marroqui, op.cit., vol.3, p.370. *Inv. Catedral Metropolitana de* 1867. *Bib.*, p.3 and *Las Artes Industriales en la Nueva España*, op.cit. Silversmith.
Montes de Oca, Juan	1842	*A.G. de la N. Padrón de establecimientos industriales. Cuartel menor núm.*1. Silver-shop.
Montes de Oca, Manuel J. de	1772	*A.G. de la N. Ordenanzas*, vol.16, p.46. 1764. Examination 29th August. Master silversmith.
Montiel, Juan	1753	*A.G. de la N. Civil indiferente*, vol.64. *Empadronamiento de* 1753. The pages of the book are not numbered. Silversmith.
Montufar, José María	1859	*El Viajero en México*, op.cit. Silversmith. 1865 *A.G. de la N. Calificación de establecimientos industriales.* Silver-shop.
Morales, Antonio	1842	*A.G. de la N. Padrón de establecimientos industriales. Cuartel menor núm.*1. Silver-shop.
Morales, José	1811	*A.G. de la N. Empadronamiento de* 1811. *Cuartel menor núm.*1. Silversmith. (24 years of age.)
Morales, José Manuel	1782	*A.G. de la N. Ordenanzas*, vol.16, p.125 reverse. 1764. Examination 13th September. Master silversmith.
Morales, Juan Joseph	1752	*A.G. de la N. Ordenanzas*, vol.11, p.263 reverse. 1723-63. Examination 4th September. Master silversmith. 1766 *Ord.*, vol.16, p.11. 1764. 12th April. Master silversmith.
Moreno, Antonio	1741	*A.G. de la N. Ordenanzas*, vol.11, p.156. 1723-63. Examination 20th October. Master silversmith.
Moreno, Bernardo	1561	*Documentos para la Historia de México*, Series I, vol.1, by Lic. Gregorio Martín de Guijo. Silversmith. (Thief).
Moreno, Manuel	1854	*Guía de Forasteros en la Ciudad de Mégico, etc.*, op.cit. Silversmith. 1859 and 1864. *El Viajero en México Años de* 1859 *y* 1864, op.cit. Setter [of precious stones] and silversmith.
Moreno, Manuel	1865	*A.G. de la N. Calificación de Establecimientos industriales.* Silver-shop. 1867 *Directorio del Comercio del Imperio Mexicano para el año de* 1867, op.cit. Silver-shop.

Moreno, Thomas	1685	*El Gremio de Plateros en las Indias Occidentales*, op.cit., p.xxix. No.9. Silversmith.
Moreno de la Cueva, Miguel	1628	*Archivo de Notarías de México*. Before Antonio Alonso, Public Scrivener. 3rd October. Goldsmith.
Morero, Sen.n	1685	*El Gremio de Plateros en las Indias Occidentales*, op.cit., p.xxix. No.9. Silversmith.
Moroso, Mariano	1792	*A.G. de la N. Industria*, vol.5, p.255. Unlicensed silversmith.
Mosqueira, Esteban Molina de	1684	*Diccionario Universal etc.*, op.cit., vol.5, p.704. Silversmith.
Mota, Constantino de la	1620	and 1625 *Archivo de Notarías de México*. Before Antonio Alonso, Public Scrivener. 20th November 1620. Master silversmith. 27th May 1625 Goldsmith.
Muicelo, Antonio	1842	*A.G. de la N. Padrón de establecimientos industriales. Cuartel menor núm.1.* Silver-work shop.
Munguía, Pedro	1796	*A.G. de la N. Ordenanzas*, vol.16, p.182. 1764. Examination 18th July. Master silversmith.
Muñoz, Thomas	1724	*A.G. de la N. Ordenanzas*, vol.11, p.9 reverse. 1723-63. Election 8th January. *Diputado*. 1750 *Las Artes Industriales en la Nueva España*, op.cit. Silversmith.
Muñoz de Luque, Diego Jph. C.	1780	*A.G. de la N. Ordenanzas*, vol.16, p.115 reverse. 1764. Examination 7th January. Master silversmith.
Murcia, Diego de	1694	*A.G. de la N. Ordenanzas*, vol.6, p.16. Years 1686 to 1698. Examination 10th May. License for silver-shop.
Murria, Diego de	1685	*El Gremio de Plateros en las Indias Occidentales*, op.cit., p.xxix. No.9. Silversmith. (Comp.a del Liz. Dn. Juan de Valdez.)
Muzientes, Alexo Elixio de	1721	*A.G. de la N. Ordenanzas*, vol.10. Years 1714 to 1722. Examination. Master sheet-beater.
N., Susano	1864	*El Viajero en México Completa Guía de Forasteros para 1864*, op.cit. Silversmith.
Nájera, Joseph de	1732	*A.G. de la N. Ordenanzas*, vol.11, p.79 reverse. 1723-63. Examination 6th March. Master silversmith.
Narbaes, Manuel	1745	*A.G. de la N. Ordenanzas*, vol.11, p.189 reverse. 1723-63. Examination 2nd January. Sheet-beater.
Nava, Baltazar	1620	*Archivo de Notarías de México*. Before Antonio Alonso, Public Scrivener. 20th November. Master silversmith.

Nava, Manuel de	1800	*A.G. de la N. Ordenanzas*, vol.16, p.186 reverse. 1764. Examination 1st February. Owner of silver-shop.
Navarijo, Ilario de	1728	*A.G. de la N. Ordenanzas*, vol.11, p.48 reverse. 1723-63. Examination 5th June. Master silversmith.
Navarro, Juan	1536	*Archivo de Protocolos. Anónimos.* 1536-43. Silversmith.
Negrete, Ignacio	1792	*A.G. de la N. Industria*, vol.5, p.255. Unlicensed silversmith.
Neyra, Alonso de	1685	*El Gremio de Plateros en las Indias Occidentales*, op.cit., p.xxix. No.9. Filigree worker.
Nieva, J.	1882	*Nueva Guía de México*, p.833. By Ireneo Paz and Manuel Tornel. Silver-shop.
Noriega, Dario	1859	*El Viajero en México*, op.cit. Silversmith. 1864. Ibid for 1864. Silversmith. 1865 *A.G. de la N. Calif. Est. Inds.* Silver-shop. 1867 *Directorio del Comercio del Imperio Mexicano.* Silver-shop.
Noriega, Dionisio	1854	*Guía de Forasteros en la Ciudad de Mégico*, op.cit. Silversmith.
Noriega, Ignacio	1792	*A.G. de la N. Industria*, vol.5, p.255. Unlicensed silversmith.
Noriega, José	1792	*A.G. de la N. Industria*, vol.5, p.255. Unlicensed silversmith.
Núñez, Matheo	1685	*El Gremio de Plateros en las Indias Occidentales*, op.cit. Silversmith.
Núñez, Vicente	1811	*A.G. de la N. Empadronamiento de 1811. Cuartel menor núm.1.* Silversmith. (58 years of age.)
Ochoa, José Ignacio	1811	*A.G. de la N. Empadronamiento de 1811. Cuartel menor núm.1.* Silversmith. (34 years of age.)
Ochoa, Juan	1852	*Guía de Forasteros de la capital de Puebla, para el año de 1852*, op.cit. Silversmith.
Ochoa, Pedro	1852	*Guía de Forasteros de la capital de Puebla, para el año de 1852*, op.cit. Silversmith.
Olaechea, Miguel de	1690	*Las Artes Industriales en la Nueva España*, op.cit. Silversmith. 1699 *Historia de la Fundación de la Ciudad de la Puebla de los Angeles en la Nueva España*, op.cit. Owner [of silver-shop].
Olaez, Ignacio	1864	*El Viajero en México*, op.cit. Silversmith. 1865 *A.G. de la N. Calificación de Est. Indust.* Silver-shop. 1867 *Directorio del Comercio del Imperio Mexicano*, op.cit. Silver-shop.
Olaez, José	1792	*A.G. de la N. Industria*, vol.5, p.255. Unlicensed silversmith.
Olascoaga, Juan Bautista de	1724	*A.G. de la N. Ordenanzas*, vol.11, p.10 reverse. 1723-63. Examination 27th April. Master silversmith.

Olguín, Augustín de	1777	*A.G. de la N. Ordenanzas*, vol.16, p.101. 1764. Examination 23rd May. Master silversmith.
Oliba, Jesús	1864	*A.G. de la N. Calificación de establecimientos industriales. Establecimientos de plateros.* Silver-shop.
Oliver, José	1753	*A.G. de la N. Civil indiferente*, vol.64. *Empadronamiento de 1753*. The pages of the book are not numbered. Silversmith. (50 years of age.)
Oliver, Juan de	1734	*A.G. de la N. Ordenanzas*, vol.11, p.106. 1723-63. Examination 18th August. Master silversmith.
Olivera, José de	1753	*A.G. de la N. Civil indiferente*, vol.64. *Empadronamiento de 1753*. The pages of the book are not numbered. Owner of silver-shop. (36 years of age.)
Ontiveros, Juan de	1753	*A.G. de la N. Civil indiferente*, vol.64. *Empadronamiento de 1753*. The pages of the book are not numbered. Unlicensed silversmith.
Orcasitas, Mariano	1829	*Correo de la Federación Mexicana. 16 de Agosto de 1829*. Silversmith.
Ordaz, José Luis	1811	*A.G. de la N. Empadronamiento de 1811. Cuartel menor núm.1.* Silversmith. (13 years of age.)
Orduño, Baltazar	1859	and 1864 *El Viajero en México años 1856 y 1864*, op.cit. Silversmith. 1865 *A.G. de la N. Calif. de Est. Indust.* Silver-shop. 1867 *Directorio del Comercio, etc.* Silver-shop.
Origuel y Guido, Juan de	1694	*A.G. de la N. Ordenanzas*, vol.6, p.16. 1686-98. Examination 10th May. License for Silver-shop. 1698 *Reales Cédulas (planta alta)*, vol.45, p.266. 1699-1707. 21st January. Master silversmith.
Oropeza, Miguel	1792	*A.G. de la N. Industria*, vol.5, p.255. Unlicensed silversmith. 1811 *Empadronamiento de 1811. Cuartel menor núm.1.* Silversmith. (45 years of age.)
Orosco, Francisco	1792	*A.G. de la N. Ordenanzas*, vol.16, p.174. 1764. Examination 14th December. Owner of silver-shop. (City of Cadiz.)
Orozco, Antonio de	1685	*El Gremio de Plateros en las Indias Occidentales*, op.cit., p.xxv. No.9. Drawer of gold wire.
Ortega, Francisco	1854	*Guía de Forasteros en la Ciudad de Mégico*, op.cit. Silversmith.
Ortega, Rafael	1811	*A.G. de la N. Empadronamiento de 1811. Cuartel menor núm.1.* Silversmith. (18 years of age.)
Ortiz.	1750	*Las Artes Industriales en la Nueva España*, op.cit. Silversmith.
Ortiz, Florencio	1842	*A.G. de la N. Padrón de establecimientos industriales. Cuartel menor núm.1.* Silver-shop.

1854 *Guía de Forasteros en la Ciudad de Mégico*, op.cit. Silversmith. 1864 *El Viajero etc.*, op.cit.

Ortiz, Florencio — 1865 — *A.G. de la N. Calificación de establecimientos industriales*. Silver-shop. 1867 *Directorio del Comercio del Imperio Mexicano, etc.*, op.cit. Silver-shop.

Ortiz, Juan — 1580 — *Libros y Libreros en el Siglo* XVI, vol.VI, p.556. By Francisco Fernández del Castillo. Publications of the *A.G. de la N.* Printer, engraver, manufacturer of silver, silversmith. French.

Orve. — 1750 — *Las Artes Industriales en la Nueva España*, op.cit. Silversmith. (From Guatemala.)

Osa, Pedro de la — 1737 — *A.G. de la N. Ordenanzas*, vol.II, p.123 reverse. 1723-63. Examination 7th September 1737. Master silversmith.

Otero, Fran.co de — 1685 — *El Gremio de Plateros en las Indias Occidentales*, op.cit., p.xxv. No.9. Silversmith.

Oviedo, Miguel de — 1753 — *A.G. de la N. Civil indiferente*, vol.64. *Empadronamiento de* 1753. The pages of the book are not numbered. Unlicensed silversmith. (25 years of age.)

Pacheco, Atanacio — 1831 — *A.G. de la N. Ramo de Hacienda*. Book which says: *Casa de Ensaye de Mexico*. 1830-31. Bundle 45. Payment for stamping silversmiths' marks.

Pacheco, José Joaquín — 1817 — *A.G. de la N. Ordenanzas*, vol.16, p.201 reverse. 1764. Examination 10th June, 1817. Owner of silver-shop.

Padilla, Juan de — 1640 — *Acta de Cabildo 26 de Marzo 1640*. Silversmith.

Padilla, Luis de — 1736 — *A.G. de la N. Ordenanzas*, vol.11, p.120 reverse. 1723-63. Examination 12th September. Master silversmith.

Palasios, Joseph — 1717 — *A.G. de la N. Ordenanzas*, vol.10. 1714-22. Examination. Drawer of gold and silver wire.

Palazios, Pedro de — 1685 — *El Gremio de Plateros en las Indias Occidentales*, op.cit., p.xxv. No.9. Silversmith.

Palomino, Manuel — 1754 — *A.G. de la N. Ordenanzas*, vol.11, p.270. 1723-63. Examination 23rd February. Master silversmith.

Paniagua, Manuel — 1753 — *A.G. de la N. Civil indiferente*, vol.64. *Empadronamiento de* 1753. The pages of the book are not numbered. Unlicensed silversmith.

Páramo, Luis — 1854 — *Guía de Forasteros en la Ciudad de Mégico, para el año de* 1854. Silversmith.

Páramo, Pedro	1864	*El Viajero en México*, op.cit. Silversmith. 1865 *A.G. de la N. Calificación de Est. Indust.* Silver-shop. 1867 *Directorio del Comercio, etc.,* op.cit. Silver-shop.
Pardo, José Luis	1811	*A.G. de la N. Empadronamiento de* 1811. *Cuartel menor núm.*1. Silversmith. (22 years of age).
Pardo, Gregorio	1685	*El Gremio de Plateros en las Indias Occidentales,* op.cit., p.xxv. No.9. Filigree worker.
Pardo de Figueroa, Juan	1745	*A.G. de la N. Ordenanzas,* vol.11, p.210 reverse. 1723-63. 5th November. Master silversmith. (Examined in Cádiz.)
Paris, Al.so de	1685	*El Gremio de Plateros en las Indias Occidentales,* op.cit., p.xxv. No.9. Silversmith.
Parra, Sebastián de la	1765	*A.G. de la N. Ordenanzas,* vol.16, p.5 reverse. 1764. Election 11th January. *Veedor* of silver art.
Patiño, Guadalupe	1852	*Guía de Forasteros de la Ciudad de Puebla, para el año de* 1852, op.cit. Silversmith.
Patiño, José Mariano	1781	*A.G. de la N. Ordenanzas,* vol.16, p.117 reverse. 1764. Examination 11th January. Master silversmith.
Pauia, Francisco	1775	*A.G. de la N. Ordenanzas,* vol.16, p.72. 1764. Examination 9th March. Owner of silver-shop.
Pavía, Miguel	1811	*A.G. de la N. Empadronamiento de* 1811. *Cuartel menor núm.*1. Silversmith. (40 years of age.)
Pedraza, Manuel	1768	*A.G. de la N. Ordenanzas,* vol.16, p.18 reverse. 1764. Examination 7th September. Master silversmith.
Pedraza, Mig.l de	1685	*El Gremio de Plateros en las Indias Occidentales,* op.cit., p.xxv. No.9. Silversmith.
Peña, José Manuel	1811	*A.G. de la N. Empadronamiento de* 1811. Silversmith. (35 years of age.)
Peñalossa, Juan de	1685	*El Gremio de Plateros en las Indias Occidentales,* op.cit., p.xxv. No.9. Silversmith.
Peña Roja, Francisco	1741	*A.G. de la N. Ordenanzas,* vol.11, p.149 reverse. 1723-63. Confirmation of examination 13th February. Master silversmith. (Examined in Seville.)
Peña Roja, Joseph	1761	*A.G. de la N. Ordenanzas,* vol.11, p.316. 1723-63. Examination 25th May. Master silversmith.
Peña Rosa, Francisco	1760	*A.G. de la N. Ordenanzas,* vol.11, p.311. 1723-63. Election 15th December. *Veedor* of silver art. 1807 Inventory Metropolitan Cathedral, p.30. 1807. *Bib.* Silversmith.
Peñuelas, Julian	1864	*El Viajero en México*, op.cit. Silversmith. 1865 *A.G. de la N. Calificación de Est. Indust.* Silver-shop. 1867 *Directorio del Comercio, etc.,* op.cit. Silver-shop.

Peralta, Carlos	1831	*A.G. de la N. Ramo de Hacienda.* Book which states: *Casa de Ensaye de Mexico.* 1830-31. Bundle 45. Payment for stamping silversmiths' marks.
Peraza, José María	1784	*A.G. de la N. Ordenanzas*, vol.16, p.135 reverse. 1764. Examination 14th January. Master silversmith.
Peres de Segura, Andrés	1745	*A.G. de la N. Ordenanzas*, vol.11, p.189 reverse. 1723-63. Election 11th January. *Diputado.*
Pérez, Antonio	1743	*A.G. de la N. Ordenanzas*, vol.11, p.177. 1723-63. Examination 19th November. Master silversmith.
Pérez, Felipe	1753	*A.G. de la N. Civil indiferente*, vol.64. *Empadronamiento de* 1753. The pages of the book are not numbered. Unlicensed silversmith.
Pérez, Gerónimo	1724	*A.G. de la N. Ordenanzas*, vol.11, p.9 reverse. 1723-63. Election. *Mayordomo.*
Pérez, Inés L. Widow of Joaq.	1753	*A.G. de la N. Civil indiferente*, vol.64. *Empadronamiento de* 1753. The pages of the book are not numbered.
Pérez, José María	1854	*Guía de Forasteros en la Ciudad de Mégico*, op.cit. Silversmith. 1859 *El Viajero en México*, op.cit. Year 1859. Silversmith.
Pérez, Manuel	1753	*A.G. de la N. Civil indiferente*, vol.64. *Empadronamiento de* 1753. The pages of the book are not numbered. Unlicensed silversmith. (25 years of age.)
Pérez, Mariano	1792	*A.G. de la N. Industria*, vol.5, p.255. Unlicensed silversmith.
Pérez, Rafael	1792	*A.G. de la N. Industria*, vol.5, p.255. Unlicensed silversmith. 1811 *Empadronamiento de* 1811. Silversmith. (45 years of age.)
Pérez, Sebastian	1764	*A.G. de la N. Ordenanzas*, vol.16, p.4 reverse. 1764. Examination 19th September. Master silversmith.
Pérez Alamillo, Joaquín	1808	*A.G. de la N. Ordenanzas*, vol.16, p.197. 1764. Examination 25th January. Owner of silver-shop.
Pérez de Salcedo, Francisco	1730	*A.G. de la N. Ordenanzas*, vol.11, p.56. 1723-63. Examination 13th January. Master silversmith.
Pérez de Villa, Joseph	1728	*A.G. de la N. Ordenanzas*, vol.11, p.46. 1723-63. Examination 16th January. Master silversmith.
Picazo, Miguel	1792	*A.G. de la N. Industria*, vol.5, p.255. Unlicensed silversmith. 1798 *Ordenanzas*, vol.16, p.184. 1764. Examination 20th March. Master silversmith.
Piérola, Pedro José	1792	*A.G. de la N. Industria*, vol.5, p.255. Unlicensed silversmith. 1800 *Ordenanzas*, vol.16, p.190. 1764. Examination 11th October. Owner of silver-shop.

Pineda, Miguel de	1685	*El Gremio de Plateros en las Indias Occidentales*, op.cit., p.xxv. No.9. Silversmith.
Pizarro, Cruz	1864	*El Viajero en México*, op.cit. Silversmith. 1865 *A.G. de la N. Calificación de Est. Indust.* Silver-shop. 1867 *Directorio del Comercio etc.*, op.cit. Silver-shop.
Pizerro, Ger.mo	1685	*El Gremio de Plateros en las Indias Occidentales*, op.cit., p.xxv. No.9. Silversmith.
Plaza, Lorenzo	1792	*A.G. de la N. Industria*, vol.5, p.255. Unlicensed silversmith.
Polanco, Cristóbal	1694	*A.G. de la N. Ordenanzas*, vol.6, p.15 reverse. Years 1686 to 1698. Examination 21st April. License for silver-shop.
Polanco, Juan José	1811	*A.G. de la N. Empadronamiento de 1811.* Silversmith. (26 years of age.)
Polanco, Marcelo	1792	*A.G. de la N. Industria*, vol.5, p.255. Unlicensed silversmith. 1799 *A.G. y P. de la N. Guía de cargo y data etc. para la cuenta del año de 1799*, p.11. 19th October. Silversmith.
Polanco, Marcelo	1799	*A.G. de la N. Ordenanzas*, vol.16, p.185 reverse. 1764. Examination 27th May. Owner of silver-shop. 1811 *Empadronamiento de 1811.* Silversmith (52 years of age.)
Polanco, María T. widow of	1685	*El Gremio de Plateros en las Indias Occidentales*, op.cit., p.xxv. No.9. Silver-shop.
Polanco, Nicolás	1685	*El Gremio de Plateros en las Indias Occidentales*, op.cit., p.xxv. No.9. Silversmith.
Polanco, XP.l	1685	*El Gremio de Plateros en las Indias Occidentales*, op.cit., p.xxv. No.9. Silversmith.
Ponce, José María	1859	*El Viajero en México para el año de 1859*, op.cit. Silversmith.
Pons, Miguel	1798	*A.G. de la N. Ordenanzas*, vol.16, p.184. 1764. Examination 16th May. Master silversmith. (City of Barcelona.)
Pontón, Antonio	1882	*Nueva Guía de México*, p.833. By Ireneo Paz and Manuel Tornel. Silver-shop.
Ponze, Francisco	1685	*El Gremio de Plateros en las Indias Occidentales*, op.cit., p.xxv. No.9.
Ponze de León, Joseph	1763	*A.G. de la N. Ordenanzas*, vol.11, p.326. 1723-63. Examination 14th September. Master silversmith.
Porta Bargas, Joseph de la	1725	*A.G. de la N. Ordenanzas*, vol.11, p.14-a. 1723-63. Election 9th January. *Veedor.*
Portocarrero, Luis	1865	*A.G. de la N. Calificación de establecimientos industriales.* Silver-shop.
Portugues, Manuel	1811	*A.G. de la N. Empadronamiento de 1811.* Silversmith. (31 years of age.)

Prado, Teodocio	1864	*El Viajero en México*, op.cit. Silversmith. 1865 *A.G. de la N. Calificación de Est. Indust.* Silver-shop. 1867 *Directorio del Comercio del Imperio Mexicano*, op.cit. Silver-shop.
Prieto, Manuel	1792	*A.G. de la N. Industria*, vol.5, p.255. Unlicensed silversmith.
Puerto y Reyes, Felipe del	1724	*A.G. de la N. Ordenanzas*, vol.11, p.11 reverse. 1723-63. Examination 11th July. Master silversmith.
Quintana, Antonio	1792	*A.G. de la N. Industria*, vol.5, p.255. Unlicensed silversmith.
Quiroga, Miguel	1811	*A.G. de la N. Empadronamiento de 1811. Cuartel menor núm.1.* Silversmith. (50 years of age.)
Quiros, Pedro	1753	*A.G. de la N. Civil indiferente*, vol.64. *Empadronamiento de* 1753. The pages of the book are not numbered. Unlicensed silversmith. (31 years of age.)
Quiroz, N.	1852	*Guía de Forasteros de la capital de Puebla, para el año de* 1852, op.cit. Silversmith.
Ramires, Gabino	1865	*A.G. de la N. Calificación de establecimientos industriales. Establecimientos de Plateros.* Silver-shop.
Ramírez, Antonio	1864	*El Viajero en México*, op.cit. Silversmith. 1865 *A.G. de la N. Padrón de establecimientos industriales.* Silver-shop.
Ramírez, Francisco	1864	*El Viajero en México*, op.cit. Silversmith. 1865 *A.G. de la N. Calificación de Est. Indust.* Silver-shop. 1867 *Directorio del Comercio del Imperio Mexicano*, op.cit. Silver-shop.
Ramírez, Ignacio	1792	*A.G. de la N. Industria*, vol.5, p.255. Unlicensed silversmith.
Ramírez, Maximino	1854	*Guía de Forasteros en la Ciudad de Mégico*, op.cit. Silversmith. 1859. *El Viajero en México. Año de* 1859, op.cit. Silversmith.
Ramírez, Nicolás	1792	*A.G. de la N. Industria*, vol.5, p.255. Unlicensed silversmith.
Ramírez de Arellano, Antonio	1732	*A.G. de la N. Ordenanzas*, vol.11, p.87 reverse. 1723-63. Examination 21st August. Master silversmith.
Ramírez de Arellano, Nicolas	1739	*A.G. de la N. Ordenanzas*, vol.11, p.132 reverse. 1723-63. Examination 22nd June. Master silversmith.
Ramos, José Darío	1812	*A.G. de la N. Ordenanzas*, vol.16, p.200 reverse. 1764. Examination 15th September. Owner of silver-shop.

Rangel, Francisco	1859	*El Viajero en México. Año de* 1859. By Juan N. del Valle. Silversmith. (Domicile 'Santa Inés.')
Rangel, Francisco	1859	*El Viajero en México para el año de* 1859, op.cit. Silversmith. (Domicile *Acequia*.)
Reavarren, Nicolás	1734	*A.G. de la N. Ordenanzas*, vol.11, p.100. 1723-63. Examination 28th January. Master silversmith.
Recarey y Camino, Antonio	1782	*A.G. de la N. Ordenanzas*, vol.16, p.122 reverse. 1764. Examination 25th January. Master silversmith. 1783 *Documentos del Archivo de la Basílica*. Silversmith.
Recarey y Camino, Antonio	1799	*A.G. de la N. Guía de Cargo y Data etc. para la cuenta del año de* 1799, p.11. 16th October. Silversmith.
Reina, José María	1859	and 1864. *El Viajero en México Años de* 1859 *y* 1864. op.cit. Silversmith. 1865 *A.G. de la N. Calificación de Establecimientos industriales*. Silver-shop.
Reinol, N.	1864	*El Viajero en México. Completa Guía de Forasteros para* 1864, op.cit. Silversmith.
Reinosso, Joseph	1685	*El Gremio de Plateros en las Indias Occidentales*, op.cit., p.xxv. No.9. Silversmith.
Rendón, Francisco	1685	*El Gremio de Plateros en las Indias Occidentales*, op.cit. Silversmith.
Resinas, Romualdo	1859	*El Viajero en México*, op.cit. Silversmith. 1865. *A.G. de la N. Calificación de establecimientos industriales*. Silver-shop.
Reyes, Isidro	1811	*A.G. de la N. Empadronamiento de* 1811. *Cuartel menor núm.*1. Silversmith. (30 years of age.)
Reyes, José María	1854	*Guía de Forasteros en la Ciudad de Mégico, para el año de* 1854, op.cit. Silversmith.
Reyes, Manuel	1811	*A.G. de la N. Empadronamiento de* 1811. *Cuartel menor núm.*1. Silversmith. (50 years of age.)
Reyes Torres, Manuel Ygn.o	1798	*A.G. de la N. Ordenanzas*, vol.16, p.185. 1764. Examination 6th November. Owner of silver-shop.
Ribera, Domingo de	1724	and 1725 *A.G. de la N. Ordenanzas*, vol.11, pp.9 reverse and 14-a. 1723-1763. Election 8th January 1724 and 9th January 1725. *Mayordomo.*
Río Diego del	1745	*A.G. de la N. Ordenanzas*, vol.11, p.189 reverse. 1723-63. Examination 6th January. Drawer of gold [wire]
Ríos, Jph. Anastacio de los	1779	*A.G. de la N. Ordenanzas*, vol.16, p.114 reverse. 1764. Examination 12th June. Master silversmith.
Ríos, José de los	1788	Romero de Terreros, op.cit., p.24. Silversmith.
Ríos, Manuel de los	1778	*A. G. de la N. Ordenanzas*, vol.16, p.112. 1764. Examination 25th September. Master silversmith. 1785 and 1787 *Ord.*, vol.16, p.145

		reverse and 149. 1764. Election 14th January 1785 and 16th January 1787. *Veedor*.
Rivera, Francisco Xavier	1774	*A.G. de la N. Ordenanzas*, vol.16, p.66 reverse. 1764. Examination 22nd August. Owner of silver-shop.
Rivera, José María	1811	*A.G. de la N. Empadronamiento de 1811. Cuartel menor núm.1.* Silversmith. (35 years of age.)
Rivera, Manuel de	1753	*A.G. de la N. Civil indiferente*, vol.64. *Empadronamiento de 1753.* The pages of the book are not numbered. Owner of silver-shop. (40 years of age.)
Rivera, Miguel Carlos de	1730	*A.G. de la N. Ordenanzas*, vol.11, p.59. 1723-63. Examination 6th July. Master silversmith. 1767 and 1768 *Ord.*, vol.16, pp.14 and 16. 1764. Election 10th January 1767 and 15th January 1768. *Veedor* of silversmiths.
Robledo, José	1792	*A.G. de la N. Industria*, vol.5, p.255. Unlicensed silversmith.
Robles, Manuel	1852	*Guía de Forasteros de la capital de Puebla, para el año de 1852*, op.cit. Silversmith.
Rodallega, José María	1772	*A.G. de la N. Ordenanzas*, vol.16, p.48. 1764. Examination 22nd October. Master silversmith. 1777 Romero de Terreros, op.cit. and Marroqui, vol.3,p.370. Silversmith.
Rodallega, José María	1781	and 1783 *A.G. de la N. Ordenanzas*, vol.16, pp.117 reverse and 129 reverse. 1764. Election 11th January 1781 and 9th January 1783. *Veedor* of silversmiths. 1788 Romero de Terreros, op.cit., p.24.
Rodallega, José María	1793	Marroqui, vol.III, p.612. 1796 *A.G. de la N. Libro Mayor, o Guía del cargo de la Tesorería Gral. Derechos del oro de azogue*, p.1r. *Derechos de oro de fuego*, p.7.
Rodallega, José María	1797	and 1798 *A.G. de la N. Ordenanzas*, vol.16, pp.183 reverse and 184. 1764. Election 12th January 1797 and 22nd January 1798. *Veedor* of silversmiths. *Principios Siglo* XIX Marroqui, vol.III.
Rodallega, José María	1804	and 1805. Marroqui, vol.III, p.375. 1810 *A.G. de la N. Ordenanzas*, vol.16, p.199. 1764. Election *veedor* of Silversmiths. 1811 5th January Election *Veedor* and *Empadronamiento de 1811*. (70 years of age.)
Rodallega, José María	1812	*A.G. de la N. Ordenanzas*, vol.16, p.200. 1764. Election 7th January 1812. *Veedor* of silversmiths.
Rodríguez, Agustin	1792	*A.G. de la N. Industria*, vol.5, p.255. Unlicensed silversmith 1795 *Ord.*, vol.16, p.180. 1764.

		Examination 27th March. Master silversmith. 1859 *El Viajero en México*, op.cit. Silversmith.
Rodríguez, Anselmo	1761	*A.G..de la N. Ordenanzas*, vol.11, p.311 reverse. 1723-63. Examination 14th March. Master silversmith.
Rodríguez, Calletano Ysidro	1781	*A.G. de la N. Ordenanzas*, vol.16, p.121 reverse. 1764. Examination 4th December. Master silversmith.
Rodríguez, Francisco	1598	*A.G. de la N. Ramo de Inquisición*, vol.160. Silversmith. (Heretic, absent)
Rodríguez, Joseph	1726	*A.G. de la N. Ordenanzas*, vol.11, p.33 reverse. 1723-63. Examination 7th August. Master silversmith. 1753 *Civil Indiferente*, vol.64. *Empadronamiento de* 1753. Silver-store.
Rodríguez, Juan Francisco	1723	*A.G. de la N. Ordenanzas*, vol.11, p.6 reverse. 1723-63. Examination 11th June. Master silversmith.
Rodríguez Alconedo, José Luis	1791	*A.G. de la N. Ordenanzas*, vol.16, p.167. 1764. Examination 24th September. Master silversmith. 1798 *A.G. de la N. Manual Común de* 1798. 22nd. February. Owner of Silver-shop in this city. Marroqui, op.cit., vol.1, p.283.
Rodríguez Alconedo, José Luis	1803	*Poblanos Ilustres*, by Lic. E. Gómez de Haro. Puebla 1810. *El Goya Mejicano* 1805. Marroqui, vol.I, p.282. Silversmith. 1814 *Poblanos Ilustres*, op.cit. Silversmith.
Rodríguez Cabesa de Vaca, Fco.	1740	*A.G. de la N. Ordenanzas*, vol.11, p.141. 1723-63. Examination 17th October. Master silversmith.
Rodríguez, Gonzalo	1536	*Actas de Cabildo*, 27 de Octubre 1536. Silversmith. (Portuguese.)
Rodríguez, Juan Antonio	1792	*A.G. de la N. Industria*, vol.5, p.255. Unlicensed silversmith.
Rodríguez, Juan Manuel	1746	*Pregones de Ordenanzas de el Nobilísimo Arte de la Platería* Mexico, 1746. *Mayordomo* of the Silversmiths' Art.
Rodríguez, Lorenzo	1859	and 1864 *El Viajero en México*, op.cit. Years 1859 and 1864. Silversmith. 1865 *A.G. de la N. Calificación de Est. Indust.* Silver-shop. 1867 *Directorio del comercio, etc.* Silver-shop.
Rodríguez, Luys	1537	*Actas de Cabildo*, 6 de Abril de 1537. Marker and *Alcalde* (appointed).
Rodríguez, Manuel	1792	*A.G. de la N. Industria*, vol.5, p.255. Unlicensed silversmith. 1859 *El Viajero en México Año de* 1859, op.cit. Silversmith.
Rodríguez, Mariano	1811	*A.G. de la N. Empadronamiento de* 1811. *Cuartel menor núm.*1. Silversmith (34 years of age.)
Rodríguez, Mrn.	1685	*El Gremio de Plateros en las Indias Occidentales*, op.cit., p.xxv. No.9. Silversmith.

Rodríguez, Sebastián	1753	*A.G. de la N. Civil indiferente*, vol.64. *Empadronamiento de* 1753. The pages of the book are not numbered. Silversmith. (50 years of age.)
Rodríguez, Sebastián	1781	*A.G. de la N. Ordenanzas*, vol.16, p.121 reverse. 1764. Examination 13th November. Master silversmith.
Rodríguez Lozano, Juan	1713	*Pleito de Rada de* 1713, pp.65-6, point III. Silversmith.
Rojas, Gregorio de	1742	*A.G. de la N. Ordenanzas*, vol.11, p.157. 1723-63. Examination 25th January. Master silversmith.
Rojas, José	1753	*A.G. de la N. Civil indiferente*, vol.64. *Empadronamiento de* 1753. The pages of the book are not numbered. Unlicensed silversmith. (23 years of age.)
Rojas, José de	1753	*A.G. de la N. Civil indiferente*, vol.64. *Empadronamiento de* 1753. The pages of the book are not numbered. Unlicensed silversmith. (48 years of age.)
Rojas, Juan de	1753	*A.G. de la N. Civil indiferente*, vol.64. *Empadronamiento de* 1753. The pages of the book are not numbered. Unlicensed silversmith. (26 years of age.)
Romero, Antonio	1737	*A.G. de la N. Ordenanzas*, vol.11, p.122 reverse. 1723-63. Examination 23rd March. Master silversmith.
Romero, Antonio	1753	*A.G. de la N. Civil indiferente*, vol.64. *Empadronamiento de* 1753. The pages of the book are not numbered. Silversmith. (35 years of age.) *Las Artes Industriales en la Nueva España*, op.cit.
Romero, Félix	1792	*A.G. de la N. Industria*, vol.5, p.255. Unlicensed silversmith.
Romero, Francisco	1859	*El Viajero en México*, op.cit. Year of 1859. Silversmith.
Romero, Ignacio	1792	*A.G. de la N. Industria*, vol.5, p.255. Unlicensed silversmith.
Rosel, Susano	1865	*A.G. de la N. Calificación de establecimientos industriales*. Silver-shop. 1867 *Directorio del Comercio del Imperio Mexicano para el año de* 1867, op.cit. Silver-shop.
Rosellon, Domingo	1864	*El Viajero en México. Completa Guía de Forasteros para* 1864, op.cit. Silversmith.
Ro.ss, Benito	1685	*El Gremio de Plateros en las Indias Occidentales*, op.cit., p.xxv. No.9. Silversmith.
R.ss, Juan Man.l	1685	*El Gremio de Plateros en las Indias Occidentales*, op.cit., p.xxv. No.9. Silversmith.

Roto, Rafael	1753	*A.G. de la N. Civil indiferente*, vol.64. *Empadronamiento de* 1753. The pages of the book are not numbered. Unlicensed silversmith.
Rubín, Camilo	1842	*A.G. de la N. Padrón de establecimientos industriales. Cuartel menor núm.*1. Silver-shop.
Rubio, Joseph	1730	*A.G. de la N. Ordenanzas*, vol.11, p.59. 1723-63. Examination 5th July. Master silversmith.
Rubio, Juan	1842	*A.G. de la N. Padrón de establecimientos industriales. Cuartel menor núm.*1. Silver-work shop.
Ruiz, Agustín	1811	*A.G. de la N. Empadronamiento de* 1811. *Cuartel menor núm.*1. Silversmith. (45 years of age.)
Ruiz, Alejandro	1852	*Guía de Forasteros de la ciudad de Puebla*, op.cit. Silversmith.
Ruiz, Alonso	1564	*A.G. de la N. Inquisición*, vol.26. Silversmith. (*Mestizo.*)
Ruiz, Feliciano	1852	*Guía de Forasteros de la ciudad de Puebla*, op.cit. Silversmith.
Ruiz, Ignacio	1792	*A.G. de la N. Industria*, vol.5, p.255. Unlicensed silversmith.
Ruiz, Juan	1852	*Guía de Forasteros de la ciudad de Puebla*, op.cit. Silversmith.
Ruiz, Juan Fran.	1721	*A.G. de la N. Ordenanzas*, vol.10. Years 1714 to 1722. Examination. Master Drawer of Gold and Silver [wire] (Born in Iscarena in the territory of the Archbishopric of Seville.)
Ruiz, Phelipe	1725	*A.G. de la N. Ordenanzas*, vol.11, p.14-a. 1723-63. Election 9th January 1725. *Maiordomo.*
Ruiz Cano, Miguel	1778	*A.G. de la N. Ordenanzas*, vol.16, p.III reverse. 1764. Examination 11th September. Master silversmith. 1791 *Ord.*, vol.16, p.162 reverse. 1764. Election 8th January. *Veedor* of silversmiths.
Ruiz Cano, Miguel	1811	*A.G. de la N. Empadronamiento de* 1811. Silversmith. (30 years of age.)
Ruiz de Santiago, Ygnazio	1724	*A.G. de la N. Ordenanzas*, vol.11, p.9 reverse. 1723-63. Election 8th January. *Veedor.*
Ruiz Flores, Phelipe	1720	*A.G. de la N. Ordenanzas*, vol.10. Years 1714 to 1722. Examination. Master sheet-beater.
Ruiz García, Sebastián	1771	*A.G. de la N. Ordenanzas*, vol.16, p.38 reverse. 1764. Examination 11th September. Master silversmith.
Ruys, Bartolomé	1536	*Actas de Cabildo*, 28th *Julio* 1536. *Alcalde* of silversmiths and marker. And *Archivo de Protocolos Anónimos.* 1536-1543. Silversmith. 1537 *Actas de Cabildo*, 13 *de marzo* 1537.
Ruys, Francisco	1536	*Archivo de Protocolos, Anónimos.* 1536-42. Silversmith.

Saavedra, Jorge	1753	*A.G. de la N. Civil indiferente*, vol.64. *Empadronamiento de* 1753. The pages of the book are not numbered. Unlicensed silversmith. (35 years of age.)
Sabedra, Manuel	1778	*A.G. de la N. Ordenanzas*, vol.16, p.iii reverse. 1764. Examination 22nd August. Master silversmith.
Sabsedo, Pedro de	1546	*Actas de Cabildo*, 24 *de Julio* 1551. 1562 *Actas de Cabildo*, 16 *de Enero* 1562. He surrendered the office to Billasana. (Sabsedo or Salzedo.)
Sáenz, Joseph	1685	*El Gremio de Plateros en las Indias Occidentales*, op.cit., p.xxv. No.9. Silversmith.
Salazar, Hilario	1859	*El Viajero en México*, by Juan N. del Valle. Year 1859. Silversmith.
Salazar, José	1865	*A.G. de la N. Calificación de establecimientos industriales*. Silver-shop. 1867 *Directorio del Comercio del Imperio Mexicano*, op.cit. Silver-shop.
Saldaña, Fran.ca V. Widow of D.	1685	*El Gremio de Plateros en las Indias Occidentales*, op.cit., p.xxv. No.9. Silver-shop.
Saldaña Tamariz, Diego de	1724	*A.G. de la N. Ordenanzas*, vol.11, p.9 reverse. 1723-63. Election 8th January. *Diputado*.
Saldívar, Sostenes	1882	*Nueva Guía de México Año de* 1882, op.cit. Silver-shop.
Salina, Salbador de	1727	*A.G. de la N. Ordenanzas*, vol.11, p.44. 1723-63. Examination 17th May. Master silversmith.
Salinas, Antonio	1744	*A.G. de la N. Ordenanzas*, vol.11, p.185. 1723-63. Examination 7th October. Master silversmith. 1753 *Civil indiferente*, vol.64. *Empadronamiento de* 1753. Owner of silver-shop.
Salinas, José	1753	*A.G. de la N. Civil indiferente*, vol.64. *Empadronamiento de* 1753. The pages of the book are not numbered. Silversmith. (26 years of age.)
Salinas, Manuel	1753	*A.G. de la N. Civil indiferente*, vol.64. *Empadronamiento de* 1753. The pages of the book are not numbered. Silver-store. (45 years of age.) 1762 *Ord.*, vol.11, p.324 reverse. Election 14th January. *Veedor* of silversmiths.
Salmerón, Cayetano de	1730	*A.G. de la N. Ordenanzas*, vol.11, p.57. 1723-63. Examination 27th May. Master silversmith.
Salmón, Simón	1811	*A.G. de la N. Empadronamiento* de 1811. Silversmith. (36 years of age.) *Diccionario Universal, etc.*, op.cit., vol.6, p.486. 1819 *Las Artes Industriales, etc.*, op.cit. Silversmith.
Salvatierra, José	1753	*A.G. de la N. Civil indiferente*, vol.64. *Empadronamiento de* 1753. The pages of the book are not numbered. Owner of silver-shop. (30 years of age.)

Salvatierra, Joseph de	1758	*A.G. de la N. Ordenanzas*, vol.11, p.295 reverse. 1723-1763. Examination 14th January. Master silversmith.
Sámano, Fernando de	1778	*A.G. de la N. Ordenanzas*, vol.16, p.iii reverse. 1764. Examination 18th September. Master silversmith. 1788 *Ord.*, vol.16, p.156. 1764. Election 11th February. Veedor of silversmiths. Romero de Terreros, p.24.
Sámano, Fernando de	1805	1809 and 1813 *A.G. de la N. Ordenanzas*, vol.16, pp.194 reverse, 198 and 200 reverse. 1764. Election 11th January 1805, 10th February, 1809 and 8th January 1813. *Veedor* of silversmiths.
San Ciprián, José	1792	*A.G. de la N. Industria*, vol.5, p.255. Unlicensed silversmith.
Sánchez, Diego	1753	*A.G. de la N. Civil indiferente*, vol.64. *Empadronamiento de* 1753. The pages of the book are not numbered. Owner of silver-shop.
Sánchez, Francisco	1733	*A.G. de la N. Ordenanzas*, vol.11, p.112 reverse. 1723-63. Examination 17th September. Master silversmith.
Sánchez, José	1859	and 1864 *El Viajero en México. Años de* 1859 *y de* 1864, op.cit. Silversmith.
Sánchez, José María	1854	*Guía de Forasteros en la Ciudad de Mégico, para el año de* 1854, op.cit. Silversmith.
Sánchez, Joseph	1685	*El Gremio de Plateros en las Indias Occidentales*, op.cit., p.xxv. No.9. Silversmith.
Sánchez, Joseph Romualdo	1763	*A.G. de la N. Ordenanzas*, vol.11, p.325 reverse. 1723-63. Examination 7th June. Master silversmith.
Sánchez, Melchor	1576	*Actas de Cabildo*, 20 *de Febrero* 1576. Silversmith.
Sánchez, Miguel	1753	*A.G. de la N. Civil indiferente*, vol.64. *Empadronamiento de* 1753. The pages of the book are not numbered. Unlicensed silversmith. (18 years of age.)
Sánchez, Miguel	1753	*A.G. de la N. Civil indiferente*, vol.64. *Empadronamiento de* 1753. The pages of the book are not numbered. Unlicensed silversmith. (36 years of age.)
Sánchez, Sebastián	1842	*A.G. de la N. Padrón de establecimientos industriales. Cuartel menor núm.*1. Silver-shop. 1854 *Guía de Forasteros en la Ciudad de Mégico para el año de* 1854, op.cit. Silversmith.
Sánchez de Chavarría, Antonio	1724	*A.G. de la N. Ordenanzas*, vol.11, p.10 reverse. 1723-63. Examination 19th February. Master silversmith.
Sánchez de Echavarría, Diego	1713	*Pleito de Rada de* 1713, pp.65-6, point III, op.cit. Silversmith.

Sánchez de Osuna, Pedro	1727	*A.G. de la N. Ordenanzas*, vol.11, p.37. 1723-63. Election 13th January. *Mayordomo.*
Sánchez Requesso, Ju.o	1638	*A.G. de la N. Reales Cédulas. (Planta Alta.) Años* 1645-73, vol.58, p.122 to 137. *Mayordomo* of the guild and silversmiths' art.
Sandoval, Miguel	1864	*El Viajero en México, Completa Guía de Forasteros para* 1864, op.cit. Silversmith.
Santa Cruz Marín, Manuel de	1724	*A.G. de la N. Ordenanzas*, vol.11, p.9 reverse. 1723-63. Election 8th January. *Diputado.* 1727 *Ord.*, vol.II, p.37. 1723-63. Election 13th January. *Veedor (Alferez.)*
Sarcedo, Pascual	1854	*Guía de Forasteros en la Ciudad de Mégico*, op.cit. Silversmith.
Sasosena, Domingo	1730	*A.G. de la N. Ordenanzas*, vol.11, p.58. 1723-63. Examination 5th June. Master silversmith.
Segura, Andrés de	1726	*A.G. de la N. Ordenanzas*, vol.11, p.43 reverse. 1723-63. Examination 29th July. Master silversmith.
Semelian, Julián de	1535	*Colección de Documentos Inéditos para la Historia de Hispano América*, op.cit., book XIII, vol.II, p.290. Silversmith.
Sendejas, José de	1753	*A.G. de la N. Civil indiferente*, vol.64. *Empadronamiento de* 1753. The pages of the book are not numbered. Unlicensed silversmith. (25 years of age.)
Senteno, Cristóbal	1792	*A.G. de la N. Industria*, vol.5, p.255. Unlicensed silversmith.
Senteno, Juan de Dios	1738	*A.G. de la N. Ordenanzas*, vol.11, p.129. 1723-63. Examination 17th July 1738. Master silversmith.
Serralde, Bernardo	1757	*A.G. de la N. Ordenanzas*, vol.11, p.293 reverse. 1723-63. Examination 29th July. Master silversmith.
Servera, Francisco Joseph	1736	*A.G. de la N. Ordenanzas*, vol.11, p.120 reverse. 1723-63. Examination 7th September. Master silversmith.
Setadul, Francisco	1772	*A.G. de la N. Ordenanzas*, vol.16, p.42. 1764. Election 8th January. *Veedor* of silversmiths.
Sierra, Felix	1852	*Guía de Forasteros de la capital de Puebla, para el año de* 1852, op.cit. Silversmith.
Sierra, Joseph Francisco de	1732	*A.G. de la N. Ordenanzas*, vol.11, p.79. 1723-63. Examination 6th March. Master silversmith.
Sierra, Juan de	1753	*A.G. de la N. Civil indiferente*, vol.64. *Empadronamiento de* 1753. The pages of the book are not numbered. Silver-shop.
Sierra, Manuel Julian de la	1757	*A.G. de la N. Ordenanzas*, vol.11, p.292 reverse. 1723-63. Examination 16th February. Master silversmith.

Sierra y Adinolfo, Juan Ant. de	1758	*A.G. de la N. Ordenanzas*, vol.11, p.296. 1723-63. Examination 4th March. Master silversmith.
Sixmundo, Salvador	1753	*A.G. de la N. Civil indiferente*, vol.64. *Empadronamiento de* 1753. The pages of the book are not numbered. Unlicensed silversmith. (25 years of age.)
Solano y Ruiz, Jph.	1770	*A.G. de la N. Ordenanzas*, vol.16, p.25. 1764. Incorporation 12th July. Master silversmith. (City of Cadiz.)
Solórzano, Cristóbal	1864	*El Viajero en México*, op.cit. Silversmith. 1865 *A.G. de la N. Calif. de Establ. Indust.* Silver-shop. 1867 *Directorio del Comercio del Imperio Mexicano*, op.cit. Silver-shop.
Somonte, Juan	1773	*A.G. de la N. Ordenanzas*, vol.16, p.54 reverse. 1764. Examination 23rd June. Master silversmith.
Soria, Juan de	1753	*A.G. de la N. Civil indiferente*, vol.64. *Empadronamiento de* 1753. The pages of the book are not numbered. Unlicensed silversmith. (30 years of age.)
Soria y Bustamante, Juan de	1736	*A.G. de la N. Ordenanzas*, vol.11, p.118. 1723-63. Examination in August. Master silversmith.
Soriano, Bernabe	1754	*Guía de Forasteros en la Ciudad de Mégico*, op.cit. Silversmith.
Soriano, José María	1852	*Guía de Forasteros de la capital de Puebla, para el año de* 1852, op.cit. Silversmith.
Soriano, Manuel	1831	*A.G. de la N. Ramo de Hacienda.* Book which says: *Casa de Ensaye de México.* 1830-31. Bundle 45. Payment for stamping silversmiths' marks.
Soto, Antonio de	1732	*A.G. de la N. Ordenanzas*, vol.11, p.78. 1723-63. Examination 16th February. Master silversmith.
Soto, Domingo	1811	*A.G. de la N. Empadronamiento de* 1811. *Cuartel menor núm.*1. Silversmith. (30 years of age.)
Soto, Mariano	1864	*El Viajero en México*, op.cit. Silversmith.
Soto, Thomas de	1723	*A.G. de la N. Ordenanzas*, vol.11, p.5 reverse. 1723-63. Examination 20th May. Master silversmith.
Soto, Valentín de	1753	*A.G. de la N. Civil indiferente*, vol.64. *Empadronamiento de* 1753. The pages of the book are not numbered. Owner of silver-shop. (32 years of age.)
Soto, Valentín Dionicio de	1723	*A.G. de la N. Ordenanzas*, vol.11, p.97. 1723-63. Examination 13th May. Master silversmith.
Spina, Pedro de	1533	*Actas de Cabildo*, 24 *de Enero de* 1533. 'He was Assayer . . . appointed *Veedor* . . . then they delivered to him the mark and die of this city.'

Suares, José María	1789	*A.G. de la N. Ordenanzas*, vol.16, p.157 reverse. 1764. Examination 3rd June. Master silversmith.
Suárez, Agustín	1753	*A.G. de la N. Civil indiferente*, vol.64. *Empadronamiento de 1753*. The pages of the book are not numbered. Unlicensed silversmith. (30 years of age.)
Tabosa, Miguel de	1730	*A.G. de la N. Ordenanzas*, vol.11, p.58. 1723-63. Examination 5th June. Master silversmith.
Talledo, José Manuel	1778	*A.G. de la N. Ordenanzas*, vol.16, p.112. 1764. Examination 3rd October. Master silversmith.
Taña, Manuel	1753	*A.G. de la N. Civil indiferente*, vol.64. *Empadronamiento de 1753*. The pages of the book are not numbered. With a silver-store.
Tejada, Juan Manuel de	1728	*A.G. de la N. Ordenanzas*, vol.11, p.49. 1723-63. Examination 26th June. Master silversmith.
Tejeda, Francisco de	1560	*Actas de Cabildo, 24 de Enero 1560*. Silversmith.
Téllez, Ana A. Widow of Juan	1685	*El Gremio de Plateros en las Indias Occidentales*, op.cit., p.xxv. No.9. Silver-shop.
Tello Maneses, Jph. Miguel	1768	*A.G. de la N. Ordenanzas*, vol.16, p.18 reverse. 1764. Examination 18th November. Master silversmith.
Tello Meneces, José	1792	*A.G. de la N. Industria*, vol.5, p.255. Unlicensed silversmith.
Tineo, Manuel	1792	*A.G. de la N. Industria*, vol.5, p.255. Unlicensed silversmith.
Toledo, Francisco de	1582	*Las Artes Industriales en la Nueva España*, op.cit. Silversmith.
Toquero, Manuel Antonio	1790	*A.G. de la N. Ordenanzas*, vol.16, p.159. 1764. Examination 7th September. Master silversmith.
Toriz, Ignacio	1753	*A.G. de la N. Civil indiferente*, vol.64. *Empadronamiento de 1753*. The pages of the book are not numbered. Unlicensed silversmith. (25 years of age.)
Torralba, Manuel	1792	*A.G. de la N. Industria*, vol.5, p.255. Unlicensed silversmith.
Torre, Francisco de la	1792	*A.G. de la N. Industria*, vol.5, p.255. Unlicensed silversmith.
Torre, José María de la	1811	*A.G. de la N. Empadronamiento de 1811. Cuartel menor núm.1*. Silversmith. (26 years of age.)
Torre, Joseph de la	1786	*A.G. de la N. Ordenanzas*, vol.16, p.145 reverse. 1764. Election 29th January. *Veedor* of silversmiths. 1798 *Manual Común de 1798*. The pages of the book are not numbered. *Veedor* of silversmiths in Puebla.

Torre, Joseph de la	1798	*A.G. de la N. Guía de cargo y data de la Tesorería General de Ejército y real Hacienda de México. Para la cuenta del año de* 1798, p.8. Silversmith of Puebla.
Torre, Juan Manuel de	1760	*A.G. de la N. Ordenanzas*, vol.11, p.310 reverse. 1723-63. Examination 11th December. Master silversmith.
Torre, Manuel de la	1816	*A.G. de la N. Ordenanzas*, vol.16, p.201 reverse. 1764. Examination 29th June. Owner of silver-shop.
Torre, Mariano de la	1792	*A.G. de la N. Industria*, vol.5, p.255. Unlicensed silversmith. 1799 *Ordenanzas*, vol.16, p.186. 1764. Examination 4th October 1799. Owner of silver-shop.
Torre, Mariano de la	1831	*A.G. de la N.* Book which says: *Casa de Ensaye de México.* 1830-31. Bundle 45. Payment for stamping silversmiths' marks. 1836 document, 21st January 1836. Owner of silver-shop.
Torres, Domingo de	1657	*Archivo de Notarías de México.* Before Fernando Veedor, Public Scrivener. Master silversmith
Torres, Miguel	1792	*A.G. de la N. Industria*, vol.5, p.255. Unlicensed silversmith. 1800 *Las Artes Industriales en la Nueva España*, op.cit. and *Diccionario Universal*, etc., vol.6, p.488. Silversmith.
Tórrez, Joaquín	1811	*A.G. de la N. Empadronamiento de* 1811. *Cuartel menor núm.*1. Silversmith. (14 years of age.)
Tovar, Miguel	1854	*Guía de Forasteros en la Ciudad de Mégico, etc.*, op.cit. Silversmith. 1859 and 1864 *El Viajero en México para dichos años*, op.cit. Silversmith.
Tovar, Miguel	1865	*A.G. de la N. Calificación de establecimientos industriales.* Silver-shop. 1867 *Directorio del Comercio del Imperio Mexicano para el año de* 1867, op.cit. Silver-shop.
Tovar, Nicanor	1865	*A.G. de la N. Calificación de establecimientos industriales.* Silver-shop. 1867 *Directorio del Comercio del Imperio Mexicano para el año de* 1867, op.cit. Silver-shop.
Trejo, Eusebio	1842	*A.G. de la N. Padrón de establecimientos industriales. Cuartel menor núm.*1. Silver-shop. 1854 *Guía de Forasteros en la Ciudad de México*, op.cit. Silversmith.
Trigo, Josep de	1724	*A.G. de la N. Ordenanzas*, vol.11, p.12 reverse. 1723-63. Examination 9th November. Master silversmith.
Trueva, Pedro	1811	*A.G. de la N. Empadronamiento de* 1811. Silversmith. (22 years of age.)
Trujano, Melesio	1864	*El Viajero en México. Completa Guía de Forasteros para* 1864. Silversmith.

Trujeque, José María	1811	*A.G. de la N. Empadronamiento de* 1811. *Cuartel menor núm.*1. Silversmith. (20 years of age.)
Turcios, Lorenzo	1823	*A.G. de la N. Ordenanzas*, vol.11, p.97. 1723-63. Examination 7th August. Master silversmith.
Ugeña, Francisco de	1628	*Archivo de Notarías de México.* Before Antonio Alonso, Public Scrivener. 18th October. Goldsmith.
Ugía, Francisco	1792	*A.G. de la N. Industria*, vol.5, p.255. Unlicensed silversmith.
Unsueta, Francisco de	1745	*A.G. de la N. Ordenanzas*, vol.11, p.189 reverse. 1723-63. Examination 6th January. Drawer of gold [wire] Election 11th January. *Mayordomo.* (Vnsueta)
Urbina, Nemesio	1842	*A.G. de la N. Padrón de establecimientos industriales. Cuartel menor núm.*1. Silver-shop. 1854 *Guía de Forasteros, etc. para el año de* 1854, op.cit. Silversmith.
Urbina, Rafael de	1792	*A.G. de la N. Industria*, vol.5, p.255. Unlicensed silversmith.
Urbina, Ruperto	1854	*Guía de Forasteros en la Ciudad de Mégico, para el año de* 1854, op.cit. Silversmith.
Urcaga, Fermín de	1811	*A.G. de la N. Empadronamiento de* 1811. Silversmith. (29 years of age.)
Uriba, José	1792	*A.G. de la N. Industria*, vol.5, p.255. Unlicensed silversmith.
Urruchi, José Mariano	1811	*A.G. de la N. Empadronamiento de* 1811. *Cuartel menor núm.*1. Silversmith. (48 years of age.)
Urttado, Diego	1685	*El Gremio de Plateros en las Indias Occidentales*, op.cit., p.xxv. No.9. Silversmith. (Vrttado)
Usegueda, Vicente	1859	*El Viajero en México*, op.cit. Year 1859. Silversmith.
Vaez, Enrique	1535	*Colección de Documentos Inéditos para la Historia de Hispano América*, op.cit., book XIII, vol.II, p.289. Silversmith.
Valdés, Nicolás de	1685	*El Gremio de Plateros en las Indias Occidentales*, op.cit., p.xxv. No.9. Silversmith.
Valdez, José Mariano	1790	*A.G. de la N. Ordenanzas*, vol.16, p.159 reverse. 1764. Examination 16th September. Master silversmith.
Valdez y Anaya, Ygnacio	1788	*A.G. de la N. Ordenanzas*, vol.16, p.156 reverse. 1764. Examination 20th February. Master silversmith.
Valera, Pedro	1802	*A.G. de la N. Ordenanzas*, vol.16, p.191 reverse. 1764. Examination 8th January. Owner of silver-shop.

Valero, José	1811	*A.G. de la N. Empadronamiento de* 1811. Silversmith. (30 years of age.)
Vallejos, José	1753	*A.G. de la N. Civil indiferente*, vol.64. *Empadronamiento de* 1753. The pages of the book are not numbered. Owner of silver-shop.
Vallido, Manuel	1758	*Documentos para la Historia de México*, op.cit., 1st series, vol.6, p.246. 1760 *Las Artes Industriales en la Nueva España*, op.cit. Silversmith.
Vallín, José María	1792	*A.G. de la N. Industria.* vol.5, p.255. Unlicensed silversmith.
Valseca, Phelipe de	1723	*A.G. de la N. Ordenanzas*, vol.11, p.5. 1723-63. Examination 23rd April. Master silversmith.
Valtierra, Sebastián Eligio	1751	*A.G. de la N. Ordenanzas*, vol.11, p.260 reverse. Examination 22nd October. Master silversmith.
Vanegas, Rodrigo de	1589	*Indice de Documentos de Nueva España existentes en el Archivo de Indias de Sevilla*, op.cit., vol.IV, p.216. Silversmith.
Vanquilla, Juan de la	1685	*El Gremio de Plateros en las Indias Occidentales*, op.cit., p.xxv. No.9. Silversmith.
Varela, Pedro	1811	*A.G. de la N. Empadronamiento de* 1811. Silversmith. (39 years of age. Italy.)
Vargas, Francisco	1864	*El Viajero en México*, op.cit. Silversmith.
Vargas, José Agustín de	1799	*A.G. de la N. Ordenanzas*, vol.16, p.185 reverse. 1764. Examination 22nd April. Owner of silver-shop.
Vargas, Vicente de	1758	*A.G. de la N. Ordenanzas*, vol.11, p.296. 1723-63. Examination 28th February. Master silversmith.
Varrera, Manuel Joseph	1723	*A.G. de la N. Ordenanzas*, vol.11, p.4 reverse. 1723-63. Examination 11th March. Master silversmith.
Vásquez, Gregorio	1796	*A.G. de la N. Derechos de oro de fuego*, p.7. Drawer of gold [wire] of this city.
Vázques, Diego	1685	*El Gremio de Plateros en las Indias Occidentales*, op.cit., p.xxv. No.9. Drawer of gold [wire].
Vázquez, Juan	1576	*A.G. de la N. Ordenanzas*, vol.1, p.117. Years 1575-76. Examination 26th January. License for silver-shop.
Vega, Emilio	1854	*El Viajero en México. Completa Guía de Forasteros para* 1864, op.cit. Silversmith.
Vega, Joseph de la	1685	*El Gremio de Plateros en las Indias Occidentales*, op.cit., p.xxv. No.9. Goldsmith.
Vega, Ignacio	1854	*Guía de Forasteros en la Ciudad de Mégico*, op.cit. Silversmith.
Vega, Pedro de	1580	*A.G. de la N. Ordenanzas*, vol.11, p.131. Years 1579-80. Examination 20th February. Master silversmith.

Vega, Pomposo	1854	*Guía de Forasteros en la Ciudad de Mégico*, op.cit. Silversmith.
Vega, Simón Lazo de la	1737	*A.G. de la N. Ordenanzas*, vol.11, p.123. 1723-63. Examination 16th May. Master silversmith.
Vega Yerque, Marcos	1721	*A.G. de la N. Ordenanzas*, vol.10, p.109 reverse. 1714-22. Examination 15th November. Master silversmith.
Velarde, Apolonio	1882	*Nueva Guía de México. Año de 1882*, op.cit., p.833. Silver-shop.
Velarde, Francisco	1852	*Guía de Forasteros de la capital de Puebla, para el año de 1852*, op.cit. Silversmith.
Velarde, Joaquín	1852	*Guía de Forasteros de la capital de Puebla, para el año de 1852*, op.cit. Silversmith.
Velasco, José	1859	*El Viajero en México*, op.cit. Diamond setter. 1864 *El Viajero en México, para 1864*, op.cit. Silversmith. 1865 *A.G. de la N. Calif. Est. Industriales*. Silver-shop.
Velasco, José	1867	*Directorio del Comercio del Imperio Mexicano, para el año de 1867*, op.cit. Silver-shop. (Velasco or Velázquez)
Velasco, Mariano	1792	*A.G. de la N. Industria*, vol.5, p.255. Unlicensed silversmith.
Velasco, Pedro	1792	*A.G. de la N. Industria*, vol.5, p.255. Unlicensed silversmith.
Velasco, Seberiano	1842	*A.G. de la N. Padrón de establecimientos industriales. Cuartel menor núm.1.* Silver-shop.
Velásquez, Cristoval Mariano	1793	*A.G. de la N. Ordenanzas*, vol.16, p.175. 1764. Examination 11th July. Master silversmith.
Velázquez, Lorenzo	1792	*A.G. de la N. Industria*, vol.5, p.255. Unlicensed silversmith.
Veles, Andrés	1735	*A.G. de la N. Ordenanzas*, vol.11, p.113. 1723-63. Examination 4th October. Master silversmith.
Vélez, Pedro	1792	*A.G. de la N. Industria*, vol.5, p.255. Unlicensed silversmith.
Veltran, Juan Joseph	1753	*A.G. de la N. Ordenanzas*, vol.11, p.265. 1723-63. Examination 14th May. Master silversmith.
Venegas, Francisco	1748	*A.G. de la N. Ordenanzas*, vol.11, p.247. 1723-63. Examination 21st August. Master silversmith.
Venitez, Manuel	1727	and 1745 *A.G. de la N. Ordenanzas*, vol.11, pp.37 and 189 reverse. 1723-63. Election 13th January 1727. *Mayordomo* and 11th January 1745 *Diputado*.
Venitez de Aranda, Manuel	1725	*A.G. de la N. Ordenanzas*, vol.11, p.34. 1723-63. Examination 12th September. Master silversmith.
Vera, José	1798	*A.G. de la N. Guía de cargo y data de la Tesorería General de Ejercito y Real Hacienda de Méjico. Para la cuenta del año de 1798*, p.13

reverse. Silversmith. 1811. *Empadronamiento de 1811.* (45 years of age.)

Vera, Patricio	1811	*A.G. de la N. Empadronamiento de* 1811. Silversmith. (40 years of age.)
Vera, Próspero	1865	*A.G. de la N. Calificación de establecimientos industriales.* Silver-shop. 1867 *Directorio del Comercio del Imperio Mexicano para el año de* 1867, op.cit. Silver-shop.
Vera Guerrero, José de	1790	*A.G. de la N. Ordenanzas*, vol.16, p.159. 1764. Examination 22nd March. Master silversmith.
Verdeja, N.	1854	*Guía de Forasteros en la Ciudad de Mégico, para el año de* 1854, op.cit. Silversmith.
Verdejo y Santa Cruz, Manuel	1720	*A.G. de la N. Ordenanzas*, vol.10. 1714-22. Examination. Master sheet-beater. 1727 *Ord.,* vol.II, p.37. 1723-1763. Election 13th January. *Mayordomo.*
Verdugo, Diego	1591	*A.G. de la N. General de Parte*, vol.4, p.73. 1590-91. Examination 11th February. License for public store.
Vergara, Josef de	1685	*La Estrella del Norte de México etc.*, p.685. By Father Francisco de Florencia. Madrid. And *El Gremio de Plateros en las Indias Occidentales,* op.cit., p.xxix. No.9. Silversmith.
Vergara, Josef de	1695	*A.G. de la N. Ordenanzas*, vol.6, p.13 reverse. 1686-98. License for silver-shop. (*Alf.r*)
Vergara, Juan de	1685	*El Gremio de Plateros en las Indias Occidentales,* op.cit., p.xxv No.9. 1701 *Pregones de Ordenanzas de el Nobilissimo Arte de la Platería*, op.cit. *Mayordomo* of the art, etc.
Vergara, Nicolás	1685	*El Gremio de Plateros en las Indias Occidentales,* op.cit., p.xxv No.9. Silversmith.
Verta, José de	1791	*A.G. de la N. Ordenanzas*, vol.16, p.166 reverse. 1764. Examination 27th July. Master silversmith. 1796 *Derecho de oro de fuego*, p.7. Silversmith of this city.
Vezerra, Fran.co	1685	*El Gremio de Plateros en las Indias Occidentales,* op.cit., p.xxv No.9. Silversmith. (Captain.)
Victoria, Juan de	1564	*Archivo de Notarías de México.* Before Antonio Alonso, Public Scrivener. 1564. Silversmith.
Victorio, Diego de	1685	*El Gremio de Plateros en las Indias Occidentales,* op.cit., p.xxv No.9. Sheet-beater.
Vidarte, Mariano de	1774	*A.G. de la N. Ordenanzas*, vol.16, p.67. 1764. Examination 10th October. Owner of silver-shop.
Vieira, Ignacio	1831	*A.G. de la N. Ramo de Hda.* Book which says: *Casa de Ensaye de México.* 1830-31. Bundle 45. Payment for stamping silversmiths' marks. 1842 *Padrón de Est. Indust. Cuartel menor No.1.* Silversmith.

Vilches, Pedro de	1744	*A.G. de la N. Ordenanzas*, vol.11, p.186. 1723-63. Examination 27th October. Master silversmith.
Villafañe, Antonio de	1803	*Diccionario Universal, etc.*, vol.6, p.487 and *Las Artes Industriales* en la Nueva España, op.cit. He engraved the Monstrance of Puebla.
Villanueva, Marcos	1854	*Guía de Forasteros en la Ciudad de Mégico, para el año de* 1854, op.cit. Silversmith.
Villarreal, Joaquín	1778	*A.G. de la N. Ordenanzas*, vol.16, p.106. 1764. Examination 28th February. Owner of silver-shop. 1781 *Documentos para la Historia de México*, op.cit., vol.7, p.115. (Joachin.)
Villarreal, Joaquín	1786	*Gazeta de México* 14th March 1786. 1799 *A.G. de la N. Ordenanzas*, vol.16, p.185 reverse. 1764. Election 9th January. *Veedor* of silversmiths.
Villarreal, Juan	1792	*A.G. de la N. Industria*, vol.5, p.255. Unlicensed silversmith.
Villarreal, Manuel	1792	*A.G. de la N. Industria*, vol.5, p.255. Unlicensed silversmith.
Villasana, Gabriel	1544	1546 and 1551 *Actas de Cabildo, 3 de Julio* 1544, *9 de Febrero de* 1546 *y* 24 *de Julio de* 1551. Named *Veedor* (Billasaña, Grabiel) 1572 *Historia de Real Hda.*, op.cit., vol.I, p.393.
Villasana, Gabriel	1587	*A.G. de la N. General de parte*, vol.III, p.59. 1587-8. *Veedor* of silversmiths.
Villaseñor, Joaquín	1882	*Nueva Guía de México en inglés, francés y castellano, etc. Año de* 1882, op.cit., p.833. Silver-shop.
Villavicencio, Joaquín	1864	*El Viajero en México*, op.cit. Silversmith. 1865 *A.G. de la N. Calif. de Est. Indust.* Silver-shop. 1867 *Directorio del Comercio del Imperio Mexicano*, op.cit. Silver-shop.
Villavicencio, Juan de	1628	*Actas de Cabildo, 23 de Octubre de* 1628. Silversmith and marker.
Villavicencio, Mariano	1805	*A.G. de la N. Ordenanzas*, vol.16, p.194 reverse. 1764. Examination 11th October. Owner of silver-shop.
Villegas, Agustín	1792	*A.G. de la N. Industria*, vol.5, p.255. Unlicensed silversmith.
Villegas, Antonio Anizeto de	1748	*A.G. de la N. Ordenanzas*, vol.11, p.238. 1723-63. Examination 12th March. Master silversmith.
Villegas, Francisco	1792	*A.G. de la N. Industria*, vol.5, p.255. Unlicensed silversmith. 1799 *Ordenanzas*, vol.16, p.186 reverse. 1764. Examination 20th December. Owner of silver-shop.
Villegas, Jph. Ant.o	1786	*A.G. de la N. Ordenanzas*, vol.16, p.145 reverse. 1764. Examination 9th February. Master silversmith.

Ximenes, Adrian	1713	*Pleito de Rada de* 1713, op.cit. Silversmith. 1745 and 1747 *A.G. de la N.*, vol.11, pp.189 reverse and 232. 1723-63. Election 11th January, 1745 and 27th January 1747. *Veedor.*
Ximenez, Cristoual	1601	*A.G. de la N. General de Parte. Años* 1599-1601, vol.5, p.277. Examination 5th February. License for store.
Ybañez, Vicente	1781	*A.G. de la N. Ordenanzas*, vol.16, p.121. 1764. Examination 13th October. Master silversmith.
Yglesias, Jph. de	1773	*A.G. de la N. Ordenanzas*, vol.16, p.51 reverse. 1764. Examination 18th May. Master silversmith. 1782 *Ordenanzas*, vol.16, p.122. 1764. Election 11th January. *Veedor* of silversmiths.
Yñigo, Diego de	1694	*A.G. de la N. Ordenanzas*, vol.6, p.16. 1686 to 1698. License for Silver-shop. 1696 *El Gremio de Plateros en las Indias Occidentales*, op.cit. Silversmith.
Yoppe, Francisco	1865	*A.G. de la N. Calificación de establecimientos industriales*. Silver-shop. 1867 *Directorio del Comercio del Imperio Mexicano*, op.cit. Silver-shop. (Yopp.)
Ysunza, José	1803	*Poblanos Ilustres*, op.cit., pp.121-2. Puebla 1910. Silversmith and *Diccionario Universal, etc.*, op.cit., vol.6, pp.484 and 487.
Ysunza y Vega, Jph. Mariano	1780	*A.G. de la N. Ordenanzas*, vol.16, p.116. 1764. Examination 29th May. Master silversmith.
Zabala, Francisco	1842	*A.G. de la N. Padrón de establecimientos industriales. Cuartel menor núm.*1. Silver-work shop.
Zaldivar, Anacleto	1854	*Guía de Forasteros en la Ciudad de Mégico, etc.* Silversmith. 1859 *El Viajero en México*, op.cit. Silversmith. 1865 *A.G. de la N. Calif. de Est. Industriales.* Silver-shop.
Zaldivar, Angel	1859	*El Viajero en México*, op.cit. Year 1859. Silversmith.
Zamora, Luis	1854	*Guía de Forasteros en la Ciudad de Mégico, para el año de* 1854, op.cit. Silversmith.
Zamorano, Antonio	1723	*A.G. de la N. Ordenanzas*, vol.II, p.8 reverse. 1723-63. Examination 26th August. Master silversmith.
Zamudio, Diego	1685	*El Gremio de Plateros en las Indias Occidentales*, op.cit., p.xxv No.9. Goldsmith. 1694 *A.G. de la N. Ordenanzas*, vol.6, p.15. 1686-98. 21st April. License for silver-shop.
Zárate, Perfecto	1864	*El Viajero en México. Completa Guía de Forasteros para* 1864. Silversmith. 1885. *A.G. de*

		la N. *Calificación de establecimientos industriales. Est. de Plateros.* Silver-shop.
Zárate, Perfecto	1867	*Directorio del Comercio del Imperio Mexicano para el año de* 1867, op.cit. Silver-shop.
Zauallos, Ramón	1685	*El Gremio de Plateros en las Indias Occidentales,* op.cit., p.xxv. No.9. Silversmith.
Zedillo, Pedro	1685	*El Gremio de Plateros en las Indias Occidentales,* op.cit., p.xxv. No.9. Silversmith.
Zendejas, Cecilio	1859	*El Viajero en México, para el año de* 1859, op.cit. Silversmith.
Zendejas, Joaquín	1854	*Guía de Forasteros en la Ciudad de Mégico, para el año de* 1854. Silversmith. 1864 *El Viajero en México. Completa Guía de Forasteros para* 1864, op.cit. Silversmith.
Zendejas, Joaquín	1865	A.G. de la N. *Calificación de establecimientos industriales.* 1865. Silver-shop. 1867 *Directorio del Comercio del Imperio Mexicano, para el año de* 1867, op.cit. Silver-shop.
Zierra, Antonio de	1761	A.G. de la N. *Ordenanzas,* vol.11, p.316 reverse. 1723-63. Examination 20th June. Master silversmith.
Zizona, José de	1783	A.G. de la N. *Ordenanzas,* vol.16, p.132. 1764. Examination 9th July. Master silversmith.
Zuleta, Filomeno	1859	*El Viajero en México. Año de* 1859, op.cit. Silversmith.
Zurbano, Antonio	1723	A.G. de la N. *Ordenanzas,* vol.11, p.3 reverse. 1723-63. Examination 14th April. Master silversmith.

Appendix II

ORDINANCES RELATIVE TO THE SILVERSMITHS' ART[1]

Lope Diez De Armendariz, Marquis of Cadereyta, of His Majesty's Council of War, his *Mayordomo*, and Substitute Viceroy-Governor and Captain-General of this New Spain and President of the Tribunal and Royal Chancery who resides therein etc. Whereas, on the twenty-seventh of August of this year, Julio Sanchez Requesso, *Mayordomo* of the guild of the silversmiths' art of this City of Mexico, in his name and that of the other goldsmiths, sheet-beaters and drawers, presented to me the petition and the command of the Marquis of Guadalcazar of September seventh one thousand six hundred and nineteen. [This command was] relative to the afore-said having their workmen and stores on San Francisco street and its other con-tents, as well as the ordinances which said guild issued last year, one thousand six hundred and twenty three. For the good use and exercise of their trades and crafts, for greater service to His Majesty, the increase of his Royal Taxes and for the good and profit of this Republic [sic], excusing and removing therefrom, as far as possible, the means and tricks which are used to defraud, the Marquis of Gelues confirmed them and approved and ordered them to be kept, complied with and executed, requesting me to please thus command; that, because said ordinances had been maliciously concealed and had not been carried out, there had resulted and were resulting greater and more considerable difficulties each day and in order to over-come such great disorder as has existed and still exists, according to my under-standing from written advices which have been given me and [also from] investi-gations conducted by my order by Dr. Mathias de Peralta, judge of this Royal Tribunal [aided by] individuals skillful in the art, zealous in the service of God our Lord and of His Majesty, [and eager to] increase his Royal Taxes in the public and private welfare; [in order] that from now henceforth these shall cease and, con-cerning a matter so grave and of such importance, the efficacious remedy required may be applied, it has seemed to me proper to confirm, in part, some of said ordi-nances, amend others and add, with heavier penalties, those which men's cunning and time have shown to be needful and necessary. [These are] stated below with complete precision and clarity and shall be executed publicly and irremissibly

---

[1] *Archivo General de la Nacion. Reales Cédulas. Planta Alta. Años* 1645-1673, vol.58, pp.122-37. Punctua-tion, almost completely lacking in the original, is the author's.

against those who transgress them as an example to the Republic and warning to those who attempt to break them.

> 1st ordinance approves the brotherhood and its devotion in
> celebrating the feast of San Eligio their patron.

First, I approve and deem fitting that the goldsmiths and silversmiths, sheet-beaters and drawers continue with their brotherhood and the devotion with which they celebrate each year the feast of the glorious San Eligio their patron, which in previous years was originated by them. [They shall] endeavor that it be with all solemnity and splendor possible for the greater service of God, our Lord, and devotion to the saint.

> 2nd ordinance, the number of officers, who, at the beginning
> of each year, are to be elected.

Furthermore, so that in this guild and craft of the silversmiths there may be good order and harmony and it may be conducted with the punctuality and legality which is right and proper, I order and command that there shall be a rector, two *mayordomos* and five *diputados*. [This] so that, in accordance with these ordinances, they may perform their duties with diligence, care and without fail. With the knowledge that, if they attempt to conceal any transgression against all or part of what is provided and ordered by the ordinances, they shall be punished according to the gravity of the offense.

> 3rd ordinance, the place and location where the election is
> to be held and the form thereof.

Furthermore, I order and command that the first day of each year, in the building where the rector resides and, in his absence or inability, in that of one of the *mayordomos*, they shall gather with the *diputados* to conduct their election. [There they] shall elect others to take the places of those holding all the offices of said guild, in order that all may enjoy them equally. They shall proceed in peace and without passion [or personal] interest, seeing only that they [those elected] be members of and experts in their craft, of good conduct and conscience and zealous of the public welfare, for they are the ones who are to approve [those] others, who shall have public shops of their trade. Otherwise said election shall be null and void.

> 4th ordinance that they shall not postpone the election of
> officers for another day nor reelect those whose terms have
> expired, except in the manner provided.

Furthermore, I order and command that, if because of illness, absence or other legitimate impediment, the rector or any of the *mayordomos* or *diputados* cannot be present the day of the election, the others who are certain of this, the day prior to the election, may name others in their place for the sole purpose of having the full number of votes and hold the election. They shall not postpone it for another day under the pretext of not being satisfied. Also those whose terms expire cannot be reelected with the exception of the rector, if they so desire, as because of his good qualities and experience this may be proper. The two *mayordomos*, whose terms expire, may become *diputados* and two of the *diputados* may be elected *mayordomos* and always, according to this order, with the understanding that they cannot enjoy these alternatives successively. If this procedure is not carried out in said election and [likewise if] the government is not asked to conform the elections within eight days, it shall be null and void, and the government may appoint others to take their places at the expiration of their terms. Penalty for non-compliance with this ordinance, shall be a fine of twenty-five *pesos* each, which I [shall] contribute towards the expenses of their brotherhood.

> 5th ordinance that, when differences of opinion arise, they
> shall gather together and summon the oldest and the others.

Furthermore, I order and command that said rector, *mayordomos* and *diputados* shall summon the oldest [silversmith], although it is not necessary that all the members of the guild be present, to treat and confer concerning what is required to mediate and settle the differences which may arise regarding their offices. Whatever is thus arranged and agreed upon, shall be complied with and executed—but not in that which relates to fraud in Royal Taxes and deficiency in the standard of purity of the metal for, however small [such fraud or deficiency] may be, they are not empowered or authorized for that purpose, even though their interest be satisfied. [In such cases] proceedings shall be instituted, before a public or Royal Scrivener of this City. Having effected the preparatory proceeding, it shall be sent and taken to the judge of first instance and a certificate shall be taken of having done this, so that he may continue the proceedings, conclude them and hand down sentence, in conformity with these ordinances, and advise His Majesty's Attorney thereof and of the gravity of the case. Thus he may be informed and the offenders shall not, through negotiations, avoid or delay their sentences. The penalty for failure to do this is a fine of one hundred *pesos* of common gold for each of the aforesaid, half for His Majesty's Exchequer and Treasury, and the other half to be divided into four parts. One [part] for the judge who hands down the sentence, two for the informer and the other for the expenses of their brotherhood and celebration of their saint's feast day; for a second infraction the fine shall be doubled and [the infractor shall be] exiled for three years from this court and twenty leagues surrounding it.

6th ordinance that the *mayordomos* shall have three books
in which to record the brotherhood alms collected and how
these are spent and account of same shall be kept.

Furthermore, that there be no error or fraud in the distribution and spending
of the alms that may be collected during the year, and of the bequests and pious
legacies which may be made to said brotherhood: I order and command that its
mayordomos shall be obliged to keep three books, with good bindings, numbered
and rubricated by them and the other officers, which shall be kept and guarded
carefully. So that in one may be recorded the members, in the other the bequests
and pious legacies and the alms which each week are solicited, with clearness and
indicating the person who begged and collected them and in the other [the third],
the account and statement of how and for what purpose they [the funds] were
spent and distributed. And, every four months, the other officers shall ascertain
whether what has thus been spent is for the profit and welfare of their brotherhood,
and, if not, shall apply the proper remedy and, when the terms of the *mayordomos*
have expired, those who are elected to take their places, shall examine the accounts
and learn whether they failed to make any entry or entries so that they [the former
mayordomos] jointly may pay the total of the penalty, in addition to the interest
and damages incurred, of fifty *pesos* of ordinary gold for each, who fail to carry out
everything embodied in this ordinance, which I apply to the expenses of their
brotherhood.

And, in as much as the mines and veins where gold and silver, mercury and other
metals and precious stones are created and the pearl fisheries belong to the Crown
and Royal Patrimony and His Majesty, with his usual liberality and kindness, in
order that the discoverers and inhabitants and those who for a period of time went
there, shall avail and enrich themselves and the land may be populated and its
provinces ennobled, gave permission for the land to be tilled and improved and for
pearls to be bartered and to have pearl fisheries, as is seen by Order of tenth of
December, one thousand five hundred and twelve and another of ninth of December, one thousand five hundred and twenty-six, which are in the third part of those
printed on pages 356-9, provided that, on everything obtained, they pay the net
Royal Fifth Tax and although this is just and right, many persons, with damage
to their consciences, by different means and tricks, defraud the [King of his] Royal
Fifth Tax, especially on gold and silver, from which they make jewels and plate for
the service of their homes, ornament and adornment of their persons and wives,
which by order, of the second of September of one thousand five hundred and
fifty-nine, is forbidden them, if said gold and silver is not taxed and marked. [There
were] heavy penalties for keeping this excess, so much so, that, in the beginning, it
was commanded that no silversmith could practice his trade under penalty of death
and by order of the ninth of November, one thousand five hundred and twenty-six

and another of twenty-first August, one thousand five hundred and twenty-eight, they were given permission, provided they did not have bellows, forges nor crucibles in their stores, or refine metals except in the mint in the presence of the *veedor* and Royal Officials under pain of death and loss of property.

Even this severity has not been sufficient; on the contrary, crime and disorder continue in the gold and silver mining districts of this New Spain, despite the kindness of His Majesty and [the leniency of the] regulating ordinances. The miners pay 10 per cent instead of the Royal Fifth Tax and because, [it is] desired that they should continue the work, performed for their benefit by the Indians and other persons in the mines, with more comfort and enjoyment of their greater advantages, the circulation of bartered silver, and that on which the 10 per cent tax has been paid, has been tolerated and allowed, in spite of the prohibition and penalty of forfeiture if it is used in other places without first having paid the Royal Fifth Tax thereon. The excessive cupidity of those who traffic in and profit by the considerable interests involved [causes them to] take advantage of secret and ingenious means, which encourage them daringly and boldly to break the laws of the Kingdom and ordinances which prohibit [such traffic] without fear of oppressing their consciences or fear of incurring the severe penalties imposed. They hide and send it to Spain and to the Philippine Islands, where it is circulated at the same value as if the Royal Fifth Tax had been paid thereon, thereby defrauding His Majesty of his Royal Fifth Tax and duties, which would pertain to him. This would amount to a large sum of thousands [of *pesos*]. I have understood, through advices and statements which have been given me, that on the metal used in this city alone by the silversmiths for plate and many large and small single pieces which they make and sell year after year, the Royal Fifth Tax thereby defrauded would amount to more than fifty thousand *pesos* and fifteen thousand more from that made and used in settings, decorations and nails for slippers and other things. This results in harm and injury to the Republic and to private individuals through purchase of these objects at their just price, although not worth it, because they lack hallmarks. This deceit and open theft requires an effective remedy and so that from now henceforth this may be, the following is ordered:

> 7th ordinance that on all kinds of gold and silver jewels the
> Royal Fifth Tax, due His Majesty, shall be paid.

First, I order and command that on all silver and gold, which from now on is fabricated or made into plate, tables, water-jugs, pitchers, railings, writing tables, small desks and candle-holders for platforms, pans, chambers, moulds, jugs, chocolate jugs, and water heaters and other plate and objects of whatsoever kind, quality and design which are used in the homes of this New Spain and other finery and adornment of any kind of images, sheets of metal, tabernacles, paintings and oratories, mirrors, bureaus, metal plates and nails for clogs, jewels of gold collars, belts, bracelets, brooches, necklaces, chains, bands, buttons, rings, or in whatsoever other manner fabricated of silver or gold, His Majesty's Royal Fifth Tax shall be paid thereon under penalties set forth in these ordinances.

8th ordinance, the method to be observed by the silver-smiths as well as the *veedor* and Royal Officials, in order that the Royal Fifth Tax shall not be defrauded.

Furthermore, in order that no one shall defraud the Royal Fifth Tax and that it be known that it has been paid, I order and command that any silversmith, sheet-beater or drawer or any other person, of whatsoever quality and condition, who desires to make or have made jewels and objects mentioned in the preceding ordinance, shall be obliged to take and shall take and present to the Royal Officials of the Treasury from the place or town where they reside, and where there are no officials the nearest ones, the silver and gold, which is to be made and fabricated into the aforesaid articles or any of them. And said Royal Officials shall see that the Royal Fifth Tax is paid thereon and [the plate] marked and, if this has not been done, to have the taxes paid, weigh, record and register in the separate book, which for this purpose they shall keep, the amount thereof and the objects and things which the silversmith, sheet-beater and drawer or anyone else registering same shall state they wish to have made and by which silversmith. And, after this has been done, the metal shall be returned with a certificate and statement of having been recorded and registered. Such person, silversmith, sheet-beater or drawer, shall obligate himself to bring the fabricated objects again to the same Royal Officials, so that their weight may be compared with that of the ingots which were stamped with the tax mark, the entry to be noted on the margin. So that there shall always be an account and statement of their value and they can ascertain whether they are of the same standard and, this being verified, the *veedor*, in the presence of said Royal Officials, shall mark same with the mark and symbol, which for this purpose they should have of a size proportionate to the object, so that however small it may be, it shall not lack hall-marks so that it may be known forever that it is of the required standard and the Royal Fifth Tax thereon has been paid, without which, the objects cannot be owned or used nor can any silversmith, sheet-beater, drawer, Spaniard, mestizo, Indian, mulatto or Negro, fabricate the metal unless they know, by the said certificate of the Royal Officials, that it has been registered with them as prescribed. The penalty, for the first infraction, is payment of the Royal Fifth Tax jointly, by the silversmiths and owners. For the second infraction they shall incur the penalty imposed on those who defraud the Royal Fifth Tax according to Royal Order of fifteenth of October, one thousand five hundred and eighty-four, of those printed in the third part, page 362.

9th ordinance that gold, of less than twenty-two carats
standard, cannot be fabricated, with penalties for infractions.

Furthermore, I order and command that no goldsmith may fabricate gold,
whether his own or another's, of less than twenty-two carats standard which is the
value of the *castellano* in this Kingdom [that is,] by Royal decree, seventeen *reales*
less two *maravedis*. For the deceit of fabricating it of the standard and carats they
may desire, from twenty-four to twelve, into objects such as chains, necklaces,
buttons, rings and any other jewels whatsoever [and the worst is that, those they
have manufactured and finished, they sell as if they were of the legal standard].
The penalty for the first sale of any jewel represented as of twenty-four carats,
which is excellent gold, if found to be of twenty-two or twenty carats, shall be the
loss of three times the doubled value of the carats which are lacking, to be paid by
the purchaser. The same penalty shall apply when it is sold for twenty-two carats
and is not of this standard. For the second infraction, the jewel [and plate] or jewels
shall be forfeited and their value applied to His Majesty's Exchequer and to Treasury,
[and to] *veedor* and informer, a third to each. For the third infraction he shall not be
allowed to fabricate nor shall he fabricate objects of gold for a period of six years. If
this penalty is not complied with, he shall forfeit all his property whose value shall
be applied in the manner above stated.

10th ordinance that the caster shall not cast any object of
gold of less than twenty-two carats standard and what he
shall do.

Furthermore, I order and command, in view of the fact that everything manufactured of gold in the silver shops is cast, such as shields, brooches, buttons and
other jewels of this kind, the present and future casters, from now henceforth, shall
not cast them of gold, supplied him by the silversmiths, that is not of the standard
of twenty-two carats and known by him to have been registered in the manner
provided by ordinances sixth and seventh. He shall have the obligation of returning it and advising the *veedor* of having done so, as well as of the objects which he
has cast and to whom they belong. He shall keep a book, in which he shall record
them clearly and precisely. The penalty for infraction being fifty *pesos* for each
object found cast of gold of less than the legal standard and not conforming to the
above mentioned requisites. For the second infraction, double the amount and for
the third, as much more and four years' suspension from office and exile from this
court and five leagues surrounding it.

11th ordinance that the jewels of gold, without diamonds,
shall be sold by weight and their fabrication agreed upon
separately.

Furthermore, I order and command that rings set with precious stones, *jazmines*,
ear-rings, rings and other jewels of this kind, shall be of gold of the standard of
twenty-two carats and in addition the artisans who fabricate them, if they are not
of diamonds, rubies, emeralds and other precious stones, shall not sell them except
by weight. The cost of their fabrication shall be agreed upon and shall be estimated
in accordance with the new Royal Ordinance by the *veedor*, rector and *mayordomos*;
the penalty being twenty *pesos* fine for each infraction, which I shall apply to the
above mentioned and to their brotherhood in equal parts.

12th ordinance that no jewels shall be made of silver or gilt
bronze with fine enamels.

Furthermore, I order and command that, as much fraud occurs when rings with
precious stones, ear-rings, buttons and other kinds of objects of silver or gilt bronze
and with fine enamels are fabricated and sold, and in order that this may not occur,
no silversmith shall make and fabricate or sell them under penalty of a fine of
thirty *pesos* for each infraction, which I shall apply in the manner stated in the
preceding ordinance.

13th ordinance that handles or double handles of silver or
gilt copper shall not be placed on objects that are fabricated.

Furthermore, I order and command that jewels of gold, fabricated by the artisans,
shall not have handles or double handles of silver or gilt copper on account of fraud
and deceit to those purchasing them, who pay their just value, as if they were of
gold of the required standard. Penalty for the first infraction is twenty *pesos* and
for the second, forty [*pesos*] and for the third, sixty [*pesos*] which I apply to His
Majesty's Exchequer and Treasury and informer, a half to each.

14th ordinance that as there are no mines of diamonds,
rubies, emeralds and other precious stones or pearl fisheries
in this New Spain, the provisions of this ordinance shall be
observed.

Furthermore, although the mines and veins where gold and silver, mercury and
other metals are created and precious stones and pearl fisheries belong to the Crown
and Royal Patrimony, His Majesty, with his customary liberality and kindness,

permitted his vassals to work them provided they paid the Royal Fifth Tax on everything extracted therefrom. And as they come [some precious stones and metals] to this New spain from *Margarita*, *Cubagua*[1], the Continent, Philippines and other provinces of the Royal Crown and should pay the Royal Fifth Tax in the places where the metals are extracted, and as the gold, pearls, jewels and other precious stones should come registered with the statement of having paid the tax, in accordance with, and in the manner provided by the orders and ordinances on the subject. These are [to be found] under the heading of the Royal Fifth Tax on gold and silver of book 30, of the printed decrees from page 357 to 390, in which are included the ordinances for the Royal Officials on the collection of the taxes in the ports and their registry as well as the courses to be followed and lacking these requisites the application to be made of the pearls and other things which have not been registered. With respect to the aforesaid and the Royal Fifth Tax which should have been paid on said goods and form of registry which they should bring, so as not to forfeit them and have them applied to His Majesty: in these ordinances no provision is made nor is anything changed of that commanded by said orders and ordinances above mentioned, which shall be kept and executed in the cases cited and these ordinances in no way alter or change anything.

> 15th ordinance that on chains, jewels and other objects of
> gold and silver which are brought from China the provisions
> of the preceding ordinance be observed.

Furthermore, in consideration of the fact that vessels, which come from the Philippine Islands every year, in addition to cargoes of rich merchandise, bring many chains, neck chains, bands, buttons, and other jewels of various kinds and makes of gold and silver without having been registered, and whose value is considerable [although their gold content is not of many carats, the highest scarcely reaching eighteen and nineteen carats], because of their extremely curious fabrication, payment of the *castellano* of said objects is made at twenty-five, thirty and forty *reales*. If registered, the duties for His Majesty at the valuation placed thereon in the Port of Acapulco would amount to a great sum. I order and command that, from now henceforth, such fraud shall cease and that there shall be no disorder and that the provisions of this ordinance be complied with and the penalties imposed in the orders and ordinances, mentioned in the preceding one, be executed.

> 16th ordinance that, although approval may have been given,
> goldsmiths shall not have stores or work-shops for jewels
> without a government license.

---

1 An island near the coast of Venezuela. The first land in that region colonized by the Spaniards. The surrounding waters were rich in pearls.

Furthermore, I order and command that, although goldsmiths may have the approval of the *veedor*, rector, *mayordomos* and *diputados*, they shall not open stores of their craft or have therein workshops of jewels without a government license. The penalty is a hundred *pesos* fine for His Majesty's Exchequer and Treasury, judge and informer, a third to each.

> 17th ordinance, that gold and silversmiths shall have a known mark and symbol to stamp on the objects made by them.

Furthermore, I order and command, in order to prevent fraud and that there may be greater facility in punishing silversmiths who make objects of gold and silver of less than the legal standard, that they shall be obliged to have a known symbol or mark of their name, which they shall register with the Public Scrivener of the Municipal Council of this City of Mexico. From him they shall get a certificate of having done this, which they shall keep for their safety and which shall also be recorded and written in one of the books of the council. On objects they make, either for themselves or others, which are sufficiently large, they shall stamp their mark and without it they can not sell, trade, raffle, exchange or donate them under penalty of incurring in the fines imposed on those who use false weight and no one may purchase the objects under penalty of a fine of thirty *pesos* applied to the Exchequer, judge and informer, a third to each.

> 18th ordinance that the *veedor* shall not receive any piece of gold or silver unless it has the symbol or mark of the artisan who made it.

Furthermore, I order and command for better compliance and execution of what is prescribed and ordered, that, at the time and whenever there are taken to the Royal Mint pieces of gold or silver, the assayer shall not receive them until he has first ascertained whether they bear the mark and symbol of the artisan who made them. Also if they agree with those in the registry and marks stamped thereon in the presence of the Royal Officials; thus preventing their being sold wrongfully in this city or outside of it—especially objects of plain silver, such as small plates and platters which under pretext of paying the tax on one piece, hide the greater number. When seized and assayed, if they are not of the standard required by these ordinances, it is ordered, that for the first infraction, they shall be broken and cut and the silversmith or owner warned not to do this again. For the second infraction, they shall be destroyed and forfeited and their value shall be applied to His Majesty's Exchequer and Treasury. For the third infraction, in addition to the aforesaid penalty, they shall be condemned to four years exile from this court and five leagues around it and suspended from their trade for this length of time and, if this penalty is broken, they shall serve double time in the Philippine Islands with the ordinary salary. Said assayer and marker shall not receive payment of the tax on pieces of gold and silver not of the required standard and, if any piece is found without the mark, he shall be fined three hundred *pesos* of common gold, which I apply to His Majesty's Exchequer and Treasury, judge and informer, a third to each. For the second infraction, the same penalty shall be imposed and three years suspension from the office of *veedor*, assayer and marker.

> 19th ordinance that the rector, *mayordomos* and *diputados* shall inspect the houses and stores of the silversmiths and shall ascertain whether they comply with their obligations.

Furthermore, I order and command that the rector, *mayordomos* and *diputados* shall have the precise obligation of inspecting the stores and workers of the gold and silversmiths, sheet-beaters and drawers, one day of each week, whichever they choose. With special care, [they shall] try to ascertain and inquire whether in the inside of their houses or in those of their friends, they secretly fabricate objects of gold and silver of any kind and sort. Also if they have bellows, forges, crucibles and other implements for refining. If this is the case, they shall know that malice and deceit exist, all of which are forbidden by these ordinances and, after imposing the fines, these shall be made effective on the transgressors. These inspections shall be made whenever it is deemed proper. At the same time, the objects being made therein shall be examined to ascertain their quantity and quality, without the owner's being able to prevent it, under penalty for each infraction of a fine of fifty *pesos* for His Majesty's Exchequer and expenses of their brotherhood, one half to each, and eight days in prison with two pairs of fetters which the *alcalde* of the jail shall not remove. They shall not be allowed to eat or sleep at home, the same penalty to be imposed for infraction. And those objects which have been finished, shall be taken, together with their owners, so that the taxes may be paid thereon. A record shall be made of the pieces half finished and of those which are being hammered into shape and the owners thereof, as well as what pieces of gold the caster has cast. The *veedor* who shall be the assayer and marker of the Royal Treasury and Mint of this city shall be informed of all this, so that he may see if they agree with the marks stamped and registry in his keeping. For carelessness or omission in carrying out this order, each of the aforesaid shall incur in the penalty, for the first infraction, of fifty *pesos* of common gold and for the second, twice this amount, which I apply to His Majesty's Exchequer and Treasury, judge and informer, a third to each. For the third infraction a hundred *pesos* fine and two years of exile from the court and five leagues from its vicinity.

> 20th ordinance that the *veedor* shall ascertain whether the
> provisions of the preceding ordinance are complied with and
> everything else.

Furthermore, I order and command that henceforth, said *veedor* shall have the obligation of informing himself whether said rector, *mayordomos* and *diputados* effectively comply with the provisions of the preceding ordinance and if he knows that they fail to comply therewith, either wholly or in part, shall execute the penalties imposed for such infractions. For this purpose, I hereby empower him as fully as required by law, the same penalty to be applied for carelessness in performing this duty.

> 21st ordinance that silversmiths shall not have in their
> houses or stores bellows, forge or crucibles for refining or
> anything else, with penalties for violation.

Furthermore, in consideration of the fact that the license and permit given by His Majesty, in his Royal Order of twenty-first of August one thousand five hundred and twenty-eight, for goldsmiths and silversmiths freely to make use of their trades [which had been forbidden under pain of death], was with the proviso that they could not have in their houses or stores bellows, forge or crucibles or any other implement for refining metals; that they could fabricate silver and gold in their stores only without melting or forging or refining it therein, as this should be done in the smelter in the presence of the *veedor* of smelters, the Royal Officials being present so that, after melting and refining it there, they could fabricate it in their houses and stores. The penalty for violating this is death and loss of property and taking into consideration that said gold and silver, at the time the silversmiths take it to fabricate it in their stores, has been refined, the taxes paid thereon and stamped after fulfilling all the other requisites prescribed by ordinance seven. I order and command that, solely for the purpose of casting and forging the small bars from which they make the objects, they may have bellows and forges required in their stores but not in their houses; the penalty being that imposed in said Royal Order which shall be infallibly executed upon transgressors.

> 22nd ordinance that the goldsmith shall not display silver
> objects, traffic or profit in silver under penalty for violation
> of this order.

Furthermore, I order and command that, in order that these difficulties shall cease, which have been experienced to the detriment and harm of the Republic and of individuals therein. Consent was given and toleration was shown goldsmiths, as the richest and most worthy of credit, to traffic and profit by fabricating many and large quantities of fabricated silver, either their own or another's, the work being done by their slaves and those of other tradesmen little knowing that, in addition to not being lawful, they lack the art and skill required and those who could work and fabricate it with sufficient knowledge because of their poverty are unable to procure orders for work. For this reason the price of fabrication has risen and excess and disorder prevail. This should be remedied and for this purpose as most fitting, from now henceforth, no goldsmith shall fabricate any kind of silver or have a worker or workshop for silver, even though his slaves may be good and skillful artisans. And likewise they shall not have a silversmith in their stores who, under this guise, serves them as a cloak and cover for continuing their traffic and profit, except when in both trades, he be a licensed expert and approved by the *veedor*, rector, *mayordomos* and *diputados* and with a government license in accordance with the provisions of these ordinances. And the same prohibition applies to the silversmith, who may not be a goldsmith, and both shall incur the penalty, for the first infraction, of two hundred *pesos* in common gold, and for the second, three hundred and for the third, the same penalty and suspension from their trades for a year, during which they shall be exiled from this court and five leagues from its vicinity. Of the fines, I apply half to His Majesty's Exchequer and the other half to the informer, *veedor*, rector, *mayordomos* and *diputados* in equal parts, as judges who carry out the execution of said penalties.

> 23rd ordinances concerning the standard of the silver which
> the silversmiths fabricate and penalties for violating this
> order.

Furthermore, I order and command that no silversmith shall fabricate silver of a standard less than eleven *dineros* and four grains, which amount to two thousand two hundred and ten *maravedis* and every *marco* of said silver is worth sixty-five *reales*. The penalty for violation being that imposed for false weights in accordance with the law of the Kingdom and payment of the silver found not of said standard and the Royal Fifth Tax unpaid. The sevenfold fine to be for His Majesty's Exchequer and Treasury and the informer, a half to each.

> 24th ordinance that no silversmith shall cast small bars, on
> which the taxes have not been paid and marked, from which
> to forge any silver object.

Furthermore I order and command that no silversmith shall make small bars for forging any silver object, unless it be from those on which the taxes have been paid and stamped in the Royal Treasury by its assayer and marker, even though, after the object is finished, he take it for payment of the tax. Penalty for each infraction is one hundred *pesos* for His Majesty's Exchequer and Treasury, judge and informer, a third for each.

> 25th ordinance that objects fabricated that are not of the legal standard and on which the taxes have not been paid shall not be sold.

Furthermore, I order and command that no silversmith shall fabricate silver plate, relief work, brooches, strings of beads, beads, girdle bands, filigree, harness work, bracelets or other larger or smaller objects of less than the legal standard of said eleven *dineros* and four grains nor shall the assayer mark them. The penalty, that all [concerned] shall incur shall be that applied to counterfeiters. And furthermore they shall not sell these objects nor shall anyone purchase them or receive them on account and in payment of a debt, under penalty of losing the debt and the objects thus purchased and received for account of same, the value of which I apply to His Majesty's Exchequer and Treasury, judge and informer, a third for each.

> 26th ordinance that all silversmiths shall congregate on San Francisco street and they shall not have their stores on any other street under penalties.

Furthermore, I order and command that no goldsmith, silversmith, sheet-beater or drawers, from now henceforth, shall have their stores any place in the city except on San Francisco street, where they shall congregate and shall be together from the entrance and corner of the plaza to that of the buildings which belonged to Secretary Ossorio, which turn towards the girls' school. [This] because of the trouble which otherwise would arise and the opportunity for more easily defrauding the Royal Fifth Tax and that the *veedor*, rector, *mayordomos* and *diputados* would not be able to inspect them and investigate their work, each and every time it is deemed proper. The penalty for infraction to be one hundred *pesos* of common gold. For each time that any of the aforesaid shall be found to have a store and workman outside of said street, which I apply in third parts to His Majesty's Exchequer and Treasury, informer and expenses of the festival of Saint and Patron San Eligio.

> 27th ordinance that nowhere in the city except in the auction places shall any object of silver and the rest be sold under penalties.

Furthermore, I order and command that no silversmith or any other person shall sell or purchase any object of gold or silver in the plazas, streets, marts and markets of this city or on stands or in small shops except [that they may purchase] in the auctions those which belonged to the dead or other private individuals, who did not traffic and profit in silver, provided the taxes thereon have been paid but not otherwise. The penalty for the first infraction being one hundred *pesos* and for the second, twice this amount and for the third, forfeiture of such object or objects thus taken to be sold, which I apply to His Majesty's Exchequer and Treasury and informer, a half to each.

> 28th ordinance that only silversmiths shall purchase that
> which is specified in this ordinance.

Furthermore, I order and command that the objects contained in the preceding ordinance, whether new, old or in bad condition, also small ingots of gold or silver bartered or melted gold, old silver illegally obtained, old gold and silver embroidery and remnants of fine cloth shall not be sold anywhere, except on San Francisco Street and in silver-stores. And only silversmiths of these stores shall purchase them from dependable and satisfactory persons and not from their officials, apprentices and slaves, who, being persons without obligations, destroy and melt them to buy them at very low prices. [The latter practice] is the result of so many thefts in the homes, ordinarily committed by domestics, servants and slaves, who can easily find someone to secretly purchase them. These, with greater boldness and without misgiving or fear of discovery continue stealing. So that, from now henceforth this shall be properly remedied, the silversmith who purchases the aforesaid objects on which the tax has not been paid, shall be obliged to inform the *veedor*, so that, on the first day that the cashier's office is working, they shall take them for marking and payment of the taxes and stamp those that should be destroyed. The penalty for each infraction is one hundred *pesos* of common gold, and for officials, apprentices and slaves, the penalty for the first infraction shall be one hundred lashes and for the second, twice this number and four years of exile from this city and five leagues from its vicinity and both penalties shall be executed invariably.

> 29th ordinance regarding the order and account which the
> *veedor* shall observe in marking and taking the gold and
> silver objects taken to him.

Furthermore, when goldsmiths, silversmiths, sheet-beaters and drawers take to the Royal Treasury for taxing the objects which they have made, drawn or beaten, whether in sheets or gold leaf, in order that they may be credited with and a record taken of their marks, [it being assumed that they have been made from the gold and silver ingots on which the taxes were paid, registered and stamped], I order and command that the *veedor*, with particular care and attention, shall not mark handles or superimposed pieces or other objects, which must necessarily be taken separately and have to be soldered, such as necks of siphons, vials, bottles and flasks, sockets of candlesticks and the upper part of salt cellars, perfume pots, pepper shakers, sugar-bowls and other similar objects. This because Royal taxes on the principal parts of the objects could be defrauded, and as these might not be of the legal standard, thereby deceiving the individuals purchasing them and failing to comply with these ordinances. In addition, I recommend to the *veedor's* conscience that he give no less care and attention to ascertaining the standard of such objects and, as they cannot be assayed, that he take a sample of each with a burin, which he shall compare with one from the paragon, which is a piece of silver shown by assay to conform to the standard, and both shall be refired. If that taken from the object become blacker than that of the paragon, it is proved that it is not of the legal standard and then it will be well to make use of the acid test, although both are doubtful, as they are subject to sight and not to truth and exactness of an assay, that said *veedor* shall be alert as he would be responsible for carelessness in this procedure. If he finds that it is not of the required standard, he shall comply with and execute the provisions contained in this ordinance and for any carelessness and negligence of which he might be guilty, he shall be punished with the same penalties.

> 30th ordinance that no silversmith shall fabricate gold or
> silver objects outside of this city and shall comply with the
> provisions of this ordinance.

Furthermore, I order and command that outside of this city, except in the other cities of this New Spain where there is a Royal Treasury, marker and assayer thereof, no silversmith shall henceforth fabricate gold or silver objects, whether his own or anothers, as it is certain these will not be of the required standard or have the taxes paid thereon, unless in making them he shall have complied with the provisions of ordinance seven. In addition to the penalties therein contained for the first infraction, he shall be fined two hundred *pesos* of common gold and for the second, twice this amount and forfeiture of said objects and shall be exiled for four years from the place where he fabricated them and from this court, five leagues from its vicinity. For the third, a public reprimand and exile from this government for six years and these shall not be broken under pain of fulfilling them at the oars in the galleys of their native land and without wages. And I command the *alcaldes mayores* and other justices that, in their districts and jurisdictions, they shall be attentive to that which is provided in this ordinance, so that they may execute the penalties therein contained on those who break them. The penalty for failure to do this or if it becomes known that they overlook them, is a fine of three hundred *pesos*, half for His Majesty's Exchequer and Treasury and half for the informer.

31st ordinance that no money in *pesos* and *reales* shall be
destroyed, for the purpose of making any object whatsoever
of silver, with penalties for infractors.

Furthermore, because many silversmiths, blinded by their excessive cupidity,
destroy coins of *pesos* and *reales* and mix them with another alloy or metal to
fabricate silver objects without fear of incurring the severe penalties imposed by
the laws and ordinances of the Kingdom as given by law 67, section 21, book 5
abridged, and by law 6, section 17, book 8 abridged, I order and command that
henceforth, neither a silversmith nor any other person of whatsoever category and
condition shall destroy or order destroyed coins of *reales* for no reason whatever,
under pain of incurring the penalties provided in said laws and ordinances.

32nd ordinance that, with regard to gilding and silvering and
making writing-tables, desks and other finery of gilded
silver, they shall be guided by the provisions of the laws of
the Kingdom.

Furthermore, as regards the making and sale of desks, writing-tables, counters,
little chests and other things of this kind, adorned with silver, beaten, gilded or
plated, iron, copper or tin, I order and command that they follow the provisions of
the laws of the Kingdom in laws 5, 6, 7, 8, 9 and 10 of section 24, book 5 abridged,
under pain of incurring the penalties imposed therein.

33rd ordinance that scales be adjusted to the official standard
of this city and set up with a fulcrum.

Furthermore, to end the fraud and deception that may exist due to the gold and
silversmiths, sheet-beaters and drawers not having their scales regulated so that
the weight of the silver *marco* be in conformity with that of the City of Burgos and
the weight for the gold *marco* be the same as that of the City of Toledo, in the form
prescribed by the laws of the Kingdom in laws 1, 2 section 13 and laws 2nd, 3, 5,
6, 13 section 22, book 5 abridged, I order and command the aforesaid parties to
have them adjusted to the official standard of this city and publicly keep them with
a fulcrum in a box in their shop and use them for weighing the objects made by
them and the gold and silver, either their own or another's, received for this purpose, and they shall not regulate them with grains of wheat because of the deception occasioned by one being larger than another, but with weights of tin of one,
two, three and six grains each indicating on top the number of grains it weighs and
they shall be in perfect agreement with the known mark of said official standard;
under pain of incurring the penalty imposed by said laws on infractors.

34th ordinance wherein it is commanded that, before granting artisans of this court license to open a store, they shall
take oath to observe these ordinances and disregard those
previously granted, until they shall have complied with
this formality.

Furthermore, for the greater safety and truth in the use and practice of the
trades and compliance with these ordinances, I command that no person shall
make use of them, unless in the manner set forth therein, under pain of incurring
the penalties imposed, which shall be irremissibly executed. And before opening
a store and obtaining the required license, they shall be obliged to take a formal
oath that they will comply with the provisions of said ordinances, under pain of
incurring the penalty imposed on those who break their oaths. This oath shall be
taken before the rector and a *diputado*, selected by him, and the scrivener in charge
of the proceedings and this being done, it shall be noted on said license. Otherwise
they shall not make use of same. And because the importance of the enforcement
of this ordinance obliges all to be alike, I cancel the licenses which up to the present
have been issued, until those holding them shall have complied with this formality
and oath and a record made of having done so, with a warning that the penalties
imposed on those who operate without a license, will be executed on those who fail
to comply. Because time makes changes desirable, I reserve the right for myself
and the Viceroys who succeed me, to alter, amend and remove from these ordinances
what they deem fit.

35th ordinance which provides that the ordinances be proclaimed by crier, recorded in the books and printed.

Furthermore, in order that the provisions of this ordinance shall be complied
with and have full force and effect as something of much importance to the service
of His Majesty and public welfare, I order and command that they be proclaimed
by crier in the principal plaza of this city and in the other places where it is customary. Also that a statement of having done this be made at the end thereof, so
that, from today until the end of thirty succeeding days, those coming under its
prohibitions in this city and district of the government shall be obliged to come
forward and comply with that which is commanded in said ordinances, with the
warning that at the expiration of the period penalties will be executed on transgressors as therein stated. And these ordinances shall be recorded in the government books and in those of the scrivener of the Royal Criminal Court and by Royal
Officials in the books they keep and by the chief scrivener of the Municipal Council
in the city books and they shall be printed and, in order that they be known to all
and no one may pretend ignorance thereof, they shall be proclaimed by crier.

Dated in the City of Mexico, on the twentieth day of October, one thousand six hundred and thirty-eight. The Marquis of Cadereita by order of His Excellency Dionissio de Juescum.

PROCLAMATION. In the City of Mexico, on the third day of the month of December, one thousand six hundred and thirty eight, these ordinances were published and proclaimed by crier twice in the public plaza of this city and on San Francisco street, many people being present and this was done by Pedro de Peres, public crier. Before Ventura de Cardenas, His Majesty's Scrivener.

Bibliography

(∗): Unpublished Manuscript

∗Abarca José Miguel, *Inventario de las alhajas de la Santa Iglesia Metropolitana, levantado por* Mexico, 26 December 1844. Manuscript. Private collection.

Actas de Cabildo de la Ciudad de México. The most complete collection is found in the Archives of the City Council of Mexico.

Actas del Congreso Constituyente Mexicano, Mexico, 1822, *Imp. Alejandro Valdés.*

Alamán, Lucas, *Obras de, Disertaciones sobre la Historia de Méjico.* Mexico, 1899. *Imp. de V. Agüeros, Editor.* 3 vols.

Almanaque Imperial para el año de 1866, Mexico, 1866, *Imp. de J.M.Lara.*

Almonte Nepomuceno Juan, *Guía de Forasteros,* Mexico 1852, *Imp. I. Cumplido.*

Archivo General de Indias, Patronato. Arch.1, Box 1.

Archivo General de Indias. 2-2-1/1, *R° 2 Patronato,* bundle 180.

∗*Archivo General de la Nación, Casa de Moneda. Registro de Nombramientos.*

Ibid. *Ramo de Hacienda.* Book which reads: 'Casa de Ensaye de Mexico.' 1830-31. Bundle 45.

Ibid. *Calificación de establecimientos industriales.* 1865. Silversmiths' establishments.

Ibid. (*Civil indiferente,* vol.64). *Empadronamiento de* 1753. (The pages are not numbered.)

Ibid. *Empadronamiento de* 1811. *Cuartel menor no.*1.

Ibid. *Empadronamiento de* 1811.

Ibid. *Derechos de oro de fuego,* p.7.

Ibid. *General de Parte,* vol.1, p.117. 1575-6. 26 January 1576.

Ibid. *General de Parte,* vol.1. 1575-6. 3 July 1576.

Ibid. *General de Parte,* vol.1. 1575-6. 30 August 1576.

Ibid. *General de Parte,* vol.3, p.59. 1587-8. 13 March 1587.

Ibid. *General de Parte,* vol.2, p.88. 1579-80. 18 November 1579.

Ibid. *General de Parte,* vol.2, p.131. 1579-80. 20 February 1580.

Ibid. *General de Parte,* vol.4, p.73. 1590-91. 11 February 1591.

Ibid. *General de Parte,* vol.4, p.119. 1590-91. 8 April 1591.

Ibid. *General de Parte,* vol.5, p.177 reverse. 1599-1601.

Ibid. *General de Parte,* vol.5, p.277. 1599-1601. 5 February 1601.

∗*Archivo General y Público de la Nación. Guía de cargo y data de la Tesorería General de Ejército y Real Hacienda de México, para la cuenta del año de* 1798, p.8.

Ibid., *Guía de cargo etc., para la cuenta del año de* 1798, p.9.

Ibid., *Guía de cargo etc., para la cuenta del año de* 1798, p.12.

Ibid., *Guía de cargo etc., para la cuenta del año de* 1798, p.13 reverse.

Ibid., *Guía de cargo etc., para la cuenta del año de* 1799, p.9. 27 August.

Ibid., *Guía de cargo etc., para la cuenta del año de* 1799, p.32 reverse. 13 September.

Ibid., *Guía de cargo etc., para la cuenta del año de* 1799. *Señoreage*, p.37 reverse. 23 September.

Ibid., *Guía de cargo etc., para la cuenta del año de* 1799, p.11. 16 October.

Ibid., *Guía de cargo etc., para la cuenta del año de* 1799, p.11. 19 October.

Ibid., *Guía de cargo y data etc., para la cuenta del año de* 1799, p.12 reverse. 23 November.

Ibid., *Indice General de los ramos que comprenden el Libro Mayor de esta Real Casa Matriz*, p.13. No year is given but the seal on the paper is for the years 1786 and 1787.

Archivo General de la Nación, Libro General de la Contaduría del Rey. 1589.

Ibid., *Indice General de los Ramos, etc.*

Archivo General de la Nación, Industria, vol.5, p.255. Mexico, 29 December 1792.

Ibid., *Industria Artística y Manufacturera.* 1746-92. vol.5, pp.241-3. vol.2, 3 October.

Ibid., *Inquisición*, vol.26. (Witness in the suit against Alonso Ruiz, silversmith.)

Ibid., *Ramo de Inquisición*, vol.160.

Ibid., *Ramo de Inquisición*, vol.161. (Accused of heresy.)

Ibid., *Ramo de Inquisición*, vol.838.

Ibid., *Manual Común de* 1798. 22 February. (The pages are not numbered.)

Archivo General y Público de la Nación, Manual Común de 1798.

13 January. (The pages are not numbered.)

Archivo General de la Nación, Manual Común de 1798. (The pages are not numbered.) 15 September.

Ibid., *Reales Cedulas (Planta Alta). Años* 1645-73, vol.58, pp.122-37. *Hordenanças Tocante al Arte de la Platería formadas por el Marqués de Cadereyta con fecha de* 20 *de Octubre de* 1638. Unpublished document.

Ibid., *Ordenanzas*, vol.6, p.13 reverse. 1686-98.

Ibid., vol.6, p.15. 1686-98. 21 April 1694.

Ibid., vol.6, p.16. 1686-98. 10 May 1694.

Ibid., vol.6, p.16 reverse. 1686-98. 10 May 1694.

Ibid., vol.10. 1714-22. *Sello quarto vn cuartillo, años de mil setecientos y diez y nueve y veinte.*

Ibid., O.O.O.O., p.46 reverse.

Ibid., *Libro Mayor ó Guía del Cargo de la Tesorería General*, 1796, p.1.

Archivo General de la Nación. Libro de Ordenanzas, O.O.O.O., p.61 reverse.

Archivo General de la Nación. Ordenanzas:

Vol. 11, p.187 reverse. 1723-63.

Vol.11, p.320. 1723-63.

Vol.11, p.121. 1723-63.

Vol.11, p.320. 1723-63.

Vol.10, p.110. 1714-22. 11 November 1721.

Vol.10, p.109 reverse. 1714-22. 15 November 1721.

Vol.10, p.110. 1714-22. 15 December 1721.

Vol.11, p.92. 1723-63. 21 January 1723.

Vol.11, p.4 reverse. 1723-63. 11 March 1723.

Vol.11, p.3. 1723-63. 18 March 1723.

Vol.11, p.3 reverse. 1723-63.
14 April 1723.
Vol.11, p.5. 1723-63. 23 April 1723.
Vol.11, p.95. 1723-63. 4 May 1723.
Vol.11, p.97. 1723-63. 13 May
1723.
Vol.11, p.5 reverse. 1723-63.
20 May 1723.
Vol.11, p.6. 1723-63. 11 June 1723.
Vol.11, p.7. 1723-63. 11 June 1723.
Vol.11, p.97. 1723-63. 7 August
1723.
Vol.11, p.8 reverse. 1723-63.
26 August 1723.
Vol.11, p.8. 1723-63. 11 October
1723.
Vol.11, p.9 reverse. 1723-63.
Election of *Mayordomos
Veedores* and *Diputados*.
8 January 1724.
Vol.11, p.10 reverse. 1723-63.
19 February 1724.
Vol.11, p.10 reverse. 1723-63.
27 April 1724.
Vol.11, p.25 reverse. 1723-63.
14 May 1724.
Vol.11, p.11 reverse. 1723-63.
11 July 1724.
Vol.11, p.12 reverse. 1723-63.
9 November 1724.
Vol.11, p.14-A. 1723-63. Election
of *Veedor* and *Mayordomos*.
9 January 1725.
Vol.11, p.15. 1723-63.
20 February 1725.
Vol.11, p.17. 1723-63. 14 July 1725.
Vol.11, p.19. 1723-63.
17 July 1725.
Vol.11, p.18. 1723-63.
20 July 1725.
Vol.11, p.18 reverse. 1723-63.
24 July 1725.
Vol.11, p.34. 1723-63.
12 September 1725.
Vol.11, p.33 reverse. 1723-63.
29 July 1726.
Vol.11, p.43 reverse. 1723-63.
29 July 1726.

Vol.11, p.33 reverse. 1723-63.
7 August 1726.
Vol.11, p.37. 1723-63. Election
of *Veedor* and *Mayordomos*.
13 January 1727.
Vol.11, p.40. 1723-63. 6 March
1727.
Vol.11, p.43 reverse. 1723-63.
12 May 1727.
Vol.11, p.44. 1723-63. 17 May
1727.
Vol.11, p.46. 1723-63.
16 January 1728.
Vol.11, p.48 reverse. 1723-63.
5 June 1728.
Vol.11, p.48 reverse. 1723-63.
18 June 1728.
Vol.11, p.49. 1723-63.
26 June 1728.
Vol.11, p.50 reverse. 1723-63.
16 December 1728.
Vol.11, p.55 reverse. 1723-63.
13 December 1729.
Vol.11, p.56. 1723-63.
13 January 1730.
Vol.11, p.56 reverse. 1723-63.
25 February 1730.
Vol.11, p.57. 1723-63.
27 May 1730.
Vol.11, p.57 reverse. 1723-63.
2 June 1730.
Vol.11, p.57. 1723-63.
5 June 1730.
Vol.11, p.58 reverse. 1723-63.
14 June 1730.
Vol.11, p.58 reverse. 1723-63.
22 June 1730.
Vol.11, p.59. 1723-63.
5 July 1730.
Vol.11, p.59. 1723-63.
6 July 1730.
Vol.11, p.61 reverse. 1723-63.
24 August 1730.
Vol.11, p.65 reverse. 1723-63.
18 January 1731.
Vol.11, p.69. 1723-63.
12 April 1731.
Vol.11, p.69 reverse. 1723-63.

3 July 1731.
Vol.11, p.72 reverse. 1723-63.
27 September 1731.
Vol.11, p.73. 1723-63.
8 October 1731.
Vol.11, p.74 reverse. 1723-63.
7 November 1731.
Vol.11, p.76. 1723-63.
17 November 1731.
Vol.11, p.76 reverse. 1723-63.
18 November 1731.
Vol.11, p.78. 1723-63.
16 February 1732.
Vol.11, p.79. 1723-63.
6 March 1732.
Vol.11, p.79 reverse. 1723-63.
6 March 1732.
Vol.11, p.82. 1723-63.
6 June 1732.
Vol.11, p.82 reverse. 1723-63.
7 June 1732.
Vol.11, p.87 reverse. 1723-63.
21 August 1732.
Vol.11, p.112 reverse. 1723-63.
17 September 1733.
Vol.11, p.100. 1723-63.
28 January 1734.
Vol.11, p.101 reverse. 1723-63.
9 March 1734.
Vol.11, p.102 reverse. 1723-63.
5 May 1734.
Vol.11, p.106. 1723-63.
18 August 1734.
Vol.11, p.110. 1723-63.
6 September 1734.
Vol.11, p.109 reverse. 1723-63.
15 August 1735.
Vol.11, p.113. 1723-63.
4 October 1735.
Vol.11, p.112 reverse. 1723-63.
20 October 1735.
Vol.11, p.116 reverse. 1723-63.
6 March 1736.
Vol.11, p.118. 1723-63.
August 1736.
Vol.11, p.120 reverse. 1723-63.
7 September 1736.
Vol.11, p.120 reverse. 1723-63.

12 September 1736.
Vol.11, p.122 reverse. 1723-63.
23 March 1737.
Vol.11, p.122 reverse. 1723-63.
8 May 1737.
Vol.11, p.123. 1723-63.
16 May 1737.
Vol.11, p.123 reverse. 1723-63.
27 July 1737.
Vol.11, p.123 reverse. 1723-63.
7 September 1737.
Vol.11, p.124. 1723-63.
September 1737.
Vol.11, p.126. 1723-63.
21 April 1738.
Vol.11, p.126. 1723-63.
May 1738.
Vol.11, p.126 reverse. 1723-63.
14 May 1738.
Vol.11, p.129. 1723-63.
17 July 1738.
Vol.11, p.132 reverse. 1723-63.
22 June 1739.
Vol.11, p.132 reverse. 1723-63.
10 July 1739.
Vol.11, p.141. 1723-63.
17 October 1740.
Vol.11, p.149 reverse. 1723-63.
13 February 1741.
Vol.11, p.151 reverse. 1723-63.
22 June 1741.
Vol.11, p.156. 1723-63.
20 October 1741.
Vol.11, p.157. 1723-63.
25 January 1742.
Vol.11, p.159. 1723-63.
12 April 1742.
Vol.11, p.177. 1723-63.
19 November 1743.
Vol.11, p.182. 1723-63.
29 May 1744.
Vol.11, p.185. 1723-63.
7 October 1744.
Vol.11, p.186. 1723-63.
27 October 1744.
Vol.11, p.189 reverse. 1723-63.
2 January 1745. Election of
Veedor, Mayordomos and

Diputados of the Silversmiths'
Trade.
Vol.11, p.189 reverse. 1723-63.
6 January 1745.
Vol.11, p.189 reverse. 1723-63.
Election of *Veedor*,
Mayordomos and *Diputados* of
the Silversmiths' Trade.
11 January 1745.
Vol.11, p.195. 1723-63.
25 May 1745.
Vol.11, p.205 reverse. 1723-63.
1 July 1745.
Vol.11, p.210 reverse. 1723-63.
5 November 1745.
Vol.11, p.211 reverse. 1723-63.
24 November 1745.
Vol.11, p.232. 1723-63.
27 January 1747.
Vol.11, p.235 reverse. 1723-63.
8 July 1747.
Vol.11, p.236. 1723-63.
17 July 1747.
Vol.11, p.238. 1723-63.
12 March 1748.
Vol.11, p.239. 1723-63.
8 May 1748.
Vol.11, p.247. 1723-63.
21 August 1748.
Vol.11, p.247. 1723-63.
27 August 1748.
Vol.11, p.260. 1723-63.
7 July 1750.
Vol.11, p.260 reverse.
22 October 1751.
Vol.11, p.261. 1723-63.
15 December 1751.
Vol.11, p.261. 1723-63.
28 December 1751.
Vol.11, p.263. 1723-63.
7 June 1753.
Vol.11, p.263. 1723-63.
25 June.
Vol.11, p.263 reverse. 1723-63.
29 May 1752.
Vol.11, p.263 reverse. 1723-63.
4 September 1752.
Vol.11, p.265. 1723-63.

14 May 1753.
Vol.11, p.270. 1723-63.
23 February 1754.
Vol.11, p.270. 1723-63.
7 March 1754.
Vol.11, p.270. 1723-63.
22 March 1754.
Vol.11, p.270. 1723-63.
27 March 1754.
Vol.11, p.292 reverse. 1723-63.
10 February 1757.
Vol.11, p.292 reverse. 1723-63.
16 February 1757.
Vol.11, p.293 reverse. 1723-63.
29 July 1757.
Vol.11, p.293 reverse. 1723-63.
2 September 1757.
Vol.11, p.295 reverse. 1723-63.
14 January 1758.
Vol.11, p.295 reverse. 1723-63.
11 February 1758.
Vol.11, p.296. 1723-63.
14 February 1758.
Vol.11, p.296. 1723-63.
28 February 1758.
Vol.11, p.296. 1723-63.
2 March 1758.
Vol.11, p.296. 1723-63.
4 March 1758.
Vol.11, p.298 reverse. 1723-63.
11 December 1758.
Vol.11, p.299 reverse. 1723-63.
13 January 1759.
Vol.11, p.301. 1723-63.
14 May 1759.
Vol.11, p.302 reverse. 1723-63.
28 June 1759.
Vol.11, p.303. 1723-63.
30 October 1759.
Vol.11, p.310 reverse. 1723-63.
11 December 1760.
Vol.11, p.311. 1723-63.
15 December 1760.
Vol.11, p.311. 1723-63.
15 January 1761.
Vol.11, p.311 reverse. 1723-63.
14 March 1761.
Vol.11, p.313. 1723-63.

12 June 1761.
Vol.11, p.313. 1723-63.
12 June 1761.
Vol.11, p.316. 1723-63.
25 May 1761.
Vol.11, p.316 reverse. 1723-63.
20 June 1761.
Vol.11, p.319 reverse. 1723-63.
3 August 1761.
Vol.11, p.323. 1723-63.
18 January 1763.
Vol.11, p.323 reverse. 1723-63.
16 April 1763.
Vol.11, p.324 reverse. 1723-63.
14 January 1762.
Vol.11, p.325 reverse. 1723-63.
7 June 1763.
Vol.11, p.326. 1723-63.
14 September 1763.
Vol.16, p.1. 14 January 1764.
Vol.16, p.1. 28 January 1764.
Vol.16, p.4 reverse. 1764.
19 September 1764.
Vol.16, p.5 reverse. 1764.
11 January 1765.
Vol.16, p.9 reverse. 1764.
14 June 1765.
Vol.16, p.9 reverse. 1764.
15 June 1765.
Vol.16, p.9 reverse. 1764.
1 July 1765.
Vol.16, p.10. 1764. 29 July 1765.
Vol.16, p.10. 1764.
3 December 1765.
Vol.16, p.10 reverse. 1764.
14 January 1766.
Vol.16, p.11. 1764.
12 April 1766.
Vol.16, p.12. 1764.
3 September 1766.
Vol.16, p.14. 1764.
10 January 1767.
Vol.16, p.14 reverse. 1764.
23 June 1767.
Vol.16, p.16. 1764.
15 January 1768.
Vol.16, p.18 reverse. 1764.
18 November 1768.

Vol.16, p.19. 1764.
10 January 1769.
Vol.16, p.18 reverse. 1764.
7 September 1768.
Vol.16, p.19 reverse. 1764.
8 March 1769.
Vol.16, p.19 reverse. 1764.
22 June 1769.
Vol.16, p.22. 1764.
10 January 1770.
Vol.16, p.24 reverse. 1764.
16 February 1770.
Vol.16, p.25. 1764. 12 July 1770.
Vol.16, p.26. 1764.
17 August 1770.
Vol.16, p.32. 1764.
9 January 1771.
Vol.16, p.38 reverse. 1764.
11 September 1771.
Vol.16, p.41 reverse. 1764.
11 December 1771.
Vol.16, p.42. 1764.
8 January 1772.
Vol.16, p.42 reverse. 1764.
10 January 1772.
Vol.16, p.46. 1764.
29 August 1772.
Vol.16, p.47. 1764. 8 October 1772.
Vol.16, p.48. 1764.
22 October 1772.
Vol.16, p.49. 1764.
9 January 1773.
Vol.16, p.51 reverse. 1764.
18 May 1773.
Vol.16, p.54 reverse. 1764.
23 June 1773.
Vol.16, p.54 reverse. 1764.
8 July 1773.
Vol.16, p.61. 1764. 9 October 1773.
Vol.16, p.66 reverse. 1764.
21 April 1774.
Vol.16, p.66 reverse. 1764.
22 August 1774.
Vol.16, p.67. 1764. 6 October 1774.
Vol.16, p.70 reverse. 1764.
25 January 1775.
Vol.16, p.72. 1764. 9 March 1775.
Vol.16, p.79. 1764.

16 January 1776.
Vol.16, p.80. 1764. 23 May 1776.
Vol.16, p.85. 1764.
6 December 1776.
Vol.16, p.90 reverse. 1764.
4 February 1777.
Vol.16, p.101. 1764. 23 May 1777.
Vol.16, p.105 reverse. 1764.
30 January 1778.
Vol.16, p.106. 1764.
28 February 1778.
Vol.16, p.106 reverse. 1764.
28 March 1778.
Vol.16, p.111 reverse. 1764.
22 August 1778.
Vol.16, p.111 reverse. 1764.
11 September 1778.
Vol.16, p.111 reverse. 1764.
18 September 1778.
Vol.16, p.111 reverse. 1764.
25 September 1778.
Vol.16, p.112. 1764.
25 September 1778.
Vol.16, p.112. 1764.
3 October 1778.
Vol.16, p.112. 1764.
6 October 1778.
Vol.16, p.113. 1764.
8 January 1779.
Vol.16, p.113 reverse. 1764.
23 February 1779.
Vol.16, p.114. 1764. 27 May 1779.
Vol.16, p.114 reverse. 1764.
12 June 1779.
Vol.16, p.114 reverse. 1764.
14 June 1779.
Vol.16, p.114 reverse. 1764.
10 December 1779.
Vol.16, p.115 reverse. 1764.
7 January 1780.
Vol.16, p.115 reverse. 1764.
26 February 1780.
Vol.16, p.116. 1764. 12 May 1780.
Vol.16, p.116. 1764. 29 May 1780.
Vol.16, p.116. 1764. 2 June 1780.
Vol.16, p.116 reverse. 1764.
17 June 1780.
Vol.16. 1764. 1780. (The page is

not numbered and it is not
dated.)
Vol.16, p.117 reverse. 1764.
11 January 1781.
Vol.16, p.121. 1764.
13 October 1781.
Vol.16, p.121 reverse. 1764.
13 November 1781.
Vol.16, p.121 reverse. 1764.
26 November 1781.
Vol.16, p.121 reverse. 1764.
4 December 1781.
Vol.16, p.122. 1764.
11 January 1782.
Vol.16, p.122 reverse. 1764.
19 January 1782.
Vol.16, p.122 reverse. 1764.
25 January 1782.
Vol.16, p.124 reverse. 1764.
18 July 1782.
Vol.16, p.125 reverse. 1764.
13 September 1782.
Vol.16, p.129 reverse. 1764.
9 January 1783.
Vol.16, p.129 reverse. 1764. 1783.
Vol.16, p.132. 1764. 9 July 1783.
Vol.16, p.135 reverse. 1764.
14 January 1784.
Vol.16, p.136. 1764. 4 March 1784.
Vol.16, p.136. 1764. 23 July 1784.
Vol.16, p.136 reverse. 1764.
11 August 1784.
Vol.16, p.136 reverse. 1764.
27 September 1784.
Vol.16, p.137. 1764.
20 December 1784.
Vol.16, p.145 reverse. 1764.
14 January 1785.
Vol.16, p.145 reverse. 1764.
29 January 1786.
Vol.16, p.145 reverse. 1764.
9 February 1786.
Vol.16, p.146. 1764.
Vol.16, p.146. 27 September 1786.
Vol.16, p.149. 1764.
16 January 1787.
Vol.16. 1764. 1780.
Vol.16, p.156. 1764.

11 February 1788.
Vol.16, p.156 reverse. 1764.
Vol.16, p.156 reverse. 1764.
20 February 1788.
Vol.16, p.156 reverse. 1764.
23 August 1788.
Vol.16, p.157. 1764.
14 January 1789.
Vol.16, p.157 reverse. 1764.
3 June 1789.
Vol.16, p.159. 1764.
13 January 1790.
Vol.16, p.159. 1764.
22 March 1790.
Vol.16, p.159. 1764. 10 April 1790.
Vol.16, p.159. 1764.
7 September 1790.
Vol.16, p.159 reverse. 1764.
16 September 1790.
Vol.16, p.162 reverse. 1764.
8 January 1791.
Vol.16, p.162 reverse. 1764.
25 January 1791.
Vol.16, p.162 reverse. 1764.
8 February 1791.
Vol.16, p.166 reverse. 1764.
27 July 1791.
Vol.16, p.167. 1764.
24 September 1791.
Vol.16, p.170 reverse. 1764.
1 July 1792.
Vol.16, p.174. 1764.
14 December 1792.
Vol.16, p.175. 1764.
3 January 1793.
Vol.16, p.175. 1764. 11 July 1793.
Vol.16, p.175 reverse. 1764.
15 October 1793.
Vol.16, p.177 reverse. 1764.
9 January 1794.
Vol.16, p.177 reverse. 1764.
Vol.16, p.179 reverse. 1764.
26 February 1795.
Vol.16, p.179 reverse. 1764.
21 March 1795.
Vol.16, p.180. 1764.
27 March 1795.
Vol.16, p.181 reverse. 1764.

9 January 1796.
Vol.16, p.182. 1764. 18 July 1796.
Vol.16, p.183 reverse. 1764.
12 January 1797.
Vol.16, p.184. 1764.
22 January 1798.
Vol.16, p.184. 1764.
20 March 1798.
Vol.16, p.184. 1764. 16 May 1798.
Vol.16, p.185. 1764.
6 November 1798.
Vol.16, p.185 reverse. 1764.
9 January 1799.
Vol.16, p.185 reverse. 1764.
22 April 1799.
Vol.16, p.185 reverse. 1764.
27 May 1799.
Vol.16, p.186. 1764.
4 October 1799.
Vol.16, p.186 reverse. 1764.
20 December 1799.
Vol.16, p.186 reverse. 1764.
1 January 1800.
Vol.16, p.186 reverse. 1764.
1 February 1800.
Vol.16, p.186 reverse. 1764.
2 April 1800.
Vol.16, p.186 reverse. 1764.
1 May 1800.
Vol.16, p.190. 1764.
11 October 1800.
Vol.16, p.190. 1764.
17 December 1800.
Vol.16, p.190 reverse. 1764.
9 January 1801.
Vol.16, p.191 reverse. 1764.
8 January 1802.
Vol.16, p.191 reverse. 1764.
Vol.16, p.192 reverse. 1764.
13 January 1802.
Vol.16, p.192 reverse. 1764.
10 February 1803.
Vol.16, p.193 reverse. 1764.
7 January 1804.
Vol.16, p.193 reverse. 1764.
Vol.16, p.194 reverse. 1764.
11 January 1805.
Vol.16, p.194 reverse. 1764.

10 July 1805.
Vol.16, p.194 reverse. 1764.
11 October 1805.
Vol.16, p.196. 1764.
7 January 1807.
Vol.16, p.196. 1764. 10 June 1807.
Vol.16, p.196 reverse. 1764.
6 November 1807.
Vol.16, p.197. 1764.
8 January 1808.
Vol.16, p.197. 1764.
25 January 1808.
Vol.16, p.197. 1764.
1 October 1808.
Vol.16, p.198. 1764.
10 February 1809.
Vol.16, p.199. 1764. 1810.
Vol.16, p.199 reverse. 1764.
10 May 1810.
Vol.16, p.200. 1764.
5 January 1811.
Vol.16, p.200. 1764.
7 January 1812.
Vol.16, p.200 reverse. 1764.
7 January 1812.
Vol.16, p.200 reverse. 1764.
8 January 1813.
Vol.16, p.200 reverse. 1764.
15 May 1812.
Vol.16, p.200 reverse. 1764.
15 September 1812.
Vol.16, p.201. 1764.
14 January 1815.
Vol.16, p.201. 1764.
23 February 1815.
Vol.16, p.201. 1764. 10 July 1815.
Vol.16, p.201 reverse. 1764.
Vol.16, p.201 reverse. 1764.
9 March 1816.
Vol.16, p.201 reverse. 1764.
10 June 1816.
Vol.16, p.201 reverse. 1764.
29 July 1816.
Vol.16, p.202. 1764. 10 June 1817.
Vol.16, p.202. 1764.
11 August 1817.
Vol.16, p.202 reverse. 1764.
22 July 1818.

*Archivo General de la Nación,
   Padrón de establecimientos
   industriales. Cuartel menor Núm.1,
   1842.
*Archivo General de la Nación.
   Padrón de establecimientos
   industriales. 1865.
Ibid. Padrones núm.105, vol.9,
   p.140 F and v. Padrón de la
   Parcialidad de S.Juan de
   México.
Ibid., Ramo de Hacienda (Planta
   Baja), bundle 161, 1842-3.
   Ensaye Mayor de la República.
Ibid., Reales Cédulas (Planta Alta).
   vol.5. 1605.
Ibid., Reales Cédulas (Planta Alta).
   1645-73, vol.58, pp.122-37.
Ibid., Reales Cédulas, vol.15, first
   book, pp.1 reverse-4 reverse.
Ibid., Reales Cédulas (Planta Alta).
   1645-73, vol.58, pp.122-37.
Ibid., Reales Cédulas, vol.52, p.324.
   file 104. 1733.
Ibid., Reales Cédulas, vol.143,
   pp.225 reverse-233. 1775.
Ibid., Yndustria Artística y
   Manufacturera, vol.5, p.224.
   1746-92.
Ibid., Yndustria Artística y
   Manufacturera, vol.5, pp.224-43.
   1746-92.
Ibid., Yndustria Artística y
   Manufacturera, vol.5, pp.237-8.
   1746-92.
Ibid., Yndustria Artística y
   Manufacturera, vol.23, pp.59-71
   reverse. 1793-1805.
*Archivo de Notarías de México.
   Before Antonio Alonso, Public
   Scrivener. 29 October 1562.
Ibid., 27 January 1563.
Ibid., Before Antonio Alonso,
   Public Scrivener. 10 April 1563.
Ibid., 15 July 1563.
Ibid., Poder. 9 November 1563.
   Before Antonio Alonso, Public
   Scrivener.

Ibid., 1564.

Ibid., Before Antonio Alonso, Public Scrivener. 20 November 1620.

Ibid., *Poder otorgado por Juan de Escobar Salcedo ante José de la Cruz. Escribano Público.* 14 May 1625.

Ibid., Before Antonio Alonso, Public Scrivener. 27 May 1625.

Ibid., Before Antonio Alonso, Public Scrivener. 3 October 1628.

Ibid., Before Antonio Alonso, Public Scrivener. 18 October 1628.

Ibid., *Poder ante Fernando Veedor, Escribano Público.* 11 April 1657.

Archivo de Protocolos. Actas de Antonio Alonzo. 1554-65. p.207.

Ibid., *Actas de Antonio Alonzo.* 1554-65. p.733 reverse.

Ibid., *Anónimos.* 1536-43.

Archivo de Tlaxcala, vol.242. 7 October 1788.

Arrillaga, Lic. Basilio José, *Recopilación de Leyes, Decretos, Bandos, Reglamentos, Circulares y Providencias de los Supremos Poderes de los Estados Unidos Mexicanos, formada de orden del Supremo Gobierno.* Mexico, 1835. *Imp. de J.M.Fernandez de Lara.* Embraces from August to December 1823.— —, *Recopilación de Leyes, Decretos, Bandos, Reglamentos, Circulares y Providencias de los Supremos Poderes y otras Autoridades de la República Mexicana. Año de* 1831. Mexico, 1835. *Imp. de J.M.Fernández de Lara.*— —, *Recopilación de Leyes, Decretos, Bandos, Reglamentos, Circulares y Providencias de los Supremos Poderes y otras Autoridades de la República Mexicana Formada de orden del Supremo Gobierno.*— Mexico, 1839. *Imp. de J.M. Fernández de Lara.* Embraces the entire year 1837.— —, *Recopilación de Leyes, Decretos, Bandos, Reglamentos, Circulares y Providencias de los Supremos Poderes y otras Autoridades de la República Mexicana. Formada de orden del Supremo Gobierno.* Mexico, 1838. *Imp. de J.M. Fernández de Lara.* Embraces from January to December 1829.

Bandelier, Ad. F., 'On the Social Organization and Mode of Government of the Ancient Mexicans.' Salem, 1879. Salem Press.

Barroso, Francisco Diez, *El Arte en Nueva España.* Mexico, 1921.

Batres, Leopoldo *Antiguedades Mejicanas Falsificadas.* Mexico [no date], *Imp. de Fidencio S.Soria.*

Beleña, Doctor Don Eusebio Bentura, *Recopilación Sumaria de todos los Autos Acordados de la Real Audiencia y Sala del Crimen de esta Nueva España y Providencias de su Superior Gobierno,* Mexico, 1787. *Imp. Don Felipe de Zuñiga y Ontiveros.* 2 vols.

Benítez, Ing. José R., *Historia Gráfica de la Nueva España, Cámara Oficial Española de Comercio,* Mexico, 1929.

Cabo, Padre D.Andrés, *Los Tres Siglos de México.* Jalapa, 1870. *Imp. A.Ruis.*

Calendario, Manual y Guía de Forasteros en Méjico para el año de—, —. By Mariano Josef de Zúñiga y Ontiveros. *Imp. en la Oficina del Autor.*

Carrillo y Pérez, Don Ignacio, *Pensil Americano. Florido en el Rigor del Invierno, La Imágen de María Santísima de Guadalupe* (1793). *Imp. por D.Mariano Joseph de Zúñiga y Ontiveros.*

Mexico, 1797.

Carrión, Antonio, *Historia de la Ciudad de Puebla de los Angeles*, Tip. Escuelos Salesianas, Puebla, 1897.

Castillo, D.Francisco Fernández del, *Algunos Documentos Nuevos sobre Bartolomé de Medina*. Mexico, 1927. *Talleres Gráficos de la Nación.*

Castro, Diego Bermúdez de, *Theatro Angelopolitano.* Year 1746. Mexico. Published for the first time by Dr.N.León, Professor of Ethnology in the National Museum.

Castro Santa Anna, José Manuel de, *Diario de Sucesos Notables.* Year 1757. *Imp. Juan R.Navarro.* Mexico, 1854.

Cédula Real de 12 de Julio de 1622 para que todo el oro y plata que se hallare en qualesquier partes de las Yndias donde no hubiere casa de fundición que no estubiere quintado, se tome por perdido. With the signature of Philip IV. Original Manuscript. Unpublished. Collection of Mr.W.B.Stephens, Mexico, D.F.

Cedulario de Puga. Provisiones, cédulas, ordenanzas, para la expedición de los negocios y administración de Nueva España. El Systema Postal Edition. Mexico, 1878, *Imp. José María Sandoval.* 2 vols.

Clavigero, Francisco J., *Historia Antigue de México y su Conquista.* Translated from the Italian by J.Joaquín Mora. 2 vols. *Imp. Dublán y Cía.* Mexico, 1883.

Colección Completa de los Decretos Generales expedidos por el Exmo. Sr. General Forey, p.48. Mexico. *Imp. de A.Boix, á cargo de M.Zornoza.* 1863. No.13 Aguila Street.

Colección de Leyes y Decretos Publicados en el Año de 1839. Mexico, 1851. *Imp. en Palacio.*

Colección de Leyes y Decretos Publicados en el Año de 1847. Lic. Carlos M. Alcántara. Mexico, 1852. *Imp. en Palacio.*

Colección de los Decretos y Ordenes de las Cortes de España, que se reputan vigentes en la República de los Estados-Unidos Mexicanos. Mexico, 1829. *Imp. de Galván á cargo de Mariano Arévalo.*

Colección de Ordenes y Decretos de la Soberana Junta Provisional Gubernativa, y Soberanos Congresos Generales de la Nación Mexicana. Second edition. México, 1829. *Imp. Galván, á cargo de Mariano Arévalo.*

Consulta hecha a la Real Audiencia Gobernadora, por el Lic. Don Joseph Antonio Lince, Ensayador Mayor de el Reyno y Juez Veedor de el N[e.] *Arte de la Platería, etc.*

Correo de la Federación Mexicana. 16 August 1829.

Cortés, Hernán, *Cartas de Relación de la Conquista de México. Espasa-Calpe, S.A.* Madrid, 1932. 2 vols.

Cubas, Antonio García, *El Libro de mis Recuerdos. Imp. de Arturo García Cubas, Hermanos, Sucesores,* Mexico, 1904.

Cuevas, Padre Mariano, S.J., *Cartas y otros Documentos de Hernán Cortés. Novísimamente descubiertos en el Archivo General de Indias de la Ciudad de Sevilla.* Seville, 1915. *Imp. F.Díaz y Comp*[a.]

Cuenta del Tesoro Federal. Mexico. *Tip. de El Gran Libro.*

Defensa Jurídica de los Missioneros de las Californias como Herederos de la D[na.] *Gertrudis de la Peña V*[da.] *del Maestre de Campo D.Francisco Lorenz de Rada.* Has no press-mark or year of publication. The Highest Council of the Indies signed the sentence 16 April 1749. The suit had continued from 1713. Mr.W.B. Stephens' collection. Mexico, D.F.

De Solís, Don Antonio, *Historia de la .Conquista de Méjico. V*ᵃ·* Baudry Librería Europea*, Paris, 1858.

Diario Oficial of 7 June 1868.

Díaz del Castillo, Bernal, *Verdadera Historia de los Sucesos de la Conquista de la Nueva España. Biblioteca de Autores Españoles. Historiadores primitivos de Indios. Colección dirigida é ilustrada por Don Enrique de Vedia.* Madrid, 1858. *Imp. M.Rivadeneyra.* 2 vols.

Díaz del Castillo, Bernal, *Verdadera Historia de la Conquista de la Nueva España.* Madrid, 1928. *Edición de Espasa Calpe, S.A.* 2 vols.

Diccionario Autobiografico de Conquistadores y Pobladores de Nueva España. Imp. de El Adelantado de Segovia. Madrid, 1923. 2 vols.

Diccionario Etimológico de Roque Barcia. Madrid, 1881.

Diccionario Universal de Historia y de Geografía. Mexico, 1854. *Imp. de F.Escalante y Cía.* 10 vols.

Documentos del Archivo de la Basílica. Año de 1783.

Dublán, Manuel y Lozano, José María, *Legislación Mexicana ó Colección Completa de las Disposiciones Legislativas expedidas desde la Independencia de la República.* Official edition. Mexico, 1876. *Imp. del Comercio, a cargo de Dublán y Lozano, Hijos.* No.8 Cordobanes Street.

Ibid., Mexico, 1878. *Imp. del Comercio, de Dublan y Chavez, a cargo de M.Lara (Hijo).* No.8 Cordobanes Street.

Dublán, Adolfo y Esteva, Adalberto A., *Legislación Mexicana ó Colección Completa de las Disposiciones Legislativas expedidas desde la Independencia de la República. Arregladas por los Lics. Manuel Dublán y José Maria Lozano.* Official Edition. Mexico, 1898. *Imp. de Eduardo Dublán.* No.7 Callejón de Cincuenta y Siete.

Dublán, Adolfo y Esteva, Adalberto A., *Legislación Mexicana ó Colección Completa de las Disposiciones Legislativas expedidas desde la Independencia de la República. Continuación de la ordenada por los Lics. Manuel Dublán y José Maria Lozano.* Mexico, 1900. *Imp. de Eduardo Dublán.* No.7 Callejón de Cincuenta y Siete.

Ibid., Mexico, 1902. *Imp. de Eduardo Dublan.* No.7 Callejón de Cincuenta y Siete.

Ibid., Mexico, 1903. *Imp. de Eduardo Dublan.* No.7 Callejón de Cincuenta y Siete.

Duran, Diego, *Historia de las Indias de Nueva España e islas de tierra firme.* Mexico, 1867-80. 2 vols. and an atlas.

Echeverria y Veytia, Licenciado Don Mariano Fernández de, (professed Knight of the Military Order of Santiago; Attorney of the Royal Councils and of the Royal Tribunal in Mexico, Lord of the noble and ancient house of Veytia in the seigniory of Vizcaya; born in the city of Puebla, in New Spain), *Historia de la Fundación de la Ciudad de la Puebla de los Angeles en la Nueva España. Su descripción y presente estado.* Puebla, 1931. *Imp. 'Labor,'* Mixcoac, D.F. — —, *Baluartes de*

México, Imp. D.Alejandro Valdés, Mexico, 1820.

Ejercicio Fiscal de 1893 a 1894 — Cuenta del Tesoro Federal formada por la Tesorería General de la Federación, en cumplimiento del artículo tercero de 30 de mayo de 1881 Méjico. Tip. de la Oficina Impresora de Estampillas. Palacio Nacional. 1895.

El Monitor Republicano — 1 January 1847.

Fernández del Castillo, Francisco, *Libros y Libreros en el Siglo XVI.* Vol. 6 of the Publications of the *Archivo General de la Nación.* Mexico, 1914. *Tip. Guerrero Hnos.*

Fernandez Villareal, Lic. Manuel y Barbero, Francisco, *Colección Legislativa Completa de la República Mexicana con todas las disposiciones expedidas para la Federación, el Distrito y los Territorios Federales — Año* 1902 — *Continuación de la Legislación Mexicana de Dublán y Lozano,* vol.34 — only official edition of the *Secretaría de Justicia. Tipografía de la Vda. de F.Diaz de León.* Cinco de Mayo Street and Callejón de Santa Clara, Mexico, 1907.

Ibid. — *Año de* 1903. *Continuación de la Legislación Mexicana de Dublán y Lozano,* vol.35 — only official edition of the *Secretaría de Justicia. Tipografía de la Vda. de F.Diaz de León.* Cinco de Mayo Street and Callejón de Santa Clara, Mexico, 1908.

Florencia, Padre Francisco de, *La Estrella del Norte de México, etc.* Madrid, 1785. *Imp. Lorenzo de San Martín.*

Fonseca, Fabián de, y Urrutia, Carlos de, *Historia General de Real Hacienda escrita por orden del Virrey Conde de Revillagigedo* — printed with the permission of the Supreme Government. Mexico, 1845. *Imp. por Vicente G.Torres,* No.2 Espíritu Santo Street. 6 vols.

Franco, Fr. Alonzo, *Historia de la Provincia de Santiago de México* (1645). *Imp. Museo Nacional México,* 1900. 2 vols.

Gage, Tomás, *Los Viajes de. Librería de Rosa,* Paris, 1838, 2 vols.

Galvan Rivera, Mariano, *Guía de Forasteros en Méjico para el año de* 1828. Dedicated to His Excellency General of Division and First President of the United Mexican States, Citizen Guadalupe Victoria. Mexico, 1828. *Imp. de Galvan a cargo de Mariano Arévalo.* No.22 Cadena Street. — —, *Calendario manual y Guía de Forasteros en Méjico para el año de* 1831. *Imp. en su Casa, a cargo de Mariano Arévalo.* No.22 Cadena Street. — —, *Calendario manual y Guía de Forasteros en Méjico para el año de* 1832. *Imp. en su Casa, a cargo de Mariano Arévalo.* No.22 Cadena Street. — —, *Guía de Forasteros en la Ciudad de Méjico, para el año de* 1854. *Publicada por Mariano Galván Rivera.*

Gazeta de México.

Gómez de Haro, Lic. Enríque, *Poblanos Ilustres,* Puebla, 1910.

González Obregón, Luis, *Las Calles de México. Imp. Manuel León Sánchez,* Mexico, 1927. 2 vols.

Guía de la Hacienda de la República Mexicana. Año de 1826. *Parte Legislativa.* 2 vols.

Guijo, Lic. Gregorio Martín de, *Diario de Sucesos Notables. Año de* 1651.

Humboldt, Alej. de, *Ensayo*

Político sobre el reino de la Nueva España. Librería de Rosa, Paris, 1822. 4 vols.

Icazbalceta, D.F.García, *Obras de.* Mexico, 1896-9. 10 vols. *Imp. Agüeros.*

Indice de Documentos de Nueva España existentes en el Archivo de Indias de Sevilla. Mexico. *Monografías Bibliográficas Mexicanas.* 1931. *Imp. de la Secretaría de Relaciones Exteriores*, vol.4, p.174.

Indice General de los Ramos, etc., p.1 reverse.

*Inventario de Alajas de Oro, Plata y Piedras preciosas de la Sta. Iglesia Metropolitana de México, Formado en el año de 1807 de orden del M.J.D.S. Dean y Cabildo por el Sr. Tesorero Dr. D.Juan José de Gamboa. Manuscript, private collection.

*Inventario de las alhajas de la Catedral Metropolitana, de 1867. Manuscript, private collection.

Las Leyes de Recopilación. Madrid, 1745. *Imp. Juan de Zúñiga.* 3 vols.

León, Nicolas, *Códice Sierra. Traducción al Español de su Texto Nahuatl y Explicación de sus Pinturas Jeroglíficas* by Dr. Nicolás León. Mexico, 1933. *Imp. del Museo Nacional de Arqueología, Historia y Etnografía.* With introduction and published by Federico Gómez de Orozco.

Lorenzot, Francisco del Barrio, *Ordenanzas de Gremios de la Nueva España*, published with introduction and under the guidance of Genaro Estrada, by decision of the Secretariat of Industry, Commerce and Labor, *Direc. de Talleres Gráficos*, Mexico, 1921.

Maillefert, Eugenio, *Directorio del Comercio del Imperio Mexicano para el año de* 1867, published second year. Mexico. E.Maillefert, No.2 Tiburcio Street.

Marroquí, José María, *La Ciudad de México, Imp.* 'La Europea,' Mexico, 1900. 3 vols.

Mendieta, Fray Gerónimo de, *Historia Eclesiástica Indiana.* Published by Joaquín García Icazbalceta, *Antigua Librería*, Mexico, 1869.

Mendoza, D.Luis Torres de, *Colección de Documentos Inéditos Relativos al Descubrimiento, Conquista y Organización de las Antiguas Posesiones Españolas, Sacados de los Archivos del Reino y muy especialmente de los Indios.* Madrid, 1869.

Montemayor y Cordova de Cuenca, Don Juan Francisco (Judge of the Royal Tribunal and Chancery who resides in the City of Mexico, by order of the Illustrious and Excellent Father Payo Enriquez de Rivera, Viceroy, Deputy of the King Our Lord, Governor and Captain General of New Spain, year 1677), *Recopilación de algunos Mandamientos y Ordenanzas del Gobierno de esta Nueva España, hechas por los Exmos. Señores y Virreyes y Gobernadores de ella.* With permission. Reprinted in Mexico by Felipe de Zúñiga y Ontiveros, Espíritu Santo Street, year 1787.

Motolinía, R.P. Fr. Toribio de Benavente, ó *Historia de los Indios de la Nueva España*, Barcelona, 1914. *Herederos de Juan Arti*, editors.

Novisima Recopilación de las Leyes de España, Madrid, 1805. 4 vols.

Núñez y Domínguez, José de J., *Un Virrey Limeño en México*,

Mexico, 1927. *Talleres Gráficos del Museo Nacional.*

Ordenanzas de el Nobilissimo Arte de la Platería. Mexico, 1746. *Imp. Real del Superior Gobierno y del Nuevo Rezado, de Doña María de Ribera.*

Orfebrería y Platería, El Estilo Renacimiento Español. Casa Editorial Felia y Susanna, Barcelona [no date].

Orozco y Berra, Manuel, *Documentos para la Historia de México.* 20 vols., 4 series, Mexico 1853-57. *Imp. de Juan R.Navarro, La Voz de la Religión, F.Escalante y Comp. Ignacio Cumplido y Vicente García Torres.*

Paredes, Julian de, *Recopilación de Leyes de los Reynos de los Indios,* Madrid, 1681.

Pasajeros a Indias. Catálogo Metodológico de las Informaciones y Licencias de los que allí pasaron, existentes en el Archivo General de Indias, vol.1, 1492-1592; vol.2, 1492-1592. *Compañía Ibero-Americana de Publicaciones, (S.A.)* Madrid, 1930.

Paso y Troncoso, Francisco, *Fr. Bernadino de Sahagún. Historia de las Cosas de Nueva España. Códice Matritense de la Real Academia de la Historia en Madrid,* Madrid, 1907. *Edición en facsímile.* vol.8 — —, *Memorial de los Indios de Tepetlaoztec al Monarca Español contra los Encomenderos del Pueblo,* Madrid, 1912. *Fototipia de Hauser y Menet.* 1st part.

Payno, Manuel, *Memoria de Hacienda por el período de Diciembre de 1855 a Mayo de 1856,* Mexico 1857, *Imp. Cumplido.*

Paz, Irineo y Tornel, Manuel, *Nueva Guía de México en inglés,* *francés y castellano, con instrucciones y noticias para viageros y hombres de negocios. Año de 1882.* Mexico, *Imp. de I.Paz.* No.7 Escalerillas Street.

Peralta, Suárez de, *Noticias Históricas de la Nueva España. Publicadas con la protección del Ministro de Agricultura y Fomento, por D.Justo Zaragoza,* Madrid, 1878. *Imp. Manuel A.González.*

Pérez, Juan E., *Almanaque estadístico de las oficinas y Guía de Forasteros y del comercio de la República Mejicana.* Official of the Treasury and an honorary member of the Mexican Geographic and Statistical Society. 6th year, 1881-2. Mexico. *Imp. del Gobierno en Palacio, dirigida por A.Sabás y Munguía,* 1882. — —, *Almanaque estadístico y Guía de Forasteros para 1874.* 3rd year. Mexico. *Imp. del Gobierno en Palacio, a cargo de José María Sandoval,* 1874. — —, *Almanaque estadístico de las oficinas y Guía de Forasteros y del comercio de la República para* 1875. Official of the Treasury and a Member of the Mexican Geographic and Statistical Society. 4th year. Mexico. *Imp. del Gobierno en Palacio, a cargo de José María Sandoval,* 1874.

Pérez y López, Don Antonio Xavier *Teatro de la Legislación Universal de España y Indias.* Madrid MDCCXCVI 1791-8. *Imp. Antonio Espinosa.* 28 vols.

Periódico Oficial del Imperio Mexicano, No.67, vol.I, p.2. Mexico, 24 December 1863.

Priestley, Herbert I., *The Mexican Nation,* New York, 1930.

Recopilación de Leyes de los Reinos

de las Indias, mandada imprimir y publicar por la Magestad Católica del Rey Don Carlos II, Nuestro Señor. 3 vols. 5th edition. Madrid, 1841. Boix, editor.

Registro Oficial del Gobierno de los Estados Unidos Mexicanos. 3rd year, vol.9, No.47, 17 October 1832.

Revello, José Torre, *El Gremio de Plateros en las Indias Occidentales. Imprenta de la Universidad,* Buenos Aires, 1932.

Revillagigedo, Conde de, *Instrucción Reservada* (1794) *Imp. de la Calle de las Escalerillas,* Mexico, 1831.

Rubio y Moreno, Luis, *Pasajeros a Indias,* 1492-1592, 2 vols. which comprise vols. 4 and 5 of the *Colección de Documentos Inéditos para la Historia de la Hispano-América.* Madrid (no date). *Imp. Cía. Ibero-Americana de Publicaciones, S.A.*

Sahagún, Bernardino de, *Historia General de las Cosas de Nueva España,* 3 vols. Published by Carlos María de Bustamante, Mexico, 1829-30.

Sanchez-Cantón, *Las Artes,* Madrid, 1920 — *Editorial Saturnino Calleja, S.A.*

San Vicente, D.Juan Manuel de, *México en* 1768. *Exacta descripción de la Magnífica Corte Mexicana.* Published in Cadiz in the 18th century and again printed by Luis González Obregón, Mexico, 1897. *Tip. El Nacional.*

Saville, Marshall H., *The Goldsmith's Art in Ancient Mexico.* New York, Museum of the American Indian, Heye Foundation, 1920.

Sedano, Francisco, *Noticias* de *México, recogidas par,* Imp.J.R. Barbedillo, Mexico, 1880.

Sentenach, Narciso de, *Bosquejo Histórico sobre la Orfebrería Española,* Madrid, 1909, *Imp. Revista de Arch. Bibl. y Museos.*

Terreros, M. Romero de, Marqués de San Francisco, *Las Artes Industriales en la Nueva España.* Mexico, D.F. *Librería de Pedro Robredo,* 1923.

Terreros, Don Manuel Romero de, Marqués de San Francisco, *Torneos, Mascaradas y Fiestas Reales en la Nueva España. Imp. Murguía.* Mexico, 1918.

Thompson, Edward Herbert, *People of the Serpent,* New York, 1932.

Valle, Juan N. del, *El Viajero en México. Año de* 1859. Mexico. *Imp. de Andrade y Escalante.* — —, *El Viajero en Méjico — Completa guía de forasteros para* 1864 — *Obra útil a toda clase de personas.* Mexico. *Imp. de Andrade y Escalante;* No.19 Tiburcio Street. 1864.

Valle, Juan N. del, *Guía de Forasteros de la Capital de Puebla, para el año de* 1852.

Valdez, Manuel Antonio, *Gazetas de México, Compendio de Noticias de Nueva España, de los años de* 1796 *y* 1797. *Imp. de Don Mariano de Zúñiga y Ontiveros.*

*Valle, Marquesa del, *Recibo dado por* — Cuernavaca, 18 December 1543. (From a manuscript in a private collection.)

Zúñiga y Ontiveros, Felipe, *Calendario manual y Guía de Forasteros en Méjico — para el año de* 1780 — *Dispuestos por Don Felipe de Zúñiga y Ontiveros, Filomatemático de esta Corte y Agrimensor titulado por S.M. (Q.D.G.) de Tierras, Aguas, y Minas de todo el Reino — Nuevamente ilustrado con varias adiciones muy útiles y curiosas — Con privilegio — En Méjico;* In his Office — Palma Street.

Zúñiga y Ontiveros, Mariano de, *Calendario manual y Guía de forasteros en Méjico para el año de 1794 por Don Mariano de Zúñiga y Ontiveros* — With permission — In the office of the heirs of Felipe de Zúñiga y Ontiveros.

Index

pectorals, 188; perfumer, 165; platters, 180 ff., 230, 243; prayer frames, 186; pyx, 165, 178; railings, 205, 219, 221; rings, 188; sandbox, 165; spoons, 179 ff., 242 n., 243; statues, 165 f., 177, 200, 206 f., 213 f., 217, 218 n., 220, 232; sword, 244; tabernacle screens, 178; tabernacles, 176 f.; throne, 167, 215; torch-holders, 205, 212 f.; *Torrecilla, La,* 213 ff.; tray, 308; vases, 205, 219. *See also* style *under* plate

marks, (1524-78) 285 ff., (1579-1732) 288, (1623) 291 f., (1649-51) 293, (1701) 294, (1733-1820) 295, (1746) 296, (1733) 297, (1750) 298 f., (1785) 300 ff., 305 f., (1733-82) 310

production: provincial, 4 ff., 9; sixteenth century, 152 ff.; seventeenth century, 159 ff.; eighteenth century, 171 ff.; (1800-1936) 237 ff.

reproductions, 267, 306 f.

silver gilt: 91, 94, 109, 110, 157, 162, 165, 166, 173, 176 ff. *passim,* 186, 187, 206, 211, 213, 216, 217, 242, 270, 306, 308, 312, 313 n., 314 n., 324. *See also* cost *above*; fire gilding (gold plating) *under* silversmiths: technique

standard of quality, 110 ff.; Spanish precedent, 111; documents, 117 f.; value in modern currency, 119 ff. *See also* standard *under* precious metals

tableware, 126, 135, 154

taxes, 122, 125, 126 f., 132, 144, 297

Plateros, Calle de, 86 f.

Potosí. *See* San Luis Potosí

PRECIOUS METALS

assay, 8, 11, 91, 98, 101, 110,

132 ff., 232, 267 n., 273, 277 f., 281, 289, 300, 343 f.; books, 114, 126, 275, 285, 300 f., 333; early legislation, 5 ff., 93, 97, 99 f., 114 f., 292 f., 300, 302; mark, 272 ff.

Chief Assayer: lists, 304 f., 310, 318, 329 f.; marks, 295 ff., 302 f., 305 ff., 311, 315 ff., 320 ff., 325 f., 328, 336 f., 340 ff., 346 f.; the office, 99, 100, 114, 282, 293, 304 f., 319 n. *See also* González de la Cueva; Lince y González; Arance y Cobos; Forcada y la Plaza; Dávila Madrid; Buitrón; Camacho; Castillo; Mucharraz; Morales; Sáyago; Obregón Morales; *Juez Veedor*

coinage, 74, 93, 113 f., 129, 171, 277, 280, 287, 292; marks, 287, 309, 324, 335; standard of money, 111, 113, 140

fraud, 80, 84 f., 98, 100, 122 f., 126, 130, 132, 136, 232, 285, 288, 291 f., 296 and n., 297

mining, 39, 55 ff., 73 and n., 122 ff., 129 f., 138 ff., 145, 153 ff., 212, 275; Indian, 55 ff., 73 n., 129

smelting, 8, 57, 92, 122, 124 f., 129, 135, 137, 139, 141, 153, 276 f., 288, 290

standards, 8, 271 ff., 300 f., 307, 333, 351; gold, 91, 112 ff., 115 ff.; laws (1381-1785), 69 f., 91, 93, 117 ff., 281 f., (1524-78) 277 ff., (1581) 112 ff., (1638-1733) 91, 93, 291 ff., (after 1821) 138, (1839) 8, (1895) 343 ff.; modern, 267 and n. *See also* coinage *above*; standard of quality *under* plate

taxes: assay, 6, 8, 97 f., 122, 124 f., 129, 132 f., 135, 332 and n.; coinage, 122, 125, 129, 131 f., 136 ff.; excise, 127 ff., 129, 139, 167; mining (Royal

Printed in U.S.A. by
NOBLE OFFSET PRINTERS, INC.
NEW YORK, N.Y. 10003

THE ART OF THE SILVERSMITH
IN MEXICO

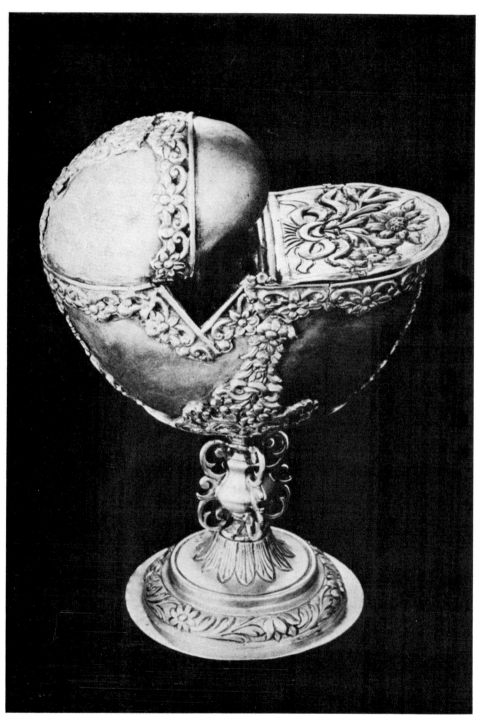

An incense boat of silver, of the XVII Century; height 8¹⁄₁₆ inches, length 6⁵⁄₁₆, width 3⅜ and base 3⁹⁄₁₆ inches in diameter. Author's collection.

THE ART
OF THE SILVERSMITH
IN MEXICO
1519-1936

BY LAWRENCE ANDERSON

Volume II
PLATE

Hacker Art Books
New York
1975

First published by Oxford University Press, New York, 1941.

Reissued 1975 by Hacker Art Books, Inc., New York.

Library of Congress Catalogue Card Number 73-81683 ISBN 0-87817-139-8

Printed in the United States of America.

This book is dedicated to the Mexican people with all affection and respect, and with the hope that it will contribute to the better understanding and appreciation of their artistic achievements.

List of Illustrations

THE ART OF THE SILVERSMITH
IN MEXICO

I

*Silver bowl of the XVIII Century, made and marked in Guatemala.
Height 2⅜ inches, diameter 5⅞ inches. Author's collection.*

2

Silver beaker 4⅜ inches in height. Made and marked in Guatemala. XVIII Century. Collection of Mrs. Concepción Gómez Farias de Carrere, Mexico City.

3

Silver bowl, height 2¹⁵⁄₁₆ inches, diameter 6⁵⁄₁₆. Unmarked. Made in Guatemala. XVIII Century. Author's collection.

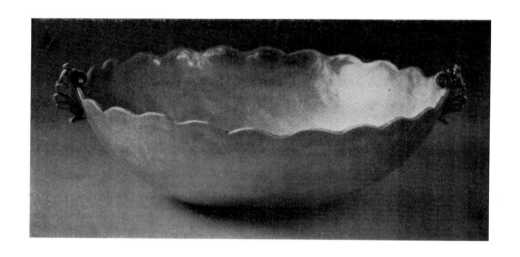

4

Ancient silver bowl, made in Peru, height 2 9/16 inches, diameter 8 11/16.
Author's collection.

5

Silver plate, 12 inches in diameter, made and marked in Guatemala. XVIII Century. Private collection.

6

Silver coffee-pot, 7⅞ inches in height, made and marked in Guatemala. XVIII Century. Private collection.

*Silver brazier, height 4⅜ inches, diameter 6⁵⁄₁₆ inches. Made and marked
in San Luis Potosí, 1827-1853. Author's collection.*

8

Silver brazier, height 4¹⁵⁄₁₆ inches, diameter 6¹¹⁄₁₆ inches. Made and marked in San Luis Potosí. 1827-1853. From the collection of Mr. W. B. Stephens, Mexico.

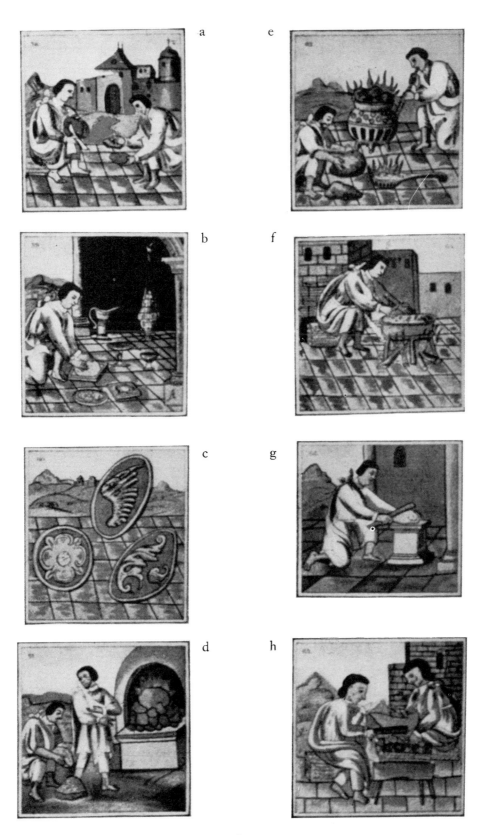

9
Indian goldsmiths at work. Florentine Codex.

10
Obverse

The famous scorpion of gold, emeralds, pearls and enamels which Hernan Cortez had made and took to Spain in 1527.

11
Reverse

*The famous scorpion of gold, emeralds, pearls and enamels
which Hernan Cortez had made and took to Spain in 1527.*

12
Silver relic case, height 12 inches, base 4¹⁵⁄₁₆ inches in diameter. Prior to 1700. From the Museum of the Metropolitan Cathedral, Mexico City.

13

Pair of silver candle-sticks. Height 14 inches, diameter at base 6⅛ inches. XVII Century. Private collection.

14
Silver ciborium, height 7⁷⁄₁₆ inches, diameter at top 4⅜ inches. Prior to 1700. Collection of the Metropolitan Cathedral, Mexico City.

15

Silver aspersorium of the XVII Century, height 14 inches, diameter 11 inches at the base. It bears the date 1792 and other letters all in modern script. Private collection.

16

Silver crucifix with bells, height 14⅝ inches, extreme width 9 inches. XVII Century. From the collection of Mr. Eduardo N. Yturbide, Mexico City.

17

Silver sauce boat, height 4¹⁵⁄₁₆ inches, length 7¾ inches. Made by silver-smith Miguel María Martel between the years 1791 and 1818. Collection of Mr. Salvador Ugarte, Mexico City.

18

Silver bowl, height 3⁹⁄₁₆ inches, diameter 18 inches. Late XVIII Century. Private collection.

19
Silver pitcher, height 10¹³⁄₁₆ *inches, diameter*
7¹⁄₁₆ *inches. XVIII Century. Private collec-*
tion.

20

Silver pitcher, height 10 inches, diameter 6⅞ inches. Third quarter of the XVIII Century. From the collection of Mr. Salvador Ugarte, Mexico City.

21

Silver relic case with relic of Saint Boniface, height 16½ *inches, extreme width* 7⅟₁₆ *inches. XVIII Century. Collection of the Museum of the Metropolitan Cathedral, Mexico City.*

22
Silver crucifix with receptacles for the Holy Oils, height 13 inches, diameter at base 7¼ inches. XVIII Century. Private collection.

23
*Bottle, mounted in silver, height 3¾ inches, diameter 2³⁄₁₆
inches. XVIII Century. From the collection of Mr. Eman
L. Beck, Mexico City.*

24
One of a set of four silver candle-sticks, height 15 inches, width at widest part 6⅝₁₆ inches. XVIII Century. From the collection of Mr. Carlos Schultze, Mexico City.

25

Silver collection-plate, diameter 14 *inches. XVIII Century.*
Private collection.

26

*Silver collection-plate, diameter 14 inches. XVIII Century.
Private collection.*

27
*Silver aspersorium for Holy Water, height 9⅝ inches, by
9⅝ inches in diameter. An excellent reproduction which
bears forged marks of Buitrón.*

28

Silver candle-stick, height 6¹⁄₁₆ inches, base 3¾ inches in diameter. A reproduction which bears forged marks imitating Buitrón's marks.

29

Silver brazier, height 3¹⁵⁄₁₆ inches; diameter 9 inches. It bears the Eagle
with the M *and small* o *above, both forged, and the mark of the Ochoa
brothers who worked in Mexico City within recent years.*

30

Silver soup tureen, height 11 inches; diameter 14⅞ inches. A reproduction bearing forged marks. Private collection.

31

Silver candle-stick, height 8⅞ inches; base 3⁷⁄₁₆ inches in width. A reproduction which bears marks, forgeries of those of Dávila and of silversmith Herrera.

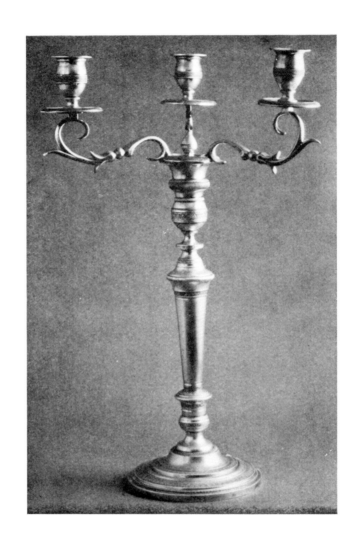

32

Silver candelabrum, height 15 inches; base 8¾ inches in diameter. A good reproduction which bears marks, forgeries of those of Buitrón. Private collection.

33

Lock with ornate silver shield, $11^{13}\!/_{16}$ *inches in diameter. A reproduction bearing the forged marks of Martínez, the* Lion Rampant *and the* M *with the small* o *above, but no mark of the Chief Assayer.*

34
*Silver key for the lock shown in
Plate 33 bearing the same marks.*

35

Silver plate, diameter 9⅟₁₆ inches, an imitation bearing marks, forgeries of those of silversmith Martínez, with the Eagle *and the* M *with the small* o *above, but no mark of the Chief Assayer.*

36

Silver tray, diameter 15 inches. A forgery which bears marks, forgeries of those of José María Rodallega and Chief Assayer Lince.

37

Modern silver platter, length 17 inches, width 11 inches, with forged marks of Buitrón.

38

Silver platter, length 17 inches, width 11 inches. A reproduction which bears forged marks of Buitrón. Author's collection.

39

Silver brazier, height 4½ inches; diameter 7¾ inches. A reproduction bearing forged marks of Buitrón.

Modern silver brazier, height 7¾ inches; length 12 inches. It bears the forged marks of Chief Assayer González.

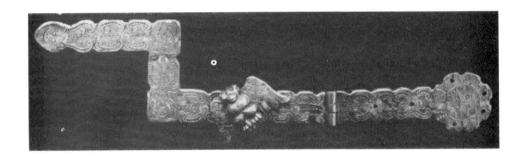

41

Silver hinge. A reproduction bearing marks, forgeries of those of Martínez,
the Lion Rampant, M *with small* o *above but no mark of the Chief Assayer.*

42

Silver bowl, height 4¹⁵⁄₁₆ inches; diameter, 16 inches. A poor imitation bearing marks, forgeries of those of Buitrón.

43

Silver bowl, a reproduction in the style of those made in Guatemala. Forged marks of Mundos y Mares.

44

Silver shell-shaped fountain, 7¾ inches in height, 14½₁₆ in length. A reproduction bearing forged marks of Mundos y Mares.

45

*Silver plate, 8½ inches in diameter. The marks were stamped
with the forged dies of Apolonio Guevara. A reproduction.
Private collection.*

46
Silver plate, 8½ inches in diameter. The marks are stamped with the forged dies of Apolonio Guevara. Reproduction. Private collection.

47

*Silver soup tureen, 13½ inches in height, 15¾ in length. The cover
dates from the XVIII Century, while the base is modern — made recently by Apolonio Guevara. Private collection.*

48

Silver box, 5¾ inches in height by 9 in length. XVIII Century.
Collection of Mr. Eman L. Beck.

49
Silver incense boat, 6⅛ inches in height, 9 in length. It bears forged marks of Buitrón and Martínez. A genuine piece of the early XIX Century. Private collection.

50

Silver incense boat, height 4¾ inches, length 6⅞ inches. Authentic piece of the early XIX Century. The marks of Buitrón and Torre, which it bears, are forgeries. Author's collection.

51

Silver bowl, height 4⁵⁄₁₆ inches, diameter 6⅞ inches. First half of the
XIX Century. Author's collection.

Silver platter, height 9⅟₁₆ inches, length 14 ³⁄₁₆ inches. 1823-1842. Collection of Mr. Carlos Schultze, Mexico City.

53

Silver ink-stand with silver gilt ornaments, 7¼ inches in height and 12¼ inches in length. The marks of Buitrón are forgeries. Genuine, early XIX Century. Private collection.

54
*Silver ink-stand, height 7¾ inches, length 12¾ inches. The marks of
Buitrón are forgeries. Genuine, early XIX Century. Private collection.*

55
Silver brazier, height 4½ inches, length 10 inches. 1830-1853. Private collection.

56
*Silver brazier, height 4¼ inches, length 7⅟₁₆ inches, width 4½ inches.
1830. Collection of Mr. W. B. Stephens. Mexico City.*

Silver brazier, 4⅜ inches in height by 9⅞ inches in length. Made by Manuel Mariano Fernández y Cartami. 1808-1843. Tolsá influence. Author's collection.

58

Silver brazier, 4½ inches in height by 9¼ in length. Middle of the XIX Century. Author's collection.

Silver tray for cruets and bell, with ornaments of silver gilt, 1⁹⁄₁₆ *inches in height by* 9 *in length.* Circa 1825. *Author's collection.*

60

*Silver brazier, 3¹⁵⁄₁₆ inches in height by 6¹⁄₁₆ in diameter, made by
A. Wimer. Circa 1830. From the collection of Mr. W. B. Stephens,
Mexico City.*

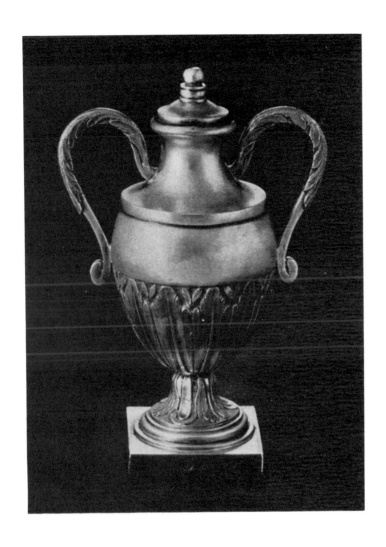

61

Silver amphora, genuine, 5¹¹⁄₁₆ inches in height, diameter 4⅛ inches. Buitrón's marks, which it bears, are forgeries. First half of the XIX Century. Private collection.

62
*Silver censer, 6½ inches in height, extreme width
4¹³⁄₁₆ inches. A genuine piece of the XVIII
Century with forged marks. Author's collection.*

63

Silver brazier, height 4½ inches, width 6⅛ inches. Late XVI or early XVII Century. Private collection.

64
*Silver incense boat, 5⁵⁄₁₆ inches in height, 2⁹⁄₁₆ in width and 6⅞ in length.
Late XVI or early XVII Century. Author's collection.*

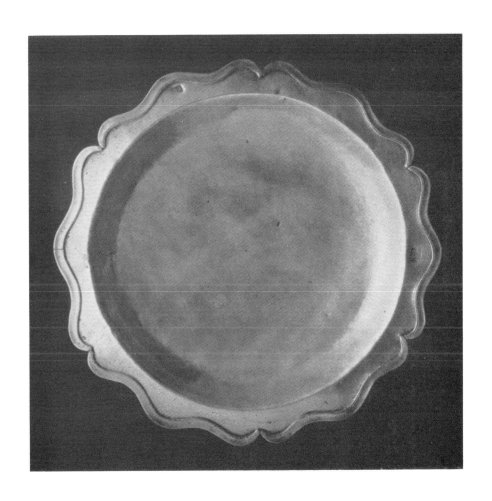

65
Silver platter, height 1⁹⁄₁₆ inches, diameter 13¾ inches. XVII Century. Author's collection.

66
Silver bowl, height 2³⁄₁₆ inches, diameter 6⅞ inches. Probably latter half of the XVI Century. Author's collection.

67

*Small silver box, with cups for the Holy Oils, width 5⅝
inches, height 5⁵⁄₁₆ inches. Probably from the latter half of
the XVI Century. From the collection of the Museum of the
Metropolitan Cathedral, Mexico City.*

68

Interior view of the box shown in Plate 67.

69

Silver pedestal with miniature, height 11
inches, diameter 6¹¹⁄₁₆ *inches. XVII Century.*
From the collection of Mr. Eman L. Beck,
Mexico City.

70

Reverse of the pedestal shown in Plate 69.

71

Silver collection-plate, height 3⁹⁄₁₆ inches, diameter 9¼ inches. A good copy of the original shown in Plate 72. Private collection.

72
Silver collection-plate, height 3⁹⁄₁₆ inches, diameter 9¼ inches. XVII Century. In the center, the emblem of 'Souls in Purgatory.' Private collection.

73
Silver incense boat, height 2¹⁵⁄₁₆ inches, length 6⅛ inches. XVII Century.
From the collection of Mr. Salo Hale, Mexico City.

74

Silver incense boat with silver spoon, height 3⅜₆ inches, width 6⅛ inches. Both of the XVII Century. Author's collection.

75

Silver pedestal for a minia-
ture, height 18⁵⁄₁₆ *inches, ex-*
treme width 7⁵⁄₁₆ *inches. XVII*
Century. From the collection
of Mr. Eman L. Beck, Mexi-
co City.

76
*Reverse of the silver pedestal
shown in Plate 75.*

77

*Silver stirrup, height 6⅚ inches, width 4⅜ inches.
Prior to 1700. From the collection of Mr. Carlos
Schultze, Mexico City.*

78

Silver chalice, height 10¼ inches, base 6⅛ inches in diameter. XVII Century. From the collection of the Museum of the Metropolitan Cathedral, Mexico City.

79

Silver incense boat, height 5¹¹⁄₁₆ inches, length 7⁵⁄₁₆, width 3⁹⁄₁₆. XVII Century. Author's collection.

80

Silver incense boat, height $5\frac{5}{16}$ inches, base $3\frac{1}{8}$ inches in diameter, with silver spoon $6\frac{1}{8}$ inches in length. Inscription with date 1702. *From the collection of Mrs. G. H. Neumegen, Mexico City.*

81

Silver collection plate, height 6½ inches, diameter 8⁷⁄₁₆ inches. XVII Century. Private collection.

82

Silver censer, height 7⁷⁄₁₆ inches, width 4¹⁵⁄₁₆ inches. Latter half of the XVI or early XVII Century. Collection of the Museum of the Metropolitan Cathedral, Mexico City.

83

Ancient 'Ciprés' (Tabernacle) of the Cathedral of Mexico. From a drawing in the 'Inventario' at the National Museum in Mexico City, Mexico.

84
Tabernacle, Cathedral of Mexico.
From a drawing in the 'Inventario' at
the National Museum in Mexico City.

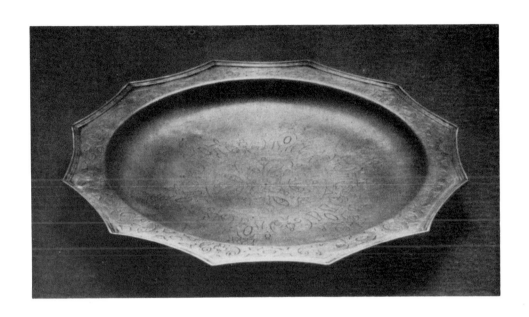

85

Silver platter, 9¼ inches in diameter. XVII Century. Private collection.

86
Silver collection-plate, 8⅞ inches in diameter. XVII Century. Private collection.

87

Silver platter, length 19¼ inches, width 13⅜ inches. Prior to 1700.
Private collection.

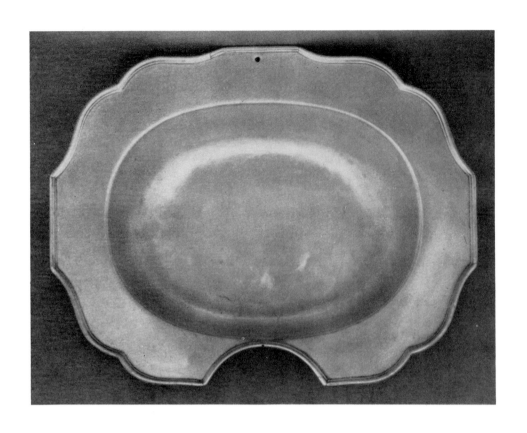

88

*Silver shaving bowl, height 2¾ inches, length 14 inches. Prior to 1700.
Private collection.*

89

Silver frame, with superimposed ornaments of silver gilt, height 11 inches, width 11½ inches. Early XVIII Century. Author's collection.

Antependium of silver, from the altar of Our Lady of Sorrows, parochial church at Acatzingo, Puebla. Made in 1761, original weight 124 marcos, 3½ ounces.

91
Silver plate, 10 1/16 *inches in diameter. XVIII Century. From the collection of Mr. Carlos Schultze, Mexico City.*

Silver plate, 12 inches in diameter. Circa 1729. From the collection of Mr. Carlos Schultze, Mexico City.

93
*One of a pair of silver candle-sticks, height
10⁷⁄₁₆ inches, base 6⅛ inches in diameter.
First half of the XVIII Century. Author's
collection.*

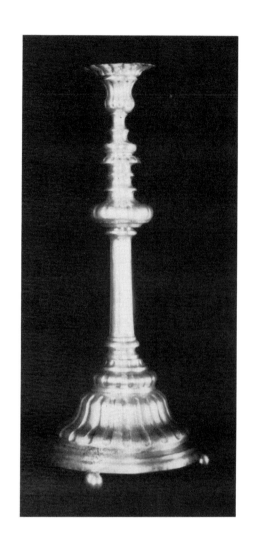

94

One of a pair of silver candle-sticks, height 27 inches, base 13 inches in diameter. Second half of the XVIII Century. From the collection of Mr. Eduardo N. Yturbide, Mexico City.

95

Jewel box of tortoise shell, with ornaments of silver gilt, height 3⅛ inches, length 3¾ inches. XVIII Century. Author's collection.

96

Jewel box of tortoise shell, with silver ornaments, height 6⅞ inches, length 7¾ inches. XVIII Century. Collection of La Granja, Mexico City.

97

Halo, for an image, of silver gilt, ornamented with colored stones, height 2¹⁵/₁₆ inches, length 7⁷/₁₆ inches. XVIII Century. Collection of Mrs. William B. Fraser, Coyoacán, D. F., Mexico.

98

Various small objects of silver and silver gilt of the XVIII and XIX Centuries. Collection of Mrs. William B. Fraser, Coyoacán, D.F., Mexico.

99
*Relic case with silver ornaments on a silver gilt
background, height 13 inches, width 8⅞ inches.
Second half of the XVIII Century, prior to the
influence of the Academy. Collection of Mr. Eman
L. Beck, Mexico City.*

100
Silver lamp, height 17 inches, width 4½ inches. XVIII Century. Collection of Mr. Mauricio de la Arena, Mexico City.

101

Silver medallion, height 5½ inches, width 4½ inches. From the best period of the silversmiths' art in Mexico, about the end of the XVIII Century, prior to the influence of the Academy. From the collection of Mr. Eman L. Beck, Mexico City.

102

Miniature with silver frame, height 11 inches, extreme width 8¼ inches. Latter part of the XVIII Century, prior to the influence of the Academy. From the collection of Mr. Eman L. Beck, Mexico City.

103

*Silver pitcher, height 9⁹⁄₁₆ inches, diameter 5¹¹⁄₁₆ inches. Work of Mari-
ano Abila. Circa 1791. From the collection of Mr. Salvador Ugarte,
Mexico City.*

104
Magnificent gonfalon of the Blessed Sacrament, of silver. Length 7 feet 8¾ inches, with banner 23 inches in width. XVIII Century. Collection of Mr. Eman L. Beck, Mexico City.

Silver medallion, height 18½ inches, diameter 15¹⁵⁄₁₆ inches. Second half of the XVIII Century. A good example of the work of that period, prior to the influence of the Academy. From the collection of Mr. Eduardo N. Yturbide, Mexico City.

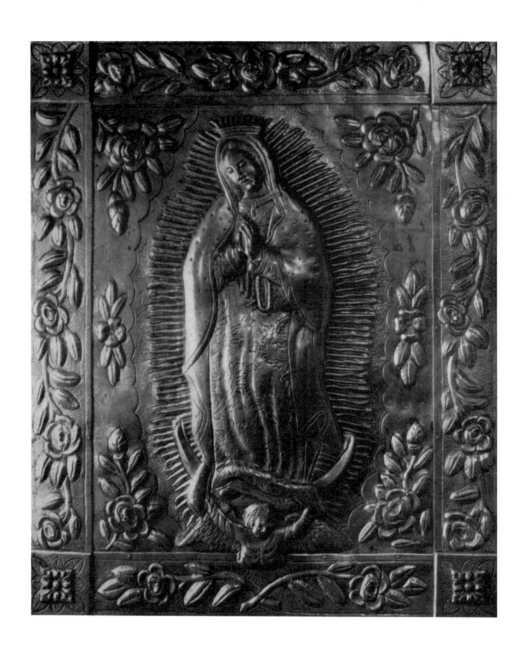

106
Silver medallion with image of the Virgin of Guadalupe, height 21⅝ inches, width 18 inches. Second half of the XVIII Century. A good example of the work of that period, prior to the influence of the Academy. From the collection of Mr. Eduardo N. Yturbide, Mexico City.

107

Silver gilt cruets, altar bell and tray. Height 5½ inches, length 9⅜ inches, width 7⅛ inches. A splendid example of the best period of the silversmiths' art in Mexico. Latter part of the XVIII Century, prior to the influence of the Academy. Made by the great master silversmith, José María Rodallega. Author's collection.

Silver basket, height 2 inches, diameter 12½ inches. XVIII Century.
From the collection of Mrs. William H. Fraser, Coyoacán, D.F.,
Mexico.

109
Silver cruet and altar bell tray, length 9⁷⁄₁₆ inches, width 6⅛ inches. Made between 1779-1789. The enamels were added later. Author's collection.

110
Head-dress of silver gilt filigree. Height 11⅝ inches, width 9⅝ inches. XVIII Century. Collection of Mr. W. B. Stephens, Mexico City.

III

Silver gilt monstrance, height 22⅞ inches, base 8⅞ inches in diameter. XVIII Century. Private collection.

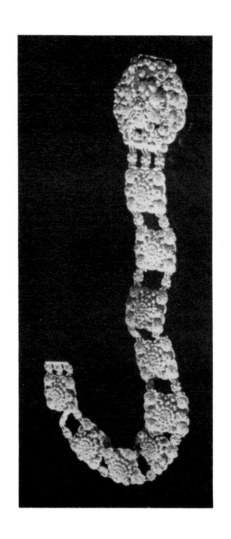

112

Magnificent silver gilt belt, 34⁹⁄₁₆ inches in length. Latter part of the XVIII Century, the best period of the silversmiths' art in Mexico, prior to the influence of the Academy. Collection of Mr. Eman L. Beck, Mexico City.

113
*Head, 4½ inches in diameter,
of the belt shown in Plate* 112.

114

Silver gilt chalice, height 10¹⁄₁₆ inches, base 6½ inches in diameter. Work of the great master silversmith, José María Radallega. Circa 1780. Collection of Mr. Salo Hale, Mexico City.

115

Silver brazier, height 4¹⁵⁄₁₆ inches, diameter 5¹¹⁄₁₆ inches. Late XVIII or early XIX Century. From the collection of Mr. W. B. Stephens, Mexico City.

116
Silver Holy Water font, height 9 inches, width 5¹¹⁄₁₆ inches. Second half of the XVIII Century, prior to the influence of the Academy. From the collection of Mr. Eduardo N. Yturbide, Mexico City.

117

Silver tray, length 14⅛ inches, width 10⅝ inches. Prior to 1800. Author's collection.

118
Prayer book with clasps of silver gilt. 1799. Author's collection.

Magnificent silver frame, height 31¹¹⁄₁₆ inches, width 25 inches. Latter part of the XVIII Century. Collection of Mr. Eduardo N. Yturbide, Mexico City.

120

Painting with silver frame, height II inches, width
7¹¹⁄₁₆ inches. Late XVIII or early XIX Century.
Collection of Mrs. G. H. Neumegen, Mexico City.

121
*Painting with silver frame, height 29⅛ inches, width 23
inches.* Circa 1790. *Collection of Mr. Eman L. Beck,
Mexico City.*

122

*Silver aspersorium for Holy Water, height 9⅝ inches, diameter
11 inches. XVIII Century. Collection of Mr. Carlos Schultze,
Mexico City.*

123
Silver missal stand, height 20 inches, width
11⅝ inches. Late XVIII Century. Tolsá in-
fluence. Private collection.

124
Painting with silver frame 53½ inches in height by 40³⁄₁₆ inches in width. Work of the great master silversmith, José María Rodallega, Tolsá influence. Probably circa 1800. Collection of Mr. Eduardo N. Yturbide, Mexico City.

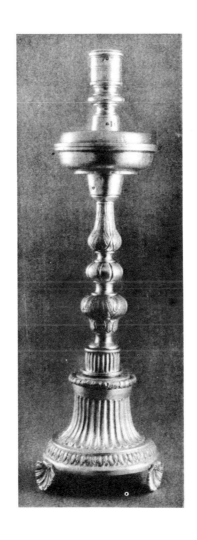

125

One of a pair of silver candle-sticks, height 20⅜ inches, base 7⅙ inches in diameter. A genuine piece, in the style of Tolsá, of the first quarter of the XIX Century. Martel's marks, the Eagle *and the* crowned M, *were stamped with the forged dies made by Apolonio Guevara.*

126
One of a pair of genuine silver candle-sticks, height 17½ inches, base 4¹⁵⁄₁₆ inches in diameter. A splendid example of the Tolsá style. First quarter of the XIX Century. The marks were stamped with the forged dies made by Apolonio Guevara. Private collection.

127

Miniature with silver frame, 11 inches in height by 7⅛ inches in width. Tolsá influence, late XVIII or early XIX Century. From the collection of Mrs. G. H. Neumegen, Mexico City.

128
Miniature with silver frame 7½ inches in height by 6⁵⁄₁₆ inches in width. Last half of the XVIII Century. From the collection of Mrs. G. H. Neumegen, Mexico City.

129
Painting with silver frame 25 inches in height by 19⅛
inches in width. Genuine, with false marks. XIX Century.
Private collection.

130

Silver sconce, 12½ inches in height by 8¾ inches in width. The marks of Caamaño and Forcada are forgeries.

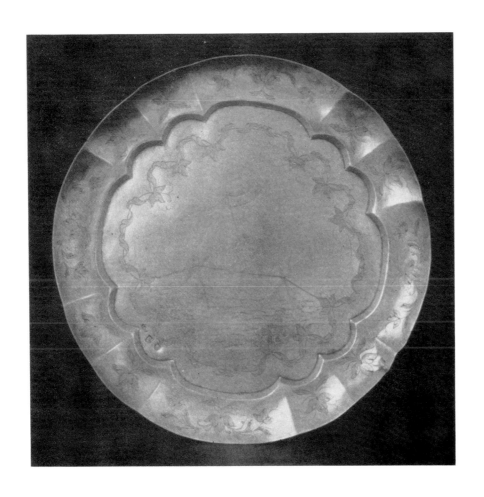

131

Silver plate, 12³⁄₁₆ inches in diameter. Both the plate and Lince's marks are forgeries.

132
Silver soup tureen, height 10 1/16 inches, length 12 inches. Genuine, but Buitrón's marks are forged. Early XIX Century.

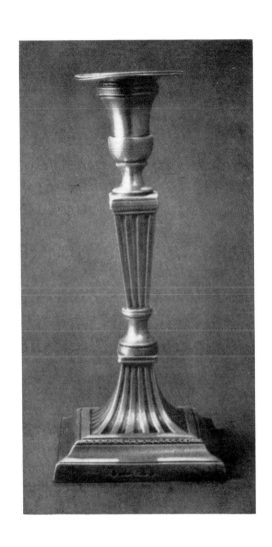

133
Silver candle-stick, height 8⅛ inches, base 3¹⁵⁄₁₆ inches in width. A reproduction bearing marks which are forgeries of those of Buitrón.

134
One of a pair of silver candlesticks, height 39¾ inches, base 8²¹⁄₃₂ inches in diameter. A reproduction bearing marks which are forgeries of those of Forcada.

135
Silver brazier, 3¹⁵⁄₁₆ inches in height by 9¹³⁄₁₆ inches in length. A reproduction with forged marks of Buitrón.

136

Silver brazier of modern manufacture, 3⁹⁄₁₆ inches in height, with tray
6⁵⁄₁₆ inches in diameter, which bears forged marks of Dávila.

137
Silver stirrup, height 8⁹⁄₁₆ inches, width 5¹¹⁄₁₆
inches. XVIII Century. From the collection
of Mr. Carlos Schultze, Mexico City.

138
Silver plate, 11½ inches in diameter. Early XIX Century.
Private collection.

139

Silver brazier, 4¹⁄₃₂ inches in height, 9¹³⁄₁₆ inches in length. Work of Antonio Caamaño, circa 1795. From the collection of Mr. Salvador Ugarte, Mexico City.

140
Silver cruet-tray 2³⁄₁₆ inches in height by 8¼ inches in length. Made by Cardona. 1800-1819. Author's collection.

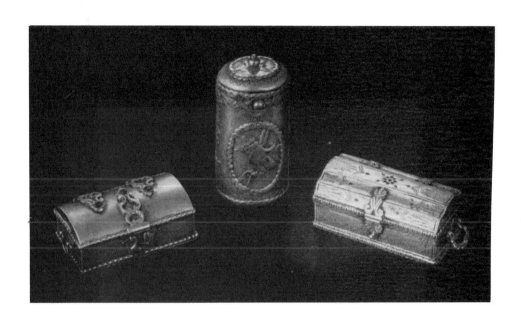

141
Boxes and snuff-box of silver. XVIII and XIX Centuries. From the collection of Mrs. G. H. Neumegen, Mexico City.

142

Silver ink-stand, 5¹⁵⁄₁₆ inches in height, 9⁷⁄₁₆ inches in length and 6¹¹⁄₁₆ inches in width. Work of Antonio Caamaño. 1810-1819. Author's collection.

143

Silver beaker, height 4⅛ inches, diameter 8¹¹⁄₃₂ inches. First quarter of the XIX Century. Author's collection.

144
Miniature with silver frame, 10¹⁄₁₆ inches in height by 6⅞ inches in width. Second quarter of the XIX Century. From the collection of Mr. W. B. Stephens. Mexico City.

145
Miniature with silver gilt frame and font for Holy Water, height 9⅝ inches, width 6¼ inches. Made by José María Martínez. 1800-1812. Tolsá in fluence. Author's collection.

146

Miniature with silver frame, height 7⁷⁄₁₆ inches, width 5½ inches. Tolsá influence. 1800-1820. Collection of Mr. W. B. Stephens, Mexico City.

147
Silver gilt ciborium, height 8 1/16 inches, diame
ter 4 15/16 inches. XIX Century. Collection of
Mrs. William B. Fraser, Coyoacán, D.F.,
Mexico.

148
Silver frame, height 49¼ inches, width 26 inches. Work of the famous master silversmith, José María Rodallega, 1800-1812. From the collection of Mr. W. B. Stephens, Mexico City.

149
Silver medallion, height 19¹¹⁄₁₆ inches, width 15 inches. Work of master silversmith José María Rodallega. 1800-1810. A good example of the Tolsá influence. Author's collection.

150
Silver font for Holy Water, height 10¹³⁄₁₆ *inches,
width* 8¹⁄₁₆ *inches. XIX Century. From the collection
of Mr. Eduardo N. Yturbide, Mexico City.*

151
Silver plate, 15 9/16 inches in diameter. Work of silversmith Alejandro Cañas. 1800-1819. From the collection of Mr. Salvador Ugarte, Mexico City.

152

One of a pair of silver candle-sticks, height 12 inches, base 6½ inches in diameter, with an inscription dated 1821. From the collection of Mrs. William B. Fraser, Coyoacán, D.F., Mexico.

153
Silver pitcher, height 10¹³⁄₁₆ inches, ex-
treme width 4¹⁵⁄₁₇ inches. First quarter
of the XIX Century. An example
showing Tolsá's influence. Collection
of Mr. W. B. Stephens, Mexico City.

154
Don Carlos Rincón Gallardo, Marquis of Guadalupe, wearing a richly adorned charro *suit of the XIX Century. The buttons belonged to the famous bandit* El Zarco, *chief of the band known as the* Plateados. Circa 1861.

155
Mexican charro *saddle, with sword, chaps and quirt, with silver ornaments. XIX Century. Collection of Don Carlos Rincón Gallardo. Marquis of Guadalupe, Mexico City.*

156
Silver nose-piece and head-bands. XIX Century. Collection of Don Carlos Rincón Gallardo, Marquis of Guadalupe, Mexico City.

157

Silver bit, length 5½ inches, width 4¹⁵⁄₁₆ inches, with chin piece, curbs, chains, throat latch, head-stall and buckles of silver, 2¹⁵⁄₁₆ inches in diameter. XIX Century. Collection of Don Carlos Rincón Gallardo, Marquis of Guadalupe, Mexico City.

158
Silver head-piece, 42⅛ inches in length. XIX Century. From the Collection of Mr. Eman L. Beck, Mexico City.

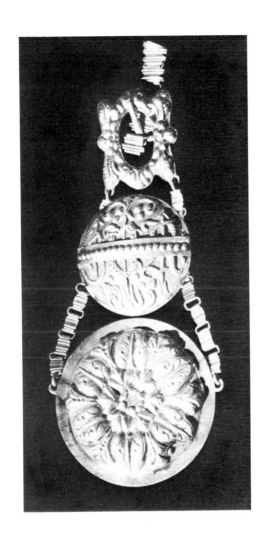

159

*Enlargement of one of the silver
ornaments on the head-piece,
shown in Plate 158. Diameter
4⅛ inches. XIX Century.*

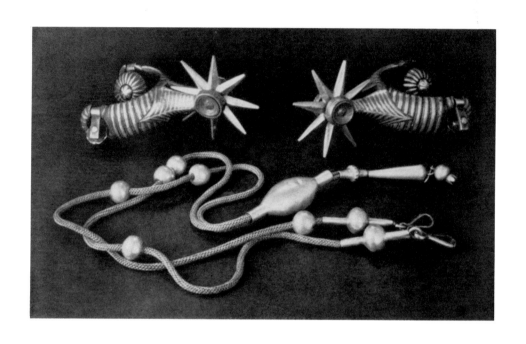

160

Silver spurs and reins, with lengths of 6⅛ and 24¹⁄₁₆ inches respectively.
XIX Century. From the collection of Don Carlos Rincón Gallardo,
Marquis of Guadalupe, Mexico City.

161
Charro *hat with silver hat band and decorations. XIX Century. Collection
of Don Carlos Rincón Gallardo, Marquis of Guadalupe, Mexico City.*

162

Silver rosette, 10¹⁵⁄₁₆ inches in diameter. Late XIX Century. Collection of Mr. Eduardo N. Yturbide, Mexico City.

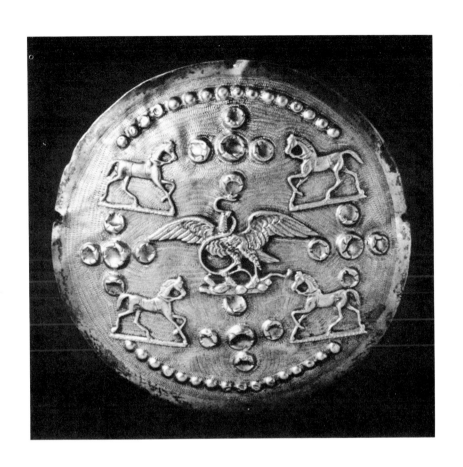

163
Silver rosette, 6½ inches in diameter. Late XIX Century.
Collection of Mr. Eduardo N. Yturbide, Mexico City.

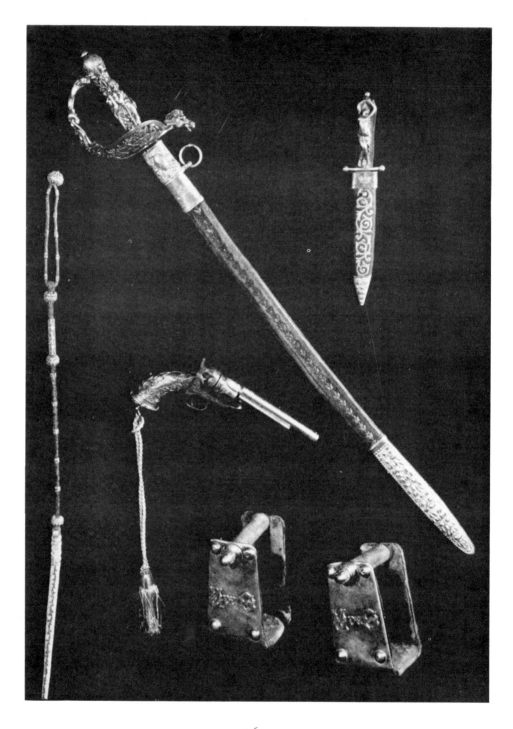

164

Quirt, pistol, sabre, knife and stirrups, with silver decorations. XIX Century. From the collection of Don Carlos Rincón Gallardo, Marquis of Guadalupe, Mexico City.

165
Silver chocolate tray, height 2⁹⁄₁₆ inches, diameter 6⅞ inches. 1823-1842.
Author's collection.

166

Silver censer, with ornaments of silver gilt, height 7⅛ inches, width 7⅛ inches. First half of the XIX Century. The chain is modern. Author's collection.

167
Silver brazier, 5¹¹⁄₁₆ inches in height by 6⅛ inches in width. Made by Eduardo L'Enfer of Puebla. Circa 1852. Collection of Mr. Salo Hale, Mexico City.

168
Silver brazier, height 4¾ inches, width 5⁵⁄₁₆ inches. Made by Eduardo L'Enfer of Puebla, circa 1852. From the collection of Mr. Salo Hale, Mexico City.

169

Silver jewel box, 10⅞ inches in height by 12⅜ inches in length. A copy of the original in the National Museum in Mexico City. First quarter of the XX Century. Private collection.

170
Silver brazier, height 5½ inches, diameter 8¼ inches. Circa 1850. From the collection of Mr. Salo Hale, Mexico City.

171
Silver frame, 19¹¹⁄₁₆ inches in height by 14⁹⁄₁₆ inches in width, with the crest of Emperor Maximilian. 1863-1867. Private collection.

172

Small silver case, 3⅜ inches in diameter, with ornaments of silver gilt and the crown of Iturbide. From the collection of Mr. W. B. Stephens, Mexico City.

173
Fork and spoons made in Mexico from French dies. 1856-1867. Author's collection.

174
Silver tray, height 1²⁵⁄₃₂ inches, diameter 13³⁄₁₆ inches. 1894-1895. Author's collection.

Silver gilt cruets, bell and tray, 6⁵⁄₁₆ inches in height, 9¹³⁄₁₆ inches in length and 6½ inches in width, 1868-1876. Author's collection.

176
Silver chamber candle-stick, height 5⁵⁄₁₆ inches, diameter 6½ inches. 1882-1888. From the collection of Mr. Salo Hale, Mexico City.

177
Coconut cup mounted in silver, 4⅛ inches in height, diameter 4⅜ inches. XIX Century. Collection of Mr. Salo Hale, Mexico City.

178
*Silver lamp, height 44³⁄₃₂ inches,
diameter 16³⁄₈ inches.*

179
Silver chandelier, height 50³⁄₁₆ inches, diameter 33³⁄₁₆ inches. A reproduction.

180

Silver pitcher, height 13⅞ inches, diameter 5⁵⁄₁₆ inches. A good example of the best of present day work. Made by Carrillo-Mendoza, 1929. Author's collection.

181
Examples of the worst type of present day work.

182
Silver sauce boat, a good example of the best present day work. Made by Carillo-Mendoza, 1929. Author's collection.

183

Silver coffee-pot made by Apolonio Guevara. First quarter of the XX Century. Private collection.

Printed in U.S.A. by
NOBLE OFFSET PRINTERS, INC.
NEW YORK, N.Y. 10003